THE TECHNIQUE
of the
SOUND STUDIO

THE LIBRARY
OF COMMUNICATION TECHNIQUES

FILM

TELEVISION

SOUND

THE TECHNIQUE OF THE

SOUND STUDIO

For Radio, Recording Studio, Television and Film

by

ALEC NISBETT

Focal Press

London and Boston

Focal Press

is an imprint of the Butterworth Group

which has principal offices in

London, Boston, Singapore, Sydney, Toronto, Wellington

First published 1962
  Reprinted 1965, 1966, 1967, 1969
Second edition 1970
Third edition 1972
  Reprinted 1972, 1974 (twice), 1977
Fourth edition 1979
  Reprinted 1981, 1983, 1986, 1987 (with revision), 1988

British Library Cataloguing in Publication Data

Nisbett, Alec
    The technique of the sound studio.—4th ed.—
    (The library of communication techniques).
    1. Sound—Recording and reproducing
    I. Title   II. Series
    621.398′3   TK7881.4

    ISBN 0 240 51003 8 (hard cover)
          0 240 51100 X (soft cover)

Printed and Bound in Great Britain by
Hartnolls Limited, Bodmin, Cornwall.

CONTENTS

6

8

INTRODUCTION

FOR the fourth edition of this book much new material was added, the remainder was thoroughly revised to bring it in line with current practice, and many passages were clarified or condensed. The result was fuller and more informative than before, but also more concise.

At each subsequent printing, further changes have been made in order to reflect current trends. These have been introduced without altering the layout, so courses in Communications based on earlier printings of the fourth edition should be substantially unaffected.

Some developments – notably quadraphonics – have proved ephemeral. But the techniques that had to be developed are still of interest and some references to these remain. The shift towards digital recording and replay has continued, and we have seen the introduction of compact disc and digital cassettes, producing a marked reduction of background noise at previously weak points in the audio chain. As a result, the sound recordist's skills are all the more important, since his errors and imperfections as well as his more subtle effects can be heard even more clearly.

Even so, some compromises are still necessary, for the end product is no better than the weakest point in the chain. Radio transmission has improved little since the advent of FM, long ago; and for both radio and television, the listening equipment and conditions may be poor, while the signal itself may have a useful dynamic range that is small in comparison with a record or recording that is being played. When they are broadcast, compact discs and digital cassettes may have to be compressed even more than is necessary for their predecessors, but mercifully this can be done without bringing up obtrusive background noise. It should never be forgotten that it is more important to satisfy the listener than to achieve the ultimate in technical perfection.

The past decade has seen an increase in the number of add-on components designed to produce particular effects without significant loss of quality. In popular music, in particular, the availability of digital circuitry has made possible a shift in emphasis toward more analytical techniques, toward perfection rather than performance. Some reversals of opinions given in previous editions have been made possible by other technical advances—for example, on continuous track faders and reverberation springs. 'Echo' devices have now reached the stage that microphones attained a generation before, where the choice of instrument was dictated by the nature of the original sound. Microphones, too, have improved a great deal since then. Some—at a price—now provide a substantially flat response throughout the audio frequency range. Here I hold to my earlier opinion that there are strong advantages to matching the frequency characteristics of sound source and microphone.

Each new edition of this book faces the same particular danger: the increasing complexity of technical equipment could all too easily be reflected in more complex technical descriptions. I have tried to avoid falling into this trap, for it would defeat the original purpose of the book, which is to explain the subject simply, in terms acceptable both to the creative people in production—including writers and performers—and to those who, more technically orientated, deal with the balance and recording of sound and with its engineering aspects. By exploring the ground common to both groups, the work of each may be interpreted to the other.

Much of this account is derived from over thirty years' experience of radio, television and film-making for Britain's public service broadcaster, the BBC.

The BBC's range of output (central, regional and local) has helped to create a body of techniques that is probably unique. Both the knowledge available to me and the opportunity to put it into practice have been as great as—indeed, possibly greater than—might have been provided in any other broadcasting organization or, for that matter, place of learning. This direct experience has been augmented by study of the many technical and operational information sheets that are available within an organization the size of the BBC: to their many (often anonymous) authors I am deeply indebted, as well as to the many individuals whose specialized expert knowledge I have consulted in a variety of fields. Where something is a matter of opinion, it is usually my own. In other cases the book reflects either a consensus or the views of an individual whose judgement I trust. For their help with this edition I offer particular thanks to Derek Taylor (operational techniques used in radio), Adrian Revill (quadraphonics), Geoff Higgs (videotape editing) and Chris Woolley (film editing).

This book assumes a need and a desire for high standards, both of technique and programme content. These may be attained with apparent ease within the large network where there is time and money to spend, but some might question whether a knowledge and understanding of these high standards is also of value at the ground-roots level—for example, in a small-town one-studio radio station with a transmitter on a rack in the corner. In my own view it is, because high-quality work sets a standard by which all else may be measured. Sometimes, particularly for the free-lance, it may make all the difference between success and failure: if you want to sell a product it helps if the quality is as high as the buyer can achieve by his own efforts. High standards are not only a matter of having good equipment; just as important is knowing how to use it.

The basic approach of this book has remained unaltered since the first edition: the emphasis has always been on general prin-ciples rather than rule-of-thumb, though the shorter routes to high quality results are not neglected. It still insists on the paramount importance of subjective judgment—of learning to use the ears properly. Above all else, the sound man needs well-developed aural perception that is allied to a strong critical faculty. So studio and location techniques are described in terms of what each operation does to the sound and why—and *what to listen for*.

Of all the chapters in this book, that which has changed least is the last, on communication itself. Happily, in the years since it was first written neither the scientific study of this human capacity nor the evolution of the media themselves have invalidated the observations made then. In one college the students are recom-mended to read that last chapter first. From another came the suggestion that it should be extended . . . But that would be another story.

13

Wee have also Sound-Houses, *wher wee practise and demonstrate all* Sounds, *and their* Generation. *Wee have* Harmonies *which you have not, of* Quarter-Sounds, *and lesser* Slides *of* Sounds. *Diverse* Instruments *of* Musick *likewise to you unknowne, some* sweeter *then any you have; Together with* Bells *and* Rings *that are dainty and sweet. Wee represent* Small Sounds *as* Great *and* Deepe; *Likewise* Great Sounds, Extenuate *and* Sharpe; *Wee make diverse* Tremblings *and* Warblings *of* Sounds, *which in their* Originall *are* Entire. *Wee represent and imitate all* Articulate Sounds *and* Letters, *and the* Voices *and* Notes *of* Beasts *and* Birds. *Wee have certaine* Helps, *which sett to the* Eare *doe further the* Hearing *greatly. Wee have also diverse* Strange *and* Artificiall Eccho's, Reflecting *the* Voice *many times, and as it were* Tossing *it; And some that give back the* Voice Lowder *then it came, some* Shriller, *and some* Deeper; *Yea some rendring the* Voice, Differing *in the* Letters *or* Articulate Sound, *from that they receyve. Wee have also meanes to convey* Sounds *in* Trunks *and* Pipes, *in strange* Lines, *and* Distances.

From *The New Atlantis* by Francis Bacon
1624

1

THE SOUND MEDIUM

SOME readers of this book will already have a clear understanding of what sound is. Others will know very little about the physics of sound, and will not wish to know, their interest being solely in how to use the medium. 'Do you have to know how paint is made to be an artist?' they might ask.

These two groups of readers can skip this chapter and go straight on to read about the operational techniques, the creative applications, and the practical problems and their solutions which are the main theme of this book.

The non-technical reader should have no difficulty in picking up as much as he needs to know as he goes along (perhaps with an occasional glance at the glossary). In other chapters most of the terms used are either understandable from their context, or are defined as they first appear. But for the sake of completeness, and for those who prefer their raw materials—or ideas—to be laid out in an orderly fashion before they begin, this chapter gives a brief introduction to the physics of sound.

The nature of sound

Sound is caused by vibrating materials. If a panel of wood vibrates, the air next to it is pushed to and fro. If the rate of vibration is somewhere between tens and tens of thousands of excursions per second the air has a natural elasticity which we do not find at slower speeds. Wave your hand backward and forward once a second and the air does little except get out of its way; it does not bounce back. But if you could wave your hand back and forth a hundred times every second the air would behave differently. It would have no time to get out of the way. Instead, it would compress as the surface of the hand moved forward, and rarefy as it moves back. In such circumstances the natural

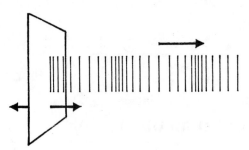

SOUND WAVE. A vibrating panel generates waves of pressure and rarefaction: sound. A tuning fork is often used for this demonstration, but in fact tuning forks do not make much noise—they slice through the air without moving it. A vibrating panel is more efficient.

elasticity of the air takes over. As the surface moves forward, each particle of air pushes against the next, which pushes against the next in turn, so creating a pressure wave. As the surface moves back, the pressure wave is replaced by a rarefaction, and that is followed by another pressure wave, and so on.

It is a property of elastic media that a pressure wave passes through them at a speed that is a characteristic of the particular medium. The speed of sound in air depends on its temperature as well as the nature of air. In normal conditions sound travels about 1120 feet in a second (about 340 metres per second).

This speed is independent of the rate at which the surface generating the sound moves backwards and forward. The example was 100 excursions per second, but it might equally have been 20 or 20000. This rate at which the pressure waves are produced is called the *frequency*, and is measured in cycles per second, now usually called *hertz*; $1 \text{ Hz} = 1 \text{ c/s}$.

Let us return to that impossibly energetic hand shaking back and forth at 100 Hz. It is clear that it is not a perfect sound source: some of the air slips round the sides as the hand moves in each direction. To stop this happening with a fluid material like air the sound source would have to be much larger. Something the size of a piano sounding board would be much more efficient, losing far less round the edges. But if a hand-sized vibrator vibrates a great deal faster the air simply does not have time to get out of the way. For very high frequencies, even tiny surfaces are efficient radiators of sound.

In real life sounds are produced by sources of all shapes and sizes that may sometimes vibrate in extremely complicated ways. In addition, the pressure waves bounce off any reflecting surfaces. Many sources and many reflections combine to create a complex field of intersecting paths. How are we to describe, let alone reproduce, such a tangled skein or sound? It seems impossible.

But consider a single air particle somewhere in the middle of this. The various pressure waves passing by cause it to move in various directions, to execute a dance that faithfully describes every characteristic of all of the sounds passing through. All we need to know to be able to describe the sound at that point is what such a single particle is doing. Its size is not critical so long as it is small compared with the separation of the successive pressure waves that cause the movement. We do not have to go *very* small; rather, we want to measure an average movement that is sufficiently gross to even out all the random tiny vibrations of the molecules of air—just as the diaphragm of the ear does.

What is so delightfully simple about sound is not what happens at each end of the chain, the production of the sound and its perception by the brain, but what happens in the middle. All we need to know about sound is stored in the motion of a single particle, complex though that motion may be. For it is such a single particle that presses against each of our eardrums.

Consideration of the ear leads us to another simplification. A single ear does not bother with all the different directional movements of the air particle; it simply measures the air pressure, which leads us to the idea that a continuously operating pressure-measuring device with a diaphragm approaching the size of the eardrum would be a good instrument for describing just about all we need to know about sound in practical audio-engineering terms. Slightly more complex calculations (involving wavelengths, etc.) confirm this, as does practical experience. For what we have described is the first requirement of a high-quality microphone.

Wavelength

Pressure waves of a sound travel at a fixed speed for a given medium in given conditions, and if we know the frequency of a sound (the number of waves per second) we can calculate the distance between corresponding points on successive waves—the *wavelength*.

Taking the speed of sound to be 1120 ft per second (340 m/sec), a sound frequency of 1120 Hz (or cycles per second) has a wavelength of one foot (about 30 cm). Sometimes it is more convenient to think in terms of frequency and sometimes wavelength.

Because the speed of sound varies to a small degree with air temperature, any relationship between wavelength and frequency that does not take this into account is only approximate. But for most practical purposes, such as calculating the thickness of

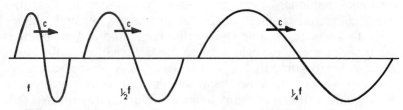

FREQUENCY AND WAVELENGTH. All sound waves travel at the same speed, c, through a given medium, so frequency, f, is inversely proportional to wavelength, λ.

sound absorber needed to absorb a particular range of frequencies, or estimating whether a microphone diaphragm is small enough to 'see' very high frequencies, an approximate relationship is adequate. Particular frequencies also correspond to the notes of the musical scale:

Note on piano	Frequency (Hz)	Wavelength	
—	14,080	1 in	(2·5 cm)
$\overline{\overline{A}}^{iii}$	7,040	2 in	(5 cm)
A^{iii}	3,520	$3\frac{3}{4}$ in	(9·5 cm)
A^{ii}	1,760	$7\frac{1}{2}$ in	(19 cm)
A^{i}	880	1 ft 3 in	(38 cm)
A	440	2 ft 6 in	(75 cm)
A_{i}	220	5 ft	(1·5 m)
A_{ii}	110	10 ft	(3 m)
A_{iii}	55	20 ft	(6 m)
A_{iv}	27·5	40 ft	(12 m)

The velocity of sound is taken to be 1100 ft/sec (335 m/sec) as it may be in cool air. N.B. metric equivalents (and shorter wavelengths) are approximate only.

The first thing to notice from this is the very great range in sheer physical size these different frequencies represent. Two octaves above the top A of the piano the wavelength is 1 in (25 mm). As it happens this is about the upper limit of human hearing; and the corresponding size is reflected (indirectly) in the dimensions

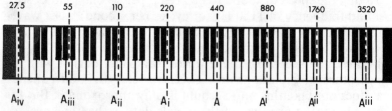

PIANO KEYBOARD. Note and frequency of fundamental.

18

of high-quality microphones. At the lower end of the scale we have wavelengths of 40 ft (12 m). The soundboard of a piano can generate such a sound, though not so efficiently as the physically much larger pipes in the lower register of an organ.

The second point to notice (and the reason for the first) is that for each equal interval, a rise of one octave, there is a doubling of frequency (and halving of wavelength).

Much less obvious is the fact that as the pitch of a sound depends on the size of the object making it, and that size remains nearly constant as temperature increases, then because the velocity of sound is increasing, the pitch goes up. The strings of violins can be tuned, but the vibrating column of air in most wind instruments cannot. So a flute, for example, sharpens by a semitone as the temperature goes up 15° C.

Waves and phase

Still considering a pure, single-frequency tone, we can define a few other variables and see how they are related to the pressure wave.

First we have *particle velocity*, the rate of movement of individual air particles. As this is proportional to air pressure, the waveforms for pressure and velocity are similar in form. But not only that: where one has a peak the other has a peak; where there is no excess of pressure, there is no velocity, and so on. The two waveforms are said to be *in phase* with each other.

The next variable is *pressure gradient*; the rate at which pressure changes with distance along the wave. Plainly, this must have a waveform derived from that of pressure, but where the pressure is at a peak (maximum or minimum) its rate of change is zero. Again it turns out that the waveform is the same, but this time it has 'moved' a quarter of a wavelength to one side. The two waveforms are said to be a quarter of a wavelength *out of phase*.

Another variable, again with a similar waveform, is that for *particle displacement*. This is a graph showing how far a particle of air has moved to one side or the other of its equilibrium position. (This is, in fact, the equivalent in sound of the wave we see on a water surface.) Displacement is proportional to pressure gradient, and is therefore in phase with it. It is directly related to *amplitude*.

These terms are all encountered in the theory of microphones. For example, most microphones are *constant-velocity* or *constant-amplitude* in operation. These names are confusing: they actually mean that the electrical output of the microphone is equal to a

19

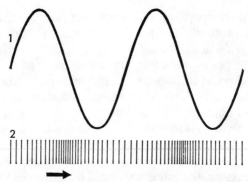

WAVES. 1. Sound waves are usually represented diagrammatically as lateral waves, as this is convenient for visualizing them. It also shows the characteristic regularity of the simple harmonic motion of a pure tone. Distance from the sound source is shown on the horizontal axis, and displacement of individual air particles from their median position is shown on the vertical axis. 2. As the particles are actually moving backwards and forwards along the line that the sound travels, the actual positions of layers of particles are arranged like this. It also shows the travel of pressure waves.

constant *multiplied by* the diaphragm velocity, or to a constant *multiplied by* the displacement amplitude. Constant-velocity microphones include moving-coil and ribbon types; constant-amplitude microphones include electrostatic and crystal varieties. From the point of view of the operator these descriptions are not particularly important: there are high- and low-quality microphones in both categories; the terms are mentioned here only because they may be met in manufacturers' literature. They are, of course, important to the microphone design or service engineer. A great deal more will, however, be heard of pressure

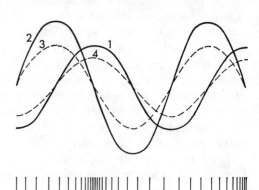

WAVEFORM RELATION-SHIPS. 1. Pressure wave. 2. Displacement wave. 3. Pressure gradient. 4. Particle velocity.

and pressure-gradient modes of operation, as these character-istics of microphones lead to important differences in the way they can be used.

The phase of the signal as it finally appears in the microphone output is clearly not always the same as that of the sound pressure measured by the ear. Fortunately the ear is not usually interested in phase, so it does not generally matter whether a microphone measures the air pressure or pressure gradient.

The only problem that might occur is when two signals very similar in form but different in phase are combined. In an extreme case, if two equal pure tones exactly half a wavelength out of phase are added together the output is zero. Normally, however, sound patterns are so complex that microphones of completely different types that are sufficiently far apart may be used in the same studio, and their outputs mixed, without too much danger of the differences of phase having any noticeable effect.

So far we have considered simple tones. If several are present together a single particle of air can still only be in one place at one time: the displacements are added together. If many waves are superimposed the particle performs the complex dance that is the result of adding all of the wave patterns. Not all of this adding

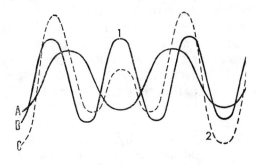

ADDING SOUND PRES-SURES. At any point the sound pressure is the sum of the pressures due to all waves passing through that point. If the simple waves A and B are summed this results in the pressure given by the curve C. 1. Here there is partial cancel-lation. 2. Here the peaks reinforce. The resultant curve is more complex than the original.

together actually results in increased pressure. At a point where a pressure wave is superimposed on a rarefaction the two—opposite in phase at that point—tend to cancel each other out.

Energy, intensity and resonance

There are one or two more concepts that we need before going on to consider the mechanics of music.

First, the *energy* of a sound source. This depends on the ampli-tude of vibration: the broader the swing, the more *power* (energy

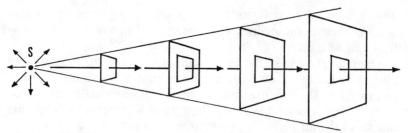

SOUND INTENSITY is the energy passing through unit area per second. For a spherical wave (i.e. a wave from a point source) the intensity dies away very rapidly at first. The power of the sound source S is the total energy radiated in all directions.

output per second) it can produce. The sound *intensity* at any point is then measured as the acoustic energy passing through unit area per second. But to convert the energy of the sound source to acoustic energy in the air we have to ensure that the sound source is properly coupled to the air, that its own vibrations are causing the air to vibrate with it. Objects that are small (or slender) compared with the wavelength in air associated with their frequency of vibration (tuning forks and violin strings) are able to slice through the air without giving up much of their energy to it: the air simply slips around the sides of the prong or the string.

If a tuning fork is struck and then suspended loosely it goes on vibrating quietly for a long time. If, however, its foot is placed on a panel of wood the panel is forced into vibration in sympathy and can transmit to the air. The amplitude of vibration of the tuning fork then goes down as its energy is lost (indirectly) to the air.

If the panel's natural frequency of vibration is similar to that of the tuning fork the energy is transferred and radiated much faster. In fact, wooden panels fixed at the edges may not appear to have clear specific frequencies at which they resonate: if you tap them they do not usually make clear musical sounds, but instead rather dull ones, though with perhaps some definable note seeming to predominate. In the violin the wooden panels are very irregular, to ensure that over a whole range of frequencies no single one is emphasized at the expense of others. The string is bowed but transmits little of its energy to the air. Instead, it is transferred through the bridge that supports the string to the wooden radiating belly of the instrument.

At this stage an interesting point arises: the radiating panels are not only much smaller in size than the strings themselves but also considerably smaller than some of the wavelengths (in air) that the strings are capable of producing. The panels might respond well

22

enough to the lowest tones produced, but they are not big enough to radiate low frequencies efficiently. And this leads us to consider several further characteristics of music and musical instruments.

Overtones, harmonics, and formants

Overtones are the additional higher frequencies that are produced along with the *fundamental* when something like a violin string or the air in an organ pipe is made to vibrate.

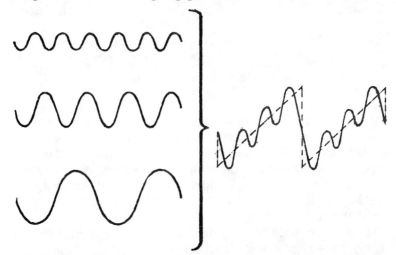

COMPLEX WAVEFORMS. Pure tones may be added together to produce a composite form. In this case the first two overtones (the second and third harmonics) are added to a fundamental. If an infinite series of progressively higher harmonics were added, the resultant waveform would be a 'saw-tooth'. When the partials are related harmonically, the ear hears a composite sound having the pitch of the fundamental and a particular sound quality due to the harmonics. But when the pitches are unrelated or the sources are spatially separated the ear can generally distinguish them readily: the ear continuously analyses sound into its components.

On some instruments, such as bells, it may be a problem in manufacture to get the principal overtones to have any musical relationship to each other (the lowest note of a bell is not even distinguished by the name of fundamental). In drums, the fundamental is powerful and the overtones add richness without harmonic quality, while from triangles or cymbals, there is such a profusion of tones that the sound blends reasonably well with almost anything.

On a string the overtones are all exact multiples of the fundamental, the lowest tone produced. It is this lowest tone which, as

23

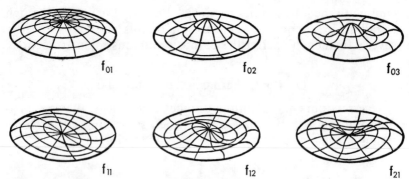

VIBRATION OF A DRUMSKIN (stretched circular membrane clamped at the edges). The suffixes refer to the number of radial and circular nodes (there is always a circular node at the edge of the skin). The overtones are not harmonically related. If $f_{01} = 100$ Hz, the other modes of vibration shown here are as follows: $f_{02} = 230$, $f_{03} = 360$, $f_{11} = 159$, $f_{12} = 292$, $f_{21} = 214$ Hz.

with most of the musical instruments, defines *pitch*. If the string were bowed in the middle the fundamental and odd harmonics would be emphasized, as these all have maximum amplitude in the middle of the string; and the even harmonics (which have a node in the middle of the string) would be lacking. But the string is, in fact, bowed near one end so that a good range of both odd and even harmonics are excited.

There is one special point here: if the string is bowed at approximately one-seventh of its length it will not produce the seventh

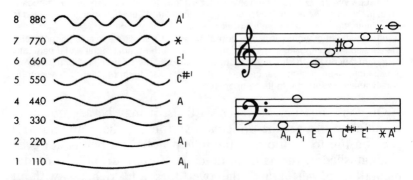

THE FIRST EIGHT STRING HARMONICS. (The fundamental is the first harmonic; the first overtone is the second harmonic, etc.) They are all notes in the key of the fundamental, except for the seventh harmonic which is not a recognized note on the musical scale (it lies between G′ and G″). If the violinist bows at the node of this harmonic (at one seventh of the length of the vibrating string) the dissonance is not excited. The eleventh harmonic (another dissonant tone) is excited, but is in a region where the tones are beginning to cluster together to give a brilliant effect.

harmonic. So this is a good point at which to bow, because as it happens the seventh harmonic is the first that is not musically related to the rest—though the sixth and eighth are both members of the same musical family, and there are also higher harmonics produced in rich profusion to give a dense tonal texture high above the fundamental. These are all characteristics of what we call string quality, irrespective of the instrument.

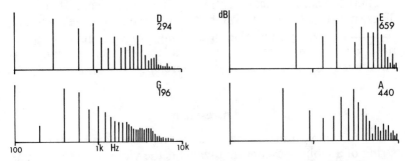

THE OPEN STRINGS OF THE VIOLIN: relative intensities of the harmonics. The structure of the resonator ensures a very wide spread—but is unable to reinforce the fundamental of the low G, for which it is physically too small. Note that there is a difference in quality between the lowest string (very rich in harmonics) and the highest (relatively thin in tone colour).

The quality of the instrument itself—violin, viola, 'cello or bass —is defined by the qualities of resonator; and most particularly by its size. But clearly, the shape and size of the resonator superimposes on the string quality its own special *formant* character-

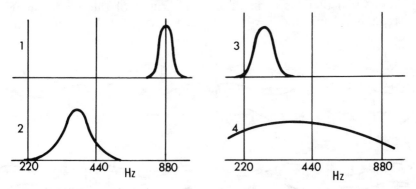

INSTRUMENTAL FORMANTS. 1. Oboe. 2. Horn. 3. Trombone. 4. Trumpet. The formants, imposed by the structural dimensions of parts of the instruments, may be broad or narrow. They provide an essential and recognizable component of each instrument's musical character.

25

istics. Some frequencies, or range of frequencies, are always emphasized; others are always discriminated against. Formants are very important: obviously, in music they are a virtue, but in audio equipment the same phenomenon might be called 'an uneven frequency response' and would be regarded as a vice—unless it were known, calculated and introduced deliberately with creative intent.

There are many other essential qualities of musical instruments. These may be associated with the method of exciting the resonance (bowing, blowing, plucking, or banging); or with qualities of the note itself, such as the way it starts (the *attack*) or changes in volume as the note progresses (its *envelope*).

Air resonance

Air may have dimensional resonances very much like those of a string of a violin—except that whereas the violin string has transverse waves, those in air, being composed of compressions and rarefactions, are longitudinal. And whereas radiating sound moves through the air forming *progressive waves*, dimensional resonances stand still: they form *stationary waves*.

These stationary or standing waves can again be represented diagrammatically as transverse waves, though here the waveform chosen is usually that for displacement amplitude. At *nodes* (e.g. at solid parallel walls if the resonance is formed in a room) there is no air-particle movement. At *antinodes* (e.g. half-way between the walls) there is a maximum movement of the air swinging regularly back and forth along the particular dimension con-

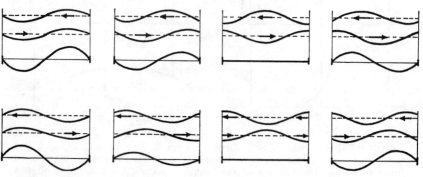

STATIONARY WAVE formed from progressive waves moving in opposite directions.

cerned. Harmonics may also be present. *Standing waves* are caused when any wave strikes a reflecting surface at right angles and travels back along the same path.

The air in a narrow pipe (such as an organ pipe) can be made to

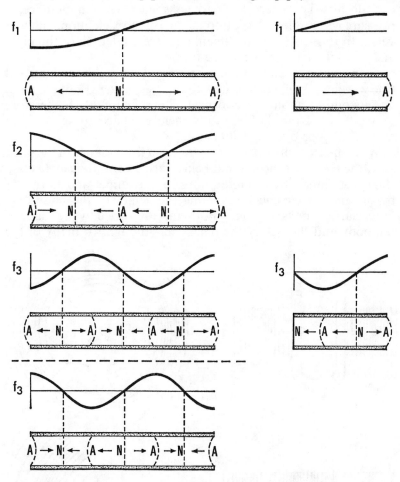

VIBRATION OF AIR COLUMNS. *Left.* For an open pipe, f_1, the fundamental frequency, is twice the length of the pipe. There is a node N at the centre of the pipe and antinodes at the open ends. The second and third harmonics are simple multiples of the fundamental: $f_2 = 2f_1$; $f_3 = 3f_1$, etc. *Left below.* The third harmonic, half a cycle later. Air particles at the antinodes are now moving in the opposite direction, but the air at the nodes remains stationary. *Right.* A pipe closed at one end (i.e. stopped). The wavelength of the fundamental is four times the length of the pipe. The first overtone is the third harmonic; only the odd harmonics are present in the sound from a stopped pipe: f, $3f$, $5f$, etc. In both types of pipe most of the sound is reflected back from an open end for all frequencies where the aperture is small compared with the wavelength.

resonate. If it were closed at both ends there would be reflections, as at any other solid surface. But if the pipe is open at the ends resonance can still occur. In a tube that is narrow in comparison with the wavelength the sound has difficulty in radiating to the outside air. The energy has to go somewhere: in practice, a pressure wave reflects back into the tube as a rarefaction, and vice versa. In this case the fundamental (twice the length of the pipe) and all of its harmonics may be formed.

If one end is open and the other closed, only the fundamental (the wavelength of which is now four times the length of the tube) and its odd harmonics are formed. The tone quality is therefore very different from that of a fully enclosed space, or again, from that of the pipe open at both ends.

Wind instruments in the orchestra form their sounds in the same way, the length of the column being varied continuously (as in a slide trombone), by discrete jumps (e.g. trumpet and horn), or by opening or closing holes along the length of the body (e.g. flute, clarinet, or saxophone). Formants are varied by the shape of the body and the bell at the open end—though for many of the

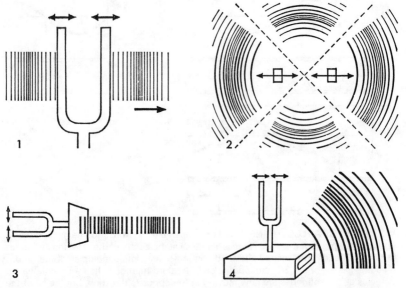

TUNING FORK. 1 and 2. Each fork vibrates at a specific natural frequency, but held in free air radiates little sound. 3. Placed on a wooden panel, the vibrations of the tuning fork are coupled to the air more efficiently and the fork is heard clearly. 4. Placed on a box having a cavity with a natural resonance of the same frequency as the tuning fork, the sound radiates powerfully.

notes in instruments with finger holes the bell makes little difference, as most of the sound is radiated from the open holes.

Another important way in which air resonance may govern pitch is where a volume of air is almost entirely enclosed and is connected to the outside through a neck. Such a device is called a *cavity* or *Helmholtz resonator*. It produces a sound of a single, distinct frequency, an example being the note obtained by blowing across the mouth of an empty bottle. In a violin the cavity resonance falls within the useful range of the instrument and produces a 'wolf-tone' that the violinist has to treat with care, bowing it a great deal more gently than other notes. Going back to the example of the tuning fork, boxes may be made up with volumes that are specific to particular frequencies. These make the best resonators of all—but each fork requires a different box.

The voice

The human voice is a great deal more versatile than any musical instrument. This versatility lies not so much in the use of the vocal cords to vary pitch as in the use of the cavities of the mouth, nose, and throat to impose variable formant characteristics on the sounds already produced. It is as though a violin had five resonators, several of which were continuously changing in size, and one (the equivalent of the mouth) so drastically as to completely change the character of the sound from moment to moment.

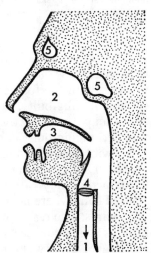

VOCAL CAVITIES. 1. The lungs. 2. The nose. 3. The mouth. This is the most readily flexible cavity, and is used to form vowel sounds. 4. The pharynx, above the vocal cords. 5. Sinuses. These cavities produce the formants characteristic of the human voice, emphasizing certain frequency bands at the expense of others.

These formant characteristics, based on cavity resonance, are responsible for vowel sounds and are the main vehicle for the intelligibility of speech. Indeed, sometimes they are used almost on their own.

For the effect of robot speech the formants are extracted from the human voice or simulated by a computer and used to modulate some simple continuous sound, the exact nature of which is chosen to suggest the 'personality' of the particular machine producing the sound. (In practice, it is a great deal cheaper to use a real voice as the original.)

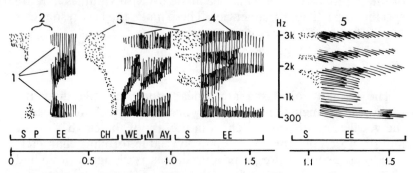

HUMAN SPEECH analyzed to show formant ranges. 1. Resonance bands. 2. Pause before plosive. 3. Unvoiced speech. 4. Voiced speech. These formants arise from resonance in nose, mouth and throat cavities. They are unrelated to the fundamental and harmonics, which are shown in the second analysis of the word 'see'. 5. The vocal harmonics are falling as the voice is dropped at the end of the sentence. But the resonance regions are rising as the vocal cavities are made smaller for the 'ee' sound.

In addition to the formants, a number of other devices are used in speech: these include sibilants and stops of various types which, together with the formant resonances, provide all that is needed for high intelligibility. A whisper, in which the vocal cords are not used, may be perfectly clear and understandable; in a stage whisper intelligibility carries well despite lack of vocal power.

The vibrations produced by the vocal cords add volume, further character, and the ability to produce song. For normal speech the fundamental may vary over a range of about twelve tones and is centred somewhere near 145 Hz for a man's voice and 230 Hz for a woman's. The result of this is that, as the formant regions differ little, the female voice has less harmonics in the regions of stronger resonance; so a woman may have a deep-toned voice, but its quality is likely to be thinner (or purer) than a man's.

For song the fundamental range of most voices is about two octaves—though, exceptionally, it can be much greater.

The human ear

The part of the ear that senses sound is a tiny spiral structure called the cochlea. It is a structure which gets narrower to one end of the coil, like the shell of a snail. But unlike the shell, it is divided lengthways into two galleries which join only at the narrow 'inside' end. The entire structure is filled with fluid to which vibrations may be transmitted through a thin membrane or diaphragm called the oval window. The acoustic pressures may then travel down one

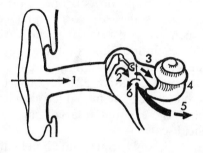

THE EAR. 1. Sound enters via the outer ear and the auditory canal. This channel has a resonance peak in the region 3–6 kHz. At the end of the auditory canal is the eardrum, which vibrates in sympathy with the sound but is not well adapted to following large low-frequency excursions. 2. The sound is transported mechanically from the eardrum across the middle ear via three small bones which form an impedance matching device converting the acoustic energy of the air to a form suitable for transmission through the fluid of the tiny delicate channels of the inner ear. The middle ear contains air: this permits the free vibration of the ear drum, and avoids excessive damping of the motion of the small bones. The air pressure is equalized through the eustachian tube, a channel to the nasal cavity. 3. The sound is pumped into the inner ear via a membrane called the oval window. 4. The inner ear is formed as a shell-like structure. There are two channels along the length of it, getting narrower until they join at the far end. Distributed along the upper channel are fine hairs which respond to particular frequencies: when the hair is bent, a nerve impulse is fired. The further the hair is along the canal the lower the frequency recorded. 5. A bundle of 4000 nerve fibres carries the information to the brain, where it is decoded. 6. Pressures in the cochlea are equalized at another membrane to the inner ear: the round window.

side of the dividing partition (the basilar membrane) and back down the other, to be lost at a further thin diaphragm, the round window.

All along one side of the basilar membrane are hairs that respond to movements in the surrounding fluid. Each hair standing

31

in this fluid acts as a resonator system designed to respond to a single frequency (or rather, a very sharply tuned narrow band). The hairs therefore sense sound not as an air particle sees it, as a single, continuous, very complex movement, but as a very large number of individual frequencies. The hairs are so arranged as to give roughly equal importance to equal musical intervals in the middle and upper middle ranges, but the separation is poor at very low frequencies: it is difficult to distinguish between very low pure tones. So (apart from indicating this lack of interest in low notes) a study of the mechanism of hearing confirms that we were right to be concerned with intervals that are calculated by their ratios rather than on a linear scale.

Growth of this sort is called *exponential*: it doubles at equal intervals, and a simple graph of its progress rapidly runs out of paper unless the initial stages are so compressed as to lose all detail. To tame such growth, mathematicians use a *logarithmic* scale, one in which each doubling is allotted equal space on the graph. The frequencies corresponding to the octaves on a piano progress in the ratios $1:2:4:8:16:32:64:128$ (see page 18). The logarithms of these numbers are in a much simpler progression— $0,1,2,3,4,5,6,7$—and these equal intervals are exactly how we perceive the musical scale.

Frequency is not the only thing that the ear measures in this way: changes of sound volume follow the same peculiar rule.

Sound volume and the ear

The hairs on the basilar membrane vibrate in different degrees, depending on the loudness of the original sound. And they, too, measure this not by equal increases of sound intensity but by *ratios* of intensity: each doubling of intensity sounds roughly as loud again as the last. It is therefore convenient once again to use a logarithmic scale, and the measure that is used is the *decibel*, or dB. This is based on a unit called the bel, which corresponds to a tenfold increase or decrease. But the bel is inconveniently large, as the ear can detect smaller changes, and it is because of this that an interval a tenth of the size—the decibel—has been adopted.

The ratio of intensities in 1 decibel is about $1\cdot26:1$. ($1\cdot26$ is approximately the tenth root of 10.) This is just about as small a difference in intensity as the human ear can detect in the best possible circumstances.

As it happens, the ratio of intensities in 3 dB is $2:1$. This is convenient to remember, because if we double up a sound source we double the intensity (at a given distance). So if we have one soprano bawling her head off and another joins her singing equally loudly the sound level will go up 3 dB (not all that much more than the minimum detectable by the human ear). But to raise the level by another 3 dB two more sopranos are needed. Four more are needed for the next 3 dB—and so on. Before we get very far we are having to add sopranos at a rate of 64 or 128 a time to get any appreciable change of volume out of them. To increase intensity by increasing numbers soon becomes very expensive: if volume is the main thing you want it is better to *start* with something more powerful such as a pipe organ, a trombone, or a bass drum!

Loudness, frequency and human hearing

The ear does not measure the volume of all sounds by the same standards. Although for any particular frequency the changes in volume are heard more or less logarithmically, the ear is more sensitive to changes of volume in the middle and upper frequencies than in the bass.

The range of hearing is about 20–20 000 Hz for a young person; but the upper limit falls with age to 15 000 or 10 000 Hz. Sensitivity is greatest at 1000 Hz and above: the auditory canal between the outer ear and the eardrum helps here by having a broad resonance in the region of 2000–6000 Hz.

Obviously *loudness* (a subjective quality) and the measurable

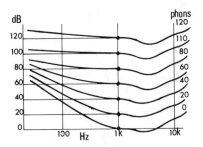 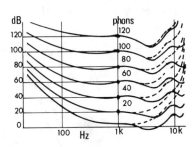

EQUAL LOUDNESS CONTOURS, measured for pure tones. *Left.* The classical curves of Fletcher and Munson, published in 1933. Intensity (decibels) equals loudness in phons at 1 kHz. *Right.* The curves measured by Robinson and Dadson take age into account and show marked peaks and dips in young hearing. The unbroken lines are for age 20; the broken lines show typical loss of high-frequency hearing at age 60. The lowest line in each case represents the threshold of hearing.

volume of a sound are not the same thing—but for convenience they are regarded as being the same at 1000 Hz. Perceived loudness in *phons* can then be calculated from actual sound volume by using a standard set of curves representing average human hearing.

Figures for such things as levels of *noise* are also *weighted* to take hearing into account. This may refer to electrical as well as acoustic noise. For example, some microphones produce more noise in the low-frequency range: this is of less importance than if the noise were spread evenly throughout the entire audio range.

The lower limit is called the *threshold of hearing*. It is convenient to regard the lower limit of good human hearing at 1000 Hz as zero on the decibel scale. There is no natural zero: absolute silence would be minus infinity decibels on any practical scale. The zero chosen corresponds to an acoustic pressure of 2×10^{-5} newtons per square metre.

The upper limit is set by the level at which sound begins to be physically felt—a *threshold of feeling* at around 100–120 dB.

The ear and audio engineering

At all times when we are dealing with the techniques of sound we will bear in mind the capability of the human ear. The objective measurements of the engineer are meaningless unless we interpret them in this way. When we fall short of what the ear can accept we should be aware of the fact and be able to give good reasons why. Usually the reason is that the difference in cost would be too great for the difference in subjective appreciation. For example, an individual may be happy to spend money on equipment with a frequency response substantially level to 20 000 Hz, but for a

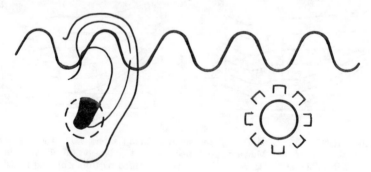

THE SHORTEST WAVELENGTH that young ears can hear defines the size of diaphragm that is needed for a high quality pressure microphone.

broadcasting organization this is too high. For most people hearing is at best marginal at 15 000 Hz; it is a waste of money to go above this figure—particularly as costs do not observe the same logarithmic law that the ear does. The octave between 10 000 and 20 000 Hz is by far the most expensive.

A microphone is simply a device for converting sound into electricity in such a way as to retain the information content. The simplest way of doing this is quite adequate: *changes in pressure become changes in voltage; the electrical waveform is the analogue of the acoustical waveform.*

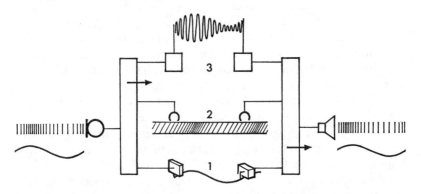

ELECTRICAL AND MECHANICAL ANALOGUES OF SOUND. Recording and transmission systems use analogues of the original sound wave. 1. Disc. 2. Tape. 3. AM radio.

In the microphone, sound intensity is converted directly to electrical energy. But energy is proportional to the square of the voltage, and it is generally the voltage that we are interested in: fluctuations in voltage are amplified and carry the audio signal.

One result is that the full range of audible sound between the thresholds of hearing and feeling, a ratio in sound intensities of a million million to one, is reduced dramatically—to a mere million to one—in the corresponding voltages. In terms of decibels it means that the 120 decibels of acoustic power, dB(A), are equivalent to only 60 decibels of voltage change, dB(V). Note that where the performance of microphones and other audio equipment is described in terms of 'decibels' that generally means dB(V), not dB(A).

The electrical signal derived from the sound can in turn be used to magnetize iron oxide particles on a moving strip of tape, or drive a cutter that physically inscribes a waveform on a disc.

35

But in these cases the exact waveform will not do. In the case of the disc, assuming that the amplitude of the middle frequencies is about right, the low frequencies would be too big and occupy too much space on the disc. Accordingly, they are reduced in amplitude. The high frequencies, on the other hand, would be of a size comparable to the tiny irregularities in the wall of the groove which are heard as noise. To improve the signal-to-noise ratio the high frequencies must be emphasized. Provided that these changes are the same for every record, there is no problem: the inverse characteristic is included in the amplifier of each record player, and the original signal is thereby reconstructed.

For tape, too, recording and reproducing characteristics are chosen that are suitable to the physical conditions of tape. Unfortunately, Britain and Continental Europe, on the one hand, and the United States and Japan, on the other, have adopted different standards, so that it is necessary when handling foreign tapes or equipment to ensure that the right characteristic is chosen. These are CCIR in Europe and NARTB in America.

For radio, amplitude-modulation transmission is given no special pre-emphasis—which is perhaps just as well, as the wavebands are so crowded together that the high frequencies often overlap. In frequency modulation, however, a true high-fidelity response is possible; but high-frequency pre-emphasis is used to combat noise, and once again this is compensated for in every receiver.

Note, however, that this book is not concerned with engineering aspects of the equipment used for recording or transmitting sound information except in so far as they affect operational techniques.

A special engineering problem that affects all aspects of operation is the efficient conversion of electrical signals back to sound energy—in other words, the design and construction of loudspeakers. Loudspeaker design (discussed briefly in Chapter 14) is probably the principal limiting factor in most sound systems, and should be studied by those with an interest in audio engineering, but is aside from the main theme of this book.

2

SOUND CONTROL

THROUGH years of intimate daily contact with the problems of the medium, through spending hours each day consciously and critically listening, the professional sound man in the radio or recording studio, or in television or film, builds a considerable body of aural experience. He becomes aware of subtleties and nuances of sound that make all the difference between an inadequate and a competent production, or between the competent and the exciting. He hears details that would pass unobserved by the untutored ear. At the same time he develops the ability to manipulate the equipment to mould sound into the shape that he requires.

The tools for recording sound continue to improve, and it becomes easier to acquire the basic skills; but because of this there is more that *can* be done. Microphones have become more specialized, creating new opportunities for their use. With tape, complex editing jobs can be tackled. Using lightweight portable recorders or tiny radio transmitters sound can be obtained from anywhere man can reach and many places he cannot.

The easy acquisition of tools, however, does not obviate the necessity for a well-trained ear. Each element in a production has an organic interdependence with the whole; every detail of technique contributes in one way or another to the final result; and in turn the desired end-product largely dictates the methods to be employed. This synthesis between means and end may be so complete that the untrained ear can rarely disentangle them—and even critics may disagree on how a particular effect was achieved. Faults of technique are nothing like so obvious as those of content. A good microphone balance in suitable acoustics, with the appropriate fades, pauses, mixing and editing can make all the difference to a radio programme—but at the end an appreciative listener's search for a favourable comment will probably land on some remark about the subject matter. Similarly, where the technique is faulty it is often, again, the content that is criticized. The sound man himself must develop a faculty for listening analytically to the operational aspects of a production, to judge technique independently of content while making it serve content.

In radio, television, or film the investment in equipment makes slow working unacceptable. Each recording, with its individual problems, has to be technically satisfactory on the first 'take'. And although each individual is concentrating on his own job, this is geared to that of the team as a whole. The major concern of everyone is to raise the programme material to its best possible standard and to catch it at its peak.

Studio operations

The operational side of sound studio work, or in the sound department of the visual media, includes:
1. Microphone balance: selecting suitable types of microphone and placing them to pick up the most satisfactory sound from the various sources, and, where this is desired, modifying the signal obtained.
2. Mixing: combining the output from microphones, tape or disc replay machines, echo device, remote studios, etc.
3. Control: ensuring that the programme level (i.e. volume in relation to the noise and distortion levels of the equipment used) is not too high or too low, and uses the medium—recording or radio transmission—efficiently.
4. Creating effects (called hand or spot effects) in the studio.
5. Playing tape and disc into programmes: this includes recorded effects, gramophone records, interviews and reports, pre-recorded sequences, etc.
6. Recording: ensuring that the resultant mixed sound gets on to the tape without any significant loss of quality.

In small American radio stations one additional responsibility may be added to this: supervising the operation of a transmitter which may also be housed in the studio area. Certain minimal technical qualifications are required.

The person responsible for balance, mixing, and control may be a balance engineer or programme engineer; in BBC radio is called a studio manager; in television may be a sound supervisor with sound assistants; in film, a sound recordist or, at the re-recording stage, a dubbing mixer. Although in many parts of the world the person doing some of these jobs is an engineer,

BBC experience indicates that in radio—and for some roles in other media—it is at least equally satisfactory to employ men and women whose training has been in other fields, because although the operator is handling technical equipment, the primary responsibilities are artistic.

Whatever his designation, the sound supervisor has an overall responsibility for sound studio operations and advises the producer on technical problems. Where sound staff are working away from the studio (e.g. on outside broadcasts or when filming on location), a higher standard of engineering knowledge is required. This is true also in small radio stations, where a maintenance engineer may not always be available. The sound man or woman in radio may also be responsible for recording items if no separate monitoring is required—though for complex recordings (and always in television) a separate recording engineer is employed. In film, recording is a primary function of the sound department around which all other activities revolve. The sound recordist may have one or several assistants: in radio these may deal with effects in the studio, and may play tapes and gramophone records. Assistants in television and film may also act as 'boomswingers', positioning microphones just out of the picture.

A convenient single term for all of these—and whether male or female—is 'sound man'.

The sound control room

In considering the layout of equipment that is needed for satisfactory sound control let us look first at the simplest case: the studio used for sound only, for radio or recording.

The nerve centre of any broadcast or recording is the control desk. It is here that all the different sound sources are mixed and controlled. In a live broadcast it is here that the final sound is put together; and it is the responsibility of the sound supervisor to see that no further adjustments of any sort are necessary before the signal leaves the transmitter (except, perhaps, for the occasional automatic operation of a limiter to protect the transmitter from overloading).

Apart from the microphones and control desk, the most important equipment in a studio is a high-quality loudspeaker system. For a radio or recording studio is not merely a room in which sounds are made and picked up by microphone; it is also a place where shades of sound are judged and a picture is created by ear.

So the main thing that distinguishes a 'studio' from any other place where microphone and recorder may be set up is that two acoustically separate rooms must be used; one where the sound may be created in suitable acoustics and picked up by microphone, and the other in which the mixed sound may be heard. This second room is often called the control room (although in BBC radio terminology it is a 'control cubicle': historically, the control room was a lines switching centre). Tape and disc reproducers, and the staff to operate them, are also in the control area, as are the producer or director (in BBC radio these two roles are combined) and the production secretary (who checks programme timing, etc.).

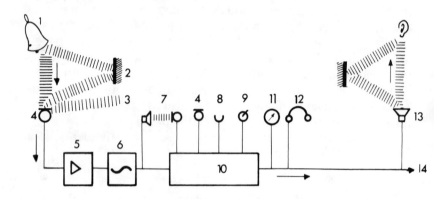

COMPONENTS OF THE STUDIO CHAIN, showing some of the symbols used in this book. 1. The sound source. 2. Direct and indirect sound paths. 3. Noise, unwanted sound. 4. Microphone. 5. Amplifier. 6. Equalizer. 7. 'Echo' path (artificial reverberation). 8. Tape head. 9. Record player. 10. Mixer. 11. Meter. 12. Headphones. 13. Loudspeaker: sound reaches the ear by direct and reflected paths. 14. Studio output.

In the simplest television studios, sound and picture are controlled side by side, but more often there is an acoustically separate sound room with much the same physical layout as it would have in a radio studio (except that it will have two picture monitors, one for programme and one for preview). The television sound supervisor does need to listen to programme sound in a separate cubicle because the director and his assistant must give a continuous stream of instructions on an open microphone, which means that their programme sound loudspeaker has to be set at a lower level than is necessary for the judgment of a good balance, and at times their voices obscure it. Their directions are relayed to the sound control room on an audio circuit, but at a reduced volume.

Studio layout for recording

It is no good finding a recording fault ten minutes after the artist has left the studio. So an important rule in studio work is that every recording must be monitored *from the tape* as it is being made. On the simplest recordings—straight talk programmes in which there are no cues to be taken—the operational staff can do both jobs, operating the recorder and monitoring the output from a separate replay head.

When the tape is monitored in this way, there is a delay of perhaps one-fifth of a second—3 i/s (7·5 cm/s)—between recording and reproducing heads at 15 i/s (38 cm/s) or two-fifths of a second at $7\frac{1}{2}$ i/s (19 cm/s). This delay makes it unsatisfactory to combine the two jobs when the programme has any degree of complexity. One-fifth of a second does not sound much—but in fact it can completely destroy the sound man's sense of timing. The perfect fade on a piece of music, for example, may have to be accurate to within one-twentieth of a second.

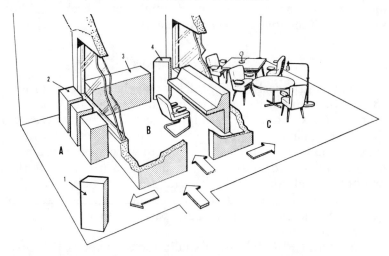

STUDIO LAYOUT FOR RECORDING. A. Recording room. B and C. Studio suite. All three sections are acoustically separate. Equipment includes: 1. Recording engineer's loudspeaker, reproducing output. 2. Tape recorders. 3. Disc and tape replay. 4. Loudspeaker for monitoring control, mixing, etc. (Small radio studio for magazine programme with interviews, etc.)

41

These requirements mean that there may be a third acoustically separate room in which the recording engineer can check the quality of the recorded sound. The most convenient plan is to group together the studio, control cubicle, and recording room as a suite. Many programmes use such an arrangement, rehearsing and recording section by section. Each few minutes of the programme is separately discussed, run through, and then recorded; and the results are edited together afterwards. This is quick, and for many pruposes the finished product is perfectly acceptable. An alternative arrangement is based on the idea that the dramatic contour of a programme is likely to have a better shape if it is fully rehearsed and then recorded as a whole, leaving any faults that occur to be corrected by retakes at the end. In this case a more economic arrangement is to divide studio time into two parts, with the recording session limited to a relatively short period. This technique is based on the way studio time is organized for live transmissions. In such cases the recording room may be remote from the studio.

There are various other possibilities, such as that commonly used for topical and miscellany programmes which go on the air in the form of a mixture of live and recorded segments. Here last-minute items are recorded in the control cubicle. The recording is monitored on headphones for an immediate check, and subsequently on the loudspeaker if time allows.

Sound control desks

Sound control desks used professionally have become progressively more complicated with time; and television desks are even more complex than those used in radio. This is partly because of the extra demands of vision; for example, movement within a single scene may require a performer to appear on a number of different microphones where in sound radio he might work to one only. In addition, television studios cannot be so specialized as those used in radio; a smaller number of very much more expensive studios must each be capable of producing a wider range of programmes.

In a typical BBC television studio the capacity of the mixing desk is conditioned by the number of possible sources—though not all will be used at once. There may be available some sixty microphones, four disc reproducing desks, two or three tape machines, a reverberation plate (and access to other echo devices), together

42

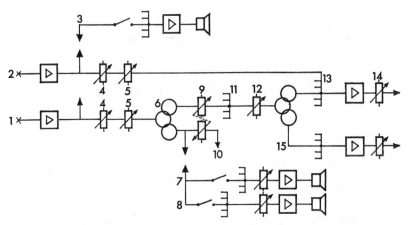

CONTROL DESK: FACILITIES ASSOCIATED WITH FADERS. 1. Normal microphone input. 2. Independent microphone (signal to be mixed in after group faders). 3. 'Prehear' side chain. 4. Microphone balance attenuator (preset). 5. Channel fader. 6. Hybrid transformer, splitting the signal. 7. Foldback side-chain to studio floor loudspeakers. 8. Public address side-chain to audience loudspeakers. 9. Echo mixture switch. 10. Echo feed. 11. Star mixer combining a group of sources. 12. Group fader. 13. Star mixer combining groups and independent sources. 14. Main gain control. 15. Clean feed chain (supplying feed of all groups except independents).

with many outside source lines. These will come from telecine and videotape sound reproducers, other studios, outside broadcasts (remotes), overseas circuits, the public telephone system, and so on. Radio has sources of all these types, though with less microphones and perhaps more disc and tape reproducers. As radio studios are more individually specialized, so, too, are their control desks. Most specialized of all is that used for popular music recording.

Much equipment is of modular construction, with units that can be used equally in radio, television or recording studio control consoles and for either mono or stereo. For each microphone there is a separate amplifier-fader channel which in some versions is very versatile and can be adjusted to accept sources that are intrinsically loud or faint, differing in their average levels by as much as 90 dB. Ancillary controls, most of which are mounted in line with their corresponding faders, provide a range of additional facilities. Where so indicated, these will be described in more detail in later chapters. They include:

Prehear. Before it is faded up as part of a programme mix, a remote source needs to be checked; so also does any microphone that has been replugged, knocked or has otherwise become suspect since

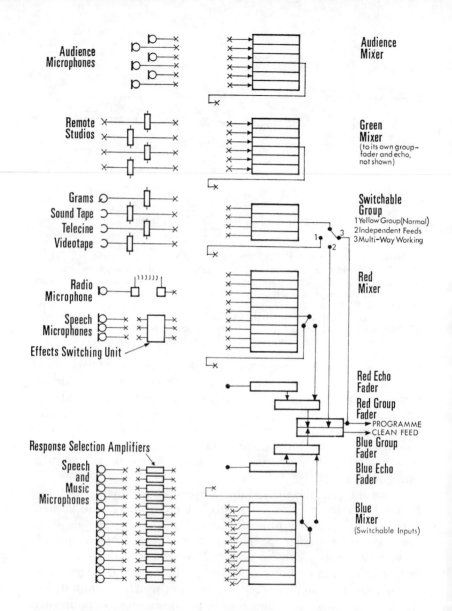

STUDIO SOURCES, SWITCHING AND CONTROL DESK. This would be a complex desk for a radio studio, but very simple for television. Note the elaborate facilities for cross-plugging (patching) which allows each source to be fed to any fader bank of the sound man's choice. In many cases the individual channel faders can be left at some chosen setting and controlled in groups. If the group faders are all close together it is possible to dispense with the main gain fader together with its associated amplifier.

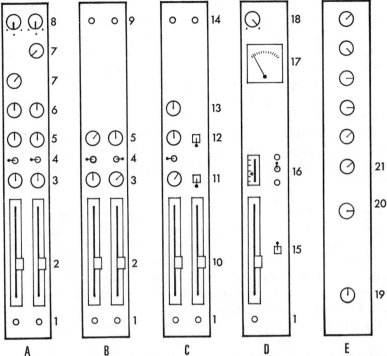

A   B   C   D   E

MODULAR UNITS FOR RADIO OR TELEVISION CONTROL DESK. Note that as each module carries two channels the basic units can be also modified for stereo sound, in which case the fader knobs will be clipped together in pairs. A. Individual source module (two channels). 1. Pre-hear buttons. 2. Slide faders. 3. Public address volume control. 4. Selector switch: public address feed before or after fader. 5. Foldback volume control. 6. Echo feed control. 7. Pre-set attenuator for coarse setting of volume from source. 8. Group selector switch. B. Group control (accepts all individual faders switched to it, plus group echo output). 1–5. Controls as for A. 9. Emergency change-over push button for group amplifier (using public address feed amplifier as spare). C. Master control module. 10. *Left.* Clean feed fader. 10. *Right.* Main fader. 11. Public address feed 'cut' switch. 12. Foldback feed 'cut' switch. 13. Pre-hear overall volume control. 14. *Left.* Main amplifier emergency change-over push-button. 14. *Right.* Split working push button—permits the two channels to operate independently, different groups being selected to each. In this condition the desk is working, in effect, as two separate control desks. D. Echo control module. 15. Echo 'cut' switch. 16. Echo plate controls (to change reverberation time), with scale. 17. Peak programme meter, indicating volume of signal sent to echo room or plate. 18. Switch selecting output from one of two groups as echo feed. E. Audience mixer. 19. Volume control for loudspeakers in audience area. 20. Group fader for audience microphones. 21. Six inexpensive faders for audience microphones. A–E represent only a selection of facilities available on a modern desk. Simpler desks often have rotary faders, turning clockwise to open, but there is no 'natural' preferred direction for a quadrant or slide fader. A practical solution to this design problem is for the fader to open as it is pulled forward: in this way the open channels are closer to hand, and closed faders are less easily knocked open. BBC designs have followed this practice, but in many commercial desks, the faders open up away from the operator.

a recording or broadcast began. Press-button operation allows such circuits to be sampled by feeding their output to an auxiliary loudspeaker. This facility is also called *prefade-listen* (PFL) or sometimes *prefade* (but this last term is ambiguous). Alternatively, a point is available before each fader at which headphones can be inserted to check that a circuit is available.

Echo mixture. A control sets the ratio of direct and echo feeds from each channel (see pp. 401–412).

Foldback. A switch (which may be preset and left) taps the output of the fader (in combination with any other selected individual or group faders) to provide a feed to a studio loudspeaker for cue (or possibly mood) purposes (see pp. 299, 428).

Public address. This, too, permits a feed to be taken from each channel, so that a selection of sources may be routed to loud-speakers in a studio audience area (see pp. 219–220, 428).

Prompt-cut. In television, it may sometimes be arranged that the output of one or several studio microphones can be interrupted by press-button from the studio floor by an assistant floor manager acting as a prompter. Performers should not need to rely on this and it should be used only as a last resort.

Stereo panning controls. These position an individual source within the stereo picture (see pp. 71–74).

Group selection. For convenience of handling, individual channels are gathered into groups, each controlled by its own group or sub-master fader. The groups are sometimes designated by different colours, such as yellow, green, red, blue, and orange. The group selection switches are used to choose the routing required for each individual channel. In music recording studios, group or individual faders are connected to recorders with 8, 16 or 24 parallel tape-tracks, or more if several recorders are synchronized. If the master (unmixed) tapes are retained, recordings initially designed for 2-channel stereo can later be remixed for quadraphony.

Independents. In radio and television desks, there is often provision for some of the channels to bypass all of the group faders or even the main control, in which case they can be used for *multiway working* with *clean feed* (see pp. 321–322).

Equalization (EQ). Most channels have controls permitting the modification of frequency response (see pp. 391–394, 397–398).

Effects units. These are sharp filters used to simulate telephone quality, public address, etc. (see p. 394). A television desk may also have a *telephone effects switching unit* linking the filters to the picture-switching buttons, ensuring that the telephone-quality sound is always associated with the out-of-vision end of a telephone conversation (see p. 395).

Compressors, limiters and expanders. These may be set to operate automatically upon the dynamic (i.e. volume) range of individual channels, groups or the fully mixed sound (see pp. 355–363).

Delay line. This is an electronic device for delaying the whole of the signal passed through it by designated intervals of time, typically in multiples of 7·5 milliseconds. Some digital delay systems are almost continuously variable (see pp. 412–414).

Flanger or phaser. The signal from a channel or group is routed through these in order to change the sound quality continuously by means of phase cancellation effects which sweep through the audio-frequency range. The effect is used as a pop music gimmick (see pp. 415–416).

Phase selection. A phase-reversing switch is provided on desks used for multimicrophone music recording. It can be used to alleviate cancellation effects that may occur when a sound is picked up on two microphones, and in any case, the more microphones there are in use, the more necessary it is to have an operationally simple system for checking phase. Out-of-phase effects may also be used deliberately.

Studios equipped for multitrack recording often have further specialized facilities that their radio and television counterparts can manage without. Every channel has an equalizer and a compressor/limiter, in addition to the normal control fader and echo feed. Then the signal is split. One part goes to the multitrack recorder, where it is retained until later, and the second undergoes further processing before being combined with other signals for monitoring. In the *monitoring circuits* each channel includes:

1. A switch to select the point at which the input to the monitoring circuit is taken.
2. A foldback fader (elaborate arrangements for fold-back to the headphones of players may be required in this type of balance).
3. The monitoring channel fader.
4. 'Solo' (sometimes called *afterfade-listen*, AFL) and 'cut' switches.
5. A second echo feed, using a separate echo system.

Soloing may be done in two ways: one diverts the channel to a separate monitoring loudspeaker, as for prefade-listening; the other suppresses the monitoring circuits of all channels but that selected. The purpose is to allow the balancer to assess the contribution of the selected channel, after treatment, and at the level that has been set. Cutting that single channel while leaving the rest of the balance intact serves a similar purpose.

This type of desk has stereo or quadraphonic panning controls (see next chapter), and these, too, operate on the monitoring circuits. *Computerized mixdown* (see p. 184) begins to be of benefit as the complexity of recording and mixdown grows.

Faders

The fader is the principal means of control provided by a mixer desk. It is the one item that is in continuous use, as the operator monitors the relative levels of the sounds from different sources, and at the same time keeps up a running compromise between the desire for a dramatic or natural contrast in levels and the need to make the best use of the medium by keeping the overall volume as high as possible—for example, by allowing the peaks of programme volume to reach full modulation of a radio carrier wave. (Volume control is discussed in Chapter 13.)

Certain types of fader are unsuited to professional use. Simple carbon-track and wire-wound resistors both rapidly become worn and subject to unpredictable crackles as the slide contact is moved. For many years, the only satisfactory high-quality alternative was a fader with separate studs that the sliders engaged in turn. Between each successive pair of studs there was a fixed network of resistors. Unfortunately, however, even with the most expensive faders it proved difficult to create studs and sliders with surfaces that always gave perfect contact, unaffected by dust, moisture, and other contaminants from the atmosphere. But a rare crackle or two seemed more than offset by the capacity for the precise setting of levels, stop by stop in stages of $1\frac{1}{2}$ or 2 dB. Further, with the advent of stereo these also provided exact matching between the two signals.

A very large number of geometric configurations of resistances is possible in stepped faders. Some of the simplest designs have been used in low-level mixers (i.e. those in which there is no preamplifier, or internal amplifiers compensating for the loss in the faders) but the results are unsatisfactory because as each additional channel is faded up it provides an alternative path for signals from the other sources. In consequence, the faders are not independent in operation: as fader 2 is brought up, there is a slight loss in signal 1, so that its fader must be adjusted to compensate.

48

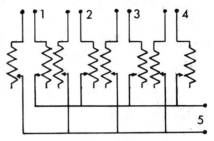

SIMPLE LOW LEVEL MIXER (an even simpler type has the fader on one wire only). 1–4. Inputs. 5. Output. One disadvantage of this layout is that the channels cannot be controlled independently: as fader 2 is opened, the signal on channel 1 finds an alternative path and is reduced.

This is undesirable in professional equipment where it is generally arranged that the channel faders present a constant, rather high resistance to other signals 'looking back' into them.

One such layout was the 'bridged-T'—which presented a constant impedance to the source and—as relatively high resistances were involved—it required more amplification in the circuit

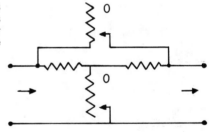

BRIDGED-T FADER. The two slides operate together: at O the fader is closed. Whatever the setting, the fader presents a constant impedance to the mixer.

than did simple faders. The bridged-T was combined with high-level mixing so that the chain consisted of microphone, preamplifier and channel fader—after which the signals from the mixers were combined to pass through the first of the main gain amplifiers, the main control, and then via the second main amplifier to the line out. In a later BBC design the fader contained two potentiometers with their operational ranges displaced, so that they were effective at different input levels. That used for most of the lower part of one fader's range was placed between two successive stages of the channel amplifier, so that for a high input signal there was no risk of the second stage overloading. The channel amplifier itself had variable gain, with the attenuation split in a complex way between the two stages.

The effect of this system—in the particular layout chosen—was to allow a control range of 90 dB by a combination of the fader itself (which in effect is continuously variable over a narrower

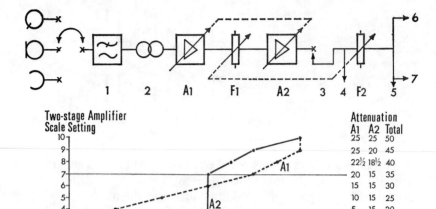

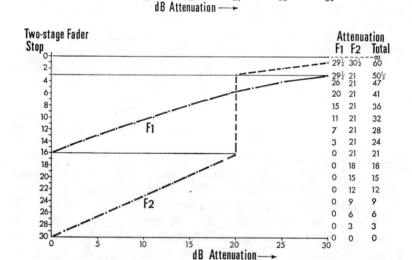

Two-stage Amplifier Scale Setting

Attenuation		
A1	A2	Total
25	25	50
25	20	45
22½	18½	40
20	15	35
15	15	30
10	15	25
5	15	20
0	15	15
0	10	10
0	5	5
0	5	0

Two-stage Fader Stop

Attenuation		
F1	F2	Total
29½	30½	∞
29½	21	60
26	21	50½
20	21	47
15	21	41
11	21	36
7	21	32
3	21	28
0	21	24
0	18	21
0	15	18
0	12	15
0	9	12
0	6	9
0	3	6
0	0	3
0	0	0

AMPLIFIER-FADER COMBINATION (A1–F1–A2–F2) used in BBC sound control desks. It is shown *(top)* in combination with other elements used with it in a microphone channel: 1. RF filter. 2. Balancing transformer. 3. Insertion jackfield (for response selection amplifier, compressor, limiter). 4. Public address and pre-hear feeds. 5. Public address, pre-hear and foldback feeds. 6. Echo feed. 7. Direct signal (to group fader). A1 and A2 are parts of a single amplifier. Attenuation is applied first to stage 2, then to stage 1, then to both together. The channel can accept both high-level and low-level sources. F1 and F2 are two tracks on a single quadrant fader: for a channel fader, F1 and F2 also operate at different settings, as shown. This extends still further the useful range of input levels that the channel will accept without distortion. But for group and main controls F1 and F2 both operate over the whole range of the fader.

50

range) and an amplifier which could be preset at 5 dB steps over a range of 50 dB. As a result, the same channel was used not only for an ordinary microphone picking up a sound of normal or low volume but also for the high-level signal from a tape or disc reproducer or outside-source line; or again, for anything in between, such as a high-level signal from a microphone balancing a trombone section or a bass drum.

In earlier BBC equipment 600 ohm junctions were used throughout, but this was abandoned in favour of high-impedance fader module outputs working in to low-impedance desk inputs: this meant that the operator could link any number of channels in to a group without appreciably affecting the levels in the circuit, and as a result the desk became more flexible.

The studs in faders that use them are separated by about $1\frac{1}{2}$ dB over the main working range, perhaps increasing to 2 dB over the lower half of the range, with broader spacing still for the two or three steps at the bottom end (to avoid too sharp a drop as the signal is cut off completely). A difference in level of $1\frac{1}{2}$–2 dB is only just appreciable on pure tones in the middle and upper middle frequency range, so nothing more precise than this is really necessary for ordinary working.

More recently, however, faders of professional quality have been made from conductive plastics or carbon compounds that do not produce the noise that marred the older types of continuous-track attenuators. It is now possible, therefore, to eliminate bulky precision resistance networks, together with the studs that have occasionally still caused crackle. These newer faders are somewhat less expensive, but they remain precision instruments: they must still, of course, be logarithmic; and it is essential that the components of a stereo signal can be controlled together, without image wobble. Note that the constant impedance requirement can also be dispensed with if the impedance of the faders is sufficiently high: fading up additional channels has no significant effect on the level of sound already being heard. The amplifiers associated with faders are as important as ever— but have become more compact and reliable.

Studio communications

In both radio and television there are sound circuits that are used for local communication only.

The use of headphones carrying an independent talkback

circuit between control cubicle and studio may help a recording session or radio transmission. Their use may range from the full-scale relaying of instructions (as occurs in television productions), through supplying a list of questions to an interviewer, to monitoring a feed of some separate event in order to give news of it. There may be both talkback (to the studio) and reverse talkback. The latter is an independent feed from the studio, sometimes associated with a microphone-cut key, so that a speaker can cut himself off the air and ask for information or instructions.

When a studio microphone is faded up it is usually arranged that the studio loudspeaker is cut off (except for talkback purposes during rehearsal). This can be done automatically by having a relay-operated switch that can be on only if all the faders are turned right out. Convenient though this arrangement is, it may mean that an artist in the studio does not hear the last second or so of his cue to speak. For most purposes this does not matter, but when the man in the studio is a regular broadcaster with a good sense of timing it is possible to dispense with signals (hand or light) and let him take his own cues—listening to the music or other recordings on headphones.

In television the complexity of the communication systems is much greater, partly because there are so many more people involved, each with a different job to do, and also because they need to occupy about half a dozen acoustically separate areas, including the studio itself and the main control gallery where the director sits and the vision is mixed. The director speaks to the floor manager over a local VHF radio circuit; the floor manager hears him on a deaf-aid type of single earphone; the cameramen and others in the studio hear him on headphones.

In his separate room the sound supervisor can hear high-level and high-quality programme sound. In addition, on a second much smaller loudspeaker (so that it is distinctly different in quality) he hears the director's instructions and reverse talkback from his own assistants on the studio floor.

Lighting and camera control also generally have a (third) acoustically separate area. They have their own talkback system to appropriate points on the studio floor; and cameramen in their turn have reverse talkback to them. In the control gallery itself the technical manager has in front of him what is in effect a small telephone exchange for communication with all points concerned technically with the programme: this includes control lines to remote sources, and also to the videotape recorder and telecine operators (who, in their own areas, hear the director's circuit as well as programme sound or their own output).

Television outside broadcast trucks sometimes have sound control, director and camera control all in the same tiny area of the vehicle: this is best for sports and other unrehearsed events where side-by-side working helps the operators to synchronize their actions. But for rehearsed events, and programmes built on location sequence by sequence, good sound conditions are more important, and these demand an acoustically separate area. This may be either in the same mobile control vehicle or (for music, where more space is desirable for monitoring) in a separate truck or, alternatively, 'derigged' and set up in some convenient room. This arrangement also reduces the distraction caused by the relatively loud voice of the director, who must compete with programme sound.

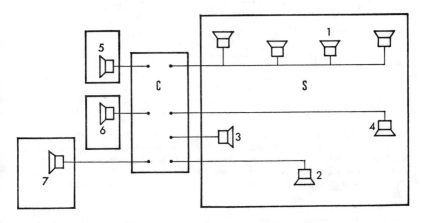

LOUDSPEAKERS IN A TELEVISION MUSICAL PRODUCTION. C. Sound control room. S. Studio. 1. Audience (public address) system. 2. Foldback of recorded sound effects. 3. Special feed of vocalist's sound to conductor. 4. Special feed of rhythm group to vocalist. 5 and 6. Echo feeds. 7. Remote studio.

In both radio and television outside broadcasts the sound man provides communication circuits between the various operational areas (e.g. commentary points) and the mobile control room. This often takes the form of local telephone circuits terminating at special multipurpose boxes which also provide feeds of pro-gramme sound and production talkback. (On television outside broadcasts the latter is particularly for the stage manager.) Additionally, field telephones may be required at remote points.

The broadcasting chain

In broadcasting, the studio suite (studio and control cubicle) may be only the first link in a complex chain. In a station with mixed output, the next link is a continuity suite where the entire programme service is assembled. The output of individual studios is fed in live, and linked together by station identification and

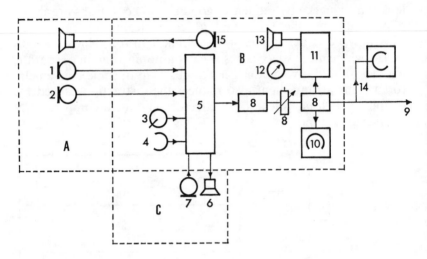

THE STUDIO CHAIN. Block circuit diagram of studio (A) cubicle (B) and echo chamber (C). Showing: 1, 2. Microphones. 3. Disc reproducer. 4. Tape reproducer. 5. Mixer. 6, 7. Echo loudspeaker and microphone. 8. Main gain amplifiers and control fader. 9. Studio output. 10. Tape recorder. 11. Monitoring amplifier. 12. Programme meter. 13. Monitoring loudspeaker. 14. Feed to external recording room. 15. Talkback circuit.

continuity announcements. The announcer on duty in the continuity studio is also usually given executive responsibility for the service as a whole, and must intervene if any contribution under-runs, over-runs, breaks down, or fails to materialize. He cues recorded programmes, presents trailers (promotional material) and also commercials where appropriate.

In small specialized stations such as those which dominate American radio, virtually the whole of the output emerges from a single room—though a separate studio may be available for news and discussion programmes or for recording commercials. In his 'electronic office' the presenter controls his own microphone and plays in the records, taped commercials, etc. For this, he should have three or more turntables, several reel-to-reel tape

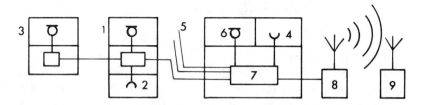

THE BROADCASTING CHAIN. The studio output may go to a recording room or it may provide an insert into a programme compiled in another studio—or it may be fed direct to a programme service continuity suite. Between studio, continuity and transmitter there may be other stages: switching centres, boosting amplifiers, and frequency correction networks on landlines, etc. 1. Studio suite. 2. Tape recording room. 3. Remote studio. 4. Tape reproducing room. 5. Other programme feeds. 6. Continuity announcer. 7. Continuity mixer. 8. Transmitter. 9. Receiver. This diagram shows the chain for radio, but the television chain is similar, though perhaps a little more elaborate. For example, the presentation studio (7) may have both a small television studio and a separate sound studio for an out-of-vision announcer.

decks for major programme segments or syndicated tapes, and three or four cartridge tape players. Cartridges (or cassettes) are used for commercials, promotional trailers, production effects and public service announcements. Several reproducers are required, as these may be played one after the other ('back-to-back'). Cartridges can be reproduced from carousels containing (in one design) 24 on a revolving drum that conveys them to a replay head. Another version has a stack of 55 that remains stationary while a replay head moves to each cartridge in turn. In addition to his microphone and reproduction equipment the presenter may also have two-way communication with news or traffic cars or helicopters, which can also be arranged to record automatically, on tape, while he is on the air with other material.

In large networks the basic service is put together in the same way, but with greater emphasis on precision timing, and the output of the network continuity appears as a source in the regional or local continuity which feeds the local radio transmitter. The links between the various centres may be landlines or radio links.

In television the broadcasting chain is substantially the same as for sound radio, except that in the presentation area there may be both a small television studio and a separate—usually very small—sound booth for out-of-vision announcements. Use of the sound booth means that rehearsals of more complex material in the main studio do not have to be stopped completely for routine, or un-scheduled, programme breaks.

Broadcast automation systems

The introduction of broadcast automation systems at many stations has meant the elimination of a large amount of routine work which can be taken over by machines under the control of a switching unit or, for the more ambitious systems, a small on-line computer. In principle, automation clears the way for a higher proportion of the jobs that remain in broadcasting to be creative in nature. In practice, however, it is equally possible for such systems to be used as an almost complete replacement for creative effort, because once they are set in operation they are capable of providing a simple basic service to a standard format with a minimum of computer programming.

A simple automated control system has manual switching. Typically a sequence of up to 24 events may be set up in advance and recycling may be started at any predetermined time. A range of replay decks or cartridge carousels is used for individual constituents of the programme. For example, a replay tape might contain a series of items—music or speech segments. In normal use one item only is played, at the end of which a 25 Hz signal cues the control unit to make its next selection (or in the event of failure, a silence sensor in the control unit exercises the same function). The tape then automatically sets up at the start of the next piece. Music programme tape services are available (often with built-in announcements over music). These tapes are replayed by the automatic reproducers with the musical numbers appearing in different combinations so that although each tape is used a number of times the same sequence is not repeated. The station may (if it so wishes) record its own local 'personality' links on a separate tape.

A further bank of controls may be manually preset for the times at which the local station must switch to and from the network. (When computer control is used, this input bank is not required, as the information is held in the computer memory.) There will also be a fill tape which is cued automatically at a given time before network switching: its starts mute (on 'deadroll' or 'prefade') and fades up when other programme material ends. A digital clock times all the switching operations.

A typical fifteen-minute sequence using a simple automatic broadcast control system might be put together using the various pieces of equipment as follows:

Equipment	Address	Event
Tape replay deck	4	Personality tape: 'mood' announcement
Tape replay deck	1	Music from 'show opener' tape
Random spot locator	6	Spot commercial
Tape replay deck	2	Music from second tape
Audio clock	5	Time check
Tape replay deck	3	Music (third category)
Filler replay deck	9	Fade-in of closing music
Random spot locator	6	Spot commercial
Audio clock	5	Time check and station identification
Time switching bank	10	Switch to network

To preselect this sequence the numbers 4–1–6–2–5–3–9–6–5 are set on the control unit; switching to and from network will occur automatically at the times that are preset.

Computer control of output

Full computer control of replay equipment is not unduly expensive: indeed, taking staff costs into account, it may actually be cheaper than automated machinery, because routine computer programming is quicker and simpler than manually setting a control unit. A real-time (process control) computer is employed,

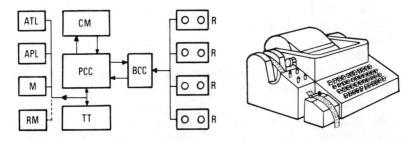

COMPUTER CONTROL OF PROGRAMME OUTPUT. PCC, Process control computer. BCC, Broadcast control centre. R, Tape reproducers, etc. CM, Computer memory. ATL, Automatic transmitter log. APL, Automatic programme log. M, Monitor. RM, Remote monitor (via telephone line). TT, Teletype (input output) employing a simple computer language (usually plain-language radio terminology). The computer is 'conversational', that is, it gives an immediate response to each instruction.

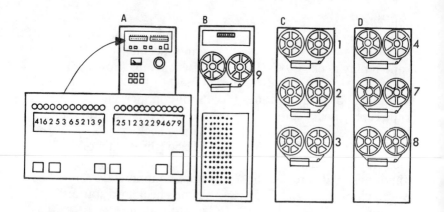

BROADCAST AUTOMATION SYSTEM I. A. Manually-set sequence of 24 events: the numbers correspond to addresses in racks B–F. Computer control works in a similar manner. B. Control unit. *Top.* Digital clock. *Middle.* Filler tape, cued to end immediately before a scheduled switchover. *Bottom.* Network time-switches, also preset manually. C, D. Playback machines. Individual items will be played on cue, and each will end with a burst of 25 Hz tone which will cue the next item in sequence; it will also set up the tape for its next replay.

and although it has a fairly large requirement for information storage, there is no need for high-speed handling of large amounts of material, so the hardware itself is relatively simple and the capital cost correspondingly low. Replay equipment of the type described above is also suitable for computer control, but in addition fast retrieval systems are available: a pair of multitrack broad tapes (of the type also used for computers) is fitted in a single rack, and any item (which may be up to 70 seconds long) can be located and set up for replay in 15 seconds. This allows continuous replay from random access. Depending on the size of the memory one or two day's programmes or a whole week can be held in the computer. Where day-to-day working is adopted, each day's schedule can be retrieved, then up-dated and re-inserted a week later.

Computer control gives great facility for commercial operations: in particular, once a given number of commercial slots has been programmed into a day's schedule, the computer can at any time be asked for information about what spots are still available. Further, this information can be requested from a distance, using ordinary telephone circuits. It also makes it possible for a roving reporter to dial in from a public telephone and by using a coded signal have his line switched to transmission at the next

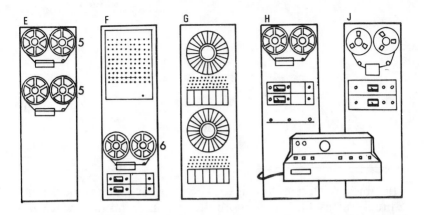

BROADCAST AUTOMATION SYSTEM II. E. Two replay machines are used for an audio clock, one covering the even minutes and the other the odd ones. F. Random spot locator. The tape contains up to a hundred items. The fifty pairs of switches allow up to fifty items to be selected in any order (including repeats). The main use for this is to allow spot commercials to be introduced into the programme material in an order that is predetermined by manual switching. After playback of each selection the next in sequence is automatically set up. G. Cartridge carousels. Each wheel holds up to 24 cartridges, and a sequence of 52 playbacks can be set up manually. Again, the main use is for replay of spot commercials. H. Recording unit (mono or stereo) with, *inset*, remote recording panel. J. Station log. Very low speed recorder notes time and transmission details.

junction. All this, together with the associated cueing systems can be achieved entirely without human intervention at the studio.

Either system may include an audio clock. Two tape transports are used: one has prerecorded announcements for every even minute of the programme day; the other covers the odd minutes. Time is given to the nearest half minute. Each of the two replay machines in turn is on standby for a minute, then, as the other takes over, it automatically moves forward to the next announcement. Alternatively, the announcement can be subdivided further. One tape provides the first half of the announcement, perhaps including a station identification with musical accompaniment, or a comment on the weather, but ending in mid-sentence, and then a second tape is cued to give the actual time. Variations on the first half can be prerecorded, along with other announcements and links, in a single session at the start of the day.

Equipment for the automatic logging of programme output is also included in a computer-controlled system.

3

STEREO

THE object of stereophony is to lay before (or around) the listener a lifelike array of sound—both direct sound and that which has been reflected from the walls of the original studio—which recreates some real or simulated layout in space.

In its simplest form, this *sound stage* is reproduced by a pair of loudspeakers, each of which has a separate signal fed to it. Sound reproduced by a single speaker appears to come directly from it. If, however, the sound is split and comes equally from the two speakers it sounds as if it is located half-way between the two. Other directions on the sound stage are simulated by other mixtures being fed to the two speakers. It is usual to refer to the left-hand loudspeaker as having the 'A' signal and the right-hand one as having the 'B' signal.

Two loudspeakers

A pair of stereo loudspeakers must work together in every sense. But the very minimum requirement is that if the same signal is fed to both, the cones of both loudspeakers move forward at the same time; in other words, the loudspeakers must be wired up to move in phase with each other. If they move in opposite senses an effect of sorts is obtained, but it is not that intended. For example, a sound that should be in the centre of the sound stage, the most important part, is not clearly located in the middle, but has an indeterminate position.

A second requirement is that the loudspeakers be matched in volume and frequency response. If the volume from one is greater than that from the other the centre is displaced and the sound stage distorted. If the difference is as great as 20 dB the centre is displaced to the extreme edge of the sound stage. The exact matching of frequency responses is less important to the average listener. Of

HEARING STEREO. The position of apparent sources is perceived by time, amplitude and phase differences between signals received by the left and right ears, and (at high frequencies) by the effects of shadowing due to the head. For any particular frequency the phase at each ear is given by the sum of the sounds arriving from the two loudspeakers.

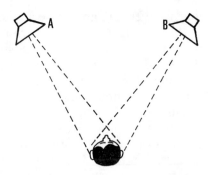

a number of possible effects, probably the most important is that the differences could draw attention to the loudspeakers themselves, thereby diminishing the illusion of reality.

In the studio, operational staff need to work in fully standardized conditions, sitting on the centre line of a pair of matched high-quality loudspeakers placed about 8 ft (2·5 m) apart. It is recommended that the home listener should have his loudspeakers between 6 and 10 ft (about 2–3 m) apart, depending on size of room. With less separation the listener should still hear a stereo effect, but the width of the sound stage is reduced. On the other hand, the loudspeakers should not be too far apart. For normal home listening if one person is on the centre line, others are likely to be 2 ft (say 60 cm) or more to the side, and the further the

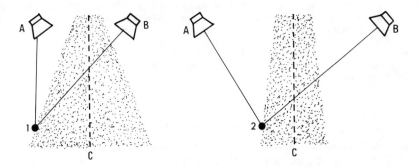

STEREO LOUDSPEAKERS: SPACING. With the closer loudspeakers, *left*, the spread of the stereo image is reduced, but there is a broad area of the listening room over which reasonable stereo is heard. With broader spacing, *right*, the stereo image has more spread, but for the benefit of a relatively narrow region in which it can be heard at its best. For listeners off the centre line C, the growing difference in distance rapidly 'kills' the stereo, due to the Haas effect. Position 1 (with a narrow spacing of speakers) has the same loss of stereo effect as position 2 (with the broader spacing).

loudspeakers are apart, the greater the loss of stereophonic effect to the outer members of the group. If the listener is as little as one foot (30 cm) closer to one loudspeaker, phase effects that distort the sound stage are already marked (see later), and as the difference in distance grows the nearer source progressively appears to capture the whole signal.

This second distortion of the sound stage—indeed, its near collapse—is induced by the *Haas effect*. This derives from the capacity of the ear to localize the source of a sound, distinguishing its direction from that of reflected sound, which is delayed by a few thousandths of a second (milliseconds, ms) even in a small room: in one millisecond sound travels just over one foot (34 cm).

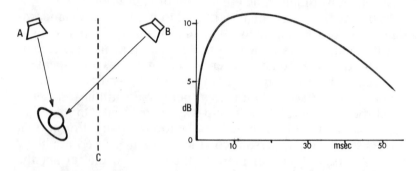

HAAS EFFECT. For a listener away from the centre line C, the difference in distances means that the sound from the farther loudspeaker arrives at the listener's ears later than that from the nearer one. The delay is one millisecond for every 13·4 inches (34 cm) difference in path-length. For identical signals coming from different direc-directions a difference of only a few milliseconds makes the whole sound appear to come from the direction of the first to arrive. The effect can be reversed by increasing the volume of the second signal: the curve shows the increase in volume required to re-centre the image.

The Haas effect is at its strongest for delays of 5–30 ms, which is produced by a difference in path lengths of some 6–18 ft (about 2–7 m). The capacity diminishes a little with increasing delay, but still remains effective, until eventually the reflection of a staccato sound can be distinguished as a separate echo.

But it is what happens at the lower end of this scale of delays and their corresponding distances that is more important for our perception of stereo. As the difference in distance from the two loudspeakers grows from zero to about 5 ft (1·5 m) the Haas effects grows rapidly and continuously to approach the maximum, where it would take an increase of 10 dB in volume from the farther loudspeaker source for it to begin to 'recapture' the source. Plainly, an optimum stereo effect is achieved only in a narrow wedge-shaped region along the centre line, and this is narrower still if the loudspeakers are widely separated.

Between the reduced spatial effect of narrow separation and the reduced optimum listening area created by a broad layout, it may seem surprising that stereo works at all. The fact is, most casual listeners happily accept a sound picture that is spatially severely distorted. This is their prerogative: the sound man should be aware that his listeners often prefer their own seating plan to his clinical ideal.

Alternatives to two loudspeakers

What alternative is there to the two-loudspeaker stereo layout?

One is to dispense with the loudspeakers entirely and to wear *stereo headphones* instead. These are convenient where people of different tastes are crowded together (particularly on an aircraft) and one advantage is that the spread of the image is the same for all listeners with normal hearing. But several characteristics of the two-speaker system are lost: one is that sound from *both* loudspeakers should reach *both* ears, and do so from somewhere to 'the front'; and another is that the sound stage is static—it does not swing around as the listener turns his head. As a result, listening with stereo headphones provides a different aural experience. But for most people this is less important than whether they are happy to spend substantial periods of time so cocooned and constrained, and whether they are prepared to accept, or perhaps prefer, the reduction in social contact that results.

The sound man should not use headphones to monitor stereo that will be heard by loudspeaker.

Stereo by wave reconstruction is a theoretical alternative to the two-speaker system in which the wave front in the studio is sensed at many points so that it can be reconstructed at a similar number of points in the listening room. This requires a large number of microphones, transmission lines and loudspeakers, so in its fullest application the idea is clearly impractical, but a modified multi-loudspeaker system is often used for stereo in cinemas—

63

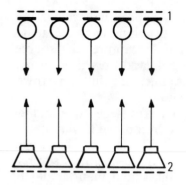

STEREO BY RECONSTRUC-
TED WAVEFRONT. 1. Sound
pressures at many points in a
large surface sampled by many
microphones. 2. The sound is
reproduced at corresponding
points in a similar surface. The
biggest practical problem in
this arrangement is the very
large number of channels of
communication required.

though for people sitting near the front or the side walls, individual or pairs of loudspeakers are bound to dominate the sound that they hear. The Haas effect is severe: most people are more than 6 ft (2 m) closer to some loudspeakers than to others.

In *quadraphony* (or 'quad') two further signals are fed to loudspeakers on the opposite side of the room from the normal A and B speakers. There are two ways in which this can be used. One is to surround the listener with direct sources, so that he is placed in the middle of the action. To bring individual sources forward they can also be 'placed' on the axis between pairs of diagonally opposed loudspeakers. The effect of being in the middle of the

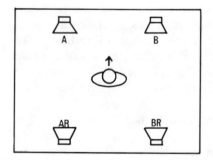
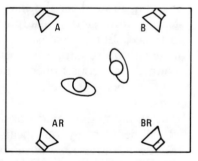

FOUR LOUDSPEAKERS. *Left.* A and B are equivalent to two-channel stereo from the front, and AR and BR are placed at the back of the listening room. (R indicates 'rear'). If most of the direct sound comes from the front and the spacing of the A and B loudspeakers is greater than for two-channel stereo, the position of the listener (close to the centre line) is correspondingly critical. If there is direct sound from all speakers the effect is multiplied: away from the centre of the room individual loudspeakers tend to dominate, and this is increased still further in the symmetrical layout, *right.*

action can be dramatic and exciting, and it has been claimed that this is the only way to sell quad to a cautious public. However, little existing classical music requires this, although notable exceptions include the Berlioz *Requiem* (which employs a quartet of brass bands) and early antiphonal church music by composers such as Gabrieli and Monteverdi.

The alternative use for the four channels is more conventional, with only the indirect sound, i.e. reverberation, spread over all of the four speakers, so that the listener is offered a sense of space in a way that cannot be achieved by the acoustics of a relatively small listening room. In fact, this in itself is more than sufficient to justify the system, without the need for more than an occasional *jeu d'esprit*. New works including drama written especially for surround-sound are another matter, but most existing music demands that direct sound should come from one sector only. Indeed, many listeners prefer that their room has some orientation, with a 'front' and a 'back'.

A further complication arises (again) from the Haas effect. For the proper placing of sounds between loudspeakers, a speaker in each corner of the room renders the position of the listener very critical, except for sources that sit unequivocally in a particular loudspeaker. If two-channel stereo (or quadraphonics in which the rear speakers carry reverberation only) is reproduced on a four-loudspeaker system it is better if the A and B channels are spaced as for conventional stereo. In this case the power handling capacity of the rear loudspeakers need not be as great as those in front (thereby saving money and making the expansion of an existing stereo system easier), and their spacing is less critical (which is often more convenient for the room layout). This arrangement is also well suited to matrixed quadraphonic sound (see p. 178). But if the governing criterion is direct sound from all sides the rear loudspeakers should be of a quality equal to those at the front, and the room layout may have to be redesigned around the four loudspeakers. A relatively small area in the centre receives the intended image. Discrete quadraphony (in which the four channels are separately recorded) gives the best positional information at the sides and back.

There has been a lack of unanimity on the objectives of quadraphonics together with a lengthy debate on technical standards (including the question of compatibility: should four-channel recordings be reproduceable on conventional stereo and mono equipment and vice versa, or not?), and this has slowed widespread public acceptance of what many may see as an expensive and not-too-easily manageable extension of home audio.

Hearing and stereo

How, in real life, do our ears and brain search out the position of a sound and tell us where to look for its source? First, the Haas effect allows us to distinguish between direct and reflected sound (except in the rare case where the reflections are focused and their increased loudness more than compensates for the delay in their arrival). A second clue is offered by differences in the signal as it arrives at our two ears: a sound that is not directly in line with the head arrives at one ear before the other. At some frequencies the sounds are therefore partly out of phase, and this may give some indication of angle. Such an effect is strongest at about 500 Hz.

The head itself begins to produce screening effects for frequencies at 700 Hz and above, resulting in differences in the amplitude of signals reaching the ears from one side or the other. Further aids to direction finding are provided by movements of the head, together with interpretation by the brain in the light of experience. Even with all these clues, with our eyes closed we might still be uncertain: we can distinguish, separate out and concentrate our attention on the contents of particular elements of a complex sound field far better than we can pinpoint their components precisely in space. The clues tell us where to look: we must then use our eyes to complete and confirm the localization . . . if, that is, there is any picture to see. In our present case there is none, and the fact that in real life we rely rather heavily on the visual cues is peversely rather helpful to us: it permits us to continue to enjoy the spatially distorted image even if we are a little off the centre line. Two-speaker stereo measures up to this specification quite well.

Assume first that the source is in the centre of the sound stage and that the listener is on the centre line. The A signal reaches the left ear slightly before the B signal, and for middle and low frequencies the two combine to produce a composite signal that is intermediate in phase between them. For the right ear the B signal arrives first, but the combination is the same. The brain, comparing the two combined signals, finds them to be the same and places the source in the centre. If the amplitude of the sound from one speaker is now increased and the other reduced, the signals combine at the ears as before, but the resultant signals

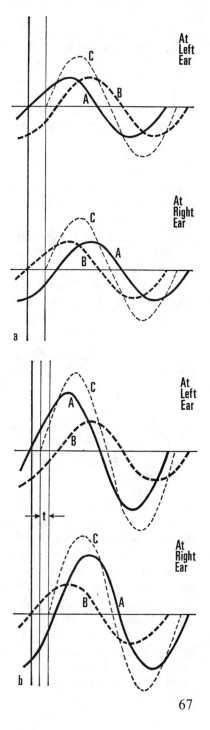

TWO LOUDSPEAKER STEREO. (a) The signals from the A and B loudspeakers are equal; the B signal takes longer to reach the left ear, and the A signal takes longer to reach the right. But the combined signal C is exactly in phase: the image is in the centre. (b) Signal A is increased. The effect of this is to make the peak in the combined signal C at the left ear a little earlier, and that at the right ear, later. There is therefore a slight delay (t) between the two signals C; this phase difference is perceived as a displacement of the image to the left of centre. In these diagrams it is assumed that the listener is on the centre line between A and B, and facing forwards. If, however, he turns his head this will cause the phase difference at his ears to change—but in such a way as to keep the image roughly at the same point in space. If the listener moves away from the centre line the image will be distorted but the relative positions of image elements will remain undisturbed. These arguments apply in their simplest form only to sound derived from a coincident pair of microphones, and to frequencies below about 700 Hz, at which the head itself causes shadowing effects.

67

differ from each other in *phase*—in effect, it appears as though the same signal is arriving at the two ears at slightly different times. This was one of the requirements for directional information.

If the listener moves off the centre line, or if the volume controls of the two loudspeakers are not set exactly the same, the sound stage is distorted, but there is still directional information that matches the original to some reasonably acceptable degree.

Microphones for stereo

For the basic stereo signal in classical music and drama, BBC radio generally uses methods which provide components that are in phase with each other throughout the frequency range, directional information being provided solely by differences in signal amplitude. These are called *coincident microphone* techniques. The two microphones feeding the A and B information are usually mounted one above the other or closely side by side and are directional, so that the A microphone picks up progressively more of

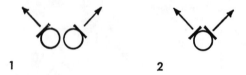

1   2

STEREOPHONIC MICROPHONE. The method of picking up stereophonic sound that will be recommended in this book is the coincident pair: two directional microphones very close together (1) or in a common housing, usually one above the other (2). The second symbol (as 2) will generally be used. The microphone elements will not necessarily be at 90° to each other.

the sound on the left and the B microphone progressively more on the right. Both pick up equal amounts of sound from the centre, the line half-way between their directional axes. Such techniques are relatively simple in theory and work well in practice. BBC stereo programmes have been widely praised; and the advice given in this book is largely based on BBC experience.

An alternative system that is widely used is based on spaced microphones. The original reason for this technique may have been an idea that the sound at two points in the studio was being reproduced at two comparable points in the listening room. The reader is not advised to try to follow the logic of this line of argument: it is both confused and confusing. What really matters is what happens at the point where the listener is sitting. And at that point there is a very complex situation indeed.

Because microphone A is physically nearer to side A its signal is greater in amplitude than that from microphone B: so far, so good. But in addition there are phase differences from subjects that

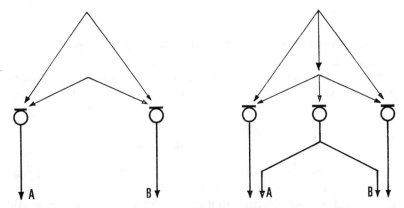

SPACED PAIR. *Left*. A technique which was sometimes used in the early days of stereo. However, for subjects along the centre line the apparent distance from the front of the audio stage is greater than for subjects in line with the microphones; and the farther forward the subject is, the more pronounced the effect. It is called 'hole-in-the-middle'. *Right*. The introduction of a third microphone in the centre does a great deal to cure this.

are off-centre, due to the separation of the microphones: these are bigger the farther off centre the subject is. In addition, the phase differences vary systematically throughout the audio-frequency range. Even so, there is plainly a great deal of directional information of one sort or another being offered to the listener, and the brain can still sort some sense out of it. Spaced microphones can be and are used successfully by many record companies.

The only test that can be applied is the practical one: does it sound all right? It was soon discovered that one pair of spaced microphones did *not* sound right: there was 'a hole in the middle'. The centre subjects appeared to be much farther away from the listener than the outer ones. In order to combat this the usual technique is to add a third microphone in the centre, the output of which is split between the A and B channels.

Another technique that has been used is a *dummy head* with two pressure microphones in the position of the ears. The analogy is obvious, but is not related to the stereo we hear from spaced loudspeakers. There is a spatial effect, because the A and B signals

69

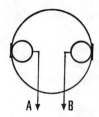

DUMMY HEAD. Microphones mounted in a solid baffle of head size. When used in combination with a two loudspeaker system this cannot be justified on theoretical grounds. For headphone listening the effect is good.

are slightly different, especially in high frequencies at which the obstacle effect of a real head helps to discriminate position. But the test is whether it works in practice and it does not, in comparison with other stereo techniques (except when heard on headphones, as in airline in-flight entertainment, in which case it is excellent).

Stereo control channels

A stereo channel into which the output of a coincident or spaced pair of microphones is fed has separate paths for the A and B signals, but with the principal faders ganged, so that the signals are automatically faded up and down together. In some older equipment the faders are stepped at intervals of $1\frac{1}{2}$–2 dB between successive contacts. If the slide on one side makes contact with a stud a fraction of a second before that on the other, the image momentarily shifts laterally. This is called fader *wiggle* or *flicker*. To minimize the danger, the operator must move the fader smoothly and never too slowly from stud to stud. Modern designs of high quality continuous track faders do not have this problem.

Additional controls are used on stereo sound channels:
1. Image width control. This cross-links the A and B signals,

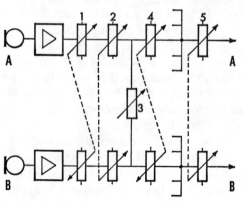

STEREOPHONIC CHANNEL. 1. Preset control to balance output between microphone elements. 2. Ganged fader. 3. Image width control. 4. Channel offset control (this displaces the complete, spread image). 5. Group fader.

feeding controlled and equal amounts of the A signal to the B channel, and vice-versa. As this cross feed is increased, the image width narrows. However, if at the same time the phase is reversed the image width is increased.

2. Displacement control. This is a ganged pair of faders, one on each path, and working in opposition to each other, so that turning the knob has the effect of moving the whole of the image on this particular channel sideways. This control can also be used to give apparent movement to a static but spread source.

In a stereo channel the main pair of faders and the width control could also be put into the circuit in a different way: by first converting A and B into M and S signals and operating on these. When M and S signals are faded up or down there is no 'wiggle'; instead, there might be minor variations in image width—but this is less objectionable. In addition, image width can now be controlled simply by changing the proportion of M to S signal. In particular, image width can be increased without change of phase. However, after passing through the channel fader and the width control the M and S signals must be converted back to the A and B form before passing through the displacement faders.

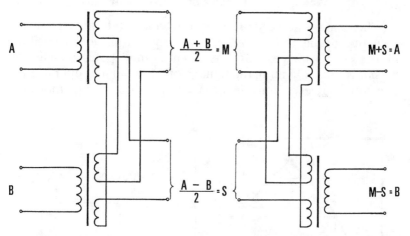

STEREO SIGNALS: an electrical method for converting A and B signals to M and S, and vice versa. 'M' is equivalent to the signal that would be obtained by directing a single suitable monophonic microphone towards the centre of the audio stage. It therefore gives a mono output which can be used by those without stereo loudspeakers. The balance between centre and side subjects, and between direct and reverberant sound will not necessarily be as good as for a normal mono balance. 'S' contains some of the information from the sides of the audio stage.

One stage in this process can be eliminated by using microphones which produce the M and S signals directly.

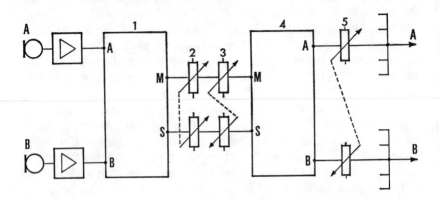

STEREOPHONIC CHANNEL WITH CONTROL ON THE M AND S SIGNALS. 1 and 4. Signal conversion circuits. 2. Channel fader. 3. Image width control. 5. Offset control. This arrangement is less subject to fader 'wiggle'—a momentary displacement of the image which occurs when contacts with A and B stud faders are not made simultaneously.

Monophonic channels in stereo: the panpot

When monophonic sources are introduced into a stereo mixer their output has to be *steered* or *panned* to a particular position in the stereo image. For this a panoramic potentiometer or *panpot* is used. Dividing the signal from a mono microphone into two equal halves is equivalent to feeding it through a panpot with

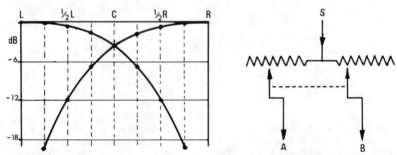

PANPOT ATTENUATION. A signal from a monophonic source is split and fed through a pair of ganged potentiometers. Step-by-step, the attenuation in the two channels is matched (*dotted lines*). The apparent volume will then be the same in all available positions across the stereo stage. L. Left. $\frac{1}{2}$L. Half left. C. Centre, etc.

its control centred; the image, too, appears in the centre. Classical music is often recorded using a master stereo pair, to which are added *spotting microphones* for some of the individual instruments or sections. The signals from these microphones are fed through panpots so that their position can be adjusted within the

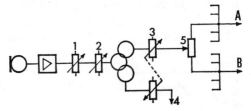

PANPOT USED WITH MONOPHONIC MICRO-PHONE IN STEREO BAL-ANCE 1. Preset control. 2. Fader. 3. Echo mixture switch. 4. Echo feed. 5. Panpot.

sound picture. For popular music there is no master pair, and panpots are used on every channel. For films with stereophonic sound tracks effects and even speech are often recorded in mono and then panned as necessary to follow action.

Where full stereo equipment such as that described earlier is not available, two monophonic channels with panpots can be linked together in pairs to form a stereo channel into which A and B microphone signals can be fed. The two channel faders are generally physically linked: adjacent quadrant faders are clipped to-together. Image displacement and width are then controlled by the relative settings of the two panpots.

If the two panpots have the same setting as each other the source has zero width and is displaced to whatever position the panpots give them. If the panpots are then moved in opposite directions from this point the image increases in width. Full width is given

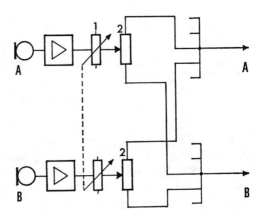

TWO MONOPHONIC CHAN-NELS USED AS A STEREO CHANNEL. 1. Faders clipped together. 2. Panpots: these will be preset to give the correct scale of width for the source covered (i.e., they are being used not as panpots, but as width and offset controls).

73

by steering one of the signals to the A side and the other to the B side in the mixed signal; but this can, of course, be done without a panpot at all.

A quadraphonic panpot is made up by combining two stereo panpots, one for side-to-side position and the other for forward-to-rear. By use of the two together a monophonic source may be steered to positions within the four corners. For special effects such as a circling aircraft or aggressive insect a joystick control gives continuous smooth movement, but for most purposes it is sufficient to have separate controls. In multitrack recordings a pair of panpots is required for each channel.

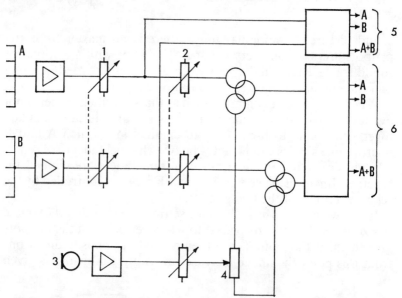

STEREO CONTROL DESK: clean feed and output arrangements. 1. Master control. 2. Main control. 3. Separate microphone (e.g. for announcer). 4. Panpot. 5. Clean feed (i.e. without sound from separate feed, 3 and 4). 6. Fully mixed control desk output. The combined A + B signals are generated in order to check the quality and volume of the compatible mono signal.

Compatible stereo

If the outputs of the two stereo microphones are added together they should provide an acceptable monophonic signal. In fact, the A and B channels can easily be combined electrically into two new signals, A + B and A − B. The first of these is taken as the derived mono signal and the second contains the information that is needed to convert it back to stereo.

74

There are advantages to using A + B and A − B signals when recording on disc and for radio transmissions.

If a disc is recorded so that A + B corresponds to lateral displacement the mono signal can be picked up on a mono record player without difficulty. To this extent *all* stereo records are compatible. However, the groove is so constructed that a stylus of smaller tip radius and lower playing weight is required—and if the

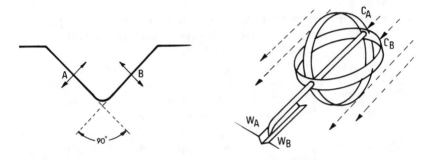

STEREO DISC REPRODUCTION. The information for channel A is inscribed in wall A, closest to the centre of the disc, at 45° to the vertical. Wall B carries signal B. A mono pick-up detects only the sideways component (A + B), disregarding the hill and dale (A − B) movement which carries the additional information for stereo. A magnetic stereo pick-up has coils (C_A and C_B) which respond directly to the signals in the walls (W_A and W_B). Quadraphonic information must be encoded into the same two channels.

second of these conditions is not met by a mono record player the record is likely to be damaged. The A − B signal is recorded in the vertical plane, by hill-and-dale signals: a mono stylus simply rides up and down but has no means of converting this information into an electrical signal.

For stereo reproduction it is not necessary to separate the signals electrically: it can be done mechanically, as the A and B signals are in effect inscribed in the respective walls of the groove, which are at 90° to each other. The pick-up has two elements, one responding to movements at 45° to the vertical on one side and the other on the other side at a similar angle: these produce A and B signals directly.

Similar advantages are obtained from using A + B and A − B signals in radio. The A + B signal occupies the place in a waveband normally occupied by a mono signal; the A − B signal can then be modulated on to a subcarrier above the main A + B band.

75

It is beyond the scope of this book to give engineering details, but briefly: frequency modulation is generally used, with a subcarrier at 38 kHz; and a pilot tone at 19 kHz is used to stabilize phase relationships (which are very important in this case). Signal-to noise ratio is slightly (but not appreciably) poorer for a compatible mono signal than for pure mono; the stereo information has, in principle, a substantially poorer signal-to-noise ratio, but as it starts off from such a high standard in FM, the loss does not matter in practice.

The normal method of recording stereo on magnetic tape is to put the A and B signals side by side on separate tracks. A full-track head reproduces both together, or alternatively the combined signal can be obtained electrically by adding the two outputs.

There has been some debate about whether quadraphonic and stereo systems should be sufficiently similar that recordings made for one will replay on the other. Should four-channel systems be compatible, or should the opportunity have been taken to improve engineering standards generally, while optimizing them for the new system? The second course would require the duplication of equipment to a degree that only the extreme enthusiast could welcome, so it is fortunate for the less dedicated audiophiles that some degree of compatibility has proved possible.

In some systems the two extra channels are encoded *(matrixed)* into the A and B stereo signals. This is done by introducing phase differences (some positive and some negative) and combining them in some proportion with the other pair of signals. The resultant signal can be recorded, e.g. on disc, in the conventional way and is compatible with two-channel stereo, although components of the direct signal are reduced if it is replayed as normal stereo. Matrixed recording systems are also called 4–2–4 systems: to reproduce four separate signals from them, existing stereo equipment may be used, adding the appropriate decoder.

4–2–4 matrixing introduces substantial crosstalk between channels. This results in some lack of positional clarity, usually at its worst somewhere at the sides or rear—the exact nature of the loss depending on the method of matrixing that is used (there are rival proprietary systems). BBC radio has adopted a system described as '4–2$\frac{1}{2}$–4' in which the loss of information is somewhat reduced. Crosstalk can be further reduced by employing *discrete* systems, i.e. those in which the four channels are kept separate at all times. In a discrete system that has been devised for disc recording, the additional channels are carried piggy-back above the normal audio frequencies, rather as the A — B (or S) channel for two-channel stereo is carried on radio transmissions. In principle, such a disc system could be compatible, but in practice anything but the lightest and most compliant of pickups would damage the higher frequencies that are inscribed in the groove.

Quarter-inch (6·25 mm) tape, recorded using a four-channel stacked head, is an excellent medium, and can be compatible. However, cassette tapes for home use present serious problems

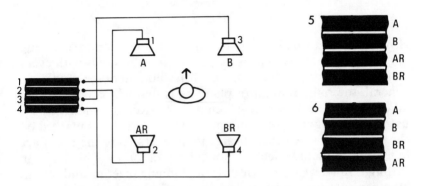

FOUR-CHANNEL STEREO. Tracks 1 and 3 feed the front A and B loudspeakers. Tracks 2 and 4 feed the rear AR and BR loudspeakers. This layout gives the greatest compatibility with existing $\frac{1}{4}$-inch (6·25mm) tape systems. In-house recordings on broader tape do not have to be compatible, and several arrangements are used: 5. BBC in-house layout permits panning between odd (left) and even (right) pairs of tracks. 6. A commercially available system has a clockwise arrangement.

if a layout of tracks offering compatibility with two-channel stereo is attempted, as this implies cramming eight tracks (four in each direction) on to half the width of standard recording tape.

The four channels are best broadcast by using higher frequency subcarriers for the additional information: the lower bands can then still carry signals equivalent to A + B and A — B, for compatible mono and stereo. The best way for quadraphonic programme material to be passed from one broadcasting organization to another is in the form of discrete four-channel recordings on standard tape.

4

PLANNING AND ROUTINE

How much detailed planning should go into the technical handling of a scripted radio or television production? It varies with every script and every producer or director who enters the studio. In general, the right amount of planning is that which ensures that all of the necessary technical facilities are available and ready for use; and the right amount of operational instructions marked on the script is that which indicates in a general way the necessary fades, mixes, sound effects, echo, and so on for a preliminary run through. In television this follows a planning meeting and (often) attendance at some rehearsal prior to arrival in the studio.

What follows applies particularly to radio or television studio work, whether for recording or broadcast, and also (with a few minor changes of terminology) to gramophone record recording sessions. Film dubbing (re-recording) is similar, but involves additional techniques that are described later (pp. 480–490).

During the first run-through of a complex programme the sound supervisor ('studio manager' in BBC radio) glances ahead down each page of script, quickly estimating what will be needed; he ensures that the right microphone channels are open and gets the feel of the overall and relative levels and such things as fades and mixes. At this first attempt the results are rarely exactly right, but each operator quickly notes down anything out of the ordinary on his script in some sort of personal shorthand: it might be the level of a recorded effect, perhaps, or the setting for the first words that are to be heard in a fade in. In radio, a few extra words may have to be written in for a fade, or a small adjustment made to an actor's distance from the microphone: such questions are referred to the producer. But in television, the sound man is more inclined to try to solve his problems with the minimum of reference to the director. Often the difficulties are more severe; generally revolving around the question of how to get adequate sound coverage without the microphone getting in the picture or throwing shadows.

Nothing should ever be too precisely set prior to the recording or transmission: in a play, for example, actors' emphases and levels may be substantially different on the 'take' as they let loose their final reserves for a performance. Where difficult sequences or unusual ways of doing things have to be fitted in, pre-rehearsals and perhaps pre-recording of the complicated parts are necessary; but these themselves can be rehearsed and recorded in the same not-too-calculated way. It is merely a question of breaking up awkward material into tractable segments.

Planning: radio or recording studios

In comparison with television, the planning that is necessary prior to the arrival of the production and sound staff and performers in the radio or recording studio is simplicity itself.

When there is a range of studios available the request for a booking is normally accompanied by a brief description of the use to which it will be put, e.g. the number of speakers or musicians, and if necessary a brief indication of the type of balance: 'discussion—6 people' or 'novelty sextet with vocalist'.

Except for the very simplest programmes, the production office prepares a running order or script which (except for very topical material) is sent to the programme operations staff in advance. Many productions follow an established routine such that the minimum of discussion is necessary before arriving in the studio; but if there is any doubt, or any unexplored aspect to the production, the sound staff should contact the producer in advance. For example, before a recording session involving an unfamiliar musical group the balancer should discover from the production office what instruments are to be expected and what sort of balance the producer wants to hear: if, for example, it were required to sound like an existing record the balancer would have to listen to it. He would want to know whether the music is to be featured, or for background use; whether it is to be brilliant and arresting in its sound quality, or soft and undisturbing; or whether it is to be heard with announcements at certain points within it, or applause (which would thicken the texture of the sound).

The recording arrangements are also discussed: the probable duration, whether it is to be stop-start or single take, the tape speed to be used for the recording and the number of copies required;

and any special arrangements for handing over the tapes, or for transfer to magnetic film stock. Any unorthodox or experimental layout has to be discussed with the musical director in sufficient time for studio attendants to be given a plan showing the provision of chairs, music stands, acoustic screens and other furniture; and studio instruments such as the piano. The balancer also sets up the microphones (or checks their layout) and arranges their output on his desk, working out and plugging up a suitable grouping of channels, with frequency correction units, compressors and limiters in the appropriate circuits and echo and tape delay or any other devices ready for use.

And finally, before the musicians arrive in the studio he checks that all of the facilities that he is likely to use are actually in working order: this also includes things like the talkback and any foldback circuits and the levels of the loudspeakers associated with them.

Television planning

For a television programme of some complexity the sound crew may be six or seven in number: a BBC team might include an operator for the tape and disc replay decks, two boom operators, and a floor assistant (who may track the boom, reset microphones, etc.). Second in command and the most versatile in his duties is the sound assistant: in some programmes he leads the sound department's forces on the studio floor, supervising the rig for musical programmes, operating the main boom on a complex play, or sitting alongside the supervisor and handling the audience microphone pre-mix, public address and foldback in a comedy show.

Representing the facilities that his team can offer, the sound supervisor attends the planning meeting (several if necessary) called by production to coordinate design and operational plans. The size of such meetings varies. For a simple programme it may involve the director, the designer, the lighting man, the technical manager (who is in direct overall charge of all technical services other than lighting and sound). More complex programmes may also require the presence of the floor manager, senior cameraman, the costume and make-up supervisors, and other people dealing with house and studio services such as audience management, the assessment of fire risks, allocation of dressing rooms, and dealing with any special problems in catering caused by breaks at unusual times or the arrival of distinguished guests.

From this planning meeting, and from subsequent contact with the director and the production team—and often also from direct observation of outside rehearsals—it is the sound man's responsibility to assess what will be required in order to arrive in the studio with all non-standard equipment and facilities booked and available, knowing how the sound coverage is to be obtained, and ready to set up the microphones and other equipment to go ahead with the rehearsal on schedule.

But the planning meeting also serves a secondary purpose: it is a forum within which ideas can be proposed and discussed and then either adopted or abandoned. There may be conflicts of interest as each department tries to do its best for the director, conflicts that must be resolved in compromise and cooperation. As the director listens to the various suggestions that are made, he generally arbitrates rapidly between conflicting aims. Sometimes he makes slight modifications to his original ideas to make things easier for everybody; but if in a complex situation he does not, it is usually the sound man who has the trickiest problems to solve —many more television directors put picture first and sound second than the other way round. Sound men who make light work of complex problems are therefore valued members of any production team—but those who accept unsatisfactory compromises and then explain after the programme that poor sound was an inevitable result are not likely to be thanked.

At the planning meeting the sound supervisor starts to build— or re-establish—a working relationship with several other members of the team that will carry on throughout the term of the production.

The sound supervisor and the television director

The sound man meets various types of director (and producer). Some are able to outline their needs concisely and precisely— and once they have said what they want they stick to it. Such directors are easy to work with and are not likely to waste others' effort, demand extra staff who are not used or cause the sound supervisor to requisition equipment and resources that in the event are not needed.

Another director may have few of these obvious virtues, but still be worthy of all the help the sound man can give him. This is the type who likes to maintain as much flexibility as possible up to a late stage in the preparation of a production. As a result, he is then able to take full advantage of elements of the production that turn out better than could reasonably have been expected, and cut his losses on ideas that do not shape up well. In these circumstances the sound man may have to plan his resources by intelligent anticipation, expecting some degree of wasted effort. With this sort of director the means can be justified by the results.

Inexperienced directors also need a great deal of help from the sound man, but should be persuaded toward simpler solutions so that things are less likely to go wrong. Then, when they do go wrong, the resulting situation is relatively easy for everyone (including the director himself) to cope with.

For certain types of production (in particular, plays) the sound supervisor sees the script even before the planning meeting, and will already have a number of questions that he wants to ask the director—who for his part will probably be ready to give the answers without even being asked. The director may start by giving a general outline of what the programme is about, and what his own production attitude is. His descriptions may be technical or artistic in style. In the first case he may not be very accurate (but do not assume that this is always so!); in the other the technical staff may require a fertile imagination to turn far-fetched analogies into concrete requirements.

The sound supervisor should pay particular attention to descriptions of the visual style: a 'strong' style with fast cutting, mixtures of close and wide shots, unusual angles and split focus (which may be adopted to establish an appropriate pyschological mood or simply to jazz up a weak story line) could require different sound coverage from a simple and more logical visual style. As he listens to this he is looking at plans—scale drawings of the studio layout—which should already be available to show the areas in which the action will take place.

At this stage the director may welcome advice on sound coverage. Effective solutions to some of the more difficult problems may, indeed, involve him in extra effort before arriving in the studio—by making pre-recordings, for example—or extra expense for additional equipment or staff; and the director should have the opportunity to decide whether the effect he is seeking is worth this.

Even before the planning meeting, the studio sound supervisor may have been consulted on ways of linking film to studio. Mismatches of background sound or voice quality can sometimes be avoided by the appropriate choice of microphone types or techniques. For example, a close balance might be possible on film but has to be avoided because it gives a bad sound cut with a related studio shot. Again, the studio sound supervisor may advise that sound effects specially recorded on a film location will help a studio sequence.

The basic running order for rehearsal and recording is also settled at the planning meeting: here the director needs to hear whether there is sufficient time allowed for the various things that he is asking for, or whether (for example) a recording break will save equipment and staff and therefore perhaps money. But to bring a television studio to a halt for ten minutes for the lack of one man may be an expensive economy. Note, however, that a sound man's desire to provide perfect results without regard to cost may conflict with the director's responsibility to make the best use of limited resources.

Actors and other performers may have a period of rehearsal before coming into the studio, towards the end of which the sound supervisor should attend and watch. At this stage, scenery is indicated mainly by floor markings, so that its detailed shape, height and manner of construction must be visualized from the designer's plan. But much of the action will already be set, so the sound man can observe speed of movement and relative positions; he can listen to the quality of the voices and note the direction of voice projection; in short he can see reasonably well whether the planned sound coverage is likely to work in practice and also how it may be affected by the evolving plans for lighting and camera movement. Any major changes in sound coverage that seem to be warranted should be discussed with the director and the other specialist departments, and then entered in the studio plan. At the outside rehearsal he can also check the way in which equipment such as property telephones or acoustic foldback will be used in the studio, and can get a feel for the timing of speech and action relative to music and effects. Sometimes recorded sound is brought to the rehearsal and tried out with the performers.

Rehearsal-quality sound equipment used outside the studio, for example to work up sequences mimed to sound replay, may be collected from the sound department and operated by an assistant floor manager. But where a sound assistant would benefit by rehearsing timing with the performers, he should operate the replay equipment himself: this may save studio time later.

Sound and the television designer

It is the job of the television designer to produce the scale plan of the proposed studio layout. The sound supervisor needs to be expert in interpreting such plans, to which symbols for his own equipment (booms, slung and stand microphones and loudspeakers) will be added later by the director after their positions, boom tracking lines, etc., have been discussed with the sound man.

Rostra, ceilings, doors, archways and alcoves are all accurately marked on the plan, as are features such as tree-trunks or columns that may obstruct a boom arm, or areas of floor covered with materials that make it impossible for sound equipment to follow. Stairs and upper working levels are also shown. Scale models are sometimes made up for complex production and can be of considerable assistance in providing an immediate interpretation of the plan.

But at this stage the plan is not final: a ceiling may be re-designed to be made of an acoustically transparent material so that a microphone can 'see' down from above; a tree may be chopped off at a calculated height so that a boom can swing over it; or a potted plant may be strategically repositioned so that it can bear improbable fruit in the shape of a concealed microphone.

Certain types of set reflect and therefore reinforce sound: this is particularly true of flattage built of wood. Such flats may help musicians or other performers, but can cause trouble if they are arranged in a semicircle so that they focus the sound. The extra difficulties in the placing of performers and microphones can generally be overcome, but an added complication is that such a setting also focuses reflected noise from other parts of the studio.

Scenic projection equipment such as that for back projection of film or television pictures (the latter derived from the output of telecine, videotape replay or other live cameras) may itself be noisy—due to cooling fans, if not the projector mechanism itself. Such noises are more likely to be intrusive if the scene is rural or from a period before the use of mechanized vehicles. The positioning of projection equipment and the need or otherwise for it to be blimped again involves both sound man and designer. Happily for television sound, direct projection has now largely been replaced by electronic colour-separation (chromakey) techniques.

Floor and other surfaces used in television are often painted or

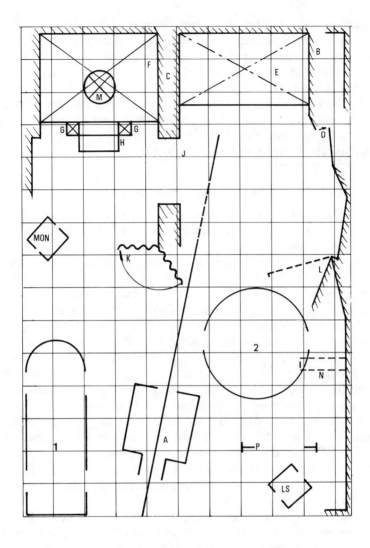

STUDIO PLAN. Corner of set in a television studio, including cameras (1 and 2), boom (A), loudspeaker (LS), and Monitor (MON) and scenery. Here, Camera 1 is a small motorized tracking camera (other cranes require much more space). Camera 2 is a pedestal camera: the circle represents the working area it requires. The boom is capable of further extension (to reach beyond the back wall of the set) if required. Details of set: B. Single clad flattage. C. Double clad flattage. E. Ceiling over (broken lines). F. Rostrum (height will be marked). G. Columns. H. Steps. J. Arch. K. Drapes on gallows arm. L. Swinger (flat which can be pivoted in and out of position). M. Slung microphone. N. Bracket. P. Lighting barrel over (these will be shown all over the plan).

made up to look other than they really are. Consequently, foot-steps are often a problem: there may be footsteps that are audible (and wrong) when they should not be heard at all, and others that are wanted but for which the natural sound is quite inappropriate to the picture. Here again the designer can help sound by the suitable choice and treatment of surfaces. This is discussed further in the chapter on sound effects, as are the sound-effects treatment of wind, rain, and fire in television, and also 'practical props', such as telephone and intercom systems.

Planning microphone coverage

In planning television sound coverage the first question is almost invariably: can it be covered by a boom? The microphone that can be swung or moved in and out on its telescopic arm, and then turned to any horizontal or downward angle, is, with its operator, a 'microphone with intelligence'. It can cope with so many situations without appearing in vision that it must be regarded as the principal method of sound pick-up in television.

Static or 'personal' microphones may also be used to augment booms, or in place of them. Also, for many types of television programme, microphones may appear in vision. The conventions that govern this, the details of different types of microphone that condition their choice, and also the techniques for their use for speech and music are all described in Chapters 6–9.

At the planning stage the sound supervisor must decide how many booms are required and how they must be moved about the studio to cover the various sequences, remembering that some sequences may require more than one boom. At this stage, too, it is necessary to anticipate minor changes in the script that could have a big effect on the sound man's ability to cover a scene. For example, it may seem reasonable to plan for speeches by two performers who are separated from each other to be covered by a single boom because the script indicates there is a few seconds between the two during which the boom can be swung. But supposing that at a late stage it becomes apparent that dramatic-ally a pause is wrong at this point and must be cut? If that happens, the sound man may find himself in a very difficult position: he is the one person who is standing in the way of a good perform-ance. Once in a lifetime is usually enough to convince any sound man that this is a problem he must plan to avoid.

A boom may require no operator (if it is simply to be placed in relation to a performer who does not move), one operator (for normal operation), or two (if it must be tracked at the same time). The sound supervisor must ensure that an operator is not placed so that he is unable to follow the action properly because the performers move into a corner of the set that he cannot see in to. He also has a responsibility for the operator's safety: he must arrange that the boom platform does not get angled so that

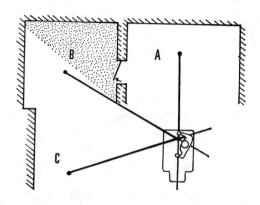

BOOM OPERATOR IN DIFFICULTIES. If the operator of a boom positioned for use in area A is asked to swing to area B, he is blind to all action which is obscured by the wall, and so cannot judge the angle and distance of his microphone. If the action continues to area C without movement of the dolly, the operator is now supported only by his boom and a toe-hold on the platform. Alternative provision must be made for coverage of B and C before the position for A is decided; this requires planning as camera positions and lighting are also involved.

as the operator swings the arm he runs out of platform to stand on; with certain types of boom this can happen very easily.

He must agree with the senior cameraman on the relative positions of cameras and boom pram; and particularly in the case where large camera mountings such as cranes need freedom of movement. He must also ensure that lighting will not throw shadows of microphones or booms on to performers or visible parts of the set.

Booms and lighting

To see how shadows may be caused it is necessary to understand a little about television and film lighting.

Performers are generally lit by two frontal lights. One, the *key*, is the main light: it is the strongest, and casts sharp-edged

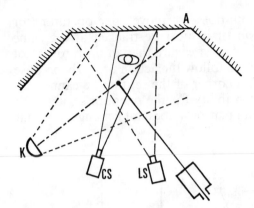

LIGHTING, CAMERAS AND MICROPHONE: the ideal situation. The close-shot camera has near-frontal key lighting (from K). The microphone shadow is thrown on to the backing at point A where it appears in neither picture. Few cases are, however, as simple as this. Cameras: CS takes close shot, LS takes long shot.

shadows. The second frontal light is the *fill*: ideally this should be from a source that has a lower power but a large area (e.g. an array of relatively weak lamps) so that it does not cast a hard-edged shadow. In addition there is *rim* lighting from the rear to outline the figure and separate it from the scenery behind (which will be lit separately).

For portrait close-ups the camera and the key light are not widely separated in their angle to the subject (though they must be far enough apart to give satisfactory modelling to a face). If the boom were also to come in from somewhere about the same angle there would obviously be a danger of a shadow being cast down on the subject's face. So the first rule for boom placing is that *the boom should come in from the side opposite to the key light* (perhaps at 90–120° to it).

Provided that the same camera is not used for wide-angle shots, there should be no danger of the shadow being seen against the

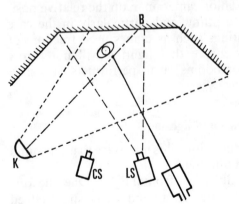

LIGHTING, CAMERAS, AND MICROPHONE: problems. The actor is too close to the backing, and the microphone, to get good sound, has followed. There is a shadow visible at B in the long shot.

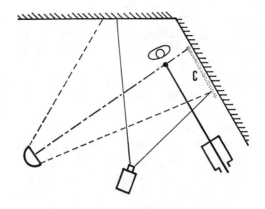

BOOM SHADOW. With a boom close to a long wall there is a danger of a shadow along it (C) on wide shots. If the boom is very close, even soft 'fill' lighting will cast a shadow.

backing. This leads us to the second rule: *long shots should if possible be taken from an angle well away from the key light.* Then, if the boom is coming in from roughly the same angle as the long-shot camera the shadow is thrown to the side of the shot and not into it.

In television, lighting often has to serve several purposes in order that a scene can be shot from a number of different angles. For example, it is often arranged for a light that is used as a key for one person to become the rim for another facing him.

But as scenes become more complex in their camera coverage, what may be relatively easy to arrange in shot-by-shot filming may become tricky in television, and compromises must be made. A third rule (which generally makes things easier) is that *plenty of separation should be allowed between the main action and the backing*, on to which a boom shadow could easily fall. This is, in any case, desirable for good back lighting. As a corollary to this,

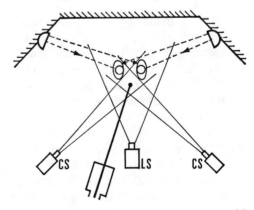

REAR KEY LIGHTING. Here two people facing each other are both satisfactorily lit, and there is no danger of microphone shadows as these are thrown to the front of the set. But this solution is less satisfactory for colour television than it was for black and white, as more light is needed than for frontal keying.

89

note that the boom arm should not be taken close to a wall or any other vertical feature of the set that will appear in vision. If the arm is close enough, even the soft fill lighting begins to cause shadows. Slung microphones may also cause shadows; again, the danger is greater if they hang close to a wall.

Occasionally there is no convenient alternative to having a microphone shadow, perhaps from the fill light, in vision: it may be the only way to get close enough for good sound. In this case the shadow is less likely to be seen if the microphone is kept still on the particular shots concerned and also if it is arranged to fall on a point of fussy detail rather than an open, plain surface.

In the planning stage, if the action seems to be getting too close to the backing, the lighting and sound supervisors are likely to join together in an appeal for more room to work. To such a strong demand the director will usually accede. The director may have several courses open to him: he may change the action or the timing of the words spoken; he may move action props away from the wall; or he may arrange with the designer for the working area to be physically enlarged.

In practice, shadow problems rarely result from bad planning—they are such a headache to everyone in a team that several people are likely to be on the lookout for any such possibility—but they can result from last-minute changes of plan on which consultation is impossible, or as a result of a series of minor compromises that finally build up to a big one. In such situations the normal co-operative spirit between sound and other departments may wear thin.

Standard routines for the recording session

Before considering individual techniques in greater detail there are a number of more or less related aspects of studio organization that should be touched on first. Apart from the placing of microphones and checks on balance and level there are a variety of other routines and practices that help to keep a recording session or transmission running smoothly. Here are some of the main elements of these:

The line-up procedure. This is to check that for a standard signal at the start of the chain all meters read the same, showing that nothing is being lost or added on the way. When extra equipment is introduced into the system this too must be lined up. For example, when a recording session or transmission follows a period of rehearsal, time must be set aside for line-up tests before the 'take' or live show. A sound studio schedule normally allows ten to fifteen minutes for this. Television line-up (involving similar procedures for the video signal) lasts much longer, so there will be adequate time for sound line-up within this. (However, in the more complex television desks provision can also be made for line-up tone to be sent to line without disturbing normal sound rehearsal circuits.) Where a recording machine is part of the studio equipment, or permanently linked to it, the line-up procedure may be abbreviated.

Timing the programme. A constant check is kept on timing, using either a script, a timed cue-sheet, or the recording form. All recording faults are noted on this, as is any other information that may be useful in editing, including all details of retakes.

Documentation. This is a chore, but may save time and avoid confusion later. On sound tapes a leader (giving summarized details of the contents) and a trailer (several feet of coloured tape—preferably red—to give a visual indication of the end) may be cut on to the recording.

Cueing. In radio a system of signals and other methods of liaison must be established at an early stage in the proceedings. In television these are passed through a floor or studio manager who is permanently on headphones.

Each of these subjects is discussed in detail in the following sections.

Line-up

Each organisation has an established routine, and so must the individual working on his own; but the exact details may vary.

The procedure adopted for a BBC sound radio recording illustrates the form that such routines may take. At the end of the rehearsal, and a few minutes before the scheduled recording time, the studio manager calls the recording room (if this is separate) on the *control line* (an ordinary telephone circuit that is called a control line to differentiate it from the broad-band *music line* along which the programme is fed). Details of the recording are checked, and the equipment is lined up by means of a 1000 Hz tone sent from the studio. The standard used in 1 milliwatt in 600 ohms: this is called *zero level* and is equivalent to 40% modulation at the transmitter (so that 100% is about 8 dB above this). At all stages in the chain the tone should give the same steady reading on all meters, and some of it is recorded on the tape, so that this process can be repeated when the tape is replayed.

Then *level* is given: someone in the studio is asked to read a few lines. This gives the recording engineer an additional check on quality, the last he will hear direct from the studio, for, just before he starts recording, he must switch over to monitor the output of his own recorder.

After a final check that everybody is ready, the studio manager announces over the studio talkback (which also goes to the recording room), 'We'll be going ahead in ten seconds from . . . now!' He switches on a red light (which indicates to people outside the studio that a recording or transmission is in progress); he fades up the studio, flicks a green cue-light—and the recording is under way.

In television the procedure is a little more complicated. In the line-up period video and sound lines are tested (again the BBC uses zero level tone for sound line-up). At the start of the actual recording a clock mounted on a board giving programme details is shown for the thirty seconds or so prior to the start of the required material. On an open microphone the floor manager calls '30 seconds...20 seconds...ten–nine–eight–seven–six–five–four–three...' and then both sound and picture are faded out for the last three seconds. As an additional sound check, ten seconds of tone (lined up to zero level at the studio control desk) is sent to line between the counts of 20 and 10, and this, too, is recorded on the tape as a final reference level.

At the end comes the reckoning: the duration is checked, and possible retakes discussed. If these are necessary further cues are given and they are recorded at the end of the main programme tape, to be edited later. Apart from documentation, the recording session is now complete.

A live transmission differs from a recording in several details, but principally in that just before the studio goes on the air the end of the preceding transmission is monitored. The sound man hears his cue and once his own transmission is under way he switches back to studio output, and since at every stage between studio and transmitter everyone is listening to the programme as it leaves his own point in the chain, the source of any fault can be rapidly located. The same switching procedure is adopted at the end of the transmission.

BBC stereo is lined up slightly differently from mono—with each channel at 3 dB below zero level. This is convenient in that at all points where the combined A + B signal is fed to mono equipment, line-up tone appears at the normal mono zero level.

The main thing to be noticed in these cases is that nothing is haphazard, though the routine may be got through in a casual and relaxed sort of way; and nothing is inessential.

Programme timing

By *timing* we mean two things: the tyranny of the stop-watch over broadcast programmes, and the artistic relationship in time of the various elements of a programme. In much radio work, particularly in America and other countries where commercials have to be fitted into the schedules with split second precision, and also where there is networking, each second must be calculated. An American director once described himself as 'a stop-watch with an ulcer'.

Today the stop-watch is probably no longer in his hands, but for some purposes is built in to the operation of an automatic control unit or possibly a computer. For the purely mechanical business of getting programmes, short items, music, commercials, time checks, and station identification announcements on the air some stations are now almost entirely automated, leaving the staff formerly occupied in this work free for more useful work, such as (according to the manufacturers of one broadcast automation system) selling more air time to advertisers, or giving news stories on the spot coverage. Or perhaps that director still has both his ulcer *and* his stop-watch—for the segments from which programmes are built still have to be created, and often to a strict overall duration: automation can—so far—only build transmission schedules from material which already exists.

This preoccupation with the value of time is not always such a bad thing. It reminds us to tighten up our programmes and make sure that every part counts (though whether we always take this hint is a different matter). The amateur is rarely under this sort of pressure, and it is perhaps no coincidence that the professional quality most often lacking in amateur work is that other aspect of time, a good sense of timing. Although 'time' and 'timing' are two separate things—and are often enough at odds with each other—they are closely inter-connected. Differences between rehearsal and transmission timings may explain a fault of pace. The relative lengths in time of different scenes or sections of a programme may throw light on faults in overall shape. So we see that the one obvious and overwhelming reason for timing radio programmes is not the only one.

When timing an item, the usual practice is to set the stop-watch going *on* the first word and not before it (not, that is, when the cue is given); and the watch is stopped after the last word is complete. The reason for doing it this way is that if various timings are to be added together in sequence, we want to count the pause between successive items once only—and it is obviously better to calculate a pause at the end than to add in an indeterminate stretch of dead air at the start.

There are various ways of marking the rehearsal and recording timings on a script. It can be done at minute or half-minute intervals, at the bottoms of pages, paragraph by paragraph, or by scenes or parts of scenes. Working in round figures makes calculation easier; but marking the time at natural junctions in the programme probably has more actual value.

If a programme is being timed in rehearsal or recording and an error occurs, so that it is necessary to break off and either go back on it at once or stop to sort the matter out, the first thing to do before dealing with anything else whatsoever is to stop the watch and mark in the script the point at which this was done, even if this is after the mistake. Then when the same point is reached again, the watch is restarted. Even if there is quite a long overlap, the true duration is probably substantially as shown on the stop-watch, despite the fact that it is the first take that has been timed, and not the second.

Where a programme consists of various individual elements— as in a magazine programme—two (or more) watches may be used including one for the overall and one for individual timings. In television this is done for videotape or film inserts, and the producer's assistant keeps everybody informed over talkback how many more minutes there are (useful if moves or microphone changes have to be made in the studio) and counts down the last ten seconds.

Another way in which a stop-watch may be used in radio is to give a speaker his last minute of air time. A stop-watch is started by someone in the studio and placed in front of the speaker, who knows that as it ticks up to one minute he must stop. It is a curious and very professional-looking accomplishment to be able to extemporize perfectly to the last second—and yet in radio circles people who can do this are by no means rare.

Documentation

After a recording is complete various details must be written up for later reference. Some of these are technical responsibilities and some production (and it must be clearly understood who does what). They may include:

1. Name and address of owner and recordist, title, reference number, date and place of recording, etc. The sample recording report on page 96 shows a layout for a sound tape recording. Similar forms are used for videotape and film sound recording.

2. Technical notes. Besides details of equipment and tape (including reel number where there is more than one, e.g. 'reel 2 of 5') the report should indicate which track was used and the position at which material is to be found; also details of any technical imperfection, fault in balance, etc.

3. Brief details of contents with durations: e.g.—

(*a*) Names and addresses, etc., of interviewees.

(*b*) Music information: composer, writer, performer, copyright owner, record numbers, etc.

(*c*) Identification of material that is not original.

4. Timed script or cue sheet, with editing notes; and details of the current state of the editing process.

5. Details required for programme costing.

6. Any extra information related to the programme, e.g. source of material used, contacts, etc.

In addition to this, summaries of the programme details may be written on the leader of the tape itself and on the spine of the box in which it is kept. The contents of the tape can then be identified immediately, whether the tape is lying loose or stacked away in its box on a shelf. For sound radio programmes the BBC uses printed leader tape: 'British Broadcasting Corporation' followed by spaces for the title of the programme, its reference number, reel number, tape speed, duration and date of recording. On the spine of the box the reference and reel numbers, title and speed are repeated. When the tape is finally wiped and reclaimed the leader is removed and a new strip of tape is stuck down the spine of the box ready for reuse.

Leader tapes are not used on film sound tapes recorded in the field; instead, it is more useful for the boxes to have the film slate numbers, etc., listed for quick reference. Video tapes may be identified by a label on the spool as well as the box, together with

OWNER				SOUND RECORDING REPORT
ADDRESS				
TITLE			REF. NO.	
SUBTITLE			REELS USED	
DATE	PLACE OF RECORDING		EQUIPMENT	
Type of Tape	Reel Size	Tape Speed	I/2/4 Track	Mono/Stereo

Report on Quality of Incoming Programme

REPORT ON QUALITY OF RECORDING/EDITING AND COPYING NOTES

Reel No.	Duration		Cues	Technical Notes
	Mins	Secs		
TOTAL			RECORDED BY	

RECORDING REPORT for a quarter-inch (6·25 mm) sound tape recording. Similar forms are used for videotape and film sound recording.

some identification written with a felt marker pen on the back of the tape itself at the start.

Radio and television stations usually log their output as it is broadcast: in the United States this is a requirement of the FCC. Such a log can be used—among other things—to check the total duration of commercials per hour, or the proportion of sustaining (i.e. unsponsored, public service) material in a schedule. But since the effort involved benefits no one at the station directly, it is not surprising that even its storage space is grudged. However, stations using broadcast automation systems can now have a very low-speed recorder for the automatic logging of programme details to comply with FCC regulations: the tapes take up only $1\frac{1}{2}$ cubic feet of space for two year's information. In computer-controlled versions the log is teletyped on demand, giving accurate times from the computer's digital clock (see pp. 57–59).

Cueing methods

The sound man in radio may be directly or indirectly involved in cueing performers; in television he may be responsible for equipment for doing so.

There are two principal systems of communication between director and performer. These are the cue-light system (used by BBC radio and adopted by many other radio organizations which are modelled on the BBC and also in film dubbing theatres), and the hand-signal system (favoured in American radio and universally in television).

BBC radio studios are equipped with green cue lights. These are operated by switches set in the control desk close to the faders. A separate cue light is provided for each studio area (or table) and is placed so that the artist does not have to turn away from the microphone to see it. One green flick means 'go ahead'. It is held on long enough for the least observant speaker to see it, but not so long as to hold up the person who thought you said 'when it goes off'. This convention is standard for all types of programme except one, the fast-moving news and actuality programme. For this the narrator is given a steady green 'coming up' cue ten or twenty seconds (as agreed) before the actual word cue is expected. The narrator goes ahead when the cue light is switched off.

Some hand signals are also used: the equivalent hand signal for 'go ahead' is to raise the arm for 'get ready' and then to drop the arm, pointing at the performer.

For radio talks, cue lights are also used to help regulate timing and pace. A series of quick flicks means 'hurry up', and a long steady means 'slow down'. A mnemonic for this is 'quicker-flicker, slow-glow'. These instructions may not be solely to adjust the programme to fit the scheduled time, but also to stop an un-practised speaker from gabbling or to get him moving. The equivalent hand cues are: hand and forefinger rotating in a small circle, fairly rapidly—'speed up'; hand, palm down, gently patting the air—'slow down'. These are both used extensively even when cue lights are available. In television the director gives the cue via the production talkback circuit to the floor manager, who signals it to the performer.

In discussion programmes the chairman may wish to use these signals and others for precise information about timing, e.g. two steadies at two minutes before the end, one at one minute to go, and flicks at thirty seconds. To give the signals by hand the director must stand where he is clearly visible, and then indicate 'minutes to go' by holding up the appropriate number of fingers; and 'half' by crossing the forefinger of one hand with the forefinger of the other.

Other hand signals sometimes used are: pulling the hands apart repeatedly—'stretch'. But have care, as it might also be taken for 'move back from the microphone'; as moving the hands together may be used to indicate 'get closer'—either to the microphone or to another speaker. Waving the arms across each other, palms down in a horizontal plane, can be used for 'stop'; and the side of the hand drawn across the throat predictably means 'cut'.

Crowd noise in a television play may be waved out; but in radio a series of quick flicks may be used to indicate 'the studio is faded out—everybody stop' and can be followed quite soon by the single flick for the start of the next scene.

There is one special case in radio: when the speaker is blind. The director, or an assistant, must stand behind the blind person's chair and give the various cues by laying a hand on his shoulder or arm. Quite complex cues can be given in this way if arranged before-hand. The blind often take more easily to radio broadcasting than do the sighted.

Cueing applause

The management of audience applause is important to many radio and television programmes.

In most ordinary circumstances an audience will wait politely until the end of a sentence and then (it what they have heard seems to call for it) they will clap or shout or do whatever seems appropriate. Through uncertainty as to whether they should interrupt the proceedings or not, the applause may be delayed a second or two and apparently, or actually, be half-hearted. They may even completely fail to applaud (particularly if the speaker is inexperienced in this branch of stagecraft). In any of these cases the effect is a lack or warmth and a failure to generate the feeling of an event with unity of location and purpose. For the home audience, the people who are watching in the studio might just as well be as far away from the action as they are themselves; as a result, there is no one with whom the viewer or listener can identify himself, to feel vicariously that he, too, is invited and actually a participant.

At the other extreme of audience reaction the studio applause may be excessive to the extent of breaking the flow of a programme in too many places. If applause is injected one sentence before the best point, then that point is not applauded at all (and might just as well be dropped), or it is given reduced applause (and appears as an anticlimax), or it receives a totally excessive reaction that simply holds up the programme in time and alienates the home audience.

Certain types of excessive applause may be inappropriate in their programme context, or simply unsatisfactory for sound— for example, young people stamping their feet on the wooden or metal rostra that support the seating in many television studios.

In Britain the overt management of applause is often viewed with disapproval. It is, however, necessary in all of the cases already mentioned where the programme becomes clumsy without it; it is particularly necessary in the case of small audiences of, say, a hundred or less, which may lack enough of those people who in any given situation help to start a crowd reaction; and it may be useful where 'atmosphere' demands that applause continues unnaturally long, such as at the close of a programme, behind closing music and titles or announcements, until sound (and where appropriate, vision) finally fades out. The management of applause is right and proper where it leads the local audience to react in places where reaction would in any case be natural, where such applause helps to interpret the material to which it is a reaction, and where it helps by pacing a programme and allowing the home audience time to absorb and assess what has gone before.

The behaviour of the audience may be partisan, either in the sense of being composed of admirers of a particular performer, of a participating team, or of a political party: in any of these cases it is reasonable to show the outward trappings of an existing genuine relationship. In all of these cases applause must be handled with responsibility towards both truth and intelligence.

Appropriate signals (in television from a floor or stage manager) might be as follows:

For 'start applauding', the stage manager stands in clear view of the audience, raises his hands high, and starts clapping. It may help to draw attention if he has a folded script in his hand. He should not be too close to a live microphone.

For 'continue applauding', the same action may continue, or be replaced by waving the script in a small circle, still well above the head (this adds variety to the stimulus and allows the other hand to be used for cueing). Both hands high, palms inwards, will also keep it going. But turning the palms outwards will bring the applause down, and waving the hands downwards at the same time, or if necessary more violently across the body, will bring it to a stop. Other signs may be used: the only requirement is that the audience understands and follows. But avoid the ludicrous 'applause' signs that are sometimes shown in old films. It is better to lead an audience than to direct it. For natural, warm applause it is often best if there is a slight overlap between speech, or music, and applause. This implies careful timing and clear understanding by the sound supervisor about whether the last words must be intelligible or whether it is permissible for them to be partly or completely drowned. He must also know whether the first words of a new cue starting over applause require moderate or high intelligibility (ideally, for 'warmth', it should be the former, with redundant information in the words spoken until the applause has almost completely died away).

The 'warm-up' is an essential part of any programme with an audience. Often the sound department play records of a suitable style until the warm-up proper, which consists of speeches giving information about the programme and the audience's important role in it, and, for a comedy show, 'warm-up' jokes.

Public address loudspeaker feeds to the audience and microphone techniques for applause are described on pp. 219–220.

Film sound recording

A film unit includes a director, a cameraman, a sound recordist and an electrician (for lighting), plus as many assistants in each of these departments as is necessary for efficient operation or to observe union rules. But using modern equipment, there are few occasions when a sound recordist actually *needs* an assistant for television film location work, except as a mobile microphone stand for certain types of dramatic subject.

The sound recordist generally has a high-quality lightweight quarter-inch (6·25 mm) tape recorder which can be used to record both the output from his own microphones and a reference signal related to camera speed. In countries where the electricity supply frequency is 50 Hz, 25 frames per second has been adopted as the standard television film speed, and the pilot tone is 50 Hz; but where the mains frequency is 60 Hz the film industry standard of 24 frames per second has been retained for television work, and a pilot tone based on 60 Hz is used for film recorders.

Many ingenious systems have been devised for combining the two signals on the one tape, of which the main aim is often to achieve the highest possible signal-to-noise ratio for the sound recording. One commercially well-established system uses a full-track recording, but with the pilot tone superimposed down the centre. There are, in fact, two narrow centre tracks each of 0·01 in (0·25 mm) with a similar gap between them. Pilot tones on the two tracks are recorded out-of-phase, so that on full-track replay of the recorded sound the two cancel and are not heard. A competing method has out-of-phase pilot tone tracks along the edges of the tape; and other systems have the tone recorded laterally. Simplest of all, the tone may be recorded half-track, with the film sound on the other half-track: this can be done with an adapted stero tape recorder.

In each case the corresponding system must be available for transfer of the tape to 16 or 35 mm magnetic film stock for editing: it is this transfer equipment which matches the speed of tape and magnetic film by scanning the pilot tone, so that the picture and sound tracks that are presented to the editor are perfectly in register, sprocket hole to sprocket hole, whatever the duration of the take.

To make this work, the camera and tape must be controlled to a common standard speed. In older equipment this is achieved by running a cable (a *sync lead*) between camera and recorder: the tone signal is generated by the camera and transmitted to the recorder. This has largely been replaced by systems in which the camera and recorder are controlled by a matched pair of crystals, vibrating at the same frequency. The camera motor has its speed accurately controlled, and the tape records the corresponding pilot tone. Note that in this case if the cameraman does not use the crystal control on his camera (if, for example, the mains frequency is used in order to synchronize with the frame speed of a television monitor) the sound synchronization may be lost.

Two other systems of recording are in use. One employs a magnetic stripe on the film itself and is suitable for news and other situations where the extreme mobility of a one- or two-man team is required. The sound is recorded in the camera itself, but displaced by about a second from the relevant picture. The remaining system is a hang-over from before the days of quarter-inch (6·25 mm) tape: a single unit acts as both camera and sound recorder, but using sprocketed magnetic film stock to run in mechanical interlock with the picture.

The film sound recordist's microphones and his techniques for using them are described in later chapters. Note also that many other techniques that are discussed primarily in terms of the studio are equally applicable in location filming.

Filming routine

Consider first the case where the director has control over the action before the camera.

Rehearsal for a film shot normally allows the recordist to obtain a microphone balance and set his recording level. In a full rehearsal the action, camera movement, and lighting are close to those to be adopted on the actual take, so the recordist has a final chance to see how close in he can get his microphone without it appearing in vision or casting a shadow. He can then judge the ambient and camera noise levels in realistic conditions.

When the rehearsal is complete and the performers are ready, the camera is normally set up for some form of identification of the shot, and the lights (where they are used) are switched to full power. While this is going on, the recordist listens for any rise in noise level due to traffic or aircraft, or people who are so carried away by the informality of the occasion as to be chatting happily but audibly in the background. If he feels that the director is likely to go ahead before any of these extraneous noises have been stopped or have died away he will warn him, ask for a delay, or possibly resort to direct action to get the offending noise stopped. When the director has checked with each department—often very informally—the camera assistant (in the conventional start to each shot) holds up a clapperboard to the camera, and the sound recordist or his assistant directs a microphone towards it.

On the director's instruction 'turn over' the tape starts: the recordist runs his tape immediately the camera operator runs the film; the recordist and cameraman then both check that their equipment has run up to speed, so that they have crystal 'lock'. Alternatively, if a sync cable is used they check that the sync pulse is reaching the recorder and that both camera and recorder have reached stable speeds. When they have, the camera assistant is told to 'mark it'. Note that although other technically ingenious systems have been devised for the synchronization of picture and sound, for example, one which puts light on a number of frames of film and a tone (or silence) on the corresponding duration of sound, the traditional sound clapper board is still preferred by many film-makers, including most of those at the BBC. It uses a little more film, which adds to its cost, but saves on editing by providing ready identification of both picture and sound (see p. 473).

Marking the shot (*boarding* or *slating* it) consists of stating clearly the shot and take numbers, e.g. 'one–two–seven take three,' while holding the board up to the camera with the bar open. The board is then clapped, the assistant and the camera operator both taking care that the action of the board closing is clearly in vision, and the recordist noting that the clap is identifiable and distinct from other sound that it could be confused with. If any fault is observed, a second board can be called for: the camera assistant puts the board back in shot, this time saying something like: 'one–two–seven take three, sync to second clapper'. He then clears the shot quickly but quietly, while the cameraman checks his framing and (if necessary) focus, and the recordist checks his microphone position for the start of the take and gives a final thought to noise problems—as the director himself may also do at this time.

The director checks that his performers are absolutely ready, waits for a signal that the cameraman has framed up and his assistant has settled himself and that there are no new shadows that will affect the start or a later part of the shot. When he is finally satisfied he calls 'action' . . . and the whole of this procedure so far may have taken only a few seconds.

At the end of the take the director calls 'cut': the camera stops running first, and as soon as it has, the recordist stops too (or if there is some continuing noise, he may signal for everyone to hold positions while he records extra sound for a fade: the director's cue might later be deleted in the editing).

If an event occurs without warning, so that camera and sound have to be run without a board (and the director should be very clear in his instruction to do this) the cameraman and recordist should continue to run after the end of the filmed action until the assistant can reach a place to mark the film with the inverted board, adding the words 'board on end' to spoken identification.

Mute shots, i.e. picture filmed without sound, are marked with an open board (perhaps held in such a way that it could not be shut without chopping off a few fingers).

Wildtracks are recordings made without a picture. The best way of identifying them is to relate them to a particular shot number, e.g., 'Wildtrack extra background of car interior with gear change for slate one–two–eight' or 'wildtrack commentary for one–three–two onwards.' Another system is to give them letters: 'Wildtrack B: atmosphere quiet classroom'.

The recordist should make a separate recording of the characteristic continuing sound of each different location unless specifically told it will not be wanted; he may also wish to rerecord important effects that can be improved by a balance in the absence of the camera, unless this is likely to hold up the proceedings—together with any specific additional noises the director wants.

In the case where the director does not have complete control over the action, it may still be predictable to the degree that a front-board is possible, or failing that, an end-board. The director (if any) may give instructions to turn over (start the camera) and cut, as before, in which case the recordist takes his cues in the normal way. (The recordist should call for the camera to keep running if the director calls 'cut' before the shot has been slated.) Alternatively the director may instruct the cameraman to take his cues from the action itself: in this case the recordist follows the lead of the cameraman, who will ask him to run (though he may have already taken his own cue directly). If the synchronising mark is missed, it is often simplest to run the shot again and board it properly, rather than leave the editor to find the sync for himself (although he usually can). This depends on the time available and the ease of repeating the shot.

Where the scene that is being filmed would be unduly disturbed by the standard procedure for marking shots, it can be simplified by starting each sync take with the recordist speaking the shot number and tapping his microphone in vision. The recordist can help the editor by leaving his fingers touching the microphone for a fraction of a second, and some confirmation of the take number may be provided by its being spoken in vision. Extra care should be taken not to get confused over shot numbers and it is advisable not to repeat any number for a 'take two': again, this is to help the editor when putting sound and picture together later.

Note that a hand clap, a pencil tap on a table or any similar action can also be used for synchronization when things are moving very fast. The procedure may also be streamlined when there is little chance of error, as in a small organization where material is unlikely to be mislaid. Then, the numbers may be omitted, leaving just the clap, tap or bump at the beginning or end of each sync shot.

Film documentation

The director's assistant, the camera assistant, and the recordist or his assistant each have their own documentation to complete. The main (director's) shot list should include the following (this is my own preference for documentary work):
1. Roll number (of film).
2. Board and take number of each shot.
3. A suffix 's' or 'm' to the shot number to indicate sync or mute; also 'eb' for end-board if appropriate (this use of suffixes is not general, but is convenient for quick reference—which is what shot lists are mostly used for).
4. Shot description with brief indications of opening frame (on start of action); the action within the shot (including camera action; pans, tracks or zooms, timed if possible); continuity points; faults or errors, including sound problems; and the overall duration of significant action. All of this should be brief and selective.
5. Overall duration or footage of film used for each take.
6. 'P', 'OK', or a tick for a shot to be printed; 'NG' for a shot that is not worth printing. Note, however, that where 16 mm film is printed to a low-cost cutting copy it may be as cheap to print everything, depending on rates charged by the film laboratories (bulk rates are usually cheaper). In this case the 'OK' or 'NG' serves as an editing guide.

7. Sound roll numbers as new rolls are started.

8. Wildtrack details (inserted in the shot list between the sync takes where the sound itself is to be found).

The film sound recordist's own report should include as many technical details of recordings as may be useful later. Each board for which sound was recorded will be listed, followed by a list of takes. A convenient way of indicating the good takes is to put rings round those particular ones but not round the others. (Note that it may cost more in manpower to supervise the transfer than is saved on magnetic stock costs, and if the editor or director later wants to double-check an 'NG' take against picture, it will cause delay if the sound has not been transferred. Again the simplest course may be to transfer all sound.) Wildtracks are included on the sound report in the same order in which they were recorded, and notes on quality are added where relevant.

In addition, the recordist identifies each new roll of tape over the microphone, with a standard list of details that might include his name, that of the film costing codes, date, location, recorder type and number, and camera speed (in countries where this might be at either 24 or 25 frames per second). He may also record a ten-second burst of reference tone at an agreed (or stated) standard volume such as 'minus 8 dB' (i.e., 8 dB below his nominal maximum volume).

The recordist is responsible for getting the tapes back for transfer within the shortest convenient time unless otherwise agreed: the simplest arrangement is for them to be despatched with the film (which is often sent for overnight processing) and then forwarded with the rushes for transfer while the picture is being viewed without sound). If so required, the synchronized rushes could then be viewed later the same day. This schedule assumes a fast, routine operation; but in a slower schedule the rush print would still be viewed for technical faults as soon as possible, though the sound might not be synchronized with it until later—perhaps at the start of the editing.

Choosing film locations

A final word about film routine takes us back to the planning stage, and the choice of suitable locations—an important first step in avoiding sound problems that may prove expensive in the loss of working time or may even make it impossible to record anything satisfactorily.

Surveys should establish that aircraft are not likely to disturb the proceedings too much. Direct observation is a good start but in addition a glance at an air traffic control map of the area concerned will show what type of disturbance there might be—jet airliners along the main airways and in the terminal control zones, and light aircraft elsewhere. The survey should also ensure that traffic noise is not obtrusive (or, if traffic is accepted as a visual element, that it is not excessive), and that machinery noise from factories, building sites, or road workings will not create difficulties —and so on.

If the investment in good sound is high, a visit to the site at the same time of day in the appropriate part of the week is a useful precaution. The story is told of a production assistant who went out on a Sunday and found a delightfully idyllic secluded rural location for a period drama—and it was not until the film unit had actually arrived and the camera was ready to turn over that the first roar of a jet engine started up on the other side of the nearest hedge. It was a busy military airfield which had just happened to be closed down for the Sunday.

In many cases where people unconnected with the film are found to be making noises that mar a performance a courteous request to stop often produces results, in which case courtesy also demands that the noisemaker should be told when filming is complete or when there are long gaps. It is, of course, unreasonable to expect people to stop earning their living in order that you may earn yours, so in such cases (or where it is the only way of gaining silence) payment may have to offered.

For interiors, acoustics as well as noise will be surveyed: what can be done to convert an interior 'location' to something approaching a studio is considered later in the next chapter.

5

STUDIOS

THIS chapter deals with studios: their purpose and layout (seen in terms of the operations that must be carried out in them); their acoustics, and treatments that can be used to modify the acoustics; and their furnishings. These are described both for radio studios and for television. Film studios are similar to but perhaps simpler than television studios: the output of a television studio is very high, and demands a high investment in equipment and working space.

How many studios and what sort?

Before considering how studios are planned to fulfil their function, it would perhaps be better to consider what are the needs for countries, regions, or communities of various sizes. Not until we do this can we see whether studios must all be for general (and perhaps limited) purposes or whether it is possible to design studios for particular specialized purposes.

The cost of television is such that the number of studios that can be supported by any given population is very limited. A regional population of 5–8 millions is generally sufficient to sustain two centres (perhaps in competition with each other), each with about three studios for major productions (including drama), for general purposes (including entertainment, with audience), and for speech only (presentation and news), plus an outside broadcast unit.

With a smaller population it would be difficult to sustain even this number: there may be only two studios or even one. But there would also be less use for an outside broadcast unit, so this may be taken for part of its time to a 'drive-in' studio—something like a film studio converted for television by the addition of the outside broadcast mobile control room, electronic cameras, videotape recorder or radio links, and so on. Such a studio centre would not be self-sufficient: it would use networked material or film for the greater part of its output, unless special local conditions required a high proportion of low-cost local material.

At the lower end of the scale towns serving areas of a million or so may have single-studio stations (again perhaps two, in competition). But these studios will be small, big enough for only two or three setting areas of moderate size.

A national population the size of Britain or the United States is sufficient to sustain three or four national networks. At the main studio centres there will be a range of studios that is broad in both size and purpose, and greater in number than for a region only. Very large conurbations can sustain both network centres and smaller local stations, particularly if these specialize to cater for substantial minorities that are disregarded by the main networks.

In radio (living, in most countries, in the shadow of television) a more confused situation exists. In the United States there is a radio station to every 25–30 000 population. Of the vast total number, half subsist on an almost unrelieved output of 'middle-of-the-road', 'conservative' or familiar 'wall-to-wall' music in some narrowly defined style. Then there are the top-forty, the country-and-western, and the classical specialists, plus stations that offer full-time news, full-time conversation (e.g. telephone chat) or full-time religion. Educational stations have a broader range, broadcasting both speech and music. In addition, a few 'variety' stations still exist, segmented in the old style and containing an integrated range of drama, documentary, quiz, comedy, news and so on; and there are also ethnic stations which may be impelled to serve the broader interests of a real, defined community. Most of these survive with low operational costs by using records or syndicated tapes for much of their output, and their studio needs are necessarily simple: perhaps no more than a room converted by shuttering the windows against the low-frequency components of aircraft noise that heavy drapes will not impede. Acoustic treatment can be added on the inside of the shutters. For some stations, a second, general-purpose studio may be partly justified by its additional use for board or staff meetings.

But looking again at our region with 5–8 million people, we now have a population which can sustain a full range of studios for all of the specialized functions that the current purposes of radio permit. These are likely to be fewer in the United States,

where radio has become more limited, than in Britain, where a regional centre may have the following studios:
1. Speech only (several),
2. Pop music,
3. Light and orchestral music,
4. Light entertainment (with audience),
5. General purpose, including dramas and dramatized educational programmes.

Smaller regions (100 000–1 million population) are capable of sustaining vigorous, but more limited, radio stations. National populations are capable of sustaining networks in about the same number as for television (though these are much more fragmented in the United States than in Britain, where they all reach almost the entire population). The BBC has about sixty radio studios in London alone, though many are for overseas broadcasting. Some are highly specialized—for example, those which are acoustically furnished for dramatic productions in stereo.

Studio design: keping noise out

When designing or choosing buildings for the installation of radio or television studios, here are some points to consider:
1. Do not build near an airport.
2. Prefer massive 'old-fashioned' styles of construction to steel-framed or modern 'component' architecture.
3. In noisy town centres offices that are built on the outside of the main studio structure can be used as acoustic screening. These outer structures can be built in any convenient form, but the studio must be adequately insulated from noise from *them*.
4. The best place to put a studio is on solid ground.
5. If a radio studio cannot be put on solid ground the whole massive structure, concrete floor, walls and roof can be floated on rubber or other suitable materials. The resonance of the whole floating system must be very low: about 10 Hz is reasonable. One inch of glass fibre or expanded polystyrene gives resonances at about 100 Hz, so care is needed. An alternative technique is to suspend the structure like a leaf from a tree.
6. Airborne noise from ventilation is a major problem. Low-pressure ducts are broad enough to cause resonance problems if not designed with care: they also require acoustic attenuation within them to reduce the passage of sound from one place to another. Grilles can also cause air turbulence and therefore noise.

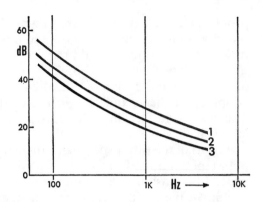

PERMISSIBLE BACK-GROUND NOISE IN STUDIOS. 1. Television studios (except drama and presentation). 2. Television drama and presentation studios. Sound radio: all studios except those for drama. 3. Sound radio drama studios.

7. High-speed ducts have been suggested as an answer to some of the problems of airborne noise, but would also require careful design, particularly at the points where the air enters and leaves the studio.

8. Double doors with a pressure seal are needed.

9. Holes for wiring should be designed into the structure and be as small as possible. They should not be drilled arbitrarily at the whim of wiring engineers.

10. Windows between studio and control area should be double and of different thicknesses, say $\frac{1}{4}$ in and $\frac{3}{8}$ in (6 and 9 mm). Contrary to what might be expected, it does not seem to matter if they are parallel. Insulation to higher standards than this is not necessary, as the higher levels of sound will be the same in both places.

11. Windows to areas outside the studio area *or to the control area if the loudspeaker is to be switched to replay during recordings* should be triple. Measures to avoid condensation will be necessary only in the case of windows to the outer atmosphere, where there will be temperature differences.

12. Any noisy machinery should be in a structurally separate area, and should be on antivibration mountings.

Although massive structures have been recommended, *extremely* massive structures may be more expensive than their improvement warrants. *Doubling* the thickness of a brick wall gives an improvement of only 5 dB.

For television studio roofs the limiting thickness for single-skin construction is about 10 in (25 cm): this gives an average attenuation of 60 dB over the range 100–3200 Hz. BBC research indicates that for noisy jet aircraft flying at 1000 ft a minimum of 65 dB attenuation is desirable. Even low-flying helicopters are less of a problem than this (provided they do not land on the studio roof), but supersonic aircraft producing a sonic boom with overpressures of 2 lb/ft² (9·6 kg/m²) would require 70 dB attenuation—particularly at low frequencies. Since a double skin is in any case desirable for more than 60 dB attenuation, it may be wisest to adopt the higher standard—70 rather than 65 dB attenuation. This results, in fact, in a structure which is little heavier than a 60 dB single skin.

As part of the BBC experiments there were subjective tests using both types of aircraft noise attenuated as if by various roofs and added to television programme sound at quiet, tense points in the action. In the limiting case the action may be part of a period drama, in which aircraft noise would be anachronistic.

Obviously, permissible noise levels depend on the type of production. For example, in television drama background noise from all sources (including movement in the studio) should ideally not exceed 30 dB at 500 Hz (relative to 2×10^{-5} N/m²). For light entertainment the corresponding figure is 35 dB. However, in practice, figures up to 10 dB higher than these are often tolerated.

Reverberation

So far all we have for our studio is a bare empty box of concrete (or some similar hard and massive material). It will reflect most of the sound that strikes it; and this will be almost independent of frequency—though very broad expanses of flat thin concrete may resonate at low frequencies and mop up some of the low bass.

When normal furnishings are placed in a room they include carpets, curtains, soft chairs. These (together with people) act as *sound absorbers*. Other furnishings include tables, hard chairs, and other wooden and metal objects. These reflect much of the sound striking them, but break up the wave fronts. They act as *sound diffusers*. Some things do both: a bookcase diffuses sound and the books absorb it.

The absorption or diffusion qualities of objects vary with frequency. In particular, the dimensions of an object condition how it behaves. A small ornament diffuses only the highest frequencies; sound waves that are long in comparison to its size simply pass round it. The thickness of a soft absorber affects its ability to absorb long wavelengths, and so does its position. At the hard reflecting surface of a wall there is no air movement anyway. So one inch of sound-absorbing material reaches out into regions of substantial air movement (and damps them down) only for the highest frequencies; to have any effect on lower frequencies it must be well away from the wall.

Sounds in an enclosed space are reflected, many times, with some (great or small) part of the sound being absorbed at each reflection. The rate of decay of reverberation defines a characteristic for each studio: its *reverberation time*. This is the time it takes for a sound to die away to a millionth part of its original intensity, i.e. through 60 dB. Reverberation varies with frequency, and a studio's performance may be shown on a graph for all audio frequencies. Or it may be given for, say, the biggest peak between 500 and 2000 Hz; or at a particular frequency within that range.

Reverberation time depends in part on the distance that sound must travel between reflections, so large rooms generally have longer reverberation times than small ones. This is not only expected but also, fortunately, preferred by listeners.

Coloration

In a large room an *echo* may be detected. If there is little reverberation in the time between an original sound and a repetition of it, and if this time gap exceeds an eighteenth of a second—which is equivalent to a sound path of 60 ft (18 m)—it will be heard as an echo.

In a small room *coloration* may be heard. This is the selective emphasis of certain frequencies or bands of frequencies in the reverberation. It is often the result of hard parallel wall surfaces which allow many reflections back and forth along the same path: at each reflection absorption always occurs at the same frequencies, leaving some frequencies still clearly audible long after the rest have decayed.

Parallel walls also give rise to *eigentones*, the natural frequencies of air resonance corresponding to the studio dimensions. If the main dimensions are direct multiples of, or in simple ratios to each other these may be reinforced.

The rate of absorption in different parts of a hall may not all be the same, giving rise to anomalous decay characteristics. For example, sound may die away quickly in the partially enclosed area under a balcony, but reverberation may continue to be fed to it from the main hall. More unpleasant (though less likely) might be the reverse of this, where reverberation was 'trapped' in a smaller volume and fed back to a less reverberant larger area.

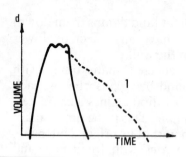
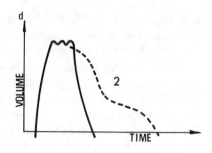

HOW SOUNDS DIE AWAY. 1. In a good music studio the sound dies away fairly evenly. 2. In a poor music studio (or with bad microphone placing) the reverberation may decay quickly at first, and then more slowly.

Resonances may interchange their sound energies: this happens in the sounding board of a piano and is one of the characteristics which we hear as 'piano quality'. In a room it may mean that a frequency at which the sound has apparently disappeared may recur before decaying finally.

Not all of these qualities is bad if present only in moderation. They may give a room or hall a characteristic but not particularly unpleasant quality: something, at any rate, that can be lived with. In excess they are vices that may make a room virtually unusable, or usable only with careful microphone placing.

The answer to many of these problems—or at least some improvement—lies, in theory, in better diffusion. The more the wave fronts are broken up, the more the decay of sound becomes smooth, both in time and in frequency spectrum.

In practice, however, if acoustic treatment has been carried out and panels of the various types that may be necessary for adequate sound absorption have been distributed about the various walls and on the ceiling, little more generally needs to be done about diffusion.

Studios for speech

Studios that are used only for speech are often about the same size as a living-room in an ordinary but fairly spacious house. But where demands on space result in smaller rooms being used, the results may be unsatisfactory: awkward, unnatural-sounding resonances occur which even heavy acoustic treatment will not kill. And, of course, acoustic treatment that is effective at low frequencies reduces the working space still further.

Coloration, which presents the most awkward problem in studio design, is at its worst in small studios, because the main resonances of length and width are clearly audible on a voice containing any of the frequencies that will trigger them off. An irregular shape and random placing of the acoustic treatment on the walls help to cut down coloration. But in small rectangular studios treatment may be ineffective, and this means working closer to the microphone. With directional microphones, bass correction must be increased and the working distance restricted more than usual (see pp. 141–144).

But coloration, as already indicated, is not necessarily bad; a natural sounding 'indoor' voice always has some. But it has to be watched carefully, and especially on monophonic recordings. Remember that even on a single voice there is a world of difference between mono and stereo: with mono all of the reverberation and studio coloration is collected together and reproduced from the same apparent source as the speech.

At first sight the answer might appear to be to create entirely 'dead' studios, leaving only the acoustics of the listener's room.

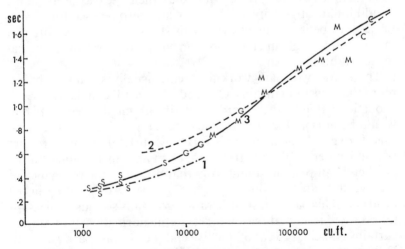

APPROPRIATE REVERBERATION TIMES FOR SOUND STUDIOS of different sizes. 1. Speech studio. 2. Music studio with 'natural' acoustics. 3. Central line shows BBC experience of good studios: S. Speech. G. General purpose. M. Music (natural acoustics). C. Concert halls. Studios for recording popular music are designed to be as dead as is practicable. Artificial reverberation is added in different proportions to the output of the microphones (10,000 cu ft is 286 cu m.)

But listening tests indicate that most people prefer a moderately 'live' acoustic—whether real or simulated. The experience of the BBC has suggested that, for normal living-room dimensions, 0·35–0·4 seconds is about right for speech when using directional microphones. A smaller room would need a lower time—a quarter of a second, perhaps.

Remembering that reverberation time is the time it takes for a sound to die away through 60 dB you can use a hand-clap to give a rough guide to both duration and quality. In a room that is to be used as a speech studio the sound should die away quickly, but not so quickly that the clap sounds muffled or dead. And there must certainly be no 'ring' fluttering along behind it.

Listening rooms and sound-control cubicles should have similar acoustics: 0·4 second is just about the maximum. BBC listening rooms are acoustically engineered for a response of 0·4 second up to 250 Hz, falling gradually to 0·3 second at 8000 Hz.

General-purpose sound studios

In Britain there is still a need for studios in which a variety of acoustics is used for dramatic purposes. In some other countries such facilities can hardly be justified by their use except, perhaps, to add interest to commercials. They may also be used for special projects to be issued as records. This studio type is therefore still important, though much less so than when radio was the principal means of broadcasting.

There are two main working areas, usually separated by no more than a set of curtains. One end, the 'dead' end, has a speech acoustic that is rather more dead (by about 0·1 second) than would be normal for its size. The other end is 'live', so that when used for speech the acoustic is very obviously different from that of the dead end. If the curtains are open and microphones in the dead end can pick up sound from that direction the resonance of the live end can sometimes be heard on speech originating in the dead end. This parasitic reverberation generally sounds unpleasant unless there is a good reason for it, so the normal position for the curtains is such as to cut off the live end (i.e. at least partly closed). However, useful effects can sometimes be obtained near the middle of the studio.

The live end can also be used for small musical groups working with speech in the dead part of the studio.

There may also be a very dead area; though if this is small it

116

may sound like the inside of a padded coffin rather than the open air it is supposed to represent. For good results the type of treatment used in anechoic chambers for sound testing would be best. These have wedges of foam extending out 3 ft (1 m) from the walls. But it would not be necessary to have this on the floor; a normal carpet would be adequate. After all, the open air usually has ground underneath it.

However, some performers find it unpleasant to work in such surroundings.

Studios for stereo speech are more dead than other general-purpose studios. The reason for this will be seen later: where coincident microphones are used, voices must be placed physically farther back than for mono; otherwise, movement is exaggerated.

The music studio

The foremost characteristic of a studio with live acoustics, such as is used for classical music, is its reverberation time. Preference tests indicate that, for any given size of studio, music requires longer reverberation than speech does. These preferences are not absolutes; but they are valid for the conventional music and musical instruments played in them during the tests. However, both music and instruments as we know them in the West today have developed in a very specialized way: in particular, our orchestral and chamber music is developed from that played in rooms of large houses in the Europe of the seventeenth and eighteenth centuries. The original acoustics has defined the music —and our music now, in turn, defines the acoustics needed for it.

That these instruments and this music are not the only forms possible should be fairly obvious—but it is only necessary to point to the majority of Eastern music, which is designed for performance in the open air, and to church music, which is at its best in highly reverberant surroundings, to show that we are dealing with a form that has been ruled somewhat arbitrarily by the acoustic conditions available. Moreover, some modern music is now written for drier acoustics than those which sound best for Beethoven. Nevertheless, the acoustics that we have been accustomed to have led to the design of instruments for which music of great beauty and power has been composed; so the studios we look for have certain specific qualities which can be judged by these subjective tests.

Listening tests are not always the best indication of true value:

they measure what we like best at the time of the test, and not what we could learn to like better if we took the trouble to change our habits. Nevertheless, several clear results appear when such tests are applied to music studios. It turns out that the ideal (i.e. preferred) reverberation time varies with the size of the studio: small studio—short reverberation; large studio—long reverberation. For the very smallest studios (e.g. a room in a private house set aside as a music room) the ideal is between three-quarters and one second. This is what might be expected if the room has no carpet and few heavy furnishings. Some authorities suggest that there should be more reverberation in the bass; but the BBC has generally adopted a response that is 'flat' at all frequencies.

An interesting sidelight on reverberation is that for monophonic radio and recording work, reverberation times about a tenth of a second lower than those for live music are preferred. The emergence of the reverberation from the same apparent source as the direct sound means that less is required. And in any case the reverberation of the listening room is added.

Apart from this, the principal quality of a good hall is good diffusion, i.e. the sound waves are well broken up and spread throughout the hall. There should be no echoes due to domes, barrel vaults, or any other concave architectural features.

Dead pop music studios

The studio acoustics play no part in much of today's popular music. The internal balance of the orchestra is deliberately surrendered in exchange for electronic versatility. A celesta, piano, or flute may be given a melody and may be expected to sound as loud as brass, and various other effects may be sought which can be achieved only if the sound of the louder instrument does not spill to the microphones set at high amplification for quiet instruments. Microphones are placed as close as may be practicable, and their directional properties are exploited to avoid picking up direct sound from distant loud sources, and to discriminate against reverberation from the open studio. Reflected sound is just a nuisance.

The solution to these problems has been to make the studio dead—more dead than is required for a speech studio. It is not just a question of cutting down reverberation. There must be substantial attenuation at a single reflection from any wall. This means much less of the sound of the brass (for example) will strike the walls and reach the flute or celeste microphone from directions that cannot be discriminated against.

There is one aspect of acoustics that is very important to pop music, not for its presence but again for its absence; this is the attenuation due to air transmission. At frequencies below about 2000 Hz absorption by the air is negligible. But for 8000 Hz, air at 50% relative humidity has an absorption of 0·028 per foot. This means there is something of the order of a 30 dB loss at a distance of 100 ft (30 m) for high frequencies. For damper air the loss is a little lower, while for very dry air it rises sharply and begins to affect lower harmonics (400 Hz) appreciably. This may make a great deal of difference between two performances using a distant balance in the same concert hall, but it does not affect close-balanced pop music, except to make instrumental quality *different* from that which may be heard normally: substantially more of the higher harmonics of each instrument are heard.

Television and film studios

Studios for television and film (and particularly the larger ones) are usually made very dead for their size. The primary reason is that if they are not to appear in vision, microphones must be

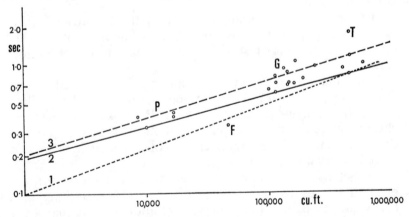

REVERBERATION TIMES OF TELEVISION STUDIOS (maximum values between 500–2000 Hz). 1. Lowest practicable limit. 3. Highest acceptable figure. 2. Normal design aim. The examples are all BBC television studios. Those above the upper line are too live (though mostly only marginally so). Group P. Presentation and small news studios. Group G. General purpose studios. F. A. converted film studio: unusually dead. This deadness has been obtained at the expense of a poor balance of frequency content. T. A converted theatre. The sound is too live for convenient use in television, but satisfactory for the audience present. (10 000 cu ft is 286 cu m.)

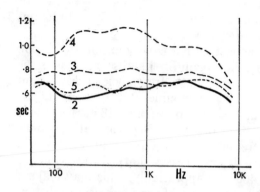

FOUR TELEVISION STUDIOS: frequency response (variation in reverberation time with frequency). BBC Television Centre Studios 2 and 5 are both 116,000 cu ft (3,320 cu m); studios 3 and 4, 357,000 cu ft (10,230 cu m). Studio 4 was designed primarily for musical entertainments, for which it is very satisfactory; it is a little live for plays.

farther away from their subjects than for other types of balance. But it also helps to reduce inevitable noise from distant parts of the studio. Noise arises in a variety of ways. For example, even with improved cameras and modern lighting, the lamps still produce heat, and the necessary ventilation cannot be completely quiet. Scenery may have to be erected or struck during the action, or props set in. Performers and staff must walk in and out of the studio, and from set to set. Cameras move close to the action: the movement itself is fairly quiet, but the cables dragging behind the cameras are not. And scenic projection equipment too, can be noisy.

The floor of a television studio must allow the smooth movement of heavy equipment. Accordingly, it is acoustically highly reflective, whereas the rest of the surfaces have to be very absorbent.

Sound that radiates upwards at any angle is reflected several times before it can reach a microphone, but sound travelling horizontally may be reflected only once. For this reason the most effective place for the absorption of sound is the lower parts of the walls; more of the treatment is concentrated here than is placed higher up.

The set itself may reduce the overall reverberation a little: braced flats absorb low frequencies, while soft furnishings and heavy drapes reduce the highs. In addition the set may have unpredicted effects on the local acoustics. A cloth cyclorama makes little difference, but if constructed of wood or plastered brick it reflects sound strongly (and curved sections focus it). Unfortunately, acoustic quality is not usually given much consideration in the choice of scenery or props, except sometimes in musical productions.

120

lios have acoustics approaching those used in
udios; they are therefore suitable for music
his type. For serious music, however, they are
able, and artificial echo must be applied liberally
for this. But this does not solve the problem of the
finds the surroundings acoustically unpleasant.
In particular, string players need reflected sound to satisfy themselves that they are producing a good tone quality at adequate
power. In its absence they are apt to bow harder, changing the
internal balance of the orchestra and making its tone harsh and
strident. The timing of ensemble playing also suffers. An orchestral
shell helps all of the players, but reinforces the brass players (who
do not need it) more than anyone else: a full shell turns a balance
inside out and should not be used. In fact, the best solution is to
design the setting to have reflecting surfaces for the benefit of the
strings. This does nothing for the overall reverberation time, but
helps the musicians to produce the right tone.

Film studios have in the past tended to be even deader than
television studios. In addition to the other problems, the cameras
are, by the nature of their intermittent action, noisy things which
are difficult to silence really effectively—though there have been
very great improvements in recent years.

Television sound control rooms and film dubbing theatres have
the same characteristics as their counterparts in radio: 0·4 second
at 250 Hz to 0·3 second at 800 Hz. But the main production and
lighting control areas should be as acoustically dead as is practicable in order that the director and his assistant and the technical
director shall be clearly audible on open microphones in an area
that also has programme sound. In fact, these rooms are not very
dead: the large areas of hardware and glass see to that.

Other technical areas, such as those for telecine and videotape,
need acoustic treatment: both machines can be noisy in operation; and both have loudspeakers for programme sound and
two-way talkback circuits. If machines are grouped in partly open
bays acoustic partitioning is necessary; in the case of telecine a
20 dB separation between one bay and the next is a suitable level
to aim for.

Acoustic treatment

Three basic types of acoustic treatment are available:

Soft absorbers. These are porous materials applied to walls:
their action depends on loss of sound energy, as air vibrates in the

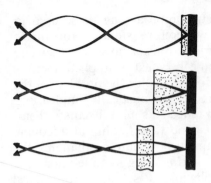

SOUND ABSORBERS. [...]
is close to a reflecting surface[...]
only for sufficiently short wave[...]
Screens with a thin layer of pad[...]
are poor absorbers at any but the highe[...]
frequencies. For greater efficiency in
absorbing a particular wavelength the
absorber should be placed at a quarter
wavelength from reflecting surfaces.

interstices of the foam, rockwool, or whatever it may be. The method works very well at high and middle frequencies, but for efficiency at low frequencies needs to be about 4 ft (1.2 m) deep. So it is reasonable to lay these at thicknesses that are efficient down to about 500 Hz and then become less so. Many different types are commercially available. Control of high frequencies (for which absorption may be excessive) is provided by using a perforated hardboard surface: with 5% perforation much of the 'top' is reflected; with 25% much of it is absorbed. Different surfaces may be alternated.

Helmholtz resonators. Cavities open to the air at a narrow neck resonate at particular frequencies. If the interior is damped they

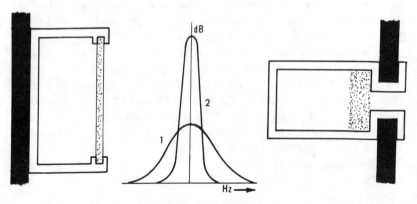

ABSORBERS. The membrane absorber, *left*, is a box covered by a panel which is fixed at the edges and weighted with some material such as roofing felt. It absorbs a broad range of frequencies (1). The Helmholz or damped cavity absorber, *right*, is, in effect, a bottle of air resonating at a particular frequency, with damping material within it. It absorbs at the frequency of resonance (2).

absorb at that frequency. Such resonators are useful for attacking dimensional resonances in sound radio studios. This is not a problem that should be overstated, however. Only about seven out of a hundred BBC studios seem to be affected; and in these it may not be the ideal solution, as it requires treatment to be fitted either at particular places that may be already occupied or some of the only places that are not.

Membrane absorbers. These are often used to cope with the low frequencies. But if the low frequencies are a problem, so too, can be the absorbers themselves. The idea is simple enough: a layer of some material or a panel of hardboard is held in place over an air space. The material moves with the sound wave like a piston, and this movement is then damped, so that low-frequency sound energy is lost.

A *combination absorber* of BBC design consists of units of a standard size—2 ft × 2 ft × 7 in deep (60 × 60 × 18 cm)—which are easy to construct and to instal; building contractors can be left to do this without constant supervision by acoustic engineers. A level response for a studio can be obtained by making (literally) superficial changes on this single design.

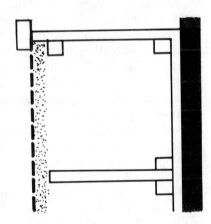

ALL-PURPOSE ABSORBER. A plywood box fitted to the wall and covered with rockwool and perforated hardboard. The response is tuned by varying a single factor, the amount of perforation in the hardboard surface layer. Combinations of boxes with 5% and 20% perforation can be used as required.

The box is made of plywood, with a plywood back. The interior is partitioned into four empty compartments by hardboard dividers 6 in (15 cm) deep. Over this airspace, and immediately behind the face of the box, is 1 in (2·5 cm) of heavy density rockwool. The face itself may be of perforated hardboard or something similar. If the open-area perforation is very small (about 0·5%) there is a resonance peak of absorption at about 90 Hz. If the perforation area is large (20% or more) a wideband absorption is achieved, but with a fall-off at 100 Hz and below. So by using one lot of boxes with two lots of facing it is possible to achieve level reverberation curves.

Using sound absorbers

If the acoustics of a sound studio are fully designed, then a mixture of absorbers is likely to be needed; and the majority of existing studios have a mixture of different types of absorber.

The *coefficient of absorption* of a material is the proportion of sound (at 512 Hz unless otherwise stated) that is absorbed in a single reflection at normal incidence. For total reflection the coefficient is zero; for total absorption it is unity. In practice the figure should therefor lie between zero and one. For example, free-hanging heavy drapes may be measured at 0·8 for 500 Hz and above. But note that for relatively small areas absorbers may have a coefficient that is greater than one—an apparent impossibility that can be produced by diffraction effects.

Larger objects have been described as the number of 'open window units' (their equivalent in the number of square feet of total absorption) that they represent. People rate about four and a half on this scale (at lower-middle to high frequencies); orchestral musicians with all their equipment can rate two or three time this, and a padded sofa may have ten times the effect of the man sitting on it. Tables of these values are available: in addition, they give values for the studio structure itself and for the volume of air within it. The calculations are complex, but here are some rule-of-thumb ideas that can be applied when attempting to correct the performance of a given room:

1. Apply some of each type of absorber to surfaces affecting each of the three dimensions.
2. Try to ensure that no untreated wall surfaces remain to face each other. (Note that a surface that is treated at one frequency may be reflective and therefore effectively untreated at another.)
3. Put the high-frequency absorbers at head level in speech studios.

The cheapest and best treatment for the floors of speech studios is a good-quality carpet and underlay (though the roof will need compensation in the bass). Wooden blocks are good on the floor of a (live) music studio.

As for the general furnishings of sound studios it is obviously

124

unwise to get the acoustics right for the studio when it is empty and then bring in a lot of items (particularly large soft absorbers) that subsequently change it. Such things must be included in the calculations from the start. But apart from this, it is not worth worrying too much about problems until you actually hear them. For example, if there is enough treatment in a room to get the reverberation low and level, and if the main rules for the layout of absorbers have been observed, the diffusion of sound is probably going to be all right anyway. So you can arrange the furniture with aesthetic and other considerations in mind: for how it looks best, makes the occupants feel happy, and gives the most convenient layout of working areas.

The use of screens

Very often the acoustics that are built in to a studio are not exactly those that are wanted for a particular programme, so ways of varying studio quality have been devised. Sometimes the acoustic treatment of a studio is set in hinged or sliding panels, so that with little effort an absorber can be replaced by a reflecting surface. But such arrangements rarely prove satisfactory: it is difficult enough getting a studio's acoustics right for a single particular type of programme, without introducing extra uncertainties into the design problem. A more flexible approach relies on various layouts of studio screens.

If padded screens are to be easily moveable (on castors), they must be light in weight (which in practice means they cannot be very thickly padded) and not too broad, often about 3 ft (0·9 m) wide. For stability they are mounted on cross-members. Individual free-standing screens are effective only for sound of short wavelengths: low-frequency sound flows round and past them as though they were not there. But grouping screens together improves things somewhat. At best, thin screens may reduce the sound flow between neighbouring areas by some 10–15 dB, while heavier screens with several inches of absorber (say 10 cm thick) will do substantially better.

Various types of screen have been designed, the most common consisting of a panel of wood with a layer of padding on one side. Such screens have the advantage of being dual purpose: used dead side to the microphone, they damp down the highs: with the bright side forward, the highs are emphasized, and the ambient sound in the studio is somewhat reduced by the absorbent backs.

125

In music studios with dead acoustics large free-standing sheets of perspex or wood are used in addition to thickly padded screens to separate instruments and their associated microphones from each other.

Whatever the type, the effect of all screens is basically the same in several important respects:

1. There are shorter path lengths between reflections of the sound in the studio: there are more reflections and more losses in a given time. This means, in general, a lower reverberation time for the studio as a whole.

2. Sound from distant sources is reduced; but sound that does get round the screens is usually lacking in top. This includes any appreciable reverberation from the open studio.

3. Coloration can be introduced by careless layout. If there are two parallel screens on opposite sides of the microphone a standing-wave pattern will be set up. On the other hand, such distortion effects may be used constructively—though this is more often done by placing a microphone close to a single screen.

4. For the purposes of multimicrophone music balances the separation of a large number of individual sources that are physically close together can be made more effective. Important enough in mono, this is vital in stereo.

In any studio it helps to have a few screens around—you never know when they may come in useful. They may be wanted to produce subtle differences of voice quality from a single acoustic, or to screen off a light-voiced songster from the big accompaniment, or in classical music for backing and reinforcing the horns.

Altering the acoustics of concert halls

Traditionally, the design of concert halls has been a fallible art rather than an exact science. In many halls of a suitable size it is difficult to pick up good sound, and even where after careful experiments a reasonable compromise is found for microphone placing, many members of the audience (whose audible enjoyment may contribute to the sense of occasion of a broadcast) may suffer poor sound in the hall itself. Fortunately it is now possible to do something about many such halls (or studios). Two that have had their acoustics physically altered are the main concert halls of London.

Ever since it was built in Victorian times, the Royal Albert Hall inflicted severe echoes on large areas of seating and its unfortunate occupants. This was partly due to the shape of the hall and partly its size. Being very large, for some seats the difference in path length between direct and first reflection indirect sound is of the order of 100 ft (30 m), resulting in a delay of nearly 0·1 second. To be absolutely sure that the reverberation is not distinct from the direct sound this interval should be 0·02 second or less. An appreciable delay between direct sound and the earliest reflections is therefore a characteristic of all halls. Whether this is acceptable or not depends on the nature of those reflections.

This is where the shape of the Albert Hall comes in: it was designed as a cylinder with an elegant dome surmounting the interior. Such concave surfaces produce focused reflections, and some of them coincided with the seating. Apart from the gallery, where the sound was clean, though distant, there were (regular concert-goers claimed) only about two places in the hall that were satisfactory. Staccato playing, including percussion and piano, were special problems. Also, the natural reverberation time of the hall is long. As a result, the range of music that could be played to really good effect was limited virtually to one type: romantic music with long flowing chords.

Attempts to improve the acoustics without changing the appearance of the hall failed. The problem was eventually tackled by suspending flights of 'flying saucers' 6–12 ft (2–3 m) in diameter: one hundred and nine of these hang just above the gallery level. Taken all together, they define a new ceiling, slightly convex towards the audience and filling about 50% of the roof area.

These polyester-resin-impregnated glass-fibre diffusers (some of them with sound-absorbent materials on the upper or lower surfaces) have largely solved the problem of echo from above and at the same time have reduced the reverberation at 500 Hz to more reasonable proportions for a wider range of music. Before, it would have been impossible to broadcast without the acoustic aid of an audience. Now something with reasonably large forces— say *Verdi's Requiem*—could be.

In London's post-war Royal Festival Hall the error was in the opposite direction. Musicians had been asked in advance what acoustics they would like to have, 'tone' or clarity. The answer came, 'tone'—but unfortunately what they actually got instead was a quite remarkable degree of clarity. The sound was much more dead—and particularly in the bass—than had been expected, largely due to the construction of far too thin a roof shell. Minor

127

measures, such as taking up carpets from walkways and making surfaces more reflective, had insufficient effect. While a cough sounded like a close rifle shot, the bass reverberation remained obstinately at about 1·4 seconds. How, short of taking all the seats out and sending everybody home, do you lengthen a reverberation time?

The answer was novel and like the hall, twentieth century in style: *assisted resonance*. Cavity resonators were used, but not in their normal form: these contained microphones, which were thereby tuned to respond to narrow bands of frequencies present and to reradiate sound through individual loudspeakers. A hundred channels could each have a separate frequency; allocating each a band of 3 Hz, the whole range of up to about 300 Hz could be boosted. In this way, reasonance was restored at surfaces at which, previously, sound energy had begun to disappear. A reverberation time of 2 seconds was now possible, but it could be varied and actually tuned at different frequencies.

Assisted resonance has since become available as a commercial package, prolonging a selected range of 78 frequencies between 50–1250 Hz by 20 milliseconds. At the Festival Hall this dealt very effectively with the balanced overall duration of reverberation, but offered less improvement in other ways: in particular, when the brass opens up or timpani start rolling, the other players are still overwhelmed and blotted out. Modern works with a dry sound remain the most successful.

In both of these places, however, the BBC had been able to get good or fairly good sound before the alterations by suitable choice of microphone and careful placing; and the balance problems (other than for reverberation *time*) have hardly been affected.

Recording companies working with London's many first-rate orchestras have found their own solutions. Audiophiles all over the world may not know it, but the acoustics *they* generally hear on record are not those of the well-known concert halls, but obscure suburban town halls at places like Walthamstow, Wembley, Watford, and Hammersmith—in buildings that were not originally intended for such a use at all. The moral of this story is that science, so far, is not doing quite so well as happy chance, the fortuitous combination of circumstances that gives perfect blending. Search until you find it.

Acoustic modelling of studios

A more scientific approach to the design of new studios—or redesign of defective ones—can be achieved by the use of scale models. If the model is made to a scale of one-eighth linear, the sound path lengths are reduced in the same proportion. With the absorbers scaled accordingly, the reverberation is one-eighth of that for the full-size studio. Variations in design can be explored at costs that are tiny in comparison with those of the older trial-and-error methods: surfaces are one sixty-fourth life size and the total volume about one five-hundredth. A special acoustically dead selection of musical recordings is replayed into the model at eight times normal speed, and re-recorded with the acoustics of the model added. This can be replayed at normal speed, and the results of various configurations and forms of treatment compared.

BBC experiments faced difficulties in the design of a suitable loudspeaker to fill the model with sound at the required 400 Hz to 100 kHz. The design finally chosen had three elements: a 11 cm thermoplastic cone (400–3000 Hz), a commercial 20 mm domed plastic diaphragm (3–21 kHz), and a cluster of 45 small electrostatic units mounted on a convex metal hemisphere giving wide-angle high-frequency radiation (21–100 kHz). Microphones to reproduce the same raised frequency band required a very small diaphragm. The smallest practicable instrument, with a diaphragm 6 mm across, was adequate, if rather large for the highest frequencies. The microphones were omnidirectional, so for a stereo pick-up a spaced pair had to be used. The tape recorder was required to cover 50 Hz–12·5 kHz at normal speeds and the 400 Hz–100 kHz band when speeded up: for this a commercially available machine was modified.

Structural components and miniature furnishings to be used in the model were first acoustically tested in a specially constructed reverberation chamber. Materials with textures similar to the full-scale object were used where possible: for example, velvet for carpets. Perforated absorbers were represented by scaled-down absorbers of similar construction. It proved essential to include miniature musicians too; an orchestra is widely spread and mops up a great deal of the sound it creates. Indeed, the early experiments were unsuccessful until the players were adequately modelled in cutouts of expanded polystyrene with 3 mm of felt stuck to their backs.

The biggest problem was the air itself—for this must also

absorb eight times more sound in transit. This was achieved by making it much drier, getting it down to 4% relative humidity (compared with a typical, though very variable, 45% in normal air). Silica gel was not good enough for the job, but an artificial zeolite dried the air in the model in only half an hour.

The first application of the technique was in the redesign of the BBC's main orchestral studio, a former ice-rink that has served the BBC Symphony Orchestra reasonably well for many years, but which had certain nagging deficiencies. A vast number of experimental modifications were tried out on a model of this hall. Absorbers were changed on the end wall, and added on the roof, then covered with a low-frequency reflective material; the choir rostra were changed, then switched to a different position, and subsequently replaced by a new design; while various shapes of wooden canopy were suspended over the orchestra. The results were compared with each other and (as was possible in this application) with the sound produced by playing the same test material through the real studio. The experiment saved more than its own cost by one result alone: it indicated that the big reflective canopy would have been a waste of money. The chosen design was built, without the canopy, and came within 10% of the performance predicted—an unusually good result in this problem-ridden field.

The second application was to the construction of a completely new music studio (in Manchester), where the question asked was: would a simple design work, using the 'combination' absorbing boxes described earlier (p. 123) to tailor its response? The answer was yes, and, surprisingly, that far fewer such boxes were required than simple extrapolation from results in smaller studios would have led the designers to expect. They had modified the absorbers a little, making them a little deeper in order to handle the low frequencies better. In the model it was found that scattered boxes absorbed more than 100% of the sound falling on their equivalent area of wall: evidently their sides made an important contribution, as well as the front. Again the initial experiments proved extremely valuable.

Ambiophony

A general purpose television studio has quite the wrong acoustics for orchestral music. The addition of artificial 'echo' is only a half-solution, because of the effect of the acoustics on the players themselves: the string and some other players may tend

130

to force their tone to hear themselves as they think they should be, thereby marring both the internal balance of the orchestra and the overall orchestral quality. Another problem for the musicians is that more distant sections that can normally be heard clearly may not be, so that ensemble playing is more difficult.

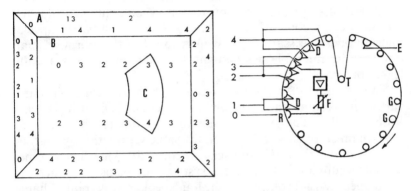

AMBIOPHONY. A. Gallery level. B. Grid level. C. Orchestral area below. 0–4. Loud-speakers with different delay times: 0. No delay. 1. 30 and 60 ms delay. 2. 90 and 150 ms. 3. 120 ms. 4. 180, 210, and 240 ms. This is a typical layout, but each actual case will be different. R. Recording head, fed from ambiophony microphone, plus feedback loop, F. E. Erase head. T. Tension pulley. G. Tape guides. D. Delay heads.

One answer that has been tried is *ambiophony*. This replaces the missing reflecting surfaces by a large number of loudspeakers —fifty or more in a studio of moderate size—fed by special microphones through a tape delay system. The delay is essential because the acoustic path lengths are shorter than the actual dimensions of the studio would suggest: the total distance from musician to ambiophony microphone, plus that from wall or roof loudspeaker to listener (or the studio microphone that represents him) is less than first reflection path via the same point on the wall. With tape delay the apparent reflective surface can be made to recede to a point even beyond the actual limits of the studio. In practice, the best result—simulating the well-diffused and open textured reverberation of a good, large hall—was achieved by introducing not just one delay system but four (plus some loudspeakers relaying undelayed sound). The four systems are derived from combinations of the outputs of eight replay heads situated at intervals on a tape loop. The sound passes repeatedly through the studio, diminishing as it does so.

In addition, variable feedback within the loop itself introduces artificial echo.

Ambiophony microphones need to be placed close to the sound source—preferably not more than 6–8 ft (2–3 m) away—so that they discriminate strongly against the relatively distant wall loudspeakers. Where close spotting microphones are used on individual instruments or sections, such as the string and wood-wind sections, an ambiophony feed may be split off using the public address controls. Otherwise, for wider shots, the special microphones necessarily appear in vision. For this purpose small electrostatic microphones hanging by their own cables are the least obtrusive.

The system is tuned by taking each loudspeaker in turn, raising its volume until a howlround occurs, then setting back a little from this. The overall master ambiophony feedback volume control must, of course, be left at the same setting throughout the process, and at the end is set back a further 4 dB. This then becomes the maximum level at which the system may be used. To achieve the highest possible output for the loudspeakers, a response shaper consisting of a system of octave (or more closely spaced) filters may be included in the circuit.

The final pick-up of the resulting sound can be made using an omnidirectional microphone placed high up, as described in the chapter on microphone techniques for music, but with the variation that the microphone is balancing direct sound against a system of apparent acoustics that it itself variable in frequency response, in reverberation time (by varying feedback within the tape delay system itself) and to some extent in overall volume. The first two of these techniques are discussed further in the chapter on echo and distortion techniques.

Once a particular distribution of loudspeakers, each with its own delay, is worked out, it becomes specific to the particular position of the sound source for which it was calculated. As a result, if additional sources are introduced (say, singers in other parts of the studio) the system may be unbalanced. In particular, ambiophony may not work satisfactorily where a boom microphone is used for a moving singer, because as the microphone is swung around, different loudspeakers are favoured.

Ambiophony creates conditions in which musicians can work comfortably, and offers a fair simulation of music studio acoustics. But the studio layout, once optimized, is inflexible, so the BBC has abandoned its use, to rely instead on the flexibility and technical skill of the musicians themselves.

6

MICROPHONES

In the simplest terms, the job of a microphone is to convert sound energy into electrical energy, and to do so without changing the sound information in any important way.

A microphone must therefore do three things:

1. For normal sound levels it must produce an electrical signal that is well above its own electrical noise level.

2. For normal sound levels the signal it produces must be substantially undistorted.

3. Together with its associated equipment, it should, for a particular sound source, respond almost equally to all significant audio frequencies present.

With today's high-quality microphones the first two objectives are easily met—though to achieve a signal that can be transmitted safely along the microphone lead, a transformer or amplifier is often required so close to the head as to be regarded as part of the microphone itself. The third requirement is more modest, and deliberately so. Indeed, until the advent of FM broadcasting there was no call in radio for microphones that could pick up the full audio range. To have demanded this would have been a waste of money. Even today it may still be unnecessary to use a microphone with a full-range frequency response for a source of restricted range.

Microphones differ from each other in the way that movement of the diaphragm is converted into electrical energy. The most important types in present-day professional use are moving-coil, electrostatic (condenser), and ribbon types. Crystal microphones have been used in cheaper equipment and carbon types in telephones. Other microphones include inductor, moving-iron, magnetostriction, and electronic types. The latter are not described here; several of them have practical disadvantages that have limited their development. Another possible principle is that of the pressure sensitive semiconductor.

Microphones also differ from each other in the way in which air

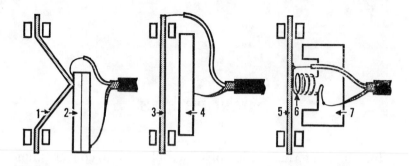

TYPES OF MICROPHONE. *Left.* Crystal. 1. Light rigid diaphragm. 2. Crystal bimorph. *Centre.* Condenser. 3. Foil diaphragm. 4. Backplate. *Right.* Moving coil. 5. Diaphragm. 6. Coil fixed to diaphragm. 7. Permanent magnet.

pressures are converted into movement of the diaphragm. These variations show themselves as differences in directional characteristics and are of great importance to the user. Although the output of a microphone may be deliberately designed to change with the angle from a given axis, the frequency response, ideally, should not. Unfortunately, however, this is an almost impossible demand, so it is usual to define the 'useful angle' within which this condition is, more or less, met; or to devise ways in which the deficiency can be turned to advantage.

Sensitivity—the strength of the electrical signal that is produced by a microphone—is also an important quality. In practice, most professional microphones have sensitivities within a range of only a few dB of each other (though this level may be at the output of a microphone head amplifier). Characteristically, rather more than 70 dB (further) amplification is required to reach a level suitable for input to a high-level mixer or for transmission by line between studio and radio transmitter—though at the bell of a trombone a microphone may also have to respond without distortion to levels 60 dB higher than that for which it is rated.

Other properties that may be of importance are:

1. *Robustness.* Moving-coil microphones in particular stand up well to the relatively rough treatment a microphone may accidently suffer when used away from the studio. Electrostatic (condenser) microphones require greater care.

2. *Sensitivity to handling,* e.g. by pop singers. Again moving-coil types score. If microphones are to be handled while in use the cables and cable connections must not produce handling noise.

A reduced low-frequency response helps. Ribbon microphones are unsuitable, as their ribbon diaphragms typically have a resonant frequency of about 40 Hz which is easily excited by any form of movement, even on a boom.

3. *Sensitivity to wind.* Gusting produces erratic pressure gradients, so microphones relying on this principle are at a disadvantage. Ribbon microphones in particular also have a relatively floppy diaphragm and so are doubly at risk in this respect, and may therefore not be suitable for outdoor work.

4. *Shape, size or weight.* Appearance matters a great deal in television, and size and weight in microphones that are held or attached to clothing.

5. *Cost.* Crystal microphones are very cheap, and good moving-coil microphones moderately so; electrostatic microphones (other than mass-produced electrets) are relatively expensive.

6. *Suitable impedance.* Nominally a microphone should be rated appropriately for the impedance of the system into which its signal is fed, otherwise the interface between components reflects some of the signal and may affect the frequency response. In practice, the impedance of a microphone should be lower than that of the system it is plugged in to. After a transformer or head amplifier (where necessary) many professional microphones have an impedance of about 200 ohms. This works well with a mixer that has a higher input impedance.

7. *Sensitivity to temperature and humidity variations.* Location filming may sometimes be undertaken in extreme climatic conditions, and heat and humidity can also cause trouble high up among the lights in a television or film studio. Water vapour condensing on to a lightweight diaphragm increases its inertia and temporarily wrecks its response. So will any moisture that impairs the insulation of an electrostatic microphone.

In a given situation any one of these points may be dominant,

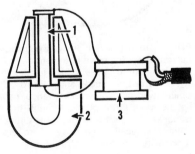

RIBBON MICROPHONE. 1. Light, conductive foil ribbon. 2. Permanent magnet (with pole pieces extending above). 3. Transformer.

135

severely restricting or even dictating the choice of microphone. Many commercially available microphones emphasize particular characteristics at the expense of others, and examples of some that have been designed for specialist uses are described later in this chapter. But more often, there is a range of possibilities.

Microphone balance means placing a microphone in relation to discriminating against noise or sources covered by other microphones, while giving a good account of the studio acoustics (or, alternatively, eliminating them). Balance itself is discussed in the next chapter: first, we must meet some of the main types of microphone that are available.

Directional response

Microphones fall into several main groups, according to their directional characteristics. Their field patterns are best visualized on a *polar diagram*, a type of graph in which the output in different directions is represented by distance from the centre.

Omnidirectional microphones. These, ideally, respond equally to sounds coming from all directions. Basically, they are devices for measuring the *pressure* of the air, and converting it into an electrical signal. Many designs of moving-coil and crystal micro-

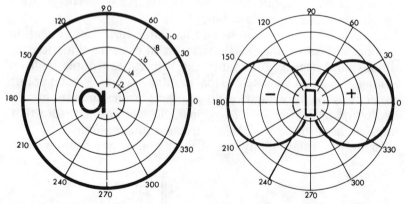

POLAR DIAGRAMS showing the field patterns of *omnidirectional* and *bidirectional* microphones. The scale from centre outwards measures sensitivity as a proportion of the maximum response, which is taken as unity. An alternative scale is in decibels: with 0dB at the outside and -25 to -35 near the centre, giving a diagram that is similar over the main working range. *Left.* A perfect omnidirectional response would be the same in all planes through the microphone. *Right.* A perfect bidirectional response, is the same in all planes through the 0°–180° axis. At 60° from the axis the output is reduced to half, and at 90° to zero. The response at the back of the microphone is opposite in phase.

136

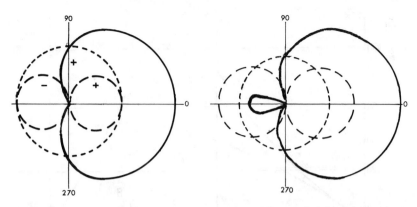

CARDIOID RESPONSE, *left*, is the sum of omni- and figure-of-eight pick-up when the maximum sensitivity of the two is equal. The front lobe of the 'eight' is in phase with the omnidirectional response and so adds to it; the back lobe is out of phase and is subtracted. The cottage-loaf shaped hypercardioid response, *right*, is a more directional version of the cardioid microphone. It is one of a continuous range of patterns that can be obtained by combining omni- and bidirectional response in various proportions. As the bidirectional component increases further, the rear lobe grows, to make the characteristic cottage-loaf shaped response.

phone work in this way, as do some electrostatic microphones. The diaphragm is open to the air on one side only.

Bidirectional microphones. These measure the difference in pressure *(pressure gradient)* at two successive points along the path of the sound wave. If the microphone is placed sideways to the path of the sound the pressure is always the same at these two points and no electrical signal is generated. The microphone is therefore *dead* to sound approaching from the side and *live* to that approaching one face or the other. Moving round to the side of the microphone, the response becomes progressively smaller and a graph of the output looks like a *figure-of-eight*, (a term often used to describe this type of microphone.) The *live angle* is generally regarded as being about 100° on each face. At the back the signal is equal in strength to that at the front, but of exactly opposite phase *(antiphase)* to it.

Ribbon microphones most often work in this way, responding to the difference in pressure on the two faces of a strip of aluminium foil. Single-diaphragm electrostatic mictophones work in this way if the air pressure can reach both sides of the diaphragm equally.

Cardioids have a heart-shaped response. This is obtained if the output of a pressure-operated microphone is added to that of a pressure-gradient microphone with a response of similar

137

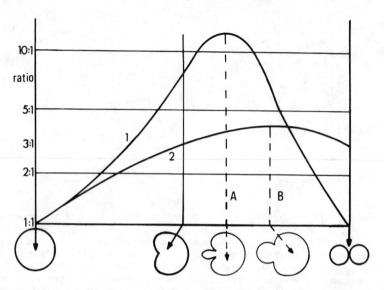

DIRECTIVITY, as a microphone ranges from pure pressure operation (omnidirectional) to pure pressure gradient (bi-directional). Curve 1 shows the ratio of sound accepted from the front and rear. The most unidirectional response is provided by the hyper-cardioid, A, for which the microphone is, essentially, dead on one side and live on the other. Curve 2 shows discrimination against ambient sound. With the cottage-loaf shaped response, B, reverberation is at a minimum and the forward angle of acceptance is narrower. In the range between omnidirectional and cardioid, direct sound from the front and sides is favoured, so a microphone of this type could be placed close to a broad source. (Note that the close balance will already discriminate against reverberation, and that this microphone will reduce long path reverberation still further.)

strength along its forward axis. Various ways of combining the two principles are possible: early cardioid microphones actually contained a ribbon and a moving coil within a single case. The output of the two is added together for sounds at the front; but at the back the two are antiphase and cancel. At the side there is no output from the ribbon, but the omnidirectional element retains its normal output. So there is a substantial pick up of sound on the front and right round to the side, but beyond this relatively little.

Hypercardioids. If the pressure and pressure-gradient modes of operation are mixed in varying proportions a range of polar diagrams is produced, passing from omnidirectional through cardioid to bidirectional. The directional qualities within this range may be described in two ways. One is in terms of the degree of *unidirectional response*, measured as the ratio of sound accepted at front and back of the microphone (i.e. before and behind a

138

plane at right angles to its directional axis). This is 1:1 for omni-directional and bidirectional responses and maximum, reaching a peak ratio of 13:1, at an intermediate setting. The second way of describing a microphone's directivity is by measuring its *discrimination* against indirect sound: in practice, this too is expressed as a ratio, here describing the proportion of the total solid angle over which the microphone is effectively sensitive to sound. It is 1:1 for omnidirectional microphones, 3:1 for both cardioid and bi-directional pick-up, and is higher (a little over 4:1) for a response half-way between the latter two.

The combination of the pressure and pressure-gradient principles in different proportions is very useful for cutting down the amount of reverberation received and for rejecting unwanted noises. Some microphones can be switched to different polar diagrams; others are designed for one particular pattern of response. When choosing between different field patterns, note that the breadth of pick-up narrows as the pressure-gradient component gets stronger. Microphones within this range are sometimes called *hypercardioid* or *supercardioid*. A *cottage loaf* pattern is most evident at the point where the discrimination against ambient sound is at its greatest; and the term 'undirec-tional' may be taken to refer to the response between cardioid and cottage loaf.

Highly directional microphones. These are substantially dead to sound from the side or rear. They are characterized by their size: either a large parabolic dish to concentrate sound for a micro-phone placed near the focus or, more commonly today, a long tube extending forward from the main unit. The frequency response is a narrow forward lobe at high frequencies degenerating into a broader response at wavelengths greater than the major dimensions of the microphone.

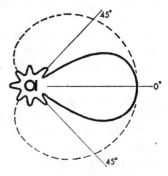

HIGHLY DIRECTIONAL MICRO-PHONE. The unbroken line shows the polar response for medium-high audio frequencies. At low frequencies (broken line) the response degenerates to the normal response for the microphone type being used (in this case cardioid).

The frequency response of practical microphones

Practical, high-quality professional microphones do not have a response that is perfectly flat. Peaks and troughs of the order of 3–4 dB are common and are to be found even on relatively expensive microphones. This is not bad workmanship: it is

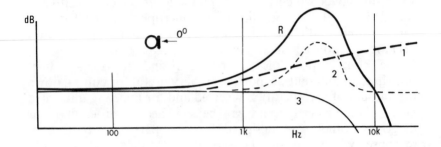

HIGH FREQUENCY EFFECTS on a microphone diaphragm. The response R at 0° (i.e. on axis) is the sum of several components including: 1. Obstacle effect (which sets up a standing wave in front of the diaphragm). 2. Resonance in the cavity in front of the diaphragm. 3. Inertia of the diaphragm as its mass becomes appreciable compared with high-frequency driving forces.

simply that it is difficult to design a microphone for a level response at all audio frequencies. In addition, an individual sample may vary by 2 dB or so from the average for its type. Fortunately, few people notice variations of this order: in a reverberant balance they will probably be overshadowed by variations due to the acoustics, anyway. But a broad peak of 6 or 7 dB in the top response of a close speech microphone will certainly be noticeable.

Some microphones have a response that falls away in the bass enough to make them unsuitable for particular orchestral instruments (or for that matter a full orchestra). But much more common is loss of top—from about 10 kHz (or even below) on some professional microphones and from 12 kHz on many of high quality. A few have an effective high-frequency response that goes well beyond this, but with these the angle at which the microphone is used may be critical: the axis of the diaphragm should point directly at the sound source. A common defect of microphones— and a serious one for high-quality work—is an erratic response in the upper-middle range. Except in individual cases where a continuous trace of the frequency response is provided with each microphone, manufacturers tend to publish data and diagrams

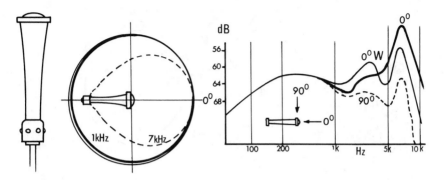

MOVING COIL OMNIDIRECTIONAL MICROPHONE of medium quality. In this example, the difference between the axial response and that at 90° is vast. The most level response is at about 45°. The presence of a windshield (0°W) further modifies the response, but may not unduly degrade speech quality (unless it is already sibilant). Variations in the frequency response of microphones are generally described in decibels of voltage, dB(V).

that somewhat idealize the performance of their products. So this defect may not be apparent from publicity material.

The size of a microphone affects its frequency response. In general, the larger the diaphragm and the larger the case, the more difficult it is to engineer a smooth extended top response (but the easier it is to obtain a strong signal).

Bass tip-up

The pressure-gradient mode of operation, by its very nature, produces a distortion of the frequency response called *bass tip-up*. A pure pressure-gradient microphone is bidirectional, so this is a particular characteristic of all ribbon microphones that work in this way. The distance at which bass tip-up begins to set in depends on the difference in path length as the signal reaches first the front then the rear of the diaphragm. Bass tip-up occurs when the sound source is close enough for the path difference to be a significant proportion of that distance, and is due to the fact that, as it radiates outward, sound dies away—in fact, as we have seen, for spherical waves diminishes in proportion to the square of the distance.

Pressure gradient is the sum of two components. One is produced by the phase difference at two points on a wave separated by the distance from front to back of the diaphragm. The other is the change in intensity with distance. For low frequencies to be

141

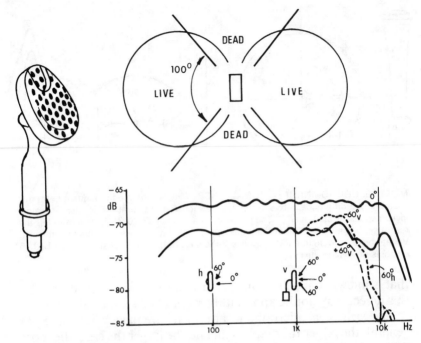

TYPICAL RIBBON MICROPHONE. Much of the casing is taken up by the magnet system, which in early ribbon microphones had to be substantial in order to provide reasonable sensitivity. An arc of approximately 100° on each side provides a 'live' working area. The frequency response at 60° to the axis is halved, but begins to depart from the common curve at about 2000 Hz, where high-frequency effects begin. Those for variation in the vertical plane (v) are more pronounced than those for the horizontal plane (h).

picked up at all by a pressure-gradient microphone it is arranged that it is sensitive to very small phase differences. As a result, when a source is close, the drop in intensity may be large in comparison. In fact, the distance at which this begins to dominate depends on wavelength. For middle and high frequencies the distances at which it becomes important are too small to be of practical importance; it is only for low frequencies that the effect reaches out to a normal working distance from the microphone. The greater the path difference the greater the frequency range over which a significant amount of bass tip-up occurs.

Bidirectional ribbon microphones require a substantial path difference to achieve adequate sensitivity, so are strongly affected by bass tip-up, in some cases with a noticeable effect as far out as 20 in (50 cm), becoming increasingly marked as the distance is reduced.

142

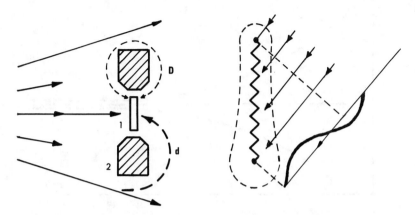

RIBBON MICROPHONE: DIMENSIONAL EFFECTS. *Left*. The sound wave travels farther to reach the back of the ribbon (1) than it does to the front. The effective path difference d is roughly equivalent to the shortest distance D round the pole-piece (2). *Right*. Vertical response: at oblique angles there is partial cancellation of very short wavelengths (i.e. high frequency) sounds along the length of the ribbon. In the horizontal plane there is little variation with wavelength.

Some directional microphones have arrangements to switch in bass roll-off to compensate for the increase that occurs at a particular working distance. Movement back and forth from this chosen position produces changes in the ratio between bass and middle frequencies that cannot be compensated by simple control of volume; to make matters worse, such movements also introduce changes in the ratio of direct to indirect sound. But, for practical purposes, bass tip-up is less troublesome with some voices: in particular, women, having higher pitched voices, may

BASS TIP-UP increases as a directional microphone approaches a sound source. For a bi-directional ribbon the curves 1–4 may correspond to distances of 24 to 6 in (60 to 15 cm).

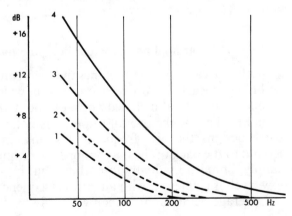

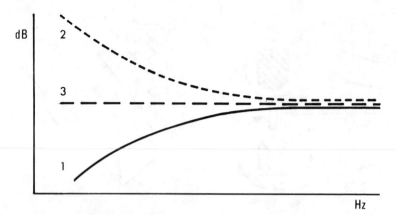

COMPENSATION FOR CLOSE WORKING. 1. Some microphones have a reduced bass response which automatically compensates for the tip-up (2) due to close working. 3. With the microphone at a certain distance from the source, its response to direct sound is level.

be above the danger zone, and so may approach to less than the usual recommended working distance without frequency distortion being apparent.

When two bidirectional microphones are placed close together a check should be made that the two are in phase. If they are not, cancellation of direct sound occurs for sources equidistant from the two (although normal reverberation is heard) and severe distortion may be apparent for other positions of the source. The cure is simply to turn one of them round (or to reverse its leads).

When two microphones are needed to pick up separate sources, ribbons may be used with each placed dead-side-on to the other source. This gives better control in mixing.

Cardioid and hypercardioid microphones

With true cardioid microphones the useful angle is a broad cone including at least 120° on the live side—but which may be taken as extending to a total included angle of about 180°, though so far round to the side the overall response is noticeably lower and in some designs the high-frequency response may be lower still. Round to the back of the microphone the output should in theory simply diminish gradually to nothing, but in practice, though at low level, it is uneven, with an erratic frequency response.

Coverage being broader than with a figure-of-eight, a cardioid

144

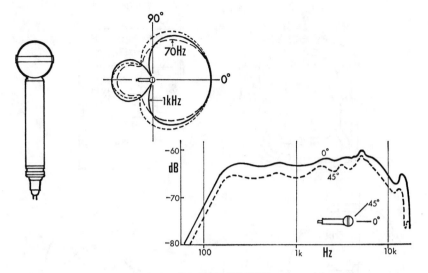

DOUBLE-RIBBON HYPERCARDIOID MICROPHONE: polar and frequency response.

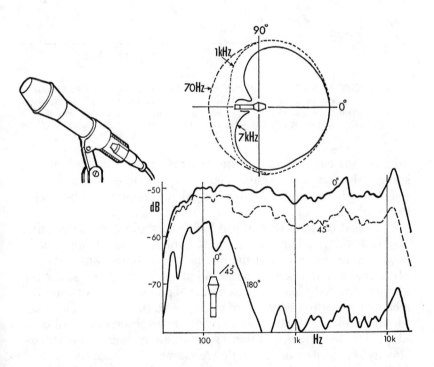

DOUBLE MOVING COIL CARDIOID MICROPHONE: polar and frequency response.

145

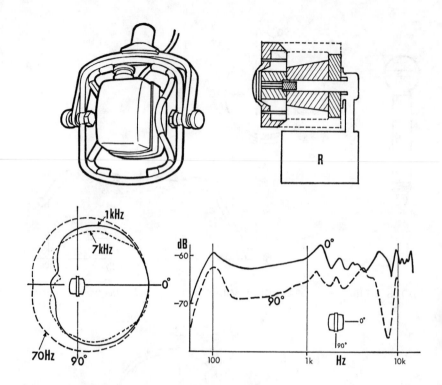

MOVING COIL CARDIOID MICROPHONE suitable for television boom operation. A complex system of acoustic labyrinths is built in to the microphone housing: the air reservoir R (shown in the simplified sectional diagram) provides the damping for one of three resonant systems which are used to engineer the response of the microphone.

microphone can be used where space is limited. When working sufficiently close there is again some bass tip-up—in fact, half as much as with a similar figure-of-eight microphone. This reflects the combination of polar responses that makes a cardioid.

The most obvious way of producing a cardioid, by connecting up omnidirectional and bi-directional units in parallel, has already been mentioned. A second method is to have both front and back of the diaphragm open to the sound pressure, but to persuade the signal to reach the back with a change of phase. For this a complicated phase-shifting network of cavities and tunnels is engineered. Moving coil, electrostatic and ribbon microphones have all been adapted to this principle. Such a system can be described mathematically in terms of acoustic resistances, capacitances, and inertiances. Using these, the pressures on both sides of the dia-

146

phragm can be calculated for a range of frequencies arriving from different directions, so that working back from the desired result— for example, a cardioid response reasonably independent of frequency—it has been possible to design a suitable acoustic network to the back of the diaphragm.

An electrostatic microphone with a pair of diaphragms on either side of a central base-plate will also work as a cardioid. In this case there is a polarizing charge between one of the diaphragms and the base-plate; but the other plate has the same charge as the base, so only one diaphragm is being used as a normal electrostatic microphone element. Sound waves cause both diaphragms to vibrate; and the resulting pressures in the cavity behind the second diaphragm are transmitted through holes perforating the base-plate: these holes are of such a size and number that they produce a phase change, and this in turn produces the cardioid response.

In recent years designers have produced a range of professional microphones based on these and similar ideas: for example, twin-diaphragm electrostatic, moving-coil, and ribbon microphones have all appeared. Not all of these microphones are pure cardioid: they can, in principle, be anywhere in the spectrum between omnidirectional and bidirectional. One microphone of this type, a double-ribbon, has a bass output which falls off below 200 Hz: this is automatically compensated by placing it at a particular distance from the sound source (such as may be arranged in a multimicrophone music balance). In another example, a double-

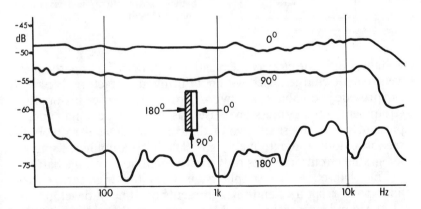

CARDIOID RESPONSE OF HIGH QUALITY CONDENSER MICROPHONE. The axial response is substantially flat to 15 000 Hz and the response at 90° almost so. The irregularities in the 180° curve are at low level and therefore unimportant.

147

moving-coil cardioid, the two capsules respond to different parts of the frequency range, allowing the front-to-rear paths to be engineered separately. The high-frequency capsule is in the forward tip, and the low frequency element is behind it, with the path to its rear passing through ports at the furthest end of the stem. The cardioid response is allowed to change to omnidirectional at low frequencies, so bass tip-up is no problem.

For an extended high frequency response, electrostatic (condenser) microphones have particular advantages. The diaphragm has an extremely low mass, so it responds readily to minute changes of air-pressure. In addition, as it has to have one stage of amplification near the microphone capsule (in order to convert the signal to a manageable form) the diaphragm itself can be made small.

In the original condenser design a polarizing voltage had to be supplied to the capsule (only a minor additional complication, as the head amplifier already required a power supply). The majority of high quality professional microphones still have the polarizing

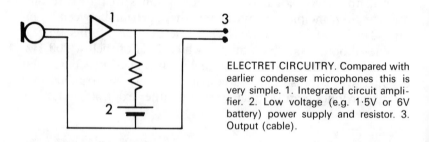

ELECTRET CIRCUITRY. Compared with earlier condenser microphones this is very simple. 1. Integrated circuit amplifier. 2. Low voltage (e.g. 1·5V or 6V battery) power supply and resistor. 3. Output (cable).

voltage, but in the *electret* the plastics diaphragm has a permanent electrostatic charge sealed within it during manufacture. Electrets can provide good quality at low cost, so are widely used in domestic equipment. One professional use has been in personal microphones, where the small size of the capsule allows it to be both inconspicuous and extremely light. The head amplifier, using an integrated circuit, requires only a very small, low-voltage battery.

The electret, by its simplicity, is ideal for engineering to a fixed polar response: and this represents one line of development of the condenser principle. Moving in another direction, the polarizing voltage has been retained and turned to new advantage —in order to make the microphone more versatile.

Switchable microphones

A microphone in which the cardioid response is directly derived from two microphones, one omnidirectional and one figure-of-eight, can be made switchable between the three conditions, and in principle also to intermediate ones, by combining the outputs of the two microphones in various proportions. However, early microphones of this type underwent so much compromise at the design stage in order to optimize their cardioid response that their performance in the omnidirectional or bidirectional condition is not as good as that of separate microphones.

In a switchable electrostatic microphone one diaphragm is constantly polarized and the other can have its polarization changed. If the two diaphragms are polarized in the same sense the microphone operates as a pressure capsule, as would two

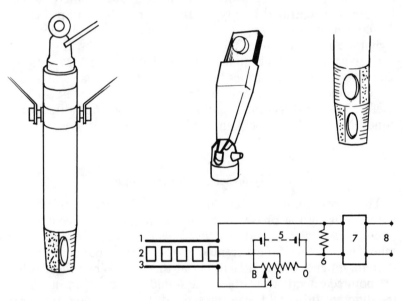

SWITCHABLE CONDENSER MICROPHONE. *Left*. The early version of a high quality variable-response condenser microphone, and, *top centre*, a later, smaller version that has replaced it. The response is varied by changing the polarizing voltage to one diaphragm. 1. Front diaphragm. 2. Rigid centre plate (perforated). 3. Rear diaphragm. 4. Multiposition switch and potentiometer. 5. Polarizing voltage. 6. High resistance. 7. Head amplifier. 8. Microphone output terminals. When the polarization is switched to position 0 the voltage on the front and back diaphragm is the same, and above that of the centre plate: the capsule operates as an omnidirectional (pressure) microphone. At B the capsule measures pressure gradient and is bidirectional. At C the polar response is cardioid. *Top right*. Two such capsules in a single casing, making a coincident pair.

149

single-diaphragm electrostatic microphones placed back to back and wired to add outputs. But if the polarizing current on one diaphragm is decreased to zero (and the centre plate has suitable perforations) the polar response becomes cardioid.

Taking this process a stage further, if the polarizing current is now increased in the opposite sense, so that the voltage on the centre plate is intermediate between those of the two diaphragms, the mode of operation of the microphone becomes pressure-gradient and its output bidirectional. That it would do so might have been expected: this is very similar to the symmetrical layout in which a central diaphragm is balanced between two oppositely polarized perforated plates.

Despite their fragile construction, the diaphragms stand up well to overloading, though the head amplifiers may not. It is in this latter field that much recent work on electrostatic microphones has been concentrated, and types using several different principles for converting the changes of capacitance to a usable electrical signal are now available.

Even with a very high-quality double-diaphragm microphone of this type some compromises have to be made. In a particular case the cardioid response is excellent and the intermediate positions useful; the omnidirectional condition is good, but the bidirectional condition has a broad peak in its high-frequency response.

Highly directional microphones

The most common way of achieving a highly directional response is by the phase cancellation method employed in *gun microphones* (also called *line microphones*). Early designs had many narrow tubes of different lengths forming a bundle, with the diaphragm enclosed in a chamber at the base. When these tubes are pointed directly at a subject the sound pressures passing along the different tubes all travel the same distance, so the tubes have no significant effect on the sound. But for sound approaching from an oblique angle many different path lengths are travelled, and as the pressures recombine in the cavity before the diaphragm there is cancellation over a wide range of frequencies. The further round to the side or rear, the more efficient this cancellation becomes; for sound from the rear the path lengths vary by twice the length of the 'barrel' of the 'gun'. But there is a limit to effective cancellation, and therefore to the directional response itself. The length of a gun microphone gives an immediate visual indication of the longest wavelength (and so the lowest frequency) at which its directional properties are effective.

In more recent gun microphones the many tubes have been replaced by a single narrow barrel, to which the sound has access at many points along the length.

One 'rifle' microphone has a tube 6 ft 8 in (2 m) long, and is therefore highly directional; indeed, as an acoustic engineering aid it has been used to pinpoint the sources of echoes in concert halls. Similar microphones have been used for picking up voices at a distance; for example, reporters in a large audience at Presidential press conferences. But the sound obtained in this way is

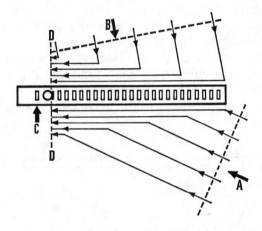

GUN MICROPHONE: phase cancellation effect. Wave A, approaching from a direction close to the axis, reaches the microphone front diaphragm D by a range of paths that differ only slightly in length. Cancellation occurs only at very high frequencies. Wave B reaches the diaphragm by a much wider range of path-lengths. Cancellation is severe at middle and high frequencies. Normal sound reaches the back of the diaphragm via port C. The polar diagram of the capsule without the acoustic delay network is cardioid; with the tube it becomes highly directional.

far from high quality, and the operation of the microphone is itself aurally distracting, as it is very obvious when it is being faded up or down, or panned to find a person who is already speaking. The speech it picks up has a harsh, unpleasant quality—but is, at least, clearly audible. A shorter version has a tube about 3 ft (0·9 m) long.

The next generation has been much shorter still, with an interference tube length of about 18 in (46 cm) on one side of a cardioid-response electrostatic capsule. It retains much of the larger instrument's directional response at high frequencies, but has a high-quality performance in the direction in which it is pointing. This has found favour with many film recordists for location work. It is sensitive to low-frequency noise from the sides, but if bass-cut can be applied (as it often can be for exterior work) traffic rumble is reduced considerably. The earlier, larger microphones had a porous material covering the entry slots and acting as an acoustic impedance. The impedance increased stage by stage along the tube, thereby progressively reducing the loss of sound and reducing the input closer to the diaphragm. For the shorter tubes this balancing act has been dispensed with, and the entry slots have no more than a light mesh to obstruct any continuous air flow and larger dust particles.

In one example there is a pistol grip below the microphone. A windshield is often used for outdoor work but its bulk may make it very obtrusive when in vision. However, a strong, gusting wind can cause break-up of the signal even when the windshield itself is protected by the body of the recordist and other screens. In this respect, however, there is little to choose between this and

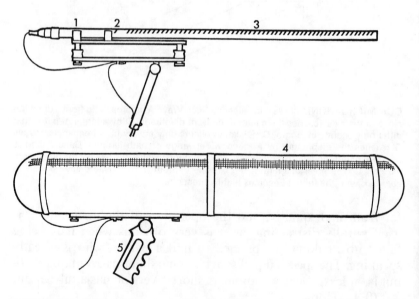

GUN MICROPHONE. 1. Head amplifier of condenser microphone. 2. Electrostatic capsule (cardioid operation). 3. Acoustic interference tube (with entry ports along upper surface). 4. Windshield for open air use. 5. Handgrip.

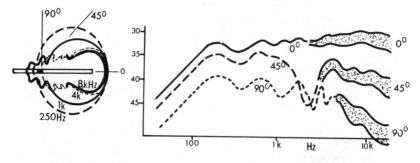

RESPONSE OF GUN MICROPHONE with 18 in (45 cm) interference tube. For high frequencies the cone of acceptance encloses 50°. The axial response is reasonably level, with some bass roll-off.

'personal' microphones (which are described later); but when used out of doors the gun microphone is preferable for its quality.

When used indoors or in acoustically live surroundings the microphone suffers partial loss of its directional qualities because the reverberation is random in phase and therefore not subject to cancellation. Indoors, therefore, the response may be no better— nor significantly worse—than the cardioid of the capsule itself. Unless the microphone is brought close to the subject (which defeats the object of using the 'gun') off-axis sound is likely to be unpleasantly reverberant.

A further development of the principle employs a 'miniature gun attachment', an interference tube that (once again) is half the length of the last, so that the strongly directional response is limited to frequencies that are higher still. In fact, the four microphones that have been described above switch from the highly directional gun response to that of the microphone capsule at approximately octave intervals. This last, the shortest, has for many purposes the best quality. It will again serve the film sound recordist as a hand-held gun microphone, in a windshield if necessary (but one that is somewhat shorter and less unwieldy). In the television studio it may be slung on a boom and used at a slightly greater distance than a cardioid, in comparison with which it gives more discrimination on the high frequency content of direct sound.

A major difference is that this short gun can also be used indoors as a hand microphone. But here again we must consider an older problem of directional microphones: bass tip-up. In

153

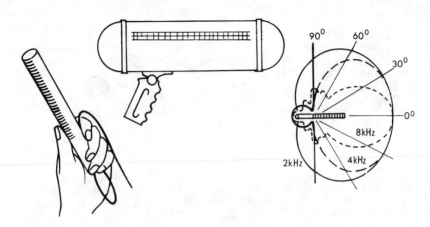

CONDENSER CARDIOID/PHASE CANCELLATION MICROPHONE, overall length about 10 in (25 cm). At 2000 Hz and below, the response is cardioid. The minimum distance from capsule to mouth is controlled by the length of the tube, so that there is little bass tip-up even when held close to the mouth. Phase cancellation due to the interference tube makes the microphone highly directional only at high frequencies. It has excellent separation from surrounding noise when hand-held by solo singers or reporters, or when used as a gun microphone for film sound recording.

this design it is controlled in part by the distance between mouth and microphone that is created by the length of the tube itself, and the remainder can be compensated by switching in the appropriate roll-off. Some examples are sold in a kit which permits the use of the capsule either by itself as an electrostatic cardioid or with an interference tube. One of these is based on an inexpensive electret with a tiny head amplifier powered by a miniature battery that seems to last indefinitely.

Gun microphones have not entirely replaced an earlier method of achieving a highly directional response. The principle whereby the parabolic microphone achieves its special properties is obvious; equally obviously these, too, degenerate at low frequencies, for which the sound waves are too long to 'see' the dish effectively. So although high frequencies may be picked up well at a considerable distance, low frequencies are not: for a reasonably manoeuvrable reflector of 3–4 ft (1 m) in diameter the directional response is less effective below 1000 Hz. Also, the microphone is subject to close unwanted noises at low frequencies, unless a bass cut is used.

For picking up faint sounds, the parabolic reflector has one great advantage: its directional properties rely on acoustic amplification of the sound before it reaches the microphone, achieving perhaps a 20 dB gain. This offers a far better signal-to-

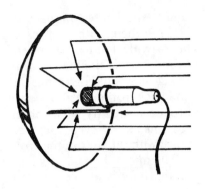

MICROPHONE IN PARABOLIC RE-
FLECTOR. The bowl may be of glass
fibre or metal (coated on the outside
with a material to stop it 'ringing').
Alternatively, if it is made of transparent
plastics the operator can see through it
to follow action, e.g. at sports meetings.
In another design the reflector is segmented and can be folded like a fan for
travel and storage.

noise ratio than could be obtained from a microphone that has a
similar capsule but which relies on phase cancellation. The
reflector has therefore found favour for recording birdsong and
for other specialized purposes where its bulk and poor low-
frequency pick-up are acceptable. The sound can be concentrated
almost to pin-point accuracy at high frequencies, or defocused
slightly by moving the microphone along the axis to give a broader
lobe of pick-up: the latter is generally preferred. An advantage
over gun microphones is that reflectors work just as well indoors
as out. Tested in highly reverberant conditions (an underground
garage) a parabolic reflector picked up intelligible speech at twice
the distance that could be achieved by the better of two gun
microphones.

It has been suggested that the microphone capsule itself should
have a cardioid response (or something similar), pointing into
the bowl, in order to avoid phase cancellation effects at frequencies
related to the size of the dish, where the reflected signal is weak
and out of phase with the direct one. But the cardioid response
should be broad, because the contribution from the rim is
is important. Indeed, where there is little sound at the limiting
wavelength (or it is filtered out) an omnidirectional microphone
would make better use of it.

Noise cancelling microphones

There are several ways of getting rid of noise: one is to put the
microphone user—a sports commentator perhaps—into a soundproof box. But commentary boxes tend not to be soundproof
against the low frequency components of crowd noise and in any
case are bound to introduce unpleasant resonances if they are

small. Another technique is to use an omnidirectional microphone close to the mouth; but in very noisy surroundings this may still not provide the ideal balance between the voice and the background sound—while the man who is controlling the sound level has no direct means of correcting the mixture. For best results the voice and background need to be almost completely separated. The one broadcast-quality microphone that can do this in almost any circumstances, even for a commentator speaking in a normal voice with the roar of the crowd all around him, is a *lip ribbon*.

The microphone, as its name implies, has its ribbon very close to the mouth of the speaker. As the ribbon is working in its pressure-gradient mode, it is, in fact, subject to very heavy bass tip-up for sound from such a close source, but there is no bass tip-up on ambient sound arriving from distant sources. If a specific distance is chosen, say a little over 2 in (5 cm), for the separation between lip and ribbon, and sufficient equalization is introduced to make the microphone response flat for a sound source at such a distance, the ambient bass noise level is also reduced by the same amount. Obviously, the closer to the mouth the ribbon is, the better—so long as the explosive sounds in speech, and streams of air from the mouth and nose can be controlled. With a distance of $2\frac{1}{8}$ in (54 mm)—fixed by placing a guard against the upper lip—these factors can be controlled by windshields (which, as they are so close to the mouth or nose, need to be made of stainless steel or plastic), and by cupping the ribbon itself behind the magnet.

Some versions have a variety of equalization settings for different degrees of bass; but in general the reduction of noise is about 10 dB at 300 Hz, increasing to 20 dB at 100 Hz. A high-frequency response of up to about 7 kHz is all that is needed for

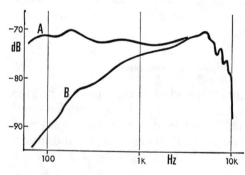

RESPONSE OF LIP-RIBBON MICROPHONE. A. Response to spherical wave at approximately $2\frac{1}{2}$ inches (i.e. the user's voice). B. Response to plane wave (ambient sound), on axis. This effect is achieved by equalization, without which B would be flat and A would be high at low frequencies, due to extreme bass tip-up at such a close working distance.

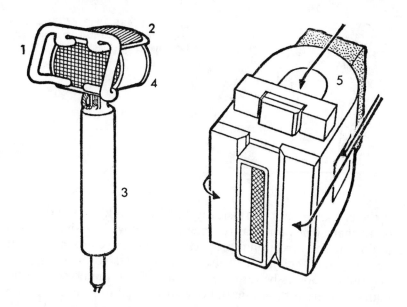

LIP RIBBON MICROPHONE. 1. The mouth guard is placed against the upper lip. 2. A stainless steel mesh acts as a windshield below the nose. 3. The handgrip contains a transformer. 4. Case containing magnet assembly. 5. Yoke of magnet is towards the mouth, and the ribbon away from it. The sound paths are marked.

speech in these conditions, so above that frequency the sensitivity of the microphone falls away. These figures are, of course, to be added to those for discrimination due to the extremely close working, and (for lateral noise) the figure-of-eight response.

It is possible that even more efficient noise-cancelling microphones could be devised. But this one—though not visually attractive because it obscures the mouth—has proved sufficient for almost any conditions of noise yet encountered in radio.

Microphones for use in vision

Everything within a television or film picture, as much as everything in the sound, adds to the total effect; and a microphone which may be in the picture or a series of pictures for a long time is an important visual element. Accordingly, many modern microphones have been designed for good appearance as well as high-quality performance. They are mid- or light-toned, often of silver-grey, with a matt finish to diffuse the reflection of studio lights.

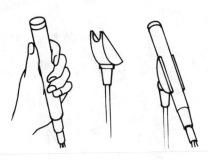

EASY-RELEASE CLIP on floor stand allows performer to take the microphone from the stand while in vision.

If the capsule is not intrinsically small it should be slender, and performers will more easily understand how they should work to do it if any directional properties it may have are in line with the long axis (*end-fire*): in use it then points towards them. A microphone looks better entering frame from the bottom rather than from the top. A microphone suspended in vision is particularly untidy and calls attention to itself: indeed, it may be used in this way for deliberate effect, to proclaim 'television studio'.

Table microphones. The condenser microphone lends itself to suitable design. A pencil shape perhaps half an inch or more (1·5–2 cm) in diameter has room for a directionally sensitive capsule pointing along the axis; the body of the pencil houses the head amplifier. The mounting, if it is to be relatively heavy and stable, and is to protect the microphone from vibration, cannot also be made small. But this, too, can be given clean lines and can

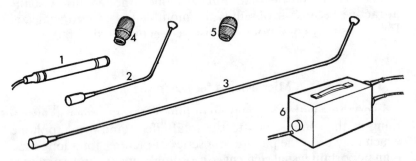

AN ELECTROSTATIC MICROPHONE, supplied with alternative capsules for cardioid and omnidirectional operation. 1. Head amplifier and capsule. 2, 3. Extension pieces (these are fitted between head amplifier and microphone capsule). 4, 5. Windshields. 6. Power supply unit.

158

often be concealed from the camera in a sunken well in the table.

Microphones on floor stands. For someone standing up, a microphone may be placed at the top of a full-length stand, which again should be reasonably strong and have a massive base. It will normally be telescopic. Whatever happens, in a long shot there is going to be a vertical line very obviously in the picture, but the cleaner this is, the better. The clip holding the microphone itself should be neat but easy to release (e.g. by a performer in vision). Some microphones have only an electrostatic capsule at face level, and are plugged in to one of a selection of thin rigid extension tubes connecting them to the head amplifier: the capacitance of the wiring is taken into account in the design. One such microphone kit comes with a choice of capsules for omni-directional or cardioid response and two different lengths of 'swan-neck' column. It is suitable for floor use with seated speakers without a

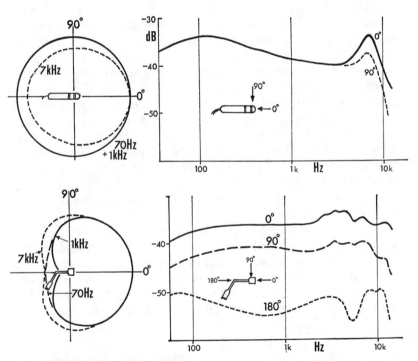

ELECTROSTATIC MICROPHONE of type shown opposite. *Top.* Response curves for omnidirectional head fitted directly to head amplifier (i.e. without the extension pieces). *Bottom.* Response obtained when cardioid head is used in combination with extension piece.

table, or alternatively may be stood on a box so that only the neck and capsule projects into vision.

Hand microphone. These generally have a 'stick' shape so that they can be held easily. If the diaphragm is at the tip, its distance from the user's mouth cannot be predicted, so in order to avoid variable bass tip-up it requires an omnidirectional response at low frequencies. An additional advantage of this is that by its pressure operation at these frequencies the microphone is less sensitive to wind noise. While a hand microphone that becomes directional at middle or high frequencies should have an end-fire response (as it is natural to point the microphone toward the mouth) the high frequency pick-up lobe must be broad enough to accommodate a good range of angles. Robustness and lack of handling noise are essential, but sensitivity is less so: the microphone is often held close to the lips, which is visually intrusive but improves separation from other sound.

Microphone mouse. Microphones can be placed unobtrusively in vision in a wide shot by inserting them within a foamed rubber or plastics pad that acts as a combined windshield and shock-absorbent mount, and simply putting them on the floor. Generally, microphones are kept away from reflective surfaces owing to the interference fields these produce. However, as the diaphragm is moved closer to the surface this effect moves up through the sound frequency spectrum, until at a distance of one inch (2·5 cm) it occurs only in the highest octave of human hearing, so that on speech and song the effect becomes unimportant. For a sound wave approaching a rigid solid surface at right angles a microphone so placed registers only pressure variations, not the pressure gradient, but for a sound travelling lengthways along the surface it measures by either method. A directional microphone is effective therefore only in directions parallel to the wall. A common arrangement is to place an end-fire cardioid microphone with its diaphragm normal to the surface, directed towards action at a distance. It may therefore be well suited to opera performed before an audience. Sightlines are unobstructed by the small, neutrally coloured, and felicitously named mice.

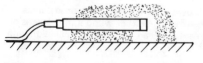

MICROPHONE MOUSE, in section. It is made of foamed rubber or plastics, moulded with a tubular slot for the insertion of microphone, and a cavity for the capsule. It is placed on the floor.

Personal microphones

A *lavalier microphone* may be suspended round the neck in the manner of pendant jewellery—but rather less obtrusively. In this case it may also properly be described as a *lanyard* or *neck microphone*. Alternatively, it may simply be called a *personal microphone*, a term with more general application, because the small capsules used today are more often simply attached to the clothing. For the best sound quality the microphone will be in vision; for neater appearance it can be concealed beneath a tie or some other garment.

The microphone should be omnidirectional because, although it is situated fairly close to the mouth, it is not at a predetermined distance. Commonly, a tiny electrostatic capsule or electret is used, or sometimes a small moving coil unit. Such microphones work reasonably well because the pattern of radiation from the mouth is also essentially omnidirectional; though there is some

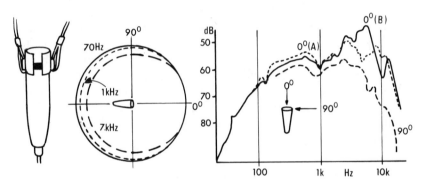

LANYARD MICROPHONE: omnidirectional moving coil. With the clip lowered (0° curve A) this is a general purpose omnidirectional microphone. With the clip raised (0° curve B) the 7 kHz peak makes it suitable for a lanyard position below the chin.

loss of high frequencies reaching the microphone, particularly if it is hidden behind clothing. A microphone with a strong, broad resonance between 2500 and 8000 Hz (perhaps produced by cavity resonance in the housing above the diaphragm) will compensate for this but is suitable for speech only. It is not very satisfactory in other possible uses for a small unit of this type, e.g. held in the hand, or hidden in scenery to cover an otherwise inaccessible position in a set, unless the cavity resonance can be eliminated. One example with a more level response for normal studio use has a sleeve or clip that can be raised around the top of

161

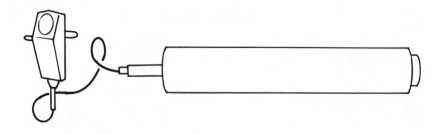

LAPEL MICROPHONE. Length 1½ in (32 mm). Diaphragm diameter, ¼ in (6 mm). Omnidirectional condenser with remote electronic section which can go in a pocket.

the unit giving a broad 'presence' peak. Alternatively (or additionally), an octave filter may be used to correct the frequency response, matching it as well as possible to that of some other well-balanced good-quality microphone.

Lanyard microphones must be very light in weight as well as being tiny (or, at least, slender), but they need to be robust, as they are easily bumped or knocked about. Electrostatic personal microphones are designed with a cable connecting the capsule to the head amplifier: this is thin (and therefore relatively unobtrusive) but inevitably it is vulnerable to damage, and is also a possible source of conduction noise when rubbed against clothing.

In the studio and on location a personal microphone may be used either with a cable (heavier beyond the head amplifier) or with a radio link.

Radio microphones

In radio or television the user of a personal microphone may need to be completely free of the cable because:
1. In a long shot the cable may be seen to drag; this is completely unacceptable in drama and is distracting in other programmes.
2. In a sequence involving a number of moves the cable may get caught on the scenery, or completely tangled up; or movement may be unduly restricted to avoid such mishaps.
3. The performer with a neck microphone may have to move about so much in the intervals between the various rehearsals and takes that it may be more desirable to give him full freedom of movement than to keep plugging or unplugging his microphone.

In these cases the cable may be replaced by a battery-powered radio transmitter and aerial. The transmitter pack should be

162

small enough to be slipped into a pocket, pinned to the inside of the clothing, or, more likely, simply hung at the waist beneath the jacket. If simpler answers fail, put it in the small of the back: a cloth pouch of the exact size, with tapes to hold and support it, is useful for this. If an external aerial (approximately a quarter wavelength long) is used, it may perhaps be allowed to hang free from the waist, or, if it would then be in shot, drawn upward within outer clothing. For studio use the screening of the microphone lead can itself be made the right length and used as an aerial.

The receiving aerial is usually a simple dipole placed so that there is an unobstructed electromagnetic path from the performer. The equipment can 'see' through sets made of wood and other nonconductive material, but is likely to be affected by metallic objects (including large camera dollies, which, of course, move around during the production).

When setting them up, i.e. before giving the transmitter to the performer, checks should be made that the dipole is suitably placed. This needs two people: one of them walks in all the places in the set or location to which the performer is expected to go, talking over the circuit to a second person who listens for dead spots. Several positions may have to be tried before a suitable one

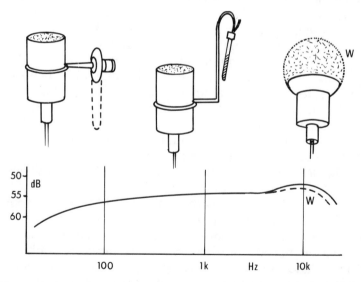

VERY SMALL PERSONAL MICROPHONE. Size: 0·7×0·42 in (19×11 mm). Weight of condenser capsule 0·16 oz (4·5 g), plus cable permanently attached to supply unit. The microphone can be used with one of several clip attachments or a windshield, W.

163

is found. Alternatively, additional dipoles may be set to see into the dead spots—in which case it is often sufficient to connect them in parallel. In a television studio, existing monitor circuits can be used to carry the signal from the dipoles to a radio receiver in the sound gallery. In order to smooth out unexpected signal variations the receiver may possibly be set for a modest amount of automatic gain (but not in cases where the performer is going to speak loud and soft for dramatic intent). As the transmitter controls have to be preset the signal can easily be overloaded, causing distortion, or undermodulated, reducing the signal-to-noise ratio. These can be avoided by introducing some degree of compression at the transmitter, too.

The transmitter should be free from frequency drift and its signal should not 'bump' if it is tapped or jolted. Battery voltage generally drops suddenly when the power source is exhausted, so batteries should be discarded well within their expected lifetime (which should itself be reasonably long). For crucial applications a log of hours of use will regulate their replacement. The BBC uses a transmitter radiating a radio-frequency power of 120 milliwatts (more in locations where greater than normal distances are involved); a practical minimum is 100 mW. Unfortunately, different wavebands are used in Europe and America so that equipment carried by film crews must be reset (not always easy) after crossing the Atlantic. The band used in Britain is allocated to television broadcasting in the United States.

Occasionally, other equipment in a studio interferes with the radio link; for example, a signal operating radio-controlled special effects. It is safest to anticipate the unexpected by having stand-by transmitter packs with different frequencies. Obvious frequencies to avoid are those used for production talkback continuously broadcast to the studio floor manager and for his switched reverse talkback (where this is used). If it is of a suitable type, the floor manager's own radio microphone is available in an emergency when all others have been used: it is therefore helpful to standardize, using the same model for both purposes.

Radio microphones can be used in filming (particularly in documentary work or news reporting); for roving reporters in television outside broadcasts; by the hosts of studio programmes, and for many other purposes. But, although the quality of the radio link may be high, it is compromised by that of the neck microphone. So alternatives should be considered: in the studio a boom, and on location a gun microphone.

164

Radio links can also be used with hand-held microphones, though in this case the sight of a cable disappearing into the clothes and not coming out again may be distracting to the audience, particularly in the case of lady singers in tight clothing.

Contact microphones

A device that is used to pick up sound vibrations from a solid material, such as a reverberation plate or the sound board of an electric guitar, is called a contact microphone. For the conversion of acoustic energy to an electrical signal, any of the methods used in microphones and record pick-ups (and conversely in loud-speakers) could in principle be used.

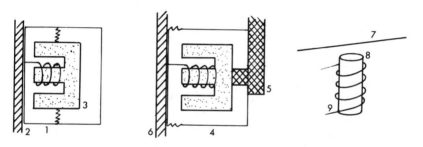

SOUND FROM SOLIDS. *Left.* 1. Contact microphone. 2. Vibrating surface. 3. The mass of the suspended magnet holds it relatively still. The mass and suspension system can be arranged so that the resonant vibration of the magnet is at a very low frequency and heavily damped. *Centre.* 4. Microphone. 5. Solid arm to which it is fixed. 6. Moving part touching the vibrating surface. *Right.* 7. Metal string vibrating in the field of electromagnet (8) modulating the current in coil (9). Other electro-mechanical principles can be used for all of these.

Contact microphones often have to be placed where it would be inconvenient to anchor them to a rigid bridge or massive arm. They are therefore supported only by the surface to which they are attched so that the casing moves with the surface. An 'active mass' inside is, however, subject to inertia and free to move relative to the casing.

This mass reacts against, say, a piezo-electric device (e.g. the ceramic, barium titanate) to generate the electrical signal. The microphone measures the acceleration of the air particles as they are moved by the sound wave and is therefore frequency dependent, but as with other acceleration microphones, this is allowed for by equalization.

165

Directional characteristics of stereo pairs

For stereo an important technique for giving positional information is the coincident pair (see Chapter 3). If separate microphones are used they should be matched by manufacture and model (at the very least), for even a minor difference in design may lead to big differences in the structure of the high frequency response. An alternative to the matched pair is the double microphone, in which two capsules are placed in the same casing, usually with one diaphragm vertically above the other, so that they can be rotated on a common axis. Sometimes (in either system) the polar responses may be switched between figure-of-eight, hypercardioid, cardioid and broad cardioid conditions (as well as omnidirectional, which has no direct use in stereo). The angle at which the axes of the two elements is set is a matter of choice: it is part of the process of microphone balance. In practice the angle may be as little as 60°–70°, but for simplicity in describing how the signals combine and cancel, let us consider the case where they are set at right angles.

A coincident pair of figure-of-eight elements set at 90° to each other have their phases the same (positive or negative) in two adjacent quadrants. The overlap of these allows a useful pick-up angle of 90°. Outside of this the elements are out of phase, so that directional information is confused and meaningless to a listener, except at the back, where there is a further angle of 90° within which the elements are in phase once again. Sound sources at the rear of the pair are introduced in mirror image into the sound stage that the listener has in front of him, so that physically incompatible objects can appear to be occupying the same point in space.

In a hypercardioid pair (crossed cottage-loaf response) the frontal lobes must again be in phase. With the diaphragms still at 90° to each other, the useful pick-up angle is about 130° at the front. The corresponding 50° at the back is not much use for direct pick-up, as the frequency response of the individual microphones is degenerate in these directions. However, if a source that is being picked up on a separate microphone is placed in this angle at least its position will not be distorted by the out-of-phase pick-up that would be found at the side.

Crossed cardioids have a maximum usable angle of 270°, but for direct pick-up the useful angle is about 180°, as the frequency response of the microphone that is turned away from the sound source degenerates at angles that are farther round to the side.

There are two ways of looking at the polar response of a co-incident pair. One uses the normal response curves for the A and B microphones. The other considers their combined signals, the A + B and A − B signals. As we have seen, the A + B signal is also called the M signal: this stands for 'main' (not 'mono', though mono usually is taken as A + B). Similarly, A − B is sometimes called the S signal ('side', not 'stereo'; stereo information requires *both* M and S signals—though 'S' represents the *extra* information required for stereo).

The M and S diagrams correspond to the polar responses of another pair of microphones that could in principle have been used to obtain them directly—a 'main' one which has a range of different polar diagrams and a 'side' one which is figure-of-eight. Sometimes A + B and A − B stereo information has been taken directly from main and side microphones, thereby cutting out several items of electrical equipment. But a disadvantage of this is that the combined frequency response is at its most erratic at the most important part of the sound stage: close to the centre—though the effect gets less as the S contribution gets smaller.

As will be seen later, crossed cardioid or hypercardioid microphones are preferred for most practical professional balances, as they permit a better use of the studio space and provide a signal that loses less when heard in mono.

Lining up a stereo pair

If coincident microphones do not have the same output level the positional information is distorted. Here is a line-up procedure that can be carried out in a few minutes by two people, one at the microphones and one at the monitoring end.

1. Check that the loudspeakers are lined up reasonably well, e.g. by speaking on a mono microphone (or one element of the pair) that is fed equally to A and B loudspeakers. The sound should come from the centre.

2. If they are switchable select identical polar diagrams for the coincident pair. These may be the ones that will subsequently be used operationally, or if this is not known, figure-of-eight.

3. Visually set the capsules at about 90° to each other. Check and identify the left and right capsules in turn. Where microphones are mounted one above the other, there is no agreed standard on which capsule should feed which channel.

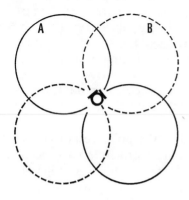

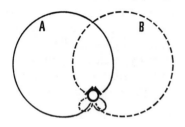

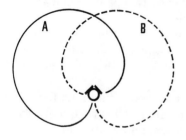

Polar diagrams for coincident pairs of microphones at 90°. *Top*. Crossed figure-of-eight. *Centre*. Crossed cottage-loaf. *Bottom*. Crossed cardioid. The M and S diagrams corresponding to these are shown opposite. Note that although the subject of crossed microphones is introduced here in terms of elements set at 90°, a broader angle is often better for practical microphone balances. 120° is commonly used.

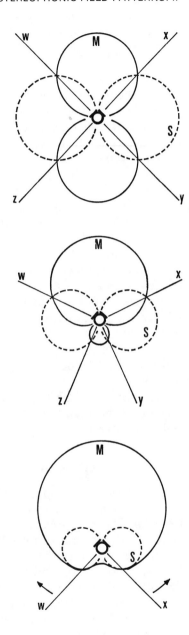

M and S diagrams for the coincident pairs of microphones shown opposite. *Top.* For crossed figure-of-eight the useful forward angle (W-X) is only 90°. Sound from outside this (i.e. in the angles W-Z and X-Y) will be out of phase. The useful angle at the rear (Y-Z) will (for music) be angled too high for practical benefit. *Centre.* Crossed cottage-loaf microphones have a broader useful angle at the front (W-X). *Bottom.* The crossed cardioid has a 270° usable angle (between W and X, forwards) but only about 180° is really useful, as to the rear of the elements the response is erratic.

169

4. Visually set the pair at 0° to each other, ensuring with micro-phones of symmetrical appearance that they are not in fact back to back (there is always some identifying point, e.g. a stud on the front, or the mesh at the back of the housing may be coloured black).

5. Listen to A − B only—or if there is no control to select this, reverse the phase of one microphone and listen to A + B.

6. While one person speaks in to the front of the microphones, the other adjusts for minimum output. If possible, this should be on a preset control for one microphone channel or the other; most conveniently, this may be a separate microphone balance or 'channel balance' control.

7. Restore the loudspeakers to normal stereo output (restoring the phase reversal to normal if necessary). As the person in the studio walks in a circle round the microphone his reproduced voice should remain approximately midway between the speakers whatever the position of the speaker. Disregarding minor varia-tions when the speech is from near the common dead axis or axes of the microphones, if there are any major shifts in image position as the person speaks from different places there is something wrong with the polar response of one of the microphones; the test must be started again when the microphone has been corrected. The earlier part of the line-up procedure is then invalid. As the person walks round loudness should vary in a way that coincides with the polar characteristic chosen.

8. Restore the angle between the capsules to 90° (or whatever angle is to be used operationally) and identify left, centre, and right once again.

Miscellaneous microphone equipment

Windshields are supplied to fit many microphones. Sometimes they may be needed even indoors to reduce breath effects in close working. These *pop-shields* can be quite small, and need not even be rounded. Generally, however, the purpose of a shield is to cut down noise due to wind turbulence at sharp edges, or even corners that are too sharply curved. To reduce wind effects proper, a smooth airflow round the microphone is required. The ideal shape, if the direction of the wind were always known and the same, would be a teardrop, but in the absence of this information practical windshields are usually made either spherical or a mixture of spherical and cylindrical sections typically of 2 in

170

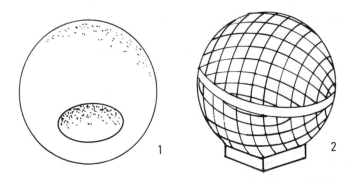

WINDSHIELDS. 1. Open cell (rubber or polyurethane foam). 2. Glass-fibre and polyester screen. Typically the diameter of these may be two inches or more for wind; or smaller if for breath. Wire mesh or other open weave or porous materials may also be used.

(5 cm) radius. The framework is generally of metal or moulded plastic, with a fine and acoustically transparent mesh, often of wire and foamed plastic, covering it.

Mountings. In addition to the equipment already described, there are many other standard ways of mounting microphones, including a variety of booms. In concert halls most microphones

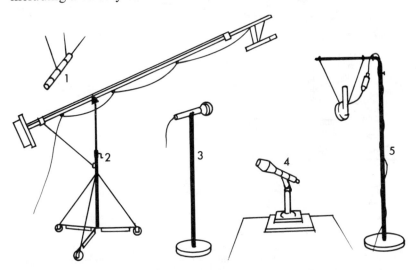

METHODS OF MOUNTING MICROPHONES (used in radio studios). 1. Suspension by adjustable wires, etc. 2. Boom (adjustable angle and length). 3. Floor stand (with telescopic column). 4. Table stand (but 1, 2, or 5 are better for table work if there is any risk of table-tapping by inexperienced speakers). 5. Floor stand with bent arm. Most methods of mounting have shock absorbers or straps.

may in principle be slung by their own cable from the roof of the hall—but for additional safety many halls insist on separate slings, and in any case guying may be necessary for the accurate final choice of position and angle.

Microphone booms. A typical boom used in television and film has a telescopic arm extending from about 7 to 17 ft (2 to 5 m). It can swing in any direction and tilt to 45°. The operator stands on the platform to the right of the boom, his right hand holding the winding handle that racks the arm in or out, and his left on a crank handle that rotates the microphone on the axis of its supporting cradle. With his left arm he also controls the angle of the boom. A seat is available but is used only for long pauses as it restricts mobility. Some television organizations provide him with a miniature monitor, which is fixed to the boom arm a little forward of the pivot. The platform and boom can be raised or lowered together: they are usually preset to a height such that the boom extends nearly horizontally, swinging freely above pedestal cameras. The whole carriage can be tracked by a second operator.

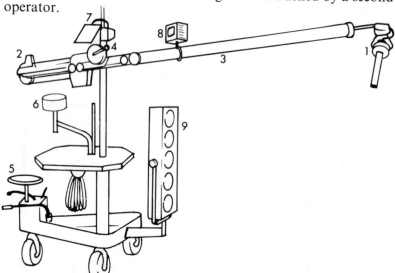

STUDIO BOOM. 1. The microphone cradle pivots about its vertical axis, controlled by the angle of the crank (2). 3. The arm pivots and tilts, and is extended by winding the pulley (4). The whole dolly may be tracked, using the steering controls (5), and the platform (and arm fulcrum) height may be raised and lowered. 6. The seat is used only during long pauses in action. The operator has a script rack and talkback microphone (7). Some television organizations provide him with a personal monitor (8) attached to the boom arm; others use floor monitors. 9. The loudspeaker feeds foldback sound to the studio floor.

A hand-held boom, called a fishing rod, offers some of these advantages, but takes up much less space and can in addition be brought in from directions that are inaccessible to the larger booms, for example, it may work close to the floor. In normal use, it is supported on a shoulder or braced under one arm for substantial periods. In exceptional circumstances it can be held high with both arms braced over the head, but directors should expect this only for short takes.

Shock absorbers. Certain microphones, particularly ribbons with compliant (i.e. relatively floppy) diaphragms, are very sensitive to vibration at resonant frequencies and benefit from the use of mountings to absorb these frequencies. Most microphones benefit from some degree of protection from mechanical vibration.

Plugs, etc. In plugs and sockets, like the colour coding of wiring and the impedances chosen by different organizations for different purposes, there has been little standardization in the past; and as high-quality equipment is drawn from a wide international field, this may lead to—to say the least—inconvenience. The vastness of the range of connectors available is the worst feature.

Microphone connections. In sound and television studios, microphone cables may be plugged into sockets (outlets) built in to the studio walls. In television it is necessary to route sound cables round or through the set (which may include extensive backings) at suitable points, and to avoid camera tracking lines and areas of the studio floor that will appear in vision. So here a very large number of points is provided: one BBC studio has over a hundred; several have over fifty. Mostly they are distributed around the walls in groups, but some are in the studio ceiling, so that cables can be 'flown', or microphones suspended from above. Some terminate in the gallery area itself. It is convenient to have several multiway single-socket outputs at the studio walls so that a single cable can be run out to a terminating box on the floor, to which, say, ten microphones can be routed. In order to minimize induction, sound wiring should be kept away from power cables (to lighting or other equipment) and should cross them at right angles. This is necessary also for wiring built in to the studio structure.

7

MICROPHONE BALANCE

THIS chapter outlines the general principles governing the relation-ship between microphones, sound sources, ambient sound (reverberation) and unwanted sound (noise). These rules are valid for speech and music (considered in detail in Chapters 8 and 9) and effects (Chapter 10).

Its surroundings may indicate the way in which a microphone is used. In a very noisy location, for example close to an aircraft that is about to take off or among a vociferous crowd, the only place for a microphone is right by the mouth of the speaker. In these and many other cases the first criterion must be intelligibility. But if clarity is possible in more than one limiting position of the microphone (or with more than one type) there is a series of choices to be made. The exercise of these choices is called *micro-phone balance*.

The first object of balance is *to pick up the required sound at a level suitable to the microphone and recording set-up; and at the same time to discriminate against unwanted noises.*

In professional practice this means deciding whether one micro-phone is necessary to cover the sound source adequately, or several, and choosing the best type of microphone, with particular regard to its directional and frequency characteristics. In addition, it is often possible to choose the position of the source or degree of spread of several sources.

Where the natural acoustics are being used, the second aim of a good balance is *to place each microphone at a distance and angle that will produce a pleasing degree of reinforcement from the acoustics of the studio*—or, in other words, to achieve an appropri-ate ratio of direct to indirect sound.

Acoustic reinforcement may, however, be replaced by artificial reverberation which is mixed in to the final sound electrically. In this case each individual sound source can be individually treated.

For this reason, and because picking up a sound on a second more distant microphone will reintroduce the effect of the studio acoustics, we have as an alternative aim of microphone balance: *to separate the sound sources so that they can be treated individually.*

For the man working on pop music the term balance means a great deal more: it includes the treatment, mixing, and control functions that are integral parts of the creation of his single composite sound. This is discussed later in the chapter.

Stereo microphone balance

Microphone balance has the same objects in stereo as in mono—but with one major addition: *to find a suitable scale of width.* Whereas indirect sound occupies the whole sound stage, it may be quite acceptable that direct sound should occupy only part of it.

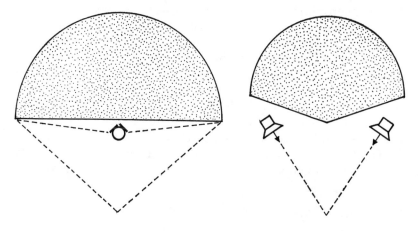

COMPRESSION OF SCALE OF WIDTH. A sound source that might be spread over 90° or more in real life *(left)* may be compressed on the audio stage to 60° or less.

A large sound source such as an orchestra should obviously occupy the whole stage and, to sound realistic, must be set well back by the use of adequate reverberation. On the other hand, a string quartet with the same reverberation should occupy only part of the stage, say the centre 20° within the available 60°; anything more would make the players appear giants. The same quartet can, however, be 'bought forward' to occupy almost all of the sound stage (provided that the balance itself is sufficiently dry). In either case, whatever reverberation there is would occupy the whole available width.

175

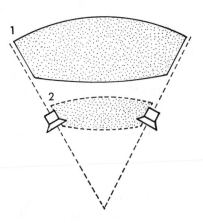

ORCHESTRA IN CORRECT SCALE OF WIDTH. A broad subject needs enough reverberation to make it appear a natural size (1); if the reverberation is low the subject appears close and under-sized or cramped together (2).

With coincident microphones, image width can be controlled in several ways:

1. The microphones may be moved closer to or farther from the sound source. Moving farther back narrows the source and also (as with mono) increases reverberation.

2. The polar response of the microphone elements may be changed. Broadening the response from figure-of-eight out towards cardioid narrows the image. It also reduces the long-path reverberation that the figure-of-eight picks up from behind and permits a closer balance. With crossed hypercardioids there is a reduction in reverberation as well as the change in quality.

3. The ratio of A + B to A − B may be changed electrically: if the A − B component is reduced the width is reduced. If the A + B

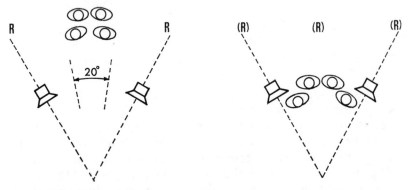

A QUARTET IN STEREO. *Left.* The quartet uses only a third of the audio stage, but reverberation fills the whole width. *Right.* The quartet occupies the whole of the space between the loudspeakers. Here the reverberation must be low in order to avoid the players appearing gross: such reverberation as there is appears from behind them.

176

component is reduced the width can be increased a little. There are two ways of doing this (see pp. 70–72).

4. The angle between microphone axes may be changed. Narrowing the angle also brings forward the centre at the expense of the wings, and discriminates against noise from the sides.

With spaced microphones, their separation and the directions in which they point have the strongest effect on image width; and the $A + B/A - B$ ratio may again be manipulated. With both kinds of stereo balance further reverberation may be added from additional distant microphones.

Where individual sources for which no width is required are balanced on monophonic (or 'spotting') microphones, the balance must be close enough (or the studio sufficiently dead) to avoid appreciable reverberation, or there will be a 'tunnel' effect—extra reverberation beamed from the same direction.

A position on the sound stage may be established by steering (or panning) portions of the signal to the A and B channels. If a second monophonic microphone picks up the same source unintentionally it joins with it to form a spaced pair, giving a false position; what is more, the degree of displacement also shifts if the level of one of the microphones is changed. Close balance, directional characteristics, layout of sources in the studio and screens may all be used to make sure this does not happen.

Monophonic spotting techniques cannot be used for subjects that have obvious physical size—such as a group of instruments or singers, a close piano, or an organ. In this case two monophonic microphones may be used to form a stereo pair.

Quadraphonic microphone balance

Quadraphonic balance is achieved in three main ways:

1. From a conventional stereo balance, direct sound (with some reverberation) is fed to the A and B channels and reverberation only to AR and BR. Direct sounds are steered to the rear channels for special effects only.

2. A multimicrophone balance is employed, using mainly mono microphone techniques but with stereo pairs for broad sources such as piano or organ. The images are steered to their desired position around the periphery. Control of depth may be achieved by splitting individual direct sounds between diagonally opposed channels (to bring the image forward) or by adding reverberation

177

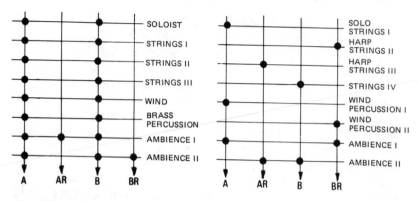

				SOLOIST	

TWO KINDS OF QUADRAPHONY (mixed down from 8-track tape). Blobs indicate a feed through the mixer. *Left:* in this example the A and B channels carry conventional stereo; reverberation only is fed to the rear channels. *Right:* direct sound is fed to all four channels, with the two reverberation tracks split diagonally, and the wind and percussion also divided diagonally. In this example a premix appropriate to the music has been planned. In practice, modern multitrack techniques will involve many more tracks than this and the mix-down will be more complex.

(to carry it back, as in two-channel stereo).
3. A cluster of four hypercardioid microphones is set in the middle and directed outward to sound sources arrayed around them. Generally these sources are all pointing inward, but a directional sense can be preserved by having the sources all directed towards the same wall of the studio.

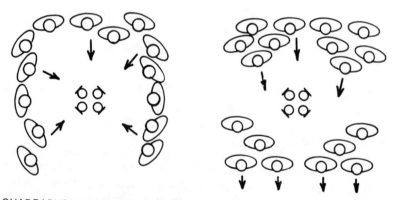

QUADRAPHONIC MICROPHONE CLUSTER. *Left.* All performers working to the centre. *Right.* All performers working in the same direction. The cluster technique works well with discrete quadraphony; less so with matrixed systems.

178

The balance test

A sound balance, whether for mono or for stereo in its several forms, may be intended as a close representation of the original sound or an adaptation of it to suit different listening conditions—or, indeed, for any effect selected from a broad spectrum of modified sound qualities that might be offered for the listener's pleasure. It is never an exact copy, but always an interpretation: it is the balancer's job to exercise choice on behalf of the listener, selecting for him from a vast range of possibilities.

Good sound is not just a matter of 'going by the book'. It is a subjective quality, but the balancer's subjectivity must be allied (paradoxically) to a capacity for analytical detachment. And whenever possible, he judges his results in the best listening conditions that the intended audience is likely to use.

The surest way of getting a good balance—or at any rate the best for the available studio, microphones and control equipment —is to carry out a balance test. Such tests are not made on every occasion: with increasing experience of a particular studio and the various combinations of sources, a balancer spends less time on the basics and more on detail. A newcomer to microphone balance is likely to see a great deal of the latter, and this apparent concentration on barely perceptible changes may prevent his discovering how the broader objective is achieved.

Consider first the single microphone (or stereo pair) picking up a 'natural' acoustic balance. The preferred technique is to rig at least two microphones in positions that (according to the general principles outlined later) should provide a reasonable sound. Compare two balances by using the mixer desk and monitoring loudspeakers to listen to each in turn, switching back and forth at intervals of ten seconds or so, considering one detail of the sound after another until a decision can be made. The poorer balance is then abandoned and its microphone moved to a position that seeks to improve on the better. The process is repeated until no further improvement is possible or time runs out. In practice, this means advance preparation, providing opportunities to move microphones with minimum disturbance and loss of rehearsal time.

For a multimicrophone balance the same process may be carried out for each microphone. Here, what might appear to be a lengthy process is simplified: there is no need for an acoustic balance between many sound sources with a single microphone, as this is achieved in the control desk; nor (in dead music studios) to balance direct with ambient sound.

Where multitrack recording is used (as in many music recording studios today) some of the balance decisions can be delayed until the recordings themselves are complete. Mixing down—still using comparison tests—is a part of balance that may be continued long after the musicians themselves have gone.

For speech, in those cases where the speaker works to the microphone (which includes most radio and some television) a similar method may be used: place two microphones before the speaker, replace that which gives the poorer balance, and so on.

A television balance in which the microphone is permitted to appear in vision may be similar to those already described. Static microphones are set to musical instruments or to speakers in a discussion; or a singer may perform to a stand microphone. But where there is movement and the microphone itself should not be seen, the process is reversed and the microphone is made mobile (on a boom), working to the performers. The balance changes from moment to moment—ideally in harmony with the picture.

In either case the visual element increases the complexity of the balance problems, to which the simplest answer may be additional microphones.

In any kind of balance here are the main things to listen for:
1. The clarity and quality of direct sound. In the case of a musical instrument this radiates from part of the instrument where the vibrating element is coupled to the air. It should comprise a full range of tones from bass to treble, including harmonics, plus any transients that characterize and define the instrument.
2. Unwanted direct sounds, e.g. hammer (action) noises on keyboard instruments, pedal operation noises, piano-stool squeaks, floor thumps, page turns, etc. Can these be prevented or discriminated against?
3. Wanted indirect sound, reverberation. Does this add body, reduce harshness and blend the sound agreeably without obscuring detail?
4. Unwanted indirect sound, severe colorations.
5. Unwanted extraneous noises.

When trying out a balance, listen to check that bass, middle, and top are all present in their correct proportions, and sound in the same perspective. If they do not, it may be the fault of the studio, in that certain frequencies are emphasized more than others, so changing both proportion and apparent perspective; or it may be more directly the fault of the balance in that a large instrument is partly off-microphone (this can happen with a close piano balance).

Here are some of the variables that may be changed during a balance test:
1. Distance between microphone and sound source.
2. Height and lateral position.
3. Angle (in the case of directional microphones).
4. Directional characteristics (by switching, or by exchanging the microphone for a different type).
5. Frequency response (by using a different microphone if an extended response is required, or otherwise by filtering).

For greater control over these variables, as few of them should be changed between successive comparisons as is feasible in the time available. Another possibility for improving a poor balance is to set in additional microphones to cover any parts of the original sound that are insufficiently represented.

The man working in a studio, having a separate monitoring cubicle, is able to use a high-quality loudspeaker to listen to the balance from the soundproof studio direct. But where these ideal conditions are not available, and artistic quality is both important and possible, balance tests should take the form of trial recordings —if necessary, a whole series of them—so that comparisons can be made on playback. Since the recordist uses these trial runs to judge how he can use the acoustics of the studio to the greatest advantage (or to the least disadvantage, if the reverberation is excessive or highly coloured), he must use reasonably high-quality equipment for playback. It must be remembered that a tape recorder's internal speaker generally has colorations (peaks and troughs in its frequency response, due to resonances, etc.) which are often severe enough to mask those picked up by the microphone.

A film recordist or radio man working on location may be at a particular disadvantage here; a disadvantage that will not be viewed sympathetically back in the studio. So skill—or in the absence of experience, very great care—is needed here

For reportage, an unchecked balance generally yields results that have an adequate documentary value. Here, experience is invaluable.

Visual conventions for microphones

In film and television the normal criteria for the placing of microphones for good balance still apply, but in addition a second set, based on what is visually acceptable, must also be considered.

One important convention concerns the match of sound and picture perspectives for speech. Obviously, a close picture should have close sound. Also, if possible, a distant picture should have sound at a more distant acoustic perspective. However, the need for intelligibility may override this: a group walking and talking across a crowded room may be clearly audible in a relatively close perspective, whereas nearer figures may be virtually inaudible; again, a reporter seen in long shot may be audible in close-up. In neither case will the audience complain—because they want to hear, and they can.

Other conventions concern whether microphones may appear in vision or not.

For dramatic presentations, the microphone should always be unseen, as its presence would destroy the illusion of reality.

For television presentations where such total suspension of disbelief is not required of the audience, microphones may be out of vision or discreetly in vision. In-vision microphones are used where better or much more convenient sound coverage can be obtained in this way; but because much of television consists of programmes in which microphones *may* appear in vision they may be seen a great deal without being noticed. However, their very ubiquity is a point against them: there is visual relief in getting rid of them if the opportunity allows.

For film, including television films, where the illusion of reality is not required, microphones may appear in vision; but the reason needs to be stronger than that required in a television studio; and the use even more discreet. This is because most film is shot in places where microphones are not part of the normal furniture; so that to show a microphone may remind the audience of the presence of all of the technical equipment (including the camera). Also, in a film there may be greater variety of picture, or a more rapid rate of cutting than may be possible in the studio; in these circumstances a microphone that is constantly reappearing is more intrusive.

When it is decided that a microphone really has to be in vision its choice depends on its appearance and also, perhaps, mobility as well as on the balance required: some of the microphone types that are available have been described in the preceding chapter, and their use is discussed in the next two. But when microphones must not be seen, the best balance will probably be obtained with studio booms, Here, too, the equipment has already been described; and as it is used mainly for speech balance, boom operation is dealt with primarily under that heading. Television musical performances present special problems: their balance should compare well with that on radio or record even though television studios are usually fairly dead. Unless a concert hall is used, this provides an extra reason for multimicrophone balance.

Multimicrophone balance

In a multimicrophone balance a broad range of techniques is drawn together: ways of handling echo, of creatively distorting sound, of building up a recording by adding track upon track, and of mixing down from 8, 16, 24 or even more prerecorded tracks to a mono, stereo or quadraphonic finished product. More detailed description will follow in later chapters, but here are brief notes on some of the techniques used:

Equalization. Nominally this means restoring a level response to a microphone that has inherently or by its positioning an uneven response. But in addition it is a second stage in the creative distortion of sound—the response of the microphone in its chosen position being the first. Equalization, whether in a separate response selection amplifier, or incorporated into an integrated fader-amplifier unit, has controls for bass response, top response, and midlift or cut. Some units have fixed bands of midlift, centred on, say, 1·4, 2·8, 4·0, and 5·4 kHz, with switched levels of increase; others have a continuously variable frequency selector and more versatile level controls. Sometimes there are also low-pass, high-pass or narrow band ('notch') filters (see p. 393).

Echo (see p. 401). This replaces the natural reverberation given by conventional acoustics. Greater control is possible, as feeds taken from individual microphones can be set at different levels. Equalization can be applied to echo, too, perhaps to give the high harmonics of direct sound greater clarity by having less echo in the 'top'.

Compression (see p. 350). Reduction in dynamic range may be used to maintain a high overall level (in order to ensure the strongest possible recorded or broadcast signal), or it may be applied to single parts of a backing sound which without it would have to be held low in order to avoid sudden peaks blotting out the melody, or to the melody itself, which might otherwise have to be raised overall, and as a result become too forward. Limiters as well as compressors are used for this.

Overdubbing. This is building up a complete sound by additive recording. For example, the instrumental backing may be recorded first; then the soloist listens to a replay on headphones and adds his contribution, the mixed sound being recorded on a second machine. Or, for a particular item, an extra instrumental track may be required from a musican who has already played in the original recording.

Post-balancing and mixing down. Music recording studios take many tracks side by side on broad tape, usually 2 in (50 mm), with 16 or 24 stacked heads to record and replay them. Most instruments are recorded in mono, but some, such as piano or a vocal backing group can be in stereo and require two tracks; some (notably drums) may have many. With 8-track recordings it is likely that some preliminary mixing of groups of instruments will be necessary, with the stereo elements remaining split across pairs of tracks. Using the monitoring circuits (see p. 47), a reference balance is obtained during the recording sessions and may be taped. At the end of the session the levels chosen for all channels are noted.

A further tape recorder taking safety tracks may be left running throughout the session, and the safety copy retained at the studio until final acceptance of the recorded balance (after which the tape is reused).

After the departure of the musicians the tapes are replayed so that the original individual tracks, perhaps with further treatment, can be mixed down (*reduced*) to the desired quadraphonic, stereo or mono result. For some purposes, for example, television mono background music with many cues, the reference tape itself may be used, perhaps with a little further additive processing or minor remixing of individual items. For the preparation of tapes as the first stage in record production a mixing-down session is usually arranged on a later day, in order to allow fresh judgment to be applied to experiments in combining and placing the sounds. Panpots can be used to position the individual tracks on the stereo stage, with components that are already in stereo being either compressed and placed within the picture or retained at their full width. Similarly the individual tracks may be placed within a quadraphonic field by pairs of panpots controlling the two dimensions. Some of the techniques used for popular music are considered further in Chapter 9.

Computer control. There are advantages to systems that

'remember' mixing instructions and can reproduce them on demand—on another day if necessary. Subsequent experiments then involve only trying out and then feeding changes to the store of mixing instructions. Internal variations in level are reliably reproduced; tracks with nothing on them for the time being are consistently faded out, and forgettable operations like briefly taking out a channel to eliminate a cough are handled automatically.

The desk has 'write', 'read' and 'update' modes and additional 'write' and 'update' buttons associated with each fader. The initial balance is made with the desk in the 'write' mode. When the tape is replayed with the desk in the 'read' condition, all the earlier fader settings and changes are reproduced (irrespective of the current fader positions). If while the mix is being read a 'hold' button is pressed, the replay continues but with the controls unchanged from that point on: this could be used (for example) to get rid of a fade-out that had been put on the end of the initial mix.

To update the mix, all of the faders are set to zero or to some nominal setting which becomes the 'null' level. After the relevant channels have been set to 'update', the tape is replayed and any changes from the null position (and their variation in time) are fed to the data store, changing the selected components of the mix by the amounts indicated. Alternatively the whole of the previous control sequence for a channel can be rejected and written afresh by using the 'write' button instead of 'update' and operating the fader normally. Also associated with each fader is a grouping switch. If several faders are dialled to the same number to form a subgroup, the 'write' and 'update' instructions for any one of them operate on the control data for all members of the sub-group.

Early computer control was applied to the faders only; later versions may include the settings for equalization, compression, echo-feed and so on, and controls for passing the signal through external processing equipment.

Artistic compatibility: mono and stereo balances

If an item recorded or broadcast in stereo is likely to be heard by many people in mono it is obviously desirable that the mono signal should be artistically satisfying. This may mean modifying the stereo version somewhat. Several problems may occur.

Loudness. Whereas a sound in the centre appears equally loud in both channels, those at the side are split between the M and S channels. As the S information is missing in mono, such subjects may be lower in volume than is desirable.

Reverberation. The S signal has a higher proportion than does the M; the mono version may therefore be too dry. A possible way round this is to make the main stereo balance drier still, and then add more reverberation on the M channel. In crossed figure-of-eight balances, in particular, there is heavy loss of reverberation due to cancellation of out-of-phase components.

Aural selectivity. Individual important sound subjects may not be clearly heard in the mono version when in stereo they are quite clearly distinct because of spatial separation. It may be necessary to boost such subjects or so place them (towards the centre of the stage) that in the mono version they are automatically brought forward.

Phase distortion. Spaced microphone techniques may not adapt well to mono, as the subjects to the side have phase-distortion effects: systematic partial addition and cancellation of individual frequencies which no longer vary with position.

In addition, there are things that are less of a nuisance in mono than stereo. For example:

Extraneous noises. Noises that are hardly noticed in mono may be clearer in stereo because of the spatial separation. Moving noises (e.g. footsteps) may be particularly distracting unless they are part of the action and balanced and controlled to the right volume, distance, and position.

8

SPEECH BALANCE

SPEECH balance depends on three factors: the voice itself, the microphone, and the surrounding acoustic conditions. In a good balance the voice should be clear and sound natural, perhaps reinforced and brightened a little by the acoustics of the room that is being used as a studio. There should be no distracting noise, no sound that is not an appropriate and integral part of the acoustic scenery.

A studio designed for speech and discussion programmes may be about the size of a fairly large living room, with a carpet on the floor, and perhaps treatment on the walls and ceiling to control reverberation. The nature, as well as the duration of reverberation should be considered: a large, open studio, even if dead enough, sounds wrong, and a speaker needs screens around him, not to reduce the studio's reverberation, but to cut down its apparent size by introducing more short path reflections. A warm acoustic might match that of a domestic sitting room; but for a film commentary an audible studio ambience might conflict with picture, so for this and certain other purposes there is more absorber, and a lower reverberation time.

Microphones for speech

Microphone and acoustics are interrelated. For a given working distance an omnidirectional microphone requires far deader acoustics than a cardioid or bidirectional microphone, which by their directivity discriminate against the studio reverberation and any colouration that goes with it. A hypercardioid, with its greater directivity, reduces these still further. On the other hand, the omnidirectional types (including hypercardioids which become omnidirectional at low frequencies) permit closer working.

MICROPHONE POSITION. Showing a good position for speech, with head well up. Script also held up and to side of microphone.

Let us consider first a microphone for which, by this reckoning, the studio acoustics are important: the bidirectional ribbon, which at normal working distances, two to three feet (60 to 90 cm), has a reasonably flat response throughout the frequency range of speech. The response tends to roll off above and below that range, but that is no disadvantage, because these limits discriminate against low and high-frequency noise. To study the interplay of voice and unfamiliar acoustics, experiment with balance tests as described in the Chapter 7. Try several voices: some benefit more by a close balance than others. But do all this well ahead of any important recording or broadcast, as a last-minute series of complicated microphone adjustments can be disconcerting.

The best way of getting a good signal-to-noise ratio is to speak clearly and not too softly. A common vice of the British is to speak too quietly; not to open the mouth wide enough. Some other nationalities, e.g. Americans and Australians, are less inclined to mumble. But whatever the nationality, very quiet speech is at a disadvantage.

Balancing two speakers on opposite sides of a ribbon is little more difficult than a single voice, unless the two speakers have radically different voice levels. In an interview, the interviewer can sometimes help by adopting a suitable voice level to ensure that the two voices balance. It has sometimes been suggested that an interviewer's voice should be slightly lower in volume than that of the interviewee. If this can be managed without the whole discussion becoming too subdued it will generally succeed, the primary aim of an interview being—as it is generally understood by most of the audience—to bring out the views and personality of the interviewee.

If the relative loudness of two voices does not sound right on the balance test it should help if the microphone is moved slightly to favour one or the other. But watch out for any tendency for the more distant voice to sound acoustically much brighter than the other; rather than allow this to happen it is necessary to introduce some control (i.e. adjustment of the gain)—just a slight dip in level as the louder speaker opens his mouth to speak—or to balance the speakers separately on hypercardioid microphones. Random variations in loudness are much less tolerable when heard over a loudspeaker than when listening to a person in the same room, so if nothing can be done to stop people rocking backward and forward, or producing considerable changes of voice level (without, for example, breaking the flow of a good spontaneous discussion) some degree of control is necessary.

It may help if the microphone is less obtrusive, e.g. mounted in a well in a table between interviewer and interviewee. Sight lines are better, but paper noise from notes lying on the table may be worse.

An omnidirectional microphone at a similar distance would give far too full an account of the acoustics, so a closer balance is employed, and the effects of movement in and out relative to a fixed microphone are correspondingly more pronounced. However, with a very close balance the importance of the acoustics is diminished, so compensation by fader alone becomes less objectionable.

In practice, omnidirectional microphones lie somewhat uncomfortably between those designed to use acoustics and those that substantially eliminate them. As a result, microphones that unequivocally de-emphasize acoustics are generally preferred. This is where hypercardioids come into their own. They have a reduced acceptance of ambient sound and allow closer balance—partly because of the reduced pressure gradient component (compared with bidirectional types) but rather more from their carefully cultivated tendency towards an omnidirectional response at low frequencies. This last may, however, begin to bring a boomy low-frequency component of the room acoustic back in to the balance which, in turn, is de-emphasized by any bass roll-off in the microphone itself. In hypercardioids there is scope for a wide range of design characteristics. Variables include angle of acceptance, the way in which the polar response changes at low frequencies, the degree of intrinsic bass roll-off, and whether additional switched bass cut is provided. At high frequencies the differentially changing response at angles of around 30° or 45° to the axis may be used for fine tuning the response to particular voices.

With early omnidirectional designs the erratic high-frequency response made it desirable to add acoustic resonance to the voice, if only to disguise the deficiencies of the microphone itself. Modern hypercardioids are more satisfactory, so many voices can be close-balanced and acoustically dead without sounding harsh. This style is suited not only to voices over film but also to radio documentary narrative, news reporting and announcements between segments with different qualities and acoustics. But it does also emphasize the mechanical noises from the lips and teeth that sometimes accompany speech, and increases the danger of blasting, particularly on the plosive 'b' and 'p' sounds. A wind-shield (or pop-shield) may be needed, if not already included in the microphone design.

Some disc jockeys prefer a close, intimate style, with very little of the studio acoustic in the sound. It is possible that the wish to work very close to the microphone is partly also psychological: the performer is helped if he can feel that he is speaking softly in the audience's ear. A disc jockey with a soft, low voice does not improve matters by gradually creeping in to an uncorrected directional microphone and accentuating the bass elements in his voice, particularly when he is presenting pop records, which have what in other fields of recording would be regarded as an excess of top. Once a good balance has been found, microphone discipline is necessary.

Interviewing with a hand-held microphone

For an interview using a hand-held hypercardioid or omni-directional microphone one of four basic balances may be adopted:

1. With the microphone at or just above waist level, so that its presence is unobtrusive. This balance is sometimes attempted for television work or where it is felt that the interviewee will take fright at a closer technique. It gives poor quality (very poor, if omnidirectional) with either too much background sound or too reverberant an acoustic. In television, however, the picture distracts conscious attention from the sound quality, so that provided speech is clearly intelligible it may sometimes be accepted.

2. Between the two speakers at chest or neck level, the face of the

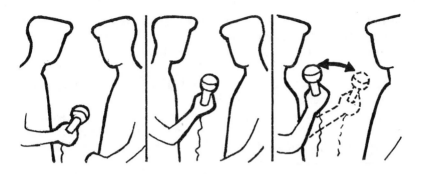

INTERVIEWING TECHNIQUES. Position 1. Microphone at waist or chest height. Sound quality: poor. Position 2. At shoulder or mouth level. Sound quality: fair; or good if interviewer and interviewee are close together in acoustically favourable and quiet surroundings. Position 3. Moving the microphone from one speaker to the other. Sound quality: good. In a fourth variant, the microphone is held to favour the interviewee most of the time.

microphone pointing upwards. With hypercardioids both speakers must be within the angle of acceptance, which may be adjusted during the dialogue to favour each voice in turn. This is preferable for television.

3. By moving the microphone to each speaker in turn, especially necessary with omidirectional microphones, the distance being judged according to the acoustics and noise (unwanted) or 'atmosphere' (wanted) in the background. The interviewee may find the repeated thrust of the microphone towards his face distracting, but the overall sound quality will be good.

4. Close to and favouring the interviewee, with only slight angling away during questions, the interviewer relying more on clarity of speech, voice quality and well-judged relative volume.

The interviewer should be close to the subject. This may best be arranged by standing at about 90° to him or sitting side by side.

Three or more voices

When three or four people are taking part in an interview or discussion—again, in good studio conditions—the ribbon microphone is useful. Although a round-table layout is not possible—four speakers must be paired off two-a side, and three divided up two and one—good sound is consistent with comfort for the speakers. The microphone can be moved a few inches, or angled slightly, to favour lighter voices; and two speakers on the same side of the microphone should be encouraged to sit shoulder to

191

shoulder so that there is no tendency for anyone to get off-microphone. The seating should be arranged so that those sitting side by side are more likely to want to talk to the speakers across the table. The change in quality that occurs when one of a pair turns to his neighbour can be marked, and if he leans back at the same time the effect is magnified.

For a discussion where there are more than four people a cardioid microphone may be suspended above the group or lowered in to a well cut into the centre of a round table between

ROUND TABLE DISCUSSION. Showing six speakers working to a cardioid microphone (1) suspended above them, or (2) sunk into a table-well.

them. The acceptance of ambient sound is the same as for a ribbon, but its proportion may be greater, because for the same working distance (which must be maintained in order to avoid crowding the speakers too closely together) the direct sound is reduced by several dBs by being some 45°–60° off-axis. The result is more reverberant unless the acoustic itself is deadened to restore the balance.

An alternative is to provide separate microphones (which can be hypercardioids) for each speaker or pair of speakers. The ambient sound pick-up is that of all the open microphones combined, and in total is broader than that of a single cardioid or bidirectional microphone, but the much closer balance can more than compensate for this. If the order of speakers is known (or

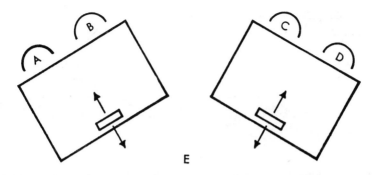

E

TWO BIDIRECTIONAL MICROPHONES. Voices A and B are on the dead side of microphone 2 and vice versa: this is a useful balance for quiz-games, etc., recorded before an audience. A voice at E would be picked up on both—provided the two were in phase.

can be anticipated by watching the discussion) some microphones can be held down a little, favouring the speakers who already have the floor.

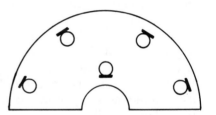

HOST AND GUESTS layout for radio show, allowing individual control of each contributor's voice. Guests take their places at the table while records or prerecordings are played.

Any nearby reflecting surface affects a balance: the reflected wave interferes with the direct sound, producing phase cancellation effects and making the quality harsher. To reduce this, tables in radio studios (and for some television programmes, too) can be constructed with a surface of acoustically transparent mesh. If a microphone well is used, it should be open at the sides. The best arrangement is a small platform suspended by springs or rubber straps. For insulation against bumps or table taps, rubber in tension is more effective than rubber in compression.

In a sufficiently dead acoustic there is one further interesting possibility: to insert an omnidirectional electret into a foamed plastic (or rubber) pad and simply place it on a table. Even a normal hard top may do, for the capsule is so close to the surface that only very high frequencies suffer interference effects.

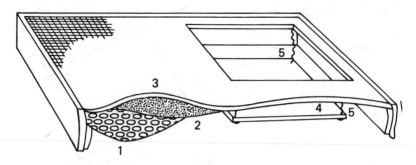

ACOUSTIC TABLE WITH WELL. The table top has three layers. 1. Perforated steel sheet. 2. Felt. 3. Woven acoustic covering (of the kind that is used on the front of loudspeakers). These are not bonded together, but held at the edges between wooden battens. 4. Wooden microphone platform, suspended at the corners by rubber straps, 5.

Studio noise

For many purposes (e.g. narration, plays, etc.) background sounds are undesirable. They are reduced to a minimum by good studio discipline, the elimination of potential problems during rehearsal, and critical monitoring. A check at the time of the initial balance will show whether *room atmosphere* itself is obtrusive. 'Atmosphere' means the ambient noise that pervades even the quietest of rooms; and some check is needed to see whether voice level or balance have to be changed to reduce it. But the sort of voice quality that stands out really effectively against background noise is more suitable for a hard-sell commercial than ordinary talk.

Even in the studios of radio stations built to discriminate against external noise, difficulties can occur: ventilation systems may carry noise from other parts of the building, or may themselves sound noisy when quite speech is being recorded—simply due to the flow of air. Structure-borne noises are almost impossible to eliminate, and rebuilding work is complicated by the need to avoid all noisy work when nearby studios are recording or on the air.

Noise may come from the speaker himself. A lightly tapping pencil may resound like rifle-fire. A slightly creaky chair or table may sound as if it is about to fall to pieces. Lighting a cigarette may be alarming; lighting several, a pyrotechnic display. Tracking fainter sounds to their source may prove difficult—embarrassing, even. A loose denture may click, a flexed shoe may creak. Many people develop small nervous habits before the microphone: for example, retractable ball-point pens can be a menace—people

194

will fiddle with them, and produce a sharp, unidentified click every ten or fifteen seconds.

There are several things that make these noises so irritating. The first is that many people listen to broadcast or recorded speech at a level that is much louder than real life; and a quiet talker is allowed much the same volume at the loudspeaker as someone who almost shouts. So the extraneous noises are loud too—and, heard monophonically, they appear to come from the same point in space as the speech. Also, whereas a visually identified sound slips immediately into place in the mind and is accepted, the unidentified one does not. Many practised broadcasters realize this and take it into account. A studio host will notice that a guest's movements are not absolutely silent and say, 'And now, just coming to join me, is . . .' and the noise is given a reason and thereby reduced to its proper proportions—so that it is not consciously noticed by the listener.

Handling a script

A frequent source of extraneous noise at the microphone—and a particularly irritating one—is paper rustle. A few comments by the producer on the handling of scripts or notes is common practice at the start of any recording or broadcast where these are used, and where the speaker is not thoroughly versed in the business. Here are a few general rules about this:

1. Use a fairly stiff paper (duplicating paper is quite good). Do not use a copy that has been folded or bent in the pocket. Avoid thin paper (e.g. airmail paper or flimsies sometimes used for carbon copies).
2. If you are sitting at a table, take the script apart by removing its paper-clip or staple. It is very difficult to turn over pages quietly, so it is a good idea to turn up two corners of the script, and then each page can be lifted gently to one side as it is finished with. Any sliding of one page over another will be audible. Better still, hold the script up, and to the side of the microphone.
3. Hold or place the script so that it is not necessary to turn or drop the head in order to read.
4. Standing at a microphone (necessary for actors with moves to make) the script can be left clipped together. The pages should be turned well off-microphone—in the case of a bidirectional microphone this means on the dead side.

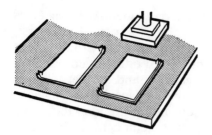

AVOIDING SCRIPT NOISE. Corners of script turned up to make it easier to lift noiselessly to one side. But script laid on the table reflects sound, affecting the balance.

5. When there are several people in a studio (as in a play) they should not all turn the pages together. If actors remember to stagger the turnover, they will also remember to turn quietly.

6. If there are only a few sheets of script they may perhaps be slipped inside clear plastic envelopes of a suitable size.

One device sometimes used is a script-rack. Sloping up toward the microphone, it avoids awkward reflections but does not prevent a persistent offender from dropping his head. Indeed, as he will be speaking more directly into the microphone at the top of the page, results may be worse than without the rack.

SCRIPT RACK. No reflections from the script can reach the microphone, but speaker may still drop his head at foot of page. The rack (as well as table surface) may be made of acoustically transparent mesh.

Speech in stereo

Much speech for stereo radio transmissions is, in fact, balanced on monophonic microphones. In particular, announcements are normally taken mono, and are generally placed in the centre, so that listeners can use this to balance the two loudspeakers. If the announcement is in a concert hall a monophonic microphone is again used with a relatively close and dead balance, but with a stereo pair left open at a distance to add stereophonic reverberation. The announcer and microphone are so placed that little direct sound is picked up in stereo; if it were (and were not central) the position of the announcer would be offset.

One reason for avoiding a stereo pair for speech balances where movement is not expected is that any slight lateral movements close to the microphone are emphasized and become gross on the sound stage.

Boom operation

In radio the microphone is usually static, and the performer works to it. In television the performer's position is determined by the scenery and lighting, and the microphone must work to him. Radio and television differ most strongly when, in addition, the microphone must be out of the television picture, and the performer moves freely. The 'microphone with intelligence' that moves and turns with him, ever seeking the best practicable balance, is the boom microphone (p. 172). Its operation is central to the subject of speech balance in television, and film, too.

From a given position the boom can cover a substantial area, and the carriage itself can be tracked to follow wider action, or repositioned between scenes. Its main positions is chosen bearing in mind the lighting (p. 88) and the fact that it is quicker to swing the arm than to rack in and out when moving from one subject to another. In addition, the operator can turn the microphone to favour sound from any one direction, or (almost as important) to discriminate against any other. Characteristically, a cardioid or near-cardioid is used, and its diaphragm must be unaffected by rapid movement and insensitive to or protected from the airflow this causes, so that the operator is not restricted in the speed of his response to action. Note that an effective windshield may be bulky, and can make movement clumsy. In practice it is best to use a directional moving coil microphone, or perhaps a condenser microphone with shock-mounting and windshield. In the ideal balance for the best match of sound to picture the microphone is above the line between subject and camera, but because of the need for clarity and internal balance between different voices (and, in addition, frequent changes in the picture itself), no single compromise position is likely to last for long.

The boom operator has a script (where one is available) and generally turns his microphone to present its axis toward whoever is speaking or expected to speak. It may be asked why, when he is using a cardioid with a good response over a wide range of directions, he needs to move the microphone at all for most work, instead of splitting the difference between two people and leaving it. The answer is that there is a 2 or 3 dB high-frequency loss at about 45° to the axis, increasing to perhaps 5 dB at 60°. The microphone will be dropped as close to the performers as the picture allows (in rehearsal he will from time to time dip his microphone into picture to locate the edge of frame), and this closeness accentuates any angle there may be between speakers. This means that by proper angling there can be not only the best signal-to-noise ratio for the person speaking but also automatic discrimination against the person who is not. If both speak it may be decided to let this balance ride to favour the person who has the most important lines, or perhaps to cover both equally. With actors of different head heights the microphone must be placed either well in front of them or to the side that favours the lower of the two.

The position for the microphone must be a compromise between the positions of the various speakers, and if they become widely separated, or one speaker turns right away, the split may become impossible to cover by a single boom. In this case a second microphone may be placed on a stand out of vision, or suspended over the awkward area, or concealed within the picture. Sometimes a second boom is used, though this is liable to cause lighting problems.

For 'exterior' scenes in plays produced in the studio the microphone must be kept as close as the limits of the picture allow. To provide a contrast with this, interiors may have a slightly more distant balance or a little added reverberation.

Because a number of different types of microphone may be used for a single voice, the control desk in a studio must have frequency correction which can be used to make microphones match as closely as possible. If correction is needed, the boom microphone is usually taken as the standard and the other microphones matched to it.

Another justification for the boom is that given suitable (rather dead) acoustics, it automatically gives a perspective appropriate to the picture: close shots have close sound; group shots have more distant sound. The boom operator uses vision monitors in the studio to check his limits (the edge of frame) during rehearsal. Then by taking a sight line again on the far backing he is able to remember the position of the microphone for the main programme.

In the days before the widespread introduction of zoom lenses it was also possible for him to see at a glance what width of shot each camera was set up for; now he has a more difficult task.

However, in television the sound supervisor can call the boom operator (and his other staff on the studio floor) over his own circuit, which cuts in on the director's circuit to the operator. (The BBC procedure is for this to be preceded by a tone-pip warning to tell them that this message is specifically for them.) During rehearsal and at such times in recordings or transmissions as the studio sound is faded out, the boom operator can reply to or call his supervisor on a separate sound talkback circuit. A boom therefore has a multicore cable, permitting communication as well as transmitting programme sound.

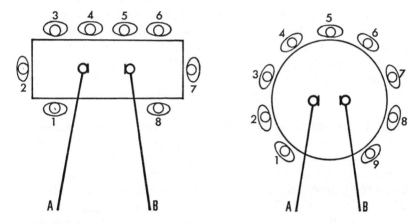

BOOM COVERAGE of a large television discussion (e.g. board meeting in a play). *Left.* Boom A covers speakers 4–8, B covers 1–5. *Right.* Boom A covers speakers 5–9 (with 1 and 4 at low level); B covers 1–5 (with 6 and 9 at low level). Cardioid microphones are used.

In certain types of television discussion programme the frame size is unpredictable, but this is partly compensated by the influence of an audience, which provides a powerful limitation on how far performers will turn. To cover situations like this, the boom may be equipped with a highly directional microphone. Although the high inertia of a gun that is nearly two feet long overall makes it a little clumsy to handle for work where gross and rapid movements from one direction to another are necessary, the fact that it can be placed farther back helps to compensate for this.

Where two people are having a 'face-to-face' discussion, but

199

are far enough apart for a boom operator to have to turn a cardioid microphone through a considerable angle to cover each in turn, it may be best to use two microphones pointing outwards at about 90° to each other. The overall effect is a very broad cardioid which is suitable for low close working. In a play such an arrangement would restrict the use of the boom for other scenes, so in a similar situation—or, for example, for a number of people sitting round a large table, two booms might be brought in.

A boom can cover action taking place on rostra built up to a height of about 6 ft (1·8 m) provided that the performers keep within about 10 ft (3 m) of the front of the high area. The boom pram, however, should be positioned as far back as possible so that the angle of the arm is kept reasonably low. For scenes on acting areas above this height it may be necessary to hoist the boom up on to rostra at a similar level (as a result of which it will, of course, be lost for scenes in the more distant parts of the studio to which it could normally be taken). Another possibility is to de-rig the microphone boom arm and attach it to fixed scaffolding. The arm will require rebalancing, and the operator will need rather more time in rehearsal to get used to the unfamiliar conditions.

The boom operator has other responsibilities. He is, for example, well placed to identify sound problems in the studio and report them back to the supervisor in the gallery. Although wearing headphones most of the time, he occasionally takes them off to listen for gallery talkback breaking through into the studio. In addition he should be aware that, unlike the cameramen, he is visible to artists, so he should react positively to their performance.

Slung and hidden microphones

In television balance one aim must be to keep the number of microphones to a practicable minimum, and the use of booms helps towards this. But unless set design and action are to be restricted there are occasionally places that are inaccessible to booms. To reach them, additional microphones may be suspended above the action—ideally, just out of frame, and downstage of the speaker's position, so that sound and picture match. If a slung microphone has two or three suspension cables, its position may be adjusted in rehearsal, and if there is any danger of its shadow falling in shot, provision should be made for it to be flown when not in use.

200

Microphones are sometimes concealed in special props that are constructed of wire gauze, then painted, covered or otherwise disguised to blend in to the picture, though with the advent of miniature condenser capsules the construction of special hiding places is less often required. When positioning such a microphone take into account any nearby reflective surfaces. An octave filter may in any case be used to match the sound to that of the boom microphone, but reflections may make a good match impossible.

One example of a small personal microphone used to good effect was provided by a play with a a death scene in a four-poster bed. Quiet speech in such a setting is difficult to cover by a boom, as the director usually wishes to include wide shots. A static microphone might be concealed in the hangings, canopy or behind a downstage pillar but for the dying pronouncements none of these were close enough, so a personal microphone was concealed in the bedclothes, which in this case were not likely to be moved so roughly as to produce rustling noises while the microphone was faded up.

Microphones in vision

The presence of a microphone in vision must be natural and undistracting. A boom microphone (for example) which is actually visible in the top of the picture can be very disturbing, particularly if it is moved from time to time to point to a different person.

Microphones used in vision are either *personal*, fixed below the neck or held in the hand, in which case they are moved around by the performer, or they are *static*, on table or floor stands.

For a speaker who is not going to move, a fixed microphone in the picture gives by far the best sound. But to do its job properly it must generally be angled to point at the speaker (or may be split between two): if this deliberately chosen angle conflicts with the designer's choice of 'line' within the picture the microphone may be more noticeable, as it will also be in a simple uncluttered design. This may not matter, but it should never be unexpected.

The base, for stability and to cushion shocks, needs to be reasonably large and can therefore sometimes appear more obtrusive than the microphone itself. Sometimes it may be recessed into a desk, but such a cavity needs to be designed with care: a fully boxed-in cavity would perhaps modify the local acoustics noticeably, so one or more sides of the recess should be left open.

The microphone capsule itself should in any case stand well clear of such a recess, so in a shot showing the table it has to be clearly in vision, unless hidden behind something standing on or in front of the table—which in turn may be a more obtrusive or unattractive element of design than the microphone itself. Alternatively, a specially designed desk might have its front continue upward a little beyond the level of the desk top. An acoustically transparent top can be included in the design.

A microphone placed to one side may be neater than one immediately in front of a speaker; normally a speaker is more likely to turn one way than another, so the microphone could be placed on that side. However, if the person does turn the other way he may be right off microphone; it is therefore useful if the next person's microphone can also pick up his voice.

Where many people are spread over a large area of studio, a microphone is often used for every individual. Even when there are pairs who are close together, the sound man may prefer to balance them individually, provided that he always known who is going to speak, either from the script or because names are used. Good quality demands that as few microphones as possible be open at any one time.

In a practical example: in a particular quiz there are three questioners and three teams, each of which may consist of anything up to six or even more people. Each team is examined in succession, but for each the questioning is limited to two of the judges, who may, however, butt in on each other at any point. In addition, the answers are limited to four spokesmen from a team (in fact, only these four have microphones), and they are always identified by name in the question. Thus the balancer has only six microphones to handle, which is just about possible without his being caught napping too often.

Using hand microphones in vision

The use of hand microphones has long been established as an accepted convention of television (and television film) reporting.

This is because it is very convenient for the two-man, reporter plus cameraman combination; and because the microphone can always be used closer if the surroundings become noisier. In two-man operation it is recorded directly on to a magnetic stripe on the film. Even if there is a sound man in the crew, the reporter may still prefer to use a hand microphone for interview work (the techniques have been described on p. 191) or in excessively noisy conditions. In one example two stick microphones were used for a discussion taking place by an electric-arc steel-melting furnace, the microphones being held very close to the lips of the two speakers. This achieved a satisfactory balance with the noise of the furnace, and was exciting to listen to. The only difficulty was a non-technical one—the two people had more difficulty in hearing each other than making themselves heard to the audience.

In extreme circumstances lip microphones may be used in vision: one was used for the commentary, at the airfield itself, for the maiden flight take-off of Concorde, and gave excellent separation of speech and engine noise. On that occasion the microphone was passed from hand to hand between commentators.

But hand-held microphones can easily be overused, particularly where they make a person look unduly dominating and aggressive: for this reason they should be used with caution by women interviewing men.

Alternative techniques, which for most purposes should be preferred, are the use of personal (lanyard) microphones, or (for exterior work) gun microphones.

Using gun microphones

The virtues and limitations of the gun microphone have already been described (p. 152). It is very useful for filming out-of-doors, held just outside the edge of frame and pointed directly at each speaker in turn. Careful working between cameraman and sound man is required to avoid the microphone getting in to picture: its windshield is very obtrusive even when still, and is even more so if it moves.

An advantage of this microphone is that it allows very considerable movement (but not of course for the subject to turn right away from the microphone while speaking). Accidentally off-microphone sound is at low level in exterior work, and very bad quality in interiors. The gun microphone can, however, be used in the relatively dead surroundings of a television studio (in an area well away from strongly reflecting surfaces) for picking up voices at a distance. But in general its directional qualities are not trustworthy in normal interiors or even reverberant exteriors.

The gun microphone can also be attached to a camera, pointing along its line. It is subject to mechanical noise from film cameras that are not well blimped and, with any camera, makes handling a matter for even greater care than normal. It picks up sound effects adequately within the field of the average wide angle lens. The principal application is to one-man news-film coverage.

When a highly directional microphone is used to cover effects such as tap dance, or to follow the action in an outside broadcast of some sport (to which it adds great realism), it is often best to filter out frequencies below about 300 Hz. A gun microphone with bass cut has sometimes been used in conjunction with other microphones to cover the press-conference type of situation, supplying presence that other distant microphones lack. For this, a parabolic reflector could also be considered: it would be out of frame, or possibly hidden behind a gauze that is lit to look solid.

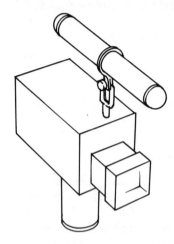

GUN MICROPHONE ON TELEVISION CAMERA. A gun microphone may be used in this way to cover sports or other events, pointing toward the same action as the zoom lens.

Using lavalier microphones

Lavaliers are another very useful type of microphone for location work: one is fixed to the clothing or hung round the neck of each speaker (but take care if two are brought close together, as this can affect the balance).

The microphone itself can often be hidden behind a tie (though some synthetics cause crackling), while a thick tie can produce a correspondingly woolly response. If it is concealed it is best to ensure that the means of suspension is also invisible—for example, by using a cord of the same tone or colour as the shirt or other clothing against which it may otherwise be seen. Many recordists do not bother with this: the results can be untidy. A microphone that is not concealed may also sometimes merge in to the tones of a tie or other clothing and not be too distracting. A slip-on cover of thin, matching material can help. Care is needed in making large or sudden movements, especially those that disturb the hang of clothes (as sitting down or standing up does with a jacket). However, the subject should not be discouraged from normal movement unless absolutely necessary; indeed, an advantage the lavalier has over the hand-held stick microphone is that it leaves both hands free. Also, if the speaker turns right away from the camera he may still be heard clearly—though turning his head to look over one shoulder may cause speech to be off-microphone.

The cable may be hidden beneath a jacket for a tight mid-shot (which probably does not warrant the use of a personal microphone anyway), but, in the more general case it will go to a hidden radio transmitter (see p. 162) or continue on its path beneath the clothing, down a trouser leg, or inside a skirt. It should have a connector not too far from the feet, so that the wearer can easily be disconnected during breaks. If the subject is going to walk it is best to attach the cable (and connector) to one foot, perhaps tying it in to a shoelace. Walking dragging a considerable length of cable is awkward, and may be visibly so—reinforcing the case for a radio link.

Because of their position, lavalier microphones have a characteristic quality. Once a sequence starts with such a microphone the speaker should continue on it until there is either a marked change of location (e.g. exterior to interior) or a very long pause before the same voice recurs. This is true also for many other microphones, though to a lesser degree. A disadvantage of personal microphones when compared with booms is that there is no change of aural with visual perspective. This is more important in plays than in other programmes. Lavaliers usually offer reasonable intelligibility in fairly noisy surroundings, or in acoustics that are brighter than usual for television. The quality gains a little from good reflected sound,

When considering the use of neck microphones it is worth remembering that most viewers assume much more spontaneity in television than can be the case. And even though the amount or work involved in pinning on a microphone may be trivial compared with the care that will often be taken with lighting or camera, its visible presence may, by drawing attention to technique, diminish the illusion. Also, a person seen to be wearing a lavalier should be unequivocally (in the mind of the viewer) a willing 'victim'. In confrontations those under attack should not be visibly anchored in this way even if they are willing.

In very long shots the posibility of using radio microphones may have to be considered even in plays (where they would be wrong for perspective unless the sound is treated with care); the radio microphone is for this purpose better than the cabled lanyard, as there can be no question of trailing microphone leads in view.

Using low-quality 'actuality' microphones

There may be occasions when the output from certain low-quality microphones may be wanted: for example, actuality intercom in an aircraft for a documentary film. In this case a feed can generally be taken from the distribution system (a suitable plug—or temporary lash up—will be required, and impedances may need to be matched). But there will still be some question as to whether the resulting recording will actually be intelligible to anyone but the air and ground crews who are used to making sense of such quality. This sort of excise is not usually tried unless no alternative exists for the recordist.

A special, but very wide, group includes transducers that can pick up sound from media other than air. A case in point was an underwater sync interview filmed at the bottom of the English Channel. The subject of the film was the method of communication used in this interview. So, as the film unit itself was to be used to illustrate the story, an underwater (aluminium) clapper-board was made, and even a metal-framed folding chair labelled 'Director'. In the standard underwater communications equipment being used a small microphone in the face mask fed speech to a waterproof 10 watt battery-powered moving-coil loudspeaker strapped to the air-cylinder back pack. Unaided underwater ears were used to pick up the sound. A microphone switch was used, both to conserve the batteries and to cut down on transmissions of heavy bubbling by both interviewer and director.

A further part of the equipment was a 'boat set': another similar transducer used alternately as loudspeaker and microphone. The sound recordist (sitting comfortably in the boat) was able to take a feed from this. The recording was moderately intelligible through marred on one take by noise from a passing aircraft, which could be clearly heard underwater. The sound-conducting medium itself was, in principle, no problem, as water is a good conductor of sound; but underwater film-makers should beware: the sea is a noisy place.

Radio drama

In many countries radio drama is still vigorously alive. Its continued existence can be justified by audience size alone, let alone the statistically measured high appreciation of the audience. As a result, stereo techniques have been developed, and have been routinely used for many years in Britain. But let us consider first their monophonic precursor.

In drama the acoustics of a studio are used creatively, the 'scenery' being changed by altering the acoustic furniture around the microphone. As early radio drama developed, specialized studio suites were designed for them, providing a basic set of acoustics for the director to work with and to adapt further as he wished.

The studio was divided into areas having different amounts of sound-absorbent or reflecting treatment; each area providing a recognizably different quality of sound. Some—the live areas— offer a more-or-less realistic simulation of the actual conditions they are supposed to represent. Dead acoustics, on the other hand, are rarely dealt with realistically—as will be shown later. In most cases the same microphone type is employed in all areas: this means that the voice quality itself does not change but is matched from scene to scene. Ribbon microphones have been widely used: their frequency range is well adapted to that of the voice, and with working distances of about 3 ft (1 m) give a generous account of the studio itself. Actors can work on either live side of the microphone, standing two or three abreast, and can move 'off' either by increasing their distance or, more often, by easing round to the dead side (or by a combination of the two). The conditions are comfortable, flexible and easily understood. The actor is working *with* the acoustics.

One factor in the aural perception of studio size is the timing of the first major reflection—so that tape delay may sometimes be used to increase apparent size without creating excessive reverberation. But the quality of the reverberation itself also plays an important part. Small rooms sound small because certain frequencies are picked out and emphasized in the dimensions between the walls, etc. A combination of reverberation time and quality suggests both size and the acoustic furniture of a room: a sound with a reverberation time of one second may originate from a small room with little furniture (and therefore rather bright acoustically) or from a very large hall with a rather dead acoustic. The two would be readily distinguishable.

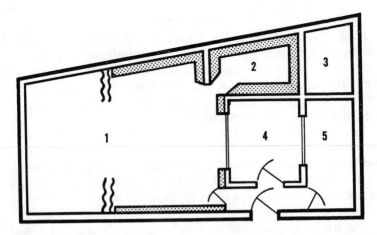

DRAMA STUDIO SUITE. This is typical of the specialized studio layouts adopted for broadcast drama in the days when radio was at its peak of popularity. Many such studios still exist (as at the BBC) and are used for their original purpose. The principles involved in the layout remain valid for many other purposes. The areas shown are: 1. Main acting area: the 'live' and 'dead' ends of the studio can be partially isolated from each other (and their acoustics modified) by drawing double curtains across. 2. 'Dead' room, with thick absorbers on walls. 3. Echo chamber. 4. Control cubicle. 5. Recording room. In this example a virtue has been made of the irregular shape of the site. The use of non-parallel walls avoids standing wave coloration.

For example, a 'bathroom' acoustic would be provided by a small room with strongly sound-reflecting walls, and can be used for any other location that might realistically have the same acoustic qualities. Similarly, a part of the main studio (or a larger room) with a live acoustic can be used to represent a public hall, a courtroom, a small concert-hall, or anything of this sort—and indeed, when not needed for drama, can be used as a small music studio. When going from one type of acoustic to another, balance (i.e. distance from the microphone) can be used to help to differentiate between them; for example, the first lines of a scene set in a large reverberant entrance hall can be played a little farther from the microphone than the main body of the action which follows—it would probably be too hard on the ears if the whole scene were played with heavy reverberation.

For a large, open acoustic with many actors, a court room, public meeting, or council chamber scene, an alternative to the ribbon is a cardioid suspended above the action. Working distances and speed of approach or departure are set by listening to the acoustic balance. An additional hypercardioid microphone can be set in for quiet asides that require little reverberation.

208

If there is a narrator as well as the 'living-room' action the two must be recognizably different. There will, of course, be differences in the style of acting, and the use of the fader at the start and end of each scene will encapsulate it, and so further distinguish between the two. But acoustics can also be used to emphasize the differences: if the scene is played well out into the open studio the narrator can be placed nearer to one of the walls and at a closer working distance to his microphone. In this case, too, a different type of microphone may be prepared: a hypercardioid or omnidirectional type, perhaps. In the studio layout, the distance between the narrator's microphone and that for dramatic action must allow for any rapid turn from one to the other. It may help to provide a satisfying contrast if there is a screen near the narration microphone.

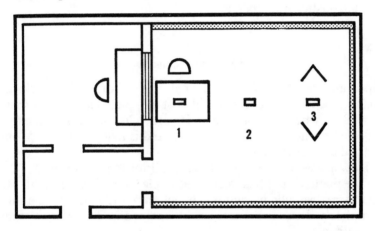

SIMPLE LAYOUT FOR DRAMA. A simple set-up using three ribbon microphones for dramatic work. 1. Narrator (close to window). 2. 'Open microphone'—for normal indoor acoustics. 3. 'Tent'—to represent outdoor quality. This is a much less versatile layout than can be obtained in a multiple-acoustic studio, and the results sound more stylized. It can be argued that this is all that is necessary for broadcasting directed to schools, because: (a) school audiences often have poor listening conditions and hear only a limited range of acoustic differences; (b) casts for a variety of reasons are small and do not need much room; and (c) educational broadcasting generally has a low budget, so studio space allocated to it is accordingly small.

It is sometimes necessary to mix acoustics—to have two voices in acoustically different parts of the same studio. There is a great deal of scope for ingenuity here; and the big problem lies in avoiding spill, particularly where the voice in the brighter acoustic must be louder than the other. Much can be done by using directional microphones, but these may not prevent the spill of

209

reverberation from the live acoustic to the dead one. Double curtains running out from the walls may help to trap the sound—or screens may be used for the same purpose—but in extreme cases separate studios or prerecordings are needed. Spill is an even greater nuisance in simulated telephone conversations, so methods of avoiding it are considered in more detail in a later chapter (p. 394).

Screens can be used to lend realistic touches to a scene. For example, the interior of a car consists of a mixture of padded and reflecting surfaces: a 'box' of screens, some bright, some padded, gives a very similar quality of sound. But one of the most common arrangements of screens—a double-V of two (or more) screens on the two sides of a bidirectional microphone—is used representationally rather than realistically to suggest an almost completely dead acoustic—the open air.

Open-air acoustics

Open-air acoustics, frequently required in dramatic work, are characterized in nature by an almost complete lack of reverberation. Even when there are walls, etc., to reflect some of it, the total reflected sound at the source is low, and is likely to produce only a small change in quality.

How are we to represent these conditions in the studio?

One method that has been tried in Germany is to simulate this quality realistically by building a section of the studio with almost completely dead acoustics, i.e. a dead-room. There are definite advantages:

1. It provides the best possible contrast to other acoustics in use, thus making a wider range of sound quality possible.
2. The muffling effect of the treatment causes the performer to lift his voice and use the same amount of edge on it as he would in the open air.
3. Effects recorded outdoors blend in easily.
4. Off-microphone voices and spot effects can be blended with on-microphone voices by using positions round towards the dead side of a ribbon microphone.
5. The amount of space round the microphone is greater than that within a tent of screens.

Unfortunately, there are also disadvantages:

1. Such an acoustic is very uncomfortable to work in, and for

those with any tendency to claustrophobia the atmosphere rapidly seems to become oppressive and unreal.

2. The transient sounds in speech peaks tend to overmodulate, even if the general level is kept low.

3. It is less pleasant to listen to completely dead sound for any length of time.

In fact, the true dead-room is not a practicable proposition, and some sort of a compromise solution has to be found. Just how far away our representational 'dead' acoustic must be from true out-door deadness depends on just how much 'open-air' there is required by the script. Where a script is set almost entirely out of doors, it is more convenient to go for a formalized style of production with an acoustic that is hardly less reverberant than a normal speech balance. On the other hand, if there are only a few isolated lines set outdoors, something fairly close to the dead acoustic may be used. In other words, apart from exceptional cases, one should usually try to set the average acoustic demanded by the script as one that is fairly close to a normal speech balance, and arrange the others relative to this.

Of the various possible sound-deadening systems, it is best to try to avoid those that give a padded-cell effect. This is, very literally, what a thinly padded dead-room sounds like, and the same sort of sound can all too easily be obtained by laying out a cocoon of screens. But probably the most satisfactory arrangement is that which employs two Vs, one on each side of a ribbon microphone.

Here are some points to remember with this layout:

1. Keep the screens as close to the microphone as is conveniently possible; try to persuade the actors to accept a little restriction on their movements. This layout keeps the path lengths short and damps out reverberation (and coloration) as quickly as possible.

2. Avoid setting the screens in parallel pairs. In fact, keep the V

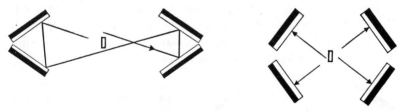

A TENT OF SCREENS. In a double-V of screens it is better that sound should be reflected twice on each side *(left)*. Standing waves cannot form unless there are parallel surfaces opposite each other *(right)*.

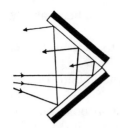

USE OF SCREENS. Double reflection of sound in a V of screens set at an acute angle. For any particular path some frequencies are poorly absorbed, but they are different for the various possible paths. Sound that is reflected back to the region of the microphone is less coloured with this arrangement than with a broad V.

of the screens fairly acute. This helps to reduce bass as well as top. Also, actors should avoid standing too far back into the apex of the V.

3. Exit and entry speeches can be awkward. In nature, distant speech is characterized by a higher voice level arriving at a lower final volume. In the studio, a voice moving off is likely to be characterized by a sudden increase in studio acoustic. So stay inside the screens at all times, and avoid directing the voice out into the open studio.

4. Off-microphone (i.e. 'distant') speeches may be spoken from the screens, speaking across the V. And if this is still too loud to mix with other voices, the actor should change his voice quality, giving it less volume and more edge. He should not try to deaden his voice by turning to face right into the angle of the screens: the only result from this will be a cotton-wool muffled quality.

All in all, the effect of screens is not that of the open air. But it is not a normal live acoustic, either. It is just different: half measures, perhaps, but acceptable as a convention. If the results seem to sound more boxy than they should it won't necessarily improve matters to play in a record of birdsong: this may just contrast with and emphasize the deficiencies of the methods.

An example of the sort of set-up that can be adopted in this type of studio is one where no less than six microphones were used for a quarter-hour playlet:

The main action was a trial scene in a criminal court at the Old Bailey, and this took three bidirectional (ribbon) microphones in the livest part of a drama studio. Counsel and witnesses worked to microphone 1 at various distances, and slight echo was added.

SPEAKING OFF MICROPHONE. No actor should go farther off than this, or turn farther into the screens. More 'distant' effects must be achieved by changes of voice quality or by adjusting the microphone fader.

The people working farther away were picked up also on microphone 2, which was about 5 ft (1·5 m) above microphone 1 and given a stronger dose of echo: perspective effects were made more real by this arrangement. A record of courtroom atmosphere completed the picture by providing an occasional cough or shuffling noise. An intermittent whispered discussion in the gallery had to be superimposed on the main action; for this, microphone 3 was 10 ft (3 m) to the side of microphone 1. No echo was used on this, and the actors worked at about 18 in (45 cm).

Flashbacks to the scene of the crime employed microphone 4, in a tent of screens representing the open air. Microphone 4 could also be used with a filter switched in circuit for the far end of a telephone conversation. Microphone 5 was for the car door (a real car door mounted on a frame) and 'body' falling (a piece of metal tubing, wrapped in thick cloth). Taken on the same microphone as the action, the car door would have been too loud and the 'body' too soft and distant. Microphone 6, at the end of the studio that had normal living-room acoustics, represented a room in a suburban house.

Use of these six microphones gave a very wide range of acoustics, and varying the combinations of microphones and echo made the illusion of tracking shots possible.

Stereo drama

In BBC studios coincident pairs are almost invariably used for the main stage; and crossed cardioid or hypercardioid gives best use of the space. The studio floor is marked up with stripes of white adhesive tape on the carpet showing the main limits of the acting area, together with any special positions or lines of movement. Movement across stage (a straight line on the sound stage) is movement along an arc of the studio: the acting area should therefore be defined by an arc at its centre, or by arcs roughly limiting it. Such arcs can be drawn either as having constant radius—for convenience—or alternatively at distances that give constant A + B pick-up. The latter is better for more complex situations, such as group or crowd scenes in which the relative distance of different voices is important. From the microphone polar diagrams it can be seen that for a crossed cardioid this arc is farther away at the centre line and loops in closer at the sides. In addition, the studio itself has an effect: unless the acoustic treatment is evenly balanced, the line may 'pull' closer to the microphone on one side than on the other. Indeed, sound stage positions may also be offset laterally from studio positions: the whole studio may seem to pull to the left or right.

Positions 'in the speaker' on the two sides may be marked: for

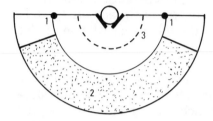

STAGE FOR STEREO SPEECH. 1. If crossed hypercardioids are used, voices in these two positions, roughly opposite to each other in the studio, appear to come from the loudspeakers. 2. Most of the action takes place in this area, at a distance of about 2–3 m from the microphones. 3. More intimate speech may be closer.

crossed cardioids, these would in principle be at the 270° limits of the theoretically available stage. But in fact, the cardioid response of practical microphones is imperfect at the rear, so the best 'in speaker' positions would usually be found at about 200°–220° separation. In practice it is often convenient to reduce this further, to 180°, by setting microphones with variable polar response one step towards hypercardioid.

In mono a long approach from a distance can be simulated by a relatively short movement by the performer, who simply walks slowly round from the dead to the live side of the microphone as he comes in to it. In stereo this space-saving technique cannot be used: long approaches, if they are required, really have to be long, and must be planned in terms of what space is available. They may, for example, be laid out to the sides, or in other particular directions from the microphone: a decision on this in advance will probably determine studio layout.

If a microphone with capsules one above the other, in the same housing, is used the difference in the height of the two capsules may cause problems in close working: a tall actor is nearer the top capsule and 'pulls' one way; a short actor is nearer the low one and 'pulls' in the other direction. Working side by side, a short and tall actor may seem to be either separated more or shifted to the same position.

But in any case it has been found that balances more distant than those that are normal for mono are necessary in order to avoid movements being exaggerated: for safety the nearest part of the real stage in which much lateral movement will occur should be at least as broad as the sound stage. In consequence, the

214

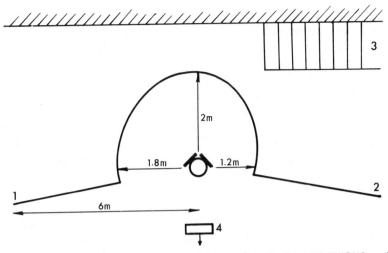

A STEREO SPEECH LAYOUT EMPHASIZING EXTREME SIDE POSITIONS and allowing long approaches from left (1) and right (2). This is taken from an actual layout in a BBC studio where, owing to asymmetry in acoustic treatment, the minimum distance for normal working was closer on the right than on the left. The positions were judged by ear and marked on the floor accordingly. Use was also made of an existing studio staircase (3) for actors to approach from mid-right, making their own footsteps. 4. The announcer, as usual, is centred.

studio must be somewhat deader than for a comparable scene in mono, and reverberation added if brighter-than-average sound is required.

For this, either stereo echo or a second stereo pair within the studio may be used. If a coincident pair is chosen, it should be placed, say, 4 ft (1·2 m) above the first pair (this is a little like the technique described for mono and provides some degree of automatic compensation as a speaker moves in close: see p. 411. An alternative arrangement is to use a spaced pair pointing back to the end of the studio that is away from the stage.

Whereas a studio for drama in mono may have several acting areas, the same studio used for stereo may have room for only a single stage (this allows for a reduction in reverberation and an occasional need for deep perspective). Therefore there may be good reason to record all scenes that have one basic acoustic before resetting the studio for the next, eventually editing the programme to the correct running order. If very different acoustics are required in the same scene—e.g. a distant open-air crowd scene including studio 'open-air' voices, mixed with close 'in-

215

terior' conversion—a pre-recording has to be made, the studio reset, and the second part dubbed in to a playback of the first.

To simulate exterior scenes in a studio it may be unavoidable to use the same basic studio acoustic. Cutting bass on the microphone output may help, but the result depends on the particular coloration of the studio acoustic. For the effect of a more distant voice in the open air, the actor himself may help by staying well forward and projecting and thinning the tone of his voice, or, alternatively, by turning away from the microphone and speaking into a screen. Ideally it is bass that needs to be absorbed more.

Stereo drama problems

New dramatic conventions have had to be established for stereo sound productions: the most important is that movement (or other sound) should occur during speech, or while other sounds —e.g. footsteps—are being made; certainly, moves should never be made in a short pause between two speeches, except for blind man's buff comic or dramatic effects—easily overused.

Problems that are met in mono drama may be greater in stereo. For example, extraneous noises are worse because:
1. There is no dead side of the microphone.
2. With a more distant balance of voices, the signal at the microphone is at a lower level. Channel gains are higher and therefore noise is amplified more.
3. Noises may be spatially separated from other action, and therefore more distant.

Particular difficulties are raised by a need for artistic compatibility between stereo and mono. Consider, for example, a conversion between two people trying to escape unnoticed through a crowd: they talk unconcernedly as they move gradually across the stage until eventually they are free of the other actors and can exit at the side. The mono listener to the stereo play needs as many positional dialogue pointers as he would be given if the production were not in stereo. Indeed, in mono the microphone would probably stay with the main subjects and other near voices would drift in and out of a clear hearing distance; in stereo this convention, too, could perhaps be established—though with greater difficulty. In such a case the producer must imagine or listen to both stereo and mono versions of his chosen convention and must decide whether changes could or should be made for the benefit of one group or the other; or whether to disregard potential mono listeners (an important part of a radio audience).

A more extreme case might be a telephone conversation: a theoretical possibility would be to split the stage, putting one actor in to each loudspeaker. This might work well in stereo, but for mono would be meaningless. In this case artistic compatibility does not just suggest, it *demands* another technique: the voice of one of the actors must be filtered, as in mono (see p. 393). The distorted voice could still be put in one of the loudspeakers, but the other, undistorted voice would probably be closer to the centre of the sound stage and in a normal stereo acoustic ambience, but offset to balance the distorted voice.

Quadraphonic drama

Experimental quadraphonic drama has employed techniques similar to those of stereo drama, but with the floor marked in quadrants and circles around a quadraphonic cluster. A practical disadvantage of this arrangement is that a studio dead enough for stereo may still need additional treatment, perhaps by importing soft screens into the studio to deaden it further. Actors' moves, such as long approaches from rear to front can become somewhat unnatural, with the actors tending to crab in a spiral around the

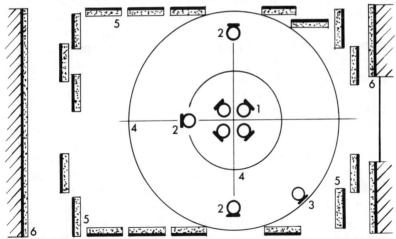

EXPERIMENTAL QUADRAPHONIC DRAMA with a cluster of four cardioid microphones (1). 2. Microphones for close 'asides'. 3. Spotting microphone for singer. The choice of these or other additional microphones depends on the special needs of the work performed. 4. Floor markings for the guidance of actors. 5. Screens, to deaden studio. 6. Studio walls, with windows to control room. This balance works well in discrete quadraphony.

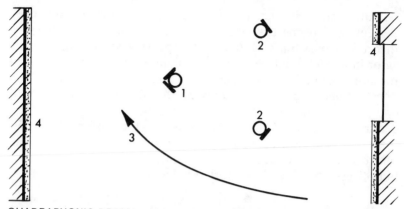

QUADRAPHONIC DRAMA with more conventional layout. 1. Main stereo pair. 2. Spaced pair. 3. Actor's long approach from the side. 4. Studio walls with window to control room.

cluster. For a BBC production of *The Tempest* further microphones were set in for whispered asides and Ariel's songs; and the maelstrom effect was enhanced by physically spinning the central cluster. Specially composed quadraphonic music (with instruments also arranged in a circle) was recorded in advance and mixed down to four tracks of eight-track tape. Speech and songs were subsequently recorded on the other four. The eight tracks were then mixed down to four for the quadraphonic experiment, and separately to stereo (compatible with mono) for regular radio transmission. Considered as a special event, the experiment was an artistic success: excellent in either discrete quadraphony or remixed stereo. But matrixed quadraphony, with its reduced positional information at the sides and rear, was less satisfactory.

Later BBC quadraphonic drama has mostly been balanced on a normal stereo pair facing the control window, with a spaced pair facing the A and B rear corners. The main stage was unequivocally at the front, while long approaching could still be made from the rear and sides. Acoustics were now little more difficult than in normal stereo, with each scene acoustically furnished for live settings (e.g. a courtroom, for which the studio carpet might be taken up and additional 'space' microphones set in), or for a normal indoor sound (no special treatment required). For a deadened outdoor quality the rear pair is faded out, except for panned approach effects. Here matrixed systems gave technically satisfactory results that would work in a wider range of home listening conditions.

218

With quadraphony, drama production is necessarily more analytical, and untoward effects that might have been masked in mono are heard clearly. Interestingly, the solutions found have often improved mono and stereo as well.

Audience reaction

Audience reaction is a vital element of many comedy programmes, while for music broadcasts it provides a sense of occasion that the audience can share. The two differ in that for the first the performers' and audience microphones must be live at the same time, while for music performances the two sets of microphones are opened one after the other.

For all types of programme, applause (and other forms of audience reaction) must be clear, without being unbalanced, that is, individual pairs of clapping hands should not be loud or dominant enough to draw attention to themselves.

In order to achieve such a response two conflicting requirements must be met: the audience must be reasonably large (ideally, several hundred strong); and the microphone coverage must not be so distant as to lose the desired clarity. In addition, there must be adequate separation between audience and other microphones that may be live at the same time. Many modern mixer desks on which all of the main channels are mixed at high level have a simple six-channel low-level submixer supplying audience as a balanced source to a single channel on the main mixer.

In stereo, applause is best spread across the full sound stage. It must be picked up on the main and any announcer's microphone only in such a way that controlling the level of the applause does not pull it to one side.

The audience reaction to a comedy show will obviously be poor if the words are not clearly audible. This requires foldback loudspeakers above the heads of the audience, so placed that the audience microphones pick up little of the foldback sound. A line-source loudspeaker radiates most strongly in a plane at right angles to its length, and a microphone placed in line with its long axis will receive its middle, and high-frequency sound only by reflection.

In television, for which the performers' microphones may be set well back from the action, the foldback loudspeakers must be brought as close over the audience as is practicable for adequate coverage. The loudspeaker volume can be raised by 3 to 4 dB without increasing the danger of howlround if the frequency of

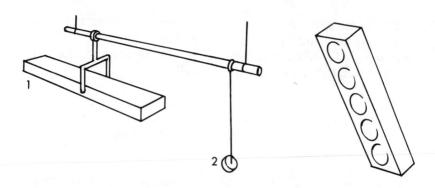

AUDIENCE LOUDSPEAKER AND MICROPHONE. 1. Line loudspeaker. Except at low frequencies the elongated source radiates at right angles to its length, and low frequencies are reduced by bass roll-off. The microphone, 2, on the dead side of the loudspeaker, is itself dead-side on to it. Both are attached to the same bar, so that their relative position is fixed.

the foldback sound is shifted by a few Hz. This requires a device which first modulates the signal to a much higher frequency, then demodulates it again, but with a slightly greater frequency change—preferably downward. Alternatively, a device which gives a modest *spread* of pitch could be used (see p. 428).

Slung microphones cover low and middle frequencies, and directional microphones add presence. If the response from a particular individual in the audience becomes obtrusive, fade down the microphones gently, in turn, until that nearest to him is located, then reset it accordingly.

The volume of applause at the end of a performance must be held back a little: prolonged clapping at high level is irritating to the listener, who may be impelled to turn it down. On the other hand, laughter within a programme may have to be lifted a little: it should be held down between laughs in order to avoid picking up coloration from the foldback, raised quickly as the laugh begins, and then eased back under subsequent dialogue just enough to avoid significant loss of clarity in speech. The performer relates his own timing to the audience's response, and sensitive control anticipates the progress of this interaction. In such cases a separate operator may control the audience and foldback volume.

It may help to have a limiter before the main audience fader. A further limiter or compressor can be inserted after mixing audience and dialogue, and used in such a way that speech automatically pushes down the audience reaction as the voice itself is compressed.

220

9

MUSIC BALANCE

THERE are two basic types of music balance. One is the 'natural' balance which uses the studio acoustics for reverberation and is generally preferred for 'serious' music. For a single instrument or for a group having perfect internal balance one microphone (or a stereo pair) may be sufficent. However, perfect balance is rare: a singer may be overwhelmed by all but the quietest of pianos; an orchestra may be (and often is) dominated by its brass. So 'natural' balance often requires additional microphones.

This first type of balance has two subdivisions: mono (still required for most television work) and stereo. In this book, coincident pairs rather than spaced microphones are recommended as the basis of acoustically reinforced stereo balance. Many excellent, commercially available stereo recordings have been made using a curtain of three or five microphones but when such techniques are copied, they may be found less flexible. For example, the control of an individual microphone to favour one of the string sections may shift the brass or percussion bodily across the sound stage. The problems are greater in broadcasting, where the dynamic range is more limited, and speed of working is at a premium, than in recording for sale as record or tape. But note also that records may also be heard by radio, and if the reception is in mono, spaced microphone balances may suffer: the greater likelihood of phase cancellation makes them inherently less compatible.

The second type of balance uses many close microphones and artificial reverberation (echo) instead of natural acoustics. It is preferred for popular and much light music. Mono balance techniques are generally used for both mono and stereo, with stereo positioning, like the reverberation, being introduced synthetically.

In this chapter the problems of each of these types of balance are considered in general terms; then taking individual instruments and groups of instruments in turn, I will show how they are applied.

'Natural' monophonic balance

In a monophonic balance that is taken basically on a single microphone, its distance depends on both the polar response of the microphone chosen and the acoustics of the studio. For many purposes it is best to use a condenser microphone with a polar diagram that can be switched by remote control. Try various distances and listen carefully to the results: the balance to seek is one where there is plenty of reverberation, but not so much that the sound becomes muddy or coloured.

A close balance sounds more dramatic; it is ear-catching, arresting. Such a balance can, in fact, help to sell a record—but may be difficult to live with. However, where the acoustics are difficult it may well be necessary to accept the brilliant close balance whatever one's personal preference, perhaps making a kind of virtue of necessity. With a sufficiently distant balance a

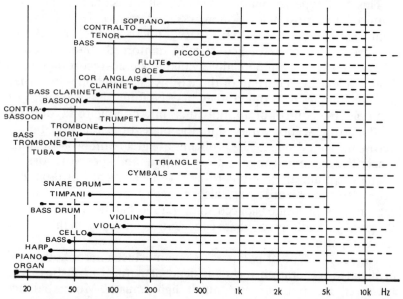

FREQUENCY RANGES. A microphone with a frequency response which matches that of the sound source will not pick up noise and spill from other instruments unnecessarily. The lowest frequency for most instruments is clearly defined, but the highest significant overtones are not. At high frequencies, an even response is usually considered more valuable than a matched one.

bidirectional response may be possible, but as the microphone is moved a progressively broader pick-up is required. In many cases the best result is achieved by a cardioid with a clean, even response (in which the polar response is independent of frequency). As spotting microphones, smooth cardioids are again favoured. Avoid hypercardioid microphones in which the directional response is engineered by means of a phase-shifting network, as these may be a little erratic at high frequencies. Ribbons are undervalued today. They can provide an excellent, smooth response in all but the extreme top—which in any case lies beyond the range of the human voice and many instruments.

Bear in mind that when they have high-quality loudspeakers many listeners *prefer* a more distant and therefore more blended sound than that which many balancers enjoy. But for listening on poorer equipment, greater clarity helps to make up for some of the deficiencies: if you can't hear everything, at least you can hear the main elements of the music. For this reason (and also because it helps to motivate close-ups), a drier balance is preferred in television.

The arrival of an audience can change the balance dramatically. Experience will show how much too live the balance must be in rehearsal for it to be correct with a full hall.

Music studio problems

In a 'natural' balance we record the characteristics of the studio just as much as those of the player.

It is rather as though the studio were an extra member of the orchestra. With stringed instruments, very little of the sound we hear is directly from the strings; what we are actually listening to is the radiation from a sounding board to which the strings are coupled. And the individual character of the instrument depends heavily on the shape and size of that radiator. In the same way, the studio acts as a sort of sounding board to the instruments: its shape and size gives character to the music. But there is an important difference. By uniformity of design, the character of all instruments of one particular type is roughly the same. But music rooms, studios, halls, and so on differ widely in character: no two are the same.

In broadcasting studios theory suggests that a monophonic directional microphone should be angled to pick up reverberation equally from all three main dimensions. Theory also suggests that a central position should be avoided, because in the middle of the room the even harmonics of the eigentones—the basic resonances of the room—are missing, thereby thinning out its acoustic response. Fortunately, in practice, the number of studios where there are serious eigentone problems in music balance is small. (Stereo microphones are usually placed on the centre line of concert halls and rarely with ill effect; though admittedly concert-hall eigentones are very low pitched.) Nevertheless, there is no harm in playing safe: a microphone position that works well for a music balance in mono can often be found somewhere along one of the main diagonals of the room. Then, using comparison tests, proceed by trial and error—remembering that if the sound is wrong wherever you put the microphone it may help to move the sound source.

In a studio that is comparatively dead for its size, an omni-directional microphone may help. But there are times when even a distant balance with an omnidirectional microphone does not do enough. Some percussive instruments, such as timpani, continue to sound for some time, and have decay characteristics somewhat similar to those of reverberation. If they tend to stand out in too dead a hall, artificial reverberation may have to be considered.

The average television or film studio is the dead studio on the grand scale. But the same problems may also arise in microcosm when one or two singers or instruments are being recorded on location—perhaps in a domestic living-room, which is not designed for music making. Here the answer is different, for taking the microphone to the other side of a small room with heavily damped acoustics only emphasizes their inadequacy. In this case the only effective solution may be furniture removal: if it is possible to get rid of heavily padded furniture—armchairs and so on—take these out first; but, in any case, rugs should be rolled up and soft drapes pulled aside. And avoid having too many people in the room.

For monophonic balance, a directional microphone gives the greatest control in cases where acoustics cause difficulty, as it allows an extra dimension for experiment: the angle can be varied, as can the distance from the source and position within the room. In stereo this facility is, however, lost: a good 'natural' stereo balance is therefore even more at the mercy of studio acoustics than is monophonic balance.

The stereo music balances recommended in this chapter,

based primarily on coincident pairs of microphones with cardioid elements angled at 90°, may be modified in practice by changing the polar diagram, or by changing the relative angle of the elements: this will have the results described in Chapter 6 (p. 176).

In particular, for two reasons the double figure-of-eight is rarely used. The most important is the poor compatibility with mono: there are bound to be some listeners to a stereo broadcast or disc who will hear it in mono, and if the A − B signal is very large they lose a significant part of the information. What happens, in fact, is that they lose far too much of the reverberation, which is very strongly represented in the A − B component of a double figure-of-eight. The second problem is that reverberation is picked up on both back and front of the microphones in roughly equal proportions, so that at low frequencies there is a phase-cancellation effect that takes some of the body out of the stereo reverberation, making it thin and harsh. This is noticeable in a concert hall and very marked in the more reverberant surroundings of, say, a cathedral. Switching the polar diagram even a quarter of the way towards cardioid reduces the effect significantly.

One microphone or many?

The alternative to studio acoustics and the natural blending of sounds is the multimicrophone balance, in which an essential, but not necessarily conventionally natural, quality is sought from each instrument or group and blended together electrically. Neither technique is any more 'right' than the other, but opinion has tended to polarize to the view that most classical music is best balanced on relatively few microphones, and that popular music demands many.

There is a rightness about this: the 'simpler' microphone technique for classical music reflects the internal balance of the orchestra and existing acoustics that the composer wrote for; whereas the top-twenty hit of the moment generally reflects the acceptance of the opportunities for experiment that are open to today's arranger. But the question, 'one microphone or many?' is still open in a number of areas lying between the extremes of orchestra and pop group: somewhere in the region between light orchestra and showband there is room for this to be a practical question.

Before choosing a single-microphone balance one has to consider how the sound source is distributed. Even if the acoustics are suitable, can it be arranged that the sound source falls within the pick-up field of a single microphone? Given a satisfactory instrument layout careful microphone placing can ensure that the distance between the microphone and each source is exactly right.

Instruments of orchestras and pop groups

Orchestral players and pop musicians play instruments that have a great deal more in common than in difference. All orchestral instruments are fair game for popular music; but there are instruments in pop or novelty groups that rarely make the journey in the opposite direction, notably the electric guitar but also some of the older sounds such as the piano accordion or banjo. Nevertheless, for all types of music balance we are dealing with the same basic sound sources, which can be treated in a range of different ways, but for which the various possible treatments required in different types of music overlap. An orchestral balance may require reinforcement of a particular instrument; a stereo balance may require individual mono spotting: both of these demand close microphone techniques which approach those used in multimicrophone balance. In serious music a distance of several feet is 'close' or even 'very close', depending on the instrument; for pop music closeness may be measured in inches. There may also be slight differences in terminology.

But there is no difference in the basic problems and possibilities. In the following sections these are explored in terms of individual instruments, sections, and combinations; and full orchestras and bands. The instruments to be examined are divided into the following groups:

1. *Strings:* plucked, bowed, or struck, and coupled to a sounding board acting as a resonator (or from which vibrations are derived electrically and fed to a loudspeaker).
2. *Wind:* where the resonator is an air column excited by edge tone, vibrating reed, etc.
3. *Percussion:* where a resonator (often with an inharmonic pattern of overtones) is struck.

This far from exhausts all possibilities: mouth organ and accordion, 'wind' machine and musical saw are further variations; as are the instruments devised in France that use longitudinal vibrations in glass rods (which are excited by stroking them with wet fingers) to cause lateral vibrations in metal rods, which are transmitted to the air by metal resonators of novel design.

226

These last, and many others, are not consiered in detail. For any instruments that have not previously been met it is useful to determine (or guess) the radiation pattern for different frequencies and try microphones in different directions and at different distances accordingly, using (wherever possible) comparison tests to find the preferred balance for a particular purpose.

It is well also to remember that such a balance is for a particular player and a particular example of the instrument: some players and some instruments produce very different sounds from others of the same apparent style or type (this is notably true of double basses and their players). It is a balance also for the particular microphone or microphones used, and in all but the closest balance, for a particular studio—and perhaps even for particular weather conditions. A humid atmosphere might be expected to affect balance, as high frequencies are transmitted better by damp air. Other factors may be its effects on musical instruments and human ears, and—perhaps even more important —subjective judgment.

Violin, viola

A violin radiates its strongest concentration of upper harmonics in a markedly directional pattern; and therefore it is to be expected that, for all but the lower frequencies produced, much of the sound goes into a lobe directed over the heads of the audience. A great deal of harsh quality, squeak and scrape that even good players produce is thereby also lost to an audience. So it must be recognized that an audience normally hears little of the high-frequency sound that is produced, as even in the reverberation it may be heavily attenuated in the air. At its lowest frequencies the radiation pattern is omnidirectional, but the violin is an inefficient radiator of sound at low frequency owing to its size: the lowest notes are heard mainly in their harmonics.

RADIATION PATTERN AND MICRO-PHONE POSITION FOR VIOLIN. 1. Low frequency radiation. 2. High frequencies. 3. Move along this arc for more or less high frequencies. 4. Move closer for clarity; more distant for greater blending.

For a concert balance the microphone is placed well back from the instrument to add studio reverberation; and the frequency content can be controlled by movement in an arc over the instrument. The upper harmonics are heard at their strongest a little off the axis, towards the E string (the top string on the violin).

To make a *close* violin sound pleasant requires more than the art of the balancer; it demands a modified style of playing in which the unpleasant but normally acceptable components are much reduced. But very close working for pop music work may be limited by the athleticism of the player. In ordinary circumstances 3 ft (0·9 m) is the minimum, for during pizzicato passages there is some danger of the bow hitting the microphone, though some players are capable of encircling it with the right (bowing) arm. The lowest string of the violin is G of which the fundamental (196 Hz) is weak, so bass tip-up is not a serious problem with directional microphones; indeed, a bass filter at 220 Hz may be used to discriminate against low-frequency sound from other sources. A high-quality ribbon microphone can give a very satisfactory response (though possibly requiring some reduction in top). Alternatively, try a lavalier microphone slung around the violinist's neck: this position will discriminate against the stridency of the instrument.

For a close balance on a violin section the players may sit in their normal arrangement of two at a desk, with the desks one behind another. The microphone is then slung directly over and slightly behind the first two players. This still favours the leader sufficiently for solos, but does not lose the rear players as a close balance farther forward would. If this balance is still too distant for adequate separation in, say, a dance band balance in live acoustics, a microphone may be placed over each desk. But some roll-off of high frequencies will be required to counter the harsher quality.

For a stereo balance either a mono or stereo set-up may be used. But a mono microphone must necessarily be used for close working, as the slightest movement near a coincident pair becomes gross. In this case the instrument has to be steered to its appropriate position on the sound stage (for a soloist on his own, in the centre) and stereo added to fill the full width with reverberation.

For a true stereo balance the microphones must be more distant. Slight movements of body and instruments then produce an effect that is pleasant, unless they substantially alter the proportions of sound reaching the microphones. This could happen very easily with spaced microphones but may still do so with a

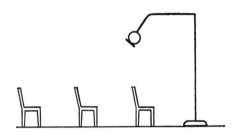

CLOSE BALANCE FOR THREE DESKS OF VIO-LINS. Alternatively, for very clean separation it is possible to work with separate microphone for each desk, but that produces a very strong high frequency response which must be discriminated against or corrected for.

coincident pair: a change in reflected sound may produce spurious movement. Once again, reverberation must be adequate in quality and distributed throughout the sound stage.

Violas may be treated in the same way as violins, except that very close working on directional microphones may produce bass tip-up, and that a filter at 220 Hz cannot be used, as this is well inside the frequency range of the instrument.

'Cello, bass

'Cellos and basses differ from violins and violas in that they are much more efficient as radiators in the lower register, because they have a much larger area of resonator to drive the air. The high, extended spectrum of resonance which makes the violin shrill and 'edgy' if heard directly above the instrument is scaled down to the upper middle frequencies in the case of the 'cello. In order to get the full rich sonority of this instrument's upper harmonics, it becomes necessary to place the microphone more directly in line with its main radiating lobe. Again with these lower strings we have a tool to aid us in balance. If we merely want to add depth to a fuller orchestral sound we may be content to balance near-sideways-on to the instrument, but if we want richness we turn the instrument to the microphone, as a 'cello is turned to the audience in a concerto.

If 'cellos or basses are mounted on light rostra, these may act as sounding boards, introducing unwanted coloration. Rostra should therefore be solidly built or heavily damped. Strategically placed, the mass of the player himself may help. If microphone stands are used, avoid placing them on the same rostra or pay particular attention to their acoustic insulation. In an orchestra, the basses in particular may be helped by a spotting microphone, placed about 3 ft (1 m) from the front desk and angled towards the bridges.

For popular music the bass, or double bass—plucked rather than bowed—is one of the three basic instruments of the rhythm group; the others are piano and drums. Of the three, the bass is the most difficult to separate: a very close balance is essential, as the level is low. Pop music balancers are disinclined to recommend any single balance that will always work, pointing out that there are great differences between one bass or bass-player and another.

The following are suggested:

1. A cardioid, 'cottage-loaf' or figure-of-eight microphone 1 ft (30 cm) from the bridge, looking down at the strings.

2. A similar microphone directed towards the f-hole at the side of the upper strings.

3. A 'personal' or small studio microphone suspended from the bridge, with the diaphragm pointing directly upwards to face the bridge.

4. A 'personal' microphone wrapped in a layer of foam plastic, suspended by its cable *inside* the upper f-hole. This gives virtually total separation.

Most directional microphones used for (1) or (2) require low-frequency equalization to compensate for bass tip-up. In general, (1) has the most to recommend it, because it hears the percussive attack quality from the string itself as it is plucked, and there can be fine control over the ratio of this to the resonance of the body of the instrument. In contrast, (4) gives a heavy hanging quality which has to be controlled to a lower level than the other balances. In stereo pop balances the bass is always taken mono and steered to its appropriate position.

More strings

Other stringed instruments, such as the classical guitar and the banjo, the violin's predecessors (the viol family), and so on, all radiate their sound in ways similar to the instruments already discussed, and the control that the balancer has over the ratio of top to bass is much the same. Groups based on stringed instruments are also balanced in a similar way.

The string quartet is a simple group to balance: if the players sit in two rows of two, the microphone can be placed in front of them at any suitable distance. Imagine a line extending forward and upward at about 30° from the middle of the group, and try a microphone position somewhere along this. Then check that

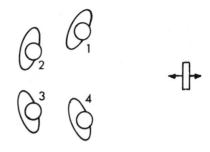

STRING QUARTET. 1. Viola. 2. Cello. 3 and 4. Violins. Similar arrangements may be made for wind and larger chamber groups.

distance, angle, and position within the studio are right for taking full advantage of the acoustics. Listen to each instrument in turn as though it were a soloist, and make sure that the cello can 'see' the microphone. The quality of sound to listen for is one which combines clarity and brilliance on individual instruments with a resonant well-blended sonority for the group as a whole. For a discussion of the string quartet in stereo, see p. 176.

As more instruments are added, a similar 'natural' arrangement may be retained, moving the microphone back if necessary in order to keep all the instruments within its field. In this way we progress through the various types of chamber group or wind band to the small orchestra.

'Electric' stringed instruments

There is, of course, an alternative way of picking up the signal from the resonating panel, and this is to attach a contact microphone to it. Alternatively the vibration of the wire itself may be sensed and amplified electrically. In either case the output is fed to a loudspeaker. The overall character of the instrument is derived from a combination of the frequency response of the loudspeaker and that of the electromechanical system generating the signal.

How are we to balance the electric guitar family? Or perhaps the first question is, *why* balance it? Why not feed the electrical output direct to the recorder? There are several reasons which favour a normal balance, and the first is that a performer needs to hear his own instrument and the way it blends with others: do not forget that more than half the job of balance is done before the sound reaches the microphone. The second reason has already been indicated: the loudspeaker provides part of the composite formant

231

characteristic of the instrument. The most flexible approach, particularly useful for the bass guitar, is to take a split feed from the instrument itself as well as an acoustic pick up from the loudspeaker. These are recombined in the mixer. Try taking the lower bass from the direct feed, and the mid-range via the loudspeaker. The two signals can be treated separately, with different equalization and added reverberation. Double-check the balance by monitoring on a small loudspeaker.

Where a feed of any electrical signal is taken directly to the desk, a radio-frequency rejection filter should eliminate unwanted police and taxi messages, and (in TV studios) radio talkback.

The loudspeaker of the pure electric guitar should be treated like any other instrument, though for the fullest high-frequency response the microphone should be exactly on the axis of the cone. A cottage-loaf microphone like that described above may be used for a close balance. If it is set at the high volume often used for stage shows, the loudspeaker itself may be overloaded. To avoid this, reduce the acoustic volume (or the bass) restoring it in the mixer.

In many cases the guitar serves double purpose as an acoustic and electric instrument. In the simplest balance the loudspeaker is placed on a box or chair opposite the player, with the microphone between loudspeaker and instrument. The player himself can now adjust the overall amplifier level, comparing it with the direct, acoustic sound. He has control of the loudspeaker volume from moment to moment by means of a foot control. A directional microphone is used for this balance, with any bass equalization that may be necessary at the distances involved. However, many pop music balancers prefer to separate the two signals, placing the loudspeaker farther away from the player and balancing as indicated above; then picking up the acoustic output with a microphone close to the bridge, angled to discriminate against noise from the finger board. This arrangement permits treatment of the two components with different echo and equalization, for example by applying bass roll-off at 200 Hz to the acoustic signal. To avoid spill on to the acoustic guitar microphone, some studios use a separate room for this instrument, with communication by window and headphones only.

An electric piano has two loudspeakers, for which separate microphones are required, forming a stereo pair. Equalization may be applied to emphasize high-frequency percussive transients or to add weight to the bass, as required.

The piano

The piano radiates in a similar manner to the smaller stringed instruments: the vibration is fed to the soundboard, from which almost the entire wanted sound is radiated although there is some contribution from the strings themselves at the higher frequencies. If the microphone were to be placed beneath the piano this higher component would be lost.

The radiation pattern from the soundboard allows a reasonable degree of treble and bass control: in particular, the bass is at its strongest if the microphone is placed at right-angles to the length of the piano. In an arc extending from top to tail of the piano, the balance with the most powerful bass is that at the end of this arc closest to the top of the keyboard. As the microphone is moved round, the bass is progressively reduced until it is at its minimum at the tail. For very powerful concert pianos the tail position may be best, but there is a slight disadvantage in that there is a loss of definition in the bass, as well as reduced volume. For most purposes, a point somewhere in the middle of this arc is likely to give a reasonable balance—and this is as good a starting-point as any for studio tests.

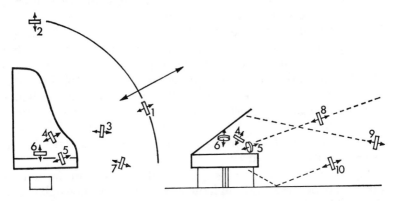

PIANO BALANCE. The best balance for a grand piano is usually somewhere along the arc from the top strings to the tail. A close balance gives greater clarity; a distant balance gives better blending. Of the positions shown: 1. Often gives a good balance. 2. Discriminates against the powerful bass of certain concert pianos. 3. Picks up strong crisp bass. A mix of 2 and 3 can be very effective. 4. Close balance (with lid off) for mixing into multimicrophone dance band balances (pointing down toward upper strings). 5. Discriminates against piano for pianist/singer. 6. (Angled down towards pianist) as 5. 7. One of a variety of other positions that are also possible: experiment rather than rule-of-thumb indicates best balance. 8. Concert balance 'seeing the strings'. 9. By reflection from lid. 10. By reflection from the floor: microphones set for other instruments may inadvertently pick up the piano in this way.

The piano is the first individual instrument that we have considered that benefits by stereo spread of the direct sound. But even for a solo the spread should not be too wide: half the stereo stage is about enough, with reverberation occupying the full width.

Distance is governed largely by the desired ratio of direct to ambient sounds. A fast piece may need clarity of detail; a gentler romantic style benefits from greater blending. A closer balance is also required where brilliant or percussive effects are wanted, and to some extent these qualities may be varied independently of reverberation by changes of microphone field patterns as well as distance. A piano used for percussive effect in an orchestra might require a spotting microphone. Pianos themselves vary considerably: some are 'harder' (more brilliant) than others, so that for a similar result greater distance is required. Conversely, a muddy tone quality may be improved by bringing the microphone closer. A new piano takes time to mature and is better reserved as a practice instrument until the tone settles down.

In a dead acoustic such as that of a television studio try using two microphones—one close to control brilliance, the other more distant and with added reverberation. To give a concert-hall scale to the sound, feed the echo via tape delay.

The height of the microphone should allow it to 'see' the strings (or rather, the greater part of the soundboard) which means that the farther away it is, the higher it should be. However, if this is inconvenient, other balances are often possible: for instance, use reflections from the lid. This is the balance that an audience generally hears at a concert. For the very lowest notes, the pattern of radiation tends to the omnidirectional; but for the middle and upper register, and the higher harmonics in particular, the lid ensures clarity of cound.

Depending on the acoustics, cardioid or bidirectional microphones may be used. Although out of favour with some balancers, a bidirectional ribbon often gives excellent results: its range is well matched to that of the instrument.

The closer one gets to an open piano, the more the transients associated with the strike tone became apparent; at their strongest and closest they may be difficult to control without reducing the overall level or risking momentary distortion on the peaks. Action noise—the tiny click and thud as the keys are lifted and fall back—may be audible, and in balance tests this and the noises from pedal action, etc., should be listened for. When a close

234

balance is employed for pop music the lid is always removed, unless this makes separation problems more severe.

A balance suitable for a piano in a rhythm group may be as close as 6 in (15 cm) above the top strings. Surprisingly, a bidirectional ribbon microphone can still be used, as the bass tip-up at this distance actually helps to rebalance the sound. The exact position finally chosen varies with the melodic content of the music being played: one criterion is that the notes played should all sound in the same perspective, which can also be affected by the manner of playing. For a percussive effect the microphone could be slung fairly close to the strikers. A baffle, perhaps a piece of cardboard, fastened to the upper surface of the outer casing of a ribbon microphone further emphasizes and 'hardens' the higher frequencies, and especially the transients.

Working at such distances, it may be better to use two microphones, one near the hammers in the middle top, and the other over the bass strings—kept separate to give appropriate breadth to the piano in the stereo picture. If the lid has to be kept low to improve separation, the separate treatment of equalization and echo makes it a little easier to cope with the resulting less-than-ideal conditions.

An alternative is to use the focusing effect of the holes in the iron frame of some pianos: the different sounds can easily be heard by listening close to them. A microphone two or three inches above the second hole from the top may give the best overall balance. With two microphones, try the top hole in combination with the fourth, fifth, or sixth hole.

Distortion (particularly of the percussive transients) due to overloading has to be avoided, and may require attenuation before the first pre-amplifier.

With an upright piano lift the lid and try the microphone somewhere on a line diagonally up from the pianist's right shoulder. But remembering that it is the soundboard that is

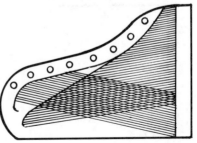

PIANO HOLES. The focusing effect of holes in the frames of some pianos can be used in a close balance. Microphones can be used singly (usually over the second hole from the top end of the keyboard) or in pairs.

radiating, an alternative is to move the piano well away from any wall and stand the microphone at the back (for a close balance), or diagonally up from the soundboard (for a more distant one). Behind the soundboard there is less pedal action noise, but also, of course, less brilliance and clarity.

One or other of these methods is also suitable for balancing a jangle-box—the type of piano that is specially treated, with leaves of metal between hammer and strings to give a tinny strike action, and with the two or three strings for each note of the middle and top slightly out of tune.

Piano and soloist, two pianos

In a studio with suitable acoustics it is possible to get good separation by turning the soloist's microphone dead-side-on to the piano and mixing in the output of a second and possibly third microphone, arranged to pick up a little of the piano. This time start by getting a good sound from the soloist, and then gradually fade in the piano just enough to bring it into the same perspective.

The normal technique in pop music recording is to employ a backing track. The soloist listens to the pre-recorded piano on headphones, and the levels can be adjusted at will at the mixer.

A slightly more tricky balance is one where the pianist himself also speaks or sings. In many such cases a singer will wish to take advantage of the opportunity to use less voice than would be possible without a microphone. A more intimate effect is achieved, but at the expense of losing internal balance. A suspended ribbon microphone. may be placed about 20 in (50 cm) from the singer (as for a speech balance), with its dead side toward the soundboard of the piano. It may be in front of the singer (tilted down) or round to his right. An omnidirectional microphone requires a much closer balance of the voice in order to discriminate against the piano.

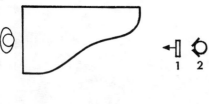

PIANO AND SOLOIST SIDE BY SIDE. 1. Mono microphones. 2. Microphones used in stereo.

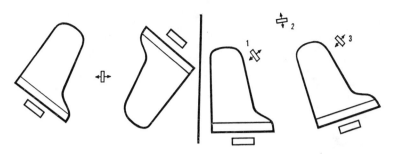

BALANCE FOR TWO PIANOS. *Left*. Two pianos on a single microphone. *Right*. Two pianos on individual microphones (1 and 3) or on a single microphone or stereo pair (2).

A two-microphone balance can sometimes be employed for this arrangement as well, using microphone 2 for piano presence. But a great deal of care should be used if either is to be faded, as the quality can change considerably.

The best way of balancing two pianos on a single microphone depends on studio layout—and this in turn is a matter where the wishes of the pianists should be observed if possible. With the pianos placed side by side, use a single ribbon or stereo pair at the tail. The equivalent two-microphone balance would use two ribbons, each in the curve of one of the pianos: these can be a shade closer than the single microphone, and give a marginally greater degree of control over the relative volumes and frequency pick-up.

Harp, harpsichord, celesta

The harp has a soundbox below the strings; in performance it is cradled by the player who reaches round on both sides of it to pluck (and otherwise excite) the strings. Owing to the relative inefficiency of the soundbox, the vibration of the strings themselves contributes relatively more than in a piano, and ideally any balance should cover both. The key of the instrument is controlled by pedals at the foot, and as these may be operated during the performance of quiet passages, their mechanical sounds may be audible. In an orchestra, the harp or harps generally benefit by spotting for presence and to locate them more clearly, usually toward the side of the stereo picture.

A microphone, about 4 to 5 ft (1·5 m) diagonally upward from the soundbox, may be directed to cover both that and the strings.

237

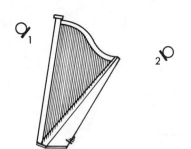

HARP. 1. Frontal coverage, looking down to soundbox. 2. Rear position for microphone favours strings, discriminates against pedal noise.

A ribbon is excellent, giving tight coverage of one or both harps on its relatively narrow forward lobe, while the rear lobe points upward into the hall. An alternative position, discriminating in favour of the strings and against pedal noise, is behind the head of the player.

A harpsichord has many of the qualities of the piano, including mechanical action noise, plus the characteristic attack on each note as the string is plucked by its quill. Where the instrument is featured, it is useful to have control over the relative values of transients and resonance. For this, set out two microphones, one above and one below the level of the soundboard. The lower microphone takes the body of the sound, most conveniently by reflection from the floor; the other, angled to 'see' down into the action, picks up the full sound but with the transients and upper harmonics somewhat over-represented. Mix to taste.

In a baroque orchestra (covered by a coincident pair) harpsichord continuo needs to be located well back, to avoid its penetrating sound appearing too dominant, and also near the basses, with which it must closely cooperate. A spotting microphone can then be used to fine-tune the contribution of continuo.

In other instruments of the same general class, such as virginals, clavichord or spinette, apply the same principles, first identifying the soundbox or board, the sources of action noise, attack transients and higher frequency components and placing the microphone or microphones accordingly.

The celesta is a rather quiet keyboard instrument. In an orchestra it benefits by spotting; the needs of separation then generally require that a close balance be employed in order to avoid bringing up neighbouring instruments with it. This has the disadvantage of accentuating the already potentially intrusive action noise. A layout in which a balance at 6 to 8 ft (about 2 m) is possible may avoid the worst of this. If a closer balance is unavoidable try a microphone either in the middle at the back or below the keyboard, on the treble side of the player's feet—and keeping well away from them.

Woodwind

Each of the wind instruments has its own directional pattern of radiation. In contrast to brass, for the woodwind with fingered or keyed holes the bell may make little difference to the sound: the main radiation is through the first few open holes. It follows that, unless we go closer we have considerable freedom in balancing woodwind; in general, a microphone placed somewhere in front of and above the player will prove satisfactory.

For wind, as with other sections of the orchestra, the transient, the way in which a note starts, is of considerable importance in defining the instrument for the listener and giving it character: as also is the breathy edge tone that we hear with the flute. These sounds must be clear but not exaggerated. The closer the balance, the stronger are the transients in comparison with the main body of the sound. Listening at an ordinary concert distance, the sharp edges of the notes are considerably rounded off. Listening to a flute at two feet, it sounds like a wind instrument with a vengeance! In close balances it is occasionally advisable to resort to devices such as placing the microphone *behind* a flautist's head, so reducing the high-frequency mouth noise and edge tones without affecting the sound radiating from the other end of the instrument.

In a close orchestral balance the woodwind may sound relatively far back, so sling any additional coincident pair or set in three separate microphones on stands at a height of 6 ft (about 2 m). These will add presence to the woodwind and bring forward the instruments behind. The extra microphones do not provide the main balance, and their signal must be added to it with discretion. But they do allow precise control of the stereo spread in the central region, perhaps broadening it a little. (The width required from a stereo pair on woodwind would still, of course, be much

FLUTE. A microphone behind the player's head discriminates against the windy edge-tone, but can 'see' the pipe and finger holes.

239

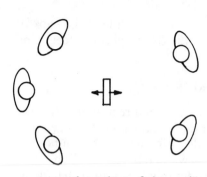

WOODWIND in dance band. Saxo-phones arranged in a group in a multi-microphone balance. The microphone stands on a box to raise it above the bell of the instruments.

narrower than that of the main pair covering a whole orchestra.)

In big band or 'easy-listening' music a commonly used 'wood-wind' section consists of up to five saxophones. These are sometimes balanced by placing three players on one side of a bidirectional microphone and two on the other, with the micro-phone raised on a box to a height such that it is in line with the bells of the instruments. The lowest saxophone (usually a baritone) should in this arrangement be at one end of the row of three. Players in this section may double on flute or clarinet, which is often also played to the same microphone.

However, for this balance on the saxophones, separation is less than it could be, as there has to be compensation in volume for the angle of the bell of the instrument; besides which the microphone is well placed to pick up sound reflected from the walls of the studio. So other arrangements have been suggested. One uses the same grouping of the players, but with two hyper-cardioids angled down toward the centre of each side.

An alternative arrangement that some balancers prefer is to place this section in a line or arc, with one microphone to each pair of musicians. This helps particularly where saxophone players doubling woodwind fail to move in for their second, quieter instrument, and also allows the height of each microphone to be adjusted more precisely to the needs of the second instru-ment. For a close balance on a clarinet, for example, it should be lower than for a flute.

The woodwind section (and particularly saxophones) may benefit from midlift at about 2·5–3 kHz.

In informal popular music the balancer will probably have no score to guide him (even if the players have), so he does not necessarily know whether a player has the melody or part of the backing. In an extreme case a woodwind player may to all appearances have an important part, which when the balancer

240

lifts it so that it can be heard, turns out merely to be fingering—the musician doubling another player at low level. The balancer may reasonably expect the musical director to indicate where the melody lies: this is especially important where particular instruments have figures or lines that are introduced into pauses in a vocal.

Brass

In brass, the axis of the bell of each instrument carries the main stream of high harmonics. Even when the music requires that this be directed at the audience, only a relatively small group receives the full blast at any one moment, the rest hearing the sound off-axis. In consequence, for all but the most exaggeratedly brilliant effects, the main microphone for an orchestral balance is usually quite satisfactory for the brass. That its distance from the microphone is greater than that for some other sections is no disadvantage, for the added reverberation conventionally suggests the sheer volume produced. Orchestral brass that is balanced well back in a spacious hall is usually easier to control (requiring relatively little manipulation of level) than when, by choice or necessity, closer microphones are used.

The range of volume from brass is wide, but there should be no trouble with this except where the output of a close balance on heavy brass is fed through pre-amplifiers of fixed gain and results in overloading and consequent distortion. Care should therefore be taken when the pre-amplifier comes before the volume control.

The balancer should not rely on rehearsal levels of big band brass players he does not know, but should allow for as much as a 10 dB rise in level on the take, which if it were a live broadcast could be disastrous. Not only might he be left without an adequate working range on the faders, resulting perhaps in distortion of the sound, but also he could find himself facing new and unrehearsed problems of separation.

A close balance on trumpets or trombones is difficult to control, but it helps if the players themselves are prepared to cooperate by leaning in to the microphone on quiet passages with mutes, and sitting back for the louder passages. The microphone must be near enough for them to reach for close work but far enough back to pick up several players equally. Players are also well aware of the directional properties of their instruments and will play directly towards the microphone, or not, as the music requires; though some bands which have done little work in studios and more in dance halls may take this to extremes—perhaps by playing soft passages in to the music stand. Here the balancer needs to remind them that a cleaner sound can be obtained if some of the control is left to him.

The height of the microphone should be such that it may be on the axis of the instruments as they can be comfortably played—though with the trombones this is a little awkward, as the music stands get in the way of the ideal position. However, the leader of the section will say whether he prefers the microphone above or below the stand. The answer probably depends on how well the players know the music. In a band where the music played is part of a limited and well-rehearsed repertoire the trombones are often held up; but musicians faced with unfamiliar music will, understandably, wish to be able to look down to see it.

Brass is one section of the orchestra that benefits from midlift, an increased response of 5 dB or more, in this case at somewhere about 6–9 kHz. But certain microphones have peaks in their response in this region and produce the effect without much need for help from an equalizing amplifier.

In the orchestra, horns are generally placed where their sound reflects from a wall or from other surfaces behind them. Such an arrangement—with a microphone looking down from above at the front—is suitable in almost any circumstances; though exceptionally, for complete separation and a strong, rather uncharacteristic quality, a microphone can be placed behind the player and in line with the bell.

Brass and military bands

Several layouts are possible for brass or military bands. In one the various groups are laid out in an arc round the conductor in the same way as a string orchestra; in the other the performers form three sides of a hollow square, with the cornets and trombones facing each other on opposite sides. In this way the tone of the horns and euphoniums at the back is not blotted out by the full blast of the other, more penetrating instruments. The microphone may be placed a little way back from the square, and off the centre line of the studio.

The main body of euphoniums and bass tubas radiate upward and can sound woolly on the main microphone unless there is a reflecting surface above them to carry their sound forward. Failing this, an additional microphone above them will add presence. A ribbon has a satisfactory frequency range. A solo euphonium player should come forward to another microphone that is set high up and angled to separate him from other instruments of similar sound quality. A solo cornet may also have its own microphone, a condenser cardioid.

The military band behaves like a small orchestra from which the strings have been omitted. There is usually plenty of percussion, including such melodic instruments as the xylophone and glockenspiel. Care must be taken that these are given full value in the balance.

Percussion, drums

Most percussion instruments can be recorded with ease. However, some percussion sounds register more easily than others, and on all but the most distant microphone set-up it is as well to check the balance of each separate item with care. Any rostra used need to be reinforced to prevent coloration. In orchestral percussion a microphone with an extended, smooth high-frequency response is required mainly for triangle, cymbals and gong.

Whereas instruments such as the glockenspiel and xylophone require no special balance, the characteristic sound of the vibraphone requires a close microphone beneath the bars, angled upward to the tops of the tubular resonators (the bottoms are closed).

In popular music percussion shows itself mainly in the form of the drum set including a snare drum, bass drum (foot-pedal operated), a cymbal (or several), a hi-hat (a foot-operated double cymbal), a large tom-tom, and perhaps a small one as well.

In the simplest balance, a single microphone (which also requires a good high-frequency response) points down at the snare drum. But any attempt to move in for a close balance from the same angle increases the dominance of the nearer instruments over the bass drum and the hi-hat. The hi-hat radiates most strongly in a horizontal plane, in comparison with the up-and-down figure-of-eight pattern of the top cymbals. So for a somewhat closer balance place a wide-frequency-range cardioid microphone at the front of the kit and at about the level of the hi-hat.

For a tighter sound move the main microphone closer to the hi-hat, also favouring the left-hand top cymbal or cymbals and some of the snare and small tom-tom, together inevitably with

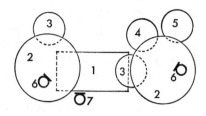

TYPICAL DRUM KIT for dance band or pop group. 1. Bass drum. 2. Cymbals. 3. Tom-toms. 4. Snare drum. 5. Hi-hat. 6. Microphones with good high frequency response used in two-microphone balance. 7. Additional microphone (moving coil) for more percussive bass drum effect. Further microphones may be added, to give each drum and the hi-hat its own close pick-up, plus two above for cymbals and overall stereo.

some bass drum; a second cardioid microphone is then moved in over the other side of the bass drum to find the other cymbal or cymbals, the big tom-tom, and again, perhaps, the snare drum. Changes of position, angle, polar diagram, or relative level give a reasonable degree of control over nearly every element except the bass-drum sound. This may also be required to fill in the texture of some pop music and can be obtained by facing the diaphragm of a moving-coil microphone toward the front skin and close to its edge, where a wider and more balanced range of overtones is present than at the centre. This is one place where one of the older, more solid-looking microphones with a limited top-response is as good as a modern high-quality microphone (which might in any case be overloaded). For the dry thud required in pop music take off the front skin (remembering to tighten up the loose lugs to avoid their rattling) and put a blanket inside.

For greater control still, use separate microphones for each component of the kit. With very close balances on the snare drum and each tom-tom as well as the bass drum and hi-hat, and with an overhead pair for the cymbals and basic stereo coverage the drum-kit alone can use up far more tracks in a multitrack recording than any other part of a group. Many pop balancers work with the drummer to tailor the sound, and in particular modify the snare drum by tightening the snare tension (perhaps also putting some masking tape on it), and may tape a light duster over part of the skin (away from where it is struck). Midlift (at 2·8 kHz) plus additional bass and extreme top may be added. The tom-toms are less likely to require attention, but the quality of cymbals varies and the application of masking tape may again help to

244

reduce the blemishes of poorer instruments. With such extreme close balancing it is wise to check the maximum playing volume in advance, and also to recheck the quality of the sound from each drum from time to time: it may change as a session progresses.

In stereo, width can be introduced by steering the various microphones to slightly separate positions.

Singers: solo and chorus

What counts as a close balance for a singer depends on the type of music. For a pop singer it may be close to the lips: for an operatic aria, at arm's length. For serious music a clean, flat response is all that is necessary; a high-quality ribbon at 3–4 ft (1 m) is excellent. But for lighter styles of music a closer balance is used, and compensation for bass tip-up is needed when working close on a directional microphone. A hypercardioid discriminates well against the background. One double-ribbon hypercardioid has a reduced bass response such that a singer can work at a matter of inches without noticeable tip-up (indeed, if the singer moves back, bass may have to be added). A singer working very close does in any case produce less of the chest tone which in serious music is used to deepen and strengthen the sound. To improve separation

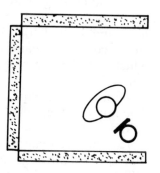

VOCALIST. When the volume of surrounding instruments is high the singer is screened. The microphone's live side is towards absorbers and its dead side towards the open studio.

the singer is often given a tent of screens, open (for visual contact with any musical director) only on the dead side of the microphone. In many pop balances a vocal guide track is recorded (on a spare track) at the same time as the main instrumental sound, and the lead and backing vocals recorded to replay.

As with speech, certain plosive consonants can cause popping noises in a close balance, and sibilants may be intrusive. A microphone chosen for inherent freedom from these effects may not have the frequency response desired, and vice versa. Use a wind-shield or ask the singer to work across the diaphragm rather than directly in to it. Some singers seem subject to a superstitious belief that close balance gives them presence. In fact if separation (the real reason for close balance) can be achieved in other ways, try setting in a second microphone a foot or two (30–60 cm) from the singer's mouth. Not only will popping no longer be a problem; it may also be found that the more distant balance is actually better, as well as easier to control. Presence can be added electronically, with midlift at about 1500–3000 Hz or more, depending on the voice. Sibilance can be cured by some combination of singing across the diaphragm, careful enunciation, high-frequency roll-off, and choice of a microphone with a smooth response in the 3–12 kHz region. Condenser cardioids are preferred for this quality rather than for their extended high frequency response, which is not needed. Limiters and tracking are also employed on pop music vocals (see later).

A folk-singer with guitar can in principle be balanced on a single microphone, perhaps favouring the voice, but two rather closer microphones mounted on the same stand give greater control of relative level, together with the capacity for separate equalization and echo if required.

Individual singers are never balanced in stereo (except where action is taken from an operatic stage). Mono microphones are used and steered to a suitable position in an overall balance. But a coincident pair is ideal for a pop music backing group, which can then be given any desired width and position in the final mix.

With choral groups, clarity of diction is the thing to aim for. The microphone must be far enough back to get a well-blended sound, but the limit for this is the lower limit of intelligibility. Spread bidirectional or cardioid microphones may cover a large chorus. This is also used for a chrous with orchestra (see below). Where a small group can conveniently work to a single microphone position use a cardioid in mono or a coincident pair for stereo, arranging the front line of singers to match the microphone field pattern (of the combined pair, if in stereo).

There is no special virtue in clear separation of sopranos, altos, tenors, and basses into separate blocks: the stereo effect may be good, but the musical quality of a layout that blends all sections may be better. As an alternative to the block layout a chorus may be arranged in rows (here even more than in the other cases the

246

microphones need to be high up in order to balance all of the voices). Better still, the singers may all be mixed up together. Opera singers must be able to do this, and so can some choirs. A high order of musicianship is required: when a group is able to and wishes to sing like this the stereo balancer should not discourage them.

Church music, and particularly antiphonal music with spaced choirs of voices, benefits enormously by being brought round the normal spread of stereo: it is here that quadraphony comes into its own without the need for special composition. A separate microphone pair for each choir can be set for its optimum width and position. For compatibility in stereo it is best that the voices do not completely surround the listener. This is also better for matrixed quadraphony; and in any case an important component of this particular sound is the sector—a full hemisphere, perhaps—in which the full richness of the reverberation alone is heard.

The orchestra

Our next individual 'instrument' is the full orchestra. And, indeed, an orchestra may rightly be considered to be an individual instrument if it is well balanced internally.

The detail of orchestral layout is far from standardized, but the strings are always spread across the full width of the stage, grouped in sections around the conductor, and with the woodwind behind them in the centre. In the older form of string layout the violins are divided, with the first violins on the left and second on the right, and with the violas and cellos between them and the double basses also in the centre. For stereo this has the advantage that the violin sections are clearly separated, and the weight is in the middle. But that the upright instruments ('cellos and basses) face forward is unnecessary for microphone or audience, as they are virtually omnidirectional radiators anyway; and there is also the slight disadvantage that the high-frequency radiation from the second violins is directed backward away from both audience and microphone. The more modern layout has the sections placed, from the left: first violins, second violins, violas, 'cellos; and raised behind the 'cellos on the right, the basses. Apart from the woodwind, which are always across the centre, there are further variations in the rest of the placings: brass, timpani, percussion, horns, piano or harpsichord (as orchestral

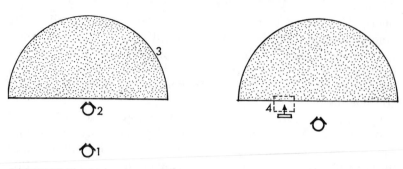

ORCHESTRAL BALANCE IN STEREO. 1 and 2. Two stereo pairs with different polar diagrams but giving the same stage width to the orchestra (3). Microphone 1 is double figure-of-eight; microphone 2 is double cardioid: a mixture of the two can be used to control and change reverberation where there is such a wide dynamic range that a great deal of volume compression is necessary. 4. For a soloist a spotting monophonic microphone is used, steering this to the same position as it appears on the audio stage established by the stereo pair.

instruments, not soloists); all of these may appear in different places.

While his job is generally to reflect what is offered to him as well as he can, a well-established and experienced balancer may also offer suggestions for improvement. Indeed, a conductor who is thorough will consult the balancer not only on matters of detail in placing but will also ask how the internal balance sounds. Many conductors, however, concentrate solely on musical qualities, so that if, for example, there is too much brass it will be left to the balancer to sort it out, if he can—though in fact the problem will be virtually insurmountable.

In a stereo orchestral balance that is based on co-incident cardioids the microphones are placed to control width rather than reverberation: for a subject that is to occupy the major part of the audio stage the microphones look down from one edge of the pick-up area. For an orchestra that is to occupy about two-thirds to three-quarters of the sound stage, they are high over and set back somewhat from the conductor.

Reverberation may be added by a variety of means. One is to have a second coincident pair set back from the first and facing toward the empty part of the hall or studio. Another has a spaced pair of cardioids at the sides of the hall, well forward again, but looking back along it. In either of these cases the two microphones must be steered to their correct sides of the studio, as some direct sound will arrive at these microphones, and even more by short-path first reflections.

248

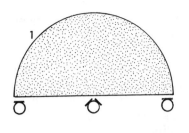
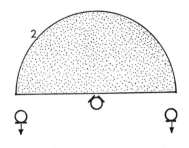

STEREO ORCHESTRAL LAYOUTS. 1. With a spaced pair to 'pin down' the corners of the orchestra (e.g. harp on left and basses on right). 2. With a spaced pair used to increase reverberation. This layout can be readily adapted for use in four-channel stereo.

These two layouts also offer the prospect of good sound in four-channel stereo in cases where the rear loudspeakers are used only for reverberation—which for conventional classical orchestral music is more aesthetically pleasing than feeding direct sound to all four speakers. References to stereo in this chapter generally assume two channels, but can readily be adapted to quadraphony in this way.

Another layout has a second coincident pair of microphones, but this time figure-of-eights looking forward and set back to such a distance that the positions of the various parts of the image roughly coincide. For an orchestra this distance may be about 10 ft (3 m). This arrangement has the additional advantages that

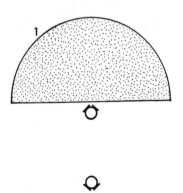
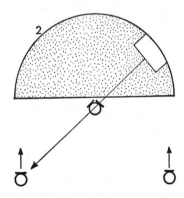

REVERBERATION IN STEREO ORCHESTRAL LAYOUTS. 1. A second coincident pair with reversed output used to control reverberation separately: can also be used for four-channel stereo. 2. Wrong: A forward-facing spaced pair set back into the hall may give false information from the brass, which, directed towards the microphone on the opposite side, may suddenly appear to be in the wrong place.

the balancer can work between the two pairs to handle extreme changes of volume, and that the second pair gives an automatic stand-by facility in the event of failure or loss of quality of the first pair during a live transmission. Such failure is very rare, but the facility is nonetheless desirable; two pairs of microphones are in any case needed for balance comparison tests. Phase cancellation on the back of the second pair does remain a problem.

Any microphone that is set up in addition to the main pair and facing toward the orchestra (or a 'bright' reflecting surface) may give false information about the position of the brass, if significant direct or strong first-reflection sound can reach it. The trumpets are likely to be directed over the heads of the strings and may be picked up on any microphone in line of fire on the *opposite* side of the studio. There is then an extra trumpet signal, pulling the section across the sound stage, perhaps to a position occupied by other instruments.

Further mono microphones are generally added. Two, one on each side of the orchestra may be placed to cover strings. They are faded up just suficiently to lend presence to their tone, and panned to their proper places in the stereo balance, which is

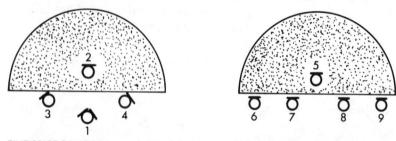

FIVE MICROPHONES, two layouts. 1. Stereo pair. 2–4. Directional spotting micro-phones about 6 ft (2 m) from string and woodwind sections, adding presence and strengthening positional information. 5–9. A curtain of omnidirectional microphones. Phase and control problems are reduced by adopting a sufficiently close balance for microphones 6–9, but the precise positioning of performers requires careful attention. Changes in the relative level of adjacent microphones can affect the apparent position of instruments equidistant from them, including loud, distant sources such as brass. Further spotting microphones would be added to both layouts.

thereby more clearly defined. Woodwind may also benefit similarly: where the main pair gives good basic stereo coverage a mono microphone is sufficient. It lends presence to woodwind solo passages. Harps and some other instruments may be given spotting microphones, but again must be used with subtlety to add clarity and positional information. Spotting microphones can also be used to a limited extent to restore the balance of sections that are weak in numbers, but that implies lifting volume more than is needed solely for a subtle increase in presence. The result may sound like a small group given solo status.

Quiet, unusual instruments such as the *mandolin* need to be brought well forward, right under the conductor's nose. Then, the instrument may not have to be spotted for stereo, but if it should prove to be necessary, it can easily be arranged.

Pipe organ with orchestra

If a *pipe organ* is used with orchestra there is a danger (in stereo) that its distance will cause its image to be too narrow.

In fact, as a good organ is laid out in the hall, it should have some width (indeed it is bound to), but not so much that the spatial separation of the various voices are marked: like a choir, organ tone is better blended than broken up into obvious sections. However, in stereo, excessive width (such as that of the Royal Festival Hall in London) is narrowed by the microphones to something more reasonable; and a good average width may appear rather narrow. A pair of microphones at such a distance that they 'see' the organ as a whole can be used to broaden it on the sound stage. They should be placed to pick up as little orchestra as possible; and the orchestra microphone itself may have to be angled to discriminate against direct sound from the organ.

Orchestra with soloists or chorus

Concert works with solo instruments placed near the centre can in principle be taken using a standard orchestral balance: the main microphones favour the soloist. However, it is usual to provide solo spotting microphones for additional presence. For a piano concerto, however, it may be necessary to angle or place the main microphones to discriminate somewhat against the volume of the solo instrument.

If there are several soloists, as in a double or triple concerto, or several solo singers, they need to be placed with a thought for lay-out on the sound stage.

In a public performances a chorus is normally placed behind the orchestra. If it is already weaker than the orchestra this position does not help; and moving the microphone in (as for stereo) only makes the orchestra stronger in comparison with chorus. Several spaced directional microphones are therefore added to

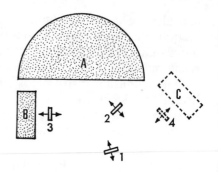

ORCHESTRA AND CHOIR (mono). A. Orchestra. B. Choir or soloist. C. Alternative position for choir or soloist. 1. Microphone position for orchestra only. This balance is acoustically similar to 2 plus 3 (or 2 plus 4) for orchestra plus chorus or soloists.

give presence to the choir. These are set on very high stands (or suspended) at the back of the orchestra. As they look down at the choir, giving it increased body, presence, and intelligibility, their dead side is toward the orchestra. In stereo the spread can be increased if on the main microphone they appear to be bunched too close together.

There are further problems in stereo when the chorus is supplying not words but orchestral texture, as in Ravel's *Daphnis and Chloë* (the difficulty here is to get sufficient spread when spotting microphones would bring the chorus too far forward), or in the last movement of Beethoven's Ninth Symphony (where the soloists would be better placed for perspective at the back, but prefer to come and stand at the front).

Opera

Opera may be recorded or broadcast in concert form; or it may be taken from a public stage performance. A range of methods has been used for each. The simplest employs a standard layout for orchestra, with chorus behind, and soloists to the fore: this remains excellent for oratorio and for concert performances of opera where there is no pretence at dramatic presentation.

For opera on records an advance was made by introducing stereo movement laterally and in perspective. Historically, a layout that produced excellent results had a line of five cardioid microphones beyond the orchestra. These covered an acting area marked in a chequered pattern. The square from which the player should sing was marked on his score; moves were similarly indicated. A disadvantage was that the conductor could not hear the solo singing as well as with the oratorio layout. An alternative was to have the singers on either side of him, but facing the orchestra, and working to cardioids which therefore had their dead sides toward the orchestra. The singers were recorded on separate tracks and their perspective and position (with movement provided by panning) was arranged at the mixdown stage. For this, less preparation was required in advance.

A similar layout provides an interesting possibility for quad: in this case the action is laid out before the listener with orchestral accompaniment behind him. This assumes equal quality for the four loudspeakers.

A further stereo layout that has been employed by BBC radio has a normal balance for the orchestra but laterally reverses the singers. With the orchestra at one end of the studio, the chorus is placed at roughly a right angle to it along one side of the studio, so that one corner of the orchestra adjoins one end of the chorus. The chorus, arranged in rows on ascending rostra work to a line of four or more microphones, as do the soloists in front of them. These microphones are 'folded' back across the orchestral sound image.

For opera from the stage, coverage is possible using a coincident pair for the orchestra and a row of cardioids along the front of the stage for the singers. Unfortunately, in its best position, the main pair may obscure sight-lines. If it is raised, close microphones are required in the orchestra pit.

For the stage itself there are several further possibilities. One has a coincident pair of cardioids at the centre of the footlights, with a spaced pair to the sides, filling in the downstage corners. By mounting them on a bracket, so that the diaphragm is low and close to the edge of the stage, the effect of sound reflections from the stage itself is minimized. The main pair also picks up some

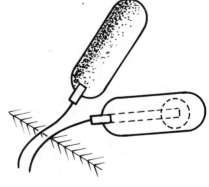

OPERA MICE. A stereo pair of microphones lies close to the stage, supported in foamed rubber pads. Sufficiently close to the reflecting surface, interference effects are small.

(though relatively little) of the orchestra. Greater separation is achieved by microphone mice (p. 160), placed on the stage itself. In one layout there is a coincident pair at the centre and single microphones at the corner, but on a wide stage three separate pairs can produce good results. The width of each pair is reduced, with the inner microphone of each outer pair steered to the same

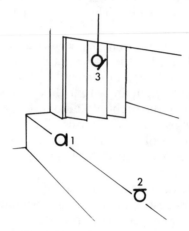

MICROPHONE POSITIONS IN THE THEATRE (e.g. for opera). 1 and 2. A pair of (cardioid) microphones in the footlights. Though very close to the orchestra their response discriminates sufficiently against this. 3. A single microphone placed high in the auditorium—but well forward. Cardioid response again favours singers.

position as the corresponding element of the central pair. In practice, this gives smooth coverage of movement across the stage. With a central prompt-box, two pairs might serve. Note, however, that if mice are placed on a flexible rather than solid surface, their directional response may change in ways not predicted by simple theory. In particular, they might pick up more orchestra, nominally in the dead sector of the cardioid, than expected. A deficiency of any footlight microphones is that they favour footsteps on the stage. If the feet approach any particular microphone too heavily, take that one out and rebalance on a microphone to one side. Check the effect on the stereo picture: it may be acceptable, or it may seem better to pan the remaining microphone to restore the image to its former position.

Important action in an upstage area that is not covered adequately on the downstage microphones can perhaps be taken on a microphone suspended by its own cable. Take care not to

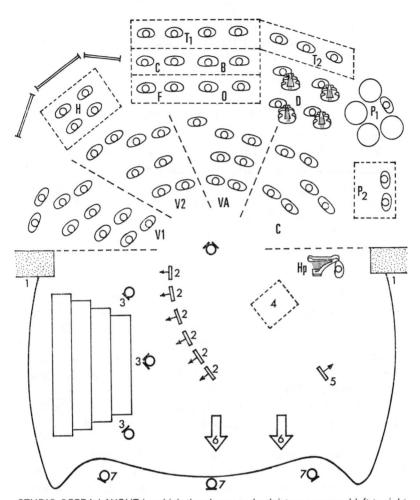

STUDIO OPERA LAYOUT in which the chorus and soloists are reversed left to right and superimposed on the orchestral stage. A converted theatre is used in this example. 1. Proscenium arch. The stage is extended into the main auditorium. 2. Soloists. 3. Chorus. 4. Conductor. 5. Announcer. This microphone can also be used for spotting effects (e.g. castanets, which can be steered to represent the movement of a dance). 6. An off-stage chorus can be placed underneath the balcony without a microphone. 7. Audience above. Orchestral layout: V1. Ist violins. V2. 2nd violins. VA. Violas. C. 'Cellos. D. Basses. H. Horns (with reflecting screens behind). F. Flutes. O. Oboes. C. Clarinets. B. Bassoons. T1. Trumpets. T2. Trombones. P1. Timpani. P2. Other percussion. Hp. Harp. Note that the harp is 'in' or near the right-hand speaker, and that the left-hand side of the orchestra and the side of the chorus and soloists nearest to it will be picked up on each others' microphones and *must* therefore be arranged to coincide in the audio stage. For the singers, examples of positioning for particular scenes using this layout are as follows: i. Part of chorus left; principals centre; off-stage chorus, right. ii. Duet at centre solo microphones; harp figures, right. iii. Quartet at four centre solo microphones.

255

overdo its use, bringing intentionally distant scenes too far forward. But in general, balance with an ear to the clarity of vocal line—even when, on television, subtitles are added.

Classical music in vision

For classical music, a television picture makes only a little difference to the type of balance that is sought. But getting a good balance of any type is a little more difficult, because:

1. Television studios are generally too dead: concert halls (or even music sound studios) are therefore to be preferred in cases where they can conveniently be used.

2. Microphones must not be obtrusive.

3. The layout must be visually satisfying; but a good rule is to adopt a layout that is as close as possible to that of a concert performance.

What is *not* needed is any attempt to make sound follow picture: where the camera zooms in to a close-up of the oboe the sound remains at the concert perspective (note that this is the exact reverse of what may be done with speech). The big close-up in sound would be permitted only for a special effect; if, for instance, someone were talking about the role of the oboe in the ensemble, or alternatively, if this were a drama and we were hearing, as we were seeing, from a position within the orchestra. Even in these cases the overall orchestral sound would be distorted as little as possible.

One slight difference in balance is desirable for television: this is marginally greater clarity at the expense of the tonal blending that many people prefer for sound radio and records. The extra presence permits individual instruments or groups to be heard just clearly enough for close shots to be aurally justified. This does not necessarily mean shorter reverberation, but simply that the attack on each note must be heard with reasonable clarity: this is usually enough to identify individual instruments. A technique that can be used successfully to produce this effect is to mix the outputs of two microphones, one closer and one more distant than would be used for a single microphone balance.

A balance with this extra degree of clarity also takes into account the different listening conditions that may exist in the home: the sound quality of loudspeakers on the majority of television receivers is rather lower than that used for radio and records by many people who enjoy listening to serious music; for this lower quality of sound reproduction a clear balance is better than a tonally blended quality.

For *ballet* performed in the television studio it is often difficult to get both the dance settings and the orchestra into the same studio: this may be a blessing in disguise, however, as the solution is to take the orchestra away to a music studio (with their own remote cameras, if required). The music can then be replayed to the dancers over loudspeakers.

Limitations (due to cost) on orchestral rehearsal time means that orchestra and dancers really need to be rehearsed separately; if this also means that the orchestra can be prerecorded the tempi are then set, and the dancers know from then on precisely what to expect. Ideally, of course, the principal dancers will have attended the recording. Piano transcriptions may have to be used for rehearsal, however, and it may be a responsibility of the sound department to make and replay a recording of this too. The dancers must have clear audio replay at all places where the action takes them, so the action studio must be liberally supplied with suitable loudspeakers. In some cases in ballet the dancers start before the music; where this happens it is up to the tape operator to be as precise and accurate as an orchestral conductor in timing the start of the music to match the action.

Effects microphones—usually gun microphones or cardioids angled to discriminate against loudspeakers—are needed in the studio to add just sufficient noise of movement (the dancers' steps, rustle of costume, etc.) to add conviction to the pictures of the dance.

For *singers*, the type of balance depends on whether a microphone may appear in vision; if not, a boom will probably be used. This may introduce separation problems: orchestral spill on to the singer's microphone can modify the balance to a noticeable degree. Normally, electrostatic cardioid microphones are preferred.

One marginal advantage of the relative deadness of television general purpose studios is that when artificial reverberation is used it can be added differentially—not simply by mixing in different proportions of echo but (where facilities permit, such as in a large studio centre) by adding echo of different durations to different parts of the sound: in general, singers require less than the orchestral music that may accompany them.

An important part of any singer's performance lies in his use of vocal dynamics. In sound radio some degree of compression may by necessary; in television the problem is made more complex by movement of both the singer and the microphone and by variation in the distance between singer and microphone to accommodate the size of shot. In these circumstances even more of the responsibility for interpretation of the artist's role may be given to the sound man than is normal: he must therefore think not only about problems of coverage but also—along with the director and the singer himself—about the overall artistic intention.

Where singers and accompaniment have to be physically separated, time-lag problems may hinder the performance, and foldback loudspeakers are needed to relay sound from the musician to the singer; the conductor, too, needs to hear how the singer's contribution fits in to the ensemble.

For wide shots pre-recordings may have to be used: timing this to work in with live action requires careful planning and rehearsal. Often the second track of a twin-track recorder is used for cues that are fed to performers but not to line.

Televised opera

There are several different ways of presenting opera on television:
1. From the stage.
2. With actors miming to prerecorded music (the actors may include some of the singers themselves).
3. With singers in a television studio and orchestra in a sound studio.
4. With both singers and orchestra in some hall of suitable (large) size with good musical acoustics.

For stage performances use a monophonic balance similar to those already discussed (p. 254). Where a televised relay is controlled from a mobile control van it is usual either to de-rig the sound equipment and set it up in more sympathetic surroundings or to use a larger, special mobile sound control room which has good loudspeakers, a reasonable volume of space, and suitable acoustic treatment.

Miming opera is a technique that has in the past been extensively used in Europe, but in Britain mime has been used less, in the belief that the singer's own performance has greater musical conviction. For many of its productions, the BBC uses a combination of two studios, each appropriate to the job that has to be

258

done in it. The orchestral studio has good musical acoustics; the action studio has all of the normal facilities for the visual and sound coverage of dramatic action. It goes without saying that in this type of production the original grand, and deliberately unrealistic style of stage opera is modified to that of music drama (the more theatrical style of presentation can, in any case, be adequately represented in direct relays from opera houses). The singers are therefore covered by boom (and, where necessary, other microphones) in a way basically similar to that for a play, while at the same time trying to maintain many of the pure musical qualities of a concert performance.

Several of the difficulties that have had to be overcome are relatively straightforward technical problems of intercommunication between studios that may be several miles apart. Picture is easiest to deal with: the conductor has a monitor for the action, and a camera relays his beat back to the action studio where a repetiteur takes it from another monitor and relays it to the singers. The latter, apparently complex arrangement presents no problems for the musicians: a similar arrangement is used in nearly every opera house.

Sound communication is a little more complicated. The orchestral sound is relayed to the action studio floor by using directional loudspeakers mounted on the front of the boom prams. As the booms themselves are moved around to follow the action, so do the upright line-source loudspeakers that are used with them. As we have seen, a line source is directional at middle and high frequencies, radiating primarily in a plane intersecting the

OPERA OR BALLET IN THE TELEVISION STUDIO: layout for conductor with orchestra in separate sound studio. 1. Line loudspeaker along top of music stand. 2. Hood loudspeaker over conductor's head. 3. Monitor for conductor to see action. 4. Camera to relay beat to repetiteur in television studio.

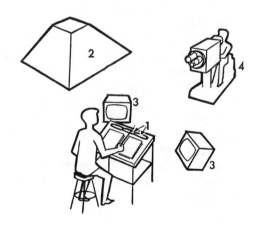

line at right-angles, so that good separation can be achieved. Relaying the voices of the singers to the conductor has been done in several ways: one employs a hood (a large pyramid-shaped baffle) with a loudspeaker in the apex and above the conductor's head. But if the conductor is to appear in vision this restricts the television lighting. The alternative is to give the conductor a line-source loudspeaker along the top edge of his music stand. In practice, three very small elliptical speakers set in a line have been used. This produces little bass and is directional at high frequencies, so once again separation is possible.

Even using this technique, it may be necessary to pre-record or film some scenes in advance. To employ an orchestra for such a short sequence may be disproportionately expensive, so a system of guide tracks may be used. Here the pre-recorded (or filmed) scenes are accompanied by a sound track consisting of bar counts or a piano version of the music, plus any useful verbal instructions such as warnings of impending changes of tempo. This guide track is fed to the conductor only (by headphones in this case). Orchestral sound is then added at the main recording.

If singers' voices are included in the pre-recording this can itself be used as the guide track or, better still, twin track sound can be used with one track for each purpose. Videotape has a separate audio cue track available, and for film a combined optical or magnetic track can be used for cue and a separate magnetic track for the sound.

Where singers' voices are pre-recorded in sound only (so that miming can be used—e.g. as the only means of satisfactorily covering very long shots), a guide track can again be accommodated if a twin-track sound tape recorder is used.

So much for the third system of presenting televised opera. Despite its complexity, this is now well established—but as with any compromise, some people are bound to find it cumbersome. And so it was that in 1969 the composer and conductor Benjamin Britten (disliking his remoteness from the action) persuaded the BBC to try an opera recorded with orchestra and singers in the same place. Accordingly, an opera was mounted with the two elements at opposing ends of the same concert hall. In this sort of production, some of the communications systems used with separate studios are still needed: for example, the time lag between the ends of the hall still requires the use of the conductor's music-stand loudspeakers. Separate rehearsal, one of the advantages of twin studios, is lost; but in its place is an enhanced unity of purpose.

Popular music groups

Having worked up to some of the largest and most complex layouts for classical music, we can now take some of the same—or similar—components and put them together again in a contrasting style.

For absolute contrast to the last musical theme, and linked to it only by the rapturous applause that is common to both, consider a typical pop group. This may consist of drums, three guitars (lead, bass and acoustic), vocalist and perhaps electric piano. In the dead acoustics of a big recording studio it is usual to place the various components in booths around the walls, with tall sound-absorbent screens on either side of the drum-kit (unless it is in a corner) and half-screens in front. Lead and bass guitar loudspeakers can be directed in to half-screened bays, and picked up on cardioid microphones, but an acoustic guitar may need a separate room. The piano is angled to radiate any acoustic output into an opposite wall, and the amount of screening depends on whether there are any further quieter instruments to be balanced; if so, heavy screening may be required. The guide vocalist is kept physically well away from all of these (the track may sometimes be used in the final mix) but in good visual contact with the other players. Considerable use is made of tracking (sequential recording) for vocals, vocal backing, additional acoustic guitar and percussion and other effects. Depending on the number of tracks available, there may be partial mixing as the session progresses, with some components 'jumping' from one track to another to leave space free for further material to be recorded. Some parts such as the main drum coverage, piano and vocal backing may appear on stereo pairs of tracks; the rest will be mono.

The session may start by recording the basic rhythm plus guide vocal, followed by additional acoustic guitar and piano. Next the lead vocals are laid down, then the backing (as separate stages if complexity warrants it). Finally, the solo guitar, electric guitar riffs, etc. are overdubbed. Reduction, a separate session, begins with checking the treatment applied to individual tracks, starting with rhythm as before, and gradually building up a stereo composite from the separate components.

To regain a sense of occasion and the feeling of a real, live performance, recordings may be made from concerts or road shows. A rock concert can itself involve a great deal of electronic rebalancing, even before any recording is contemplated. A group of three or four players may have some thirty channels linked to its own travelling mixer desk feeding the stage loudspeaker system; indeed a hundred channels is not unknown, with a separate desk for the drummer alone. To record from such a concert it is usual to take a feed from each channel by means of a passive splitter near the microphone. This is a low-level feed via a resistor. The increase in signal strength available in an active splitter (i.e. using an amplifier) is not needed and might even result in distortion, as the volume is so high to start with.

Depending on the number of tracks available on the recording tape, some of the channels may have to be combined at the time of the performance—for example, the drums could be reduced to four channels, with all but the snare and bass mixed down to a stereo pair. The recordings are taken back to the studio and reduced in the normal way. Records produced from concerts are sometimes proudly marked 'no overdubbings'.

When recording on location, whether from a rock or classical concert, time is limited and it is sensible to establish a routine, setting microphones or taking split feeds as early as possible, then laying the cables back to the mixer. Microphones are identified by scratching them and indicating what instruments they cover. Radio microphones may be used for direct communication between stage and mixer. The recording arrangements are set up and checked out last. A mobile sound control room is sometimes used.

In music recording studios there will be monitoring arrangements for quadraphonic balance to be checked in stereo and for stereo to be heard in mono. In addition there may also be provision for the studio output to be switched to small domestic-quality loudspeakers: studio communications loudspeakers may be suitable. It should not be below the notice of the balancer that this is how many will hear his work.

Light music and jazz

A basic component of much popular light music and jazz is the piano trio, i.e. piano, bass and drums, which forms the nucleus of most larger groups. To this may be added, stage by stage, guitar (acoustic/electric), brass, woodwind (primarily saxophones), vocalist and other instruments for particular effects. These might include celesta, violin, horn, harp, electric organ or any other

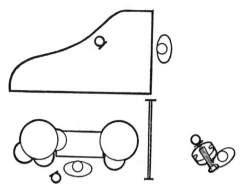

RHYTHM GROUP. The drum kit and bass are separated by a low acoustic screen. A range of positions is possible for each microphone.

instrument that interests the arranger. Once again, mono balances are normally used for most purposes, but stereo pairs might be tried on trumpets, trombones and woodwind as well as piano and vocal groups. Here, too, tracking is often used, but economics may demand that a substantial amount of music be recorded in a single session. Or there may be limitations on the number of microphones, the mixing or recording equipment or in the studio

SMALL BAND. Rhythm group with 1. Guitar (acoustic/electric). 2. Trumpet. 3. Trombone. 4. Woodwind (saxophones). Rhythm group microphones not shown.

acoustics. Despite such deficiencies it is often possible to achieve a balance that makes satisfying listening—even if not to the pop-music balancer's taste.

Normally the studio is dead, but sometimes only bright surroundings are available. In this case some spill may be inevitable, and it might be best to modify the ideal fully separated balance.

Even in good conditions there may be enough spill in the studio to dictate some elements of the layout of the stereo sound picture. However, certain relationships will appear in both the real layout and its image, for example, the piano, bass, and drums will always be close together. These might be steered to centre and left of centre with electric/acoustic guitar near the left speaker, vocalist and woodwind right centre, and brass on the right. The actual layout in the studio is governed not only by the need for separation (so that this or some other stereo picture can be achieved, and so that all of the sounds can be individually treated), but also by a number of practical considerations—such as whether the players can hear or see each other.

Multimicrophone layout

When the musicians arrive in the studio they expect to sit at positions already arranged for them, with chairs, music stands, screens, piano, boxes for such things as guitar amplifiers, and microphones all (at least roughly) laid out. They will have been set according to the balancer's instructions; and in the case of the microphones he or an assistant will have actually placed them himself. What guides the balancer in the various choices he can make in his layout?

Three different situations may occur:

1. The group may already have a layout used for stage shows. In this case the balancer finds out in advance what this is and varies it as little as possible (but as much as may be necessary for good separation) with the cooperation of the musical director.

2. The group may have done previous recordings or broadcasts with the same organization. The balancer finds out what layout was used before, and if it worked well uses it as a basis for his own layout. The group will not expect to be in different positions every time they come to the studio. However, minor changes for the purposes of experiment, or to include ideas that the balancer is convinced work better than those already used may be tried— with the cooperation of the individual instrumentalist, leader of a section or musical director, as appropriate. Major changes may be dictated by the use of additional instruments (of which the balancer should have been informed), or particular new problems created by the music itself (which will become apparent in rehearsal).

3. The group may be created for this session only, in which case the balancer—having found out the composition from the producer or musical director—can start from scratch.

Even starting afresh, the balancer can apply certain rules that make the musician's job easier. For example:

1. The bass player may wish to see the pianist's left hand, to which his music directly relates. This is particularly important if there may be improvisations.

2. The drummer, bass player, and pianist form a basic group (the rhythm group) who expect to be together.

3. In a piano quartet the fourth player can face the other three in the well of the piano; everybody can see everybody else. But a guitar player may be working particularly with the bass, so could be placed at the top end of the piano keyboard in order to see across the pianist to the bass player.

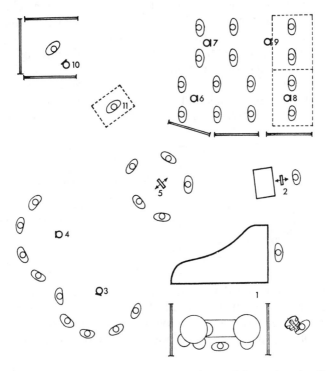

SHOW BAND WITH STRINGS. 1. Rhythm group. 2. Electric/acoustic guitar. 3. Trumpets. 4. Trombones. 5. Woodwind. 6. lst violins. 7. 2nd violins. 8. Violas. 9. 'Cellos. 10. Vocalist. 11. Musical director. Variations must be made for acoustic difficulties: in one regularly used BBC layout it was found necessary to bring the bass forward to the tail of the piano and separate him by acoustic screens from brass, drums and woodwind (the trumpets having been moved farther away). Additional forces also complicate the layout still further. For example, the pianist may need an additional keyboard for organ or celesta: this could be placed to his right and the guitar moved forward. A wide range of different microphones is used: see the notes on individual instruments for details of type (including frequency and polar response) and position (distance, height and angle).

4. When the bass player has fast rhythmic figures he needs to hear the drums, particularly the snare drum and hi-hat; these can be heard well on the drummer's left.

5. Any other two players who are likely to be working together on a melodic line or other figures need to be close together.

6. Where players double, e.g. piano with celesta, the two positions must be together.

7. All players, including a saxophone (and woodwind) group which may be split with up to three and two facing each other, need to see the musical director or conductor.

8. The musical director may also be a performer playing a particular instrument. But if it has been arranged that all players can see each other, condition 7 is still satisfied.

This may appear to make the original idea of building up a lay-out according to good principles of separation less feasible. But in fact, although compromises may be necessary, careful use of directional microphones and screens should make a good sound possible. A low screen is needed between bass and drums, and

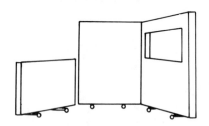

STUDIO SCREENS, absorbers about 4 in (10 cm) thick. A dead music studio has a supply of full and low screens that are easily moved on rollers to provide acoustic separation without loss of visual contact. Vocalist's screen may have a window of stiff transparent plastics.

another to separate drums and brass. Particularly quiet instruments, such as strings, celesta, etc., will probably also require screens. A vocalist may be provided with a tent of screens well away from the players, but so positioned that he can see them.

Popular music in vision

Obviously the recording-studio layout for pop music cannot be adopted in vision—though a band wholly or largely out of vision certainly can, and probably will use it. But apart from layout—which may produce some problems of separation—all other elements of the balance and treatment will be as close as possible to that of the recording studio, which after all, provides the standard by which the television sound will be judged.

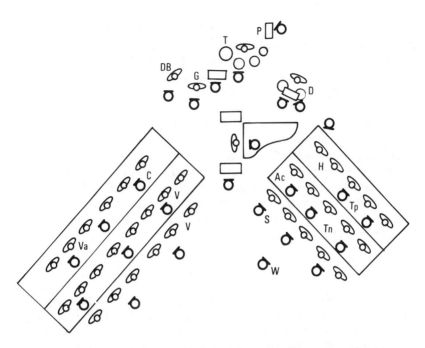

SHOW BAND appearing in vision and giving support to singer or other featured acts. Typical layout: V. Violins. Va. Violas. C. 'Cellos. DB. Double Bass. G. Acoustic guitar. T. Timpani. P. Percussion. D. Drum kit. H. Horns. Tp. Trumpets. Tn. Trombones. Ac. Accordion. S. Saxophones, doubling woodwind. W. Overall wind microphone. All microphones may be condenser cardioids except for a moving coil on bass drum.

Low microphones in among the instruments are generally not obtrusive; indeed, they are readily accepted as part of the pop paraphernalia. Microphones at about or just above head height (particularly if they would be between the cameras and the front line of players) are avoided if possible; as are large microphone booms and stands. Indeed, there are more differences in mountings than in positioning.

The pop singer's hand microphone is accepted as a prop and not merely something to sing into—though some experienced singers also use it to balance themselves with skill. For the less mobile singer a stand microphone is an accepted convention.

For any popular music television programme it is essential for the control desk to have all of the equalization, compression and echo facilities of the recording studio. Today most television studios have these available on a sufficient number of channels as a matter of course. A capacity for pre-recording some tracks may also be necessary even to a live performance if a group is to match its expected sound. Miming to playback of records is a cheap and easy way of creating television—though some would call it cheap and nasty: the sense of occasion is prejudiced, and the audience may quite justifiably feel cheated. Such devices should be kept to a minimum.

Television has to a large extent adapted its pictures to the sound needs of popular music, rather than the reverse; nevertheless, occasions still occur where a singer must appear without a microphone in vision—so booms are still used, but perhaps with a high quality gun microphone to improve separation. Only where separation cannot be achieved by these means, or in complex song and dance acts should the music be pre-recorded and vision shot to playback of sound.

Music on film

Most of what has gone before applies also to music on film (including film for television); though generally there is a somewhat greater effort to eliminate microphones from the picture.

Although multiple-camera techniques have, at times, been used, close-ups are normally shot separately, taking sound, but only as a guide to synchronization with a master recording. More is shot than is actually required, so that actions before and after the cuts will match. Occasionally film shot in sync for one sequence is eventually synchronized to the sound from another part of the work. Here the beat or action (e.g. drum beat) is marked on the track and matched to a close-up of the action. Or, for example for a marching band, the beat in two different sections may be synchronized and the film transposed from one part of the music to the other, provided that the right players are doing the right things in the picture.

Largely due to the technical problems involved, stereophonic music on film has rarely achieved its full potential. A single song—superb in every department—from *Seven Brides for Seven Brothers* stands out and will serve as an example of what can be done in the way of combining picture, song, and musical effects (chopping logs) in vision. The whole number was, incidentally, filmed in a single extended mobile shot.

10

SOUND EFFECTS

Sound effects are of three basic types, 'spot' effects, 'library' recorded effects and actuality recorded effects.

Spot effects are those that are created live in the radio studio at the same time as the performers speak their lines, out of vision in a television studio, or live in a film dubbing theatre to match action on the screen. They include such noises as doors, telephones, bells, tea-cups, letters being opened, crashes, bangs, squeaks, footsteps, and even that old standby, horses' hooves. They include sounds it just is not worth recording, and sounds that are so much part of the action that to have them anywhere but in the studio would leave the actor confused and uncertain of his timing.

Recorded effects consist principally of those that cannot conveniently be created in the studio: cars, aircraft, birdsong, weather, crowd chatter, and so on. Their field overlaps with that of spot effects in many instances: for instance, as an alternative to coconut shells, a recording of real horses' hooves may be used. But curiously enough, some very realistic horses' hoof sounds were actually recorded using coconut shells. It may seem odd that an effect may be created by an apparently—and in the case of coconut shells, even ludicrously—inappropriate sound source. But it is important to realize that the purpose of sound effects is not, in general, to re-create actuality, but to *suggest* it. Realism is not always necessary, and indeed at times may even be detrimental to the final result, in that some inessential element of the 'real' sound may distract the listener.

Library effects are those already available on disc or tape; *actuality effects* are those specially recorded (more often for film than for any other medium).

For any radio production in which effects appear, it is probable that both spot and recorded effects will be needed, and a brief examination of the script will indicate into which category most

269

cues fall. The division of labour will probably work out about fifty-fifty, with most sounds obviously belonging in one group or the other. In a few cases the final decision depends on factors such as whether the studio is equipped with the heavier pieces of spot effects furniture or whether a particular recording is available.

The semi-realistic use of effects

Effects are rarely used in a strictly realistic way—and even when this is attempted, it is generally a heightened realism that owes a great deal to art. This is true enough in film or television; it is particularly the case in radio.

As an example consider an eye-witness account of a 'Viking Raid'—a highlight of a traditional festival on the Isle of Man. The tape received was not usable in the form in which it had been recorded. The reporter had, very rightly, concentrated on getting good speech quality, so that the background noises were too low. There were some good shouts, screams, and crowd noise, but when the words 'You can probably hear the clash of their swords now' came up the swords themselves were neither clear not close enough. Also, there were breaks in recording; the loudspeakers were being used to explain the scene to onlookers, and whenever these were switched on the atmosphere of the event was lost.

To re-create the event in a form acceptable to the listener, the tape had first to be cut together into the form of a continuous narrative, deleting inessential expressions of enthusiasm—the report conveyed this without the necessity for words. As reconstructed the first sound heard was a recorded sound effect, heavy breakers on the beach (the report referred to gusts of wind up to forty miles an hour), and these were held behind the studio narrator as he quickly sketched in the necessary background information. Toward the end of this the actuality screams were faded in, and the tape report took over. The effect of sea-wash was gradually lost as the description of the invasion brought the Vikings on to and up the beach, but an occasional angry-sounding seagull was touched into the clamour to keep the sense of location strong. After the first reference to swordplay the sentence starting 'You can probably hear . . .' was cut and in its place the clash of swords was inserted in a much closer perspective. The final result was highly realistic: an actual event (with the actual shouts and screams) had been brought into sharp focus by a little touching up on the sounds which could not have been recorded at the same time without an array of microphones dotted about the beach, and a complicated piece of mixing.

So much for the neo-realist technique, one which is well suited to the sound medium when a programme consists largely of edited actuality. But where the programme is created entirely in the studio, we must live by a series of highly artificial—but effective—conventions; we rarely strive after the sound that would be found in a recording of an event as it happened.

The conventional use of effects

Sound effects are usually held quite deliberately to an unrealistically low level. There are many reasons for this, apart from the risk of overmodulation. One is that, for many listeners, sudden loud noises are unnerving or irritating, and not just dramatic.

A second reason for holding effects back—and a very important one for all continuous effects—is the masking that is caused by even moderately quiet background sound. The *cocktail party effect* is often quoted as a demonstration of one of the basic qualities of binaural perception: this is the ability of the ear and brain to fasten on to a single sound source in a crowded room, rejecting and almost ceasing to be aware of the excessive surrounding noise level. But if a monophonic link is introduced into the chain (microphone, recorder or loudspeaker) a great deal of this ability to discriminate is lost, and the effort to concentrate on the main stream of dialogue becomes a very conscious one. To demonstrate this in a programme about hearing aids, I plugged one into a recorder to pick up a discussion between six people in a half-empty bar. As may be expected the din as it appeared on the tape was appalling, with only a word here and there intelligible. It was clear why my deaf friend preferred to switch it off and lip-read.

This, then, is the cocktail-party effect in reverse. Set up an open microphone in a noisy location without attempting to discriminate against the background and you will be lucky if you can make out more than an occasional fragment. Record in stereo and the situation is vastly improved: one of the greatest benefits that stereo offers to drama is freedom from the absolute necessity to hold effects so far back as to separate them from the rest of the action. Unfortunately, the need for compatability with mono often makes it impossible to take this advantage.

Loudness is only one element in the make-up of a sound, and one that is nothing like so important as its *character*, the evocative quality that makes it visual in effect. This is true even of effects for which loudness appears to be a particularly important part of the sound—for example, a car crash. Analysis of a car crash shows that it consists of four separate elements: skid, impact, crunching metal, and broken glass falling to the ground. In a real crash the second of these is the loudest part: so loud, in fact, that if it were peaked exactly to the loudest permissible volume for no appreciable distortion the rest of the sound would be much too quiet and lacking in dramatic effect. So the whole sound has to be reorganized to ensure that no part is markedly louder than any other. But, even more important, during this recomposition certain of the characteristics have to be modified to create the right mood for the sound to fit into its context. The effects man is a good way along the road to mastering his craft when he realizes that a dizzy blonde driving into a brick wall makes a different noise from a payroll bandit doing exactly the same thing. For the former we would try to create (or select) a funny sound; for the latter, one that is vicious and retributive.

The various stages of the crash would be made up as follows:
1. The skid. This is essential for a dramatic effect: a crash without a skid is just a noise that is half through before we can decide what is going on. The scream of tyres is a distinctive noise that may or may not happen in real life: whether it happens in radio depends on mood. The skid is nemesis, doom closing in on the bandit and preparing to take him.
2. A pause. The listener, having been drawn to the edge of his seat, must be given half a second to hold his breath and . . . wait for it. . . .
3. Impact. A hard, solid thud: very difficult to get just right, but fortunately not so important as the other sounds.
4. Crunching metal. In a real crash this usually sounds like a couple of dustbins being banged together, a ludicrous enough sound for the dizzy blonde, but not sinister enough for the bandit. A more purposeful and solid sound, and one with less of the empty-tin-can quality, is needed.
5. Glass. Like the skid, this is an identifying sound, and also one which clearly puts an end to the sequence of noises. For the listener it plays an essential part in the dying away of sensation.
6. A period of silence.

The car crash provides a good illustration of the general principles underlying the creation of sound effects. No drama sound effect should be simply the noise that would naturally accompany

272

the action being played, unless it is merely included as part of the counterpoint of sound and silence, i.e. for variety of backing. Rather, it must be related to the dramatic content. This applies just as much to the more important actuality sound effects used in film. They must be recorded and treated with creative care if they are to work well.

Unrealistic and surrealistic effects

Effects that are intended to be funny are very different from normal dramatic effects. The latter may be exaggerated, but this is done in a subtle way, by slightly emphasizing the characteristic qualities and cutting away the inessentials; but in the comic effect the same process of emphasis of character is carried to its illogical extreme. A whole canon of what are sometimes called *cod effects* is created by this method, and in a fast-moving comedy show every sound is deliberately overdone—even including the way a door is opened in radio comedy programmes such as the old Goon Shows.

In fact, the cod 'door opens' is typical of the way all of these sounds are created. An ordinary door opening may or may not produce a slight rattle as the handle turns, but for dramatic purposes this characteristic is seized upon; indeed, if it were not for this, it would be difficult to find any readily identifiable element in the otherwise rather quiet sound—a faint click would be meaningless. But for a cod door the volume and duration of this identifying characteristic is exaggerated beyond all normal experience—though not so much as to obstruct the action.

Such a method of codding effects works only if the normal spot effect makes use of some slightly unreal element; where the natural sound cannot be conveniently exaggerated, other methods have to be found. For example, little can be done with the sound 'door shuts', which in any case has to be toned down slightly to prevent overmodulation. So other methods must be examined: for example, the creation of completely different and totally unreal sounds. These might include such cod effects as a 'swoosh' exit noise (created, perhaps, by speeding up the change of pitch in a recording of a passing jet plane). Or an object (or person) being thrown high into the air might be indicated by the glide up and down on a swannee whistle (which has a slide piston to govern the pitch). This is just one example from the rich field of musical spot effects: the villain in a comedy show may be dealt a sharp tap on the Chinese block; or in a children's programme, Jack and Jill may come tumbling down a xylophone arpeggio.

As with dialogue, timing can be used to make noises comic. Typical of this is the way many a crash ends. Don Quixote being thrown from his horse by a windmill offered an example of this: after the main pile of 'armour' had been thrown to the ground and stirred around a little there followed a slight pause, and then one last separate piece of 'armour' was dropped and allowed to rock gently to rest. For this effect a pile of bent metal-based 'acetate' records was used: they were threaded at intervals along a piece of string—except for the last single. Any similar pile of junk might be used. The timing of such a sequence is its most vital quality; the essence of its humour could almost be written out like music—and, indeed, an ear for music is very useful to an effects operator.

For one Goon Show the script demanded 'a 16-ton, $1\frac{1}{2}$-horse-power, 6-litre, brassbound electric racing organ fitted with a cardboard warhead'. Here anything but sheer surrealism was doomed to remain stickily on the starting-line. The first stage in the creation of this sound was to dub together a record of an electric organ playing a phrase of music first at normal speed, then at double, and finally at quadruple speed. Three spot-effects enthusiasts dealt with gearchanges and backfires, engine noises and squeaks, and hooters, whistle, and tearing canvas—mostly produced by rather unlikely looking implements. The whole effect was rounded off by a deep, rolling explosion.

Spot effects

A radio studio needs a supply of 'sounds' readily available. At the BBC certain items are kept permanently in each drama studio; and others may be obtained from an Aladdin's cave of sound-making equipment—a spot-effects store.

The studio equipment may include a spot door, a variety of floor surfaces, a flight of stairs, a water tank and perhaps a car door. It is difficult to find an adequate substitute for this last, though a reasonable sound can be got with a rattly music stand and a stout cardboard box. Place the stand across the top of the box, and bang the two down on the floor together.

A well-filled store may take on the appearance of a classified arrangement of the contents of an upper-crust rubbish tip. The shelves are loaded with stacks of apparent junk, ranging from

274

realistic effects such as telephones, clocks, swords, guns (locked away in a safe), teacups and glasses, door chimes and hand-bells—none of which pretended to be other than they are—to musical sound sources such as gongs, drums, blocks, glocks, tubular bells and the rest of the percussion section—which may appear as themselves or in some representational capacity—and then on again to decidedly unobvious effects, such as the cork-and-resin 'creak' or the hinged slapstick 'whip'. In this latter field, ingenuity —or a rather tortured imagination—pays dividends. One can, for example, spend days flapping about with a tennis racket to which thirty or forty strands of cloth have been tied (to represent the beating wings of a bird) only to discover later that the same sound could have been obtained with less effort by shaking a parasol open and shut. A classic example is the French Revolution guillotine: slice through a cabbage.

But whether or not such ingenious improvisations are beginning to be old-fashioned, there are certain basic qualities of spot effects that are at least as valid today as they were forty years ago. Indeed, the acoustic requirements of effects are now, in the days of high-quality radio transmission, a great deal more stringent than they have been in the past. Good timing, however, is the most important quality of a well-performed spot effect—the more so because it is now likely to be a staccato interjection, the continuous background sounds being more often in the form of recordings.

Where feasible, the operator works with the actor, at his side or behind him (relating to his position in a stereo or quadraphonic field): this helps to match acoustic and perspective, as well as timing. Even large pieces of equipment can often be set in in the correct perspective. Where this proves impossible—for example for footsteps that are restricted to an area where a suitable surface is provided, or for water effects that depend on the use of a tank—the effects have to be panned to the correct position and if necessary given stereo spread by using a pair of microphones.

The following descriptions of spot effects indicate the ways in which the commonplace bread-and-butter sounds should be organized and timed. Most are described in the form of radio effects, but may equally apply to out-of-vision effects in television or to the film dubbing theatre.

Door effects

The basic item of studio spot-effects equipment is a large

square box on castors, generally having a full-size door set in it. The handle is allowed to be just a shade loose, so that it can be rattled a little as it opens. A variety of other items of door furniture may also be fitted, including a lifting-type latch, a bolt, a knocker, etc. There can be a sash window fitted in the back of the box.

The sound of opening has to be exaggerated somewhat, as in real life it may be too quiet to register. The sound of closing may have to be quietened down a little to avoid overmodulation. Close the door lightly but firmly. The characteristic sound is a quick double click. Being quiet does not mean slowing the effect down to 'click-pause-click'.

Bad timing can impede the flow of a programme. The sound of a door opening should generally come slightly ahead of the point at which it is usually marked in a script; this allows dialogue to carry straight on without any undue pause. If the scripted cue follows a completed line of dialogue, superimpose the sound on the last word, unless there is some good reason for leaving that word cold (e.g. to follow a direction to enter). If the door is going to be closed again, allow sufficient time for the actor to 'get through' it. Also, the perspective of actor and door should match, and they should stay matched until the door is shut again, if he is supposed to shut it behind him.

Some types of door have to be pre-recorded: prison-cell doors, castle gates, and so on. Sometimes heavy doors of this sort can be made up from an ordinary sound by recording it with reverberation and playing back at slow speed. Halving the speed doubles the size and weight of the door (but does not change the basic quality of it being a wooden door).

For such things as knocking, take care to find a place where the door or frame sounds solid enough. Metal knockers, bolts, latches, lock and keys, etc., should be heavy and old-fashioned; they are

SOUND EFFECTS DOOR, used in radio drama studio.

best attached to the effects door or, if loose, held against it. The larger area of wood acts as a resonator for the sound and gives it true solid quality. Loose bolts, etc., should be screwed on to at least a small panel of wood.

One last note about doors: when in doubt, cut. Some script-writers seem to go mad on the mechanics of exits and entrances. An approach on dialogue is often quite as effective as door-plus-approach. It is better to keep doors, like all other effects, for the occasions when the sound has some actual significance in relation to the story. Otherwise, when the time comes that it does, it will not be so easy to establish its importance.

Footsteps

What was a footnote when dealing with doors becomes a point or primary importance with footsteps. Are your footsteps really necessary? Go through a script with a blue pencil, if it appears to be full of feet. Make sure that every footstep that remains has a direct relevance to the action. In films this effect is often used merely to fill a silence, to reassure the audience that the sound has not broken down at a time when attention must be concentrated on the picture. There is no direct equivalent to this in the pure sound medium—and when footsteps are used here they will far too often draw the listener's attention in the wrong direction.

Such footsteps as remain may be created as spot effects or played in from a recording—the former is preferable, for the sound effect should tie in exactly with the mood of the moment. If the effect is created in the studio this means not only that the exact pace may be found easily but also that changes of pace and a natural stop can occur exactly on cue. In the studio or not, the most satisfactory sound is obtained when the effects man (or woman) is walking about fairly freely, and not just treading the same tiny patch of studio floor. This leads to the major dis-advantage of using a studio effect: that an adequate amount of studio space is not ordinarily available, and if it is, more than

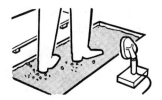

GRAVEL 'PIT' for footstep effects—in this example, it is built in to the studio and concealed below the wooden floor.

six paces are difficult to balance on a static microphone unless the man is walking in a circle.

A well-equipped drama studio has a variety of surfaces available for footsteps: the most important are wood, stone and gravel. Boards or stone slabs (laid out on top of the studio carpet) should be as hefty as is convenient, in order to give weight to their resonance—and the carpet prevents them from ringing too much. The gravel effect can be obtained by spreading sand and gravel on the stone slabs.

On these surfaces long sequences of footsteps are particularly difficult: they have to be done either by walking on the spot or by using pre-recordings. Walking on the spot is not really a very satisfactory way of creating footsteps, as it takes an expert to make them sound anything like real steps. Walking along, the foot falls: heel, sole; heel, sole. When walking on the spot it is natural to put the foot down sole first, so a special heel-first technique must be worked out: a fairly crisp heel sound, followed by a soft sole sound. This is not at all easy to get just right. Even when the foot action is the same, the two are still readily distinguishable by the fact that the surface 'ring' sounds different on every step when walking along, but is monotonously the same when the foot keeps landing at the same place.

Walking or running up and down stairs are also better done with real steps: there is a very different quality for every step. But if the effect has to be simulated, the correct foot-fall is with the sole of the foot, going up, or sole-heel, going down. But again the result is right unless there is some variety of surface.

Some attention should be given to the footwear used. Leather heels and soles are best for men's shoes. High-heeled ladies' shoes are usually noisy enough without special care in their choice. If only one person is available for footstep effects, remember that it is easier for a girl to simulate a man's footsteps than vice versa. It is not easy to get the right weight of step if shoes are held in the hand. The best way of getting two sets of footsteps is to have two people making the sound: one person cannot conveniently do the job—particularly as the two are not generally in step. But two sets of footsteps will stand for three, and three will stand for a small crowd.

Telephone, bell and buzzer effects

For electric bells and buzzers it is useful to make up a small battery-operated box that can be used to give a variety of sounds

278

(or make up several boxes, each giving a different quality). The mobility of such a box allows it to be placed at any appropriate distance, in any suitable acoustic, or against any surface that will act as a sounding board to it.

EFFECTS BELL with two press-button controls.

For telephones in radio a standard hand-set can be adapted, so that the bell may be worked by a press-button. In order to suggest that the ring is stopped by picking up the hand-piece it is usual to finish up with half a ring. For example, the ringing tone in Britain being buzz-buzz . . . buzz-buzz . . ., the ideal amount of ring is one which goes buzz-buzz . . . buzz-b . . . followed quickly by the sound of the hand-piece being lifted. As this last sound is much quieter than the ringing, two things can be done to make it clear. First, the rattle of picking it up should be emphasized a little, and second, the telephone can be brought closer to the microphone at the end of the effect. The first ring is fairly distant (e.g. partly on the dead side of a ribbon microphone). This is doubly convenient in that it may be interrupting speech, and it is better not to have a foreground effect in this case. The second ring is closer, rather as though a camera were tracking in to the telephone, to become very close as it it picked up. The words following must, of course, also be in close perspective.

At the end of the conversation the action of replacing the receiver may be balanced at a greater distance: for one thing it is a sound that is naturally rather louder than picking up, and for another, it is an expected sound that fits neatly in the slight pause after the end of the telephone.

Dialing is more of a performance than being on the receiving end of a phone call, simply because most dialing codes are much too long: for example, even the seven figures used for local calls in London can be a considerable embarrassment, and if there is any way of cutting this sort of hold-up from the script it should usually be adopted, unless dialogue can continue while the dialling is done. The effect cannot be shortened by cutting down the number of figures dialled: for a given location it should be assumed that this will be known by at least some of the listeners, and this is the

279

sort of 'mistake' that is quickly spotted and spoils the illusion. But it is well to dial only low numbers. Push-button phones are a mercy.

For television, telephones are used so often that it is worth making up 'specials'—a portable kit using real telephones, properly (and permanently) polarized so that they are fully practical, and linked together. This is necessary because good sound separation between the microphones picking up the two halves of the conversation may make it difficult for the parties to hear each other clearly without a telephone. Indeed, if one of the speakers does not appear in vision it is best to place him in an acoustically separate booth.

If both speakers do appear in vision at different times their voices are balanced on normal studio microphones, but that of the speaker who is at any particular time out-of-vision must have telephone quality distortion (see p. 393). Manual switching is risky, as the result of the slightest error may be very obvious. A better arrangement is therefore for the distortion circuit to be linked to the camera cut buttons so that the two ends of the conversation are automatically reversed on a cut. But note that when there are more than two cameras (i.e. one at each end) it is necessary to make sure that *any* camera that can possibly be used in the sequence is linked in to the switching system.

In the kit used by the BBC up to six telephones are connected through a box that is effectively a small telephone exchange that

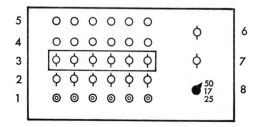

TELEPHONE CONTROL UNIT for operating and interconnecting telephones used in television plays. 1. Input sockets for up to six lines. 2. Keys to select mode of operation (manual or automatic) for each line. 3. Line keys: down-select, up-cancel. 4. Indicator lamps: 'line called'. 5. Indicator lamps: 'line calling'. 6. Ringing switch for use by operator: up—automatic ringing; down—manual ringing. 7. 'Auto-dial' switch. When 'on', this permits extensions having dialling facilities to ring each other automatically; in addition normal dialling tone is heard when a receiver is raised. In all other forms of operation the switch is left 'off'. 8. Ringing frequency selection. This apparatus is similar to several used in BBC television studios; but for most purposes a simpler arrangement for interconnecting telephones is adequate.

can produce either manual or automatic ringing tones at 17, 25 or 50 Hz, as required. Lights above each key show the condition of the associated line, showing 'called' or 'calling'. When the automatic button is pressed the selected telephone rings immediately, starting with the start of the first buzz; and it goes on automatically (using the proper ringing tone for the country represented) until either the operator's finger or the phone itself is lifted—when the ringing stops in the proper realistic manner. The use of such an automatic telephone also ensures that the bell itself is heard in the same acoustic and perspective as the actor.

Most 'far end of the telephone' dialing, ringing or engaged tone effects can be provided by the use of a buzzer, etc., on strong filter or by the use of a recording.

Personal action effects

I use this heading to include various sounds that are so individual in their application that it would be almost ludicrous to attempt to use recordings: sounds of a newspaper being folded, a letter being opened, or a parcel undone; or eating and drinking effects.

First, paper noises. Newspaper makes a characteristic noise, but as a spot effect it is as well to treat it in a fairly formalized way, e.g. shake slightly, fold once, and smooth the page. Opening a letter should be similarly formalized into two or three quick gestures, the last action, smoothing out the paper, being tucked under the dialogue (reading, or comment on contents) that follows. The balance needs to be fairly close to the microphone. The type of paper used should be thin but hard surfaced: thick brown paper crackles like pistol shots, airmail paper sizzles like a soda syphon, and duplicating paper provides a somewhat dull sound. With the right sort of paper, the effect is simple but definite. And it is the same with undoing a parcel: a cut, perhaps, then two deft movements to smooth away the paper, and a final slower crinkling noise trailing into the speech that follows.

Many sounds, such as an orchestral conductor tapping his baton, can be made quite realistically (using a music stand); similarly for the chairman's gavel and block (though here it may be as well to soften the quality just a little to avoid sharp peaks, e.g. by binding a layer or two of electrician's tape round the face of the gavel). And again, the quality of surface struck is important: it will not do to hold a small block of wood up in the air; it should be lying on something solid.

Pouring a drink is also inevitably a spot effect. The sound of pouring is itself not a very definite one, and for all but the longest of drinks is over too quickly to establish itself properly; so a clink of bottle on glass helps. But even without this clink it is important to use the right thickness of glass. Health salts do fine for fizzy drinks. A pop-gun may be a shade less acceptable as a champagne cork than the real thing—but it is a degree or two more predictable. If 'tea' or 'coffee' is to be poured into a cup, the effect can be confirmed by placing a spoon in the saucer afterwards—and again the right thickness of china for the occasion is essential.

Sometimes a scene is set at a meal table. For this the complete noise-making set consists of knife, fork, plate, cup, saucer and spoon. It is a good idea to give the noise a rest from time to time—and the right points to choose for this depend on the mood and pace of the script. At any point where the tension rises, stop the effect; as the mood relaxes again, the knives and forks get back to work. It takes only a little of this noise to suggest a lot: listen to a recording of a tea-party for six and you will find that it sounds like crockery noises for twenty.

Gunplay

A rifle shot is one of the simplest sounds you can meet. It is an N-shaped wave like that from a supersonic aircraft: a sharp rise in pressure is followed by a relatively gradual drop to as much below normal pressure. Then there is a second sharp rise in pressure, this time returning it to normal, then nothing—of the original sound, at any rate. The length of the N (its duration in time) depends on how long the object takes to pass a single point. For a supersonic airliner this is short enough—for a bullet it is practically instantaneous. There is just amplitude and brevity. A rifle shot travels at something like twice the speed of sound, and that from a smaller gun at about the speed of sound. Whatever the speed, any loudspeaker would have a hard job to match the movement, however simple. It is perhaps fortunate that what happens after the double pulse is a little more complicated.

In fact, the very size of the initial pulse is itself, in recording or broadcasting, unacceptable; everything must be done to discriminate against it. One way of doing this is to fire (or simulate) the shot on the dead side of the microphone; another is to take it outside the studio door—or into some small room built off the studio—and the door can then be used as a 'fader'. Very often a script calls for loud shouts and noisy action when shots are being fired, which clearly makes it a little easier to deal with the sheer loudness of the effect than if the microphone has to be faded right up for very quiet conversation. The balance used varies from case to case, and experiment is always necessary to check this, so that in each particular case the shot is as loud as the equipment can comfortably handle.

Experimentation is also necessary to judge the appropriate acoustics for the shot: for the sound to be picked up is a picture of the acoustics in their purest form. Shots recorded out of doors are all bang and no die-away, which means that at the level at which they must be replayed they sound like a fire-cracker. So always check the acoustic when balancing a studio shot, and watch out for colorations and flutter echos that may not be noticeable on a more commonplace sound.

A third element in the sound is (or may be) a ricochet—the whining noise made by the jagged, flattened, spinning scrap of metal as it flies off some solid object. And whereas the previous sound is just a noise of the purest type, the ricochet is a highly identifiable and characteristic sound. Even if in reality ricochets are rarer than they might appear from Westerns, they may be used in practically any outdoor context, i.e. anywhere where there is space for a ricochet to take place.

Here are some of the techniques that have been used for gun effects:

1. A real gun. A modified revolver is better than a starting pistol, which some times tends to sound a little apologetic. Legal regulations must be conscientiously observed, and, needless to say, care used in handling the gun. Even blanks can inflict burns. Guns for BBC radio are modified to allow the gas to escape from a

Gun and other
Percussive effects.

point along the bottom of the barrel, and not from the end. The microphone balance adopted is generally that for a maximum ratio of indirect to direct sound.

2. An electronic gunshot generator. This consists of a white noise generator which when triggered into action can produce 'bangs' with a variety of decay characteristics, ranging from staccato to reverberant. In a BBC design (see below) several settings have associated circuitry to produce some very acceptable ricochets.
3. A slap-stick. This is a flat stick with a hinged flap to clap against it. Depending on balance and acoustic conditions, it may sound like a gunshot (though not a good one), the crack of a whip, or just two flat pieces of wood being clapped together. Narrow strips of thick plywood are as good as anything for this.

GUNSHOT EFFECTS
GENERATOR used
in BBC studios.

4. A long, fairly narrow piece of wood, with a string attached to one end. Put the wood on the floor with a foot placed heavily on one end, then lift the other end off the ground with the string and let go. The quality of the sound depends more on the floor surface than it does on the type of wood used. A solid floor is best—stone or concrete.
5. Cane and chair seat. The sound quality again depends on the surface struck. Padded leather gives a good crisp sound.
6. A piece of parchment on a frame, with an elastic band round it: the band can be snapped sharply against the resonant surface. This method is included as an example of the kind of improvisation that the effects man might invent.
7. Recordings of real bangs or of any of the above. The apparent size of any *explosion* can be increased by slowing down a recording. A sharp clap may become a big, rumbling explosion if dubbed down to an eighth or a sixteenth of the original speed.

If the gun itself is used in radio there is no problem in taking it well away from the action. But for television this may not be possible: particularly if the gun is to be fired in vision, perhaps several times, with realistic flashes and smoke and perhaps with dialogue before, between, and after. In this case two microphones are used. The close (dialogue) microphone has a limiter set for 2 dB below 100% modulation; the second is distant and is balanced for a high proportion of reverberation, and may also have echo added

For television gunshots out-of-vision or for radio the BBC uses its own design of generator linked directly to a studio loudspeaker that is balanced acoustically. As they can hear the bang the actors are able to react satisfactorily. The basic sound is provided by a

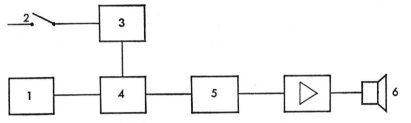

GUNSHOT EFFECTS GENERATOR. 1. White noise generator. 2. Push button. 3. Impulser relay. 4. Gate. 5. Low pass filter. 6. Loudspeaker. The special equipment includes only items 1–5. An existing good quality studio amplifier and loudspeaker unit is used in combination with it.

white noise generator. It passes through a gate (operated by the 'trigger', a push button) and a low-pass filter. The gating circuit allows the white noise passing through to rise sharply from zero to a predetermined peak, is automatically followed by an exponential fall that eventually shuts off the white noise once again. A low-pass filter set for 5 kHz cut-off gives a quality simulating the close shots of a revolver or automatic; set to remove all but the lowest frequencies, it gives distant heavy gunfire—a 'cannon' quality.

A machine-gun effect can be obtained by using an impulser which operates the gate at regular intervals for as long as the button is pressed. In this case the exponential decay is made faster in order to keep the shots separate and distinct. Ricochets are produced by a separate pulsed oscillator, the output from which is rich in harmonics and falls in frequency with time. This oscillator works from the same initial trigger action, but delayed a little.

Creaks, squeaks, swishes, crashes and splashes

Creaks and squeaks offer rich opportunities for improvisation. Over a period of time the enterprising effects man can assemble an array of squeaky and creaky junk just by noticing the noises when they happen and claiming the equipment that makes it. Wooden ironing boards, old shoes, metal paper punches, small cane baskets; anything goes in a collection of this sort.

But there are two rather more organized ways of producing creaks and squeaks:

1. String, powered resin, and cloth. The resin is spread in the cloth, which is then pulled along the taut string. If the string is attached to a resonant wooden panel the sound becomes a creaky hinge. Varying pressure varies the quality of sound.

2. A cork, powdered resin and a hard surface, e.g. polished wood, a tile or a saucer. Place some resin on the surface and slowly

CREAKS AND SQUEAKS, using resin and string; or cork, resin and tile.

grind the flat of the cork into it. Again, the squeak varies in quality with pressure and speed, and with the type of surface and resonator, if any.

The swish of a javelin or arrow may be simulated by swishing a light cane past the microphone. In real battles the arrows must have bounced off stone walls and parapets, making an undramatic clatter. An arrow landing in wood is, however, more satisfying aurally, so convention demands that all the best misses land in wooden panelling and tree-trunks. For this, throw a dart into a piece of wood close to the microphone. Proximity makes a sound grow bigger—so the twang of an elastic band may do well enough for the bow.

Crashes are another reason for hoarding junk—ranging from empty tin cans up to pretty well anything that makes a resonant noise when dropped. But glass crashes demand care. For these, spread out a heavy ground sheet and place a stout cardboard box in the middle. Sprinkle some broken glass in the bottom and place a sheet of glass across the open top of the box. Give this sheet a sharp tap with a hammer, and as it shatters it should all fall inside the box. Have a few odd pieces of glass in the free hand to drop in

286

immediately afterwards. Not difficult—but it may still be just as well to pre-record such a crash, if only to save the worry of having broken glass around on the take (and the same goes for footsteps in broken glass). An additional reason for pre-recording is that successive crashes may not be predictable in quality and volume.

One of the fittings for a well-equipped drama studio is a water tank. If convincing water effects are to be obtained the tank must be nearly full, to avoid any tinny resonance of the space at the top. For any but the gentlest water effects it may be a good idea to protect the microphone—which may have to be close—by hanging a gauze in front of it, or putting it in a plastic bag.

Horses' hooves

Horses' hooves are included as an example of a highly specialized spot-effects technique that dates back a long way but is still valid today. For coconut shells really can be as good as the real thing, if not better—and certainly they are a great deal easier to fit to dialogue.

The secret of a good sound lies not so much in the shells (one shell sawn neatly across the middle) as in the surface. Start with a tray about 3 ft (1 m) across and several inches deep (e.g. a

HORSES HOOVES, traditional method: a pair of half coconut shells.

baker's tray). Fill the bottom with a hard core of stones and put gravel and mixture of sand and gravel on top. For a soft surface place a piece of cloth or felt on top of this at one end of the tray, and bury a few half bricks at the other end to represent cobbles. This will give the qualities of surfaces ordinarily needed for horses' hooves. For horses' hooves (or human footsteps) in snow a tray of broken blocks of salt may be used.

There are three basic actions to simulate: walking, cantering, and galloping, and the rhythm is different for each. When a horse is walking, the rhythm goes clip, clop . . . clip, clop . . . With a shell in each hand use them alternately, but with alternate steps from each shell move forward, digging in the 'toe' of the shell, or backward, digging in the 'heel'. The sequence is left forward, right back (pause), left back, right forward (pause) . . .

In this way a four-legged rhythm is obtained. For the canter the same basic backward and forward action is used, but the rhythm is altered by cutting the pauses to give a more or less even clip, clop, clip, clop, clip, clop, clip, clop. In galloping the rhythm alters to a rapid clipetty clop . . . clipetty clop . . . 1, 2, 3, 4, . . . 1, 2, 3, 4, . . . But there is now no time for the forward and backward movements.

For jingling harness try a bunch of keys and a piece of elastic: the keys hang between the little finger and a solid support to the side of the tray, and jingle in rhthm with the horse's movement.

A special spot-effects microphone is needed for hooves. This should not be too close, and the acoustic should match that used for dialogue.

Obsolescent effects for weather and fire

At one time rain effects were regularly produced by gently rolling lead shot (or dried peas) around in a bass drum; sea wash was produced similarly, but rather more swooshily, while breakers could be suggested by throwing the shot into the air and catching it in the drum at the peak of the swoosh. But high-quality reproduction would reveal the device for what it is, so nowadays a recording of the real thing is likely to be used. However, a bass drum remains a useful item in a spot-effects store—a noise produced by something placed on top of it is given a coloured resonance that may be particularly useful in overemphasizing the character of a sound for comic effect. For example, brontosaurus' footsteps can be made by grinding coconut shells into blocks of salt on a bass drum.

A bright, crackling, spitting fire may be simulated by gently rolling a ball of crinkled cellophane between the hands.

A wind machine consists of a weighted piece of heavy canvas hung over a rotating, slatted drum—but again it is better to use a record of wind, except where the noise is wanted for an orchestral work such a Ravel's *Daphnis and Chloë*, where the ability to control pitch is valuable. But wind comes in many qualities, and its tone should suit the dramatic context. A good recorded effects library has gentle breezes, deep-toned wind, high-pitched wind, wind and rain, wind in trees, wind whistling through cracks, and blizzards for the top of Mount Everest or the Antarctic. A wind machine produces just one sound, wind; and the same applies to thunder sheets. They are not convincing except for comic effects.

The recorded sound picture

There are two distinct types of actuality sound recording: those that create a *sound picture* in themselves, and those that are selective of some particular *sound element* to the virtual exclusion of all others. These two general categories are not only different in content but are based on totally different concepts of sound programme work. The sound picture is the complete picture, a programme item in its own right. But the true recorded sound effect is, like the spot effect, heightened reality; it is the distilled, essential quality of the location or action. It is a simplified, conventionalized sound, the most significant single element of the complete picture.

A sound picture of a quiet summer countryside may have many elements, with plenty of birdsong, perhaps the lowing of cattle a field or two away, and in the distance a train whistle. A beach scene may have voices (shouts and laughter), the squawk of seagulls and distant rush of surf on shingle, and, beyond that, the popping exhaust of a motor boat. As pictures in their own right these may be delightfully evocative, but how would they fit into a play?

In either case it is easy to imagine dialogue to match the scene— but, significantly, it is the speech we have to fit to the sound effect, and not the other way round: in the countryside picture the cows might play havoc with an idyllic love scene, and the distant train whistle would add a distinctly false note to Dick Turpin's ride to York. Similarly, the beach scene is fine—if we happen to be on the sand and not in the boat. And suppose we want to move about within this field of action? With a sound picture we are severely restricted: the only view we ever have is that seen by the artist from the point at which he set up his canvas; we cannot stroll forward and examine one or another subject in greater detail unless he has chosen to do so for us. But if we ourselves are given paints and canvas in stead of a finished picture we can recompose the scene in any of a hundred ways. The true sound effect is the pigment, not the painting:

In a play or in any other programme where recorded effects are to be combined with speech, the final composition of the mixture will at many points be very different from that of a sound picture that has no speech. Consider the beach scene. The first sound to be heard might be a surge of surf on shingle, and, as this dies, the hoarse cry of a gull; then, more distantly, a shout and answering laughter. The second wave does not seem so close, and from behind it emerges the distant exhaust note of the motor boat for a few moments. Then the first words of scripted dialogue are superimposed at a low level upon this picture, and gradually faded up to full. Now the composition of the effects alters. Staccato effects, such as gulls and shouting, must be, in general, rather more distant, and timed with the speech, being brought up highest at points where the dialogue is at its lowest tension, or where characters move off-microphone, or where there are gaps in the dialogue (other than dramatic pauses). The motor boat, too, may go completely or be missing for long stretches, appearing only as a suggestion in such a gap. The individual elements can be peaked up much more readily than the waves themselves, which cannot be subjected to sudden fluctuations in volume without good reason.

When using effects in this way avoid those that have become radio clichés. Because of a programme called 'Desert Island Discs', which starts with seagulls, seawash, and a record of 'The Sleepy Lagoon', it has been difficult to use seagulls and seawash together on British radio. Another warning concerns authenticity in such matters as the location of birds and railways. There are so many experts on the sounds of these things that it is as well to try to get the region right—and in the case of birds the time of year as well.

The use of recorded effects

As the aims differ, when recording a sound picture or sound effects, so also must the recording methods. For effects, the backgrounds must not be obtrusive, nor must the acoustics be strongly assertive on effects that are of a continuous nature; the levels must not be subject to sudden high peaks, and there must be no unexpected changes of character.

A suitable microphone placing for an effects recording may not be the most obvious one. For example, a microphone placed inside a modern, closed car may not pick up any clearly recognizable car sound, so for a car recording—even for an interior effect—the microphone must be deliberately placed to emphasize the continuous engine noise. The mechanical noises associated with gear changes, on the other hand, should not be emphasized (except for starting and stopping), as their staccato quality may interfere with the flow of the script.

An effects sequence, like the composite sound picture, is best constructed from individual elements. Take, for example, a sequence with dialogue in which a car stops just for a short while to pick up a passenger. The elements of this are as follows:

1. Car, constant running.
2. Car, slows to a stop.
3. Tick over.
4. Door opens and shuts.
5. Car revs up and departs.

Of course, a recording could be found with all of these in the right timing and in the right order. But:

1. If there is any considerable amount of dialogue before the cue to slow down, the timing is more flexible if the slowing is on a separate disc or tape. The cue to mix from one to the other should be taken at a point in the dialogue some ten seconds or so before the actual stop, or there will be too marked a change in engine quality. As the sound of a car stopping is lacking in identifiable character, a slight brake squeal or the crunch of tyre on gravel helps to clarify the mental image. The overall level of effects may well be lifted a little as the car comes to a halt.
2. The tickover may well be part of the same recording as the stop. But the microphone balance for a good clear tickover is so different that it may be just as well to record it separately. Fade in the tickover just before the car comes to rest—the point at which the engine is slipped out of gear and begins to idle.
3. Doors opening and slamming must be timed to fit in with dialogue. A real car door shutting is very loud indeed compared with sounds such as the door opening and the tickover, so it needs a separate recording and separate control.
4. Departure could be on the same recording as the tickover, but timing is more flexible if the two are separate and the departure can be cued precisely.
5. Extraneous noises, such as shuffling on seats, footsteps, etc., may well be omitted.
6. Additional sounds—e.g. another door, a motor horn or the characteristic sound of the meter of a London taxi being set— may be cued in at will.

This example is just one of a multitude of such sequences—and each should be thought through as fully as this if the result is to blend into the landscape of sound.

The best way of putting together such sequences depends on the facilities available. At the BBC the tried and trusted way over many years has been to use effects records and a bank of turntables. Tape cassettes are used in a similar way. The flexibility of such a technique is beyond question, and it is necessary to pre-record only the most complex sequences.

An alternative method, using two tape reproducers, is to pre-record into short tailor-made sequences and assemble these in the form of two insert tapes, which can then be used to mix from one to the other at the points where flexibility of timing or of the level of individual components is required. If only one tape reproducer is available, then all the tailoring must be done on a single tape by editing—trimming the tape to fit the dialogue—and it is best to record the effects sequence specially for the programme in which it is to be used.

Recorded effects in stereo

Ideally for stereo drama it is best to use an effect actually recorded in stereo, steering it to its appropriate position and width. Where no suitable recording is available and it is impracticable to make one specially, it is often possible to adapt existing monophonic sounds.

With continuous noises such as rain or crowd effects a stereo picture can be created by using several recordings played out of sync (or one, passed through delay lines with different time delay settings) and steered to different positions within the scene. This works in quadraphonics, too. Rain or crowd scenes could also be fed through an electronic device called a *spreader*, which

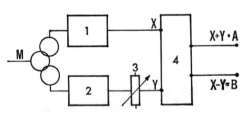

SPREADER CIRCUIT. The monophonic input (M) is split equally between paths X and Y. 1 and 2. Delay networks producing differential phase shift. 3. Spread control fader. 4. Sum and difference network producing A and B components from the X and Y signals.

distributes a mono sound over the whole sound stage like wallpaper. For a distant, moving sound in the open air (or one that passes quickly) panning a mono source is satisfactory. A larger object such as a troop of horses passing close would require a

292

spread source to be panned across, with the spread broadened as the troop approaches and narrowed again as it goes. This effect could also be achieved by panning two mono troops across one after the other; while a coach and four might benefit by spread horses from one recording being followed closely by wheels from another.

In an example illustrating all of these, a horse and carriage may be heard to pan through a spread crowd, until a shot is heard from a particular point, its reverberation echoing over the whole of the sound stage. Note that in stereo sound drama there is a danger of lingering too long on movement that is meaningless in mono: for the sake of compatability this should be avoided.

Similar devices can be used for effects in stereophonic film.

Changing the speed of a recorded effect

The range of sound compositions available from a given set of effects recordings can be increased if the reproducers have more than just a single standard replay speed. The best sort of turntable for disc effects has a continuously variable range of speeds.

Nowadays, however, most high-quality domestic turntables have only certain specific speeds. In musical terms the changes of pitch obtained by switching from $33\frac{1}{3}$ to 45, and again to 78, may appear somewhat irrational; but in terms of changing the quality of sound effects they do amount to a certain degree of versatility. Tape speeds, too, can usually be lifted or dropped an octave and, although this is rather a drastic speed change, an otherwise unavailable effect can sometimes be created.

Equipment designed to operate at given fixed speeds can sometimes be modified to provide speeds that are continuously variable between, say, half and double the nominal speed. This is done by powering the drive motor from a three-phase variable-frequency oscillator.

When the speed of an effect is changed the first difference in quality that presents itself is a change of *size*: slow down the two-stroke engine of a motor lawn-mower and it becomes the lazy chugging of a motor boat—or a small motor boat becomes a heavy canal barge. In the same way, water effects are increased in scale by slowing down the recording—just as filming a model boat in slow motion provides a substitute for the full-size real thing.

As a by-product, it may sometimes happen that reducing the speed gets rid of some unwanted rumble or resonance in the bass.

Speeding up an effect produces the reverse change of quality, e.g. mice talking, and so on. These points should be borne in mind not only to extend the range of already available material but also when planning new recordings. The use of these methods can sometimes save a lot of work.

A change of speed also changes the apparent size of the room in which an effect was recorded: the characteristic colorations go up or down in pitch with everything else. This means that recordings made out of doors may be more conveniently speed-changed than those with indoor acoustics attached. A good subject for drastic transformation is wind. Record a good deep-toned wind and double its speed, and you get a high, stormy wind; double its speed again, and the result may be used for a biting, screaming Antarctic blizzard.

There are times when it seems to be a very good idea to vary the speed of effects while they are being played, but the results often sound weird. Nearly every sound contains some coloration that is essentially fixed in frequency. For example, footsteps should not be bought to a halt by slowing down the last couple of steps, as it will result in a sudden apparent enlargement of the feet (this may be partly compensated for by lowering the volume) and a deepening of the tone quality of the surface.

Speed transformations are considered further on p. 423.

Speed transformations are considered further on p. 423.

The effects library: contents

The contents of an effects library fall into a variety of general classifications.

First, and most important, there are *crowd* effects—a crowd being anything from about six upward. It may seem odd that the very first requirement among recorded effects should be the human voice in quantity, but the fact remains that the illusion of numbers, the cast of thousands, is often essential if a programme is to be taken out of the studio and set in the world at large. The classifications under this general heading are many and various: chatter, English and foreign, indoor and outdoor; the sounds of fear, apprehension, agitation, surprise, or terror; people shouting, whispering, rioting, laughing, booing, applauding, or just standing there and *listening* . . . for the sound of a crowd that is silent except for the occasional rustle, shuffle or stifled cough may at times be as important as the roar of a football crowd. A subdivision of crowd effects is *footsteps* . . . in this case a crowd being anything from two pairs of feet upward.

Then there are *transport* effects: cars, trains, aircraft, boats and all the others (such as horses), doing all the various starting, carrying on, and stopping things that are associated with them, and recorded both with the microphone stationary and moving with the vehicle, and with interior and exterior acoustics where these are different.

Another important group that has links with both of the above is *atmosphere of location* recordings. Streets and traffic (with and without motor horns), railway station, airport or harbour atmosphere of various types and places; all these are needed, as well as the specific identifying noises of London, Paris and New York; also the atmosphere of schoolroom, courtroom, museum, shop or concert hall, and the distinctive sounds of many other locations.

The *elements*—*wind*, *weather*, *water*, and *fire*—provide another vital field. Then there are the sounds of all branches of human activity: *industrial* sounds, *sport*, *domestic* effects from the ticking of clocks to washing up, and the sounds of *war*. There are *animals*, *birds*, *babies;* and dozens of other classifications of sound, such as *bells*, *sirens*, *atmospherics*, *electrical* sounds, etc.

The effects library: disc or tape

An effects library may be built up using disc or tape—or both.

The disc effects library. One or more copies of a wide variety of records is kept (these may be purchased from a variety of commercial sources, or, as at the BBC, specially pressed). The records from such a library get a great deal of use in the process of selection and rehearsal, and so must be replaced frequently. In a large library it is easy to sift through a dozen different recordings that are nominally suitable to find out which is best and which will not do at all. It is possible to go to the studio with two or three specimens of each sound: one the likely best bet, and others sufficiently different in character to provide alternatives in case, on adding the sound to dialogue, the first turns out to be wrong in mood, level or timing. A different disc can be readily substituted at any point in a production. But some expertise in disc-playing is needed for programmes with complex effects. The recordings on BBC effects discs are laid out in bands, and each is preceded by a burst of tone, growing in volume, then cutting off sharply. Accurate cueing is made possible by the quick-start techniques described later (pp. 315–317).

The tape effects library. When tape is used there are two conflicting requirements. One is for the storage of a wide selection of effects; the other is for immediate accessibility, both for sampling and for rapid setting up in the studio. To store a very large number of effects normal (but small) spools may be used, with many recordings each identified by a separate spacer or some other marking on the tape. Such a store is, however, inconvenient for operational use and is likely to hinder a thorough search for the exact sound. It might perhaps be used by dubbing the sounds required in sequence on to a programme tape (or alternate effects to two tapes). But the result is inflexible: if even one effect proves unsatisfactory or is dropped, the system is disrupted much more than if each effect were handled individually.

Small *tape cassettes* are much more satisfactory than normal spools. No time is spent in lacing up, and they can be automatically reset to the start. But for a store of substantial size a very large number of cassettes is required. A possible compromise is to hold permanently on cassette those effects that are most in demand; complementing them with effects transferred to cassette from the larger library (tape or disc) or specially recorded either in the studio or on location.

It may be noted that cassettes are particularly suitable for short running effects that start abruptly on cue: in other words, they provide a very convenient tape equivalent to what I have previously described as studio spot effects. As a result, the designers of the various types of automatic effects-reproducing machines that use tape as a medium have tended to emphasize the 'spot' facility rather than continuous running as their major advantage.

Automatic replay devices

Of a very large range of possible effects-playing machines using tape and with some degree of automatic operation, I will describe two that are representative of different approaches to the problem. Neither requires manual threading of tape; both set themselves up automatically at the start of the tape. As it happens, neither of those described here can automatically set themselves up at a given point within a recording (this is in marked contrast to the ease with which this can be done by most manually operated systems—both tape and disc), but instead they can be used for re-recording the given feature at the start of a section of tape. They reproduce the required effect almost instantaneously on pressing the start button or key, and can also be used for standard spot announcements, jingles or radio commercials.

The continuous-loop cartridge. Loops of various lengths are used—say of ten, twenty or thirty seconds. This allows sounds of various durations to be recorded (and, in principle, steady continuous sounds). When the replay button is pressed the loop is played through until the starting-point is reached again, when it automatically stops to await further replay. The cartridge is engaged by being pushed into the slot: when pressed fully home it is immediately ready for replay. To disengage the cartridge a 'reject' button is pressed: the cartridge emerges partly from the

ENDLESS TAPE. 1. The tape is lubricated with graphite so that it slips easily when on the spool. 2. Drive roller. 3. Output from reproducing head.

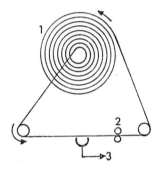

slot and may now be removed by hand. Reset time depends on the length of tape that remains to be played through after the required effect has been reproduced. This is the reason for having a range of cartridges of different durations, rather than using a single length of loop for all purposes.

The keyboard effects console. Looking rather like an electronic organ (or harmonium), this type of replay machine has a tape associated with each key, which is played for as long as the key is pressed. On the machine to be described here, the Mellotron, each key has the tape physically below it, and pressing the key presses the pinch roller down against the tape and drive capstan, which is already turning as long as the machine is switched on. The key also mechanically operates a pressure pad to hold the tape against the reproducing head.

297

At any particular time 6 ft (1·8 m) of tape lies between two storage rollers, which remain static during replay of the effects on the section lying between them. When the key is pressed a spring-loaded loop of tape in front of the head is drawn over the reproducing head and dropped into a tape storage box on the other side. When the key is released the tape is drawn rapidly back to the starting position by the return spring. Again, the reset time depends on the duration of the effect, but this time in a different way: the starting position is resumed in a fraction of the replay time, and the shorter the replay, the faster the reset. This means that repeated staccato sounds, e.g. hammer blows or (using pairs of adjacent keys) left foot, right foot sequences of footsteps can be run in any rhythm, and if necessary (and given an adequate sense of timing by the operator) synchronized with picture.

The Mellotron replays at $7\frac{1}{2}$ i/s (19 cm/s), with a facility for variation a little either way—giving at normal speed a usable eight seconds only. (Longer continuous sequences can be put together, but not always very successfully when the sound is supposed to be smooth and continuous—a disadvantage of this design.) A non-standard tape width permits three normal 'half-tracks' to be accommodated side by side, any one of which can be selected

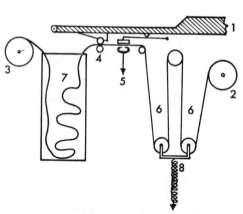

MELLOTRON EFFECTS CONSOLE. 1. One key and its associated tape. 2 and 3. Store. The effect required is selected in advance from those available; the storage rollers do not move when an effect is being played. 4. When the key is pressed the pinch roller holds the tape against the capstan. 5. Reproducing head. 6 and 7. The tape is transferred from two deep loops to the storage bin. When the key is released the pulleys and spring (8) draw the tape rapidly back into its original loops. The Mellotron has a keyboard like a harmonium.

by sideways movement of the replay head. Also, the total length of tape under each key and the associated storage spools is sufficient for six effects tracks to be recorded along the length of the tape; so that each key has 18 effects available to it. As there are 70 keys the machine holds a total of 1260 effects—a number that sounds a lot, but may be found to be curiously limited in practice.

Acoustic foldback

In certain cases, usually where lively acoustics are being used, it is possible to route prerecorded sound effects through the studio via a loudspeaker. It is of greater advantage to do this when the pre-recording is very dry—for an outdoor recording, perhaps, or one made with a very close balance. Passing the sound through the studio adds the same recognizable acoustic qualities that are on voices present in the studio. An additional advantage is that actors have something to work to, and can pitch their voices against the sound or react to it in a realistic way. The main danger with this technique is that the loudspeaker/microphone combination can all too easily introduce excessive coloration or even distortion.

There is not usually room for the loudspeaker at the same microphone as the actors, so a specially placed microphone is often necessary. A close balance should generally be adopted. Foldback is fed via a separate fader on the control desk. The volume of the studio loudspeaker amplifier should be set at such a level that most of the range of the input fader is in use. These two controls are used in combination to set the sound level in the studio; what comes out of the studio is governed by the position of loudspeaker relative to the microphone, and the settings of the microphone faders on the mixer. A little experiment is necessary to find the optimum settings for the various elements in the chain—if a satisfactory result can be obtained at all. This technique will not improve the match between effect and studio if the effect is already brighter than it should be and the studio is dead.

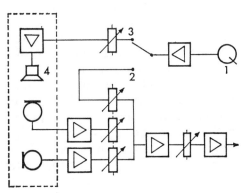

ACOUSTIC FOLDBACK.
1. Tape or disc reproducers, which are normally fed direct to the mixer via switch contact (2), may sometimes be switched (3) to provide an acoustic feed to the studio loudspeaker (4).

Sound effects for television and film

All the effects that have been described here work well out-of-vision on television. Recorded effects are likely to be preferred to spot effects, which in turn are more often recorded in advance and played in from a sound tape: this helps to limit the number of open microphones and produces more predictable results when the director has many more elements to watch and listen to at the same time. However, in-vision sound effects are still produced by some practical props. These need the same care in balancing that they would be given in sound radio, but here in more adverse conditions.

Often an effect that can be picked up satisfactorily on a speech microphone sounds much better if given its own close effects microphone. For example, a studio discussion about radioactivity using a geiger counter could have a small 'personal' microphone hidden near the loudspeaker of the counter. In this example a recorded effect could not have been used successfully because the rates would not have varied realistically; because the people present would not have been able to react properly to the rates; and because a meter was sometimes shown in close-up, working synchronously with the clicks. The effects microphone made it possible to vary not just the volume but also the quality of the sound at appropriate points in the discussion, so that the clicks could be soft and unobtrusive at points where they were not central to the discussion, and hard and strong when they were the centre of interest. This is an extreme example of one use for effects, but there are many others: for example, where clear, crisp action noise enhances an otherwise quiet sequence.

As in sound radio, recorded effects are used to suggest atmosphere. Effects plus a camera track in over the heads of six extras may convince the viewer that he has seen a shot of a crowded bar; or film may establish a street scene and the sound may continue over a shot in the studio set showing a small part of the street.

Television introduces an extra dimension to sound effects that radio never had, the ability to jump easily between different viewpoints—say, between interior and exterior of a car or train. For fast-cut sequences it is convenient to use a twin track effects tape with interior on one track and exterior on the other. The operator simply fades quickly from one to the other on each of the appropriate cuts or uses a device that automatically links sound with vision cuts (as in the telephone effects switching unit, p. 395). It

300

is in any case useful to pre-record effects sequences for complex scenes in television, for which little rehearsal time is available in the studio itself.

Footsteps in vision

Where footsteps are to be heard in the studio, the television or film designer must help sound by providing suitable surfaces. Rostra, in particular, cause problems. Stock rostra are generally made with a folding frame supporting a wooden surface which gives a characteristic hollow wooden sound to footsteps. An action area on rosta should therefore be treated to reduce this to reasonable proportions: a suitable treatment would be to 'felt and clad', i.e. to surface the rostra with a layer of thick felt with hardboard on top. On this, footsteps are audible but no longer have the objectionable drumming sound. If little or no footsteps are to be heard a further soft layer of rug or carpeting is needed.

For 'outdoor' areas the use of a sufficiently large area of peat not only deadens the surface but may also deaden the acoustic locally. But certain materials commonly found out of doors cannot be used in television studios. *Sand* cannot be used, as it spreads too easily, gets in technical equipment, and makes an unpleasant noise when a thin layer is ground under the feet. Sawdust is a convenient substitute. For similar technical reasons salt and certain types of artificial snow cannot be used: again substitutes may be found that do not cause sound problems.

Rocks are rarely used in studios, because they are too heavy and inconvenient. Wooden frames covered with wire netting and surfaced with painted hessian have been used, as have fibreglass mouldings or expanded polystyrene carved into suitable shapes. Unfortunately, none of these has a satisfactory sound quality, so any climbing, rubbing or bumping must be done with the utmost care by the performers—and then preferably only at places that have been specially arranged not to resonate, perhaps by using peat or sawdust either as a surface layer or packed in sandbags. Falling 'rocks' of expanded polystyrene must have recorded sound effects exactly synchronized—which is easier if the action is seen in big close-up, with the rocks falling through frame, rather than wide-angle. Film gives a better guarantee of achieving realistic effects, as individual elements of the sound can be precisely positioned on the track. Expanded polystyrene can sometimes squeak when trodden or sat on, and particularly when small pieces are ground against the hard studio floor. Problems of this sort can be so difficult to overcome that it is always worth considering filming or pre-recording on location.

Sidewalk *paving stones* are often simulated by fibre-glass mouldings, as these are light and convenient to hold in stock. When laid in the studio they should stand on cloth or hessian to stop any rocking and to damp the resonance somewhat. If, in addition, performers are wearing rubber-soled shoes and there is recorded atmosphere the results should be satisfactory. But if synchronous footsteps are to be heard there is no satisfactory alternative to the real thing, despite the inconvenience and weight.

Stone floors can be simulated by the use of a special $\frac{1}{2}$ in (12·5 mm) simulated stone composition sheeting laid on underfelt. But 'stone' steps that are actually constructed of wood are very likely to cause trouble if the sound effect is required (and often if it is not). If a close effects microphone with good separation can be used for the footsteps there is some chance of improvement, as heavy bass cut can then also be used.

A play series centred on a prison camp in a castle had trouble throughout a television season with its simulated cobbles and fibreglass doorsteps around the courtyard. For a second run the film-set was constructed using real cobbles and stone—which, to everyone's surprise turned out better not only for sound, but also for the programme budget.

Wind, rain and fire in vision

The sound effects for wind, rain, and fire create no problem: recordings are used as in radio. It is when they must be combined with visual effects that the trouble starts: the usual problem is that the device that makes the right picture sometimes makes the wrong noise, which must therefore be suppressed as much as possible, to be replaced by the proper recorded effect.

Wind is generated by machines varying in size from the very large aircraft-propellor-type fans about 8 or 9 ft (2·5 m) in diameter, through medium sizes 3 or 4 ft (1 m) in diameter and which can be moved round on a trolley, down to small machines about 18 in (45 cm) in diameter, which can be set on a lamp stand and used for relatively localized effects.

The large and medium sizes are very noisy and push out a large volume of air over much of the studio (if they are used indoors). Windshields are needed for any boom or other microphones within range. The largest size may be used for the controlled single shots of a film, but is inconvenient in the television studio, where the smallest size is best. When run at a relatively low speed, the noise produced actually sounds like wind (at higher speeds blade hum is heard). The visual effect is localized and controllable, so that microphones may be avoided.

Rain, when produced in the television studio, may be far too noisy, so it should be arranged for the water to fall on soft material in a tray with good drainage. Also, if it is being used in the foreground of the shot the feed pipe may be close to the ideal microphone position, making balance on a boom difficult. Another problem is that it takes a little while to get going and even longer to stop completely, to the last drip. This may be overcome either by slow mixes to and from effects (including recorded effects) accompanying the transition to and from the rain scene or by discontinuous recording and subsequent videotape editing.

Fire—including coal and log fires—in television studios is usually provided by gas (with visual flicker effects added by lighting.) Unfortunately, gas does not burn with a sound appropriate to other flames, so again recorded effects have to be used (though usually at a very low level). Any hiss of the gas tap can be prevented by leaving the tap fully open at the burner, controlling the flow instead from the tap at the studio wall.

Sound equipment in vision

When radios, television sets, record players and tape machines are used as props by actors in television programmes they are rarely practical—obviously, the sound gallery want to retain control so that the most suitable sound balance can be maintained at all times, and also so that there is perfect sound cueing in and out. This means that careful rehearsal is necessary for exact synchronization of action.

The actors rehearse in advance without cameras, so there is a tendency for them to slide in to sloppy visual habits—and particularly with tape recorders. Everyone who has ever used a tape recorder knows that to spool fast backward or forward and always land on the right word without any cueing aids is virtually impossible; but actors, assisted by the sound gallery, do it all the time; and rarely with even a hint of awareness that the writer is asking them to be just a little lucky in their guesswork.

Writers generally show more awareness with radios and television sets, though all too often we hear half of a previous sentence and then go straight in to the item that is required for the plot. This is one of those places where téchnique all to easily becomes noticeable—and if it is added to clumsy programme construction it makes it much worse.

Occasionally such items are read live from a microphone in a distant part of the studio, but pre-recording is generally preferred, because control of sound quality (by filtering) is easier. Where it is necessary for cueing the actors the sound is fed at low level to a studio loudspeaker.

Pre-recordings using the studio itself are sometimes used for out-of-vision sound. This may allow the correct perspective to be obtained or, more often, it is used simply to fix one element in an otherwise all-too-flexible medium. Music is often pre-recorded where complicated song and dance numbers are to be performed— and frequently in a different acoustic and with a close balance, both of which create matching problems.

Sound effects on film

In film, effects are used in the dubbing (see p. 481) to maintain a continuous background of sound, or to define a particular quality of near silence. But in addition, effects of the 'spot' type are made easier by the process of synthesis that is used to create films from many individually directed short scenes, within each of which the sound element may be given greater care than in the continuous take of the television studio. A live action effect recorded synchronously as a scene is filmed may be enhanced in a number of ways:
1. It may be changed in volume at the dubbing.
2. A second copy of the effect may be laid alongside on another track, so that it can be changed in quality and volume to reinforce the original sound.
3. The timing may be altered, e.g. for an explosion filmed from a distance the noise can be resynchronized visually, and not left trailing behind as in the original recording (which is out of synchronization because of the time taken for the sound to reach the microphone).
4. The original effect may be replaced or overlaid by a totally different recording, again in exact synchronization with picture.

In the film industry, the provision of footsteps and other spot effects may be a separate stage in post-production, and is the province of specialists called foley artists in America. Their skill

304

permits the film director to concentrate on picture and action in locations where there is extraneous noise from traffic, aircraft, production machinery or direction; or where the acoustics or flooring (for footsteps) are inappropriate (see page 277 for techniques). The tracks are recorded or laid to picture and can be adjusted, treated and pre-mixed as required, before the final re-recording session.

Even if a particular staccato sound works well on the speech microphone, it may be better if recorded wild-track (i.e. without picture) and given its own special balance. But when neither work satisfactorily, some other spot sound simulating the proper noise may be tried.

For example, take the case of a bulldozer knocking down a street sign. In the main synchronous recording the dominant noise is the engine and machinery noise of the bulldozer: the impact of blade on metal is hardly heard. So a second version of the noise of impact is simulated, e.g. by using a brick to strike the metal, recorded separately and without any bulldozer engine noise. This is then added in the dubbing. If the bulldozer is knocking down a wall the sound is complicated still further, and the dramatic importance of three sounds may be the inverse of their actual volumes: impact noise may once again be the most important; then the sound of falling masonry; then the bulldozer engine and mechanical noise. In this case several recordings of the principal event could be made with different microphone positions (on either side of the wall), perhaps with additional sounds recorded separately to be incorporated at the dubbing stage. Obviously if this much effort is to be worthwhile, the sound effect being created must be one that really adds to the dramatic experience of the audience.

Commercials and documentary features sometimes make use of punctuating sound effects. An item of equipment built up stage by stage by stop-action techniques, for example, has a series of parts suddenly appearing in vision: each time this occurs there may be a staccato noise in the sound that might be a recorded 'plug-in', or something tapped on a metal surface, or indeed any other sound that may be felt to be relevant. Cash-register noises accompanying messages about the amazingly low price of a product have been overdone: such music may delight the man who pays for the commercial more than the customer whose money is taken. But there is a vast potential for non-representational, comic or cod effects in commercials.

11

RECORDED AND REMOTE SOURCES

RECORD players and tape reproducers (plus, in television, video-tape and film sound) together with lines from other studios and remote locations, are all fed to the control desks of radio or television studios. They are programme sources comparable to the studio microphone and have their own operational routines. The techniques for tape and disc replay described here are valid equally for monophonic or stereophonic sound; they are valuable to television and in the film dubbing theatre, and vital to radio. In radio, in particular, many programmes consist of a sequence of records or recordings.

Each small segment of this type of programme is collected, selected or pre-recorded individually. The creative process is spread out in time, and each element may have lavished upon it all the care that it demands for perfection—within the limits of human fallibility and commercial pressures. So far, the technique is very similar to that of film making and indeed the final putting together of the programme has much in common with the film dubbing session. With a sound production there often comes a stage where all the pre-recording is complete, and all the 'insert' material is taken back to the studio to be re-recorded into a complete programme, using live links.

In order to match levels, mix in effects, introduce fades and avoid abrupt changes of background atmosphere, tapes where possible should be played in, not cut in to the programme. Each insert must be controlled afresh, so that it is fully integrated into its new setting—and particularly in terms of the relative levels at the beginning and end of each insert. The subtler points of mixing from one sound into another are considered in the next chapter; here we are more concerned with the operation of the reproducing decks and turntables themselves. Perhaps the most important aspect of this is good timing, for where successive sounds are linked by mixing it is unlikely that faults of timing can be put right by subsequent editing; in any case, on a radio transmission there is no calling back miscues.

In broadcast automation systems tape replay is controlled by cueing systems that sense tone (or silence). In one example each recording has, superimposed at the end, a 25 Hz signal that provides two cues. As the sensing amplifier detects the beginning of the 25 Hz tone it starts the next tape in the playback sequence; and at the end of the 25 Hz signal it stops the first playback. But should that system fail, or should a playback break down in the middle, another sensing system takes over. In this a second amplifier is used to listen for any period of silence: this, too, cues the next channel to start.

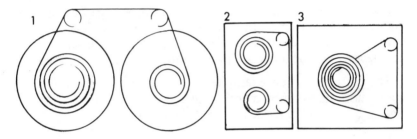

TAPE TRANSPORT SYSTEMS. 1. Reel-to-reel. 2. Cassette. 3. Cartridge, a continuous loop. Pressing the cartridge record button automatically puts a tone (below the audible frequency range) on the tape. On replay, when this point on the tape returns to the head, the tape is stopped automatically, then recued ready for immediate replay. The recycling time depends on the length of tape in the loop. In a four-track configuration the first two tracks are available for programme material, the third has auxiliary tone or data as required, and the fourth has the stop tone. On a cassette, the auxiliary tone can be used to stop the tape and switch to rewind back to the leader, at which point the tape stops and runs forward to recue at the first stop tone. Tape cue tracks may also have time code recorded on them for automatic synchronization with videotape, etc.

These devices are capable of cueing the routine transmission of a large number of items of a random nature very effectively; but in this and the next chapter the older, manual techniques are described. These are the techniques still used for most creative production work—in fact, to build the programmes or items that can subsequently be broadcast automatically—and they are also the techniques that, in their most developed form, the automatic equipment must try to simulate, or against which it must, in the final resort, be judged.

'Live-and-insert' programmes

The linked actuality programme is a typical example of what might be termed 'live-and-insert' type of work. Here on-the-spot recordings in the form of sound effects and interviews are collected and arranged in a sequence that helps to tell a story. Unless a concentrated effort is made to ensure that each collected item leads into the next—i.e. unless a certain amount of stage-managing is done at the time—linking narration is almost certainly necessary.

Another type of programme that is very similar in construction is the illustrated report, in which summary, comment, and discussion in the studio are mixed with extracts from recordings of the events that are being dealt with (parts of the talk and discussion may also have been recorded in advance). Disc-jockey shows, whether of pop or serious music, may also be regarded as live-and-insert programmes. In this case we can be sure that exquisite care has been exercised at the time of recording the 'inserts'; their arrangement in the form of a programme deserves some care, too.

These are just a few examples of the technique, and there are many more that combine both tape and disc with live narration. The script of such a feature might look like this:

1.	TAPE	(BELLS. *Actuality: Peal from beginning. 15″ and fade under.*)
2.	NARRATOR	Bells. Bells to proclaim to the world that a new cathedral stands ready for the praise of God.
3.	TAPE	(HYMN, *Actuality. Lose bells behind. Fade singing on end of first verse, and out before start of second.*)
4.	NARRATOR	But this is a story which began one quiet night (*Begin to fade in grams*) in 1940.
5.	GRAMS	(NIGHTINGALE. *Fade in drone of* BOMBERS *until nightingale drowned out. Add some distant* ANTI-AIRCRAFT FIRE. *Hold bombers behind speech.*)
6.	NARRATOR	The bombers swept across the quiet countryside to the city. In the centre of the city, the old cathedral . . .
7.	GRAMS	(BOMB *screams down and explodes.*)
8.	NARRATOR	. . . a glory of Gothic architecture. Windows of richly stained glass, set in delicate traceries . . .
9.	GRAMS	(BOMB, *tinkle of* BROKEN GLASS.)
10.	NARRATOR	. . . carvings and statuary that were the life-work of countless medieval craftsmen . . .
11.	TAPE	(*Prerecorded effects sequence: 2* BOMBS, *begin to fade in* FIRE: *hold this, but gradually lose record of bombers.*)

308

12.	NARRATOR	. . . the hammer beam roof a triumph of human ingenuity . . .
		(*Effects sequence continues: several* FALLING TIMBERS *followed by* CRASH *as roof falls in.* FIRE *up to full, and fade to silence.*)
13.	NARRATOR	With the cathedral had gone many other buildings. The centre of the city was largely a wasteland. Rebuilding could not be started until after the war. But nothing could stop people dreaming of the future . . . and planning for it in practical terms.
14.	TAPE	(*Interview, as edited. Quick fade in on atmosphere.*)
		At first there was quite a lot of opposition to the idea of a new cathedral: well, of course, people said houses first and the new city centre, shops; the cathedral could come later . . .

This script requires two tape insert machines, a bank of turntables, and a microphone. Given such resources, the results might be very effective—but remember that it is the subject that provides the greatest strength, not just the techniques; and among the techniques the most important is the one that costs nothing—good timing.

Preparing tape inserts

Each insert must first be considered as though it were a programme in its own right: it must go through all the processes of rough and fine editing that are needed to give it point and clarity of expression. One can often afford to be more drastic at this stage than would be possible in editing a complete programme. For anything that does not quite come off may be cut out without necessarily being completely lost; the essence of confused or muddled actuality can generally be tied into the script in a way that makes it both lucid and concise.

Heavy background effects should be recorded for long enough before and after speech to allow for fades (or, alternatively, a loop or an effects record can be used to cover the ends and provide the fade). Indeed, it is not a bad idea to allow a second or two of atmosphere at the end, if not at the beginning, even in cases where this is not heavy. The intake of breath before the speaker's first word may be left on the tape. At normal listening levels neither atmosphere nor breath are particularly noticeable, but their absence might be. Special care is needed when recordings of speech are interpolated between music recordings or gramophone records, on which the background of studio atmosphere may be very low indeed.

All the various pre-recorded segments of the programme can be made up into a single insert tape (omitting only the items that have to be mixed or crossfaded from a separate replay machine). Short spacers, one or two seconds long, give a visual indication of where one insert ends and the next begins. If atmosphere has been left on the front of the inserts some sort of mark is necessary to indicate the point at which the tape should be faded full in. Use a felt marker pen or a wax pencil. The end of the spacer indicates only the point at which the fade-in starts.

At this stage of a production a convenient form of script is one that gives the narration in full but the inserts in cue form (and also showing their duration)—something like this:

NARRATOR	. . . spoke on his return to London Airport.
TAPE	*Insert* 10. *Dur: 27″* *In:* What we all want to know . . . *Out:* . . . or so they tell me (laughter)
NARRATOR	The minister stressed the need for unity between the two countries and then said:
TAPE	*Insert* 11. *Dur: 30″* *In:* It's all very well to be critical . . . *Out:* . . . there's no immediate danger of that.

Note that on this script there are two different types of cue-in from the narration. The first needs about the length of a normal sentence pause. But the second piece of narration ends with a *suspended cue*, which demands to be linked closely to the sentence that follows. In the first case the fade-up of atmosphere may follow the cue; in the other it needs to be tied under the last words of the cue. In the second case the timing also depends on the pace of the first sentence recorded on the tape. For instance, 'It's (pause) all very well . . .' would sound ludicrous if tied too close to the cue '. . . and then said:'.

I have been assuming that what is wanted here is the simplest form of fade, but there are various circumstances in which more complex joins between narration and insert might be needed for the most tidy, or artistic effect. How such fades and mixes can best be arranged is considered in more detail in the next chapter.

At this stage the thing to note is the importance of marking up the script to indicate in some sort of bold private shorthand all the peculiarities of each individual cue. The purpose of a rehearsal is to examine these in detail, and unless the programme is being

310

assembled by a trial-and-error method, or in short sections, cues come up so thick and fast on the actual take that some quick visual reminder of what is needed for each one should be kept at hand in all but the simplest sequences, and used as a musician uses a sheet of music. This marked-up script is in a very real sense the score—and there is no real virtue in trying to play it from memory.

The main things to mark on the script are as follows:
1. Location of material.
2. Any peculiarities of timing.
3. Volume control settings and type of fade in.
4. Duration (or other means of noting in advance when the out-cue is coming up).
5. Type of fade-out.

When the tape is being played in there is no obligation to hold exactly to what has been worked out, but by using this method you have a standard to work from and perhaps to improve on.

Cueing tapes

First, it is necessary to check how long the tape takes to come up to speed. There are two conditions that one may start from:
1. Motor switched off. In this case the flywheel attached to the drive motor has to be set in motion. Check the run-up time by using a recording of pure tone; set the start of the tone back at various distances from the head, and then switch on. If the setting is too close the tone will be clearly heard climbing to its true pitch; whereas if it is back a long way there will be no appreciable wow. Find the point at which for pure tone a very slight slide-in is just noticeable, and this is the amount of setting-back needed for speech and most music.
2. Instantaneous start—by means of pause control, etc. The drive motor is left running, but the idler pulley is lifted from it. Here mechanical considerations no longer apply and the set-back distance can be short. Tight cueing is the best safeguard against last-second changes of pace in a live cue.

In either case it is worth practising and getting the feel of the timing. Set up the tape, start it, and fade up. Remember not to start up until the run-in is complete: there must always be that pause—however short it may have been made—between starting the tape and the beginning of the fade-in. This pause must certainly be observed if you are not coming in at the start of the tape;

otherwise you will get a wow (if only on atmosphere), or for the 'instantaneous' start we might hear the tape jerk into motion. Do not get trigger-happy; it is as much a fault to flick the fader open too quickly as it is to be slow off the mark.

Again, do not rely entirely on remembered timing to give the delay between start and fade: watch as the tape runs up to speed and fade up as the marker passes its reference point. In this way you can use different machines without being thrown by differences in run-up time. With many reproducers the whole operation can be performed with one hand. The free hand may then be used for other operations which have to be carried out at the same time —as when mixing from one tape to another.

A typical case for a mix is presented by speech tapes with different background effects. Assuming for a moment that the changeover point is internal to both tapes, there are several ways of doing the mix, depending on the lengths of pauses between words on each of the two tapes. In the simplest case there is a full sentence pause or paragraph pause on both tapes, and we have the option of retaining the whole of this at its natural length.

In preparing to make the mix, first examine the length of the pauses in both cases (and if in doubt mark their beginnings and ends). Set back the normal run-up time from the start of the pause on tape two. Now, watch or listen to tape one carefully as the cue comes up, and at a predetermined point in the last words that are wanted run tape two, so that the start of the pause arrives on both reproducers at the same time. Then fade in tape two to full (or nearly full) before starting to fade the other one out. (If the two fades were made simultaneously there would be an unwanted dip in atmosphere.) By varying the time of entry of the second tape the pause can be lengthened or shortened. And if one or other of the originals has no pause, it should still be possible to arrange a tidy mix; for example, if there is no pause at the outpoint of the first tape, then the second can be cued in and faded up early. Where there is no pause available on either side, it is necessary to fill in with matching atmosphere from somewhere else on the tape.

In all of these cases care must be taken to match levels (this is one of the reasons why it may be necessary to mix, rather than edit) and one of the commonest ways of doing this is to edge one side of the join in or out a few dB to avoid a sudden doorstep effect on the voice. The same technique can be used where heavy atmosphere is cut off close to the last, or first, word.

Preparing disc inserts

With disc (usually music or effects) there is no arrangement directly comparable with the insert tape, so it is much more important to be able to find a place on a disc very quickly; to be able to put the disc on the turntable, locate the right groove, and the right part of that groove, and set the record up ready for playing in, all in a matter of a few seconds. There are special quick-start techniques for playing discs in accurately, but in all other matters of cueing and timing there is no essential difference between tape and disc.

In a complex programme there may be many cues, creating extra problems of storage and location of material; for instead of one or two pre-edited tapes, there may be a large number of discs, some of which may have to be used several times at different places in the programme. Some simple system of quick identification is necessary. Start by numbering the spaces in a record rack, and then as the sequence of discs is established number these too, and also the script at the corresponding points. Except for the times when they are actually needed for playing, keep the discs on the rack. In any case, they should be treated with care: to avoid touching the grooves hold a record with two hands by the outer edge, or one-handed by supporting it at the label with the fingers at the rim with the thumb.

For numbering discs, use a wax pencil, and write on the smooth part of the record just outside the label, so that the number can later be rubbed off with a paper tissue. If you do not expect the rack to be more than half full, number only alternate spaces so that if extra discs have to be put in there will be spaces for them.

One property of disc is that successive excerpts can be found quickly without having to run through intervening material: the head is lifted, relocated and the stylus lowered. With a steady hand it can be placed manually within a few grooves of a predetermined cue. It is convenient to have a design in which the stylus is easily visible.

Another advantage of disc is that modulation of the groove can be seen. A point source of light reflected in an unmodulated part of the record shows up as a characteristically smooth-edged radial line. As the modulation of the groove becomes heavier, the light is more diffused, and the reflection becomes smudged at the sides of the radial line. The progress of a symphonic work can be 'read' as easily as the volume markings in the score.

In the days of 78s it was possible to mark the actual groove with a wax pencil sharpened to a knife edge. For microgroove, however, some additional location device is necessary. BBC studios are equipped with record players which optical groove-locating units: a mirror is fixed beneath the pivot and throws the

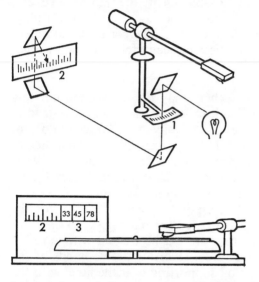

OPTICAL GROOVE LOCATOR. 1. Scale fixed to the pick-up pivot. 2. Ground glass screen displaying projected image of scale. This indicates the exact position of the needle on the radius of the disc. It is accurate to within the error produced by groove-swing (which can also be seen very clearly). 3. Il-luminated panel indicating the speed chosen.

image of a scale on to a ground-glass screen. This also shows any 'swing' in the record due to the grooves not being accurately centred on the hole, a condition that can cause wow on sustained notes of music.

The type of locator which sits on the spindle and extends in an arc round in front of the pick-up head (the other end being held in

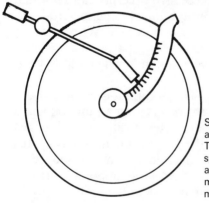

SIMPLE ARC SCALE LOCATOR for finding a position rapidly within an unmarked disc. The scale is rested over the turntable spindle at one end and in the hand or on a block at the other. Such scales have been manufactured in plastic, but can also be made very simply from card.

the hand), although not very satisfactory for quick operational work, is useful for scripting disc programmes where selection work has to be done on a record player away from the studio. A ruler, indicating distance from the centre, is better than nothing.

Cueing discs

To get a clean start in the middle of a work it may be necessary to fade up within a fraction of an inch of the start of a note. For real accuracy of timing the disc is stopped in preparation for the cue, and then, on cue, the disc is set in motion and faded up, as with tape.

Having found the place roughly, lift the stylus back a few grooves and run up to the point again, switching off the motor before reaching it, and bringing the turntable to halt as the in-cue passes under the stylus. Indicate the start of the required sound by putting a mark opposite it just outside the label. For this, use the soft wax pencil again. Check the mark by running the disc again: the sound should start just as the mark is opposite the stylus. The head is then set back once again and the disc stopped at a distance appropriate to the run up time that will be required. It is necessary to be able to hear output on headphones before the disc is faded up (either locally or at the main desk) and also whether or not the drive motor is switched on.

Quick-start techniques fall into two categories, depending on the type of drive employed by the turntable. These represent the extremes, and others fall between them.

1. Rim drive. The turntable gets up to its full speed quickly after the motor is switched on. Set up with the drive disengaged and then re-engage with the motor switched off. On cue, switch on and as the mark passes the stylus, fade up. Do not leave the turntable standing with the drive engaged for long periods: this can cause a 'flat' on the idler wheel. Alternatively, have the turntable running, but hold a slip mat with the record on it, then release it on cue.

2. Centre drive. Here the turntable acts as a large flywheel (to even out any short-period speed variations). The flywheel is driven by a motor that may be small compared with the power needed to get the turntable quickly to speed. One method for dealing with this is a spin start—a sort of assisted take-off. The disc is set up and left with the motor off. On cue the motor is switched on with one hand and the turntable flicked into motion

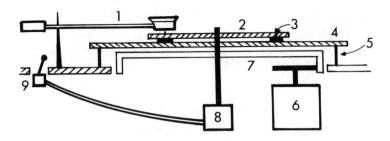

QUICK-START DEVICES. Form of drop-start mechanism in which turntable and motor assembly can be lowered away from the record. When a record is set up the pick-up (1) is at rest in groove of the record (2) which in turn is supported by rubber studs (3) on aluminium plate (4). This rests on tripod (5) when motor/turntable assembly (6 and 7) is dropped away by raise/lower cam (8) operated by lever (9). In other designs there is no aluminium plate and the record itself is raised and lowered on a moving tripod.

with the other; then the first hand fades up at the marked point. Alternatively, have the turntable running and with the stylus resting in the groove raise the disc a little from it, then drop it on cue. Many of the record players in BBC studios are equipped with a mechanical drop-start apparatus that makes the accurate cueing of gramophone records and effects very easy.

Among archive material an operator may encounter discs with *overlap changeovers*. Before recording tape came into wide use recordings were made on direct-cut discs that lasted between four and five minutes. About half a minute before the space on one disc ran out another was started, and the overlap was marked on both by a *scroll*—advancing the groove a little to mark the end section on one and the matching opening section of the other. To replay, the second disc is set up near to the start on a recognizable cue, and started as this comes up on disc one. The two are now running almost in synchronization. To complete the job, the speed of disc two is varied slightly by hand, or by the speed regulator: listening to this disc on pre-fade, the operator brings it into step with disc one. When the two are synchronized number two is faded in and number one out.

An alternative method of replaying an overlap is to convert it into a *butt changeover* by setting up for a drop start just before a pause, and changing over during that pause. This method is not satisfactory for continuous music or absolutely continuous speech, unless the timing of the drop can be made perfect.

Butt changeovers on disc are necessary for playing records of works that continue over several sides. The timing between movements of a symphony must remain consistent and (if possible) the fades linked, again bringing in the second almost to full volume before fading out the first. A well-produced recording should in principle have sufficient atmosphere recorded to fill the gap. Where orchestral movements or operatic scenes are split internally, perfection counsels that a score should be consulted to check the timing: does the next side follow after a beat, or a bar; or is the last note on one side repeated at the start of the next? A score was essential with 78s, and blanks, discs of unmodulated surface noise, were sometimes used to ensure continuity of imperfection in the gaps between movements. For butt-joins that are internal to one or both discs, the cueing is as for tape.

There is one other event that the disc-player must always be prepared for, and this is the repeating groove. If it occurs during a radio transmission the cure may have to be as violent as the effect: quickly fade out, jump the stylus on a groove, and quickly fade up. Alternatively, as the stylus generally requires very little persuasion to return to its original path, or at worst to jump forward, simply rest a pencil very gently across the pick-up arm or head and 'squeeze' the stylus toward the centre of the record.

Cueing videotape and film

Videotape machines are generally allowed a 10 second run up. Though the speed pick-up is almost instantaneous, time has to be allowed for the picture to stabilize, and then to be locked to the same picture scan as the studio, so that a dissolve is possible or a cut is clean without a picture bump. Telecine machines move into action more lumberingly but stabilize picture quicker; they are normally run from the figure 10 on the leader. This means 10 '35 mm-feet', i.e. ten measures of sixteen frames, and is the same for both 16 mm and 35 mm film. It is equivalent to about 7 seconds, to which an extra second is added for reaction and run-up time. There is no sound or picture before 0, as this defeats the object of the exercise: you might just as well have run off some other figure —as in fact you can if the machine is always stable in less than 10 feet.

This long run-up makes exact cueing difficult: it is generally done on word counts in the first instance (two words per foot or three words per second for a fairly fast speaker with no pauses), and corrected after each rehearsal. This method of successive approximations goes for nothing if the performer suddenly produces a performance on the take that has radically different (and usually slower) timing. The director has either to make sure this will not happen or to outguess the performer.

Even where the rest of the material is ad-libbed, the film or videotape cue is generally scripted and learned, or perhaps written out on cue cards and held near the camera; or run on one of the systems for unrolling cue script close to or optically superimposed in line with the camera lens. Alternatively, with very practised performers, a cue to run is agreed, and then the performer, watching a monitor showing the videotape or film run-up out of the corner of his eye, exactly matches his introduction to the time available for it.

All of these systems fail occasionally, so there is a tendency to allow a 'soft' start rather than one that crashes in with important picture and sound from the first second as a disc or sound tape can.

What this means for the sound mixer (who has nothing to do with the cueing) is that he has to be prepared to do either a straightforward match of sound to sound or a first-aid rescue job.

The easiest line is to follow the picture: fade in if the picture fades in or mixes; or make a quick mix if the picture cuts (on a miscue, a planned mix may be changed to a cut). But this assumes that no essential sound information is going to be lost by waiting for picture; sometimes it is best to anticipate by fading up the new sound in advance of a delayed cut. On an overlap of different voices it may be best either to clip a few words of the incoming speech or, more likely, to hold the first word or two at low level behind the last words of studio. Neither is elegant, but the latter makes it easier to make sense of what is said subsequently and is therefore preferable.

Where 'hard' cues are needed within a recorded programme because the insert just has to start with a bang and exact cueing cannot be guaranteed, the whole of this clumsy prodedure is thrown overboard, the cue made loose, and the two parts subsequently edited together (which means that the sound change will probably have to be resynchronized with the cut: see page 457 for the videotape editing techniques that are used for this).

In other circumstances the cueing is predetermined by cue dots. When switching from one reel of film to the next cue dots are shown in the top right-hand corner. The first is the cue to run film and the second to switch over sound and picture together. This is not a procedure that concerns the sound man; it is done by a film projectionist. Cue dots in the top left of frame are used in television for continuity purposes, giving exact synchronization to everybody on 'stand-by', 'run', and 'fade-up' cues.

Outside sources—remotes

Another type of source that may appear on a desk at a radio or television station is a line from some other studio or remote location (in Britain these are called *outside sources*). A local radio station might have lines to the regional weather bureau and recreational areas, local government offices, traffic monitoring points and vehicles, sports arenas and concert halls, together with other information centres for news, business or entertainment reports. Long distance and international links, network lines, other local studios and the telephone system may also be used. Contact between the central studio and the remote source may take a number of forms. Sometimes there are, in fact, two lines: the programme circuit, which may be one- or two-way, plus a control line which is effectively a telephone link between the control points at the two ends.

Consider first the case of a one-way *music line* (i.e. broadcast quality line) plus control circuit.

Often it is posible to prove the line fully before the programme goes on the air. In such a case contact is first established on the control circuit, and the distant contributor is asked to send line-up tone and to identify the programme line by speaking over it. Both of these can be checked with the channel fader open, so that the level of the incoming material can be accurately set and its quality is known.

In the event that the line is not available until the programme of which it is to form part is on the air, the line can only be fully tested to the last switching point prior to the active part of control desk. But the routing can be checked right up to the channel fader input if the desk has *prehear* (sometimes called *prefade*) on the channel used. If this facility is not available it should still be possible to listen to the circuit in the sound-control area at the last point before it is patched through to the control desk. Head-phones or a small loudspeaker could be used.

The control line may be made double-purpose: as well as being used for general communication between the two points before, during, and after the contribution, the return circuit may have cue programme fed to it at all other times. Other switching arrangements can also be made—for example, for the producer's talkback circuit to be superimposed on cue programme. In each of these cases the cue feed and the results of any other switching are checked by the contributor as part of the line-up procedure.

What happens at the contributor's end is again a matter for local arrangement: it depends, for example, on whether the contributor is on his own in a self-drive studio or not. If there is a separate, manned control point the cue programme may terminate there and the contributor be given a cue to start by the operator. Or it may be fed to the studio for the contributor to hear on headphones or a deaf-aid type of earpiece (better than headphones in television, but still inelegant). Either of these should be preferred to a loudspeaker, which might cause coloration. In such cases the feed might be for just the beginning and end of the contribution, or it might be left open all the way through. Obviously, the latter will be necessary in the case of an interview. If there is no alternative to a loudspeaker being on while the microphone is open, ask the contributor to use the directional properties of both to minimize spill, and then to reduce his loudspeaker level until it is only just clearly audible to him. Then, as he speaks, test the circuit by raising the incoming level until coloration occurs: this is the level it is desirable to stay below. During the programme it may also be possible to reduce the volume of the cue feed while the distant contributor is speaking, but be careful not to give him reason to fear that he has been cut off. Anti-feedback pitch-spreading (see p. 428) would also help.

An apparently simpler arrangement is for there to be not three channels of communication but two: a music line in each direction, instead of a single music line and a two-way telephone circuit. However, this is a more expensive arrangement (unless, instead, telephone circuits are used for contributions to a broadcast—of which more later). The system using two music lines is therefore used only if there is a need for high-quality sound to be transmitted both ways (as when the programme is being simultaneously broadcast or recorded at both ends), or when the facility is in any case available on stand-by. The arrangements prior to and during the broadcasts are broadly similar to those already described, except for the obvious proviso that it is not possible for a line to be used for control purposes when it is on the air.

A further possible arrangement is for there to be two-way programme lines with a completely independent control circuit. This, the most versatile arrangement, is also the most expensive.

320

Clean feed and multiway working

So far, *cue programme* has been mentioned without any indication being given as to what point in the control desk this is derived from.

Normal cue programme consists of the output of the mixer studio fed to all participants; but if, say, a speaker at the New York end of a transatlantic discussion were fed the full programme from a mixer in London he would hear his own voice coming back, delayed by the time it takes for a telephone signal to travel there and back—by cable, a thirtieth of a second. This is enough to make speech decidedly uncomfortable, and if the return signal is loud enough it becomes impossible to carry on without stuttering. Satellite links introduce delays of a quarter-second in each direction.

The alternative to this is *clean feed* or *mixed-minus*, an arrangement whereby participants hear all of the programme except their own contribution. Clearly, special circuit arrangements must

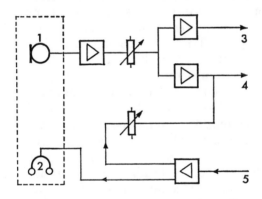

CLEAN FEED CIRCUIT. For multi-studio discussion a speaker in the studio can hear a distant source on headphones without hearing his own voice. 'Clean' cue is also provided. 1. Microphone and 2. Headphones or 'deaf aid' for speaker in studio. 3. Clean feed to distant studio. 4. Combined studio output. 5. Incoming line. This arrangement is essential for both radio and TV when studios are linked by satellite, which introduces a relatively long delay to any sound that is returned to its point of origination. A loudspeaker used in place of headphones could easily wreck the arrangement unless it is carefully placed for minimal pick-up on the studio microphone and kept at low level.

be made in the control desk. For two-way working where the outside source line is added to the studio output after the main gain control, a clean feed can be taken off just prior to the main control and fed via a parallel fader. If the studios are far apart—

at continental distances—the time delay problem makes the use of clean feed essential to any discussion; if it is unavailable, the return feed must be faded down at all times when the distant contributor is talking. If the studios are closer together clean feed may be used for comfort and convenience (some people are put off by hearing their own voice on headphones). A third use is to provide an actuality feed of an event to which various broadcasters add their own commentary. The actuality sound is fully mixed at the originating control desk, at which the commentary for the home audience is added through an independent channel which is fed in to the mixer output after the master control (or after the appropriate group fader, if the clean feed is taken from this point). This arrangement is similar to the provision of mixed music and effects tracks in film dubbing: there, too, commentary may be added separately by the user, perhaps in a language different from that of the original production.

A complex form of clean feed is used when recording sporting and other events of international interest. Picture and sound are recorded on videotape and a synchronized multitrack sound tape. Many commentaries in different languages can be recorded at the same time and then recombined individually with the actuality sound on replay of the tapes.

A totally different arrangement of studios and feeds has its application in an 'independent evidence' type of programme where a compere questions two people in separate studios who cannot hear each other (e.g. to examine the reactions of various partners who knew each other well: brother and sister, secretary and boss, or husband and wife). Three studios are required: one for the compere, who, listening on headphones, hears the full programme output, and two remote studios in which the victims sit, and are fed nothing of the other person's answers, and only that part of the questioning that is directly addressed to them. Typically the switching may be done by two sound assistants, one in each of the two remote studios.

Telephone circuits used in radio and television programmes

Telephone circuits are not routinely used in all broadcast programmes for several reasons:
1. The speech quality of the microphone is satisfactory for communication but below that normally required in broadcasting.

Distortion and noise levels are relatively high, and the frequency response is not flat. Nor are telephone lines designed to the same sound-quality standards as are those intended specifically for broadcasting.

2. The band width is relatively narrow: 300–3000 Hz in America and 300–3300 Hz in Britain. This contains more than enough of human speech to permit full intelligibility, but, again, less than is required in broadcasting.

3. The telephone system cannot reasonably be expected to guarantee the same standards of freedom from interruption that are required on lines used for broadcasting.

4. Connection by automatic equipment at any given time cannot be guaranteed: junctions, overseas circuits—or the number itself—may be engaged.

Clearly, since broadcasting is geared to different technical standards, telephone circuits are not used except for very good reasons—which should not normally include the economy of operation necessary to a telephone system. Valid reasons are:

1. Extreme topicality. With no time to arrange high-quality lines or to get a recording or the man himself to the studio, this is the only way of obtaining his contribution. The justification here is that the same programme value could not have been obtained in any other way.

2. Extreme remoteness. Here physical inaccessibility is the problem: the speaker may be in a distant country from which high-quality lines are not available or would be so prohibitively expensive or inconvenient as to limit the availability of information. Or he may be in a place that is cut off from outside other than by telephone (or a variant of it). For example, the speaker may be aboard a boat, train or aeroplane; or in an area that has been struck by natural disaster.

3. Audience participation. Here the justification is that the ordinary citizen in his own home may without elaborate pre-planning be invited to take a direct part in the proceedings of which he is normally only a passive witness.

Any of these may be used to justify the remote voice being heard with telephone quality. They cannot, however, excuse a change in quality of the studio voice, which is what would happen if a normal two-wire circuit, carrying both the 'transmit' and 'receive' elements of the connection, were used on its own for both sides of the conversation. In practice, a feed is taken from the telephone circuit through an amplifier to the studio sound-control desk,

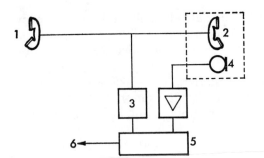

BROADCASTING LIVE TELEPHONE CONVERSATIONS. 1. Remote telephone. 2. Studio telephone. 3. Constant volume amplifier. 4. Studio microphone. 5. Mixer. 6. Studio sound output.

where it is mixed with normal studio output to add the full frequency range of the voice at the near end of the conversation.

Obviously, for the studio sound to mask the telephone quality version of the same voice the latter must not be mixed in at too high a volume. Special measures may be necessary to avoid this, for it is all too likely that, tapping directly from the telephone circuit so close to the studio, the volume of the distant voice will be reduced by losses on the line, and may therefore be low in comparison with the near voice. For a long-distance call this depends on the line quality and the distance between the last signal amplifiers and the studio. In certain studio situations it may be better not to use the local exchange, but instead to have a low-loss line installed to a point nearer the centre of an area system.

But the most important measure that may be employed is a constant-volume amplifier or (essentially the same thing) a combination of amplifier and limiter to ensure that incoming speech is as loud as that originating locally. Note that the gain of a simple limiter should not be set too high, say, a maximum of 8 dB, or line noise may be boosted to an objectionable level during pauses in the conversation. However, if a noise gate is also incorporated in the circuit (and assuming that there is adequate separation between speech and noise level) the gain of the limiter can be substantially increased (see p. 362).

The line may be specially provided for programme use, and have its own number independent of that listed for the studio and office complex, or it may be routed through the local switchboard. In either case it is advisable that rather than go directly in to the studio proper the line should terminate at a control point under the supervision of the sound man. He may then switch it either to a control telephone, which may be used for engineering tests or production purposes, or to the performer in the studio and, in parallel, the control desk.

In this system the control phone is used to establish the call, which is then checked for quality before transmission: in particular, it is essential to establish that no cross-talk is intelligible. When the circuit is finally switched through to the studio it must be arranged that the control telephone microphone is out of circuit, or noise from the control point will also be heard. As the call is switched to the studio it is also fed in parallel via the 'receive' amplifier to the control desk and to a separate loud-speaker or headphones to pre-hear the incoming circuit, so that while the circuit is faded down it may still be monitored.

It should be arranged that the call will remain connected as long as it is routed through to the studio, even if the studio telephone is not picked up, and will not be disengaged at the end of the conversation by putting the studio phone down. It is finally disconnected by switching back to the control phone when this is down (and therefore open-circuit) or by the other party replacing his receiver.

Special services may sometimes be arranged; in particular, fixed time calls may be booked in advance. Or timing pips that would normally be superimposed on a call may be suppressed by special request.

From the point of view of the engineers of the telephone service there are two rules that must be observed:

1. No equipment from which there is any possibility of a dangerous high-voltage signal arising should be connected to the line.
2. No unusually loud signals should be transmitted as these would inconvenience other users of the system by inducing abnormally high cross-talk levels.

The way in which calls are used in programmes is normally subject to some code of practice that is agreed with the telephone administration office. Whether the following are regarded as rules or merely as suggestions for such a code depends on factors such as the arrangements between the broadcasters and the telephone service concerned, and regulations imposed by the licensing authority. This may vary from country to country and also with the method of use (recording or live broadcast) and to a lesser extent the type of programme. Some are formulations of common courtesy or common sense; others are designed not to bring into disrepute or draw complaints to cooperating organizations whose service is inevitably seen at a technical disadvantage; yet others are designed to limit intrusion:

325

1. Obtain the consent of the other party before a broadcast is made.
2. Avoid the use of party lines.
3. Do not, in the context of a call, broadcast any criticism, or any comment that may be interpreted as criticism of the telephone service.
4. If calls become unintelligible or subject to interference do not persist with their broadcast, but bring them to an end as quickly as possible.
5. Immediately abandon calls that are interrupted by the operator or by a crossed line. Someone should ring as soon as possible to explain to the other party what has happened.
6. Do not broadcast telephone numbers, or permit them to be broadcast, except by prior arrangement. Special measures may have to be taken to avoid exchange congestion and the blocking of emergency calls: this may prove expensive.
7. Do not involve operators or other telephone service staff in the broadcasting of a call. In Britain the Post Office requires that no reference should be made on the air to Post Office approval having been given either to the transmission or to the equipment used for it.

Where a conversation is recorded the same result must be achieved as if the item were live—but in this case editing may be used to help achieve it.

In order to ensure that quality is as high as possible, speakers at both ends should be asked to speak clearly but without shouting, not too fast, and with the mouthpiece by the mouth and not under the chin. Broadcast sound should not be audible at the position of the telephone. And if there are parallel extensions at the telephone subscriber's end these should not be used by others listening in to the call, or this, too, will reduce the quality.

12

FADES AND MIXES

THE fade is one of the simplest operations but, as much as anything else, it is the way that fades and mixes are carried out and timed that distinguishes the polished, finished recording from the one that sounds amateur—in the worst sense of the word. Not every fade consists of a slow, steady movement in or out. A fade has to sound right and not just look smooth. Everything from disc-jockey shows to high drama on film or television depends on a sensitive hand on the sound fader. A good fade has the qualities of a well-played piece of music. A good operator does not wait for a cue and then act on it; he anticipates, and to the onlooker cause and effect often appear to coincide—but it is, after all, the purpose of rehearsal to ensure that they do.

What constitutes a smooth fade? We know that the ear detects changes of volume according to a logarithmic scale (the decibel scale). This means that a linear potentiometer faded out at a steady rate would produce very little drop in volume at first, followed by a much quicker fall away at the lower end. If, on the other hand, a logarithmic potentiometer is divided up into equal segments, each represents the same number of dB. So, for a steady fade-out of an even sound source to sound smooth, a fader that is logarithmic over the greater part of its range is used.

Over the greater part, but not all; for at the lower end of a fade, as the listener's interest is withdrawn from the sound, the ear accepts a more rapid rounding off. The fade is, in fact, a device for establishing a process of disengagement between listener and scene: once the process is accepted, it only remains to get rid of the tail-end as quickly as possible. Taking this extra condition into account, it seems that the ideal fader should be logarithmic over the upper two-thirds of its range, with a gradually increasing rate of attenuation at the lower end, until at the bottom stop there is complete cut-off.

A more complex form of fading is the mix. The film sound recordist working on location often has a small portable four-channel mixer. The sound supervisor in a television studio generally has literally dozens of faders beneath his hands.

The fade in radio

Consider first the use of fades in radio drama, where the convention is that each scene starts with a fade-in, and ends with a fade-out. Narration, on the other hand, is cut off almost square—so that there need never be any difficulty in distinguishing between story and storyteller. The type and rate of fade, and the length of pause, each have their own information to give to the listener; so the man taking on the job of creating a sound picture must start out by deciding just what it is that he is trying to convey. The means at his disposal are much more slender than those available for film which can employ cuts, fades, dissolves and wipes, plus all the elements of camera technique: pans, tracking shots and so on. A lot has to be conveyed in sound radio by slight variations in the technique of fading.

When a situation calls for a scene change the simplest form that this can take is a slow fade to silence over about seven seconds, a pause of two or three seconds, and an equally slow fade-in. Such a fade implies a complete discontinuity of time and action.

Faster versions of the simple fade imply shorter lapses of time or smaller changes of location. For instance, the 'Maybe its down in the cellar, let's go and see if it's there . . . well, here you are, have a look round' type of fade can consist of a very quick out and in, just enough to establish that a slight time lapse has taken place, and not just a move off microphone and on again.

Moving off and on, perhaps helped by small fades, is used for still smaller changes of location—say, from one room to the next. In general, it is convenient to assume that a microphone is static within the field of action, although this itself may be moving, such as a scene in a car. Any departure from this convention must be clearly signposted with dialogue or effects, otherwise the listener will be confused. Even a scene that starts near a waiting car which then moves off, may create a moment of confusion during which it is not clear whether the microphone is with the car or not. But the use of suitable dialogue pointers ensures that the listener has some guide as to what is going on. The deliberate misuse of pointers can be funny, as in the ancient gag:

FUNNY MAN	Quick, drive to Tunbridge Wells.
EFFECTS	(*High-powered car departs and fades out.*)
	(*Pause.*)
FUNNY MAN	He might have waited for me to get in.

To a limited extent, moves on and off microphone are interchangeable with fades. According to tests carried out in the United States listeners found that a fade gave just as good an impression of moving off as did actual movement. However, it only works this way round: if a move is used to represent a fade the change in acoustic perspective usually shows, and makes the effect sound rather odd. Occasionally quite complicated faking has to be worked out in the studio; for example, where a fade is combined with increasing artificial echo to suggest a move off in reverberant surroundings.

Depth of fade

How deep should a fade be? Obviously, if a scene has a good curtain line it must not be faded very much; or if the first line of a new scene contains important information a quick fade-in is necessary. In both cases we have to ensure that the adjacent fade is of the conventional slow-fade type, otherwise the impression of a scene change is completely lost—the result could easily sound like a pause in the conversation.

But apart from such special cases, most fades fall into one of two main groups, or programme types. First, there are the full-

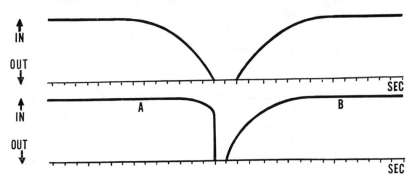

FADES IN DRAMA. *Top.* Simple fades between scenes: smooth fade out, smooth fade in. *Bottom.* Fades between narration and scene. Slight edge out at end of narration (A) and smooth fade in (B). (In these diagrams, the base line represents silence and the upper limit is normal volume.)

scale dramatic productions: these tend to have long, deep fades, taken almost to inaudibility before being cut off. Second, there are feature programmes in the form of narration and actuality recordings (or narration and dramatic scenes presented in a documentary style): in these, partial fades are common, as against the complete fades found in plays.

Schools broadcasts in Britain employ relatively shallow fades, whether they are dramatic or documentary in style. Part of the cause lies in the listening conditions in classrooms; the receiver may be poor, and the room boomy. The producers of these programmes make a point of listening under the same conditions as school audiences from time to time—and as a result tend to prefer a high-intelligibility type of construction, with low dynamic range and background effects held well down so that they do not interfere with speech.

Average listening conditions in many parts of the world may be expected to be poor, either because crowded short or medium wave transmissions are heard by many at the limit of their range, or because car or small 'transistor' radios are largely used by the audience. If this is the case, a form of presentation that uses fairly shallow fades is necessary.

Difficulties arise when a scene starts off with some such stage instruction as 'Enter Wilberforce'. The trouble is that it is not really possible to establish a location clearly, and the entry of the first speaking character into it, in just a few seconds. To make it quite clear what is going on, it is necessary to fade in on effects or other people talking, and *then* 'Enter Wilberforce'. But such a radio script probably has to be reinterpreted; and here the likely solution is simply to forget the instruction and rely on the text, acoustics, and effects to establish the situation instead.

It is better, in fact, to go to the other extreme with fades, exits and entrances, and be very deliberate about them. This often means breaking a fade up into several parts, for there is not much point in fading during a pause—which may seem obvious, but in practice it is often ignored. So, if Wilberforce has two lines to speak during his approach, most of the fading in should be done while he is doing the talking and not during the intervening line.

This is true of any fade-in: it is better to hold it momentarily if there is a pause in the speech. It may even be necessary to reset, jumping up or down in level between lines from different speakers if the overall effect of the fade is to be smooth. A graceful fade

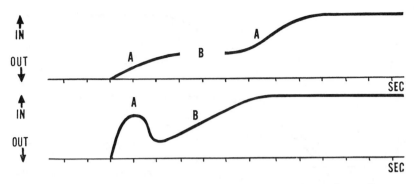

COMPLEX FADES. *Top.* A. Speech. B. Silence. Do not fade in on silence. *Bottom.* Complex fade to accommodate quiet effect at start. At (A) fader is open for 'Door Opens' then taken back for fade-in (B) on speech.

during a pause, or an actor stalking menacingly up to a microphone in silence means nothing in radio.

'Door opens' is another instruction that may head a scene. If such an effect is to be clear it has to be recorded at getting on for normal level, and the fader then has to be taken back a little for the fade-in proper. In general, a short spot-effect of this sort is not recommended for the start of a scene.

Mixing in effects

If a convention is adopted in which each scene opens and closes with a fade it is apparent that some sound is required for the fade in each case—and this usually has to be an unimportant throw-away line from one of the characters. Dramatically this is rather weak construction. To fade out on laughter (where appropriate) is better. But more generally useful are background effects. As the scene comes to a close the speech is faded down and the effects are lifted to swamp the line. Then after the effects have been peaked for a few seconds they too can be slowly faded out.

Similarly, a continuous background of sound may be used for a fade-in—such effects are very useful indeed for establishing new localities—and here again the sound may be peaked for a short while, and then faded gently down as the dialogue is brought up.

Another way of handling a fade in is to bring up speech and effects almost together, though here again the effects should be slightly ahead of speech—sufficiently so for it to be clear to the listener what they represent. Otherwise they may distract his

331

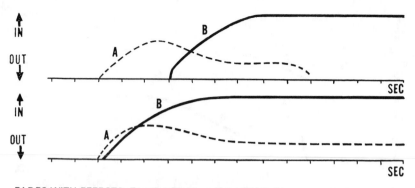

FADES WITH EFFECTS. *Top.* Establishing effects (A) before speech (B), on separate faders. *Bottom.* Fading up effects (A) with speech (B), and then holding them back to avoid an excess of distracting backing sound.

attention from the first words that he should be hearing. The more complicated the background effects, the more likely it is that they will need to be established first, though the final decision necessarily depends on the story. In either case they nearly always have to be dropped to a lower level behind the main body of the scene than they are at the beginning and end. The level may in fact have to be unrealistically low (this is one of the ways in which mono differs from stereo, where the spread background can be much louder without interfering with intelligibilty).

It is a good idea to vary the levels of effects behind a long scene almost continuously—just enough to prevent the sound from becoming dull. The backing should be lowest behind speech that it is important to 'get over' for the plot, and loudest when dialogue is inconsequential, or there is reference to the backing sound, or when characters are pitching their voices against it. In any case actors should be encouraged to sharpen the tone of their voices if in similar natural circumstances they would do so.

Effects can often be peaked as a bridge between two parts of the same scene: different conversations at a party can merge into and emerge from a swell of background chatter. In film terms, this is the equivalent of a number of different camera treatments, such as a slow pan or a tracking shot from one group to another; or one group moving off and another group on before a static camera.

Note how easy it can be, when constructing a scene for radio, to imagine that you are being more precise in terms of movement than in fact you are. Fortunately it is not usually very important if the listener has a different picture from you. Nevertheless, it is

332

sometimes possible to be little more precise and to give the impression or a tracking shot, by peaking effects and then gradually changing their content; you can, for example, move from general chatter to a relatively quiet 'balcony scene'; and the best way of doing that is by means of an effects mix.

Beware of over-use of background effects. Used for occasional scenes, they enliven a production. Used for every scene, they become tedious—the more so if they are too loud. Some relief from distracting backings is necessary now and then. Do not be too busy.

Fades in television and film

The techniques of fading so far described apply particularly to sound radio. For television and films the rate of fade and timing of any pause is normally set by the picture: in the simplest case a fade of picture is matched exactly by fade of sound. This is made slightly more complex if there is a low level but significant sound during the fade; the sound can be emphasized disproportionately. Similarly, if there is an effect of little significance, but which would be too loud, it can be reduced. Minor variations of this sort are normally fairly obvious both in the television studio and in the film dubbing theatre.

Hardly less obvious are the uses that can be found for effects and music during fades of the picture. For example, to bridge a time lapse in a party scene, it may be appropriate to peak the chatter background up, rather than fade it out. It is then firmly implied that action and location are unchanged during the time lapse. If the new scene then turns out, in fact, to be a different party a deliberate incongruity is introduced. A change of scene from one noisy location to another might be made by peaking effects against the fade and mixing while the picture is faded out. This works best if the two sounds are characteristically different.

This technique should be used only with calculated and deliberate intent. It is self-conscious in that it draws attention to technique as such—at least for as long as it takes to establish a convention. The dramatic reason must therefore be strong, and the sound important to the action.

The rather less obvious use of effects as already described for fades in radio also have their uses. When mixing from one picture to another it is normal to mix backgrounds (or fade the louder of the two in or out) to match picture. Here a slight peaking of effects to bridge the mix may be readily accepted.

333

Location cuts

More interesting—because more open to the creative use of sound—is the picture cut from one location to another. The simplest case, however, uses a straight cut with dialogue (or strong action) to carry it. For example:

Vision:	Sound:
Midshot oilman: turns on first words to see distant figure striding out towards burn-rig	*Effects: Burning oil rig* OILMAN: Sure it's easy. When you've stayed alive as long as this boy has the hardest job is working out what to write on the paper.
Paper in manager's hands: fast tilt up to C. S. face	MANAGER: Two and a half million!...

Here the effects behind the first scene must disappear very fast. They should not be cut in the physical sense of cutting tape or film sound, or there will be a click as they go. Anything just short of this is satisfactory. If the scenes are staged in a television studio the background to the first shot will perhaps be on back-projection with effects from sound tape or disc (or the whole action of the first shot might be on film). The effects would be whipped out *on* the cut. This is difficult to time accurately, and there is a danger of damaging the dramatic effect.

An alternative is to introduce a recording cut at this point—usually done by electronic (copy) editing (see p. 457).

If both of the shots in the sequence above are on film a quick fade is used. The first effects track will probably be laid (see p. 481) to overlap into the next scene. The dubbing mixer then rehearses the cut using the picture and footage counter until he can fade on the cut and not a few frames after.

The next example uses a variety of techniques on three shots:

Vision:	Sound:
Through archway to cathedral tower; tilt down to low angle, boys walk through arch and past camera.	*Effects: Singing of distant choir; chatter, footsteps.* COMMENTARY: In the shadow of the mediaeval cathedral this group's interest in electronics complements traditional activities like choral singing. . . . RUGGER PLAYER: Break!
Wide shot, football field, cathedral, and old school buildings in background; pan left as ball and players cross diagonally towards camera; when centred on science block, zoom past and in to windows.	COMMENTARY: . . . and Rugby football. Perhaps rather surprisingly, the work we're going to see started not with physics, but here in the chemistry lab.
Wide high shot, inside laboratory; two boys and glassware, dominating foreground.	BOY: Oh, no! If we've got to do this, it's set all wrong. . . .

The picture has been shot with the commentary in mind (indeed, the second shot would have been meaningless otherwise). The music was recorded separately; but chatter and footsteps, football effects and laboratory sound were all recorded in sync with the picture. The chatter and footsteps track was, however, displaced a few frames because the approach matched better with the tilt down when this was done. The music was held low from the start and chatter and effects faded in to dominate it with the tilt down. The shout 'break' cued the cut to the football field and killed the music. The football effects that continued on the same track had therefore been brought up to their full volume before the picture cut. With the first zoom the effects dipped sharply to a level matching that of the laboratory, so that a quick mix on the cut was all that was required.

The key device here was that of sound anticipating picture. Here the result was natural—rather like someone hearing a noise in a street and turning to see where and what it was. It can also be used for strongly dramatic cuts. More noticeably to the viewer,

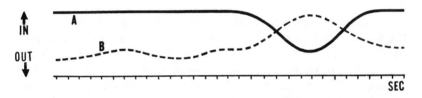

MIXING EFFECTS. Background effects (B) can often be varied continuously and can sometimes be peaked to bridge scenes, as fader for speech (A) is dipped.

the anticipation of sound can be used stylistically, as when the football fan who is talking about the big match, lapses into a daydream during which we hear the sounds of the crowd distantly as though in his thoughts, followed by a cut to a crowd scene at the match and the roar of the crowd at full volume.

The whip pan

A whip pan generally implies a spatial relationship and as such may offer interesting possibilities for the use of sound (this refers to to the whip pan proper and not the flashing blur that is sometimes cut between static scenes to give an illusion of pace in moving from location to location).

335

Here is another example:

Vision:	*Sound:*
Low angle through rigging to flag on mast	Music: military band starts playing
Low angle, figurehead of Nelson, band crossing R–L	COMMENTARY: And the martial music, the uniforms, the discipline, and the impressive reminders of a glorious past,
Closer shot figurehead . . . whip pan R, tilting down	all tell us that this school trains its boys for the sea. . . .
Cut in to matching whip pan to boys turning capstan	Effects: capstan, footsteps, creaking ropes
Closer shot, pairs of boys on spokes of capstan, passing through shot	Their project, too, is suitably nautical.
M.S. boy; in background, boat being hauled up slipway	BOY: With two of our boats at school we had a problem. . . .

In this case the whip pan was not a single shot of the two objects: the figure-head and the capstan were in fact separated by about half a mile. But they were all part of the same general location which was being suggested by a series of atmospheric detail shots rather than a wide shot that would have been relatively dull.

Sound overlaps were used in this case. The sync music from the second shot was laid back over the first (mute) shot and also carried on through the whip pan, though dropping sharply during the camera movement. On the capstan shot the associated effect (which had been recorded wild-track) was allowed to dominate, and the music eventually faded out under the boy's speech. The noise, which was relevant to what he was saying and to subsequent shots, was held low behind him.

The use of sound in these various ways is suitable to both television and film. So, too, is the use of music links between scenes. Indeed, the music bridge is a device common to radio, television, and film.

Theme, background and linking music

Few things about radio or television plays attract so much controversy as the use of music. This is because to be really effective—and indeed, to get a return on the cost and effort of using specially composed music—it is often reasonably loud. In the home, on the other hand, many people like speech loud and music soft (the cinema audience, however, is less likely to complain). Most people agree that where it succeeds, music helps to create

336

works of the highest quality; but at worst it may merely be used to smudge a little elegance over a scene that would have been as effective with good natural sound.

In so far as television shows works that are the product of, or derived in style from the older traditions of the film industry, music is still definitely 'in'. With financial economy as the keynote of modern television, simpler styles have been evolved, artistically justified and found to be effective. An increased use of well-recorded effects is linked with this. Effects are cheaper, and can serve many of the purposes that music was formerly used for. So it follows—even more than ever it did—that music must be selected with the utmost care (and rejected if the perfect fit is not forthcoming), and it must be integrated into programmes with considerable delicacy.

The ideal, for those with sufficient resources of money or talent, or both, is specially recorded music; but links or background music may be found in the 'mood' record catalogues. However, it is as easy to lose tension and coarsen the texture with music as it is to enhance it. So the number one rule about using music is: when in doubt, don't.

One should, of course, avoid popular and recognizable music unless it is to be featured as itself—and remember that all but the most out-of-the-way records are likely to figure as popular and recognizable to some people in most audiences.

Signature tunes or theme music must be in harmony with or provide a counterpoint to the qualities of the programmes they punctuate. In fact, at the start of a programme they must help to define the mood of what is to follow, and at the end, sum up what has gone before. But another criterion that might well be applied to choosing linking music is 'fadeability'. Whatever other quality it may have, it is important that there are points at which it can be got in and out tidily—and this in a piece of the right duration.

Clearly there is no necessity to use the same section of a work at both the beginning and end of a programme (if, indeed, the same work is used at all). As the ideas have progressed in the intervening time, so it is reasonable to have a piece at the end that is a fairly complex development of that heard at the start. For some works this rather conveniently means that the end of the record can be used for the end of the programme. But it is not so common for the start of a record to provide a good crisp opening signature; more often it is necessary to disregard any introduction and start clean on the main theme.

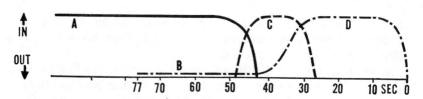

PREFADING MUSIC. The prefade time is the number of seconds from the scheduled end of programme (in this case 77 seconds). A. Last item of programme. B. Closing music playing but not faded up. C. Announcer. D. Music faded up to close programme.

For the close of many radio programmes *prefaded* music is used: this is a device which is used to ensure that a programme space is filled exactly to the last second. The term 'prefade' here means 'not yet faded up'. Another word for this is *dead-roll*.

In the case of a typical prefade (that used for the BBC's Radio Newsreel) it was known that the duration from a certain easily recognizable point to the end of the record was exactly 1 minute 17 seconds. So the record was started exactly 1 minute 17 seconds from the end of the programme. It was usually arranged that no more than about 15 seconds to 30 seconds was actually needed; and this last remaining part of the record was faded up under the announcer's last words—or a little earlier if a suitable phrase presented itself to the disc player, who listened on headphones.

Obviously, vocal music is not usually suitable for prefading, and is therefore rarely used for a closing signature tune.

Mixing from speech to music

To examine the manner in which music and speech may be linked together consider first a few of the ways in which it can be done in a disc-jockey show. The treatment of music in dramatic or magazine programmes is similar in many respects—subject to the rule that in such cases music should not be obtrusive and should be at at much lower level than featured music. In practice, this means that almost every fade or mix is different and must be judged according to the individual needs of the situation. For this the factors to be taken into account include not just the immediate context, but the mood, pace and style of the programme as a whole.

Within a single programme, many different types of fade may

338

be used. Taking a typical case of a pop vocal with a short instrumental introduction, here are some of the ways in which the transition from speech to music may be arranged.

1. *Straight—or nearly so.* The 'intro' on the record is now no longer an introduction: it has become a music link between the preceding speech and the vocal that follows, and its level can often be altered with advantage to match the speech better. After this has been done, the record may be faded up or down to a suitable overall level. The first notes of the intro can sometimes be emphasized to give bite to an unusual start.

2. *Cutting the introduction.* The first word of the vocal follows the cue fairly quickly, as though it were a second voice in a briskly conducted argument. The exact timing is determined by the pace and inflection of the cue. It may be necessary to edge the record in a little.

3. *Introduction under speech.* Here the start of the music is timed

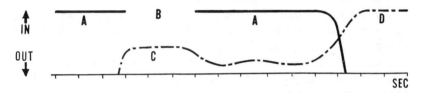

MIXING FROM SPEECH TO MUSIC. A. Speech. B. Pause in speech. C. Music 'intro'. D. Music at full volume. During the pause the music is started and then dipped behind continuing announcement. It is finally lifted on cue to its full volume.

and placed at an appropriate point under the cue, which must be specially written. The intro has to be played at a fairly low level, so that it does not distract from the intelligibility of the speech; and there may be a break in the cue in which the music may be heard on its own for a few seconds—it is *established*. The fade-up generally starts just before the final words and is then lifted to be at or near full volume for the start of the vocal, which should follow the cue after no more than a breath pause.

A coarser technique employs compressors (see p. 355) arranged so that speech pushes down the volume of music. With good quality reception, the effect is unattractive, but it is suited to transistor radio background listening or car radio reception in noisy conditions and is operationally simple.

339

Joining music to music

A link from one piece of music to another can be complicated—or very simple. The simplest case is the *segue* (pronounced 'seg-way' and meaning follow-on), in which the new number follows either after a very short pause or in time with the previous piece. Sometimes an announcement may be spoken over the intro at a convenient point, or over the join.

In some cases it may be better to avoid endings and introductions by *mixing* from one number to another. Each two- or three-minute number on a pop record is, naturally, written and recorded as though it were a complete programme in itself. It has, like any other complete and individual work, a beginning, a middle and an end. But in a fast-moving record programme it may be only the middle that is wanted, or the intro (or ending) may be too big or weak to go into the programme without throwing it out of shape. If the rhythm is strong in both pieces perfect timing is essential. It is easier if the music reaches a point where its form is not too definite; where, for example, one number can be faded on a long sustained note and the other brought in on a rising arpeggio or glissando. But whereas this sort of programme can be great fun to put together it may not give the listener an increase in listening pleasure, so do not mess discs around just for the sake of doing so.

A segue or mix is only possible if keys are the same or suitably related. Indeed, it may be that keys that are nominally the same are not close enough in pitch without a slight adjustment of the playing speeds. Expert musical knowledge is not necessary for this; though a reasonably good sense of relative pitch is essential.

In any record programme it is a good thing to give an occasional thought to the key sequence (this also can be done by ear): a lively variety of keys helps to give vitality to the overall picture. The question is, how to get from one key to another. In a single piece of music it is generally done through a progression of related keys. That may not be possible when linking together several pre-recorded items, so unless a deliberate dissonance is wanted, some other means of softening the transition must be found. There is a story of a music-hall conductor who, whenever he was faced with the problem of a quick modulation, simply wrote in a cymbal crash and immediately led off in the new key! The cymbal crash—a sudden loud noise of indefinite pitch—was designed to make the listeners forget the key that had gone before. In radio work a marginally more subtle means to the same end is used—the announcement.

With an announcement between two items, even a very short one of five seconds or so, difficulties over pitch tend to disappear. The ear does not register a dissonance if the two sounds are spaced out and the attention distracted by speech. Happily this means that programmes can be compiled according to content, with suitable contrasts of style and pace between items, and without worrying too much about keys.

But there is one special case of a linking announcement that does take key-change very much into account, a technique adopted by a disc jockey who, taking up the key at the end of each record, 'doodled' on the piano until the end of his spoken comments and then finished up in the right key for the next record. The adjustment of levels between live piano and record requires even more care than usual, if the transition is to sound smooth.

Adding speech to music

Where speech is added *to* music, as in the case of theme music with announcements or introductory comments superimposed, the voice is normally chosen for high intelligibility. The music can therefore often be given its full value and dipped only just in time to accommodate the first words. Similarly, ensuring only that the last word is clear, the music is brought up close on the tail of speech.

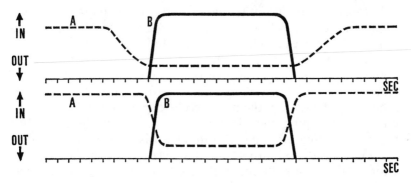

FILM MUSIC AND COMMENTARY. *Top.* Normal cueing. Music (A) is gradually adjusted in volume so that commentary or other speech (B) is clearly audible when it starts. After the speech ends, the level is adjusted gently. Alternatively the music may be written or chosen specially to give this effect. *Bottom.* Newsreel cueing. Music (A) is held at high volume until a moment before speech (B) starts, and is raised to high level again immediately speech ends. Adjustments are rapid.

341

Also, in anything longer than a breath pause in speech, the music is peaked up. This is called a 'newsreel' commentary and music mix after the old style of filmed newsreel in which the inconvenience of synchronized speech—or even sound effects—was avoided.

At the end of a programme an up-beat finish may demand that music, applause, and speech all fight each other: here, similar techniques may again be used. But in neither case should it be forgotten that for many of the audience disengagement is accelerated only by what at home just sounds like a loud and not particularly pleasant noise.

An alternative, and much more relaxed way of mixing music and speech is to employ gentle music fades before and after the speech.

Superimposition

There remains one final method of adding sounds together—superimposition. If a second recording is made on a tape that already has a recording on it (i.e. where the initial recording is not wiped by the erase head) the result is a composite sound consisting of a high-quality superimposed foreground mixed with background remnants of the first recording. The high-frequency bias that accompanies the second audio signal acts as an inefficient erase current and partially wipes what was already on the tape. One way to control superimposition is to vary the strength of the erase current.

Because the quality of the initial recording is impaired, superimposition can hardly be regarded as a valid professional technique unless the exact effect is known and is actually desired.

A related effect is sometimes involved when new material is copied in to the middle of a recorded tape with the intention of leaving the old material joined on before and after it. After rehearsing the timing, the new piece is copied normally, with the erase head wiping the old recording ahead of the new. Just before switching off, a piece of thin card is slipped between tape and erase head, so that old and new recordings overlap slightly. Skilfully done, this eliminates the gap and click that might otherwise mar the effect.

13

CONTROLLING VOLUME

FOR controlling volume, meters can prove misleading because they indicate peak volume not loudness. Some instruments, such as bagpipes, harpsichords, clavichords and virginals, sound very loud compared with the meter reading. So does much pop music. Balance of these against less noisy music and speech can and must be judged by ear—and this is only a particular case of a general rule: meters are a guide, but ears must be the judge.

Not only must levels be set correctly for the various technical processes that the signal undergoes; individual passages may also have to be compressed (restricted in dynamic range) so that they are neither too loud not too quiet in comparison with the rest of the programme. Controlling and compressing is one of the sound man's most important jobs; and one that is not undertaken solely for technical reasons.

There are few really dependable short cuts: automatic volume control, for example, would ruin Ravel's *Bolero*. Nevertheless automatic devices have become increasingly sophisticated in recent years, to the extent that some are capable of controlling specific types of programme material with a reasonable degree of adequacy. A disadvantage is that different control characteristics are required where several types of output are heard in succession, and that for some types of music in which subtle dynamic control by the performers is important to the artistic effect (this includes some light music and jazz as well as most serious music), no compressor can do an adequate job unless it can be specially set for the individual item. Automatic control lacks intelligent anticipation.

The uses for compressors and limiters include short-wave radio where a continued high-signal level is necessary to overcome static and other noise; certain other types of high-intelligibility radio where a limited range of output is broadcast to a maximum service area for a given transmitter strength; and certain purposes within programmes themselves, e.g. as an element of pop music balance, or to even up the two voices of a telephone conversation used as programme material (see pp. 322–324).

For the purposes of this chapter, however, the main theme is the manual control of volume using the ear, the eye (for meter, script or score, and to observe events in the studio), and genuine intelligent anticipation. Most of what follows applies almost equally to radio, television and film sound, and to the music recording studio.

Programme meters

Although a meter cannot be used to judge such things as the balance of one voice against another or speech against music, it is nevertheless an essential item of studio equipment. It uses are:
1. To check that there is no loss or gain in level between studio, recording room and transmitter (see p. 91).
2. To provide indications of levels that would result in under- or overmodulation at the recorder or transmitter.
3. To compare relative levels between one performance and another.
4. To check that levels meet the prescribed values for good listening.

There are several types of meter that can be used to line up equipment or check for overmodulation, but a *peak programme meter* (PPM) is among the most satisfactory instruments for the above functions. As its name suggests, it indicates not average levels but peaks. Essentially the PPM is a special type of volt-meter that is arranged to read logarithmically over its main working range. It has a rapid rise characteristic and a slow die-away which makes it easy to read. The BBC version has a rise time constant of 2·5 milliseconds, giving 80% of full deflection in 4 milliseconds (the ear cannot detect distortion of such short duration), and a slow die-away (time constant, 1 second; giving a fall of 8·7 dB/second). Other European meters usually have different rise and fall times and face-scales from those favoured by the BBC.

The *VU meter*, widely used in American equipment, has two scales, percentage modulation and decibels, and is different in operation. It is fed through a dry rectifier and ballast resistance, and draws from the programme circuit all the power needed to

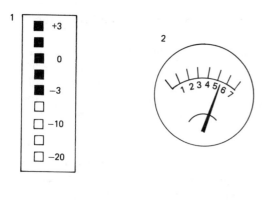

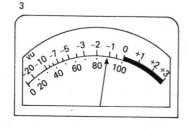

VOLUME INDICATORS. 1. LED meter. Light-emitting diodes respond to changes in volume. Wearing to watch, these are not used professionally. 2. Peak Programme Meter, PPM. In this example 6 on the meter represents full modulation and the four divisions below 6 are each of 4 dB. 3. VU meter. The lower scale indicates percentage modulation and the upper scale dBs relative to full modulation. 'Full modulation' is the level above which distortion is to be expected.

operate it. For cheaper models the ballistic operation may allow the needle to peak substantially higher on programme than on steady tone. However, the more expensive, studio quality VU meter overshoots by only a small amount when a pulse signal is applied (in which it compares favourably with a PPM). But the time constant of 300 milliseconds prevents transient sounds from being registered at all, and the meter underreads on both sharp percussive sounds and speech (at its '100% modulation' level, these are distorted).

Though it may have a linear calibration in percentage modulation (the rectifier characteristic should ensure this), more than half the scale is taken up with a range of 3 dB on either side of the nominal 100% modulation. Little programme material remains consistently within such a narrow range, so the needle is generally either registering only small deflections or flickering bewilderingly over the full range of the scale. For maximum volumes, continuous sounds (including most music) may read '100% modulation' on the VU meter; however, for staccato sounds such as speech a true maximum volume is given by an indicated '50%', because the meter does not have time to register

345

a full swing to the 100 mark on the louder individual constituents of speech.

Note that only those meters which conform to the relevant American standard can be used to compare programme material.

On a radio control desk, the meter (of whatever type) is centrally placed; a television sound meter is mounted close to the transmission monitor and, to avoid eye fatigue, at the same distance from the operator.

In music recording studios, multitrack techniques ideally require separate metering of each channel that is being recorded. It has been suggested that eight is about the limit for convenient monitoring if the meters have the conventional type of display. They are easier to observe if they are in two rows of four, but this divorces them from their associated channel or group faders. The corresponding 16-channel layout could be 8×2 or 4×4. A better arrangement where there are many channels is to have them in a line but with the needles rising on a vertical scale; the needles form themselves into an easily read graphical display and any that is consistently too high is soon noticed.

Other forms of presentation include optical spot, cathode-ray tube (CRT) and LED (light-emitting diode) displays. These are to be judged by their ease of reading over long periods without eye fatigue.

Controlling stereo

Where the stereo broadcast is on FM, control is easy. It can be shown that the deviation (size) of the signal does not exceed the greater of the A and B channels, so all that is necessary to avoid overmodulation is that these do not exceed their normal limits. The same is true for recordings on magnetic tape, where the A and B channels are kept separate. BBC stereo equipment has a double-reading peak programme meter on which both A and B signals can be seen, in addition to a combined A + B PPM.

In broadcasting, however, several problems may arise:
1. In a large network some of the transmitters may be in mono.
2. Some of the listeners to the stereo broadcast have mono receivers.
3. Some of the items on the stereo service may be broadcast in mono only.

For practical purposes it is assumed that the average level for A + B is 3 dB higher than A or B on its own; accordingly, the stereo and mono parts of the system are lined up with a 3 dB

346

difference in level. Unfortunately this is not a complete answer to the problem of relative levels.

There would be no difficulty if the signals added together simply, so that the maximum volume of A + B really were always no more than 3 dB higher than the separate maximum volumes for A + B, but in fact this happens only for identical sources, for tone or for a signal in the centre of the sound stage. If A and B are both at the same volume but are different sounds, the sum varies from + 0 dB to + 6 dB. So where A and B are at maximum volume, the A + B signal may be overmodulating by 3 dB. This should therefore be controlled for the benefit of mono systems.

On the other hand if the signal is being controlled primarily on the A + B signal, the stereo signal can overmodulate. This happens when A + B is at its maximum and all of the signal is in the A or B channel, which is then 3 dB over the top. So again there is a case for control.

Fortunately these control problems occur only in this mixed mono and stereo situation: controlling stereo for a single medium is much simpler.

Programme volume: relative levels

A peak programme meter can be used to suggest or check levels. For example, if ordinary talk or discussion is allowed a normal dynamic range with occasional peaks up to the maximum, then newsreaders (who generally speak very clearly and evenly) usually sound loud enough with peaks averaging about 6 dB less.

A whole system of such reference levels can be built up; and the following are some specimen PPM peak levels for speech and music that experience indicates are about right for listeners hearing radio programmes under reasonably good conditions (the values shown are peak levels in dB relative to the maximum that may be fed to the transmitter).

	PPM PEAK LEVELS
Talk, discussion programmes	0
News and weather	−6
Drama: narration	−8
Drama: action	0 to −16
Light music	0 to −16
Serious music	0 to −22 or lower
Harpsichords and bagpipes	−8
Clavichords and virginals	−16
Announcements between music (depending on type of music)	−4 to −8

Even if such a list is adopted as a general guide, it does not solve all the problems posed by junctions between speech and music or, on the larger scale, between programme and programme. For radio stations with a distinctive personality in the American style (i.e. a restricted range of programme material) there are a limited number of types of junction, and it is fairly easy to link item to item. For BBC listeners in Britain, where a single service includes news, comedy. light and serious music, religious services, magazine and discussions programmes, and so on, problems of matching between successive items can become acute.

A slight complication to this question of matching was suggested by the results of a BBC survey on listeners' preferences for relative levels of speech and music. Taking a large number of pieces in different styles (but excluding modern pop music) and with different linking voices, the results were:

Speech following music to be (on average) 4 dB down;
Music following speech to be (on average) 2 dB up.

At first sight these results appear to present a contradiction, but in fact this is easy enough to resolve: it simply means that announcements linking music items should be edged in a little.

In this experiment the listeners were giving the music and speech their full attention. This leads to a second inference from these results: that if you listen to music deliberately and consciously you probably set your loudspeaker volume fairly high, with the result that announcements may appear unpleasantly loud. Had they been using the music for background listening only, it is unlikely that the participants in the experiment would have wished for a similar balance between music and speech.

Maximum volumes

When a broadcast or recording is being made the balancer monitors at a fairly loud listening level, and is giving it his full attention. This is true in the television studio and film dubbing theatre too. So it must always be remembered that the state of affairs at the listening end may be very different.

Some further experimental results underline this: tests were made on the maximum sound levels preferred by BBC studio managers, musicians and members of the public. It was found that studio managers preferred louder levels than the musicians, and very much louder than the general public:

PREFERRED MAXIMUM SOUND LEVEL
(dB, referred to 2×10^{-5} N/m²)

| | Public | | Musicians | Studio managers | |
	Men	Women		Men	Women
Symphonic music	78	78	88	90	87
Light music	75	74	79	89	84
Dance music	75	73	79	89	83
Speech	71	71	74	84	77

These figures were obtained in 1948, before the advent of FM broadcasting. But the picture has probably changed very little.

The figures for the public correspond reasonably well with what they would hear in real life in a seat fairly close to the players. Musicians, who in real life would be much closer to the sound sources, might reasonably be expected to choose higher levels. But the studio managers (sound balancers) choose unrealistically high levels. Why?

Part of the reason for the diversity must be that people professionally concerned with sound are extracting a great deal more information from what they hear, and the greater volume helps them to hear the finer points of fades and mixes, etc., and check technical quality. Musicians, on the other hand, draw on a vast fund of experience of musical form and instrumental quality, and are listening for performance, often disregarding technical quality almost completely.

Loudness and listening conditions

These preferred maximum levels refer specifically to the case where the listeners, like those concerned in creating the programme, want to listen attentively and have reasonable conditions for doing so. But there are very many occasions when this is not the case. For example, part of many people's early evening listening may be done while driving or working in the kitchen. In such cases, where the listeners' attention is limited, and background noise may be high, speech may be peaked 8 dB higher than music. If, when listening to a programme controlled in this way, you decide that a particular item of music appeals to you and you turn it up, you will find that the announcement following appears unduly loud. As a general rule, the listener can do little to combat the levels as transmitted.

Television sound in the home is often set at levels comparable to that which would be appropriate to background radio listening. This may be satisfactory for some programmes, but if there follows a play with a wide dynamic range of sound, the overall level drops still further, and may remain uncorrected by the viewer. The sound man for the play (who is monitoring at high level) may well have set relative levels of speech to effects, or singer to accompaniment, that are inappropriate to such quiet listening. Alternatively, the viewer may raise the volume, and then the subsequent announcement and following programmes too loud for him: indeed, they seem all the louder because of his irritation that he has to adjust the level at all. For the broadcaster, all this requires a fine judgment of the compromises involved. A start may be made by listening to part of the rehearsal, or a recording of it, at realistic domestic levels on a small loudspeaker.

Linking together speech items of varying intelligibility presents a special problem—particularly in the case where an item containing a great deal of noise and distortion has to be matched to good studio quality. Here, the least unsatisfactory solution is found if the noisy item is matched for loudness at the beginning and end, and lifted for intelligibility in between: the item must be slightly faded in and out.

There is a further way in which listening conditions may vary. On the one hand, there are small portable radios that demand high intelligibility and, on the other, wide-range hi-fi, demanding not only high-quality transmission but also a wide dynamic range. The two sets of requirements are largely incompatible. In the United States there are different radio stations tailored to fit the two audiences and Britain and many other countries have gone most of the way in following this lead.

But where different types of programme material still form part of the same service, what is the solution? Unfortunately there can be no rule-of-thumb answer. It is a question of judgement; of trying to imagine what the audience will hear when listening to your programme for the first and (almost certainly) only time. Remember that your own ideas are considerably coloured by long acquaintance with the material: familiarity breeds acceptance.

Dynamic range—and the need for compression

The ear can accept an enormous range of volumes of sound. At 1000 Hz the threshold of pain is 110 dB or more above the threshold of hearing—that is, a sound that is just bearable may be over a hundred thousand million times as powerful as one that is just audible. For neither a recording nor a broadcast is such a range practicable. Some sort of compression of the signal is usually necessary: the question is, how much?

In inexpensive equipment there may be only 40 or 50 dB between the noise and distortion levels, and the user wants to keep well above the noise for the most part. Professional equipment generally has a better signal-to-noise ratio, but in broadcasting there are many more links in the chain. In general, a signal-to-noise ratio of at least 50 dB throughout the chain is regarded as desirable; but fringe area radio or television sound reception with a range as poor as 25 dB may also have to be catered for.

Also, as we have seen, much depends on listening conditions. For example, for an orchestral concert that is being heard on a good FM receiver, a fairly wide dynamic range is desirable—but nothing like the 60 or 70 dB that may separate the loudest and quietest passages in the concert hall. A relatively narrow range is suitable for listening under domestic conditions: indeed, only 45 dB separate the average listener's preferred maximum listening level and the noise level of a quiet living-room. A recording or broadcast that is to be heard under such 'average' conditions must take this into account. BBC practice for broadcast concerts is to keep peak levels generally within a range of 22 dB, with quieter passages not exceeding half a minute at a time. Popular music is kept to a very much narrower range, and so is speech.

Some gramophone records, it is true, have a wider dynamic range than broadcast concerts, in order to cater for those who can listen under ideal conditions; but an adequate signal-to-noise ratio must still be maintained for the quieter passages.

An AM transmitter has to be protected by limiters against sudden overmodulation. FM transmitters and receivers also run into distortion at some level, and in Britain the maximum frequency deviation is set at 75 kHz; this means that radio engineers and receiver manufacturers can work to the same standard, above which distortion may be expected. The degree of pre-emphasis set on British FM transmissions makes the high-frequency component rather vulnerable to distortion. It may be noticeable on speech sibilants, and other material with a strong high-frequency content should also be held back a little, especially where limiters are used to maintain an overall high level.

Transmission lines and links, too, can be overloaded, or will drown too low a signal in noise. The usable range on tape recordings is bounded below by the tape-hiss due to the grain structure of the oxide coating and above by the level at which printing between layers sets in. Between these two the range that is available for recording depends on noise reduction systems (p. 363) and the grade of tape. Further, if a programme has to be replayed rather quietly (and it is generally true that other people do not wish to listen to a work as loud as will its creator) careful compression ensures that it is all still audible.

Controlling a programme

As has already been seen, the control desk is essentially just a very high-quality mixer unit, with logarithmic faders for each source, for groups, and for the main gain, marked off in 'stops' which are each, in BBC practice, equivalent to $1\frac{1}{2}$ or 2 dB (over the main working range). This allows the operator a very convenient means of checking and correcting his levels. He will have a script or full score to guide him, and during the rehearsals he can use this to note his settings and other information that will be useful on the take.

Having set his gain at a suitable average level for the type of programme, and adjusted his loudspeaker to a comfortable volume, he can carry on and listen under conditions reasonably close to those of a domestic living-room. He judges divergences from his average level on the grounds of relative loudness and intelligibility (sometimes these two factors do not suggest the same results, as we have seen) and he does not have to worry about his meter too much except to watch for very quiet or loud passages. When recording, the effects of any particularly high peaks can be checked on the tape, to see whether there is appreciable distortion. On a broadcast, too, an occasional peak may be risked in preference to reducing the effective service area of the transmitter by undermodulating a whole programme; limiters deal with any peaks big enough to damage equipment. On speech programmes the sound man also checks his levels on the meter from time to time to see that he is maintaining the same average volume. The ear is not reliable for this—it tires. At the end of the rehearsal of a record programme, say, it is worth checking the levels of the first few records again, to see if one's judgment of the appropriate level for them has changed. It often has.

Compression of music

Overmodulation on music must be avoided not by 'riding the gain' but by careful preparation—gradually pulling back on the gain control for half a minute or so before the peak is due. During

MANUAL CONTROL OF PRO-GRAMME VOLUME. 1. Highest permissible level. 2. Lowest acceptable level. Method of compressing a heavy peak to retain the original dramatic effect and at the same time ensure that the signal falls between maximum and minimum levels. Steps of about 1½–2 dB are made at intervals of, say, ten seconds.

the rehearsal, the appropriate setting for handling the peak will have been noted on the score, and after the loud passage there is a slow return to the average level. Each operation should consist of one or more steps of about 2 dB. A similar procedure may be used to lift long periods of low level.

Often it is found best to vary the level continuously throughout a programme, so that all the elements of light and shade fall within the acceptable dynamic range.

Such techniques as these are most likely to be necessary when recording orchestral works, but (and this depends on the nature of the music and the closeness of the balance) control may also be needed with smaller combinations or groups, or even a solo instrument, such as a piano.

There is one other possible way of dealing with the control of orchestral music, and this is to leave it in the hands of the conductor. It has even been known for a conductor to have a meter on his desk as he rehearses and records; but this technique has not been generally adopted. On the whole, it seems preferable that the conductor should concentrate on the performance, bearing the limitations of the medium in mind if he can, but leaving control to the balance engineer.

However, music programmes specifically designed for background listening may have some measure of compression built in by the arranger; and also, of course, smaller musical forces will be employed.

The farther the microphone is away the easier it is to control music: studio or concert hall acoustics smooth out the peaks. The balancer who adopts a bright, 'tight' balance has more work to do without necessarily earning the thanks of listeners—many of whom prefer a well-blended sound for classical music, as BBC listening tests have shown.

Control of music affects the reverberation just as much as the main sound. The effect may be disconcerting: the microphone moves closer, but the perspective remains the same. The two may be controlled more effectively by using two microphones, one close and one distant, and working between them on changes of music volume. This can be done in stereo too, with two coincident pairs, one almost over the conductor's head with a double cardioid pick-up; the other on double figure-of-eight and so placed (farther back) that the various parts of the orchestra are reasonably coincident. Alternatively there may be reverberation microphones facing away from the orchestra: they are controlled independently of the main pair to achieve the best effect as the acoustic volume of the music varies.

Compression: speech and effects

In controlling speech the problems are somewhat different, as are the methods employed for dealing with them. In real life speech and noises might occupy the full range from the threshold of hearing to the threshold of pain. This would be quite intolerable on tape, even if it could be recorded.

Studio interviews and discussions for radio and television also benefit by careful control, particularly if one voice is much louder than the others, or habitually starts off with a bang, and then trails away. Here, control is a matter of intelligent anticipation: whenever your needle-bender opens his mouth to speak, drop the fader back—sharply if he does so in a pause, but rather more gently if someone else is speaking: a slight dip in level is more acceptable than the risk of a sudden loud voice. Laughter may have to be treated similarly if the general level is being held well up. But edge the fader up again as quickly as possible after the laugh.

Careful control should be unnoticeable: the way *not* to do it is to miss the first high peak and *then* haul back on the fader. No control at all is better than bad control.

Do not discourage speakers from raising their voices, unless they actually ask for advice; even then the best advice is, 'Be natural.' A natural but controlled programme is much superior to one in which voices are never raised and the programme meter never has any bad moments. It is sometimes said that the sound engineer's idea of a perfect programme is pure tone at a constant level—because it never does anything it should not. Speakers who never do anything they should not sound just as dull and un-interesting as that pure tone.

A good programme depends on variety of pace and attack. It should not be necessary to hold the overall level back in order to accommodate possible overmodulation. But if much editing is envisaged it would be better to deal with the more violent fluctuations of level after the editing session, otherwise there may be difficulty even in the case that we have been considering so far, a studio in which extraneous noise is kept at a low level.

A completely different situation arises when recordings are made on location, whether for radio, television, or film *when subsequent editing is envisaged* (as nearly always is the case when filming). In this case it is better that a level should be set so that background remains constant throughout a sequence. If necessary, some control can be exercised by slight movement of a directional microphone held by hand.

For scripted drama the BBC regards something like 16 dB as being an adequate range for peak values of speech—the average being about 8 dB below the maximum permissible. The main effect that this has on speech is that scenes involving shouting have to be held back, possibly making them sound rather distant—which is fine if this fits in with the picture that is wanted. But for cases where close shouting must be mixed in with more normal levels of speech it is up to the actors to hold back on volume, and project their voices.

This upper limit makes even more difference when it comes to loud sound effects—a gunshot, for example, or a car crash. Even a sharply closed door is too loud.

It is therefore fortunate that radio and television drama have established a convention in which such effects are suggested by character rather than by volume. Volumes have to be controlled; they have to be evened out and held back—which explains why extremely unlikely-looking methods for making sound effects often produce the best results.

Compressors and limiters

The terms *compressor* and *limiter* are sometimes used as though they were entirely different devices. In fact, as will be seen,

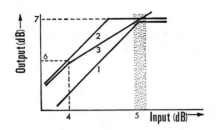

they are not: there may be considerable differences in design between two different types of compressor, either of which, with minor modifications (or simply by switching to a particular setting) can be used as a limiter.

Essentially, a compressor works like this:

Below a predetermined level (the threshold or onset point) the volume of a signal is unchanged. Above this point the additional volume is reduced in a given proportion, e.g. 2:1, 3:1 or 5:1. For example, if the threshold were set at 8 dB below the level of 100% modulation and 2:1 compression selected, it would mean that signals which previously overmodulated by 8 dB were now only just reaching full modulation. Similarly if 5:1 had been chosen, signals which previously would have overpeaked by 32 dB will now only just reach 100%.

What this means in practice is that the overall level may be raised by 8 dB or 32 dB, so that relatively quiet signals are now making a much bigger contribution than would otherwise be possible.

Suppose now that the compression ratio were made large, say 20:1, and the threshold level raised to something very close to 100% modulation (because there would now seem to be little point in leaving it at 8 dB below, unless a signal about 150 dB above normal levels were expected). The result of this is that the compressor now acts as a limiter. And in this condition it can be used

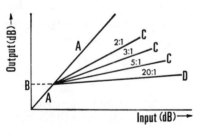

COMPRESSION RATIOS. A. Linear operation, in which input and output levels correspond. Above a given threshold level (B), various compression ratios (C) reduce the output level. In the extreme case (D) the compressor acts as a limiter holding the maximum output volume close to the threshold level, but still permitting a small proportion of any high peak to pass.

356

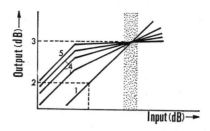

INCREASING THE VOLUME OF LOW-LEVEL SIGNALS by the use of a compressor. 1. With the compressor out of circuit only a small proportion of the input range goes in to the desired narrow dynamic range (2–3). 4. With increasing degrees of compression more can be accommodated. 5. The effect of a limiter. In these examples the choice of threshold setting has been governed by arranging for the expected maximum level to produce full modulation. The greater the compression, the less the effect of overmodulation beyond this expected level.

either to hold individual unexpected high peaks *or* to lift the signals from virtually any lower level into the usable working range of the equipment, though not without causing problems with high level signals that are being excessively compressed, and background noise, which will be lifted as well—of which, more later.

The effect of a 2:1 compressor with a threshold at 8 dB below 100% modulation is to compress only the top 16 dB of signals while leaving those at a lower level to drop away at a 1:1 ratio. An

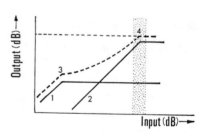

COMPRESSION BY A COMBINATION OF TWO LIMITERS. 1. Effect of low level limiter. 2. High level limiter. When the two signals are combined, the resulting compression characteristic is different from that of a normal compressor which would give a straight line from 3 to 4.

interesting variation on this would be to place two limiters together, working on a signal in parallel but with the threshold set at different levels. If one is set for 2 dB below 100% and the other for (say) 24 dB below, but raised in level, the effect is to introduce a variable rate of compression that is greater at the lower end of the range than toward the top, where something approaching the normal dynamic range is used until the upper limiter operates. A further variation is that the lower limiter could have a weighting network to arrange that quiet high- or

357

low-frequency signals were lifted more than those whose power was primarily in the central (500–4000 Hz) part of the audio range.

Originally, the main purpose for limiters was to protect equipment from excessive signals. The final power-amplifying tube in an AM transmitter was at particular risk: it was undesirable to increase the capacity and cost of such a large and expensive piece of equipment much beyond that required for the nominal full modulation. The difficulty was that once this level was reached, only a few decibels were required to raise the power passing through the value to double its normal maximum level, or even more.

Compressors and limiters work by sampling the signal at a particular point in the chain, and if it is above a designated level, deriving a control signal which is fed back through a side chain to

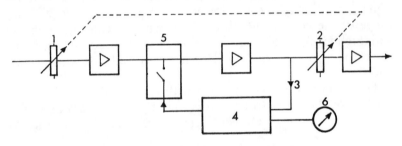

SIMPLE COMPRESSOR/LIMITER. 1 and 2. Threshold level control (ganged). 3. Sample signal fed from the main programme chain. 4. Side chain with compression ratio and recovery time controls. 5. Control element operating on the main programme chain. 6. Meter showing the degree of attenuation.

reduce the overall volume at an earlier point in the main programme chain. It is usually arranged that this control signal operates with a fast attack and slow decay—though both 'fast' and 'slow' may have a very wide range of actual durations in different circumstances.

One modern compressor/limiter reduces the power of a signal by earthing (grounding) it momentarily at intervals of 250 kHz. At 6 dB above the onset point the selection of a 2:1 compression ratio means that half the power must be removed from the signal— to reduce it by 3 dB. It is arranged, therefore, that the control switch spends half of each successive 4 microseconds open and half closed. Such a high rate of switching has no audible effect on the signal, but simply reduces the total power transmitted. A signal 12 dB over the threshold has to be reduced by 6 dB, so

358

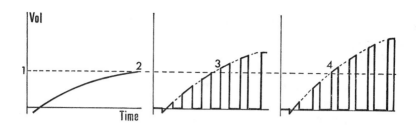

SIGNAL CHOPPING reducing the power of an audio signal. 1. Compressor threshold. 2. When the signal does not exceed this, the compressor remains inoperative. 3 and 4. For higher signals progressively more of the power is removed. Note that the chopping frequency is high compared with the highest audio signal and that it operates over the whole waveform, not just on the peak.

that the switch must be closed for 3 microseconds of every 4; for signals at or below the threshold it does not operate at all.

In the feedback side chain there are controls for varying the compression ratio and decay time, and also a circuit for driving a meter that shows the degree of attenuation at any moment.

Other systems have also been used for compressing and limiting signals: but a necessary criterion for any is that it should not operate selectively on that part of the wave which exceeds the threshold level (which would introduce harmonic distortion), but should reduce the whole wave in proportion. Perhaps the simplest way of doing this is to rectify part of the excess signal, store it in a capacitor and use it to provide a DC control bias until such time as the charge has been allowed to leak to earth.

Compression: attack and decay times

Early limiters were operated by the first half wave of the over-load signal—which meant that this first half wave itself got through undiminished. For a very low frequency such a signal could send a considerable amount of power to the transmitter, so that, for example, someone kicking a table supporting a microphone could produce a bump big enough to cause damage. It was therefore necessary to provide additional protection in the form of a trip that would stop the signal reaching the transmitter in extreme cases—which meant in effect that overloading would put the transmitter off the air until the mechanism operating the trip had had time itself to recover.

Later designs such as that already described were more sophisticated in that they were capable of chopping the signal and sampling it for a shorter period, allowing an attack time of something of the order of tens of microseconds. This, however, introduced a new problem, because such a very sharp change of level is liable to introduce an audible click.

The answer is to delay the whole signal for about half a millisecond and then make a gradual change of level over the same period—in advance of any sudden heavy peak. This eliminates the click as the background changes level, but cannot affect the fact that if the background *is* there, it *is* suddenly going to change level—and that this is bound to be in some degree objectionable. The particular quality of unpleasantness is also affected by the rate of decay of the control signal. Heavy limiting, or strong compression with a moderate recovery time produces a 'pumping' effect that is mechanical-sounding and ugly.

Early limiters had gain-recovery, or control signal decay rates of the order of seconds: this allowed a reasonable time for the overload condition to pass so that it would not be pumped by too rapid a train of high level signals. The more sophisticated limiters (described above) have a selection of decay times available (100, 200, 400 and 800 milliseconds, and 1·6 and 3·2 seconds).

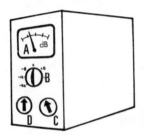

SIMPLE COMPRESSOR/LIMITER. A. Attenuation meter (scale: 0—24 dB). B. Threshold setting, −24 to +16 dB relative to nominal 0 dB setting. C. Compression control 1:1 (i.e. no compression), 2:1, 3:1, 5:1, and Lim (20:1, i.e. acting as limiter). D. Decay time control: 0·1–3·2 seconds.

The fastest of these can hold isolated brief excessive peaks without having a severe effect on the background; but they are not so satisfactory for a rapid series of short peaks: any background is given an unpleasant vibrato-like flutter.

However, if there are only occasional peaks, and they are not too big—say, of not more than about 3 dB or so—the recovery time is probably not critical, and something like half a second is generally adopted: it is only at high levels of compression that the exact choice of recovery time becomes important. One very satisfactory type of limiter used for gain reductions of up to 16 dB has automatic variations built in: varying, in fact, between about 30 milliseconds and 10 seconds according to the level and duration of the overload signal.

360

Compression using digital circuitry is very versatile. One such device, called an *Omnipressor* has simple controls that can be set for expansion, compression or dynamic inversion. The expansion ratio starts at 1:10 then proceeds by discrete steps to 1:1 after which it becomes normal compression. The scale continues to infinite compression (i.e. a ratio of 1:0, a 'perfect' limiter) beyond which the ratio becomes negative, so that the quiet sounds are made louder and vice versa. This carries the compressor principle into new realms, as an instrument of creative sound treatment and synthesis.

The use of limiters and compressors

We have already noted that the purpose of control is three-fold: to avoid overmodulation, to maintain a good signal-to-noise ratio at the lower end of the dynamic range, and—within these extremes—to ensure that all dynamic expression is appropriate to the nature of the programme.

Clearly, considerable advances have been made in automatic control of the first two of these variables: it is the third that remains the problem. It has proved difficult enough to design a device that will discriminate quickly between speech and music— and even then it is nothing like so fast as the human brain—so it would be much more difficult to discriminate quickly (if at all) between different types of music or different situations in which speech is used (though there has been some success in recognizing the total structure of certain irritating and insistent types of commercial). Yet a human operator would unhesitatingly apply different measures of control in such apparently similar situations. It may be emphasized again: heavy automatic control should be applied only in those situations where systematic errors do not become too obvious, or where very strong advantages outweigh the disadvantage of artistic ham-fistedness.

Short wave radio, and commercial radio stations determined to obtain the maximum service area from a given transmitter power, form a special case. Here control is used only to ensure that the average level is as high as possible, consistent with a distortion of peaks that is not excessive. How acceptable this is to the listener depends on conditions in the main service area. If a broadcast is intended to be heard a long way from the transmitter and is likely to have to compete with heavy static and possibly even jamming by unfriendly natives, the intending listener will welcome a heavy use of the limiter.

If the main service area is the town round the transmitter and there is little or no interference the listener will find all but the lightest touch of the limiter objectionable; if he is listening on a car radio and the signal is subject to moderate interference and fading he would welcome more.

A completely different use for compressors and limiters is that adopted in pop music balance. Here the technical possibilities are being used as creatively as the musical instruments themselves: the use of compression is assumed in the composition of the music.

Discrimination against noise

A major problem with limiters and compressors working on high gain is that background noise is lifted as well, unless something is done to prevent it. In particular, when there is no foreground signal to regulate the overall level, that is, during a pause, the noise is liable to rise by the full permitted gain. Such noise will include ventilation hum and studio clocks, movement and other personal noises, traffic or other more distant sound, electronic or line noise, and so on. Even where such sounds are themselves not raised to an objectionable level certain consonants at the start of subsequent speech are not powerful enough to trigger the compressor, the most unpleasant result being the excessive sibilance at the start of certain words, though this can be avoided by high-frequency pre-emphasis in the input to the limiter: this is sometimes called 'de-essing'.

One device that can be used to discriminate against noise is a *noise gate*. In this, when the sound level falls below a second, lower threshold setting the gain is allowed to fall to a parallel but lower input/output characteristic: this might, for example, be

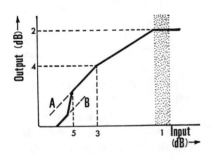

COMPRESSOR/LIMITER WITH NOISE GATE. 1. Range of maximum expected input level. 2. Corresponding maximum output level. 3. Lowest level of interest. 4. Lower end of designed dynamic range. 5. Gating level: if level of signal drops below this, the input characteristic falls from level A to level B.

8 dB below that which would apply without a gate. At this setting, a device that could not previously have been used for more than 8 dB compression on a particular signal without the background noise becoming excessively loud in the pauses could now be used for 16 dB compression.

Noise gates are often made fast operating, so that in even the slightest pauses between the syllables of a word the noise is sharply reduced. But for such an operation to be successful, the device has to be set up with care: the gate must be *below* all significant elements of speech, but *above* all of the basic noise. Indeed, if both of these conditions cannot be met the result could be unpleasant, with either the speech or the noise wobbling up and down on the edge of the gate. But in any case any extraneous staccato sound of a higher volume or a rise in the background to an unexpectedly high level will fool the gate; as also (in the opposite sense) would a very quiet passage at the start of a piece of music.

In the 'automatic level control' available on some high quality portable recorders used for professional sound radio and film location work, yet another type of limiter is used: one that avoids most of the rise and fall of background noise that is heard with other limiters. A short delay is introduced before the control signal begins to decay. The duration of this delay can be adjusted to allow for different lengths of pause between syllables or words as spoken by different individuals or in different languages, but is normally 3 seconds—after which the 'memory' is erased and a new level of adjustment selected. This same recorder has a separate circuit for the control of very brief transients, which do not therefore affect the basic level. Obviously, such a device still has limitations: there would undoubtedly be many cases where a human operator would adjust the level, for example, on a change of voice; so it will probably only be used where it is inconvenient to employ a human operator. Like the fast-operating gate, the device can all too easily be fooled by unexpected events.

Noise reduction systems

In one commercially available noise reduction system the signal is split by filters into four frequency bands: 80 Hz low-pass; 80 Hz–3 kHz; 3 kHz high-pass; and 9 kHz high-pass. Each band is separately compressed, so that very low level signals (40 dB down) are raised to 10 dB, while signals from 0–20 dB down are virtually unaffected. The recovery time is 1–100 milliseconds, depending on the signal dynamics. There are also limiters in each channel: these are simple peak choppers. An exactly matching network is used to reconstitute the original signal on playback. The principle of the system depends on the fact that noise similar in frequency to the louder components of the signal is masked by it, while that which is widely separated in frequency from the louder components is reduced in level: the improvement is therefore partly real and partly apparent. As the system produces a coded signal which must then be decoded it cannot be used to improve an already noisy signal. It is widely used to improve the quality of tape recordings, where an overall improvement of 10 dB in the signal-to-noise ratio is used partly to reduce hiss, hum and rumble and also, by lowering recording levels a little, to produce less distortion and to lower the danger of print-through. It is particularly valuable for multitrack recordings but can in principle be used around any noisy component or link. The signal is, of course, unusuable in its coded form: characteristically it sounds 'bright, breathy, and larger than life'.

A simplified system for domestic tape recorders is used to reduce tape hiss. For professional use a range of competing noise reduction systems is available.

Noise is an inherent defect of analogue recording. A way of by-passing the need for noise reduction is to use digital recording instead: this offers a 90 dB signal-to-noise ratio without further treatment. It is very convenient for multi-track work, as 32 tracks will fit on a 1-inch (25 mm) tape, though at a high playing speed of 45 i/s (114 cm/s). Harmonic and intermodulation distortion and interchannel cross-talk are all very low; while wow, flutter, print-through and erasure problems are avoided completely.

14

MONITORING QUALITY

DURING rehearsal, recording or broadcast, the ear should be constantly searching out the faults that will mar a production; certainly there are plenty of things to listen for—here are just a few that affect sound whether in radio, television, or film:

1. *Production faults:* e.g. miscast voices, stilted speaking of the lines, uncolloquial scripts, bad timing.
2. *Faulty technique:* e.g. poor balance and control, untidy fades and mixes, misuse of acoustics.
3. *Poor sound quality:* e.g. distortion, resonances, and other irregularities in the frequency response, lack of bass and top.
4. *Faults of the equipment or recordings:* wow and flutter, hum, excessive tape hiss, noises due to loose connections, poor screening, or mis-matching.

Of these, the faults in the first group are certainly the most important. They are also, perhaps, the easiest to spot. As for techniques: the ability to see faults there comes with the practice of the techniques. But the various things that can be wrong with the quality of a sound—objective, measurable things—appear, somewhat surprisingly, to be the most difficult for the ear to judge in other than subjective 'I-know-what-I-like' terms.

Quality and the ear

The quality of sound that the ear will accept—and prefer—depends almost entirely on what the listener is used to. Very few people whose ears are untrained can judge quality in reasonably precise and objective terms. Given a choice between qualities, listeners are generally prepared to state a preference, but experiments in the United States have indicated that as many will prefer medium quality as prefer the best.

There was a demonstration of this at an Audio Fair in Britain when a manufacturer of loudspeaker enclosures invited members of the public to judge and compare the quality of three different stereo speaker systems, without being able to see which was playing or being told the prices until afterwards. To a trained ear there can surely have been little doubt about the order. A large number of people, most of them presumably audio enthusiasts, took part in the tests. Their votes split evenly between the three systems.

At first sight the results of such experiments may appear rather depressing for the high-quality-sound enthusiast. Even among people who claim to like hi-fi (a term which seems to cover any sound equipment from medium quality upwards) the real preference is often for a box that sounds like a box; the sort of quality that turns a living-room into one corner of a great concert hall is found to be somewhat disturbing. It is an attitude that must be respected; but it must nevertheless be true that quality and enjoyment are often closely related. The high-quality performance of a musical work gives more *information* to a listener who is new to it; and it is often a technically superior disc that first 'sells' music content, and interests a listener in something new.

The difference between a good loudspeaker and a poor one boils down to this: that the good one allows more of the original conception of the sound to reach the listener. Potentially it permits greater enjoyment of the programme—or anyway a more sophisticated enjoyment of it. On the technical monitoring side it would appear obvious that a high-quality speaker is essential.

High-quality sound is not—as with, say, wide-screen film—an advance that imposes a new set of limitations. Different degrees of quality may be acceptable to the same person when applied to different programme ends. For example, high quality may be best for brilliant modern music (or for any orchestral music heard as a concert); medium or low quality can be satisfactory for ordinary speech, where the primary reason for listening is usually to hear what is said; and 'mellow' quality is often felt to be less obtrusive when music is required for a companionable background noise. On high-quality equipment these different types of programme are all available at the appropriate levels of quality; on poor equipment they are all debased to the same indifferent standard.

So it is undoubtedly worth persevering with the education of one's ears, and allowing other people the opportunity of listening to sound that is of rather better quality than they are used to.

366

Nevertheless, any organization that is conscious of cost must decide what is to be the practicable economic upper limit to the audio frequency range to be offered. Tests have been carried out by the BBC in which the audio frequency range was restricted to 7 kHz, 10 kHz and 12 kHz. Sounds heard within the test material included tubular bells, brass, cymbals and triangle, snare and military drums, maraccas, handclaps, and female speech. The listeners were all under 40 years of age, both male and female and included a number of people who were experienced in judging sound quality. The results of the tests suggested that:

1. Only a few critical observers hear restriction to 12 kHz.
2. Many inexperienced listeners can detect restriction to 10 kH; experienced listeners do so readily.
3. A filter at 7 kHz could be detected even by inexperienced observers.

In fact the BBC broadcasts up to 15 kHz on VHF/FM.

Loudspeakers

The main obstacle to good sound has nearly always been the loudspeaker. It is, in principle, fairly easy to get good middle range and high-frequency response, but efficient production of bass requires either a fairly large surface area to push the air, or a horn with an equally large aperture.

One apparent alternative to this is to have a relatively small area driving the air and to boost the bass so that the inefficiency of the

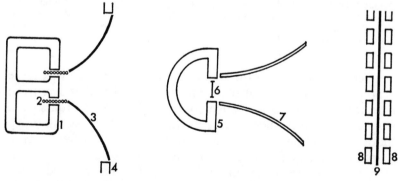

LOUDSPEAKER TYPES. *Left.* Moving coil. The most commonly used for all purposes (bass, treble and wide range). 1. Permanent magnet. 2. Moving coil. 3. Cone. 4. Baffle or enclosure. *Centre.* Ribbon unit. Sometimes used for treble. 5. Permanent magnet. 6. Ribbon (seen in plan view). 7. Acoustic horn. *Right.* Electrostatic. 8. Perforated fixed electrodes. 9. Diaphragm.

coupling is compensated for in advance. But there is a limit to this, as the excursions of the diaphragm get so big that it becomes a complication in itself, as does the extra power that is required from the amplifier.

Most loudspeakers use a stiff diaphragm working as a piston. It is operated by an electromechanical device that is usually very similar in principle to those used in microphones—except, of course, that it converts an electrical signal back into physical movement. The most common type is the moving coil; but electrostatic, ribbon, and other types are sometimes used.

It is not easy for a single diaphragm to respond equally well to all frequencies: sometimes the signal is split and fed to separate loudspeakers covering two (or even three) different parts of the

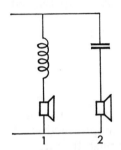 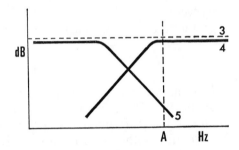

LOUDSPEAKER: SIMPLE CROSS-OVER NETWORK. 1. Bass unit. 2. Treble unit. 3. The total power is divided evenly between the two units 4 and 5; for each it falls off at 6 dB/octave beyond the cross-over point. This is a very satisfactory type of network provided that there are no severe irregularities in the response of the cone itself that are close enough to the cross-over point to make a significant contribution even though attenuated. For example a very severe fluctuation in the bass cone output at A will still affect the overall response: the answer is to make the cross-over point lower (if the response of the high frequency unit permits) or to use a more complex dividing network with a steeper cut-off at the cross-over point.

frequency range. When the sound is divided up in this way there is no need for a sharp cut-off as one loudspeaker takes over from another, so long as the acoustic output adds up to a full signal. But careful relative positioning of the two units is necessary, so that there is no phase cancellation at the switch-over frequencies. At other frequencies it does not matter.

For the low-frequency unit a cone of paper may be used as the diaphragm. This has to be corrugated concentrically in order to stop unwanted harmonics from being formed (these may include a subharmonic that is actually below the main frequency at which the cone is being driven). Cones or pistons of other materials are

368

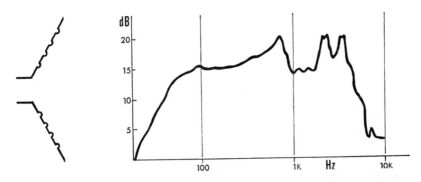

LOUDSPEAKER CONE WITH STRAIGHT SIDES of corrugated paper felt. The performance diagram shows axial frequency response with output in dB (arbitrary scale), taken from a particular example.

also used. They must be stiff but have adequate internal damping or they may ring like a wineglass at certain frequencies. The cone, of whatever construction, must also be of low mass or its inertia may affect the response.

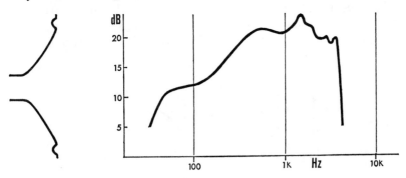

LOUDSPEAKER CONE: BBC DESIGN, 1967; at which time it was claimed to be better than any other commercially available cone of equal size (12 in, 30 cm) or larger used in a bass unit (with cross-over at 1600 Hz). The material used is Bextrene (a polystyrene/synthetic rubber compound), with a PVC surround.

A problem with a cone—or any other diaphragm—is that as it radiates the wanted signal from the front, a second signal, in the opposite phase, is being radiated from the back; and if there is nothing to stop it, some of this back-radiation leaks round the sides and join the sound from the front. The long-wavelength low frequencies are most affected by this: as the two signals combine, they are still partly out of phase and therefore tend to cancel a signal that is already weaker than it should be because

369

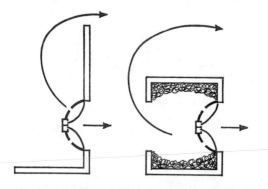

LOUDSPEAKER HOUS-INGS. *Left.* Baffle. *Right.* Enclosure with opening at rear. These reduce the frequency at which sound radiated from the back of a cone can recombine with and cancel the direct sound. A box may have internal resonances which need to be damped by lining it with absorbent material.

the cone is too small for effective low frequency work.

There are several partial cures for this. One is to house the loudspeaker in a baffle of relatively large area. The size determines the limiting wavelength, below which cancellation still occurs: a baffle some 30 inches (75 cm) square is about the minimum for a moderately good low frequency response. A second technique is to turn the space behind the cone into a low frequency resonator with a port that radiates some of the power. It can be arranged that by phase change this boosts the response in the region in which it previously fell off. But this bass reflex loudspeaker (as it

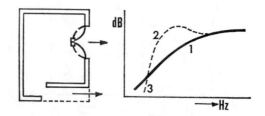

BASS REFLEX LOUDSPEAKER: this uses the internal cavity and a port at the front as a Helmholz resonator with a low frequency resonance peak. Added to the normal bass response of the loudspeaker (1) it can be used to lift the bass for about one octave (2). But below this (3) the cut-off is more severe.

is called) is bulky, may be subject to cabinet coloration in the bass, and below its resonant frequency cuts off even more sharply than before. In fact it has a characteristically recognizable quality —which is hardly a recommendation for any loudspeaker. Yet another idea is to try to lose the back radiation completely. Simply feeding it out into another room would be the best way, but as there are usually objections to this the next best answer is generally adopted: to try to stifle it within the box in such a way

370

that the diaphragm is not affected by reflections or by the 'stiffness' of the enclosed air.

The design of high-quality loudspeakers is undoubtedly a difficult problem to which there have been many other ingenious

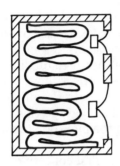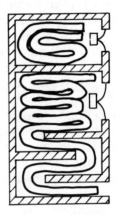

LOUDSPEAKER ENCLOSURES. *Left.* Infinite baffle. The sound from the rear of the speaker is trapped and much is absorbed. In practice the stiffness of the air within the box somewhat restricts the movement of the speaker. The cavity contains folded sound absorbent material. *Right.* The tweeter (h.f. unit) has an infinite baffle and the woofer (l.f. unit) backs on to an acoustic labyrinth (also called transmission line or pipe). This introduces both phase change and attenuation. Again, both cavities are padded.

part-solutions attempting, in particular, to get round the difficulty of the sheer size that is naturally associated with the longer wavelengths of sound. This is a very big subject, and one that is beyond the scope of this book.

Monitoring arrangements

The best distance to place a loudspeaker for monitoring programmes is probably 3–6 ft (1–2 m). Closer than this the sound has a somewhat unreal quality owing to standing waves close to the cabinet; at a greater distance the acoustics of the listening room begin to take over. It is desirable that these acoustics should be more or less the same as those of a domestic living-room. But it is important to produce a well-blended signal and to know whether some minor fault is due to the studio or listening room; and the only way to be sure is to sit rather closer to the loudspeaker than one does when listening purely for pleasure at home. This is, however, possible only for mono.

For monitoring stereo the listener should be at the apex of an equilateral triangle, or perhaps a little closer. The speakers will be about 8 ft (2·5 m) apart and the listener therefore 6 ft or more from them. The producer sits immediately behind the balancer. In a studio layout the ideal arrangement is one in which the balancer and producer do not see directly in to the studio as they face the sound stage, but can do so, to sort out positioning or other problems, by simply turning round.

For four-channel stereo two additional loudspeakers are placed behind the listener, forming a balanced set of the same type. For domestic listening it is not usually essential to have rear speakers that are as powerful or of such high quality as those at the front. Indeed, because the total power is now being split four ways, if a room were being equipped afresh, all four loudspeakers could be of a matched set that may be (individually) less powerful than would be desirable for mono or two-channel stereo.

As we monitor a sound for quality our first concern must be to recognize faults when they occur—and this is the reason why most of the main headings of this chapter are the names of forms of distortion or faults. Once the fault and the conditions in which it occurs are observed we are a long way toward a cure though there is no pretence that the details given here are exhaustive—particularly where defects of components may be the cause.

Also, various faults can occur in recording that may pass unnoticed at the time. Methods of correcting faults in recordings are indicated wherever they are feasible.

Noise

Noise, for our present purpose, may be regarded as random sound of indefinite pitch. There are plenty of other forms of 'unwanted sound', but they can each be treated separately.

All irregularities in the structure of matter cause noise: the separate particles of iron oxide in magnetic tape, tiny roughnesses in the wall of a record, the granular structure of carbon in a resistor, the random dance of individual electrons in a metal or semiconductor; all of these are bound to produce some level of noise in a recording or broadcast. The only question is, how low can it be kept in relation to the signal? For most purposes a ratio of 55 dB or more throughout the chain may be regarded as reasonably good; and, as we have seen, this provides an adequate range of volumes even for programme material that in real life would demand wider dynamics.

Noise becomes serious when components before the first stage of amplification begin to deteriorate; at a later stage, when there are more drastic faults (e.g. a 'dirty' fader or a 'dry' joint); where vibration reaches a transducer (e.g. record-player motor rumble at 25–2000 Hz); or where there are long lines or radio transmissions broadcast in unfavourable circumstances.

In recording or transmission systems where noise levels increase with frequency in a predictable manner the high-frequency signal is increased *(pre-emphasized)* before the process and reduced *(de-emphasized)* after it. Such systems require national or international standards, so that professional and domestic equipment produces complementary effects. Multitrack recording techniques, with successive stages of re-recording have been made possible by the noise reduction systems already described (p. 363).

One form of noise that does have define pitch is *hum*. This nuisance is caused by the mains frequency (and its harmonics) getting into the audio signal. Mains hum may be caused by inadequate smoothing of the electrical power supply when it has been rectified from alternating to direct current, or by lack of adequate screening on the wires carrying audio signals (particularly those at low level, or in high-impedance circuits such as those from electrostatic or crystal microphones before the first amplifier). Magnetic microphones can be directly affected by nearby electrical equipment, such as mains transformers or electric motors. Hum may also be caused by earthing faults: either the simple lack of an earth or at the other extreme, the connection of an item by separate paths to a common earth, thereby causing an earth loop, which like any other loop can pick up signals from wiring or equipment carrying mains

The second harmonic of mains hum is generally the most serious component except in certain types of hi-fi loudspeaker cabinet that provide a high output at low frequencies, so most hum filters concentrate on getting rid of 100 or 120 Hz. More elaborate 'notch' filters take out narrow slices of a wide range of harmonics without substantially affecting music.

It is, however, better to avoid hum in the first place. It can be a particular problem when recording pop music from public performances, where feeds are split from the system set up for the stage foldback loudspeakers. To identify the source of hum quickly, fit the earth (ground) leads for each circuit with a switch so that each can be individually checked. In the theatre, lighting is the main culprit, and particularly certain types of dimmer. A full rehearsal will show up the danger points; but failing that, ask for a quick run through the lighting plot and see what it does to open microphone circuits.

Distortion

If at any point in a broadcast or recording chain the volume is set too high for any stage that follows, the waveform is changed—distorted. Typically the peaks are flattened, introducing new frequencies that are harmonics of the original frequencies present. In musical terminology, new overtones are produced. However, most are added at precisely those frequencies that are already present in much sound, and most music. The introduction of harmonic distortion is therefore to some extent masked by sound already present; and where it is not is made somewhat more acceptable by its pseudo-musical relationship to the wanted sound. Speech sibilants, not already having a harmonic structure, bring it out strongly. Note, however, that human hearing is itself subject to distortion at high acoustic intensities.

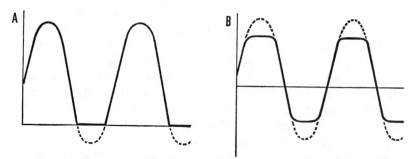

HARMONIC DISTORTION: the dotted portion of the signals is flattened. A. Bottoming causes each alternate peak to be clipped. B. Both peaks are flattened, as excessive swings in each direction cannot be followed by some item of equipment. In both cases the distortion produced includes tones which are exact multiples of the frequency of clipping.

Small amounts of distortion may be more acceptable than a high noise level: 2% harmonic distortion is generally noticeable and 1% represents a reasonable limit for high quality.

Unduly high distortion may be due to actual equipment

374

faults. For example, it occurs if the moving parts of a transducer have worked loose or are in the wrong place, e.g. a ribbon or moving coil hanging out of the magnetic field, or if too much or too little bias is used when recording on magnetic tape.

Intermodulation distortion is far less tolerable than harmonic distortion: it occurs when two frequencies interfere with each other to produce sum or difference products. High quality sound equipment is designed to avoid the production of intermodulation effects that occur in the audio range.

Distortion may arise right at the start of the chain, at points that are—in theory—under the control of the balancer. Some air pressures (perhaps caused by wind, or due to explosive consonants in close speech) may be such as to move a microphone diaphragm outside its normal working range. Or the output of the microphone may be at too high a level for the first pre-amplifier. Amplifier stages have a linear response to changes in volume (i.e. their output is proportional to input) only over a limited range. The sensitivity of professional microphones is related to the volume of expected sound sources in such a way that they mostly feed signals to the mixer at about the same range of levels. But there are notable exceptions in such sound sources as the bass drum, brass and the electric guitar, the loudspeaker for which may be set very high. If the preamplifiers are of fixed gain, a 'pad' (a fixed-loss attenuator of, say, 12 dB), may be required between microphone and amplifier. Alternatively, a microphone of low sensitivity may be selected; or one with a head amplifier that can be switched to accept different input levels.

Another example of this form of distortion may occur in very close piano balance. Used for pop music in this way, pianos may be regarded as percussion instruments, deriving a great deal of their effect from the attack transient. The brief, very high volume of this transient may not be apparent from a meter that takes time to respond—but it is there, and is liable to distort if the signal is not reduced again by perhaps 6 or 12 dB before preamplification. In such a case the amplifier works on the lower part of its range for the main signal, and the overall signal must be lifted again later in the chain—where the same damage may still occur. There has therefore been controversy as to the value of this technique.

The deliberate distortion of frequency response for subjective reasons—paradoxically called 'equalization'—is discussed in the next chapter.

Loss of high frequencies

Most of the links in an audio chain are capable of distorting the frequency response; and this is usually worse at the higher end of the scale. High frequencies can be lost in a variety of ways, and whether or not anything can be done about it depends on whether or not there is a frequency at which the signal is totally extinguished.

When a signal passes along a line, the capacitance between the two wires carrying it provides a path whereby the high frequencies are selectively lost, but the damage can be repaired by boosting the high-frequency response from time to time—and the signal-to-noise ratio is substantially maintained because high-frequency noise is first reduced and then boosted in the same proportions. But the amount of high frequency loss depends on distance, and with long lines one has to make a compromise somewhere. Taking a particular quality of line, we may decide that 8 kHz, say, is all that can be economically maintained; and then install equalizers at the various distances where the signal-to-noise ratio has fallen, say, from 55 to 40 dB at this frequency. Nor is this a complete cure, because at every stage where the frequency response is corrected a little of the noise on the line is boosted, and at the same time the many stages of distortion and subsequent correction inevitably begin to make the top end of the frequency spectrum erratic, so that eventually the signal begins to get lost even below the nominal 8 kHz.

In a building the size of a broadcasting studio centre there is a danger not only of high frequency losses due to capacitance, but also induction of programme signals, hum, etc., from other lines. One way in which this is kept at least partially in check is by the use of standard impedances, usually of several hundred ohms. If a low impedance system is adopted, the resistance and capacitance of the wiring itself becomes significant in comparison, simply because there is so much of it.

The exact matching of impedances is important when *power* is being transmitted, e.g. to a loudspeaker, as mismatching produces power losses. Where the significant part of a signal is its *voltage*, mismatching may matter less. Low in to high may go; high in to low may not: this is the rule. If a high-impedance input such as a crystal pick-up is fed to a low-impedance input there is loss of bass: if the output from a magnetic pick-up or microphone is fed into lower than its rated impedance there is loss of high frequencies.

Even more important, do not feed a high-level signal (e.g. from a tape deck or a record player) to a low-level input (such as that for a microphone) without appropriate attenuation or there will be severe overloading, with consequent distortion.

Magnetic tape

Briefly, recording tape consists of a strong plastics support (the backing) and a coating of finely divided iron oxide (or chromium dioxide) dispersed in a further binding material, also of plastics.

The particular form of iron oxide used is the ferric oxide, Fe_2O_3. This is chemically the same as jeweller's rouge, but in its physical form and magnetic properties it is different (jeweller's rouge is non-magnetic). Typically in the manufacturing process acicular (needle-like) crystals are formed: these are about one micron long and have to be dispersed as evenly as possible throughout the binding material without being broken into smaller fragments. Then, when the coating has been applied to the backing and while it is still in the form of a liquid emulsion, these crystals are orientated magnetically so that they are lengthways along the tape.

The oxide concentration in the coating is between 20% and 40%, and its sensitivity as a recording medium depends on both concentration and orientation. The thickness of the coating, too, has an effect: as the thickness of the emulsion (or the concentration of oxide) increases, low-frequency sensitivity increases, but high-frequency sensitivity goes down. In thick coatings, self-demagnetization is troublesome at high frequencies.

The range of levels available between that at which distortion (measured as 2% third harmonic distortion) is produced and that as which there is appreciable noise should be above 50 dB.

Background noise produced in the process itself depends not only on the degree of dispersion of the oxide throughout the emulsion, but also on its surface quality: tapes are improved by polishing.

In fact, to record the full range of audio frequencies efficiently it is necessary to add a high frequency bias (upwards of 50 kHz) to the signal. The most important result of this is to reduce distortion and noise at low and mid-range. To get the most satisfactory signal-to-noise ratio the bias level must be set with care. As bias amplitude is increased from zero, the percentage distortion decreases as the strength of the recorded signal goes up. The

377

recorded noise level also rises, but not so fast as the programme signal: these two both reach a maximum together, but as the bias strength increases beyond this point the signal-to-noise ratio continues to improve.

In the case of one good-quality recorder the signal-to-noise ratio is 52 dB at maximum output, rising to 54 dB as the bias is increased by just enough to reduce output by 1 dB. But if the bias is increased still further the output decreases sufficiently for the percentage distortion to become more of a nuisance. So the optimum bias setting is chosen as that at which the output has increased to a maximum and then dropped away again by 1 dB.

Faults in tape manufacture can occur: one serious defect is *drop-out*, a coating flaw that results in momentary recording loss. For crucial professional uses, tapes that have been pen-tested throughout their length are more reliable.

A recording head that has become permanently magnetized will itself magnetize the crystals of iron oxide more in one direction than the other when it is used for recording. At high levels it therefore over-records on half the cycle, and introduces distortion. This tendency is cured by the use of a tape-head demagnetizer (or 'degausser'), effectively a mild steel horseshoe magnet with a fairly small gap, energized by mains voltage. The gap of the demagnetizer is drawn along that of the recording head and removed to a distance before the energizing current is switched off. A degausser such as this may also be used to remove clicks and bumps from a recording (which may be caused on some equipment by switching on and off). At the same time, however, it removes background atmosphere.

Tape bases

Tape is available with three widely used backing materials (bases) and four thicknesses. The materials are:

1. 'Acetate' (cellulose triacetate or diacetate). This will snap rather than stretch (extending perhaps 0·5%, which is tolerable in speech). Repair is easy: a simple splice is usually sufficient. However, it also tears easily and is damaged by excessive humidity.

2. PVC (polyvinyl chloride). This is much stronger but when damaged may stretch too much for adequate repair. It is also sensitive to heat (particularly above 80°C).

3. Polyester. This is stronger still, but more expensive; it is

therefore most suitable for the thinner backings. Like PVC, it is liable to stretch extensively before breaking.

The four thicknesses are:
1. Standard play ($1\frac{1}{2}$ mil, 37 micron).
2. Long play (1 mil, 25 micron).
3. Double play ($\frac{3}{4}$ mil, 18 micron).
4. Triple play ($\frac{1}{2}$ mil, 12 micron; polyester only).

Standard play tape is normally used for professional studio work as it is best able to stand up to rough treatment—including fast rewind. It is also less subject to print-through (see below). Long-play is used where lightness is at a premium.

Two speeds now used professionally are:
1. 15 i/s (38 cm/s) for high quality music recordings.
2. $7\frac{1}{2}$ i/s (19 cm/s) for other good quality recordings (but mainly for broadcast speech).

Further lower speeds are adequate when intelligibility is required but technical quality is unimportant.

Tapes are usually wound on spools with side flanges, though in some parts of Europe tapes may be wound on cores without flanges. Apart from the obvious possibility of dropping the whole thing on the floor, these are subject to uneven spooling in fast rewind. Acetate tape with a matt backing surface gives a more even wind, presumably by maintaining a steady tension without slippage.

Where a tape has spilled and wound round the spindle and become crumpled, speech recordings are often still playable, but music recordings are not. The smoothing effect of a tight wind may help, and so may backing the worst parts with jointing tapes, but where the output is still breaking up after these measures the only answer is surgery: first cut out the damaged parts, and then edit to restore continuity (or revise your programme to incorporate a link at that point).

Stereo tape recordings

In tape recording, a defect of quality peculiar to stereo is *crosstalk*. This is measured as the level at which tone recorded on one track can be heard on the other. It may vary for different frequencies: the levels regarded as acceptable within the BBC are -38 dB at 1 kHz, rising to -30 dB at 50 Hz and 10 kHz. These figures compare very favourably with the -25 dB (at middle frequencies) of stereo disc reproduction.

If stereo recordings are made with the same tape and recording conditions as mono, there is a poorer signal-to-noise ratio, because part of the tape—a track along the centre line—must remain unused to allow physical separation of the A and B information. Two standards are used for the width of this guard track:

1. Narrow guard track. This is roughly one eighth of the full width of the tape. Only 1 dB of signal-to-noise ratio is lost on tapes of similar quality, but cross-talk may be higher than with the other standard.

2. Broad guard track. Nearly a third of the tape is unrecorded, but the effective loss is even greater: the signal-to-noise ratio drops by 3·5 dB. Cross-talk is low, but if other standards are to be maintained a more sensitive tape is required than for mono.

For stereo the BBC uses a tape that can be recorded 6 dB higher than that used for mono (the upper limit being that which can be recorded without exceeding acceptable distortion). In practice only 4 dB of this is used: this more than compensates for the loss due to the presence of a broad guard track, and allows something in hand for the less controllable conditions of stereo.

Discrete quadraphonic recordings have four tracks side by side. Cross-talk is inevitably higher than with stereo but far less than when matrixed to a two channel system. In commercial matrixed systems the cross-talk at the sides may reach levels as high as −10 dB.

Inconstant pitch

Variable speed is a fault afflicting battery tape recorders when the batteries are failing. Each take starts off at something close to the correct speed, but the tape soon slows down to fluctuate about whatever speed the battery is able to sustain. Any brief break in recording is followed by another surge of speed. Faulty motors may produce a similar effect.

Speed correction may be required for a variety of other reasons, e.g. to match music pitches exactly, or to resynchronise film picture and sound in cases where the sync pulse has failed. One system employs an oscillator that is plugged in to replace the mains supply. The drive frequency can then be varied by manual control by ±20%.

It is possible to correct tape-speed faults only if they are slow and regular enough to be adjusted by manual control. If possible compare the recording with one of the same voice at the correct speed. A methodical way to go about the job is to prepare a cue sheet, taking four or five words at a time every ten or fifteen seconds; then check the amount of correction needed at each of these points. This provides reference points to work to.

Stop and reset every time you reach a point at which the machine stopped during the recordings (or, alternatively, spacers can be cut in, to give a chance to reset while still running). These methods are suitable for speech only and are used only on recordings that are unreplaceable or unrepeatable at other than prohibitive cost.

High frequency losses on tape

Severe loss of high frequencies occurs if the tape is not in close contact with recording or replay head. A gap of one micron (a twenty-five-thousandth of an inch) has been shown to produce a loss of nearly 4 dB at 12 kHz (recorded at $7\frac{1}{2}$ i/s, 19 cm/s).

On some recorders, pressure pads are used to ensure that contact is complete; professional machines are engineered to ensure that the back-tension on the feed spool is sufficient but not enough to stretch the tape. If either of these devices fails, and the tape buckles away from the head, the gap produced may cause noticeable losses. To record through the thickness of the backing is sufficient to ruin the quality completely, so tapes of unfamiliar design should be checked to ensure which side is which: it is not always obvious.

Losses can also be due to magnetic dust from the tape coating collecting in crevices around the gap of a tape head, which should therefore be cleaned regularly. Such crevices are minimized in the manufacture of tape heads by filling the gap with a shim of material that is harder than the metal of the head. Wear is thereby kept even.

Where high frequency losses are progressive, measures may be taken to equalize for them. But where complete extinction at some frequency occurs no amount of boosting can restore it. Again the tape head proves an important example of this: if the wavelength to be replayed is an integral multiple of the gap width the two opposing half-cycles of the signal exactly cancel each other out. Clearly, such a signal cannot be restored in the reproducing amplifier. However, this does not imply that nothing can in this case be done, as the gap width of the recording head is not directly related to scanning loss (recording is achieved at

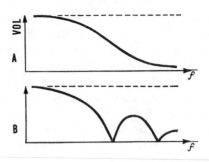

RESTORING HIGH FREQUENCY LOSSES. A. Top can be boosted and effectively restored. B. H.f. extinction at two frequencies: top cannot be restored effectively.

the trailing edge of the gap). So scanning by a replay head with a narrower gap might extract a signal.

A replay head scans a slightly greater length of tape than would be suggested by the size of the gap; but for a recording head the effect of high-frequency bias is to narrow the effective gap width. So, if a separate head is provided for monitoring the tape on replay, its gap width should be half that of the recording head.

The gap of a tape head is very much narrower than it is high; and it follows that if the line of the gap is only a very little out of its true 90° to the direction of travel, then the head is, in effect, scanning a much broader segment of the tape. Whether it is in fact the head that is out of true or the tape that is being pulled along at a slight angle, a tape that has been recorded in this way suffers a serious loss in top response when replayed on any correctly adjusted replay head. The fault is called *azimuth misalignment*.

If this fault is suspected when a tape is played back on a second

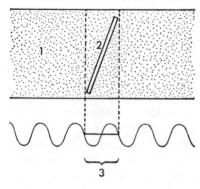

AZIMUTH MISALIGNMENT. 1. Tape. 2. Misaligned recording or reproducing head. 3. Extinction wavelength.

382

machine, try varying the angle at which the tape is traversing the head by pushing the point of a pencil between the tape and the deck. If it is possible to achieve some improvement in top response by doing this, then there is an azimuth fault which may be either on the recording itself or only on the replay machine.

If it is on the original, correction can be made by:
1. Copying from the original recorder (and head) to another machine.
2. Replaying on a machine with a variable azimuth setting.
3. Replaying only part of the full recorded track width: e.g. replay a full-track recording half-track. This will improve the effective frequency response, but the signal-to-noise ratio will go down by about 4 dB.

Tape print-through

Print-through is a tape storage fault in which the strongest effect occurs soon after recording—although sheer length of time in storage adds to it. It also increases with temperature, and if this is far above the optimum 55°F (13°C) the effect can be serious —so tapes should not be left on top of radiators. Other causes are electrical fields (keep tapes away from the magnets of loud-speakers, etc.) and physical shock. The distance between successive magnetic layers on the spool also comes into it: the thinner backing of extended and double-play tape permits a higher print level.

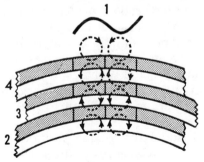

TAPE PRINT-THROUGH. Printing depends on the thickness of the tape base layer, as well as temperature and physical shock. 1. Wavelength of original and printed signal. 3. Layer with original signal. 2 and 4. Adjacent layers with printed signals.

If caught early enough, much of the printing effect may be removed by a partial wipe using a very light erase current: the erase is more marked on the small printed signal than on the main body of the recording (the print-through being reduced by perhaps 16 dB, as against 3 dB off the main signal). But after two weeks the fixity of the print increases rapidly, and this method becomes ineffective.

On recordings of speech, printing is most noticeable in the gaps between words, so a noise gate, set to operate just above the level of the printed signal, eliminates it where it is not masked by speech. But it also clips reverberation, which may be restored by the judicious use of 'echo', and atmosphere. A loop of atmosphere recorded at the same location will refill the gap: for film sound these processes are undertaken at the dubbing stage (see p. 481). Film location recordings are inevitably subject to greater hazards than those made in the controlled environment of the studio, but this is just one of many reasons why a wise recordist tapes wild atmosphere in addition to sync speech.

Printing is a common problem with sound on videotape. It does not occur, however, with magnetic film stock (used in film sound editing) of which the backing is thicker.

Film sound

The coating on 35 mm and 16 mm magnetic film is the same as or very similar to that on sound tape. The difference is in the backing, which must be relatively thick to withstand the sprocket-hole drive of the camera.

When playing acetate-based tracks relatively high tension is required to maintain adequate contact between film and heads, and this in turn can cause rapid wear and low life both for film and for heads. Low tension may permit the film to buckle away from the head at tape joins, resulting in drop-out. Doubling the thickness of jointing tape (by adding an extra layer) usually prevents this. Polyester-based tapes are more flexible, and so make better contact with the heads, which improves high-frequency response. But they stretch rather than break cleanly, and are more difficult to peel back from a joint that has to be remade.

Standards for the positions of tracks on magnetic film vary. The BBC records centre-track on 16 mm film and edge-track on 35 mm. In both cases the track width is 200 mil (5 mm)—only a little less than that for full-track tape. American 16 mm film normally uses edge-track.

The 35 mm edge-track position corresponds to that used on 35 mm combined magnetic film, except that the presence of a picture limits the latter to 100 mil (2·5 mm).

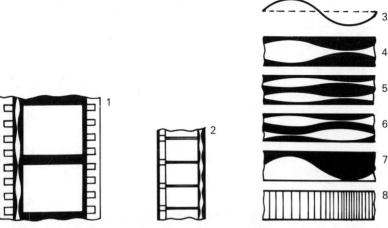

OPTICAL FILM SOUND TRACK. 1. 35-mm film. 2. 16-mm film. 3. Original sound signal shown in optical recordings 4–8. 4. Bilateral variable area track. 5. Double bilateral variable area track. 6. Push-pull track (a special sound reproducing head is required for this). 7. Unilateral, or 50/50 track. 8. Variable density track. The principal problem with optical sound is noise due to dirt and scratches on the track; also distortion in early optical recording systems. For reproduction a lamp is projected through a slit which is then focused on wanted section of film. The transmitted light is picked up by a photocell. Other recording systems are also available.

The optical sound of old films can be noisy, low quality or both. When replaying them on television, the simplest thing is to put in a filter at 5 kHz and to forget it. In an ideal world, the optical master would be found, transferred to separate magnetic track and then treated with modern equalization techniques, re-dubbing effects and even re-recording music. An ageing masterpiece can be marvellously enhanced by such restoration.

Records

Discs, either specially cut 'acetates' (as they are sometimes called—although in fact the material used is cellulose nitrate) or commercially pressed gramophone records, may be important to the tape recordist for a variety of reasons. Radio stations, of course, use records as an important source of programme material. Direct-cut 'acetates' can make—and stay—very good recordings. Cut by the hot-stylus method, which helps to smooth the wall as the cutter moves on, and subjected to no more than medium to low playing weights a microgroove direct-cut disc can survive very many replays without appreciable signs of wear—although it is always very susceptible to physical damage to the grooves.

385

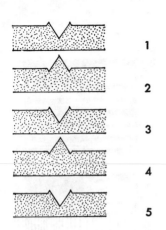

1

2

3

4

5

PROCESSING DISC RECORDS. The five stages of processing: 1. Original recording. 2. Master. 3. Mother. 4. Stamper. 5. Record. Note that any shoulders thrown up by the cutter stylus are faithfully reproduced at each stage. If only a small number (say, up to 50) is required, two of the stages are omitted.

From the cellulose nitrate original recording, records are produced by a four-stage process. First the surface is made conductive by blasting it with a finely divided metal (e.g. gold) and a copper *master* is grown on to it electrolytically. Then the two are stripped away from each other. In the second stage a *mother* is grown, again electrolytically, on the master and the signal is now once again in the form of a groove. A *stamper* is produced from the mother (with ridges instead of grooves), and can be used to press a thousand or more records.

Distortion on discs

The ability of l.p. styli to track and extract a signal from a kink in the groove that is of the same order of size as the stylus tip is quite remarkable, in view of the fact that it is being thrown from side to side under forces that are enormous in comparison with the area of contact. But as the stylus moves toward the centre of the record, the recorded wavelengths of the high frequencies close up and become progressively more difficult for the stylus to track. This gives an imperfect match in quality when changing over from the inner edge of one disc to the outer edge of another. Wear too is more rapid toward the centre of the disc than at the outer edge.

Another characteristic of records is *pinch effect* caused by the different actions of cutter and replay styli: the cutter is chisel shaped and produces a groove of which the cross-section along the radius of the disc is constant. But the replay stylus has a rounded tip and simply rides between points on the lateral cross-section of the groove. As the modulation twists the groove

386

to its greatest angle the stylus is squeezed upward to ride higher in the sharper angle of the walls. With two such 'bumps-up' to each cycle recorded in the groove, the second harmonic of the recorded signal is produced in the vertical plane. For mono records played with mono equipment, pinch effect is not serious with the light compliant stylus mountings of today. But for mono records played on stereo equipment it introduces a spurious stereo signal which, as it is out of phase with the main signal, should be suppressed.

Hill-and-dale recordings, i.e. those in the vertical plane, are subject to mechanical distortion effects different from those that affect lateral recordings. This is one reason why stereo is recorded with each channel at 45° to the vertical: the two forms of distortion are split evenly between the two channels.

Heat affects discs less than tapes—at any rate, as far as the recorded signal is concerned—so discs have been preferred for despatching transcription programmes to tropical countries. But heat makes PVC soft, so that a record may warp if left lying on a radiator, on shelves above an amplifier, or in a closed car left in the sun. A record standing on edge on a hot surface will be flattened along the rim enough to make the first few grooves bump so much as to be unplayable.

Wow and flutter

A form of distortion affecting records is *wow*, a regular steady variation in pitch that occurs once on each full turn of the disc. The smallest change of pitch that can be distinguished by most people is less than one twenty-fifth of a semitone at middle frequencies; for low frequencies the interval is much greater. Consequently, we may expect wow to be a great deal more apparent on middle range notes than on those that are low in pitch.

The ability of the ear to detect wow depends not only on the amplitude and frequency but also on the character of the instrument and type of note played. With the human voice and many stringed instruments the tones produced are not of fixed pitch, and there is, therefore, a subjective tendency to blame the performer, instead of the mechanics. But on wind instruments (which mostly produce notes of fixed pitch) and on the decay tones of plucked and struck instruments wow may be more painfully obvious. Piano and organ are particularly affected.

If notes are sustained on fixed-pitch instruments over a period long enough for wow to produce a pitch variation of more than about 0·25%, the effect begins to be appreciable; and if it reaches 1% the results are, to most ears, excruciating. But this also means that passages of moderate pace can take rather more wow than slow ones. Briskly played passages can stand even more distortion, because the ear tolerates a certain inaccuracy of pitch on notes that are held for only a very short space of time.

One cause of wow in record reproduction is a faulty turntable. This can be detected easily enough by the use of a stroboscopic disc. Another cause may be eccentricity of the groove on the pressing, often due to the hole not being in the centre of the disc, or being larger than the spindle; or it may be due to the disc being warped, or physically deformed.

To check whether the fault lies with the disc of the turntable, first note the way in which the cycle of the wow is related to the position of the label, and then stop the turntable and turn the disc through 180° relative to it and play the disc again. It should then be obvious which the wow is associated with. The magnitude of wow can be measured using an optical groove-locating system (see p. 314), or by an instrument specially made up for the job. Attach a small mirror above the pivot of the tone arm and use it to reflect light from a fixed source on to screen. As the turntable rotates and the needle tracks a faulty disc the spot of light swings from side to side. The screen can be calibrated for lateral movement of the needle and percentage wow calculated in terms of groove radius (it will be worse close to the middle of the disc).

Wow can also occur on tape, owing to a buckled spool, but is less common.

Flutter, a related fault, is a much more rapid fluctuation, in which the speed variation is sufficiently fast to impose a change of quality on any sound—and again, most noticeably on steady notes. Woodwind is particularly susceptible. This fault may be caused by a turntable rim-drive spindle being off centre.

Picture and sound quality in television and film

Television and film are nearly always conceived primarily in terms of picture: it is important therefore that the needs of sound restrict it as little as possible. Nevertheless, it is essential that, despite the presence of the camera and the constant attention paid to picture, sound quality should be high. It goes without saying that the reader of this book shares this view, but as the problems of practical film and television production pile up, it may appear that only the sound man appreciates the point. However, he may rest assured that the experienced director will—given time to think—agree with him.

It is the sound man's responsibility to any production to obtain the best sound that he possibly can in whatever circumstances he is presented with. If the quality of sound falls below that which might reasonably be expected—and nothing can be done about it—he must warn the director. In extreme cases, where sound is not suitable for use he must say so. When he *has* said so the responsibility then becomes the director's

However, the sound man must be sensible in his judgment of what is good, barely acceptable or totally unsatisfactory; and this must reflect the director's intentions for the sound, which he has a right to know about—if, indeed, the director has made up his mind. A director is also within his rights to ask for sound to be taken with the intention of making a decision later on how it might be used, if at all. The sound man is not within his rights to refuse to record on the grounds of low quality though he may protest strongly: the director may still be able to use the sound at low level behind another high-level track, or as a guide track for post-synching or for other use in dubbing. Indeed, there are some circumstances in television where on important material poor quality sound is unavoidable and therefore simply has to be used, though perhaps with an apology to the viewing public if the reason for it is not obvious.

A subjective scale for quality check

The BBC operates a system for checking programme quality (for our purposes, sound; in television, picture is also checked). Observations are made on general sound quality; background hum, noise, or hiss; change of sound level at programme junctions; and interference. In this last category is talkback induction which can sometimes be heard on radio as it is transmitted, but much more often on television because of the continuous stream of instructions and information that is being fed from the gallery to the studio floor.

Sampling is done for periods of five minutes on a wide range of material, including the programmes as they are transmitted (both before the transmitter and off the air), studio output (but taking in to account conditions that may exist early in rehearsal before all adjustments have been made), material incoming from other areas (by landline, radio link or satellite) and all recordings.

These are two subjective scales that are used:

Scale 1: Assessment of degradation
    1.1. Imperceptible
    1.2. Just perceptible
    1.3. Perceptible but not disturbing
    1.4. Somewhat objectionable
    1.5. Definitely objectionable
    1.6. Unusable

Scale 2: Assessment of quality
    2.1. Excellent
    2.2. Good
    2.3. Fair
    2.4. Fairly poor
    2.5. Poor
    2.6. Very poor

These divisions may at first glance seem coarse, but are readily assessed and easily understood. The scales are, in fact, a useful, practical tool.

15

FILTERS AND EQUALIZATION

CHANGES in audio frequency response, commonly called frequency distortion, might more properly be described as attenuation distortion, because it is the relative volumes of the signal at different frequencies that change, not the actual frequencies present. Whatever we call it, the effect has been one of the most important obstacles to be overcome as audio engineering has developed. Once it is in the form of an electrical signal, audio information can be handled with little significant change, or with changes that can readily be compensated. On the other hand, transducers—devices that convert the signal from one medium to another—often introduce marked changes, differentially responding to the frequencies present. The worst problem is presented by conversion of the electrical signal back to sound. All loudspeaker designs differ, and domestic loudspeakers are totally outside the control of the professional originator of the sounds they reproduce. Further selective emphases are imposed by the rooms in which the material is finally heard.

In fact, the expected variability of acoustics, together with the wide range within which sounds remain recognizable for what they originally were, is a psychological asset that makes or excuses changes that have occurred not only at the domestic end but also earlier in the chain. Indeed, the untrained ear is remarkably tolerant of this form of distortion when it affects the sound as a whole. The tone controls of early audio equipment were blunt instruments, coarse in their operation, accommodating the need to eliminate hiss or rumble, or to excise frequency bands containing other forms of distortion that were far more annoying than simple truncation of the reproduced audio range.

The ear is more objective about direct comparisons between sounds with different distributions of frequency distortion (as I suppose we must continue to call it) if they are presented one immediately after the other or both at the same time. Historically, the most fallible items of equipment have been microphones, and their matching became an important component of radio and television sound technique. For example, for a long time BBC radio used little but ribbon microphones for speech: monophonic drama was balanced using several, differing in their acoustic surroundings but not in their basic response. Stereo drama has used one main matched pair of microphones throughout a production, but changing the acoustics from scene to scene. These techniques remain valid. For television drama, the main boom microphone is the standard against which other sound is judged by the listener. Other microphones picking up the same voices have to be matched to that standard or the transition is obtrusive. This demands a capacity for changing each microphone's frequency response in detail. In both radio and television, a more drastic effect is the simulation of telephone quality, for which the normal frequency range is curtailed by means of filters.

For music, it became part of the balancer's skill to choose a microphone with frequency characteristics complementing those of the instrument. Today, many pop music balancers use an expensive condenser microphone with a response that is substantially flat throughout the audio range for nearly all instruments. Comparable results can, in fact, often be achieved at lower cost by the earlier technique, with the added advantage that the microphone's response is reduced outside the wanted frequency range of the instrument, thereby discriminating against noise and spill. Pop music balance takes the greatest liberties with frequency response, with bass and treble emphasized or rolled away, and selected bands of midrange frequencies lifted to lend presence to particular components of the mix. If frequency bands containing the characteristic elements of musical quality of each instrument are raised (which is the same as taking down the remainder of each sound), the result is a musical caricature or cartoon. In fact, that is precisely the object intended —and when it succeeds, the selected essentials do, indeed, seem to press themselves upon the listener. Historically, the capacity to achieve such effects was provided by equipment originally designed to correct the deficiencies of microphones, and to allow for their matching more smoothly, one to another. It is curious, indeed ironic, that deliberate distortion of the sound of an expensively engineered smooth response has usurped the name of *equalization* (EQ).

In this chapter we are concerned with equalization and related techniques, and their creative use in radio, television and music recording.

Filters

Older audio equipment often had bass and treble tone controls, as they were called, to add or subtract 10 dB (or more) at 100 Hz and 10 kHz, doing so in continuously variable or switched increments. The name has gone, but the function remains. There may also be a range of sharper top- and bass-cut filters (with or without variable slope). We have already met the notch filters for eliminating mains hum at 50 and 100 Hz, or 60 and 120 Hz, and also the television line frequency at about 15 kHz. It is also convenient to have a switch so that direct and corrected sound can be quickly compared. In most audio control desks there is provision for varying top and bass as part of the equalization equipment in each channel, while other filters with more limited uses are provided as patch-in facilities as, for example, in the case of the sharp filters that are used in drama to distort speech.

Telephone circuits usually have a band-width of some 3000 Hz with a lower cut-off at about 300 Hz, but this should not necessarily be copied when simulating telephone quality. The selection of suitable settings for bass and treble filters should, as always in such cases, be made by ear. And the degree of cut that seems most

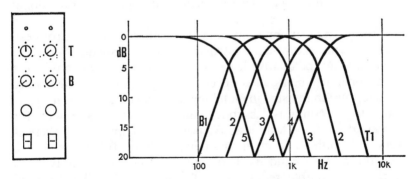

EFFECTS UNIT MODULES in BBC control desk (each module contains two units). Four degrees of bass cut-off (B1–4) and five degrees of treble cut-off (T1–5) are provided. In BBC-TV control desks one pair of units is used in conjunction with a camera channel switching unit for reversing telephone effects.

appropriate will vary from one play to another—or even between different simulated telephone conversations in the same play.

One factor that has a bearing on this is the difference in voice quality between male and female speech; and between different examples of each. If the fundamental of a male voice is at 110 Hz, then a cut at 220 Hz will give a small but appreciable change of quality. For a female voice with a fundamental an octave higher, a 440-Hz cut is more suitable. In fact, 440 and 880 Hz are more often used: the loss of bass is stressed for dramatic effect. A microphone used in conjunction with such circuitry is called a *filter microphone*, or in BBC jargon a *distort microphone*.

In a full-scale studio telephone conversation set-up it is usual to have two microphones, one normal and the other with a filter in circuit. In radio, these two can be placed in different parts of the same studio, the idea being that they should not be separated so much that the actors cannot hear each other direct. This arrangement avoids the necessity of wearing headphones.

In such a set-up it is important to avoid acoustic spill, which in this case means pick-up of the supposedly distorted voice on the normal microphone: otherwise the effect of telephone quality will be lost. If the 'near' microphone is directional (e.g. a ribbon), and it is placed with its dead side toward the 'far' voice, the pick-up of direct sound is effectively prevented. But discrimination against reflected sound presents more of a problem, so it sometimes helps to use the deadest part of the studio for the filter microphone. As spill from the full-range to the filter microphone does not noticeably change the quality of the 'near' voice, it does not really matter very much whether the second microphone is directional or not.

The two microphones are mixed together at the control desk (in some studios the filter controls are also conveniently built in to the desk) and the relative levels are judged by ear. When this sort of distortion is being introduced into a programme, meters are even less use than usual in matching the two voices, as the narrow-band input contains less bass, and therefore less power, for similar degrees of loudness. At normal listening levels there is very little difference in intelligibility between full-range speech and the narrow band used to simulate telephone quality, so a fairly considerable reduction in the loudness of the distorted speech may be tolerable in the interests of creating a feeling of actuality.

In a television studio the microphones should be well separated in space. Then, as the picture cuts from one end to the other, the normal distort arrangement can be reversed, without spill in either direction. It is useful to have the selection linked to the vision cutting buttons so that sound and picture changes are synchronized. But it is best to avoid cutting during a word as this sounds unpleasant and draws attention to the technique being used (see pp. 280–281).

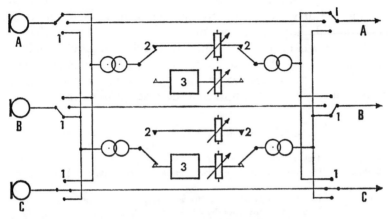

TELEPHONE EFFECTS SWITCHING UNIT for use in television. 1. Pre-selector switches. 2. Switch linked to video cut buttons: any sound routed through this is automatically switched in and out of the 'distort' condition as the pictures are cut. 3. Bass and treble filters. In this example, microphone A is undistorted only while B is filtered and vice versa; and microphone C remains undistorted whatever the picture.

As distorted sound must be held at a lower level on the meter than untreated sound great care must be taken not only in balance, but also before that, in studio layout. If the two performers cannot be acoustically completely separated, because both must appear in vision and must therefore be in the same studio, it should be arranged for the two sets to be as far apart from each other as possible. If they are not, coloration can affect both artists (distant, reverberant but otherwise undistorted sound is superimposed on the telephone quality speech). Also, if one performer speaks more loudly than the other his voice is likely to be heard over the quiet speaker's microphone. It may help for the speakers (in their separate sets) to be facing each other in the studio layout, so that cardioid boom microphones are directed away from each other. On the other hand the use of wide shots makes matters worse, because boom microphones have to retreat

395

from the speaker, thereby making it more likely that the distant voice will be heard as the channel gain is raised.

Background effects added to a telephone conversation may make a considerable difference to the necessary balance between voices. The degree of distortion and its volume relative to the undistorted speech must depend on both the loudness of the effects and their quality. In particular, background sound that is toppy in quality tends to blot out quiet speech; whereas if the backing is fairly woolly or boomy the shriller telephone effect has little difficulty in cutting through it. In either case, the mix must be very carefully monitored to check that intelligibility is reasonably high—unless, of course, the script requires otherwise.

A fairly complicated scene may require varying degrees of intelligibility—as for example in a radio script like this:

EFFECTS	(*Loud party chatter background; phone dialling close, ringing heard on line: it stops.*)
GUEST	Hey, is that you, Charlie?
CHARLIE	(*On distort, barely audible against the party chatter*) Yes. This is Charlie.
GUEST	Say, this is a great party; why don't you come on over?
CHARLIE	What are you at, a football game or something?
GUEST	What am I what?
CHARLIE	I'm in bed.
GUEST	Hang on, I'll shut this door. (*Door shuts; chatter down.*) S'better! Now what was all that about a football game? It's three in the morning.
CHARLIE	(*Now more distinct*) Yeah. It's three in the morning. I'm in bed.

Two quite different mixes are required for this; and the balance and pitch of the near voice must change on the cue 'door shuts'. In addition, the backing should change in quality, too: heard through a real door, such effects would become muffled and muddy, as well as being reduced in volume. Some degree of top cut might well be introduced at this point.

There are many other uses for filters besides telephone quality: for example, to simulate station or airport announcements (adding a touch of echo), or intercom (at the same time simulating a poor radio link by playing in a crackling, hissing background). A radio play (or recording) may include the effect of a radio announcement (or a tape recorder) for which a convenient convention is that the reproducer has little better than telephone quality. This again is a caricature in which one type of distortion, reproduction of sound through a single loudspeaker, is represented by another, limitation of frequency range.

396

Midlift

We have already met midlift in Chapter 9, as a component of music balance. For example, a singer's voice may be raised by 6 dB at 2·5–3 kHz. A snare drum or woodwind might also benefit from lift within the same frequency range. In the end the effect is selected by ear, in the light of the characteristic qualities of the

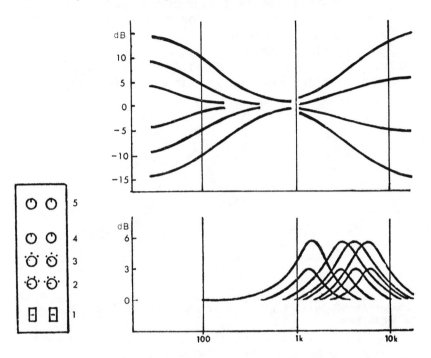

SIMPLE RESPONSE SELECTION AMPLIFIER CONTROL MODULE (two units in single module). 1. Bypass switch. 2. Mid-lift selection (1·4, 2·8, 4·0, 5·6 kHz in this example). 3. Presence control (3 and 6 dB lift). 4. Bass lift and cut control. 5. Treble lift and cut control. *On the right, above:* typical response curves for bass and treble controls. *Below:* presence peaks.

instruments, the relationship of one to another, and the overall melodic or harmonic effect desired.

Midlift is a name that is appropriate only in the sense that above and below the frequency at which it is applied, the response returns to normal. The middle of the audio range is generally taken to be around 256–440 Hz; but midlift is usually applied a few octaves above that, acting on the harmonics of the notes produced, perhaps enriching and extending them. As different

397

notes are played by a particular instrument, the midlift frequency remains constant, so it behaves rather like a physical part of that instrument, creating a formant—or, more likely, enhancing a formant already present that helps to define the character of the instrument.

Vocal formants, in the middle range, are changed continuously in the process of speech, but the higher ones resonate in cavities of less flexible or fixed size; and for midlift on vocals it is this upper range that is enhanced.

Early midlift devices had a simple range of possibilities, offering perhaps four or five nominal frequencies separated by intervals of rather less than an octave, together with several

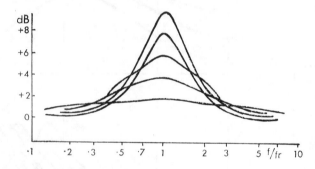

MID-LIFT. Response curves for a simple mid-lift tone control unit. In a typical unit a range of frequencies f_r = 2, 3, 5, 8 Hz (approx) may be selected; also several degrees of lift, as shown.

degrees of lift, switched at increments of 2 or 3 dB. Later designs have made the range more flexible in both frequency selection and volume, and may also allow for a dip instead of lift: by analogy with *presence* the effect would be *absence*, and this too may be used in popular music mixes. The nominal frequency is now often chosen by setting a slide control (like a small fader), which may be continuously variable. Some balancers prefer an arrangement with definite, closely spaced settings at which the slider clicks into place, as this makes notetaking easy. A desk in which equalization is programmed digitally can have virtually continuous settings that it can reproduce reliably. In early midlift systems there was no choice of the width (known as the Q) of the peak; in a more flexible system this, too, may be varied.

398

Graphic filters

Even in combination with bass and treble filters there is a limit to the flexibility of equalization based on a single midlift control. In a television studio or when filming on location, the

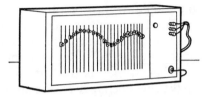

GRAPHIC FILTER. In this design the slide faders may be at, say, third or half octave intervals and the band between successive slides is attenuated according to their volume settings. The shaping shown here would have very little effect on the intelligibility of speech.

degree of mismatch between microphones may be more complex. For this we must take the principle of midlift a stage further and split the whole spectrum into bands of an octave or less and apply correction separately to each.

If all the controls are set at zero, forming a horizontal line across the face of the panel, the response, too, is level throughout the audio range; if individual levers are raised or lowered their

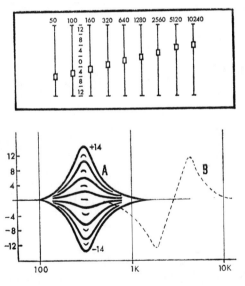

AUDIO RESPONSE CONTROL. Octave filter with slide controls marked in decibels. *Top*. Desk control panel. *Bottom*. A. Typical response curves for a single selector. B. Response obtained by setting adjacent selectors at −14 dB and +14 dB.

399

associated circuits form peaks or troughs that overlap, each blending into the next. The selection of the desired effect is made by setting the slides for the various component bands to form what appears to be a graph of the new response. In fact, the actual response achieved may be different: it depends on the design of the filter and the size of the fluctuations set. The true arbiter—once again—must be subjective judgment.

Graphic filters are required in film dubbing theatres (p. 489), on television control desks, and also in creative sound studios such as the BBC's Radiophonic Workshop (Chapter 17).

When speech is put through a graphic filter it is possible to make severe changes, for example, several dips of 30 dB, without significantly reducing intelligibility. If the filtering is intended not simply to restore the deficiencies of a balance made under adverse conditions, but instead to achieve some positive and marked dramatic effect, the imposed distortion has to be drastic. However, the selective emphasis of particular frequency bands is noticeable where a dip would not be. This is because the brain reconstructs defective harmonic structures, perceiving the sound as experience says it should be, but finds it somewhat more difficult to disregard that which should not be there, but manifestly is.

16

ECHO AND DELAY

'ECHO' is something of a misnomer for a studio technique that serves to extend reverberation without (it is hoped) introducing any actual echoes, but the name has stuck. It is used on occasions when more reverberation is wanted than the built-in acoustics of a studio can supply, or (for music) when a multi-microphone close-balance technique has been adopted. Various forms of artificial reverberation are used, including echo chambers, plates, springs and, more recently, digital electronic devices. They differ in quality from each other, and also from the real thing. Compare their development with that of microphones. Those, too, were available at first with limited capacities, and you took whatever served most efficiently. Later, microphone designs proliferated, and you selected that with the characteristics (including character-istic deficiencies) that best fitted the task in hand. Finally (though at some cost) an ideal of perfect response could be approached, so that the choice of microphone depended less on the character of the sound itself. Artificial reverberation, following a generation behind, is still at the second of these three stages of development.

A true *echo* may be heard when reflected sound—a discrete repetition—is delayed by some twentieth of a second or more. As the separation is reduced there comes a point when even a staccato original and its repetition are no longer perceived as separate entities, but as a single sound, a composite that is different in character. There is, in fact, partial cancellation at certain fre-quencies. *Delay* effects may fall into either category: they may be short, to make use of the phase cancellations; or long, producing perceptibly separate echoes, perhaps with further repetitions.

Natural *reverberation*, as we have seen, begins with first reflections that arrive from the roof and walls—in the centre of a concert hall, after a substantial delay—followed at progressively shorter intervals by many more, smaller products of multiple reflections until, vast in number, they trail away below the threshold of hearing. This is the process that most of our musical instruments and ensembles were designed to exploit: it is an unwritten part of the music itself. When considering alternatives to natural reverberation we must therefore ask how their decay

ECHO MIXTURES. 1. Original signal. 2. Reverberation. With separate control of direct and echo feeds, a wide range of effects is possible. A reverberation dominates the sound. B. Reverberation tails gently behind it.

processes compare with the natural form. In the music room or concert hall, some frequencies are absorbed more readily than others at each reflection; if after multiple reflection some frequency bands are sustained while others diminish, the result is coloration.

Coloration occurs in both natural and artificial reverberation, but note that the build-up and blending of natural reverberant sound depends on a three-dimensional system of reflections and decay which greatly enriches the quality at just that stage when coloration is likely to be most severe. When the artificial reverberation differs from natural acoustics its use is justified if the new pattern of coloration and density of decay products is still perceived as musical in quality (and if its origins are not obtrusively apparent). In many cases the natural acoustics are themselves unsatisfactory, and at worst, the artificial reverberation available to augment them may be justified only on the grounds that it is better than nothing; at best, it may be indistinguishable from the real thing. In some cases, it may provide a distinctively different, but desired effect.

Most control desks have provision to split the feed from each fader, diverting part to an artificial reverberation ('echo') chain. In the simplest case the echo feeds from all faders are combined in a single line to the reverberation device; more generally they can be grouped and fed to any one of several devices. It is best to feed echo at fairly high volume so that noise from the system itself is relatively low. After each channel fader there is a control selecting

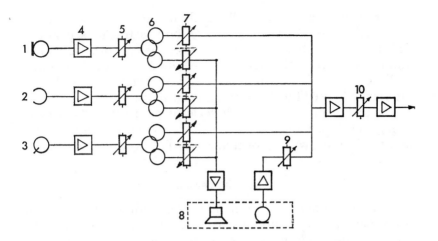

SPLIT FEED SYSTEM FOR ECHO. 1. Microphone. 2. Tape reproducer. 3. Pick-up from disc. 4. Preamplifiers. 5. Source faders. 6. Hybrid transformer giving independent feeds. 7. Echo mixture switches (ganged). 8. Echo chamber. 9. Echo fader. 10. Main control.

the amount of the echo feed and therefore the relative proportions of the several signals that are being passed to each device; there may also be simple tone controls to shape the frequency distribu-

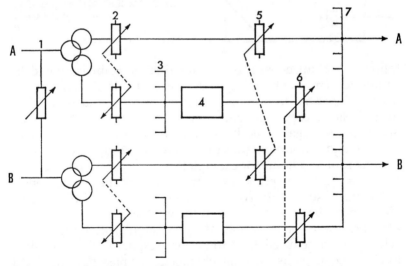

STEREOPHONIC ARTIFICIAL REVERBERATION—using separate echo devices (e.g. spring systems) on A and B channels. 1. Width control. 2. Echo mixture switches. 3. Echo feeds from other sources in the same group. 4. Echo devices. 5. Channel offset control. 6. Echo fader. 7. Group star-mixer.

tion. For stereo echo, A and B signals are often combined before being fed in, but A and B reverberation is extracted separately. This also means that mono sources taken as part of a stereo mix automatically have the stereo reverberation that is essential to a realistic sound. For quadraphony, separate stereo echo systems are generally used for the front and rear pairs.

The reverberation from each device is returned to the desk as a single feed for a mono mix or pair for stereo. It is then treated as a new source, with its own fader (or faders) and equalization.

The echo chamber

An echo chamber is a room or corridor with 'bright' reflecting walls, perhaps with 'junk' littered about at random to break up the reflections and mop up excess mid-range reverberation. The room may have a wall down the middle, so that sound has to

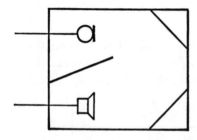

ECHO CHAMBER. A U-shaped room is often used to increase the distance the sounds must travel from loudspeaker to microphone.

follow a U-shaped path, or a disused stone staircase could be employed. The loudspeaker itself can be made directional (an open baffle is bidirectional) so that no direct sound is radiated toward the microphone; and that in turn can be directional, discriminating against both sound from the region of the loudspeaker and coloration due to structural resonances (between parallel roof and floor, for example).

A humid atmosphere gives a strong high-frequency response; a dry one absorbs top. An echo chamber linked to the outside atmosphere therefore varies with the weather.

In fact, when a large hall is being simulated, there should actually be a reduced high-frequency response, corresponding to the long air-paths. In some chambers, the bass response itself may be too heavy; or alternatively the original sound may already have sufficient bass reverberation, so that none need be added. Tone and bass-cut controls allow the necessary adjustments.

Note, incidentally, that if less bass is fed to the chamber, its loudspeaker can be used more efficiently, but if bass is reduced for this reason it needs subsequent equalization.

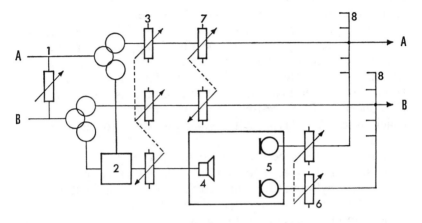

STEREOPHONIC ARTIFICIAL REVERBERATION—using echo room. 1. Width control. 2. Echo selection (A, B or A+B). 3. Echo mixture switch. 4. Echo room loudspeaker. 5. A and B echo microphones. 6. Echo fader. 7. Channel offset control. 8. Group star mixers.

We have seen that the strong advantage of the echo chamber over its competitors is that its decay is natural, three dimensional. But as it takes up valuable space within a building it is often made rather small, about 4000 ft³ (113 m³) or even less. As a result there is broadly spaced coloration, due to the natural room resonances in the lower middle frequency range.

Another element to add to the cost of these rooms is that, like radio studios, they need to be isolated from structure-borne noise. Otherwise—even at best—whenever alterations are being carried out, even in distant parts of the same building, the echo chamber will be out of commission unless all noisy work is stopped; at worst it could resonate to every footfall in the rooms above or around.

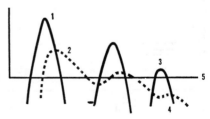

THE EFFECT OF LEVEL. 1. Loud direct sound. 2. Audible reverberation. 3. Quiet direct sound. 4. Reverberation now below threshold of hearing (5).

405

A further disadvantage of using a chamber is that, once laid out, its reverberation time is fixed. If this is about two seconds it may be suitable for music but less satisfactory for drama: a little echo goes a long way on speech. If, however, only a touch of echo is used it is noticeable only on the louder sounds; a situation that corresponds well with what we hear in real life. In this case the rather overlong reverberation time is apparently reduced.

For music the reverberation time itself may be right, but with too early a simulated first reflection (because the shortest path-length between loudspeaker and microphone is far less than in the concert hall). To restore both clarity of attack and a sense of spaciousness, a delay circuit may be inserted into the echo feed (see later).

Improvements in performance could also be obtained by using a full-sized hall as the echo chamber (which is rarely possible), or in principle by miniaturization, so that the true characteristics of a larger hall are accommodated in a smaller volume. This requires a medium in which sound travels slower than it does in air, and with correspondingly scaled transmission characteristics. One possible pitfall is a reduced signal-to-noise ratio.

The reverberation plate

Another device—more versatile than the echo chamber because its reverberation time may be varied—is the reverberation plate. In principle, this plate is rather like the sheet of metal that used to be used in the theatre to create a thunder effect, except that, instead of being shaken by hand and delivering its energy directly

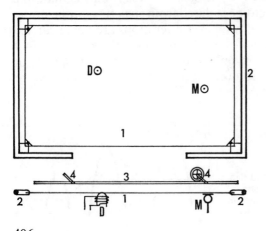

REVERBERATION PLATE. 1. Metal sheet. 2. Tubular steel frame. 3. Damping plate, pivoted at 4. (Here the spacing is shown as being set by the hand-wheel, but many damping plates are motor driven from a point on the sound control desk.) D. Drive unit. M. Contact microphone. For stereo, two are required, assymetrically placed.

to the air, it has two transducers. One vibrates the plate, rather as the coil vibrates the paper cone in a moving-coil loudspeaker; and the other, acting as a contact microphone, picks up the vibrations.

Reverberation plates have a tinned steel sheet suspended in tension from a tubular steel frame at the four corners. To reduce the metallic quality of the resonance to proportions that are acceptable for most purposes a minimum size of 2 square metres is combined with a maximum thickness of half a millimetre. This thickness of steel plate has good transverse vibrational properties (other metals are internally damped too quickly). Unlike the echo chamber effect, these natural resonances at low frequencies do not thin out to sharp peaks in the bass, but are spread fairly evenly throughout the audio range.

Coloration may also be caused by any irregularity in the flatness of the sheet. In the early days of production this was a major problem, as steel sheet rolling mills did not work to the very close tolerances that are required. Samples had to be held in suspension for several days before tests for suitability could be carried out, and many had to be discarded at this stage. In addition it was established that the contact microphone and the brass rod from the drive unit need to be of low weight and must be spot welded to the sheet (the use of bolts or rivets will not do).

A moving coil drive unit is anchored to a bridge across the frame and a piezo-electric contact microphone is used to pick up the sound; the two are asymmetrically placed on the plate. For stereo, the A + B input is fed to the same drive unit, but two pick-ups are used, so placed that they do not respond to a common set of vibration antinodes of the plate. The frequency characteristic of the plate itself, the two transducers and their amplifiers are arranged to give a response that has its maximum duration at mid-frequencies, with some roll-off in the bass and rather more at higher frequencies (15 dB at 10 kHz), thereby simulating the high-frequency absorption of the air of a room of moderate size. To achieve this, some damping has to be applied: without it, the response of the plate would rise to very high values in the extreme bass.

To produce this damping, and to control the reverberation time, a thin, stiff, porous foil is rigidly held at a controlled but variable distance from the plate: 0·8 mm of a compressed glass-fibre material is is used (light textiles would move with the air and thicker fibrous materials give an unsuitable frequency characteristic). The mechanism of absorption depends on the fact that although there is little acoustic radiation from the reverberating plate, standing waves are set up near the surface, with the result that if the damping plate is in the way, energy is absorbed and the reverberation time thereby reduced.

With the broadest separation of the damping plate (120 mm) there is a reverberation of 5·3 seconds at 500 Hz, dropping to 1·5 seconds at 10 kHz: this is similar to the response that may be found in excessively reverberant large spaces such as some cathedral interiors. The narrowest separation between the plates is as small as 3 mm: this gives a nominal reverberation of 0·3 second. In practice that figure may prove optimistic; if so, the plate is better used with reverberation times suited to music rather than speech. The damping plates may be operated mechanically or motorized, with push-button control and a reverberation time indicator on the control desk: this allows experimental changes to be made at any time during rehearsal. During a take any change would normally be made with echo faded out—though, in fact, the motor noise is not loud.

It is an advantage of reverberation plates that their two-dimensional structure allows the wave to radiate outward and break up, producing reflections that arrive in increasing numbers as reverberation continues and dies away, though this effect is not so marked as with three-dimensional reverberation.

In practice, plates vary both in the quality of the sheet and in the tension that may have been applied to them when they were set up. This is something of a specialized skill—the instructions might well read 'increase tension until the wires break, then slacken off a notch'! As a result, individual plates have their own characteristic response. More generally, some balancers dislike the way the plate treats string tone.

With a plate, having a short direct path between the transducers is unavoidable, so, once again, to simulate a large hall tape delay can be introduced into the echo feed.

There may be difficulties in finding a suitable place to stand the plate: it needs to be kept fairly quiet as it picks up noise from the air. In particular it cannot be kept in the control cubicle, as with very high loudspeaker levels howlround may occur at 200 Hz. The studio lobby is a reasonable place if there is room; or some separate quiet room—perhaps with other plates for other studios (they do not affect each other).

In an attempt to overcome some of the deficiencies of the plate, steel has given way to gold foil, produced electrolytically in sheets some 30 cm square. Even inside its double casing (with shock- and vibration-absorbing springs between the two) it occupies much less space than the steel plate, and is less susceptible to noise. The first-reflection delay is three times longer than that of the plate (but that in fact, is extremely short, being equivalent to about 2 m in air). A far better overall response is claimed—but at substantially greater cost.

In practice, users find that a well set-up steel plate is good enough for most purposes, but the improved control of short reverberation times gives the gold foil an advantage for speech—to which its first reflection delay time is well suited. It is therefore particularly useful for radio drama and for improving the necessarily dead acoustics of television studios.

Springs

A third medium for artificial reverberation employs what are usually described as 'springs'. The term is actually somewhat misleading, for although that is what they look like, they work quite differently: the axial tension and transmission characteristics of a spring are not used. Instead, the acoustic input is applied torsionally to one end of the helix, and sensed in the same manner at the other. The metal is differentially etched and notched along its length, so that its transmission characteristics change, with the effect that at each discontinuity there is a mismatch, and part of the sound is reflected. Each such reflection fathers its own family of subsequent echoes from all the other irregularly distributed discontinuities, and so the characteristics of reverberation are produced.

Separate springs are required for the stereo A and B channels, and these can either be totally independent of each other or their inputs may be linked so that A + B is fed to both. One example has a built-in effective first-reflection delay of 20 to 50 msec. When set to have a nominal reverberation time of 2 seconds, its response is level to 5 kHz (the reverberation time itself gets shorter at 5 kHz and above).

Early systems of springs were developed for use in electric organs. They were relatively inexpensive, but at that time did not find favour for professional use in many other applications. It was found that the longitudinal mode of vibration could also be set up, so that staccato sounds might be followed by a series of

409

direct reflections: this was particularly hazardous to percussion. But the principle of the device was sound, and well-engineered modern systems produce a quality of reverberation that is comparable with chamber and plate; also, being readily portable springs are well adapted to work outside the studio. With reverberation times of 2·0 to 4·5 seconds they are not suited to speech— a quoted 1·5 seconds minimum setting on one example proved optimistic. On the other hand, their treatment of string tone can be more pleasant than that of rival devices. However, springs do still have their own recognizable character, particularly when overdriven.

Digital techniques

A number of other principles are also possible. That with the greatest potential is digital echo, using the processors and *random access memories* (RAMs) developed in computer technology. In addition to a form of artificial reverberation, digital techniques offer a wide variety of other facilities: initial delay is a simple programme to add, while stereo and quadraphony are both provided readily. A 10-second science-fiction reverberation effect is no additional problem. Further, an individual source can be converted into a spread chorus by applying tiny random delays before recombining the sound (this also acts as a digital stereo spreader: see p. 292 for other systems). Then there is recombination with phase-cancellation, a recognized pop music gimmick (p. 415)—the possibilities proliferate. Unfortunately, the richness of conventional reverberation is one of the more complex of the digital programmes, but rapid progress in this field, too, is to be expected. The earliest commercial device was equipped with reverberation settings ranging from 0·4 to 4·5 sec at convenient intervals. Further controls permitted the bass reverberation time to be halved or increased relative to this figure, and the reverberation time of high frequencies to be reduced in three stages.

In a music balance, where the deficiencies of any of the different types of artificial echo become apparent, it is sometimes possible to improve the quality of reverberation by using two different types in parallel and mixing their output, or alternatively, by feeding the output of one device through another. But it may be better to use such extra equipment in other ways, for example, to apply a shorter reverberation to song (which may require verbal clarity) than to its instrumental accompaniment.

410

Using 'echo' on speech

The best choice of an echo system for speech—usually for dramatic effect—depends on its performance at short reverberation times. Echo chambers (and springs, too) usually have an intrinsically over-long decay and if allowed full rein can sound bathroomy. The steel plate is better, but at the shorter end of its range can sound metallic. A cleaner effect comes from gold foil; but digital systems show promise.

Reverberation is added by an echo device in direct proportion to the volume of sound fed into it. If an actor works close to the microphone and whispers, he will, for the same setting of the echo

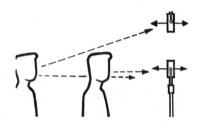

ECHO FOR PERSPECTIVE. The use of a second bidirectional microphone, suspended above the main and having a stronger echo feed, helps to create perspective on crowd scenes.

fader, produce just as much reverberation as he would when standing ten feet away and shouting. So watch perspective effects: as an actor moves in toward the microphone the echo has to be faded down.

However, if there are other voices or sound effects in a different perspective to be taken at the same time a more complex set-up is necessary. One useful arrangement has a second bidirectional microphone, with a strong echo feed, suspended above the main working microphone, which itself has little or no echo. Then, as the actor moves in close to the lower microphone, he moves out of the field of pick-up of the upper one. Thus, perspectives can be emphasized without constant resort to the echo fader. This refinement is more likely to be of use in radio than in the visual media where there are restrictions on the ideal placing of microphones.

When echo is wanted on only one voice, as, for example, in a conversation between two people, one of whom is at the bottom of a well, control can be exercised with the echo feed switch. With the echo fader left at a pre-determined setting, the switch is snapped in and out between alternate voices. If the echo fader is

411

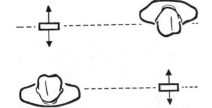

ECHO ON TWO VOICES. If differing amounts of echo are needed on two voices taking part in a conversation, it helps if opposing microphones and voices are placed dead-side-on to each other. This layout might be adopted in a radio studio; in a television studio there is normally more space available, making separation easier.

used instead of the feed switch the timing of the operation is different: the fader must not be taken in or out until the new voice has begun speaking. A third method is to place the two speakers on separate microphones, dead-side-on to each other or sufficiently separated that there is little spill. This permits completely independent control of the echo feeds from each.

Delay and spin

The need for delay as a precursor to artificial reverberation for music has already been mentioned. It enhances the realism, and also shares with reality the virtue of letting the transients through first, so that the characteristic attack of a note is heard clearly. Delays of 50–100 msec extend the apparent first-reflection pathlength by 55–110 ft (17–34 m) in fair simulation of music room or concert hall. An early method of achieving this was to put the sound through a tape recording and reproduction system at a playing speed of 15 i/s (38 cm/s). The spacing of the heads might give a delay of 150 msec, representing a substantial hall. For more flexibility, a range of tape speeds was desirable, and for this the motor speed could be controlled by a variable-frequency oscillator.

Another way of delaying an audio signal was to employ certain electronic circuits. By the standards of human perception the delay achieved in a single stage was rather small, but it could be extended by arranging the circuit elements in series. They now provide great flexibility, offering delays that can be set at multiples of, say, 5 or 7·5 msec from zero to several hundred milliseconds. In these, the first few settings permit effects that depend on differences of phase.

To ensure that delay is independent of frequency the signal is converted to a digital form in which the original waveform is represented by a series of numbers. Typically, these may be the amplitude, sampled at at least twice the rate of the highest

412

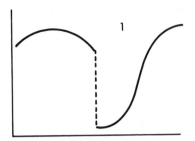
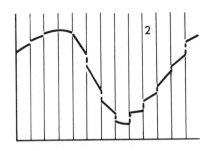

RATE OF SAMPLING. 1. A low rate of sampling introduces marked discontinuities in the signal that are clearly audible. 2. A high rate of sampling introduces many small discontinuities in the signal: if the rate is high enough the effect is not audible.

frequency required. Each item of information is coded as a succession of zeros and ones: by analogy, a switch is off or on, or an answer is 'no' or 'yes' (binary digital circuitry handles all signals in this form). This number, in computer jargon called a 'word', is fed to an electronic device called a shift register which briefly stores and then regurgitates it into the next register in line, and so on. At the end of the line the signal is changed back to a waveform—a process that is called 'digital-to-analogue conversion'. Back at the start, the original audio signal is filtered to remove frequencies above the audio range, as components close to or related to the rate at which the original waveform is sampled would produce spurious effects in the delay line, and at the end a second filter removes unwanted products of the reconversion process.

The total delay achieved is calculated by dividing the number of storage locations by the sampling frequency. Delay lines of this type may be of a single fixed duration, or may be grouped to provide extended delays of different lengths. It is, however, difficult to tap the component lines internally without degrading the signal.

A later development again uses random access memories instead of shift registers. Each RAM component may contain several thousands of 'addresses' at which information can be stored in binary form. To use them for delay, it is arranged that information is located at a known sequence of addresses. After the desired interval, the addresses are examined in the same order, the information extracted and the signal reconstructed. Then new signals are fed to the memories (thereby erasing the old) and the process repeated. The maximum delay is again determined by the number of addresses available and the sampling

413

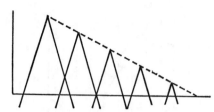

APPARENT REVERBERATION BY TAPE FEEDBACK. A hard mechanical quality is generally obtained.

frequency, but in this case smaller delays can readily be selected: this form of digital delay is (to well beyond the limits of human perception) continuously variable. In one example the delay can be changed by 20 microsecond increments from 0 to 320 milliseconds, with an option of doubling those figures at the cost of distortion above 10 kHz owing to the reduced sampling rate. In some cases it is arranged that memories can be sampled at two places, so that delays of different duration are obtained, and this may require what is described as three-state logic: the analogy is to a question with three possible replies—yes, no, or no answer.

If (in the original tape-deck version of delay) the output is mixed back in to the input, the sound circulates, dying away if the feedback signal is attenuated, or becoming a howlround if the signal is amplified. This effect is called recirculation, *spin* or sometimes *slap echo*, and has a mechanically repetitive quality. The effect depends on the delay interval: at a fifth of a second, for example, there is a marked flutter effect.

It is possible to start with a staccato effect such as a tap on a water-glass and let it spin indefinitely by controlling the feedback level manually. Any slight unevenness in the frequency response of the circuit is quickly disclosed: using tape, even a high quality professional recorder soon discloses its deficiencies and within half a minute the characteristic of the system completely swallows the original sound. Digital delay techniques are, of course, more flexible than tape delay, and the signal itself is not altered while in digital form in the same way that a waveform is distorted. However, any defects that do exist are multiplied on each tour of the circuit.

In addition to the effects already described, delay can be used to 'double' instruments; to space out the signal to rear quadraphonic loudspeakers that may be nearer to the listener than those in front; or to resynchronize sounds that have been produced a little out of step owing to the time a sound cue takes to travel through air.

414

Phasing, flanging

The short-delay effects in which phase is important were explored in pop music by tape techniques before pure electronic devices were introduced. Two recordings were played, initially in synchronization, then one was slowed by hand against the flange of the tape spool—from which the technique took the name of *flanging*. The sounds were separated by a progressively increasing interval, causing phase cancellation to sweep through the audio range. This could be made more manageable first by the use of variable speed control, and then by switching to fully electronic techniques.

One device produced a shifting phase-cancellation effect without the use of delay. The signal was fed through a series of simple circuits (rather like filters) which passed all of the frequencies present but changed their phase relationship. When this output was recombined with the original signal there was partial cancellation at some frequencies, which could be altered continuously by varying the components of the phase-change circuit. An interesting side-product was that the frequency of the signal as a whole also shifted a little while any change in the phase-shifting network was being made, so permitting deep vibrato effects. But the phasing effect was different from the 'flange' effect in other ways, too, of which the most important was that cancellation was distributed through the audio range in an exponential manner (in the ratios 1:2:4:8:16 etc.) compared with flanging's arithmetical array (1:2:3:4:5 etc.). The flanging effect was therefore directly related to the harmonic tone structure used in many

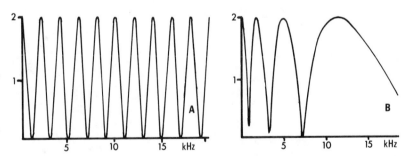

PHASING. The change in amplitude (vertical scale) with frequency. A. The effect of flanging—here with a delay of 0·5 milliseconds—is evenly distributed throughout the frequency range, but is not related to the musical scale, which is logarithmic. B. Cancellation and enhancement produced by the use of a phase-changing network: the dips are distributed evenly over the musical scale.

415

strong, dense, high-frequency overtone structure whether it is harmonically related or not.

With techniques based on the use of delay circuits, phasing reverted to the pattern of cancellation originally found in flanging, which many users still preferred. One example, called an 'Instant Flanger', employs random access memories, and has two outputs. One of these has constant delay and the other, which is continuously variable, can be swept through it, with the signals either added or subtracted. Note that when delay is changed, some data is either sampled twice or omitted and that this produces a characteristic form of distortion (see p. 427).

Flanging is most effective when the interval between the signals lies in the range from 50 microseconds to 5 milliseconds; as it increases beyond this to about 15 milliseconds the two signals separate completely to give a doubling effect. The technique works well with sounds that are sustained and have a broad frequency spectrum: guitar, cymbals or vocal-backing chords are typical applications. Other interesting effects are found when it is applied with a 1–5 msec delay to transients.

Like all gimmicks in pop-music, phasing can easily be overused; it is perhaps most effective when applied to a single phrase in a piece, repeated only when that phrase recurs.

17

SHAPING SOUND

ONE aim of audio engineering has been to approach ever closer to the ideal of perfect fidelity in sound recording and reproduction. But as our technical grasp of the means of eliminating distortion in all its forms has been extended, so also has our ability to use and control distortion for creative purposes. We have seen that, today, distortion of the sound as picked up by the microphone is deliberately introduced into many recordings and that in such cases recording, editing, and dubbing may become part of the process of composition, of creating music. A further type that illustrates this is *musique concrète*.

Techniques based on musique concrète have been used, often with considerable effect, in the theatre; and what are called *radiophonic* effects and music have been included in many BBC radio and television productions and for special signature tunes that can cut through the noise of short wave radio reception. There is also great scope for musically organized sound effects in a variety of media, including commercials.

Any amateur with a microphone, recorder and razor blade can demonstrate that the formal organization of any sequence of sounds has some resemblance to music, although its quality depends on the musical sense of the person making the arrangement. A musical intention is more obvious if the sounds themselves originate from some recognizably musical source, while if the starting-point is noise or a series of noises the effect is often comic. Comedy—and comedy timing—is relatively easy to achieve. Serious composers have experimented with the treatment of pure tones and white noise; no less seriously, but rather more commercially minded, others have explored the aptitudes of a variety of sound synthesizers—in some cases, to a counterpoint of protest from those whose livelihood is invested in the more conventional musical skills. Happily, these seem little threatened at present.

Distortion and sound conventions

Practically every sound we hear reproduced—however high the quality—is a rearrangement of reality according to certain conventions. For example, monophonic sound is distorted sound in every case except the one where the effective point source of the loudspeaker is being used to reproduce a sound that is itself confined to a similarly small source. Every balance—every carefully contrived mixture of direct and indirect sound—is a deliberate distortion of what you would hear if you listened to the same sound live. But this distortion is accepted so easily as the conventional form of the medium that very few people are even aware of it. Perhaps distortion would be better defined as 'unwanted changes of quality', rather as noise is sometimes defined as 'unwanted sound'. But in the broader sense of the term, distortion is for ever with us. Sound is continuously being shaped in some degree, and the listener is constantly being required to accept one convention or another for its use.

A point that immediately presents itself concerns listening conditions: the use of good equipment is much more important when we listen to 'new sounds' than it is for conventional music.

When a listener with good musical imagination hears instruments he knows and musical forms he understands, he is able to judge the qualities of writing and performance in spite of bad recording and bad reproduction. And although they may reduce his enjoyment, noise and distortion are automatically disregarded. The musical elements are identified according to the listener's previous knowledge and experience, and so in his imagination he reconstitutes the original musical sound without too much difficulty.

But, obviously, this does not happen on the first few hearings of a piece of music in which the new sound is produced by what, in other situations, would be regarded as distortion. Thus we reach the novel situation in which any imperfections produced by the equipment are, for the listener, indistinguishable from the process of musical composition, and indeed become part of the music. Many items of concrete or electronic music are highly effective (although perhaps an acquired taste), but one may wonder how many people have been put off by the diabolical noises for

418

which their own equipment may be responsible; or which may have been produced by the poor acoustic properties of some theatre, or by a sound system over which even a symphony by Mozart sounds like musique concrète.

Differences between the various forms

When a composer sets pen to paper he knows that he has a large number of independent variables at his command. He specifies each instrument and the way in which it is to be played; the pitch of each note and its duration; the relationship in time and pitch between successive notes and between different instruments. However much is specified, there is always room left for interpretation by the performer.

This leads to the first and most obvious difference between conventional music and taped new forms, for an electronic or concrete composition exists only in its final state, as a painting or carving does. It is not performed, but merely replayed. In this one respect, at least, musique concrète is like electronic music, from which it otherwise has certain fundamental differences.

Musique concrète is made by recording the ready-made timbres of some particular group of sound sources, transforming them in various ways, and then cutting and assembling them in a montage. Electronic music starts, as might be expected, with electronically generated signals such as pure tones, harmonic series or coloured noise (noise contained within some frequency spectrum). This basic divergence in technique produces results that are characteristically different—although in theory the concrete sounds could be imitated by electronic synthesis, and, indeed, an oscillator is a valid 'concrete' sound source.

One characteristic quality of musique concrète is that the pitch relationship between the fundamental and the upper partials of each constituent sound remains unaltered by transformation unless any frequency band is filtered out completely, or certain rather exotic types of transformation are introduced. This in itself is both a strength and a restriction: it helps to give unity to a work derived from a single sound or range of sounds, but it severely hampers development.

In electronic music, on the other hand, where every sound is created individually, the harmonic structure of each new element of a work is completely free. Where musique concrète has restrictions, electronic music offers new freedoms—and this is the essential difference between the two. And although it is yet to be established that either electronic or concrete music have any real lasting importance as forms in their own right, the two techniques really do have a proven value in extending the range of sound comment—that is, in providing radiophonic effects (to use the BBC term).

This is the field in which sound effects take on formal musical qualities in structure and arrangement; and musical elements (whether from conventional or electronic sources) complement them by taking on the qualities of sound effects. Radiophonics does not in general attempt to assert itself as an art form in its own right; it is always an element in a larger picture, and indeed rarely even moves into the foreground of the audience's attention. It is best to avoid latching too firmly on to any particular musical style. One extremely valuable attribute for anyone working in this field is, I would say, a strongly self-critical sense of humour.

The construction of musique concrète

Musique concrète is built up in three distinct phases—selection, treatment and montage.

The first characteristic of the form lies in the choice of basic material: a concrete sound is one which from the start is complete in itself. In the early days of musique concrète the emotional associations of the original sound were incorporated into the music. There was a later reaction away from this idea, for the lack of an immediate mental association can lend power to sounds. The basic materials may include tin cans, fragments of human speech, a cough, canal boats chugging or snatches of Tibetan chant (all these are in an early work called *Etude Pathétique*).

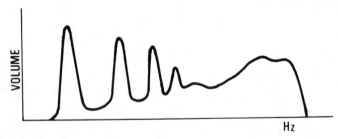

LINE AND BAND SPECTRA. Instantaneous content: this sound is composed of individual tones superimposed on a broad spectrum band of noise.

Musical instruments are not taboo; for instance, one piece uses a flute—both played and struck. And there are other things besides the natural sound qualities of an object that may affect a recording: such things as differences in the balance or 'playing' of a sound help to extend the range of sound materials enormously.

This preliminary sound recording may be considered analytically in terms of a variety of qualities:

1. The instantaneous content of the sound, its frequency spectrum or timbre (this may contain separate harmonics, bands of noise or a mixture of the two).
2. The melodic sequence of such sound structures.
3. The dynamics or envelope of the sound (by this is meant the way in which the sound intensity varies in time).

The second stage in building musique concrète, and the second characteristic of it, is treatment of the sound materials to provide a series of what may be termed 'sound-subjects'. The bricks from which the work is to be constructed must be fashioned from the raw materials selected. A wide range of technical operations is now available, and in France the *Groupe de Recherche de Musique Concrète* has distinguished between various types of manipulation:

1. *Transmutation of the structure of sound*—that is, changing the instantaneous sound content in a way that affects its melodic and harmonic qualities, but not its dynamics. Included in this category of manipulation are transpositions of pitch (which may be continuous or discontinuous) and filtering (to vary the harmonic structure or coloration).
2. *Discontinuous transformation* of the constituent parts of a sound by editing. An individual sound element may be dissected into attack, body and decay; and particular sections subjected to reversal, contraction, permutation or substitution. This form of manipulation varies the dynamics of the sound, though on any given scrap of tape the instantaneous sound content is not altered.
3. *Continuous transformation* in which the envelope of a sound is varied without editing, by the use of faders, by adding reverbertion, or by some more out-of-the-way technique.

Here is an example of what a complex operation might involve. Starting with, say, a recording of a piano note, it might be decided that the effect required by the composer could be obtained by replaying through a frequency filtering network, at the same time varying the speed of the re-recording machine, the result being edited by chopping a piece out of the middle and placing it at the end, and then joining the ends together to form a tape loop that

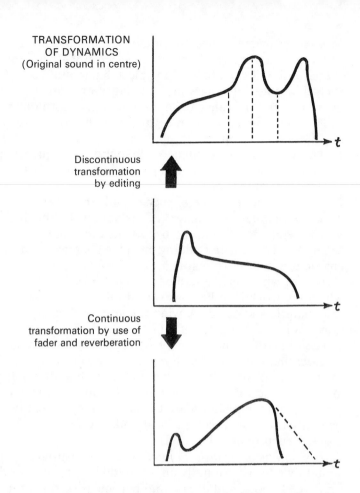

TRANSFORMATION
OF DYNAMICS
(Original sound in centre)

Discontinuous
transformation
by editing

Continuous
transformation by use of
fader and reverberation

is played backwards, twice, through an echo chamber. The result of this (or any other arbitrarily selected series of manipulations) might sound horrible or, just possibly, it might be exactly what the composer wanted.

The third phase in the manufacture of musique concrète is that of construction; the sound-subjects are put together piece by piece, like the shots of a film.

Several techniques are available for construction. One is to edit a single tape by cutting and joining pieces together (montage); another is dubbing and mixing in the same way that sound-effects sequences are put together. More satisfactory, however, is to lay tracks, and to mix them down.

422

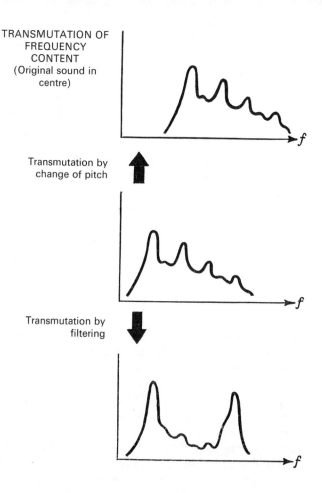

TRANSMUTATION OF
FREQUENCY
CONTENT
(Original sound in
centre)

Transmutation by
change of pitch

Transmutation by
filtering

Some of the relevant techniques have already been discussed: these include filtering (pp. 391–400), artificial reverberation (pp. 401–412), delay (p. 412), spin (p. 414), phasing (p. 415), compression and expansion (pp. 351–362) and dynamic inversion (p. 361).

Transposition of pitch by changing the tape speed

When a sound is originally being made its creator generally has a fair degree of control over various characteristics of the sound— its pitch, timbre, duration and envelope (i.e. the way in which the attack and decay are related in intensity to the main body of the

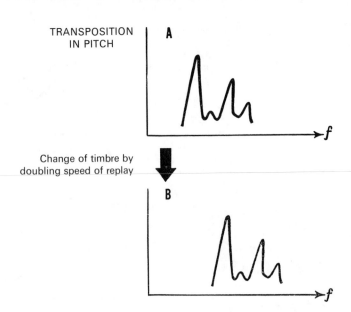

TRANSPOSITION
IN PITCH

A

Change of timbre by
doubling speed of replay

B

note). It is usually possible to exercise a greater degree of independent control of these variables if a musical instrument is
chosen as the sound source, rather than some 'concrete' sound
effect. But once the original recording has been made, all of the
formerly independent variables are locked together. For example,
speed up the replay to increase the pitch by two octaves, and the
duration comes down to a quarter, the attack and decay characteristics change so that the sound is a great deal more percussive
and dry than before, the timbre changes to that of an instrument
a quarter of the size, and so on. Everything is changed together.

One way of achieving some degree of control over the final result
is to alter the quality of the original sound material before recording—i.e. having seen what is wrong with a transposition, to go
back to the beginning and try to compensate for it in the creation
of the sound. But the method is less effective than one would
wish: speed transformations easily swamp all but the most
emphatic differences in the raw material. Not surprisingly, some
of the most successful results in musique concrète are obtained
when the composer does not try to impose his will too strongly on
the source material, but instead listens to it together with its most
effective-sounding transformations and then lets these suggest
their own arrangement.

When treating actuality sound, e.g. a foghorn, any background

424

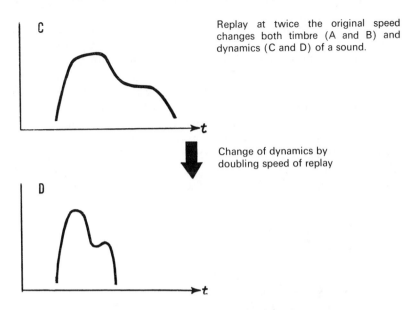

Replay at twice the original speed changes both timbre (A and B) and dynamics (C and D) of a sound.

Change of dynamics by doubling speed of replay

sound recorded with it that cannot be filtered out is treated as well. Such a background may be hardly noticed with the ordinary sound, because it is natural, but treatment may make it vividly apparent. Close microphone techniques, providing good separation, are desirable.

A simple example of pitch change is that of a double-speed piano mixed with normal piano. On the first recording the piano is played with slow deliberation, to avoid the appearance of a totally inhuman virtuosity when the tape is speeded up. This initial recording is then played back at double speed, and a conventional piano accompaniment added. The double-speed piano sound on which the composition is based is no mere variation on this instrument's ordinary quality. It sounds like a new instrument, and must be treated as such in the musical arrangement.

When a singer's voice is subjected to a speed change the result can sound particularly odd. This is due to vibrato, the cyclic variation in pitch that gives colour and warmth to a singer's sustained notes—a technique that is copied on orchestral instruments such as the violin. Analysis of voices that are generally considered beautiful suggests that pitch variations of as much as 8% may not be excessive (a semitone is about 6%). But the really critical quality of vibrato is the number of these wobbles that occur in the second. The acceptable range is narrow: it seems that

425

to create an attractive sound the vibrato rate must fall somewhere between about 5 and 8 Hz. These characteristics of vibrato are more or less independent of the pitch of the note sung.

Outside the limits of 5–8 Hz the effect resembles wow or flutter: the vibrato range can be taken as dividing the two. Clearly, only small speed changes are possible without taking the vibrato outside its normal range. If this is exceeded a vibrato that did not previously call attention to itself may suddenly become both obvious and ugly. Doubling the speed of a sustained note automatically produces a characteristic effect: it sounds like a small, vibrant-voiced animal (which is fine if that is the effect required).

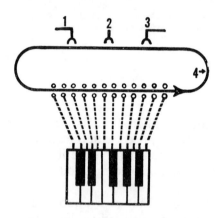

CHROMATICALLY CONTROLLED TAPE MACHINE. There are twelve keys, twelve spindles, and a 2-speed motor. 1. Recording head. 2. Erase head. 3. Reproducing head. 4. Tape loop.

Tremolo, a similar variation on the volume of a note is also dramatically affected by speed changes; so also is *portamento*, an initial slide into a note, or from one note to another which, if slowed down, changes its character, or if speeded up, almost disappears.

Whereas a male and female voice may differ in fundamental by an octave, the *formant* ranges (i.e. those parts of the vocal sound emphasized by the throat, mouth and nasal cavities and used to give the main characteristics of speech) are, on average, only a semi-tone or so apart, and vibrato ranges are also little separated. Small changes of pitch therefore tend not to change the apparent sex of a voice, but rather to de-sex it. As an illustration of some of the odd-sounding effects that one can get, try listening to the voice quality produced by playing 33's of languorous male singers at 45 rpm; the effect sometimes becomes that of a vibrant female . . . but not always.

426

Special equipment for transmutations

It is possible to make radical changes in pitch without introducing a host of awkward side effects by means of a device that is like a normal replay machine except that, instead of the tape being drawn across a single replay head, it passes round a capstan into which several replay heads are fitted. The capstan can be rotated so that the heads 'chase' the tape (and thus reduce the pitch of replay without affecting duration), or it can be rotated in the opposite direction, lifting the pitch. Owing to the discontinuity that is created when one replay head takes over from another a characteristic form of distortion is produced. But depending on the type of music and the degree of change this may be almost unnoticeable to the listener. Pitch can be varied continuously without affecting duration, or alternatively the replay can be slowed or speeded without affecting pitch.

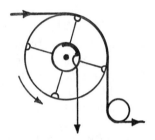

TEMPOPHON. Changes duration and pitch independently. Head assembly can rotate either way: *If sense is opposite to that of tape, pitch increases; if heads chase tape, it decreases.* Signal is fed from whichever head is in contact with tape, via commutator and brushes, to a second recorder.

Pitch can also be changed purely electronically by digital circuitry—a development from the digital delay techniques described earlier. The signal is fed to random access memories that are scanned in groups at a different rate. As with the mechanical tape-chasing device, there are overlaps if the pitch is reduced or tiny segments missing if the pitch is raised, in this case typically with durations of the order of hundredths of a second. So a similar characteristic form of distortion is induced, with the danger of transients being lengthened or repeated in overlap or nipped out completely, and whether this is important again depends on the nature of the sound and its use. One device of this type is called a *Harmonizer*: it can change internal pitch (with all of the internal harmonics remaining in their original relationship) by up to an octave in each direction, with continuously variable control, or by keyboard selection if this is preferred. The instrument has a read-out indicating the pitch change ratio; showing 1·06 for a semi-tone up, and so on. In this case, duration can be

427

varied independently of pitch by controlling the tape replay speed by means of a variable frequency oscillator. To change duration without changing pitch the two controls are given reciprocal settings.

As with some other digital adaptations, 'random access' offers a mixed bag of additional blessings. It includes some of the delay devices described earlier and also feedback, providing a form of artificial reverberation which is rather mechanical in quality. And delayed feedback can be combined with pitch change to create trails of ascending or descending sound.

The Harmonizer has a capacity for slightly spreading its designated pitch, and the control for this is designated 'anti-feedback', which is one of its applications: if the treated signal is returned (without additional pitch-change) through a studio by an acoustic feedback or public address circuit (pp. 43, 53, 219, 299), the loudspeaker level can be raised substantially. Unlike the frequency-shifted feedback sometimes used for public address (see below and p. 220) it can be fed to musicians, too, as the spread is centred on the original frequency.

An older device for changing pitch independently of duration is the *ring modulator*. It allows a fixed number of cycles per second to be added to (or subtracted from) all frequencies present (e.g. components f_1, f_2, f_3, become $x+f_1, x+f_2, x+f_3$; whereas simple alteration of speed multiplies all frequencies by a common factor). Alternatively, frequencies can be inverted ($x-f_1, x-f_2$, and so on) so that high frequencies become low ones and vice versa. By means of this type of transmutation certain curious qualities of consonance and dissonance can be obtained. These are of a type that do not occur naturally, i.e. in conventional music, but which have been a feature of the development of electronic music.

Modulators are regularly used in telephony, so that narrow-frequency bands containing the main characteristics of speech can be stacked one above the other on a line capable of carrying a broad band. In their modulated form some of the speech bands may be transmitted in an inverted form—and it is in fact possible to bring them back down to normal frequencies but still have them inverted. For example, a band of speech might be inverted so that what was 2500 Hz becomes zero, and vice versa. The most important effect of such a manipulation is to invert the three most important bands of formants, so that the speech is translated into a sort of upside-down jabberwocky language—which curiously enough it is actually possible to learn.

428

But this is only one very pedestrian example of what can be done with modulators: if both signals are complex the results may be a great deal more complicated. For example, in the field of sound effects, a filtered human voice can be used to modulate a train siren to make it talk. The effect of machine or computer voice can be obtained by modulating an actor's deliberately mechanical-sounding speech with a tone of 10 to 20 Hz. In electronic music, two relatively simple sound structures can be combined to make a much more complex form. After use of a modulator it may be necessary to filter to get rid of unwanted products.

The Harmonizer, too, can produce a useful hollow sounding alien voice effect when feedback (without delay) is used in conjunction with pitch change.

Pure tones and white noise

In creating *electronic music*, the composer has complete control of his resources, synthesizing every first and last detail of the sound. With no performer to get between him and the final product, he has the whole responsibility for the work, and more freedom than any other composer—subject only to the limitations of time, patience, and his equipment.

The basic equipment for producing electronic sound includes generators for producing pure tones and combinations of tones, which are normally required in quantity: perhaps as many as a dozen sine or square wave generators may be needed at once. For the most part these need not be of high quality, although at least one of them should have a high degree of accuracy in calibration. If musical instruments are off pitch it is only one performance that is affected, and the score itself remains unaltered; but in the case of electronic music the first 'realization' will in all probability be the only complete evidence of the composer's intentions.

One of the most characteristic sounds of early electronic works has been the use of short bursts of tone at various frequencies, sounding like a series of pips, beeps and bloops. If a work was assembled from a series of short lengths of tape to give this effect, variations in attack and decay could be introduced by varying the angle at which the tape is cut. A 90° cut gives the strongest effect of a click at beginning or end; other angles of cut soften it.

Today, however, a synthesizer would be used to provide not only the tone, together with conventional harmonic coloration, if required, but also a range of different qualities of attack and

429

decay. These are often described by relating them to some musical instrument of similar attack and tone quality.

White (and *coloured*) *noise* is another type of sound that is peculiar to electronic music and radiophonic sound, as this incorporates electronic techniques. It can be produced in several ways—for example, by amplifying the output from a noisy vacuum tube. Special tubes are made for the purpose. Another good, even source is the amplified output of a VHF receiver tuned off-station.

White noise is in itself not particularly useful; but in combination with a versatile filter it can be used to produce 'colours' that can be of indeterminate pitch, or related to any desired musical scale by placing peaks at particular frequencies and troughs at others, or by using bands of particular widths. Electronic wind effects can also be manufactured in this way. Another effect is achieved by imposing a sinusoidal envelope, or any other waveform on the noise so that it becomes a series of puffs of sound. If this is speeded up sufficiently it is transformed into a tone that can be used musically—then on slowing down again the granular structure of the original sound may be observed. The principle behind this sort of sound is very similar to that of the siren.

In cases where conventional harmonic structures are required, a useful source is a *sawtooth* or *square-wave generator*. A sawtooth-shaped wave contains a full harmonic series, while the square shape includes only the odd harmonics, like those of a clarinet. These are subsequently treated by *subtractive synthesis* (filtering, etc.), which in appropriate cases is less time-consuming than an additive process.

There are many *electronic organs* available, with names like Monochord, Melochord, Spinetta and Ondes Martenot, besides the more conventional Compton and Hammond organs. The Trautonium is one of a group of instruments that can be used (and played, live) to provide notes of any pitch, not just those corresponding to a keyboard. Organs, as one class, shade gradually into another, synthesizers, which includes instruments such as the Moog and the Yamaha. The Arp synthesizer seems remarkably like what in former times would have been called an electronic organ. It has a conventional keyboard and instrumental tone colours, but an added facility for frequency slewing (portamento), in this case a slide in pitch from one note to another as successive keys are pressed. The rate of slew can be varied.

Most of the electronics of early *synthesizers* has been 'analogue'

430

in form in that the instruments copied or reconstructed the required wave forms or noises by means that provided a continuous shape, which could also be continuously modified from the start. The next stage of development was to add digital circuitry—for example by using a digital control device to programme musical sequences of treated sounds. This is only the beginning of the digital invasion, for in practice, there is no significant difference between a signal from an oscillator and one produced from a succession of on-off switches, provided the switching is fast enough. Once that is achieved, the most important considerations that remain are the facilities a machine provides for a given cost, together with its compactness and ease of performance.

The Moog (pronounced to rhyme with vogue) was a revolutionary design of analogue synthesizer relying on compact multifunction voltage-controlled oscillators and amplifiers making possible a generous capability for the modification of sound structures in interesting ways. Increased versatility has been one line of development, but this has been parallelled by a feeling that that which can do anything does nothing in particular: in the workshop a vast available range of functions may for the most part be rarely used, with the composer seeking out a synthesizer mainly for its more unusual qualities. More recently there has been a tendency toward design for specialized purposes; for electronic instruments that can be used with conventional orchestral instruments in performance, or perhaps for reccreating classical sounds such as that of the baroque organ.

It remains legitimate to use the simplest means that offer the desired effect, so many workshops also use such sources as the electric guitar and autoharp, zither, harmonium, and piano, among other musical instruments, conventional and rare.

Radiophonics

Where a work is being synthesized from basic sources it is obviously a major task to treat and assemble them. A radiophonic workshop must have filters of many different kinds, envelope shapers, ring modulators, compressors and limiters, several types of echo equipment, and control desks with conventional operational facilities. Many of the facilities peculiar to radiophonic or electronic music workshops are now available as packages such as those manufactured by Electronic Music Studios (EMS) of London, combining electronic sources (such as pure tone, square wave or sawtooth, noise and so on) with the commonly used treatments (attack, decay, sustain, ring modulator, filters, reverberation, and a variety of other functions). Sources and functions are linked via a pin-matrix patchboard: the connection is made by putting a pin into a two-dimensional layout of holes. At the heart of such a system is the sequencer, which is digitally encoded to remember the order and timing of events, and when so programmed, to control the rhythm and rate of replay of material that has been set up note by note using the standard treatments and sources from the control panel or keyboards. Concrete or other external sources can also be fed in; or the material from the synthesizer fed out for external treatment and then returned. The limitations on what may be achieved at any one time depends on the range of hardware provided and the fact that each facility can be selected only once. The more frequently required items are, of course, duplicated or multiplied.

A workshop requires multitrack recorders (eight tracks or more) as a matter of routine, if possible with one multitrack recorder that can run at a variable speed. To this must be added record and replay machines for standard-width tape, ideally including one with chromatically controlled speeds. There will be a control desk with facilities similar to those for the recording and mixdown of popular music. For monitoring, at least three loudspeakers are needed: two for the stereo mix and one for individual guide, cue or click tracks. For work of this sort the whole studio should be made independent of mains frequency variations.

The BBC's Radiophonic Workshop has elaborate stereo panning and spreading equipment, including a keyboard-operated device for placing individual monophonic sources (such as successive speeches on a mono tape) at a range of left-to-right positions selected by keyboard and cued from a memory store. Some degree of 'overpanning', to place a source out to the side beyond one of the speakers is achieved by feeding an out-of-phase signal to the speaker on the opposite side. Continuous-track faders are essential for sound that includes pure tones, as this shows up discontinuities and crackle that would be imperceptible in more complex signals. At a time when the BBC generally used elaborate faders, its Radiophonic Workshop had photosensitive ('glowpot') faders, until the advent of plastic and improved carbon-track faders made them unnecessary.

The range of conventional synthesis is extended further by the digital envelope shaper. An envelope is drawn by light-pen on to

432

a display tube, and then converted by a processor to digital form at, say, sixty points along its length (which represents a duration that in principle is of any chosen magnitude). This is a powerful tool: earlier so-called shapers have defined no more than some four parameters of the treated sound.

The *Vocoder* offers changes of a more dramatic nature. It is designed to encode the basic parameters of speech, including the tonal and fricative qualities, so that they can be imposed on any electronic, or other, source and thereby impart to it the characteristics of a voice, including intelligible speech and song. This extends the range of technique available to television programmes that specialize in alien voices and mechanical monsters, which have previously depended heavily on ring modulators and swept filters (the latter usually wobbles a filter up and down in frequency). The Vocoder also offers possibilities for humanizing electronic music by encoding some of the characteristic 'imperfections' of musical instruments and operating with them on electronic (or other) source material. Used in conjunction with a device that changes pitch and duration independently, the opportunities are vast.

When there is picture as well as sound, it is possible to link the two directly, deriving or modulating an audio signal from some characteristic of the (electronic) video signal; or alternatively, allowing the audio to modulate video or to control the generation or selection of picture elements.

Radiophonics demands an unusual combination of skills, both operational and creative, and it is difficult to predict whether any particular individual will have either the aptitude or temperament. It is best to create ways for aspirants to try their hand before any commitment is entered into. At the BBC (as distinct from some electronic music studios) the product of its Radiophonic Workshop is applied to the needs of general radio and television programming; it is not a 'pure' experimental music laboratory. Where the latter exist there is a tendency for them to produce extreme avant-garde or computer music, much of which deserves to be played only to other computers.

New laws for music

Most radiophonics is based on the conventional musical scale in some form: this is directly related to human powers of perception and appreciation, which are attuned to harmonic structures that arise naturally. But by starting from pure electronic sources the musical 'laws of nature' can be relaxed somewhat. In view of the way in which human minds work, whether or not this is much use depends on what is offered in specific cases. Unfortunately there is little incentive to other than the more remote experimental musicians to work in this field, so little has been done to establish its broader value.

But before we can begin to examine the freedom the composer is allowed in this new medium, and in particular his freedom to create new harmonic structures and scales, we shall have to take a look at the concept of scale as we know it, and the restrictions that this imposes.

All of the scales that have ever been devised for conventional music have one thing in common—the interval of an octave, in which the frequency of the upper note is exactly twice that of the lower. If the two notes are sounded together on orchestral instruments the combination sounds pleasant because of the concord between the fundamental of the higher note and the first harmonic of the lower; and there are also many other harmonics in common. If, however, one of the notes is shifted slightly off-pitch these various concords are lost—they are present only when the frequency of the two fundamentals can be expressed as a ratio of small whole numbers.

Without the harmonics, there would be no sense of concord or discord, unless the fundamentals were themselves fairly close together. If we start instead with two pure tones at the same frequency, and then increase the pitch of one of them, the first effect that we hear is a beat between them. As the difference becomes greater than 15 Hz (twice or three times this at high frequencies), the beat is replaced by the sensation we call dissonance. This increases to a maximum and then falls away again, until as the frequency ratio approaches 5:6 it is no longer apparent. For pure tones dissonance occurs only within this rather narrow range. There is just one proviso here: that the tones are not loud. If they are, the ear begins to generate its own harmonics.

Some experimenters with electronic music, noting all this, have concluded that our conventional concept of scale is merely a convenient special case, and that if only we could create harmonic structures that were not based on the conventional 1, 2, 3, 4 . . . series, completely new scales could be devised—as, indeed, they have.

434

Stockhausen's 'Study II'

The way in which electronic music can be based on a totally new concept of scale is made easier to explain by the fact that a complete score has been published, showing everything that had gone into the making of a particular work: Karlheinz Stockhausen's '*Study II*'. When the tape of this is played to a listener with perfect pitch, or even good relative pitch, it seems immediately that 'something is wrong'—or at the very least, that something is different. And indeed, by all conventional musical standards, something is; the arrangement of musical intervals is such as could never have been heard before the introduction of electronic sound synthesis.

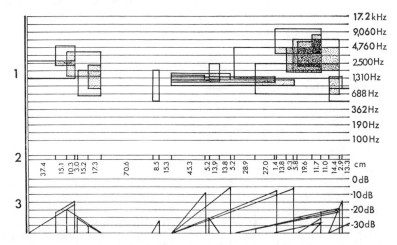

ELECTRONIC MUSIC. Score of the type devised by Stockhausen to show the structure of his 'Study II'. 1. Pitch: showing the groups of tone mixtures used. Each block represents a group of five tones (see opposite). 2. Intervals of tape measured in cm. Tape speed: 30 i/s (76 cm/s). 3. Volume: dynamics of the tone mixtures.

Now, in order to accommodate as many small-whole-number relationships as possible, the conventional scale is based on a division of the octave into twelve equal, or roughly equal, parts. Each note in the chromatic scale is roughly 6% higher in frequency than the one before, so that the product of a dozen of these ratios is two—the octave. But Stockhausen, in his '*Study II*', dispenses with the octave completely, and takes instead a completely new scale based on an interval of two octaves and a third, which is the interval between a note and its 'normal' fifth harmonic, or, to put it another way, the interval between any two notes whose

435

frequency ratio is five. This large interval he subdivided into twenty-five equal small intervals, which means that each successive note on his scale is about 7% higher than its predecessors. So it is only to be expected that very few of the intervals based on this scale correspond to anything in the previous musical experience of the listener.

If music written to this scale were played on almost any conventional musical instrument, almost any combination of notes attempting either harmony or melody would be dissonant because of the harmonics present. Violins and trombones are examples of instruments that *could* be immediately adapted to playing in it; others, such as trumpets and woodwind instruments would have to be specially made. The only feasible way of attacking the problem is to use completely synthesized sound derived from electronic sources, but the labour involved in this is bound to be immense.

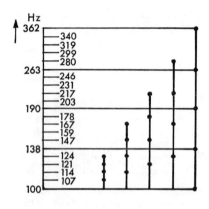

TONE MIXTURES. Five typical mixtures used in Stockhausen's 'Study II'. 193 were used in all.

Stockhausen, having devised his new scale, proceeded to construct new timbres in which the partials would all fit in with each other on the new scale. He limited himself to five basic sound groups, each composed of five tones. The most compact of these contains a group of five successive frequencies or 'notes' from the new scale. The quality of this first group could be described as astringent, as it consists of a series of dissonant pairs. The next group contains members spaced two notes apart, and the internal dissonance has now almost gone; in the other groups, whose members are spaced at three-, four-, and five-note intervals, it has gone completely, and the difference in character between them depends solely on the width of their spectrum. Before use, each of

436

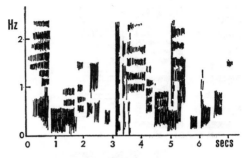

ELECTRONIC MUSIC AND REVERBERATION. Spectrogram of part of Stockhausen's 'Study II' showing the softening effect of reverberation.

the 193 basic groups were replayed through a reverberation chamber and re-recorded, in order to blend the sound.

Using these basic tones, Stockhausen proceeded to experiment with different shapes, durations, combinations, sequences, and so on—and the final work lasts just long enough for the composer to explore and scout around a variety of the possibilities that have occurred to him.

Animated sound

The use of optical sound tracks for animated sound has been going on intermittently almost as long as film has carried sound. Animation, in this sense, means photographing drawings or inscribing them directly on to the sound track either frame by frame, in convenient lengths of track or continuously (using rotating wheels with cog patterns).

Attempts to simulate actual waveforms are less interesting than experiments using common graphic forms. Sometimes sound was constructed by filming series of rectangles, triangles, ellipses, etc., pitch being controlled coarsely by using different-sized versions of the shape filmed, and finely by varying the distance of the camera. Volume could be controlled by exposure, and double exposure could be used to add one sound to another. Other graphic material has included lettering, fingerprints and facial profiles. Light slits linked to simple and complex pendulum systems have also been tried.

One group used shapes which again, by repetition, produced a pitch. A range of tone colours was drawn and filed away for use as required. Some quite simple drawings were very rich in harmonics; so that strident or harsh as well as simple sounds could be selected. Volume was controlled by varying exposure or the area of card exposed. Frame by frame exposure was used, sometimes being

437

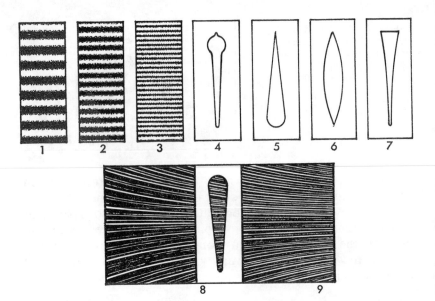

ANIMATED SOUND. 1–3. Cards from a set giving different pitches. More complex patterns of density give richer tone colours. 4–8. Masks (to be superimposed on tone cards) giving dynamic envelopes of a particular duration. Long durations are obtained by adding together cards that are open at the ends. 9. A card giving a range of pitches of a particular tone colour. Those sounds are all photographed directly on to an optical film track. A wide range of similar techniques have been employed, using both variable density and variable area.

extended over several frames to produce a continuous or mandolin quality. For silence, or a pause, black card was photographed. Reverberation was sometimes produced by photographing diminishing series of similar images—though this is tedious in comparison with rerecording using normal echo.

The most interesting part of the technique was the use of tone contouring masks. A tone colour was selected and over it would be superimposed a cut-out having an attack, a mid-note dynamic contour and a decay. At times, fascinating and in their context very appropriate sounds were produced: blips, clunks, and splinges, tone colours squirted in blobs or squeezed out like toothpaste. The difficulty in describing them illustrates the degree of success that was achieved in getting away from orthodox sound.

Notation

It has been said that there are as many systems of notation as there are electronic or concrete composers. As there is little scope

438

for interpretation, there is little practical use for a published score: notation is normally used only as a mnemonic by the composer or as a guide to his technical assistants.

This second use presents one slight difficulty, for the medium is one in which two distinct groups of people must learn to speak a common language and possess a knowledge of each other's problems.

How is the music to be written down? In conventional notation, harmonic content and, in fixed-pitch instruments, scale as well, are determined by the instruments written for; while many other details are left imprecise, to be filled in by the interpreter. But in the radiophonic forms there is so much more to be described; and

CLASSIFICATION OF SOUND. The dynamics or envelopes of sounds: classifications devised by musique concrète composers and engineers as a first step towards a system of notation. The terms shown here could represent either the quality of an original sound or the way in which it might be transformed.

ATTACK. 1. Shock—bump, clink, etc. 2. Percussive—tapping glasses, etc. 3. Explosive —giving a blasting effect. 4. Progressive—a gradual rise. 5. Level—full intensity from start.

INTERNAL DYNAMICS. 1. Steady—an even quality. 2. Vibratory or puffing. 3. Scraping—or tremulous. 4. Pulsing—overlapping repetitions blending together. 5. Clustered —subjects placed end to end.

DECAY. 1. Reversed shock. 2. Accented. 3. Deadened. 4. Progressive. 5. Flat—cut off sharply.

439

while for any particular work certain basic facts or rules of composition may be stated which remain true for the whole work, so that no reference need be made to them in the detail of the score, different works are likely to have different sets of variables.

Works based on electronic synthesis usually require representation throughout a very broad frequency band, and therefore for these the conventional stave will probably have to be discarded, as with Stockhausen's '*Study II*'. For music based on concrete sources (or any other work in which harmonic content is determined by stating the source), it may perhaps be retained where those with a musical training find it desirable.

In Paris a certain amount of work was done in the way of writing down some of the more essential characteristics of concrete sounds. A note can be described in terms of its qualities of attack and decay, the pitch and volume of the body of the note and its reverberation, and variations in these within the duration. Symbols have been suggested for such subjective qualities of sounds as 'fatness', 'thinness' and 'hollowness', and attempts have been made to give precise meanings to these terms. Other symbols describe harmonic content and the granular structure of treated sounds. But these do not add up to a system of notation. Each score or extract published has to be heavily annotated if the reader is to derive from it any knowledge of the actual content of the music, or—more important—how each effect was achieved.

18

TAPE EDITING

'EDITING' can mean various things: physically cutting and rejoin-
ing a tape; *copy editing*, in which selected sections from originals
are copied in a required sequence on to a make-up tape; and
mixing, (or *film dubbing*) where several magnetic tracks and other
sound sources are combined in a final mix.

Rough editing is assembling the main body of a programme or
sequence in the right order and taking out the longer stretches of
unwanted material. *Fine editing* is tightening up this assembled
material to provide for the best continuity of action and argument,
at the same time deleting where possible the fluffs and other minor
irrelevancies that distract the attention and reduce intelligibility.
Reclamation is the process of wiping recordings that are no longer
required and preparing the stock for reuse—if this is economically
or technically feasible. Even if the reclaimed material is of a
quality that is too low for professional recording, it can sometimes
be employed for secondary purposes such as local review or
audio transcription.

All of these apply to audio tape, videotape, and film sound.

Reasons for editing

Editing is generally undertaken for one of four reasons:

1. Getting the *programme timing* right. The duration must be
adjusted to fit the scheduled space. In radio or television this is
often the overriding consideration, whether or not editing
improves the programme.
2. *Shaping* the programme: giving it a beginning, a middle and
an end, and ensuring that the pace and tension varies, and does
not drop too low. Awkward parentheses, repetitions, phrases,
whole sentences and even paragraphs have to go if they obstruct
the flow of the argument.

441

3. *Cutting fluffs*, etc. Minor faults can lend character to speech, but too many make it difficult to follow. Mistakes in reading a script do not often sound like natural conversational slips.

4. For *convenience of assembly:* to combine film or material recorded on location with studio links, to allow material of different types to be rehearsed and recorded separately, or to pre-record awkward sections.

Techniques that aim to avoid editing presuppose either that the broadcast has a well-rehearsed and perfectly timed script or that those taking part are capable, in an unscripted programme, of presenting their material logically, concisely and coherently (or that they are under the guidance of an expert interviewer or chairman who will ensure that they do). In fact, such self-control under the stress of a recording session is rare except among experienced broadcasters. Even when a sound recording or film is made in familiar surroundings, the presence of the microphone, even more than the camera, produces an unreal situation with, very often, stilted and uncharacteristic reactions on the part of speakers. One purpose of editing is to restore the illusion of reality, generally in a heightened form.

Naturally this process of editorial selection imposes a considerable responsibility on the producer, which is not met if the result distorts the character or the intention of the speaker. If a contributor hears a playback he should recognize the essence of what he said (within the limits of what was needed for the programme, which should have been made clear to him) and feel pleased that he had expressed himself so clearly.

Nearly all recordings benefit from, at the very least, a little tidying up. Do not expect editing to accomplish the impossible: it makes things a lot easier if right from the start of the first recording you are constantly checking in your mind what might be needed later. There are lots of things to watch for: just what these are, depends on the type of programme. For example, if a fluff occurs in speech, will it be desirable or even possible to edit, or would a retake be advisable?

In film the error may occur at a point when a cutaway (in vision) is intended, or can easily be arranged. In this case the fluff may simply be left for the editor to remove, or if this is likely to be awkward the retake may be taken in sound only (*wildtrack*). If a retake in vision is necessary the director has to decide whether to go again from the start of the scene, whether to vary the framing of the picture (usually, if possible, to a closer shot or to a

442

different angle), or whether the same framing can be continued after an earlier cutaway. The sound recordist should also (and generally without being asked for it) supply background atmosphere at the same recorded level in sufficient quantity to be cut in to or recorded over any gaps that may be introduced in the editing at points where there are more pictures than synchronous sound. This saves time and effort later, at the film dubbing session.

In a radio discussion between several people, the director should be asking himself whether the various voices have identified themselves, each other, and the things they are going to talk about sufficiently clearly. If not, he might record a round of names and subject pointers in each voice so that these can be cut in where necessary. Watch for continuity of mood: if the point you are likely to join up to ends with a laugh, try to start the new take with something to laugh about (which can be cut out). Discreetly discourage phrases like 'as I've said', and retake if they are not clearly editable.

When editing radio programmes, 'pauses' may be required. So, here again record 15 seconds of atmosphere (although atmosphere for pauses can generally be picked up quite easily from hesitations between words at other points on the tape, it is better to be safe). Do this while your speakers are still there: after they have gone the sound may be slightly different. If much editing is likely to be required, don't be too clever in your control of levels; it can make for difficulties with the background atmosphere. If the background is heavy, record a spare track of perhaps 20 seconds. Longer periods than 20 seconds can perhaps be dealt with by making a loop of tape or, at a film dubbing session, a loop of magnetic film.

At a recording session for serious music it is again useful to record a few seconds of atmosphere at the end of each item in order to have something to join to the start of the next piece. Music retakes should be recorded as soon as possible after the original, so that the performers can remember the exact intonations at the link point, and also so that the physical conditions of the studio are as close to the original as possible. An orchestra quite literally warms up; its tone changes appreciably in the earlier part of each session in a studio.

In describing the techniques used I shall deal first with editing on standard sound tape, then videotape (with sound tapes as an accessory). The next chapter deals with film sound editing techniques.

443

Tape editing equipment

Electronic editing can be used with quarter-inch (6·25 mm) sound tapes (as with videotape), but physically cutting the tape is more convenient except when the levels have to be adjusted. So this account of the techniques begins with tape splicing. Of the two basic types of splicer one gives 'temporary' and the other 'permanent' joints. For the latter the tape is overlapped and stuck together, which means that a small part of the tape (and anything recorded on it) is lost with each cut. Here we shall deal only with techniques where there is no overlap, and no tape is lost when a joint is made. In the event of an unsatisfactory edit it should always be possible to get back to the starting point and try again. This encourages experiment and, in general, a more adventurous approach to editing.

For speed and accuracy, the following tools are all that are required:

1. A simple block with a channel to hold the tape. The channel is lapped slightly so that tape smoothed into it with a fingertip is gripped firmly. The block also has an angled cutting groove that can be used for mono but a groove at 90° may be necessary for stereo. It should be fixed firmly to the near edge of the tape deck.

2. A fairly sharp stainless steel razor blade. Use the one-sided type to avoid cut fingertips, and only fairly sharp for the same reason. Change the blade as soon as it begins to get blunt, however, because it then drags on the tape and may prevent butt ends

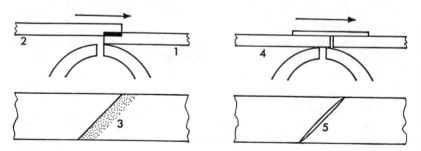

LAPPED AND BUTT JOINS. The overlap on a lapped join must be so arranged that the first part (1) of the tape or film past the head lies on top of the second part (2), so that contact is quickly regained as the second part drops on to the head. If the join is angled (3), the temporary loss of contact is less important as its effect is spread over a length of tape. If, however, a butt join is made (4) there is no loss of contact at any time unless the butt is imperfect (5). Again, the effect of any slight gap or overlap is minimized by angling the join.

matching correctly.

3. A soft wax pencil (yellow or white) or felt-tipped pen for marking edit points.

4. A roll of jointing tape slightly narrower than the recording tape to allow for a little inaccuracy in use without overlapping the edge of the tape.

5. As an optional extra: leader and spacer tapes. It is convenient to standardize: white for leaders, yellow for spacers and red for trailers. Green is also used to mark the head of a tape.

Non-magnetic scissors can be used instead of a razor blade but rarely are. Similarly, the accidental magnetization of non-stainless-steel blades is an uncommon event. A dusting powder such as French chalk is sometimes recommended but should not be necessary if genuine jointing tape is used, except in hot climates, where the adhesive may ooze a little. It is, nevertheless, important that tape should not be sticky, or layers will pull as they come off the spool, drag on tape guides and clog the heads.

Many freelance contributors to radio programmes prefer to do their own editing before submitting their tapes to programme editors. There are good reasons for this, so in the following I assume that the editing may be undertaken either on recorders of professional quality or on cheaper domestic equipment. With skilful editing there should be no difference in the result.

Preparing to cut

First, play the tape to the point at which the cut is to be made, and then switch from replay to a condition in which the tape can be spooled by hand with the tape still in contact with the head. The appropriate method for this varies from machine to machine.

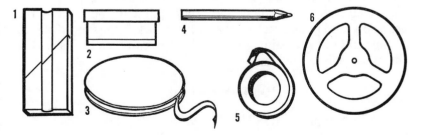

EQUIPMENT FOR JOINING TAPE. 1. Splicing block. 2. Blade. 3. Leader tape. 4. Wax pencil. 5. Jointing tape. 6. Spare spool.

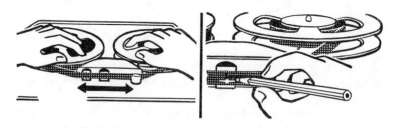

TAPE EDITING 1. *Left.* Move the tape backward and forward over the heads, by hand, in order to find the exact point. *Right.* Mark the tape with a soft wax pencil.

In some cases there is a 'pause' control, in others it is 'replay/off', and so on. Sometimes the best way is to pull against the spool clutches or brakes (but only if they are fairly loose and there is no risk of stretching the tape). The exact point can then be checked by hand (suggestions for finding this in difficult cases are given later). When in doubt about a mark, set up the tape with the mark at the replay head, switch to 'replay', and run. If the machine has a quick start it should be clear whether the mark is correct or not. Alternatively, pull quickly up to speed by hand.

Always mark the cut in the same way, e.g. along the lower edge of the tape. This is the quickest way of ensuring that a scrap of tape that is transposed, or cut and then reinstated, is put in the right way round.

Some recorders in the low- to medium-price range have pressure pads, and the head assembly is fitted with a protective cover that completely surrounds it. If much editing is to be undertaken, remove this cover to get at the replay head (if necessary by lifting the pressure pad) and mark the tape at the intended cutting point. An alternative, almost equally convenient method does not require access to the replay head. For this, measure the tape distance from the replay head to the first rigid guide pillar to the right of the assembly, and put a notch on the editing block at the same distance to the right of the cutting groove. The tape can then be marked at the guide pillar.

Making a joint

A 'temporary' joint is made like this:

1. Locate and mark the joint, as already indicated.
2. Switch the recorder to whatever condition allows the tape to

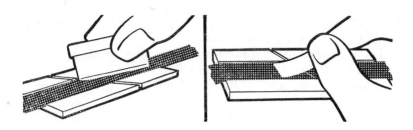

TAPE EDITING II. *Left.* Cut the tape diagonally using the groove in the block. *Right.* Butt the two wanted sections together in the block and join with special adhesive tape.

be lifted from the heads, and place the tape coated side down in the editing block.

3. Cut. The razor blade should be sharp enough not to drag when drawn lightly along its guide channel. It should not be necessary to apply pressure.

4. Then, if a fairly long piece of tape is to be taken out, replace the take-up spool by a 'scrap' spool and wind off to the new 'in' point. Mark this, cut again, and swap the take-up spools.

5. Now place the two butt ends of the tape coated side down together in the block (and a little to one side of the cutting groove) so that they just touch each other.

6. Cut off an inch or so of jointing tape, taking care not to finger-print the tacky side more than is necessary, and lay it over the butt, using one edge of the channel to steady it and guide it into place.

7. Run a finger along the tape to press the joint firm. If it seems advisable, dust with French chalk by dipping a finger in the powder and running it along the tape again.

After a joint has been made, place the tape back on the heads, and spool back a foot or so (again, this can usually be done by hand against the braking effect of the clutch plates), then play through the joint checking that:

1. It is properly made.

2. The edited tape makes sense—and that you have in fact edited at the point intended.

3. The timing is right: that the words after the joint do not follow too quickly or too slowly on those before.

4. The speaker does not take two breaths.

5. Neither the perspective nor volume of voice takes an un-natural jump.

6. There is no impossible vocal contortion implied.

447

7. The tone of voice does not change abruptly, e.g. from an audible smile to earnest seriousness.

8. The background does not abruptly change in quality; nor is any 'effect' or murmured response sliced in two.

9. (For stereo edits.) No 'flicker' has been introduced by an imperfect butt.

It is worth studying this list of possible errors with care, not because you will overlook them once they are made (they will probably shout at you) but to bear in mind both when recording and when selecting suitable points at which to cut. After a little practice, very few of your joints will have to be remade. In fact, occasional very minor faults can be tolerated, as few people will notice them unless they are watching out for them. However, they should only be tolerated if a remake, or a repair by the insertion of a section of tape from somewhere else in the recording is impossible.

You may need to cut down a gap that is too long; or insert a pause or breath or even an 'um' or 'er' to cover an abrupt change of subject or mood; or you may have to reinstate part of what was cut. After marking any new point at which you propose to cut, undo the old joint. To do this turn it over and break it; you will be able to get a grip of one of the points of the butt and pull it away from the jointing tape. If it is a fresh joint and separates cleanly you may be able to use the same piece of jointing tape a second time; so, having cut the other side to the right point, slide the two butts together in the break and reseal by smoothing along the joint with your fingertip. Alternatively, strip off the old piece of jointing tape completely and start afresh.

Rough editing: sound radio

In rough editing the objective is much the same in sound radio, television and film: it is simply to assemble the material in its intended order, so that the effect, logical or artistic, can begin to be seen. I will deal first with the case where sound only has to be considered.

In the first instance, as you cut your programme into rough shape, you may perhaps start by putting in spacers to indicate where there will be a studio link.

Remember that you can *transpose*. This is of considerable importance when several unrelated subjects have arisen in an unscripted discussion. The factors that governed the order of record-

448

ing may not hold for the finished programme. You will want to start with a bang, with something that may not be of vital importance, but which engages the listener's attention and gives him a sense of involvement. The middle should, while progressing logically, have light and shade: there should be variety of pace, of speech lengths and rhythm and of mood. And the tension should build to an effective 'curtain': for example something that contains in a few lines the essence of all that has preceeded it, or will offset and illuminate it.

As you select material, feed it on to your make-up tape in programme order, with transpositions and retakes in their proper place. At this stage try to cut at 'paragraph pauses'. If you have specially recorded any fades of background noise you will need to cut or transpose these to their proper places at the beginning and end of the section. Rejoin the unwanted material after each cut, by feeding it on to a reject spool which should be kept until the programme is complete.

Even at this stage exercise care: do not cut in the middle of a breath, or too close to the first word when there is a heavy background. If you come back to the same speaker, check that voice quality, mood and balance are sufficiently similar: it is all too easy for the listener to get the impression that someone new has entered the conversation and to wonder who it is instead of listening to what is being said.

When an additional replay machine is available the rough editing stage can be done by copy editing. In this way the original tapes can be kept intact, which will be of advantage if you want to arrange the same material differently for another programme later. It also allows for levels to be matched and provides insurance against possible mishaps. The selected programme material is re-recorded to a make-up tape in the appropriate order, perhaps taking a little more at the beginning and end of each insert than will be required. The inserts are then cut together on the make-up tape in the normal way.

Fine editing for radio

After your rough editing give thought to the shape of the programme as a whole, to the intelligibility and conciseness of individual contributions, and also to whether the character and personality of the speakers is adequately represented. The first of these considerations may mean that you have to make severe internal cuts in one section and not in another; you may have to cut out repetitions or verbal embroidery. Try to keep the theme of what remains tight and unified.

Here are some other things you may wish to cut:

1. Heavy coughs, etc. These hold up the action and may cause the listener to lose the thread. But if the speaker has a frog in his throat (and this section of the recording cannot be cut) it does no harm to leave in the cough that clears it—just for the psychological satisfaction of the listener!

2. Excessive 'ums' and 'ers' (or any other vocal mannerism that runs to seed). They should cut if it improves intelligibility—which it often does if they appear in the middle of a sentence. But some actually *improve* intelligibility by breaking the flow at a point where it needs to be broken. So be careful: there are people who use these noises as an important integral part of their vocal sentence, and while the result may not read well, it sounds right. Others seem to express character in these punctuating sounds. In these cases, do not cut. An 'er' moulded into the preceding or following word often cannot be cut, anyway.

3. Excessive pauses. In real life pauses can often afford to be relatively long, because we watch the speaker's face as he thinks. On a tape a pause is just a pause, unless it lends real dramatic emphasis to its context. But pauses should not be cut down to nothing if the effect is of impossible vocal contortions. To see what I mean, record the sentence 'You (pause) are (pause) a (pause) good (pause) editor' and then cut the pauses out completely. The result sounds like a case of hiccups. The minimum gap depends on how much the mouth would have to change in shape during the pause. This applies to 'ers', too.

4. Superimpositions. Two people talking over each other are irritating. But edit with care: it is generally necessary to leave a partial overlap, or to take out part of the sentences before and after.

5. Fluffs, where the speaker has gone back on himself. Again an edit generally improves intelligibility. But take care here too: the first word of the repeat is often overemphasized, so try to find some place to cut after or in the middle of this word.

Each different speaker presents a new set of problems and decisions on whether to cut or not. For example, an interview may begin hesitantly and gather speed and interest as it progresses. This is completely wrong for the start of a new voice in a programme tape, where the listener's attention and interest must be caught in the first few words. If you cannot cut this warm-up period it may be necessary to tighten up the opening sentence: this matters more than hesitations at a later stage, when the voice and personality are accepted by the listener.

In certain cases, particularly where the recording is of importance as a document, no editing should be done at all (with the possible exception of cutting down really excessive pauses), and the greatest care should be exercised if any condensing is to be attempted. If in doubt, resort to a studio link.

In any case do not go mad with your razor blade. It is very useful to have good ideas about where to cut; but it is just as important to know where *not* to cut.

Finding the exact point

There are two places to cut at in a 'sentence' pause. One is after the word (and its associated reverberation) has finished and before the breath; the other is after the breath and before the next word. For most purposes it is best, and safer, to choose the latter. You retain the full natural pause that the speaker allowed, and you can cut as close as you like to the new word which helps to mask any slight change in atmosphere.

Cutting between the words of a sentence is trickier. In addition, the words themselves sound very different when they are wound through slowly by hand, so that a suitable point is more difficult to locate. But certain characteristics of speech can soon be recognized, e.g. the 's' and 'f' sounds. And the explosive consonants 'p' and 'b', as well as the stopped 'k', 't', 'g' and 'd' are easy to pick out (though not always as easy to distinguish from each other) because of the slight break in sound that precedes them on the tape (see diagram, p. 30). In a spoken sentence the words may be run together to such an extent that the only break may be before such a letter—perhaps in the middle of a word.

Do not assume that because a letter should be there it will be. Complete vowel sounds may prove to be absent. The personal pronoun 'I' is typical of many such sounds. In the sentence 'Well I'm going now' it may be missing completely. If you try to cut off the 'well' you may even find the 'm' was a vocal illusion, no more than a slight distortion of the end of the 'l' sound. Similarly, in 'It's a hot day', spoken quickly, there is probably no complete word 'hot'. Nor is it possible to isolate the word from 'hot tin roof', as the first 't' will be missing and the one that is there will be joined on to the following vowel sound in such a way as to have no separate existence. Before going in for a lot of fine editing it is worth doing a little research into what the beginnings and ends of words sound like at slow speed, and where words blend into each other and where they do not.

In cutting between words, cut as late in any pause as possible. When searching for the right pause on a tape do not be misled by the tiny break in sound that often precedes the letter 't' and similar consonants. You can often cut *in* to a continuous sound (e.g. where several words have been run together), provided that the cut is at an angle, but do not attempt to cut *out* of one, unless you join straight on to a sound of equal value (one for which the mouth would have to be formed in the same shape). It is very difficult to insert missing 'a's' and 'the's'; these are nearly always closely tied with the following word, so that unless the speaker is enunciating each word clearly and separately, it is necessary to take this in combination with the sound that follows. The letter 's', however, is somewhat easier to insert or (sometimes) remove.

I quote these few cases as examples of the verbal surgery in which the tape editor sometimes finds himself involved when trying to make a difficult transition. Experience gained in this kind of editing is a great time-saver later on, as you can quickly locate each cut. These principles apply equally to videotape and film sound editing; though in the latter case the cut is normally made at discrete points defined by the frame interval.

Editing music

These are various reasons why we may wish to edit music: to cut out a repeat, or one verse or chorus; to cut in a retake; to cut everything up to a certain point so that we hit a certain note 'on the nose'; to condense or extend mood music to fit the action of a play, and so on. Most of the skill lies in making sure you are marking the right part of the right note, and this requires practice. Remember also when handling music tapes that damage due to spillage or stretching, etc., is more noticeable than on speech.

The important thing in music editing is not that the next note after each of the two points marked should be the same, but that the previous one should be—that is to say, when cutting between two notes it is the quality of the reverberation that must be

452

preserved. Any retake should start before the point at which the cut is to be made: there is nothing so painfully obvious as a music edit where a 'cold' retake has been edited in, resulting in a nasty clip on the reverberation to the previous note. It might be supposed that if the new sound is loud enough the loss may be disguised, but this is not so unless it is cut so tight as to trim away part of the start of the note. This attack transient is particularly important to the character of a sound.

So unless the cut is made in a pause that is longer than the reverberation time of the studio, the first requirement for a successful joint is that the volume and timbre preceding both the 'out' and 'in' points on the original tape should be identical.

But it may be possible to make an exception to this rule when cutting mood music to fit behind speech and effects: if the level of the music can drop low enough the whole business may often be treated fairly casually. For preference, choose a rest to cut out on and something rather vague to come back to, and if necessary dip the music level at the edit point. However, no such liberties may be taken with foreground music. For example, when linking music is being trimmed to length, any internal cuts must be made with the same care that would be given to featured music. And speech recorded over music is often practically impossible to edit, because an untidy join in the music may coincide with a slight gap in the speech.

When everything up to a certain point in a piece of music is cut, in order to create a new starting-point—e.g. when you want to come in on a particular theme—the effect of the tail of reverberation under the new first note is often unimportant. Except in the case when this tail is loud, and contrasts strongly in quality with the first wanted sound, it will be accepted by the ear as a part of the timbre of the note. However, in such a case a sharp manual fade-in often sounds better than a cut. For getting out of a piece of music at a point before the end (where there is no pause) there is no alternative to a fade.

When the cut is to be made at a place that is not clearly defined by the music itself it is often possible to identify and match the cutting points by: (a) measuring off the distance on the tape from a more easily located point, or (b) marking out the rhythmic structure of the music with a wax pencil or felt pen on the back of the tape. Of the two methods the second is possibly the better guide, as the easily located note may not have been played exactly on the beat.

Complex editing problems

Editing staccato effects and absolutely regular continuous effects presents no problems. But effects that are continuous yet progressively changing in quality can be difficult to edit, as can speech accompanied by heavy but uneven effects or speech in heavily reverberant acoustics.

Rhythmic effects on their own are fairly simple, as they can be treated rather like music; and so, possibly, in its different way can reverberant speech. But with the more uneven type of noise it may be difficult to find two points sufficiently similar in quality, and in this case we must again resort to mixing. Editing applause is typical of the type of problem that seems as though it ought to be simple, but is not. A burst of applause lasting, say, ten seconds is difficult to cut to five without a slight blip at the join. But to do this with two copies of an effects disc or tape is easy.

Sometimes the change of quality behind a speech edit can be covered by mixing in some similar, but heavier, effects afterwards, using an effects disc or tape, or a loop. Even so, a change of quality can often show through unless the added effects are substantially heavier than the earlier backing, or are peaked at the point of the join.

There are certain cases where the untidy effect of a succession of sharp cuts in background noise can be tolerated. It may be accepted as a convention that street interviews (*vox-pop*) are cut together by simple editing, with breaks in the background appearing as frank evidence of the method of assembly.

Why cut at an angle?

It is always recommended that monophonic tape should be cut at an angle—the exact angle is not vital. A 90° cut has the disadvantage that any sound on the tape, even atmosphere, starts absolutely 'square' at the point of cut; and any sound that cuts in at full volume seems to start with a click. Examples are time signal pips or 'beep' tones: the very words 'pip' or 'beep' suggest the effect that is heard. To demonstrate this for yourself record a pure tone and cut in a short length of spacer at 90°. Then try the same thing with angled cuts.

It can be demonstrated experimentally that if a fade-in or -out exceeds 10 milliseconds in duration there is no click. In fact this is over twenty times more than is actually needed in most circumstances. This duration corresponds to 0·15 inch of 15 i/s tape (i.e. 0·38 cm of 38 cm/s tape). As a 45° cut on full track tape extends nearly twice this length along the tape there will therefore be no click. Similarly, 10 milliseconds corresponds to 0·075 in of 7½ i/s tape. A half-track recording fades in or out over 0·1 in for a 45° cut, so again there is no click.

The standard angle of cut provided on some joiners used for magnetic film sound is 10°. A recording on separate magnetic film track is 0·2 in (5 mm) wide: a cut therefore fades in over about 0·02 in (0·5 mm); for 16-mm film the corresponding duration would be 2·5 milliseconds, and this too should be quite long enough to avoid a noticeable click.

Tape recorded at 7½ i/s (19 cm/s) full track is the most convenient for editing when using cine spools. Lower speeds give reduced quality and less precision in marking, and higher speeds make it more difficult to pull the tape over the heads by manually rotating the spools against the clutch or brakes. Using the larger NAB spools 15 i/s (38 cm/s) is a convenient recording speed for editing.

For stereo an angled cut cannot be used except when editing between identical sounds or in a pause, otherwise a momentary change of position (flicker) will occur. When a 90° cut is unsatisfactory for the reasons already given, mixing techniques must be employed.

Videotape sound

Videotape of professional quality is 2 in (51 mm) wide; domestic-quality tapes are narrower. As will be seen, the latter have certain uses in editing as well as for programme review, even though they should not be used for master recordings or broadcast replay.

On the standard professional equipment the picture is recorded in tracks that run laterally across the tape. A drum with four recording heads rotates at high speed and is positioned in precise contact with the tape by suction. Recorded lengthways along it are a 250 Hz control track (marking the frames in a manner similar to the pulse on separate magnetic film sound though with more pulses per frame) and two further tracks, one for programme sound and the other for cue signals or auxiliary sound. It is physically impracticable for the picture and its associated sound to be recorded side by side; instead, the vision is recorded before

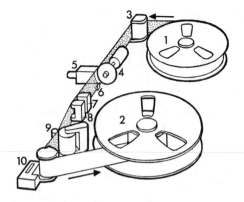

VIDEOTAPE RECORDER. 1. Feed spool. 2. Take-up spool. 3. Master erase head. 4. Drum motor and rotating recording head. 5. Tape guide (tape held in position by suction). 6. Control track recording head. 7. Sound and 'cue' track erase heads. 8. Sound and 'cue' sound recording heads. 9. Drive capstan. 10. Tape timer.

the sound. In the 625-line system the 0·6 second displacement amounts to 15 frames; in 525 it is 18 frames. This is sufficient for approximately two words of speech.

Early videotape editing systems required that the tape be physically cut and the displacement of the recorded sound meant that the final segment of tape before a cut carried sound related to picture that has been removed. Often a splice could be made at a point where the studio overlap was of no consequence, or if noticeable, perhaps even artistically desirable. However, in cases where an overlap was inappropriate a sound dub would usually

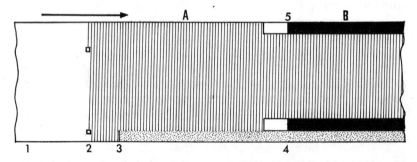

VIDEOTAPE (2 inches wide) visualized during recording, and as seen from the backing side of the tape (i.e. with recording heads on far side). 1. Unrecorded videotape. 2. Video recording heads (two of four set at 90° to each other on a rotating disc). Each line recorded on the tape represents a group of lines in the television picture. 3. Control track recording head. 4. 'Cue' track recording head. This can also be used as an additional sound recording head. 5. Main sound recording head. As the picture and sound recording heads are displaced by $9\frac{1}{4}$ inches the sound is not directly related to the picture lying alongside it, e.g. the sound at B belongs to the picture not at B but at A, which trails $9\frac{1}{4}$ inches behind it. A physical cut across the tape at B would include more sound than picture: in terms of dialogue, one or two more words would be heard after the picture had gone.

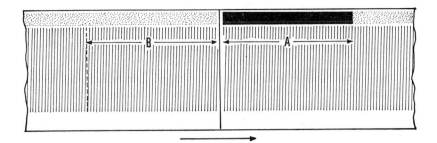

CUTTING VIDEOTAPE WITH SOUND DUB—so that sound and picture change together. The sound corresponding to section B of the picture has been copied to ¼ inch tape and then re-recorded parallel to picture section A. When the tape was cut, the dubbed sound became resynchronized with its original picture. Electronic editing (in which each required sequence is copied from the original tape to assembly tape) is in principle simpler and uses up less tape; but more capital equipment is required.

be made. Sound related to the incoming picture was transferred via a quarter-inch (6·25 mm) tape to the appropriate length of audio track on the videotape before the cut, so that the sound cut (or mix) would occur at the standard displacement or at such other point as the production required. To make a clean sound join many editors would copy sound from both outgoing and incoming scenes, edit them together by manually splicing the quarter-inch tape, then play the edited sound and outgoing picture together, synchronizing their sound manually well before the edit point. In this way the edit could be rerecorded cleanly on to the tail of the outgoing picture, continuing for a second or two past the selected picture edit point. The sound copying would then be stopped either by halting the videotape or by switching off its audio recording system. The same sound now appeared at two places on the tape and the vision edit, made by the two physical cuts in the tape, was within that repeated material.

Electronic videotape editing

In time, tape cutting was replaced by electronic editing. This conserved expensive tape, which could be reused, but employed two machines, at higher capital cost. The original material was replayed from one machine and assembled on the other. After the first section had been copied the second was chosen, and then both machines were set back ten seconds from the cutting point, marked and run up together. It was checked that the cut would be in the right place; if it was, the machines were set back again, run

457

up, and this time the second machine was switched to record at the editing point, and a second segment of programmes was joined on to the first without physically cutting tape. Sound and picture cuts were automatically coincident and sound levels could be adjusted during the transfer (this was also possible to a more limited degree with the sound-copying method previously described).

Alternatively, the automatic system could be set up to edit vision only, leaving the audio switchover to manual control. Sound mixes were also possible, if one of the sections was transferred to quarter-inch tape as before. To this stage in the development of editing techniques all cueing was manual, and its timing depended on rehearsal and then the precise repetition of the rehearsed cue on the take. The shift from physical to electronic editing did, however, require an increase in sophistication in the equipment itself, in order that the transmission between the replay and recording modes could be accomplished without disturbance of the picture—a bump. An electronic editing sequence had to be initiated 15 frames before the actual cutting point: this allowed the old picture to be erased first, and then as the edit point reached the recording drum the machine automatically switched to record. An 'out' edit (i.e. one in which new material is joined to the front of an existing recording) was still made simply by stopping the recording, an operation that could create sound problems.

Subsequent stages of automation involved equipment to control the electronic editing sequence. The BBC tried a system in which the two tapes were set up on a mark well before the desired edit point; the control equipment then counted 485 frames, switched into the electronic edit sequence and, as before, the edit occurred automatically after a further 15 frames. The whole sequence of events was repeatable (subject to some slight variability in machine run-up times) and prior to the actual edit it could be rehearsed with the change-over of picture appearing on the monitor only. The start marks were adjusted as required after each attempt. A single button governed replay of both machines, and others determined whether a rehearsal or edit would take place and whether both vision and sound would switch at the selected point, or vision only, leaving the sound edit to be made manually. As an added refinement, three-machine editing (with two for replay) permitted picture and sound mixes, if these were required.

A further and more generally available improvement allowed the edit point to be marked by a sound pip on the cue track. Because the cue-track recording head is 15 frames *after* the picture recording drum, a special new reading head had to be fitted in order to pick up the cue signal much earlier—in fact, 33 frames in advance, or 3 frames before the video erase head. On replay, the editing sequence was initiated 18 frames after the cue pip was read and the picture cut followed automatically a further 15 frames after that, as the pip arrived at the cue head. Adjustments to the editing point could be made without shifting the electronic marker, by setting the appropriate increments or decrements on the control panel. In the PAL system the relationship between the tapes can be altered only in multiples of two frames; in NTSC by single frames. For adjustments of more than 18 frames either way the cue had to be remarked.

In addition to improvements in picture stabilization during run up, still somewhat erratic at that time, the next major step forward required a new device, the time code.

Time code

A *time code* is an eight-digit number indicating hours, minutes, seconds and frames. It can be linked to a 24-hour clock (and so reset to zero at midnight) or started from zero at any arbitrary time. Recorded on to the videotape cue track it provides a method of individually marking every frame. A tape can be so marked in real time, so that sequences separately recorded over a long period are marked with the actual time of recording and so can be identified simply by consulting a programme log, or it can be built up, so that as new material is edited in sequence the timing is cumulative.

Time codes can be read out through a character generator and superimposed on the picture, or fed to number displays of various types, either set in a control panel or appearing on a *visual display unit*, VDU. It is often arranged that at the press of a button the real-time flow of numbers can be stopped, so that the time of a particular event can be logged; when the flow is restarted it returns to the advancing real time display. If a suitable (wide-band) amplifier is used time code continues to be read as a tape is spooled fast, and can also be held when it is parked. In this way logged material can be readily relocated. More important, however, it also means that automatic, or computer controlled, operations can be initiated and related to any given frame on a tape. In most editing systems using time code any required number can be punched into the memory and the control system set to search for that address, as it is called. Once found, the tape automatically sets itself back and parks, ready to run up and display the required material.

For time-code editing to work, times must be recorded on both replay and recording tapes, which are addressed separately. When 'out' and 'in' points have been selected and checked by replay the tapes are commanded to 'reset', when they automatically go to their start positions. On the command 'replay' the tapes start up one after the other, lock, and the edit is rehearsed. Adjustments of suitable numbers of frames can be made before or after the switch-over point, or both, and the rehearsal repeated. When a satisfactory edit has been demonstrated, the tapes are reset once again and the edit command is given. Auxiliary registers can be used to switch the sound at a different point from picture if this is required, or to control external equipment, such as audio-tape replay. Three-machine editing can similarly be controlled, and this allows both picture and sound to be mixed instead of cut. The mixes themselves may be set for automatic or manual control.

These advances in automation were based on editing techniques that restricted the points at which an automatic cut could be made —particularly in the case of the PAL system. Further, there have been anomalies between vision cuts made in the studio, which change the picture between frames, and those made in editing where the switching may have been designed to occur between the two fields of a single frame. This would sometimes lead to the otherwise undesirable loss of small amounts of material—sometimes with knock-on effects in the sound. In any case, it would often turn out that the sound cut was better made at neither frame nor field change but at some intermediate place. Then it might be necessary to handle the tape, manually rocking the signal over the audio head, to find and mark the exact point, or, better, to transfer the sound to quarter-inch (6·25 mm) tape, where it could be marked and without further recourse to complex electronics.

With this one reservation, time code remains a powerful tool with many uses beyond simple editing. It provides an accurate measure of programme length. It can be used for time-cued playback in automated broadcasting systems. It synchronizes video with multitrack tape, or tapes, to carry separate sound tracks (e.g. the commentaries made for different users of a common picture of some event or sporting fixture), or for stereo sound broadcast simultaneously by radio. Some helical scan recordings, employing narrower tape and a different video recording ge-

460

ometry, and which are below the technical quality that is required for broadcasting, can also accommodate time code on a second sound track. Such low cost review copies can be used for the selection of material and editing points, and so for the generation of computer programmes that can subsequently be used to control the editing of the original two-inch tapes.

With videotape editing we have reached the point where the possibilities for further advance are limited more by capital cost than by human ingenuity. One prospect is to use film as the original material and to transfer the film masters to videotape for editing. An advantage of this is that it may permit the professional use of 8-mm quality. A classic example was a documentary shot mostly during a single-handed Atlantic crossing. The transferred 8-mm originals were used in conjunction with time code, and the technical quality of the result was satisfactory—indeed, very satisfactory considering the intrinsic interest of the material that could be obtained by means of the light-weight equipment. In such cases initial editing can be done on inexpensive 16-mm black-and-white film recordings made at the same transfer session and with time code recorded on the optical sound track. In film editing, sound is normally edited on separate magnetic film stock that is run in sync with the picture (see p. 464). The time codes on the rough-edited film are used to find the corresponding points on the master videotapes.

Often, when the picture editing is complete the sound needs no further attention, but in many cases commentary or other speech, music or incidental effects is still needed, and some method of post-mixing is required.

Videotape sound post-mixing

The most straightforward method of adding to a videotape sound track is to replay it via a mixing desk to a second, intermediate, videotape recorder. When a satisfactory rebalance has been achieved, the intermediate sound is copied back to the original tape, erasing the previous recording.

But because of the capital cost of videotape recorders, and the many stages at which one or two machines are required, the search for economy is essential. A substantial reduction in the use of high quality video recorders can be achieved by rehearsing on domestic-quality cassette recorders. As the original tape is reviewed it is also copied to a narrow, helical-scan tape and this is used throughout the rehearsal period, and the more expensive equipment is brought into play again only when the rehearsal is complete. The sound is then rebalanced and recorded on the intermediate tape as before; and that in turn is reviewed, and copied back to the original. A disadvantage is that continuous-take rerecording is required.

A still less costly and far more flexible arrangement is possible: this makes videotape sound remixing comparable to that used for film (see pp. 480–490). At the BBC it is called *sypher* (*sy*nchronized *p*ost-dub with *h*elical-scan and *e*ight-track *r*ecorders). Once again time code provides the key. When the edited videotape is reviewed, the picture is copied to a helical-scan machine and at the same time the sound is transferred to one track of a multitrack tape recorder. Subsequent resynchronization is ensured by recording time code simultaneously on all three tapes: the domestic-quality video recorder should have a second sound track that can be used for this. Alternatively a continuous time code previously recorded on the original can be copied. The next stage employs specialist professional sound equipment, but without also tying up a high-cost video channel. Picture and sound can now be run in synchronization, with normal stop, start and rewind facilities. Using a character generator the time code may be superimposed on the monitor picture and will also appear electronically on the desk. Given the appropriate controls, time cues can be inserted and the tapes will find them and reset. Discontinuous rehearsal and recording is possible.

There are two main methods of remixing. One simply feeds the initial sound through a desk where additional sound is balanced and mixed with it, and the result is returned to the tape on a different track. The second uses the full range of the recording system to lay tracks of speech, music and effects, which are mixed down at the next stage. By the use of the time code and an automatic track-switching mechanism it is possible to cue sound and picture cuts or mixes to coincide. Beyond this, the desk and sound studio may be as simple or complex as desired and standard sound-mixing techniques are employed.

After the mixed sound has been reviewed, still with the helical-scan picture, the sound is copied back to the original high-quality videotape, erasing the original sound. Note that a single-machine video channel is required for little more than twice the duration of the edited programme length or three times if a separate review is required and that the specialized sound-dubbing costs are comparable to those for film.

19

FILM SOUND EDITING

THE standard professional film gauge is 35 mm. However, throughout the world there must today be much more 16 mm shot, edited, and shown to the public than there is 35 mm. The reason for this is television. In Britain, the BBC alone keeps about a hundred cutting rooms permanently in business. This is a gigantic output of film by any calculation—and nearly all of it is 16 mm. Most of the techniques described in this chapter apply equally to 16 mm and 35 mm, but in view of the vast increase in the use of 16 mm where slight differences do exist I have described the method used for this gauge.

I shall completely disregard the older methods of joining film, those involving the overlap of part of a frame (or on 35 mm, the frame bar) and the use of cement to join the two. This has now been superseded by butt joining, for which the most convenient method is the guillotine type of tape joiner—this requires no precise registration of pre-perforated tape. The advantages of using this type of joiner for the magnetic track are described in detail; but equally great advantages are found with the picture. Indeed, the joiner has facilitated a new type of film-making based on the freedom to experiment during editing. Cement joins are, however, still used to join cut negative or reversal camera master.

Another sweeping decision, and one that may offend many experienced editors who still swear by them, will be to disregard almost all editing and viewing machines that are based on intermittent action. The normal film projection method claws up each successive frame, pins it firmly in the gate for a forty-eighth or a fiftieth of a second, illuminates it, and then moves on jerkily to the next frame. In projectors this system is good enough, but in the cutting room it is arguable that such equipment is outdated.

In this book we are concerned with good sound quality. Now that equipment exists that allows editors the better to judge such quality, it should be used. The equipment I favour has systems of prisms rotating with the film, and reflecting light in such a way as to project a static image on the screen. These include viewing tables for the selection of shots and picture-synchronizers for its assembly. Both have facilities for running sound with picture; the synchronizer normally has provision for several rolls of sound to run together.

At this point I will go back a little in the order of events and describe how the picture and sound got to the cutting room.

Film: sound and picture as shot

Synchronous film sound can be recorded directly on the same film as the picture—normally on a magnetic stripe running down the side of the picture, a system that has to a considerable extent taken over from optical sound tracks for projection.

A displacement between sound and picture of rather less than a second for 35 mm and rather more for 16 mm is dictated by the amount of film transport mechanism required to guide the film and smooth its flow between the intermittent movement at the camera or projector gate and the flutter-free motion required at the sound

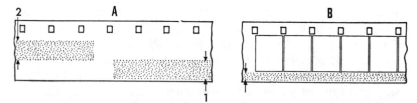

RECORDING ON 16-MM FILM. A. Separate magnetic film. 1. Edge track used in US and Canada. 2. Centre track used in Europe. The full width of the film is coated, and can therefore be used for either system. B. Combined magnetic film with narrower edge-track recording. The magnetic stripe occupies the space formerly used for optical sound. Sometimes the coating is applied to the surface of the film (in which case a narrow strip is also applied to the edge close to the sprocket holes in order to ensure even winding); sometimes it goes into a groove in the film, so that the surface of film and magnetic track is flat.

head. Optical sound came first and has the position closest to the gate. On the 16 mm gauge, provision for magnetic sound recording and replay was subsequently made at a different position, with the result that projectors could be modified to have the two heads permanently in position on the same film path. For 16-mm film, optical sound is $25\frac{1}{2}$ or 26 frames ahead of the picture, and magnetic sound 28 frames ahead; for 35-mm film, optical sound is recorded $19\frac{1}{2}$ or 20 frames ahead of picture.

For television news, 16-mm striped stock is often used. In principle, the film, once it has been developed, can be transmitted immediately, with its own sound and without any danger of loss of sync in the rush. Difficulties begin to pile up as soon as the film has to be edited, for the sound displacement is gross. On few occasions, and particularly on news, would a picture cut precede a sound cut by well over a second. It is, however, about the length of a reaction shot—so a reporter's nod may bridge the gap. Even so, the result is often awkward and untidy. The better alternative, if time permits, is to transfer all sound to separate magnetic film stock and edit on that.

The alternative and preferred system of film sound recording employs ordinary sound tape, but with a sync pulse (*pilot tone*) that is related to the camera speed superimposed on the required signal. This tape is never edited: it is used as a master for transfer to magnetic stock and for finding extra wanted sound if required at the dubbing session, when tape may also be played as an unsynchronized sound source. For the transcript of unscripted dialogue (useful in editing), tape or cassette copies are made.

Sound transfer

Film sound transfer has (apart from the normal business of maintaining sound quality from one generation of recording to the next) one major concern: to provide separate sound that is absolutely synchronous with the film so that they will run together, sprocket hole to sprocket hole. In transferring from stripe, or in making a new copy from existing magnetic stock, the problem could in principle be solved simply by interlocking the two films mechanically. When tape is transferred to film an electrically interlocking system is preferred. In this the recording speed is controlled by the sync pulse on the original tape. So satisfactory is this form of synchronization that it is generally used even in cases where mechanical systems would be feasible, e.g. in multichannel dubbing suites, and in film projectors used in television.

Film and equipment in the cutting room

For safety the original camera negative or reversal master may be stored at the labs where it was processed. The film editor gets:

1. Film positive, 'rush prints'.
2. The original sound tapes.
3. Sound transfers of the good takes, on the same gauge as the original film.
4. Documentation on film and sound, provided by cameraman and sound recordist; and perhaps also laboratory and viewing reports on the rushes.
5. A shot list.
6. A script, or sometimes a transcript of the sound.
7. Alternatively or additionally, a cutting order, which may have shot descriptions taken from the shot list and dialogue copied from the transcript.

To this list may be added: the frequent presence of the director. The creative talent of the film editor should be subordinate to that of the director. It follows that creative editing devised in the cutting room takes the form of suggestions to the director,

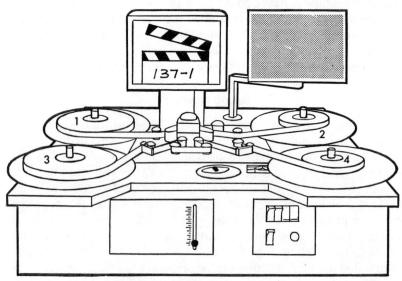

FLAT-BED FILM VIEWER. The simplest and most convenient equipment for viewing 16-mm film to give normal playing speeds and picture or sound of medium quality (i.e. the best, short of projection in a theatre). 1, 2. Picture feed and take-up plates. 3 and 4. Sound feed and take-up plates. Lacing is simple, with drive spindles on either side of the sound and picture heads (which are in the centre). The sound path has additional, tensioning rollers. It is not necessary to have rolls of film as shown here; the machine requires only enough head or tail of film to be held by the drive rollers. Typically the film can be run at normal and 'fast' speeds, and either forward or backward. In addition to the heads shown there is normally a further group to the right of the picture column, to replay combined magnetic or optical sound.

perhaps in the form of a trial cut, and whether the director accepts these depends on how well they follow or fit in with his overall artistic intention. Apart from such experimental work, editing in the absence of the director must be according to established techniques for cutting pictures or pictures and sound together, of which the editor must be the master. These will follow either the generally accepted conventions of film editing, or some style agreed with or expected by the director. As a general rule, progress towards a final result is faster if a director is present for some part of the editing.

The cutting room has the following equipment: a viewing machine; an assembly bench, synchronizer, a small amplifier and loudspeaker, a tape joiner, wax pencils, trim bin, blank spacer film, leader film and a waste bin.

On the *viewing machine* the picture and sound can be run together or separately. It should provide a projected picture and sound reproduction of moderately good quality.

An *assembly bench* has two canvas-lined bins into which picture and film sound can fall without coming to harm, and be-

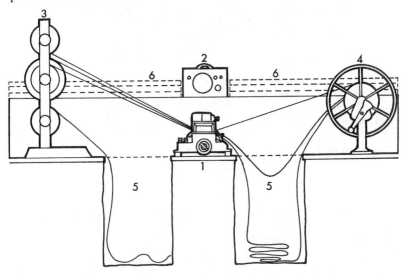

EDITING BENCH. 1. Picture synchronizer. 2. 'Squawk box'. 3. Horse, supporting rolls of film and spacer. 4. Winding spindle with 'split' reels fitted. 5. Bins, lined with canvas, to hold excess film that has not been wound up. 6. Racks for small rolls of film awaiting selection of material. A tape joiner is on the bench, but not fixed; and also a supply of wax pencils and felt marker pens. This bench does *not* give full picture detail or high quality sound. Where these are important they must be checked on other equipment.

tween them a flat platform wide enough to hold the synchronizer. The platform has an illuminated plate of frosted glass against which film may be seen and identified (more useful for 35 mm than for 16 mm, for which, as will be seen, alternative provision must be made). On either side of the bench and outside the bins are supports for the rolls of film to allow it to pass across the bench from left to right. On the left-hand side is a 'horse', several uprights with holes, so that rolls of film can be supported freely on spindles passed through the centre of the plastic cores on which film is generally wound. On the right is a take-up spindle to hold a number of split spools, with a winding handle to take up film.

The *synchronizer* has, perhaps, four sprocketed wheels all rigidly mounted on the same axle so that they are always mechanically synchronized. Each wheel is one foot in circumference, so

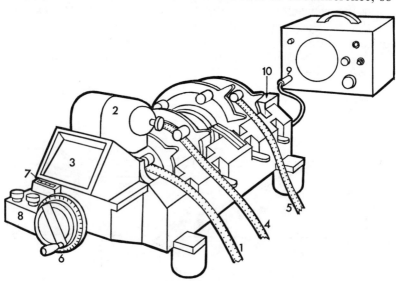

SYNCHRONIZER. Picture synchronizer with 'squawk box'. 1. Track one (picture) passes below lamp (2) which projects a picture via a system of rotating prisms on to the screen (3). 4 and 5. Two of the three sound paths. These pass over the sound heads, which are on the centre line behind the frame through which the lamp is projected. Each path passes over a one-foot diameter wheel with 40 sprockets. 6. The wheels are fixed to a common axle turned by hand at the front. Some models have a motor and clutch plate, to enable edits to be checked by running them at normal speed. A disc attached to the axle indicates the frame within each foot, and a nearby digital counter (7) shows the number of feet from the point at which the counter was set at zero. The reproduced sound signal is fed through a simple low-level mixer (8) to the loudspeaker input (9). Power is fed to the projector lamp through a transformer (10) which also has a switch on the far side. Other picture synchronizers have different numbers of sound paths or may have two picture heads.

that for each revolution 1 foot (16 frames of 35 mm or 40 frames of 16 mm) of film passes through the synchronizer. There is a counter showing feet of film. Sometimes, in BBC practice, this uses the 35 mm measure for 16 mm film: i.e. the counter is calibrated in '35-mm feet', which means that 16 frames equals one digit on the counter. '35-mm feet' are a finer measure in dubbing than 16-mm feet. There is also a disc that gives a number to the separate frame positions on the circumference of the wheels: on 16-mm equipment these run 1–40. There should also be internal provision for display of the picture, generally on the front film path and sometimes on the second as well. On all but the picture tracks there are sound replay heads that may be lowered or turned so that they do not press against the film if the path is being used to measure a length of picture (the head might scratch the film). The sound signals from the replay heads are fed through a small, simple low

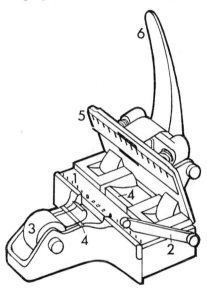

TAPE JOINER. The film (picture or magnetic track) to be cut is placed on the lower plate (1) and located precisely over the sprockets which stand along one edge. The knife is brought down on the film. The cut end is then moved to the centre of the plate and the film to be joined with it butted to it. Again, the sprockets hold the two ends precisely in position. A strip of adhesive tape is drawn from the roll (3) and placed across the butt and stuck also to the bars (4) on either side of the base plate. The upper head (5) is then brought down on to the film and the arm (6) pressed down. This causes two guillotines to cut the tape on either side of the base plate, and a punch to perforate the adhesive tape at the three sprocket holes nearest the centre of the plate. For simplicity the second, angled knife sometimes used for sound cuts has been omitted from this diagram. It is located to the right-hand side of the main knife.

level mixer built into the equipment. Some synchronizers are now fitted with motors, which can be engaged by means of a small clutch, so that picture and sound can be run at their normal speed.

A *small amplifier and loudspeaker* is the 'squawk box', to which the output of the synchronizer is fed. A small battery-powered transistorized unit is often used but any amplifier and loud-speaker system will do.

A *tape joiner* (guillotine splicer) cuts film (with a stainless steel blade) and then holds the two ends in position while tape is stuck across the join. The tape recommended for joining the film is similar in appearance to transparent plastic domestic tape but is of polyester; it is very thin, very strong, and has a non-oozing adhesive. The tape is used for picture as well as sound: the transparent base permits normal projection. As there is no overlapping of the film, and the tape is much more flexible than the film itself, joins held slackly are liable to appear to 'break' to an angle at the line of the join. The join will, however, hold in normal use with greater reliability than a cement join unless there is any way in which butted film can catch on a projection in defective equipment, or if it is replayed on certain old types of machinery for which it is unsuitable. In the latter case matters may be improved by taping the film on both surfaces and double backing each sound join to stop it bending so easily. Tape joins can be undone easily for remaking edits, and for many other purposes, without the loss of frames. The only regular maintenance required for the joiner is a change of blade after a long period of use.

Wax pencils for writing on film 'cel' are available in colours such as white, yellow, red or black.

A *trim bin* is for hanging up sections of picture and sound that have been cut. Sound trims, in particular, are valuable and may be needed later for overlapping sound in order to cross-fade between scenes.

Blank spacer film is used for insertion in the sound assembly where no sound is available or in the picture assembly where a shot is missing. Spacer is also used to protect the ends of rolls of assembled film. Note that spacer is made opaque by coating one side of the film support with a suitable material. Allowing this to run on the sound head can cause unnecessary wear, so it is usual to cut spacer in to sound with the coated side away from the head. Rough and smooth sides can most easily be distinguished by touching them with the tip of the tongue.

470

Leader film for picture and sound is printed with start marks and 35-mm footages counting down from twelve to three, after which the print is black to the point at which the film starts (which is where zero would be on this count). Sometimes a frame of tone at 1000 Hz (for 16 mm) or 2000 Hz (35 mm) is cut in on the sound leader at '3', or at '4' in BBC practice, to allow greater latitude in fading up sound at the start of a programme. As it passes through the projector or telecine prior to this being switched, the presence of the tone confirms that sound is live on the replay itself.

A *waste bin*, specifically for inflammable film waste, should be made of metal and have a lid that will exclude the air in case of a fire in the bin. As a further safety measure all technical equipment should be on a single circuit with a readily accessible isolator switch.

In addition to all of these items of equipment, there will be an adequate supply of plastic cores and split spools; perhaps a fast rewind bench; spare lamps, and so on.

The mechanical operation of most of this equipment is fairly obvious or self-explanatory; and its use closely follows the routine described for other editing jobs. These are rough assembly (p. 448) and fine editing (p. 450). It is not the purpose of this book to describe the cutting of picture: the literature on this is vast. The cutting of sound is, however, very much our business, and here many of the principles of cutting sound tape carry over virtually without modification. But extra problems (and possibilities) arise from the combination of sound with picture.

Cement joiners are obsolete and should no longer be used in editing. The lapped join necessitates the loss of a frame on each piece of film joined—and this was permissible only when it was essential. The value of trims is shown below: for many purposes they should be complete, without loss of frames for the out-of-date technical reasons.

Picture and sound in the cutting room

Film picture available to the editor includes:
1. Film shot with synchronized sound:
   (**a**) lip-sync sound,
   (**b**) synchronized effects or music,
   (**c**) material where picture and sound are related, having been shot at the same time; but for which there is no need to maintain perfect sync.

471

2. Mute or silent film, for which no directly useful sound could be recorded in sync, or for which a quiet camera could not conveniently be used. Sometimes this may have been shot to playback or wildtrack commentary or other sound (see below).
3. Library film for which suitable sound may or may not exist, or only in a technically imperfect form (e.g. optical track).

Film sound available to the editor includes:
4. Sync material as in (1) above.
5. Wildtrack commentary or dialogue that will generally be played only with pictures that do not show the speaker's mouth.
6. Wildtrack effects that will be synchronized to action in mute film (e.g. a gunshot) or sync film for which the effects recorded at the time were inadequate (e.g. too distant).
7. Location atmosphere tracks.
8. Library sound effects: atmosphere or music recorded originally on disc or tape but selected and transferred to magnetic film stock.

The editor will later have the advantage of all the extra sound that can be provided in a dubbing theatre: out-of-vision commentary, post-synchronized dialogue, spot effects, recorded effects, specially composed music and recorded music. Some of these, particularly post-synchronized dialogue, must be recorded separately and early; much of it may be left to the day of the final mix.

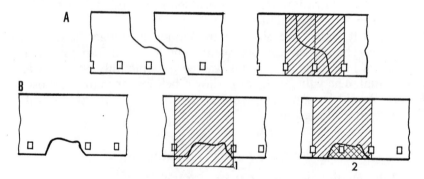

REPAIRING BROKEN FILM WITH A TAPE JOINER. A. A simple butt and rejoin. B. Torn sprocket holes with film missing: for picture the damaged section is simply taped on both sides, turned over again and the sprocket holes punched through. For sound film the tape is stuck to the upper (uncoated) surface only but is cut with a razor blade or scissors a little way from the edge of the film (1) before the guillotine is brought down. The loose edge is then doubled under, on to the coated side of the film (2), but will not reach as far as the recorded track. If time permits, the original sound is re-transferred, and the damaged track replaced.

To the dubbing theatre the editor takes a cutting copy of the film and as many rolls of sound as the dubbing mixer needs for separate control of the levels and quality of the various constituent parts of the final sound. In the first instance the editor works with one picture and one sound track.

If at this or any other stage a magnetic sound track is broken, it can often be repaired quite easily by using the tape joiner. Broken or torn sprocket holes may also be repaired by similar means.

Cutting picture and sound together

The editor's first responsibility, in practice usually undertaken by his assistant, is to synchronize the rushes. He runs film and sound, finds the frame where the clapperboard closed and uses a wax pencil to mark it with a boxed X and the corresponding frame of sound with three bars, III. He then writes the shot and take number ahead of these marks in both picture and sound. For convenience of continuous replay the spacing is then adjusted so that this picture and sound follow in the same synchronization as that of the preceding shot. If preferred, intervening mute film shots and wildtrack sound may be cut out at this stage and wound on to separate rolls: all of the good takes of sync material can then be seen in the sequence in which they were shot.

While it is in this form, the film may be viewed by the director

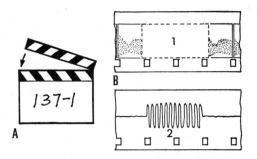

SYNCHRONIZATION OF SEPARATELY RECORDED SOUND. A. Clapperboard. In addition to the scene and take number there is other information on the board. B. Simple 'blip-sync'. In this case after the camera and sound have both started to run (so that the camera has a picture) a light is flashed to blank out the picture (1) for the same duration as a buzz (2) is recorded on sound. More complex systems have provision for varying the marking, so that scene numbers from one to ten (but not take numbers) are allocated in rotation. This still lacks the precision of identification given by the clapperboard, but is compensated by the increased operational flexibility, and reduction in film stock used.

and editor together, so that the content, intention and cutting style may be discussed. Meanwhile the assistant logs the material (see below) and breaks down the rolls that have been viewed into single shots or related groups of shots and rolls them up with picture and sound, if any, together. These are kept in large film cans: each can contains a substantial number of small rolls each of which is labelled with its shot number. The can itself is labelled

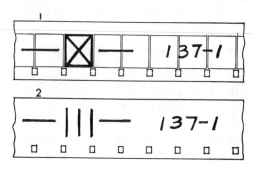

SYNCHRONIZATION MARKS on picture (1) and separate magnetic sound (2). In the conventional clapperboard system these are marked at the picture and sound of the board closing, and in the case of electronic synchronization, with the flash on the picture and the corresponding buzz on sound.

on the edge with the shot numbers it contains. The assistant looks after this rough filing system from which material can be taken, restored, and retrieved as necessary.

The editor begins by making a rough cut—almost invariably at this stage cutting sound and picture parallel, making a 'straight' or editorial cut. A methodical editor (or his assistant) will mark the sound trims with wax pencil so that they can easily be identified later. Inked-in code-numbers serve the same purpose (see below).

At the fine cut, as further sound and picture is trimmed away, sound overlays (where the sound from one shot runs over the next) may be allowed, but the cut in picture is marked on the sound track. Before any complex non-parallel cut is made, the editor ensures that he can easily find sync again both before and after the region of the cut: he can then satisfy himself that the same number of frames have been cut from both picture and sound. Most of this work is done in the synchronizer, with only occasional excursions to the viewing machine to check points where better quality of picture or sound is required, or where the editor wishes to view or hear at normal speed (if this facility is not available on the synchronizer).

474

Sync marks follow the editor's private code of letters or symbols, the same one being marked on corresponding frames of sound and picture. It is essential for an editor to be able to hold synchronization with both accuracy and the sort of confidence that does not waste time unduly: an automatic part of this is a quick check on sync after every cut is made. Fine-cut trims often require to be carefully marked and kept, and although there is a limit to the time that can be spent on this sort of detail, they should certainly be kept with or close to the rest of the trims of the associated shot.

When handling picture, the editor is helped by the fact that professional film stock is edge-numbered: to do this, the manufacturer optically exposes the edge of the film to serial numbers at intervals of 20 frames. These numbers are later used by the negative (or camera master) cutters when the edited film is ready to be printed, as those on the master will necessarily correspond to those printed from them on the rushes. Only in exceptional circumstances do the neg-cutters ever have to look at the picture to 'eye-match' original and print.

As film arrives in the cutting room, the editor's assistant logs the edge numbers of each roll. As a result, any length that is not too short to have a single complete edge number on it can later be identified, even if the editor has omitted to mark on it what part of what shot it is.

This idea can be extended to sound by using a service that provides inked code numbers ('rubber numbers'). After the rolls

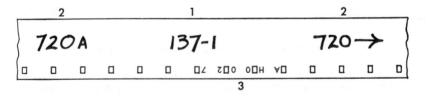

IDENTIFICATION MARKS ON A MAGNETIC SOUND TRIM. 1. The number on the clapperboard: scene 137, take one. 2. Numbers identifying position in the cut film: here the numbering system depends on the editor. And in this case the figures and letters refer to the points at which the film is cut. Note that the scene (137–1) may appear in the film in several different places or not at all. 3. Code numbers—which can be printed on both picture and sound after the rolls have been fully synchronized; using these, sound and picture trims can always be matched (however, the numbers are repeated at intervals of 40 frames on 16 mm, so that on very short trims they may not be present). The letters identify the roll; the numbers, 16-mm feet within the roll. All of these systems are optional, but for films of more than a few minutes duration they are very useful both in any subsequent recut and in tracklaying prior to the dub.

of picture and sound have been synchronized in the normal way, and the synchronization checked by the editor, possibly when he and the director view the rushes with sound, the film is run again with the sound and picture rolls in synchronization, through a machine that stamps a new set of corresponding numbers on the two. The rolls themselves are numbered AA, AB, AC, and so on, and then each foot (i.e. 40 frames) is given a serial number AA0001 and so on. Each group of letters and numbers is split into three pairs which appear between successive sprocket holes. The code numbers serve two purposes:

1. They provide a rapid means of finding the original synchronization between sound and picture. (If, in editing, the cutting copy sound is deliberately displaced relative to the picture it has to be marked clearly on both tracks, so that the code numbers do not cause any confusion later.)

2. They provide an easy check on the identity of trims—now including the sound trims. (The shot number is also useful for this.)

Over a long period of editing it is possible to wear magnetic track enough to lose sound quality noticeably—and particularly on musical items. To avoid this, two transfers from the original tapes can be made at the same time and given identical rubber numbers. One of these can be held in reserve until the editor lays tracks prior to the dub.

Code numbers are printed on to cutting copy, so the show copy, which is printed from the original negative, does not have them; nor does the final mix of the sound made at the dubbing session. The transmission film can therefore be numbered as a new roll or rolls without risk of any confusion by double numbering.

Cutting unsynchronized elements together

At the rough assembly, spacers will have been cut in, so that at some places where there was picture the sound had a spacer inserted in to it, and at some places where sound ran on, there was no picture. Indeed, even after the first rough cut, some of these spacers may still have been left in. Also, at some points where sound and picture were running side by side, one or the other will have been marked for later deletion or perhaps even replaced by spacer. There could be several reasons for this.

First, the usable or wanted lengths of sound and picture may be different from each other even within the same sync take. The film may have been shot with this intention, or there may be some imperfection in sound or picture only, or it may be that continuity of action does not coincide with continuity of sound.

Secondly, where mute film and wildtrack sound have been shot for a particular sequence they are unlikely to be exactly the same length. A careful director plans picture and sound to be the same length as it is finally to be cut together; but the pictures may turn out to be very good or very bad, so demanding a longer or shorter use of the visual element. The experienced documentary director normally has an excess of material to choose from; and perhaps an excess of good sound to cover.

Where unsynchronized picture and sound differ in length, matching is sometimes just a matter of making the longer one equal to the shorter with a parallel cut. Sometimes picture is longer than the sound intended to cover it: in this case the picture can usually be allowed to run its proper length, and the sound filled out with matching atmosphere or effects. This is done when the tracks are laid, i.e. when the sound is prepared for remixing; until then spacers will probably be left in. If sound (e.g. commentary) is longer than the picture it is intended to cover, things are more complicated. If the difference is small, the number of frames of overrun can be counted and the same number removed at some point in the commentary track: there must, of course, be no important lip-sync or synchronized effects between the two points where the cuts are made and it must be checked that looser points of synchronization (e.g. in commentary or out-of-vision dialogue referring to the picture) are not seriously affected.

Cuts may also be made by removing lengths of sound or picture, including spacing that has been inserted to maintain sync, and, having found another suitable length from the other track, simply measuring one against the other by hand, marking and cutting. It is easy to check that the lengths are the same, frame for frame, by matching the sprocket holes by eye.

A useful method for cutting sound to match a shorter picture involves looping the sound back on to another path through the synchronizer. The first thing to do is to mark sync before and after the sequence affected, noting the last frame at which synchronization is essential at the front and the first that follows. The unwanted length of picture, or spacer, is then removed and the film rejoined. Picture and sound are now in sync at one end only. The excess sound on the unsynchronized side is now looped back on to the next sound path through the synchronizer and the second sync mark is located to coincide with the corresponding mark on

477

the film. The length of sound in the loop is that which has to be cut, and by running the film and sound backward and forward between the two sync marks and using both sound heads in turn a suitable sound cut can often be found. Before the cut is actually made the remaining sound can be heard against the picture it will accompany and the words before and after the cut can be heard in sequence.

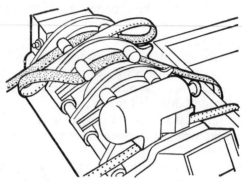

LOOPING BACK. Here sound and picture are synchronized on both sides of the picture synchronizer; but at the join there is an excess of sound, and this has been taken up in a loop between two of the sound paths. Picture and sound can now be rolled backward or forward together until suitable points for cutting the sound are found. If some of the sound in the loop is still required to be overlaid at the picture join, it is marked and retained for reinstatement on another track when additional tracks are laid prior to the dub.

This is only a particular case of a more general idea: obviously, given two picture heads in the case of 16 mm, it can be done the other way about, looping picture back instead to match a sound track that is shorter.

In another example, it may be desired to cut both sound and picture by the same amounts, but not at the same point. In this case neither is cut; but both are looped back the same amounts so that two picture paths and two sound paths are used as the film is run backward and forward to find matching lengths to cut. If required, the effect of using shorter or longer, but still equal, loops can also be investigated before making the cut.

These looping techniques are still very useful, although they are now used rather less than they were before the advent of the tape joiner, which permits experimental cuts to be remade without harm.

Note that a short cut in picture can often be accommodated by

478

making *several* shorter cuts in sound, perhaps hesitations or inessential words, that add up to the same length. Picture can also be opened out for sound by the use of freeze frame or slow motion —both of which can be processed from existing film by film laboratories, and sound can be opened out for picture by the insertion of effects or atmosphere either on the track or later at the dub.

Opening out sound, in particular, wildtrack commentary, to match picture is a common and often desirable device, because it is better to have more picture than words; but lengthening picture to match sound is an exceptional measure—and one that should have a better reason than solving an editing problem.

In all cases, the timing of speech—both in its spoken rhythm and in its cueing—must remain comfortable and natural.

Film sound cutting in detail

Here, much of the technique is identical to that used for sound tape (see p. 450). The mechanics of choosing the place are just the same; joining the magnetic film is governed largely by the same principles with one exception noted below; and the things to listen for in checking a join are precisely the same (see p. 447).

Here are a few additional points to note:

Words, syllables or pauses can often be transferred from rejected takes, replacing the same number of frames as are inserted. If this results momentarily in an apparently inappropriate mouth movement it is still worth considering whether this may be preferable to inappropriate words. This is a real question: sometimes it is preferable, but very often it is not—it depends on the individual circumstances.

A change of sound that happens with a cut is much more natural and acceptable than an unexplained change at another point.

Short gaps in background atmosphere created by lengthening the picture (e.g. with a cutaway that needs to be seen for longer than the master action it replaces) should be filled in with sound as closely matching it as possible. This is preferable to leaving it to the dub and hoping; it takes a lot to obliterate a drop-out of atmosphere, particularly where there is a continuous steady noise such as machinery hum or the whine of jet aircraft.

Guillotine tape joiners have two blades, one cutting at a right angle to the edge of the film, so that the picture can be cut between successive frames, and an angled blade that is used for sound. The angle involved gives a quicker fade up or down than that used when editing sound tapes, but is just sufficient to avoid the effect of a click on the end of material containing continuous tones. However, it does not avoid the effect of sound drop-out unless a correspondingly abrupt picture change explains the difference.

Track laying

When the fine cut is complete, the constituent parts of the cut sound are separated on to several tracks. For so long as the sound continues at the same level and quality, whether of the main or background sound, it is retained on the same roll; but at points where these change, the sound is switched to another roll. If by simple adjustments of level and tone quality settings the sounds can then be matched, a parallel shift from one roll to the next is all that is necessary. But if there is a more drastic change that is not immediately explained by an equally strong change of picture, then extra sound must be found for the dubbing mixer to fade in on or out of, or both. These fades are generally made quickly, but it is better to have too much than too little to fade on, or the sound may be heard starting or finishing at low level. Such chopped off sounds appear unnatural because they do not occur at a cut.

During the editing, extra tracks that had to be synchronized with action could not be cut in because of other synchronous material already present; these were marked and put to one side. At the track laying they can go in on their appropriate rolls.

Music may also be laid: where it is dominant it will already have been arranged for the picture cuts to be related to it, or alternatively for specially composed music to match the picture. The precise manner in which picture and music should be co-ordinated is a complex study; but a strong rhythm demands that some, but not too many, of the cuts are made on the beat; similarly, individual strong notes may cue a cut. The recording of special music is described in Chapter 9 (see also p. 79).

As many of the sound effects as possible are accurately laid by the editor; this includes both library effects, which should be selected and transferred for the purpose, and wildtracks which were specially shot during filming.

Some continuing sounds may be formed as loops: lengths of recorded track made up with the end joined back on to the beginning. Loops with strong distinguishing features must be long, so that the regular reappearance of such a feature does not become

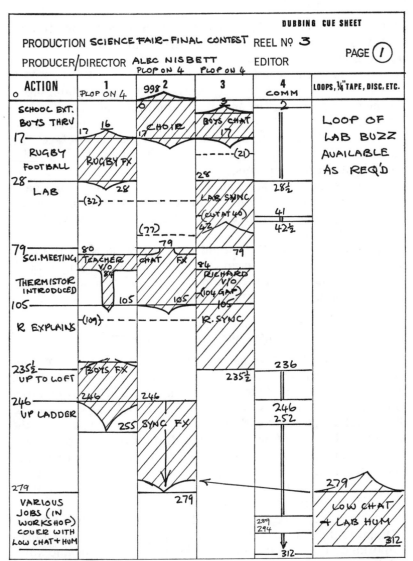

DUBBING CUE SHEET. Note the original on which this was based has provision for more sound rolls. The action column does not list every picture cut, but only sequences within which sound should remain roughly the same. In some cases sound has been laid to several feet beyond a picture change but will be faded out quickly on the cut (this is represented by the shallow V). Fine points are discussed or decided by consultation on the spot. For example in this case it was not made clear on the chart, but the choir was taken behind the boys' chatter between 3 and 17 and was faded quickly after 17 although it was originally laid as far as 32. The rugby football sound (at 16) preceded the cut at 17 and, in effect, killed the sound on tracks 2 and 3. 'V/O' means 'voice over'. At 80–84 the teacher's voice was to be heard over background chatter and effects and from 84–105; this in turn was taken to low level while Richard's voice was heard (out of vision) talking about what is happening at this point in the story. 'Hum' and 'buzz' are terms used here to indicate 'low-level background sound'. The commentator's voice has been recorded in advance and has also been laid (on track 4). The final words of each commentary section may be marked in this column.

apparent. If it is likely to, it could perhaps be trimmed out, though this would shorten the loop still further. Also, in joining the ends of loops together care must be taken to find points where volume and quality are matched.

The editor or his assistant prepares a chart with a column show-in the main points of the action, and opposite this the sound on each roll, showing the cuts in and out of sound with symbolic indications of fades and mixes and clearly marked footages, together with notes on loops and tape and disc effects that may also be used at particular points.

Commentary that has been prerecorded is also laid; but many directors prefer to cut the film completely before the final version of the commentary is settled. The exact length and value of each picture is then known.

Remember also that as an aid to synchronization a frame of tone (a 'plop') will have been cut in at '3' in the leader, or at '4' in BBC practice. Where there could be ambiguity the convention is indicated on the rerecording cue sheet.

Shot listing and commentary writing

A shot list giving footages is usually made for other reasons besides commentary writing. It can conveniently be combined with a script of the dialogue as finally cut and notes of other important sound: in this case it is laid out to look like the standard film or television script with picture on the left of the page and the corresponding sound on the right. A draft of this may be derived from the cutting order or shooting script by rewriting it to include the changes introduced in the editing; this can then be checked in detail by running the film, the completed cutting copy, on the synchronizer before the tracks are laid.

Footages should be noted not only at cuts in the picture but also at important points within the action of a shot e.g. when a detail of importance first appears in vision. Footages at the start and finish of dialogue should also be noted; and also those of important effects or dominant music.

Commentary can then be accurately written to picture: for a fast-speaking commentator allow about three words per second (or, measuring by footages, two per 35-mm foot or five per 16-mm foot). Where a speaker is slower or more expression is wanted these figures must be reduced. It is better to write too little than too much and have to rush the words; and in any case strong or exciting pictures are often better without any words at all.

The audience's primary need from a commentary is that it should interpret the picture: in the short term this is a more effective use of the medium than when the reverse is attempted. The worst possible case is when pictures and words do not agree, either because the commentator wants to talk about something else or because he wants to continue about something that is no longer in the picture. In these cases an even averagely interesting picture demolishes the commentary entirely: the words are simply not heard. It is the same as with the words and figures on a cheque: commentary and pictures must agree, or the value is lost. Only if the commentary satisfies this primary rule may it go on to give additional information.

There is one particular danger that is encountered when part of a commentary is recorded in vision, either in the studio or on location, and another part, using the same voice, is dubbed on later in the confined acoustic of a commentary box: there may be a series of abrupt changes of acoustic. Short links should if possible be planned in advance, and recorded at the location; if at this stage doubt still exists as to the best form of words, a variety of versions should be recorded. If the same voice must appear successively in location sound and as dubbed sound, one possibility is to allow a period of time, a music link or a burst of some sound effect to intervene; the change may then be less noticeable.

If it is obvious from the picture that the dubbed voice is not that filmed on location the change in quality may be an advantage: the commentator finishes speaking in vision, turns and walks in to the action; and his dubbed voice takes over: here, at least, a clear convention has been adopted, and the change of acoustic actually helps.

But nothing is more clumsy than a rapid succession of different acoustics on the same voice for no apparent reason. At best it is mildly distracting (and certainly destructive of artistic unity); at worst it is actively confusing, with the viewer having moments when he is not sure whether the new sound is the same voice or a completely new and unexplained character.

Post-synchronization

Post-synchronization is a specialized job that must be done well if it is to be really effective. It is often done very badly even by professional actors.

In particular, many continental films have been shot on location and the dialogue then badly rerecorded later. English audiences, which are very sensitive to accents often prefer to have foreign films in the original, and as a result get the worst of all worlds: a picture that can claim only part of the visual attention because of the sub-titles, and 'original' dialogue that flaps slackly toward and away from lip-sync. It is perhaps fortunate that the former deficiency must to some extent distract attention from the latter.

Good post-synchronization has to be done phrase by phrase using (for foreign language originals) words that give reasonable approximations to the original mouth movements. A loop of film should be played round and round again until the best match is obtained; then the next phrase is taken with the next loop. Technically, there are several variations on the 'loop' idea, including systems for high-speed rollback that are very similar in effect to a loop, but do not involve cutting picture and sound. Any final trimming that is necessary to match lip movements perfectly must be done as the whole is finally cut together.

Post-synchronization of spot effects is—for a few talented individuals—a well-paid job in the film industry. These experts are capable of seeing through a reel of film a couple of times, then collecting together a pile of odds and ends which they manipulate in perfect timing to movements both in and out of picture, giving it a convincing simulation of the casual sounds of live action. The best spot operators are well worth their apparently high rate of pay: they save days of special recording and editing. The techniques of producing the sounds themselves were described on pp. 274–288 but the greater skill lies in the timing of effects to picture.

A complementary technique is shooting picture to playback of prerecorded sound. This is regularly done for musical production numbers (miming), where the quality and the integrity of the sound is of primary importance. It also permits action (such as dancing) to be combined with song in a way that would be difficult if not impossible in real life. In miming, the illusion is, however, easily shattered by the sudden change of acoustic between dialogue and song, emphasizing and making awkward a transition that should be smooth.

In documentary work, close shots such as hands indicating detail are often shot to playback of the master sound take. In this case exact synchronization is unlikely, but a good match between sound and picture is fairly easily found by the editor.

484

The dubbing theatre

A film-dubbing theatre has equipment to display picture and run several synchronized sound tracks, plus a recorder. There is often a recording studio if only for a single commentary voice, and provision for playing records, tapes, cassettes, etc., together with additional facilities on the control desk that can make operations simpler and more flexible. Let us consider these in more detail:

Picture display. Many rerecording studios still have big theatre-style projectors. However, so long as a picture is plainly visible to operators and commentator, and there is sufficient detail to see all significant action, high-quality projection requiring specialist staff is a waste of money. In any case the cutting copy, or a low-quality black-and-white reversal 'dupe' of it is often used. Alternatives are a very simple optical system, or a low-cost tele-cine and monitor or both; a monitor provides a picture for the commentator if he cannot see the main screen.

Footage counter. A footage counter in 35-mm or 16-mm feet (i.e. with 16 or 40 frames to each digit) as preferred should be displayed close to the picture, perhaps with repeaters on the desk and in the studio. A commentator or musical director works to these numbers in conjunction with other cues. The numbers themselves are generated by the film projector and may be distributed to the other points by several means. One is to have an electronic display of some sort. Simpler, however, is to place an inexpensive black-and-white video camera in front of a simple mechanical counter linked to the projector, feeding monitors wherever they are required. The counter may be zeroed by the projection staff, but in an operationally simpler routine it is directly controlled from the desk; projection staff are then responsible only for setting up the film (normally on a start mark fifteen 35 mm feet, 240 frames, before zero) while the dubbing mixer himself sets the counter at the corresponding point. For an instrument that advances by one digit every sixteen frames, it will have been arranged that the mechanical zero is fifteen digits before the displayed zero: a four-figure display would start from 9985. (Alternatively, the counter may indicate time.)

Film sound replay and recording equipment. These are available in various layouts. One that is convenient to operate has provision for two decks, one behind the other on a single horizontal bench. A total of four to six (including a recorder) is required.

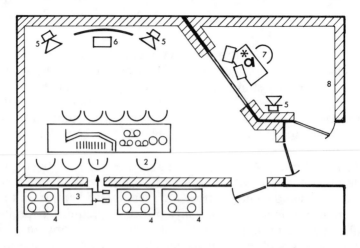

RE-RECORDING STUDIO (DUBBING THEATRE). 1. Mixer at mixing desk. 2. Assistant, with tape, cassette decks, turntables, etc. 3. Film projector and footage counter (here with video cameras to relay picture and footage as required). 4. Magnetic film sound reproducers and recorder. 5. Loudspeakers. 6. Screen and footage monitor. 7. Narrator with desk, microphone, cue light and monitors for picture and footage. 8. Acoustic treatment.

The machines are under local control while they are being loaded, but are then switched to 'remote' operation so that synchronous replay of picture and all the replay and recording machines are controlled from the desk. There is provision for discontinuous recording, sometimes called 'rock and roll'. The mix continues until errors are made, when the sound and pictures are stopped and run backward until well before the point at which rerecording must start. The footage counter runs back in synchronization with sound and picture. Then the whole system is run forward once again, and the mixer checks his levels by switching the monitor rapidly between the input and the previously recorded signals, adjusting his faders to match them; then he switches back to record, and from that point the new mix replaces the old. The switch should not operate instantaneously, of course, or a click might be introduced.

Monitoring equipment. This must be of high quality, and is usually set loud so that imperfections in the original material or of the mix itself can readily be heard; but as usual, the sound should also occasionally be heard at normal levels and perhaps on a lower quality monitor to check what most of the audience will be hearing. The sound recordist listens to replay in an

486

acoustically separate cubicle, because there is a delay, typically of five frames (one fifth of a second), between the recording and replay heads. Alternatively, the picture may be set back the same number of frames and the sound mixer himself monitors replay, which is now synchronized with picture. An advantage is that if there is any fault in the final recording its quality is immediately apparent to the sound mixer and he can stop without delay. He then runs sound and picture backwards listening to the input sound and, if the fault is not repeated, he diagnoses a fault in the recording system—it might be a clogged recording head, which must be cleaned, or drop-out on the magnetic recording stock, which could be replaced. A second advantage is the elimination of a boring job and reduction in operating costs. A disadvantage that might be thought great is that the input tracks are now several frames ahead of picture and that all operations affecting the mix must be aniticipated by the same amount. Surprisingly, the skill is not too difficult to acquire.

Ancillary replay equipment. There must be the normal provision for replay of tape (for original recordings, etc.) and disc (for music and effects records). Cassettes may also be used for a library of standard effects, while cartridges may replay continuous or staccato effects, including recorded spot effects that must appear accurately on the footage cue. Cartridges with loops of various durations are available. There should also be provision for the replay of tape or magnetic film loops, plus microphones and a range of floor surfaces for spot effects, often in an acoustically separate booth.

Commentary box. A commentary is usually recorded in a rather dead acoustic. This ensures that it does not carry with it an ambience that is alien to the picture it accompanies, for example, by overlaying a live, indoor acoustic on to an exterior scene. It also seems to help the voice to cut through background effects or music, perhaps, in part at least, because a higher level for the voice can be set. The commentary is sometimes recorded in advance of the main dub and taken back to the cutting room to adjust each cue precisely to the frame at which it has the best effect. If the possibility still exists (that is, if the negative or master has not already been cut to match the cutting copy) fine trims of the picture may be removed or restored: sometimes the strength of the word enhances a picture to an unexpected degree and demands that it remain on the screen a little longer. The commentary track is then returned to the dubbing theatre along with the other

487

tracks, although its addition is often the last stage of the mixing process. If, on the other hand, the commentary is not recorded in advance and laid by the editor, the discontinuous rock and roll facility is used not only to obtain improved performances, but also in an attempt to cue the words ever more accurately to match picture. However, even with a commentary that has been recorded in this way it may still prove an advantage to adjust the position of the track in one direction or the other in the dubbing theatre itself. To this end it is helpful if one replay machine can be advanced or retarded against the others. If it can be set using a servo control from the desk itself there should also, of course, be a counter indicating the number of frames the track has been shifted. This makes it easy to reset the track to normal.

Cueing systems. There should be provision for the commentator to be cued from the desk. The usual system is 'green for go'. As the reader has to follow his script and may also wish to glance at the picture and footage counter, the cue light should be close to his sight line. The director, editor or assistant editor, or the dubbing mixer himself may press the cueing button, as is felt to be appropriate. The footages corresponding to the cues are usually marked on the commentary script, which omits most of the picture details and carries only the most significant details of other sounds, such as the in- and out-cues of dialogue already on film, or featured sound effects that the reading has to fit. The cues have to be given a little ahead of the marked footage, to allow the speaker time to respond. It is best if the narrator speaks immediately on cue or with a consistent delay, for erratic cue takers are a nuisance even when the recorded commentary can be laid precisely to picture in the cutting room. There is also keyed talkback between desk and studio: the director uses it to advise on the reading and the sound mixer to say when recording is about to begin and to confirm the starting point. Sometimes reader and director are placed so that they both see the same picture display, but it may be better if the reader has his own monitor and is seated in direct visual contact through the double-glazed window with the director and sound mixer—this adds to the quality of communication and gives the reader an audience to work to. The commentator will often require a headphone feed of music, dialogue and effects, with or without his own voice (whichever he prefers). Before the rehearsal begins it should be checked with him that the sound level fed to his headphones is comfortable.

The desk. This has the usual fader channels, each with its echo feed and fixed or patch-in facilities for frequency correction, in the proper sense of that term. Frequency correction can usually improve the clarity and naturalness of sound that has been recorded in adverse acoustic conditions and, in addition, helps to match the quality of one recording with the next. The standard top, bass and midlift units are adequate in many cases, but sometimes the versatility of a graphic octave filter gives a better match. Compressors, limiters and expanders are available, and a noise gate (which may also be useful for eliminating the effects of tape printing when they appear in the gaps between speech). Documentaries are often mixed in stages, with a so-called music and effects (M and E) mix being made first (in fact, this would also include any sync speech, and there might be no music). The final stage is to add the commentary; but the M and E track should be retained against the possibility of changing the commentary later, or making versions in other languages, or for use when extracts from the film are taken for other programmes.

Prereader. For the final mix the dubbing mixer may have an accurate note of recorded commentary starting points; and the ends of intermediate cues may be anticipated by following the script—but even so, shorter gaps may take him by surprise and he may miss the opportunity to lift an intervening effect. This increases the time required for rehearsal and rollback. But there is one device that provides nearly all he needs to know about commentary without any additional rehearsal and with little or no need to follow a script. This is a prereader, an extra replay head fixed to the commentary deck picking up sound several seconds before it appears at the normal replay head. The output from the prereading head is fed through a gating amplifier which converts it to a signal that is on or off according to whether there is speech on the track or not. When there, it lights an indicator bulb on the desk for a fraction of a second, then another to its right and so on, so that the signal is passed along a row of, say, sixteen indicators arriving at the last at the exact moment that the track itself took to pass from prereader to the replay head. The display appears as a constant flow of light and dark passing from left to right. As the lights come on, the operator prepares to drop the level of the premixed M and E; as the dark approaches, he gets ready to bring it up. This allows him to give more of his attention to the quality of sound and its relationship to the picture.

Stereo equipment. For television, dubbing theatres do not need stereo equipment, but for the big screen they may, in which case

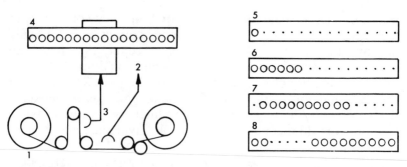

PREREADER. 1. Deck for magnetic film track. 2. Output to mixer. 3. Prereader feeding separate amplifier-oscillator which acts as a gate to detect presence or absence of signal. 4. Display on desk: a signal lights the first indicator immediately, then each successive indicator in turn. The final indicator is lit as the corresponding signal reaches the main reproducing head. 5. Signal has reached prereader head. 6. Signal is still being registered at prereader head. 7. Signal has ceased: an illuminated strip is passing to the right. 8. Strip reaches right, indicating arrival of signal at main output head. The prereader can be used for a narration track, indicating where background sound must be reduced, and (for sufficiently long pauses) where it may be raised.

there are all of the usual facilities, including stereo channels and pan pots. But while stereo, potentially, can add much to the finished product, in practice the results are often spectacular but gimmick ridden. Indeed, apart from film music there is little approaching true stereo to be heard on film. The sound for stereophonic films is still largely recorded and edited monophonically; then at the dub the various sounds are apportioned between the final film tracks by the judgement of the dubbing mixer. The process is extremely laborious and is far from being as convincing as true stereo.

After the dub

The film editor's responsibilities continue after the dub. If the film is to be a television programme it is normally transmitted with the film and sound on separate tracks. The editor cuts a leader on the start of the final mix. The show print is prepared by cutting and assembling the negative to match the finished cutting copy, often with alternate pictures on separate A and B rolls, and then printing. The sound is despatched for transmission with the show print of picture.

Synchronization of picture and separate magnetic sound may be lost temporarily or permanently during transmission, owing to

490

any of the following:

1. Runaways. Picture and sound are linked electrically and not mechanically: it can happen on some systems that the sound becomes synchronized at double the speed.

2. Wrong start marks. If the editor has put proper leaders on this is not likely. But sometimes wax or other marks are used and there may be confusion if there are several marks.

3. Unauthorized removal of picture. While a film is laying in a library or film vault it may by error or stupidity get into the hands of unauthorized people who remove sections of film or break the film and repair it, losing some frames, in neither case correcting the sound to match.

4. Faulty editing: a shot or sequence has got out of sync and this has never been put right; or the new faults have been introduced when opticals have been put in after the dub, or when other changes or corrections are made at a late stage, and when there is no time for a further technical review of the finished product.

5. Faulty negative cutting: frames may have been omitted or inserted in error, or the wrong section of film used. This, too, would normally be noticed at the review of the show print.

6. Lost loop of the picture (when played on an intermittent projector), or slippage of film or track due to damaged sprocket holes.

7. Wrong sound track played.

Some problems of loss of synchronization can be cured only by stopping the film, adjusting the picture or track by what appears to be the right amount, checking it, correcting again if necessary, rechecking, and starting again. For an organization with network breaks to meet this may result in a disastrous delay—particularly if the breaks contain commercials. If the film and track have been code-numbered, resynchronization is easy.

If the film is to be projected in the normal way (or is a television commercial) a combined sound track is required. The show print is made on magnetically striped stock, which is then recorded with the final sound mix. Alternatively an optical track may be printed. These measures ensure that whatever misfortune in handling may occur later to the film it cannot be shown out of synchronization, except for the second or so after a break and rejoin where frames have been lost, or if the loop is lost in an intermittent projector. The use of flying spot telecine machines —in which the film runs continuously and smoothly—also avoids the latter possible fault. Nor is such a film likely to be shown with the wrong sound.

20

COMMUNICATION IN SOUND

JUST how important is technique? Let us seek a perspective.

The mechanics of programme work must be seen in their true relationship to the full process of creation, and they should be given neither too much deference nor too little. Obviously I think technique *is* important, otherwise this book would not have been written. But technique is a means to an end, not an end in itself: and its major object must be to concentrate the audience's attention upon the content, and to do so in a particular way, with particular emphases. In such a supporting role technique is indispensable.

When combined with picture, in television or film, sound should always support, occasionally counterpoint, and rarely dominate; its most effective role is to extend, strengthen, and more closely define the information that comes first through vision.

It is relatively easy for the skilled professional to make technique serve the programme; and work is very rarely, if ever, done merely to display the operational ingenuity of those involved. But for the newcomer much of his work must necessarily also serve as exercises in handling sound. To the novice, technique is a vital need; perhaps even his most vital need—because he may have no lack of ideas, but little or no knowledge of the means of expressing them. He must learn the techniques, not merely of construction, but also self-criticism and correction. Once he has mastered the techniqies he must learn to apply them—to make them serve the needs of each successive production. The medium itself is *not* the message.

What makes a good production? The answer is of importance not only to the writer or the person who is directing a programme but to everyone in the studio. It concerns them all in two ways: first, so that they can see their own contribution in perspective, and to know in what ways this must be subordinated to the whole; and secondly, as the programme's first audience.

Over the years people in daily contact with a medium become sensitive to virtues or defects that even the director himself may be unsure of; and this front-line audience can be of immense value to him in cross-checking his calculation or intuition.

The things that matter most in any programme are the ideas within it (its content) and the way they are presented to the audience (its form). Some subjects are better for sound than others, because they make contact more easily through the listener's imagination. Others are more suitable for television or fiilm, demanding the explicitness or possibilities for visual imagery that these media give.

Many subjects can be treated adequately in any medium—adequately but differently, because the medium dictates certain possibilities and impossibilities; or it presents alternatives, where one path presents only difficulties, while another luxuriates in opportunities for attractive or artistic results. To this extent at least the medium does condition and reflect itself upon the message.

But so far as technique is concerned there is one major condition which, in conventional (if not in modern experimental) terms, must be fulfilled: whatever the choice of subject, it must be presented in such a way as to create interest and maintain it throughout the production.

Sound and the imagination

The greatest advantage of the pure sound medium lies in its direct appeal to the imagination. A child once said that he liked sound better than television 'because the scenery is better'. Of course the scenery is better: it is built in the mind of the listener. It is magic scenery, which can at times seem so solid that you feel you could bang your head against it; but in a moment it may dissolve into an insubstantial atmospheric abstraction. It is scenery within which not only people can stand but also ghosts. Ideas, emotions, impressions can be conjured up as easily as the camera can show reality.

Well, perhaps not quite so easily, because sound does require a greater contribution from the listener. To compel this involvement —and to deserve it—the material coming from the loudspeaker must maintain a high level of interest throughout. If it drops for one moment the imagination is turned off like a light, and all real communication is lost. The magic scenery is built and painted by the artists and craftsmen in the studio; but it is illuminated by the imagination of the listener.

The ways in which the imagination can be stimulated are many. To some extent they depend on form, which depends in turn on techniques. Apart from this, what is done, rather than the way it is done, is a matter for individual judgment or intuition.

In our analysis of the qualities of any programme we should perhaps take 'interest' as our starting point, because the one factor that all successful productions have in common is the ability to engage and retain the listener's interest. For a start, it is clear that interest depends on previous experience. What we know, we like; what we do not know leaves us relatively indifferent: this is true even of most people who regard themselves as being 'interested in anything'. For very few people indeed are interested in subjects that cannot be explained in terms of things that are already understood.

The reason is simple enough: any reference to something within the listener's experience can call up an image in his mind. When we listen to somebody talking we soon forget such superficial qualities as accent and voice timbre (unless we are forcibly reminded of them at any point); we do not listen closely to the actual words, but go straight to the meaning. The words we forget almost the moment they are spoken; the meaning we may retain. This meaning, together with its associations in the listener's mind, forms an image that may be concrete or abstract, or a mixture of the two. And if it is possible to present a subject in terms of a whole series of such images a considerable amount of interest may be aroused.

The audience

When a radio or television producer starts work he must bear in mind not only what he wants to say but also who he wants to say it to. This is not merely a matter of the listener's intelligence, but also of what sort of background he has; what sort of things he is likely to have learned at school and in later life; what sort of places he knows and people he has met; what sort of emotions he is likely to have experienced, and so on. It is also related most powerfully to the things he would *like* to do, consciously or not—ranging from taking up a life of meditation and prayer to winning a thousand pounds for saying that the Eiffel Tower is in Paris.

In practice many programmes develop a distinctive personality according to the characteristics of the audiences at which they are aimed, and may be further modified in style according to the time of day at which they are transmitted. But, all in all, the dominant factor in programme appeal is the previous background and knowledge of the listener; and failure to take proper account of this is one of the most serious mistakes any producer can make—if his aim is communication. I am not really concerned here with works of art where the artist is *not* interested in communication, I am certainly not decrying them. But if they are works of importance to anybody but the artist himself, teachers and critics busy themselves with explaining and relating until in the end communication between artist and public is established, just as though it had been intended.

In a study that was made of a number of BBC educational broadcasts in 1950, intelligibility was the main issue, but a few sidelights were thrown in 'interestingness'. It was noted that while too many main 'teaching points' (say six or more in a fifteen-minute programme) were definitely bad for a programme, the presence of what sometimes seemed to be an unduly large number of subsidiary points did not seem to result in the confusion that might have been expected; and also whereas long, complex sentences with difficult vocabulary (for this particular audience) and lots of prepositions (used as an index of complexity of construction) did appear to have a slightly adverse effect on intelligibility, the presence of a large number of adverbs and adjectives did not.

It seems reasonable to conclude that an apparent excess of facts, figures, and descriptive terms is no disadvantage, because although they may not be assimilated themselves, they help to maintain interest during the necessary gaps between the teaching points. Apart from any other function they may serve, these are the things that provide 'colour'; they are part of that vital series of images that the listener's imagination needs. And remember here that what is true for educational programmes is also true in the broader sense for a much wider range of programmes (on the larger canvas we can take 'adverbs and adjectives' to include any descriptive, or even simply amusing, piece of illustration in sound or picture).

For the particular audience of this survey (listeners to Forces Educational Broadcasts) concrete subjects were preferred to abstract ones; and, when ideas were being explained, concrete examples—references to people, incidents and actions—were preferred to high-flown 'clever' metaphors. This, too, must be a more general requirement. For apart from the genuine absent-minded professors of this world—the people for whom the world of the mind is more real than the world of reality—there can, I think, be few people for whom abstractions (except those dealing with the emotions) are more telling than are concrete references. Indeed, one danger was noted in the study: that well-developed illustrations can sometimes be so effective as to attract the attention away from the main point.

Obviously, this business of creating interest in the audience can be something of a struggle; but there need be no reason to regard it as a mystery.

If there's no picture—where is everybody?

Some problems in communication apply to one medium more than another. Before we turn to the more general case, let us consider one or two that apply particularly to the pure sound medium.

We have established that an advantage of sound lies in its direct appeal to the imagination; and that the really successful programme has one quality above all else—the ability to conjure up an unbroken succession of powerful images in the mind of the listener. These are not just imagined visual images, there to replace the concrete visual evidence that the eye is denied: they are a great deal more. Nevertheless, we must now recognize that some of the main limitations and disadvantages of sound do stem from the confusion caused by the lack of exact pictorial detail.

In our ordinary life we take this detail for granted in so many ways: when we take part in a conversation with half a dozen other people we are never in any doubt as to who is talking at any time; our eyesight combines with our faculty for judging direction aurally, and no thought is necessary. Indeed, we would have no difficulty in coping with almost any number of people; the ears localise and the eyes fix on the speaker immediately.

Without vision, the number of voices that we can conveniently sort out is reduced very considerably. In the case of stereophonic sound, half a dozen people, spread out and not moving around too much, should be fairly easy to place; but with more people (or with more movement) the picture becomes confusing. When this happens the imagination fails to do its stuff; the voices no longer appear as identities. And instead of a mental picture of a group of individuals, we merely register the sound as a quantity of de-personalized speech coming from various points in space.

In monophonic sound the picture is even more restricted: we have room for only three or four central participants in any scene at any one time, and even then the voices and characters must be very clearly differentiated. Further voices may come and go, provided that it does not matter if they do so in a fairly disembodied sort of way. The butler who comes in to say 'My Lord, the carriage awaits' does not count as an extra character to confuse the ear; he is hardly more than a sound effect. But the basic group must be small.

It must also be remembered that the moment a character falls silent, the audience 'loses' him. Leave him out of a conversation for half a dozen or more lines and he becomes invisible, so that when he speaks again his sudden re-entry into the middle of things can come as a shock; he seems to leap in from nowhere.

From this we already have one considerable restriction on subject and treatment. So beware: any feature that involves many-voiced scenes is going to sound terribly vague. And a discussion programme involving half a dozen speakers should not be embarked upon if it really matters that the listener should be able to sort out who is who—he will probably identify only about two or three speakers clearly. The extreme case is an open debate: this will be merely a succession of voices, though it may help a little if each speaker in turn is named. For clarity this must generally be done even when a voice has been heard before.

Often, of course, it does not matter that voices are not identified individually by the listener; but the producer must know what effect he is aiming for—and getting. If the voices are not pin-pointed, and especially if this is permitted without the producer being aware of the fact, then the audience will be living in a place of shadows when the artist thinks he is communicating a world of imagined substance. There is a great deal of difference between the two.

The next difficulty with sound is a related one: that of establishing location. This must be fixed as early as possible, and then constantly reaffirmed by acoustics, effects, references in the text—anything to prevent the scene slipping back into a vague grey limbo and becoming once again no more than a set of voices from a box.

On the other hand, it is often a positive advantage that the listener is not unnecessarily burdened by pictorial detail. During a television talk the eye is captured by the picture but may wander within it. It may shift to the clock on the shelf behind the speaker: it may be distracted by the shape of a lampshade, or the pattern on wallpaper. Without all that—given sound alone—the speaker becomes part of the atmosphere of the listener's own living-room.

These weaknesses and strengths must be seen before the treatment of a subject is chosen; it is important to allow for the frequent reiteration of locale in the scene of a play, or the formal disregard of surroundings in a straight talk.

It is obviously impossible to establish one picture, and one only, in the mind's eye of every single listener. So it is wise to avoid subjects that require precise pictorial detail, or treatments where the impact of a thing that is seen has to be explained in dialogue—in fact, any stories that depend heavily on visual information. Let us take as an example of this, the first meeting of boy and girl in a crowded room: eyes meet, fall, and meet again... it needs a Shakespeare to express verbally the magic of such a moment; and even in *Romeo and Juliet* the visual element adds immeasurably to the impact. Supress it, and the shape of the whole scene is altered.

And this example also illustrates another point: that direct emotional effects are best expressed visually. The close-up of the human face, and most particularly the eyes, can touch the audience directly. In terms of pure sound, using only the voice, parallels are are not easy to find.

The emotional link between screen and viewer can be very strong indeed. Vision is the dominant faculty, and it must be either fully engaged or completely suppressed if the audience is to identify itself with the actor. With film or television the link is simple, direct, and potentially compulsive. In sound only, the link has to be established indirectly but no less firmly through the imagination. The results may be quite as effective, but they are a great deal more difficult to achieve.

The time factor

As a medium, sound has a great deal in common with print. Both printed and spoken word can be presented as straight argument (or narrative) or as dialogue. There are comparable forms of illustration: the sound effect and the graphic display. And further, because of the restriction to a single channel of of communication, neither medium can engulf the senses without first making an extremely strong appeal to the imagination. The analogy is so good that it is worth considering where the differences lie: the more so as there is inevitably a tendency to assume that what can be done in print can also be done in sound.

The great difference lies in the dimension of time. The printed page leaves the time element in the hands of the reader. He can read at any speed he likes. He can read a novel in a few hours, or take weeks over a textbook. He can read one paragraph quickly and the next slowly. He can stop and go back when the meaning of something is not clear at first reading. In the process of reading the eye can afford to run on ahead in order to see how a sentence is shaped, and to take in its meaning as a whole.

For the radio (or television) audience the time relationship between successive elements of story is fixed absolutely. Similarly, once a listener has decided *when* he is going to play a record he has virtually no further control over any other aspect of time: for technical reasons, the interrelation of speed and pitch, he may not play the record faster or slower than was originally intended; nor should he be expected to jump on or back, or to stop and start as with a dictating machine.

To avoid ambiguity and aid understanding (if that is the intention), ideas must be presented in a clear logical sequence. And it is not only the order of the arguments that must be clear: the style in which they are presented must itself be lucid and lively. If possible, that is, if the subject matter does not militate against it, and sometimes even if it does, speech should be grammatical, as well as vivid in expression. Realistic dialogue, with its broken sentences, repetitions, fractured logic, and other inconsistencies, is often regarded as essential to modern writing. But if used carelessly it can also confuse the listener; and when this happens he will hear not meanings but words, and particularly any imperfections in the way they are spoken. The most frequent complaint about this sort of dialogue is 'inaudibility'—even when the sound would be adequate in other circumstances. This is not to say that it should never be done, only that it should be done only for good reason; and the degree of communication calculated.

Going to the other extreme, in the 'radio talk' by a single speaker with a prepared script, good delivery is still important. For some listeners, a bad speaker, obviously reading, and doing so from material written in a flat literary style that makes no concession to colloquial speech, will seriously diminish enjoyment. The listener may well ask, 'Why bother to present this in sound at all, when it is so obviously designed for print?' But this may be a minority view, for the quality of delivery has very little effect on intelligibility, and does not worry the majority of listeners any more than would any other relatively unimportant fault of technique. For example, many of the film-stars of the 'thirties now seem curiously stilted when we see revivals of their films; but this never prevented huge audiences from adoring them. Only if a programme is thrown completely out of balance, as, for example, by speech that is too fast, is faulty or 'unrealistic' delivery found upsetting.

It is reasonable to demand that the basic message of a piece should be understood in a single hearing—for both sound and television are basically one-shot media. By all means include deeper layers of meaning for the benefit of the people you hope will be shouting for an encore—or for whom your main points may be old hat. But a good basic assumption to start from is that no one will ever hear your creation twice.

If you find yourself donning a weak smile and saying to a fairly baffled audience, 'You'll probably see what I'm getting at if we hear it through again', then you may take it that you are almost certainly on the wrong lines. Only if you recognize this, is it at all likely that anyone will *want* to hear you twice. Of course, there are many important exceptions; and it is always tempting to assume that one's own work is such an exception. This is almost invariably a major error: so aim to make a major impact at the first hearing.

Understanding and remembering

Control over the rate at which ideas are presented is completely in the hands of the creator of a programme, so he must be particularly careful not to use this power in such a way as to impair intelligibility. There are two ways in which a producer may be tempted to disregard this need. The first of these is the quest for 'pace'—but as we shall see later, pace is not achieved by over-condensing vital information.

The second factor that may influence a producer is a more subtle one: it is his wish to present a subject in a tidy, well-shaped sort of way—in itself an unexceptionable aim. But, being by nature and education a fairly literate person, he all too often falls into the trap of assuming that what looks well shaped in the form of a script will also appear as a neat construction in its finished form, once such minor details as logical presentation and colloquial speech values have been attended to.

Unfortunately, this may not be the case. For the producer must also study one further vital factor: the rate at which new ideas are being presented. To take an extreme case: on the printed page, a concise, elegant argument can be presented neatly, tautly, as finely shaped as a mathematical theorem—and the eye will dwell on it until it is understood. In a broadcast, such a construction is out of the question.

In order to ensure at least a moderate degree of intelligibility in this constantly progressing medium, the argument must sometimes be slowed down to what in literary terms will often seem like an impossibly slack pace. The good magazine programme, play, or documentary may appear in script form to have a much looser construction than a well-written article or short story: there may perhaps be an apparent excess of illustration and padding. This is necessary because it seems that the brain will accept and retain material that is new to it only if that material is presented at no more than a certain speed. Even if a listener is intellectually equipped to follow a concise complex line of argument he needs time—more time than it takes to present the bare bones of the argument—if it is to sink in. He needs time to turn it over in his mind.

There is a clear analogy with the teaching process here. But learning—in the sense of the *permanent* retention of fact and argument—may not be the immediate result. *Repetition* plays an important part in learning; if something that is clearly understood in the first place is repeated after a few days, and once again after a few weeks, there is a reasonable chance of it being retained for a long time. Nevertheless, radio or television may help in the learning process, for although very few individual items will be given a second hearing by the audience, their content may be related to what they have read somewhere or heard in a previous programme, or know already. In such a case the content of the programme stands a much better chance of being understood and making some impact.

Clearly, learning is very much a matter of chance, or perseverance on the part of the audience. But the immediate effectiveness of any particular item is, or should be, more predictable: the producer must calculate his effects: he must allow sufficient time for the audience to take each point as he makes it. Certainly, this will affect the amount that remains in the mind after a programme is over, or the following day—but that is only half the story. If there is a logical argument or a narrative line involved, a single failure may render the whole programme incomprehensible, or considerably change its meaning. In the action of a play, for example, an understanding of points made early on is often essential to being able to follow developments at a later stage. Fail to establish a single important plot point and the play fails as a whole.

This is a matter of vital importance to a broadcasting organization such as the BBC, and it is perhaps not surprising that a number of experiments have been carried out to determine the intelligibility of programmes and the rate at which fact and argument can be absorbed.

One test was made with news bulletins to determine how many items and how much detail could be recalled by an attentive listener immediately after the end of the news. It turned out that only a small proportion was retained. Anyone with a tape recorder can very easily prove this for himself. Record ten minutes of news and then, before playing it back, try to write down all the items of news in as much detail as possible; the exact words are not important; the gist will do. Playback will confirm what will by then be pretty clear, that by far the greater part was missed. News on radio is the most convenient for this.

Another way of trying this experiment is in a group, as a sort of party game; if no recorder is available, one person should take down the subject matter and timings for particular items on a piece of paper. After listening to the news bulletin, try to reconstruct it by discussion and without help from the running order. And, incidentally, if a recorder *is* available it may be instructive to record the discussion as well as the original news; and then play them both back together; this will make it doubly clear just how vague one's memory is.

These experiments are called aural assimilation tests. Marks are awarded for major and minor points that are recalled, and are subtracted for errors. Many tests of this sort have been carried out, and the marks have always been low. The ear is not efficient at taking in ideas.

The other main enquiries were into the intelligibility of educational and current affairs broadcasts. One series of five-minute programmes called 'Topic for Tonight' was studied exhaustively. The aim of the item was to be simple and straightforward; to be understood without undue difficulty by the greater part of the mass audience. At the time of the survey, getting on for a third of

Britain's adult radio audience listened to this programme every week. It was respected and enjoyed by the vast majority. It was, on the whole, listened to attentively and thought to be interesting and informative.

The enquiry, which was thorough, showed that for the average case hardly more than a quarter of the talk sank home. Each talk was divided up into main and subsidiary points and marks were allocated according to their importance. Individual talks scored between 11 and 44%. The average was 28%.

It was quite clear that, simple as these talks already were, they could with benefit be simplified still further. If this could be done without giving an appearance of talking down—always to be avoided at all costs—the intelligibility could be increased a great deal. Direct faults in presentation were found in some cases: such things as taking too much background knowledge for granted; the use of unfamiliar words, or jargon, or flowery analogies or abstractions; poor logical construction or unnecessarily complex sentences. One of the major conclusions was that the presentation of the more important points should be better organized. Major points should be emphasized and repeated in such a way that it is quite clear which, out of all that is said, is the important part to grasp, and a summary at the end would improve things still further.

This particular survey was carried out for a specific programme aimed at a specific audience. But I think that the results would be valid for almost any type of programme (not just serious ones) and for any audience, provided account is taken of possible differences in background knowledge, literacy and intelligence.

The communication of ideas

Experience, together with the above experiments, seems to suggest this working rule: that *not less than three or four minutes of programme time should be devoted to any point of importance.*

This is very much a generalization, but if it errs, it is on the side of allowing too little time: these are pretty definitely *minimum* times for points of average complexity. Of course, for a fairly simple point it may be possible to get away with spending less than three minutes; and, on the other hand, a particularly complex point may need much longer to establish fully. But in this latter case it may be advisable to break the argument down into stages.

In a seven-minute item, for example, I would say that it is

503

possible to make two major points. The rest of the seven minutes must be spent in supporting and linking those points. There may be many minor points, but if a further major-point is introduced, then it is likely that one of the three will be lost. To take an extreme case, if the seven-minute piece is made to consist of seven important points, then nearly all of them will be lost, and the listener may be left with a frustrating feeling that he has missed something. Or alternatively, he may, perhaps, remember just one of the points that happens to appeal to him, plus the thought that this was part of a pattern that included half a dozen other points which on first hearing seemed plausible. But one cannot in this highly condensed case have an exact or predictable control over what the listener picks out and takes away with him. It may, in fact, be something totally unsuitable from the point of view of the producer, writer or speaker.

One can point to Sir Winston Churchill as a broadcaster who triumphantly mastered the technique: a study of recordings of his wartime speeches shows how he took each point in turn and attacked, analysed and presented it in a variety of ways before moving on to the next. Despite a difficult voice and an almost complete refusal to make any concession to radio (oratory is one of the 'dont's' of the medium) the results remain masterpieces.

So all broadcasters who want to get something over to their audience must follow these rules; they must, in fact, imitate the methods of a schoolteacher—though not too overtly, for unlike the teacher, they have no captive audience. A good teacher, at whatever level, aims to lay out his subject in just the way I have described. However, in the classroom his pace is subject to immediate correction by his pupils; with the constant reminder of their presence he is on the whole more likely to stick to the correct rate of presentation than is the man who talks to an invisible audience, who may feel himself under pressure to 'get on with it' because everyone about him is behaving as though air time is valuable (which it is) and because he feels he has more to say than time to say it.

This rule about good layout is more clearly valid for programmes that seek to educate and inform; it is also true for most of those whose outward purpose is solely to entertain, and in particular those with a narrative element; stories, plays, and so on. I say outward purpose, because most writers, whether serious or comic, are at heart moral people (in one sense or another), and whatever they write expresses something of their system of values.

504

At this deeper level, the level of the writer's basic philosophy, whether homespun or sophisticated, whether noble or just plain anti-social, the same rule applies: time is necessary for communication.

Pace

The term *pace* has already crept into this discussion: let us attempt to define it more precisely.

To maintain interest, a story or an argument must be kept moving at a fairly brisk rate. So the secret of pace is *to allot just sufficient time to each point for it to be adequately understood—and then move on*. Pace is impossible without intelligibility. It is perhaps odd that it should depend to such a degree on *not* going too fast. But there it is: pace is a sort of shaping of the programme in time, and it provides the basic foundation on which the finer details must be built.

When we talk of lack of pace, we are often thinking of another, seondary, defect which frequently afflicts the work of those without access to skilled critical analysis: a sort of superficial slackness that has as its origin the lack of an adequate sense of timing. But it is the other more subtle fault, lack of organization in the underlying shape, that is more likely to mar professionally produced shows that are slick enough to all outward appearance.

To sum up: in the construction of almost any successful programme we must have a series of basic units each occupying a few minutes. Each of these should contain one major point and sufficient supporting detail to help establish it as clearly as possible. There may also be material that retains the attention of the listener in between the major points that are to be made, but which may not be of direct importance to them, and which must not actively draw the listener's attention away from them. Quite apart from anything else, this sort of construction helps to provide necessary light and shade within a piece—that is to say, some variation in the pressure of attack. And that again is absolutely essential to a feeling of pace in the final product.

All this affects the choice of form for the presentation of a particular subject. An argument that is by its nature concise may have to be filled out by extra material: illustration perhaps, repetition in a different way, anything. Or an extra point that seems to be creeping in may have to be cut, because it is interesting enough to distract the listener from the main line that is being followed, but cannot be allowed its own full development.

Certain types of construction, whether in radio, television or film, simply do not work: they contain too much argument in too little time. The cool, swift logic of a mathematical theorem, or a solid, indigestible, encyclopaedic mass of essential detail are both death to clear, intelligible construction in sound.

Of course, there are exceptions to all such rules. As a television producer, director or writer who enjoys dealing with complex themes, I never construct by rote, but instead work outward from the story, the meaning, the material itself. Often the results may be criticized as overturning some of the tenets of communication, and testing others to the limit, which at least avoids deadening uniformity or predictability. But I believe that the programmes that seem to have succeeded despite breaking all the rules invented are in reality those that stick most closely, if subtly, to the ideal form.

GLOSSARY

As well as short definitions, some indication of the context in which terms may be used is given. Unless otherwise indicated, the term is usually in international use, although local variants may exist. Where usage in Britain (*Br.*) and America (*Am.*) differs markedly both forms are given. Certain expressions that seem to have originated in BBC usage are so indicated. No attempt is made here or elsewhere in this book to enter into a study of basic electrical theory, or to describe equipment or circuits in technical detail.

A   'A' SIGNAL. In stereo, the signal to be fed to the left-hand loudspeaker of a two-speaker system.

ABSORPTION COEFFICIENT. The fraction of sound absorbed on reflection at any surface. It therefore takes values between 0 and 1, and unless otherwise stated, is for a frequency of 512 Hz at normal incidence. *Soft absorbers* depend for their action on such things as the friction of air particles in the interstices of the material. This friction increases with particle velocity, and the absorption is therefore greatest where particle velocity is greatest, i.e. at a quarter wavelength from the reflecting surface. Soft absorbers (glass wool, fibre board, etc.) in layers a few cm in depth are poor absorbers at low frequencies and are fair to good at middle and high frequencies. If the outer surface is hard (e.g. painted) and unperforated, the high frequency absorption will deteriorate. *Membrane and vibrating panel absorbers* are, in effect, boxes with panels and cavities that can be tuned to resonate at particular frequencies or broad frequency bands. They readily remove sound energy from the air at their resonant frequency and this is then mopped up within the absorber by various forms of damping. Such absorbers may be efficient at low and middle frequencies. *Helmholtz resonators* respond to narrow bands and if damped internally remove them selectively.

ACETATE. (*a*) Cellulose acetate, a material used as a tape base (i.e. the backing on which the magnetic oxide coating is carried). Tends to break rather than stretch when subjected to excessive stress, and so can be mended easily. (*b*) Colloquial term for direct-cut lacquer disc.

ACOUSTIC REPRODUCTION OF EFFECTS, ETC. (from tape or disc). A feed of prerecorded sound to a loudspeaker in the studio instead of directly to the mixer. The sound picked up by the studio microphone depends on the characteristics of the

507

loudspeaker and microphone, and the studio acoustics and balance. It may be noticeably different from the original sound even if a close balance is used (often the loudspeaker is balanced at a separate microphone). Acoustic reproduction techniques may be used either to modify the sound or to provide cues when no other method (headphones, cue lights or hand signals) is possible. In the latter case volume should be kept as low as practicable, otherwise there may be a noticeable change of quality due to acoustic coloration. See FOLDBACK.

ACOUSTICS. The study of the behaviour of sound. The acoustics of an enclosed space depend on its size and shape, and the number and position of absorbers. The *apparent acoustics* of a studio depend on the effect of the acoustics on the indirect sound reaching the microphone, and also on the ratio of direct to indirect sound. Thus, apparent acoustics depend on the microphone position, distance and angle from the sound source (i.e. the balance) and also on the level of sound reproduction. Besides this, the actual acoustics of the studio may be modified close to the microphone by the placing of screens, etc.

ACTUALITY. Recording of the actual sound of an event, as distinct from a report, interview or dramatized reconstruction.

AMBIENT NOISE. In any location, from quiet studio or living-room to busy street, there is a background of sound. In a particular location the ear automatically adjusts to and accepts this ambient noise in all except the loudest (or quietest) case. In a monophonic recording, however, noise at a natural level generally sounds excessive. One purpose of microphone balance is to discriminate against such noise, where necessary. Unexplained noises in particular should be avoided. See also ATMOSPHERE.

AMPLIFIER. A device for increasing the strengh of a signal by means of a varying control voltage. At each stage the input is used to control the flow of current in a circuit that is carrying much more power. Precautions (feedback) may be necessary to ensure that the degree of amplification does not vary with frequency. In successive stages the magnification of the signal (i.e. ratio of output to input) may be much the same, so that the rise in signal strength is approximately exponential. Relative levels may therefore conveniently be measured in decibels (q.v.).

AMPLITUDE MODULATION (AM). A method whereby the information in an audio signal is carried on the much higher frequency of a radio wave. The envelope of the amplitude of the radio wave in successive cycles is equivalent to the wave form of the initial sound. Historically, AM is the method used first and such transmissions now crowd the short, medium and long wave bands. This crowding restricts the upper limit of the frequencies that can effectively be broadcast without the transmitter bandwidth overlapping an adjacent channel. The random background of radio noise that a receiver is bound to pick up at all frequencies also appears as minor fluctuations in the amplitude of the carrier wave, and cannot be distinguished electrically from the audio signal. For high quality transmission AM has largely given way to FM (frequency modulation).

ARTIFICIAL REVERBERATION ('echo'). Simulation of the natural die-away of sound that occurs in a room or any other enclosed space (e.g. in a cave, down a well, etc.). Such techniques are used when the available studio acoustics are not reverberant enough. Multi-microphone techniques for music need 'echo', as the studios used are normally much less reverberant than those used for natural balance. The technique is used to permit different treatment to be applied to each microphone output: after separate control of individual instruments or groups, their sound is fed at appropriate levels to the echo device.

508

ATMOSPHERE. The background sound at any location. This may not be un-desirable, in that such atmosphere lends authenticity and gives listeners a sense of participation in an event. Even so, it may be advisable to discriminate against back-ground sound in the main recording, and record atmosphere separately for subsequent mixing at an appropriate level (which may not be held constant). When proper monitoring conditions are available at the time of recording (or broadcast), separate microphones may be set up and the mixture again judged by ear. *Studio atmosphere* is the ambient noise, and it may at times be obtrusive even in a soundproofed room—particularly if omnidirectional microphones are used for other than close balances. The slightest movement, the flow of air for ventilation or even heavy breathing, may create problems for the balancer. See also AMBIENT NOISE.

ATTENUATION. Fixed or variable losses (usually in an electrical signal). As with amplification it is convenient to measure this in decibels (q.v.). See FADER.

AXIS (of microphone or loudspeaker). Line through centre of diaphragm and at a right angle to it. It is usually an axis of structural symmetry in at least one plane, and thus an axis about which the polar response is symmetrical. Also, it is generally the line of maximum high frequency response.

AZIMUTH. The angle that the gap of a recording or reproducing head makes with the line along which the tape moves. This should be exactly 90°. Misalignment may be due to incorrect setting of the head, or to the tape transport system not being parallel to the deck, and may be corrected by adjustment to either. Adjustment of a reproducing head may be made using a standard recording of high frequency tone (i.e. one recorded with a correctly adjusted head). Maximum output, which may be judged by ear or by meter, occurs when alignment is correct. A separate recording head may then be adjusted by recording tone with it and checking for maximum output from the reproducing head. Alternatively, satisfactory adjustment can usually be made using speech or music recordings. Azimuth misalignment produces a recording (or reproduction) apparently lacking in top. Although it is a common fault, many owners of cheaper tape recorders may not be aware of its presence, because tape replayed on the head used for recording does not exhibit faults that would be at once apparent if the tape were replayed on most other machines.

B 'B' SIGNAL. In stereo, the signal to be fed to the right-hand loudspeaker of a two-speaker system.

BACKING. The base on which the magnetic coating of tape is carried. It gives strength and permits flexibility, and although it has no screening effect its thickness ensures that the physical separation of successive layers of the magnetic coating is sufficient to maintain printing at a low level. Common materials are cellulose acetate, PVC and polyester.

BACKING TRACK. Prerecording of the accompaniment to a singer (etc.) who then listens to a replay on headphones as he contributes his own performance. At this stage the two are mixed to give the final recording. The performer's (and other musicians') time is saved, and adequate separation is achieved without the use of separate studios. *Back tracking* is the technique in which a preliminary recording by the same artists is used as the accompaniment.

BAFFLE. (*a*) A rigid screen around a loudspeaker diaphragm, extending the acoustic path from front to rear in order to reduce the flow of air around the edge of the speaker at low frequencies—an effect that causes serious loss of bass. (*b*) A small acoustic screen that causes a local variation in the acoustic field close to the micro-phone diaphragm. A baffle of hardboard, card, etc., when clipped to a microphone sets up a standing wave system at the diaphragm, distorting the sound. In some microphones, gauze baffles are used as an integral part of the design to improve the response.

BALANCE. The relative placing of microphones and sound sources in a given acoustic, designed to pick up an adequate signal, discriminate against noise, and provide a satisfactory ratio of direct to indirect sound. This is the responsibility of a *balance engineer, sound supervisor* or (in BBC radio) a *studio manager*.

BALANCE TEST. Consists of one or a series of trial balances which should preferably be judged by direct comparison.

BAND. Separately recorded section of a disc, of which there may be several on a side. By extension, the term may also mean an individual section of a tape recording bounded by spacers. Locations may be indicated on a script in shorthand form, e.g. 'S2B3' = side 2, band 3.

BASS. Lower end of the musical scale. In acoustics it is generally taken as the range (below 200 Hz, say) in which difficulties (principally in the reproduction of sound) are caused by the large wavelengths involved. Loudspeakers that depend on the movement of air by cones or plates (e.g. moving coil or electrostatic types) become inefficient in their *bass response* at wavelengths greater than their dimensions. This is due to too small a piston attempting to drive what is at these frequencies too pliant a mass of air. Certain systems of mounting (or cabinets) extend the bass response by means of a resonance in the octave below the frequency at which cut-off begins, but this results in a sharper cut-off when it does occur (e.g. bass reflex and column resonance types). *Bass lift* may be resorted to, but requires a more powerful amplifier (most power is concentrated in the bass of music, anyway) and a loudspeaker system capable of greater excursions without distortion. An efficient way of producing bass is an acoustic exponential horn with a low rate of flare. This ensures that coupling between the moving elements and the air outside is good, up to wavelengths approaching the diameter of the mouth of the horn.

BASS TIP-UP. This occurs with directional microphones when they are situated in a sound field that shows an appreciable loss of intensity in the distance travelled from front to back of microphone. The operation of the microphone depends on the pressure gradient and is exaggerated at low frequencies. At middle frequencies the effect is masked by the phase shift that occurs in this path distance in any case; and at high frequencies the mode of operation is by pressure and no longer by pressure gradient.

BEAT. If two tones within about fifteen Hz of each other are played together the combined signal is heard to pulsate, or beat, at the difference frequency. Two tones may be synchronized by adjusting the frequency of one until the beat slows and finally disappears.

BIAS. A carrier frequency with which the audio signal is combined in order to reduce distortion during tape recording. Its importance is greatest in recording low frequencies. It is generally of the order of 50–100 kHz and is produced by an oscillator associated with the tape recorder amplifier. It mostly vanishes from the tape soon after recording, by a process of self-demagnetization. However, a little of the bias signal can still be heard if recorded tape is pulled slowly over the reproducing head. The bias oscillator also supplies the erase head.

BIDIRECTIONAL MICROPHONE. One that is live on the front face and back, but dead at the sides and above and below. The polar response is a figure-of-eight.

510

BOARD, CLAPPERBOARD, SLATE. In film, a means of marking the start of each shot with scene and take numbers. It is held open for mute scenes (those shot without sound); for sync takes the scene and take number are identified on sound and then the board is clapped in vision so that sound and picture can subsequently be matched. When large quantities of film are handled in the cutting room, this method of marking is more convenient than electronic techniques.

BOOM. A telescopic arm (attached to a floor mounting) from which a microphone is slung.

BOOMY. Subjective description of a sound quality with resonances in the low frequencies, or a broad band of bass lift. Expressions with similar shades of meaning are tubby or, simply, bassy.

BRIGHT SURFACE. Strongly reflecting surface, particularly of high frequencies.

BROADCAST CHAIN. The sequence: studio—continuity suite—transmitter—receiver, together with any intermediate control or switching points, through which a signal passes.

BULK ERASER. See ERASER.

BUTT CHANGE-OVER. A change-over in mid-programme from one tape or disc to another, the second being started as the cue on the first is about to come up. The cross-over from one reproduction to the other should not be noticeable.

C   CANCELLATION. Partial or complete opposition in phase, so that the sum of two signals approaches or reaches zero.

CANS. Headphones.

CAPACITANCE. The ability of an electrical component, or components to store static charge. Charges present in a conductor attract opposite charges to nearby but not electrically connected conductors; changes of charge induce corresponding changes of charge in nearby conductors. A signal may therefore cross between components where there is no direct path. Capacitors are used in electronics for coupling, smoothing and tuning purposes. In lines, capacitance is the mechanism whereby the signal is gradually lost (capacitance between the wires or to earth). Capacitance varies with distance between plates, or other components: this variation is used in electrostatic microphones and loudspeakers. *Stray capacitances* form the mechanism whereby audio signals or mains hum is transferred unintentionally from one component to another nearby.

CAPSTAN. (*Am.:* Puck.) Drive spindle of tape deck: the tape is driven between the capstan and an idler pulley which presses against it when the machine is switched to record or replay. The diameter of the spindle and the motor speed determine the speed of the tape. It is possible, by fitting a sleeve of twice the diameter of the spindle to double the top speed of replay; sleeves of other diameters may be used to produce other speeds, a device that has been used in radiophonic work. If the rotation of the spindle is eccentric there is a rapid fluctuation in tape speed, causing a flutter in the signal.

CAPSULE. (*a*) Removable pick-up head. (*b*) A condenser microphone capsule is the diaphragm assembly.

511

CARBON MICROPHONE. Microphone in which the audio signal is produced by varying the resistance of a button of granular carbon to which a polarizing voltage is applied (a diaphragm presses on the carbon button). It has been used as a telephone microphone, and at one time (in a slightly different design) in radio. Not now used for high quality work.

CARDIOID MICROPHONE. Microphone with a heart-shaped polar diagram (arrived at by adding omnidirectional and figure-of-eight responses together, taking into account the phase reversal at the back of the latter). Some microphones consist of the two component types together in a single case, and working in parallel. In electrostatic (condenser) microphones (q.v.) the combination occurs in the principle of construction. See PRESSURE GRADIENT.

CASSETTE, CARTRIDGE. A fully encapsulated tape system that does not need to be laced up. It employs a special narrow tape. For half-track mono recordings the layout of the two tracks is the same as for standard spool-to-spool tape, i.e. the top track is played from left to right, and then the cassette is turned over so that the other track may be played in a similar manner. The stereo cassette recording layout is different from that on standard tape: A and B information is carried on tracks 1 and 2 and can therefore be reproduced on a mono replay machine, which scans both tracks to produce an A + B signal. Cassettes (or cartridges) are also used for endless tape loops, in this case often employing standard-width tape. To avoid confusion it is probably best to use the term cartridge for the endless loop system, and cassette for the encapsulated double-spool system.

CCIR CHARACTERISTIC. In tape recording, the pre-emphasis and subsequent equalization standard used in Britain and Continental Europe (set by the Comité Consultatif International des Radiocommunications.) See also NARTB and RIAA.

CEMENTED JOINT (permanent joint). A method of editing tape in which the two ends are overlapped and fixed together by an adhesive or bonding agent. As there is a slight step in the tape, this type of joint is marginally more likely to cause a momentary loss of signal on subsequent re-use than is the butt joint, which leaves the surface smooth and substantially continuous.

CERAMIC MICROPHONE OR PICK-UP. This is similar in principle to a crystal type, but its barium titanate element is less sensitive to temperature and humidity.

CHANNEL. Complete set of (professional) recording equipment. Recording room (or part of recording room that can operate independently to record a programme). See also MICROPHONE CHANNEL.

CINÉ SPOOLS. See SPOOLS.

CLEAN FEED (*Am.:* mixed-minus.) A cue feed back to a programme source that includes all but the contribution from that source.

CLEAN SOUND. Actuality sound of an event, without superimposed commentary.

CLOCK. See VIDEOTAPE CLOCK, TIME CODE.

COATING (emulsion). The layer of finely divided magnetic material, bonded in plastic and polished to allow smooth flow over the tape heads, that carries the magnetically recorded signal. Ferric oxide and chromium dioxide are both used as the recording medium, the latter having the better performance (thereby permitting lower tape speeds, narrower tracks, etc.).

512

COCKTAIL PARTY EFFECT. The means whereby a listener can concentrate on a single conversion in a crowd depends largely on the spatial spread of sound, a quality that is lost in monophonic recording—so that if a cocktail party type of background sound is recorded at a realistic level it is not only unpleasantly obtrusive but also seriously impedes intelligibility of foreground speech.

COINCIDENT PAIR. In stereo, a pair of directional microphones or a double microphone with two directional elements mounted close to each other (usually one above the other) and at an angle to pick up the A and B signals. This technique avoids the phase interference effects produced by a spaced pair.

COLORATION. Distortion of frequency response by resonance peaks. Marked acoustic coloration in a studio may be due to the coincidence of dimensional resonances, to wall-panel resonances, or to frequency-selective excessive absorption of sound. Some mild acoustic coloration may, however, be beneficial. Coloration is often exhibited by microphones and loudspeakers, and in these is generally unwanted. Nevertheless, many people, preferring what they are already used to, 'like a loudspeaker to sound like a loudspeaker', i.e. to exhibit cone and cabinet resonances, rather than the disembodied perfection of a smooth frequency response. Coloration may also be caused by loud distant sound spilling to a microphone set for a quiet source.

COMMAG. Combined magnetic film sound, i.e. with the sound on a magnetic track running beside the picture, and recorded 28 frames ahead of it. Note: wide screen combined magnetic prints have their sound recorded after the picture.

COMOPT. Combined optical film sound: the sound track is recorded beside the picture, but advanced from it by $19\frac{1}{2}$ or 20 frames (35 mm) or by $25\frac{1}{2}$ or 26 frames (16 mm). See OPTICAL SOUND.

COMPACT DISC. Commercially-available recording which is digitally coded and read by laser. Since the noise level is low, a greater dynamic range is available – which may show up problems at other points in the audio chain.

COMPATIBILITY. In stereo, the requirement that a recording or broadcast can also be heard satisfactorily in mono; in quadraphony, that satisfactory stereo and mono are obtainable. Special measures may be needed for the *artistic compatibility* of stereo or quadraphonic recordings or broadcasts.

COMPENSATION. Control of levels. e.g. between the voices of a duologue, in order to place them in a suitable sound-volume relationship. Compensation is an imprecise term, and may also refer to other forms of adjustment of imbalance.

COMPLIANCE. The ease with which a stylus can be displaced sideways: the ratio of displacement to applied force. It is the inverse of the (mechanical) stiffness of the system. Vertical compliance is also necessary in order to reproduce a stereo signal. Compliance is the acoustical and mechanical equivalent of capacitance and also enters into the theory of microphone and loudspeaker construction.

COMPRESSION. Control of levels in order to ensure that (*a*) recorded or broadcast signals are suitably placed between the noise and distortion levels of the medium, and (*b*) the relationship between maximum and minimum volumes is acceptable to the listener who in his own home may not wish to hear the greatest volume of sound that he would accept in a concert hall, and who may be listening against background noise. *Manual compression* seeks by various means to maintain as much of the original dynamics as is artistically desirable and possible, and varies in degree with

513

the expected listening conditions. The purpose of *automatic compression*, in short wave transmissions, is to bring peak volumes consistently to full modulation of the carrier. It is also used in the transmitter of radio microphones to prevent overloading at a point where volume cannot be controlled, and in pop music to limit the dynamic range of the voice or a particular instrument. Above a selected onset volume, say 8 dB below full modulation, compression is introduced in a ratio that may be selected: e.g. 2:1, 3:1, 4:1, or 5:1.

COMPUTER MIXDOWN. See MIX, also DIGITAL AUDIO TECHNIQUES, PULSE CODE MODULATION.

CONDENSER MICROPHONE. See ELECTROSTATIC MICROPHONE.

CONE. A piston of stiff felted paper or possibly of plastics. It should be light and rigid. Paper cones are often corrugated to reduce any tendency to 'break up' radially and produce sub-harmonic oscillations. Elliptical cones give a greater spread of high frequencies out along the minor axis: they should therefore be mounted with the major axis vertical.

CONTACT MICROPHONE. A device for picking up sound transmitted within a solid: an important application is in the reverberation plate.

CONTINUITY. Linking between radio programmes, including opening and closing announcements (when these are not provided in the studio), station identification, trailers and other announcements.

CONTINUITY SUITE. A centre through which programmes are routed or where they are reproduced to build a particular service ready for feeding to a transmitter or to provide source material for other programme services.

CONTROL. The adjustment of programme levels (in the form of an electrical signal) to make them suitable for feeding to recorder or transmitter; where necessary, this includes compression. Mixing involves the separate control of a number of individual sources. At a *control desk* there are faders (individual, group and main control), associated cue systems, echo and equalization controls, etc., (where required) and a variety of communications equipment. A *control line* between one location and another is a telephone circuit on which programme details may be discussed, and is so called to distinguish it from the broad band (i.e. high quality) 'music line' along which programme is fed. A control line may, of course, be narrow-band, but for outside broadcasts it is safer to use lines of equal quality so that the two are interchangeable.

CONTROL CUBICLE (*BBC radio*). The soundproof room occupied by production and operational staff and equipped with control desk, gramophone and tape reproducers and high quality loudspeaker.

CONTROL ROOM. In BBC radio, a switching centre; otherwise, the sound mixing room.

COPY EDITING. The copying of selected extracts from recorded material into sequence on a main programme assembly tape.

COPYRIGHT. The law in relation to the ownership of creative works, which is initially vested in the author, composer or artist. In Britain this extends to 50 years after the author's death (expiring at the end of the calendar year). For private study, research, criticism or review, 'fair dealing' provisions generally permit extracts without payment. Otherwise payment must always be made, the details being arranged by negotiation with the author or his agent. Sound recordings, films and broadcasts are also protected by copyright and are not subject to the 'fair dealing' exceptions. Thus a gramophone record may have two copyrights, that of the composer and that of the company that made the recording, and the two may extend from different dates. Public performance of music and records, etc., is easy to arrange, and fees are small (usually paid through the Performing Rights Society) but recording or re-recording—except of music recorded specially for the purpose (mood music)—is permitted only with elaborate safeguards, and even so permission may be difficult to obtain. Copying of records and films for private purposes is not permitted. In Britain, the BBC and its contributors' unions do permit the recording of schools and further education programmes by schools and colleges, provided that the recordings are used only for instructional purposes and that they are destroyed at the end of specified periods. There is no copyright in events: e.g. an impromptu speech or interview without a script or casual sound effects (though recordings of them are). Dramatic or musical performers are also protected; their permission must be obtained before a record is made of their performances other than for private or domestic purposes. Copyright laws are easily evaded and owners are justly concerned at the losses they undoubtedly sustain. Copyright laws vary considerably in detail from country to country—the above comments relate mainly to British law.

COTTAGE LOAF CHARACTERISTIC. See HYPERCARDIOID.

CRAB. Move camera or sound boom sideways relative to the performing area.

CROSSED MICROPHONES. See COINCIDENT PAIR.

CROSS FADE. A gradual mix from one sound source or group of sources to another. During this, both faders (or groups) are open at the same time. The rate of fade can be varied manually if desirable for artistic effect.

CROSSOVER. The frequency at which a signal is split in order to feed separate parts of a loudspeaker. *Crossover network*. The filter that accomplishes this.

CROSSTALK. In stereo, the breakthrough between channels. The separation (in dB) between wanted and unwanted sound is checked by feeding tone at zero level through one channel and measuring its level in the other. Outputs of -37 dB at 1 kHz rising to -30 dB at 50Hz and 10 kHz are reasonable. Crosstalk also means breakthrough (or 'induction') of signal between any other pair of lines, e.g. on a telephone circuit.

CRYSTAL MICROPHONE OR GRAMOPHONE PICK-UP. This generates a signal by means of a crystal bimorph—two plates cut from different planes of a crystal such as Rochelle salt and held together in the form of a sandwich. Twisting the bimorph produces a voltage (termed a *piezo-electric* voltage) between foil plates on top and bottom surfaces of the sandwich. The principle is well suited to use in a gramophone pick-up, as the frequency response is a fair match to the characteristic needed to reproduce gramophone records. This means that the output level after equalization is higher than it would otherwise be and smaller amplifiers are needed. The whole assembly can be very light in weight and may be cheap to produce. Crystals are widely used in inexpensive equipment in such a way as to obtain maximum output. Alternatively, at the loss of some output, a crystal assembly with a smoother response may be engineered. Rochelle salt is affected by temperature and humidity, so that in the past crystal microphones and pick-ups have not been used in the tropics. However, the crystal can now be effectively protected.

CUE. Signal to start. This may take the form of a cue light or a hand cue, or may be related to a pre-arranged point in a script. Headphones or, exceptionally, a loudspeaker may also be used for cueing.

CUE MATERIAL. Introductory matter supplied with a recording for the scriptwriter to fashion into a cue for announcer or narrator to read.

CUE PROGRAMME. A feed for cueing purposes.

CUT (*Am.*). One of several separately recorded bands (q.v.) on a disc.

CYCLE. One complete excursion of an air particle when vibrating in a sound, or the corresponding signal in electrical or any other form.

CYCLES PER SECOND (cps). Now written Hz. See FREQUENCY, HERTZ.

D DB. Decibel (q.v.).

DEAD ACOUSTIC. One in which a substantial loss is introduced at every reflection. For studio work this is the nearest approximation to an outdoor acoustic (in which little or no sound is reflected).

DEAD ROOM (anechoic chamber). Has very thick soft absorbers (typically about a metre) and is used for testing the frequency response of microphones and loudspeakers. Such an acoustic is unsuited to use as a studio because of its claustrophobic effect.

DEAD SIDE (of microphone). The angles within which the response of a microphone is low compared with the on-axis response. In figure-of-eight microphones this is taken to be about $50°-130°$ from the axis; in cardioids, the entire rear face. In the dead region there may be rapid changes in response with only slight movement of position, and the frequency response is more erratic than on the live side(s). In a studio these effects may be masked by the pick-up of reflected sound on the live sides.

DEADROLL (*Am.*). See PREFADE.

DECAY CHARACTERISTIC (of studio). The curve that indicates how the sound intensity falls after a steady note is cut off. It is generally slightly erratic. Plotted in decibels against time, decay should (roughly) follow a single straight line, and not be broken-backed.

DECIBEL (dB). A measure of relative intensity, power or voltage. Sound intensity is the power flowing through unit area and is calculated relative to a reference level of 2×10^{-5} N/m^2 (Newtons per square metre, q.v.). The threshold of hearing at 1000 Hz is at about this level for many young people. However, the aural sensation of loudness is not directly proportional to intensity (I) but to the logarithm of the intensity. It is therefore convenient to measure differences in intensity in units that follow a logarithmic scale, i.e. decibels. Differences of intensity in decibels are calculated as $10 \log_{10}$ (I_2/I_1). Thus, a tenfold increase in intensity is equivalent to a rise of 10 decibels (i.e. 1 Bel). Doubling the intensity gives a rise of almost exactly 3 dB. In a circuit the power is proportional to the square of the voltage, so that for a particular impedance a power ratio may be expressed in decibels as $10 \log (V_2{}^2/V_1{}^2)$, or $20 \log (V_2/V_1)$. This means that a range of $1:1,000,000,000,000$ in intensity is equivalent to $1:1,000,000$ in voltage. Note that the voltage scale dB (V) is used for microphones, and that this is not the same as the acoustic intensity scale dB (A). In acoustics the decibel is also

516

convenient in that it can be regarded (very roughly) as the minimum audible difference in sound level. A change in speech or music level of 2 dB or less is not ordinarily noticeable to anyone who is not listening for it. Loudness levels are measured in *phons* (q.v.). For dBA, dBN, and PNdB, see NOISE.

DE-GAUSS or DE-FLUX. Demagnetize (e.g. a tape recording head, or scissors or blades used for cutting tape). Wipe or erase (tape) in bulk.

DELAY LINE. Device that electronically delays a signal—for example by (switched) multiples of 7.5 milliseconds.

DIAPHRAGM. The part of a microphone upon which the pressure of a sound-wave acts. In size it should be small enough not to suffer substantial high frequency phase cancellation for sound striking the diaphragm at an angle, and big enough to present a sufficiently large catchment area to the pressure of the sound wave. In microphones working on certain principles the diaphragm mass may be small. In such designs (e.g. the condenser microphones) there are minimal inertial effects and therefore a very good transient response.

DIFFERENCE TONE. A perceived frequency 'heard' when two tones are played together, e.g. if 1000 Hz and 1100 Hz are played, 100 Hz may also be perceived.

DIFFUSION OF SOUND. The degree to which sound waves are broken up by uneven surfaces, and by the placing of absorbers more or less equally in all parts of the studio rather than allowing them to cluster in one particular part. A high degree of diffusion is desirable in a sound studio.

DIGITAL AUDIO TECHNIQUES. In these, an audio signal which was initially obtained as an electrical *analogue* of the sound is converted into binary form, in which form it may be operated upon, fed to random access memory stores, etc. While in this state the signal is not subject to the characteristic degradation of signal-to-noise ratio that occurs with an analogue signal. It is therefore well suited to the recording or transmission of sound in cases where this would be troublesome. The signal must be converted back to analogue form before it is broadcast or fed through components designed to operate on the signal in that form.

DIN (Deutsche Industrie Norm). German industrial standard. Most commonly met as a film rating, but standard are also applied to tape equalization characteristics and items of equipment such as plugs and sockets.

DIRECT-CUT DISC. One made by cutting the groove, rather than by pressing in plastic material by means of a stamper. These are made of cellulose nitrate (which contains a castor oil plasticizer to soften it for easy cutting) but are often referred to as 'acetates'.

DIRECTIVITY PATTERN. Polar diagram (q.v.).

DISC. Record, either direct-cut or pressed. The latter is also called a pressing, or, when commercially sold, a gramophone record.

DISCRETE QUADRAPHONY. Four-channel sound in which the four signals are kept separate. See also MATRIXED QUADRAPHONY.

DISSONANCE. The sensation produced by two tones in the region of about a semitone or full tone apart. As the tones get closer together they beat together and finally become concordant; as they get further apart the dissonant sensation disappears, and for pure tones does not return with increasing separation. However, dissonances and concords also arise from the presence of harmonics. The sensation of dissonance is sometimes described as unpleasant, but 'astringent' would perhaps be a better antithesis to the sweetness of consonance.

DISTORTION. Unwanted changes of sound quality, in the frequency response, or by the generation of unwanted products. *Harmonic distortion* is most easily caused by flattening of peaks in the waveform. The human voice and nearly all musical instruments possess a harmonic sound structure that tends to mask the distortion unless it is very severe. 1% harmonic distortion is not usually noticeable. *Intermodulation distortion* is, however, more serious, because it includes sum and product frequencies that are not necessarily harmoncally related to those already present.

DROP-OUT. Loss of signal due to a fault in tape coating.

DRY ACOUSTIC. Lacking in reverberation. By way of mixed metaphor, the opposite is 'warm' or 'bright.'

DUBBING. Copying, to arrange for material to be available in convenient form, e.g. transferring music from disc to tape. Also, copying together and combining effects or music with pre-recorded speech. In film, the mixing of all sounds to a single final track (or the several stereo tracks).

DUSTING POWDER. A fine powder that adheres to tacky points after a tape joint has been made, and ensures that the tape unwinds without pulling and does not drag as it passes over the heads and guide pillars.

DYNAMIC LOUDSPEAKER, MICROPHONE OR PICK-UP. See MOVING COIL.

DYNAMIC RANGE is the range of volumes in a programme. It may be measured as the range of peak values (i.e. the difference between the highest PPM readings at passages of maximum and minimum volume) or, alternatively, the range of average volume. It may refer either to the range of the original sound, or to what remains of it after compression.

DYNAMICS. The way in which volume of sound varies internally within a musical work (or in a speech or speech-and-music programme). It may refer to the variation of levels within the work as a whole, or from note to note, or in the envelope of a single note.

E   EARPHONE, EARPIECE. One side of a pair of headphones (q.v.), for placing close to the ear. Alternatively, an ear-fitting of the hearing-aid type may be used.

ECHO. Discrete repetition of a sound, produced by a single reflected sound wave, or a combination of such waves whose return is coincident in time and at least 0·05 second after the original sound. Colloquially, 'echo' is used to mean the sum of such reflections, i.e. reverberation.

ECHO CHAMBER. A room for producing or simulating the natural reverberation of an enclosed space. Ideally, the walls (and floor and ceiling) should not be parallel. It has sound-reflecting walls and such treatment as is necessary to break up the sound, and produce a fairly flat frequency response. A reverberation time of about two seconds may be suitable.

ECHO PLATE. Better known by its proper name, reverberation plate.

'EDGING IN . . .', 'TAKING THE EDGE OFF . . .'. A technique to ensure that, for example, programme inserts with heavy atmosphere or rough quality do not hit the listener with too much of a bang. Once the first word has been heard at a little below the volume of the preceding speech the level of the insert can be very rapidly adjusted to be the same as earlier speech (or higher, to compensate for any deficiency of intelligibility). Similar techniques can be used to smooth a wide range of transitions. Another example is the case where an outside source of unknown volume is inserted into a live programme. It is much better that the first word should be a shade too quiet rather than too loud, so the initial level is set at perhaps 4 dB below the expected setting, and adjustment made (as it can with practice) within the first half second. Edging in and out may also be used more formally in dramatic work, where it is the same thing as a slight fade.

EDITING BLOCK. In its simplest form, a metal plate with a channel the width of magnetic tape running along the centre, with lapped edges to grip the tape, and an angled cutting groove to guide a razor blade across it. More complex (but not necessarily more helpful) blocks are also available.

EFFECTS. Simulated incidental sounds occurring (*a*) in the location portrayed (usually *recorded effects*) or (*b*) as a result of action (usually *spot effects*—those created on the spot). A heightened realism is generally preferred to the random quality of naturally occurring sounds; but effects taken a stage further and formalised into musical patterns are called *radiophonic effects* (*BBC*) or *musique concrète*. *Comedy* or '*cod*' *effects* are those in which some element, a characteristic natural quality of the sound, or a formal element such as its attack or rhythm, is exaggerated for comic effect. In this category are simple *musical effects*, in which a sound is mimicked by a musical instrument.

EIGENTONE. The fundamental frequency that belongs to any dimensional resonance of a room. Its wavelength is twice that dimension. It can form effectively only between parallel surfaces.

ELECTRET. Condenser microphone capsule in which the diaphragm has a permanent electrostatic charge and therefore requires no polarizing voltage. The principle is used in inexpensive domestic equipment and also for very lightweight personal microphones.

ELECTRONIC MUSIC. A work constructed from recorded electronic source materials by arranging them in a formal pattern (which may be beyond the range of conventional instruments or musicians).

ELECTROSTATIC LOUDSPEAKER. An application of electrostatic principles to the movement of air in bulk. This is done by means of a large charged diaphragm suspended between two perforated plates. As the alternating signal is applied to the outer plates, the diaphragm vibrates; and so long as the excursions are not too large the transfer of power is linear (the use of two plates rather than a single backplate helps considerably in this respect). The problem of handling sufficient power and transferring it to the air at low frequencies is not fully solved in any such speaker of convenient size (though baffles reduce the immediate losses). Electrostatic loudspeakers should not be placed parallel to walls, or standing waves will form behind them. With careful positioning, however, the quality of sound achieved is very clear. As with a number of other transducer principles this can also be applied in reverse, as a microphone.

ELECTROSTATIC (CONDENSER) MICROPHONE. In this, the signal is generated by the variations in capacitance between two charged plates, one of which is rigid and the other flexible, acting as a diaphragm in contact with the air. If the space between the plates is enclosed, the air vibrations can affect one side of the diaphragm only and the microphone is pressure operated (and substantially omni-directional). If the backplate is perforated the diaphragm is operated by a modification of the pressure gradient principle. It can be arranged that the distance that sound has to travel through the backplate (via an acoustic labyrinth) is the same as the effective path difference from back to front of the plate: in this case the pressure gradient drops substantially to zero for signals approaching from the rear of the microphone, and a good cardioid response is obtained. If two such cardioids are placed back to back, the characteristics depend on the sense of the potential between centre plate and the two diaphragms. The doublet can become bidirectional, cardioid or omnidirectional, simply by varying the size and sense of the potential on one of the diaphragms. Condenser microphones have to be fitted with a head amplifier (a single stage is sufficient) in order to convert the signal into a form suitable for transmission by line. A further complication of design of both electrostatic microphone and loudspeaker is that a high polarizing voltage has to be available. See also ELECTRET.

END-FIRE. Orientation of the diaphragm within a long microphone such that the axis of directional pick-up is along the main axis of the casing. An end-fire microphone is therefore 'pointed' toward the sound source, an arrangement easily understood by performers.

ENCLOSURE. A loudspeaker cabinet. Its most important function is to improve bass response. It may do this by acting as a baffle and increasing the distance rear-emitted sound has to travel before it can combine with and cancel or reinforce forward sound (thus lowering the frequency at which cancellation occurs). It may be a ported or bass-reflex cabinet, from which a low-frequency resonance is emitted more or less in phase with the forward output from the cone. In another design the box entirely encloses the rear of the loudspeaker; in this 'infinite baffle' the rear-emitted sound is supposed to be absorbed entirely within the box.

ENVELOPE. The manner in which the intensity of a sound varies with time. Graphical representation of the envelope (or dynamics) of a single note may show separate distinctive features in its attack, internal dynamics and decay. The term may also refer to the envelope of frequency content, or of an imposed frequency characteristic, as in a formant.

EQUALIZATION (colloquially, EQ). The use of a filter network to compensate (a) for any distortion of the frequency response introduced by a transducer or other component (e.g. a landline), or (b) for a recording or transmission characteristic employed to ensure an efficient, low-noise use of the medium (as in disc recording or FM transmission).

ERASURE. The removal of recorded signals from a tape so that it is ready to re-use. This is done automatically on most machines as the tape passes the erase head, which lies between the feed spool and the recording head. The erase head is similar in structure to the other heads except that the gap is wider. The pure bias signal fed to it magnetizes the tape first in one direction and then the other until it approaches the end of the gap, when the magnitude of the oscillations dies down, and the tape is left demagnetized. With a *bulk eraser*, the tape as a whole is given a similar washing treatment, being physically removed from the region of the alternating current before switching off. In very powerful bulk erasers it is not necessary to remove the tape to complete the wiping action.

ESTABLISH. Establishing a sound effect, etc., is allowing it sufficient time (and volume, which may be greater than that subsequently used) for it to register in the listener's mind. Establishing a location may be helped by the above technique, but equally it may be a matter of supplying sufficient 'pointers' in scripted speech.

EXPONENTIAL. An exponential curve is one that follows the progress of natural unrestrained growth or decay. If, in exponential growth, something has doubled in time t, it doubles again in further time t, is eight times its original size at time 3t, and so on. Exponential growth inevitably overhauls all other forms of regular growth (unless as happens in nature, some regulating factor intervenes). Exponential decay that halves in time t, halves again in a further time t, and so on. This must eventually become the slowest regular form of decay. A *logarithmic scale* (e.g. on a graph) is one in which the scale is gradually reduced according to the same principles. The spaces between 1, 2, 4, 16, 32 . . . are all equal. This form of representation reduces an exponential growth to an apparently linear growth. However, the ear judges both changes of volume and changes of pitch by ratio; thus a logarithmic scale is more relevant than any other to perceived sound. The doubling of sound frequency is equivalent to an interval of one octave. A tenfold increase in the intensity of a sound is equivalent to an interval of 1 Bel (10 decibels).

EXTINCTION FREQUENCY. Frequency at which there is complete loss of signal due to the dimension of a component being exactly equal to signal wavelength.

F FADE. Gradual reduction or increase in the signal. This is accomplished by means of a *fader* (i.e. a potentiometer—or 'pot' for short). A *logarithmic fader* is one in which the ratio of gain or loss is the same for equal movements of the fader throughout its main working range. Such a fader may be marked off in a linear scale of decibels. All faders used in audio work should be logarithmic over their main working range.

FEEDBACK. The addition of some fraction of the output to the original; this in turn may contribute to a further addition, and so on. If the feedback is mixed in at a higher level than that of the original signal, a howlround occurs; if at a level that is sufficiently lower, it gradually dies away. See also SPIN. In amplifiers a signal may be fed back to an earlier point: *negative feedback* (in which the signal fed back reduces output) is used to control distortion introduced by the amplifier.

FIELD PATTERN (*Am*.). Polar response (q.v.).

FIGURE-OF-EIGHT. See BIDIRECTIONAL MICROPHONE.

FILM INSERT. Filmed sequence played in to a television programme.

FILM LEADER. Section of film used at the head of picture or magnetic track showing a common 'start mark' and footage marks at 16-frame intervals between 12 and 3 after which the leader is black until the first frame of the film. The same intervals (representing feet on 35-mm film) are used for all film footages. Television films with synchronous sound are usually run off 10.

FILTER. A network of resistors and condensers (inductances could also be used) that allows some frequencies to pass and attenuates others. The simplest form of filter (one resistor and one condenser) rolls off at 6 dB/octave above or below a certain frequency. There is an elbow in the curve at the turnover point: the nominal cut-off frequency (which may be calculated easily) is that at which the loss is 3 dB. For many audio purposes this gentle form of filter is quite as satisfactory as the sharper cut-off that can be obtained with a more complex network. The terms *bass*- and

521

top-cut filter and *stop-* and *pass-band filter* are self-explanatory. An *octave* filter is one in which the signal is divided into octaves whose levels may be controlled separately. Again, the simpler circuitry, providing smoother slopes at the boundaries may be just as satisfactory.

FLANGING. Effect produced by playing two recordings almost in sync but with one running slightly slower than the other, so that phase cancellation sweeps through the audio-frequency range. Originally produced by manual drag on the flange of one of the spools.

FLAT. (*a*) On a stylus, a surface of wear that appears on the two sides of the tip after some period of use. Seen under the microscope, the surface really is flat. These areas gradually become larger, the angles at their edges sharper, and the tip shape more like that of a chisel moving end-ways on in the groove. (*b*) On the rubber tyre of an idler wheel, a flat is an indentation that may form if the idler is left parked in contact with drive spindle, etc. It causes a momentary flutter in recording or replay.

FLICK (*BBC*). Flash of about one second on cue light, as signal to start.

FLUTTER. Rapid fluctuation in pitch having a warble-frequency of, say, 8 Hz or more due to a fault in equipment such as an eccentric drive-spindle.

FOLDBACK. A feed of selected sources to a studio loudspeaker or headphones at suitable levels for the benefit of the performers. It may be fed from outside sources, tape or disc, or from a microphone in a distant part of the studio to overcome problems of audibility or (in music) time lag. See ACOUSTIC REPRODUCTION OF EFFECTS, PUBLIC ADDRESS.

FOLEY ARTIST. US film industry term for specialist in matching footsteps and other sound effects in post production. Tracks are laid to replay of edited picture, and may be further edited, adjusted or treated before the final mix. See SPOT EFFECT.

FOOTAGE. Length of film expressed in feet: either in terms of its own gauge or the equivalent for 35-mm film. One 35-mm foot is 16 frames; one 16-mm foot is 40 frames.

FORMANT. A characteristic resonance region: a musical instrument may have one or more such regions, fixed by the geometry of the instrument. The human voice has resonance regions associated with the nose, mouth and throat cavities, which are capable of more or less variation in size and shape, permitting the formation of the vowel sounds and voiced consonants. The range of the formant regions is not directly related to the pitch of the sound on which they act. If the fundamental is well below or low in the formant range, the quality of sound produced is rich, as harmonics are clustered close together within the formant; if the fundamental is relatively high, there are less harmonics in the range and the quality is thinner.

FREQUENCY. The number of complete excursions an air particle makes in one second (formerly described as cycles per second, c/s or cps, now as Hertz, Hz). The only sound that consists of a single frequency is a pure (i.e. sinusoidal) tone. This corresponds to the motion of an air particle that swings backward and forward in smooth regular cycles (simple harmonic motion). The velocity of sound in air is about 1120 ft/s (340 m/s), depending on temperature. Frequency (f) and wavelength (λ) are related through the velocity of sound (c) by the formula $c = f\lambda$, so any frequency can be represented alternatively, but with a little less precision, as a wavelength. A complex sound can be analyzed in terms of its frequency components, and plotting volume against frequency gives the *frequency spectrum*. A sound which is composed of individual frequencies (fundamental and harmonics or partials, or a combination of pure tones) has a *line spectrum*. Bands of noise have a *band spectrum*.

FREQUENCY CORRECTION. The change required in the frequency characteristics of a signal to restore it to its original form; but the term is sometimes ambiguously used to indicate the application of desired deliberate distortion of the response (often a peak in the upper middle frequencies). A *linear response* in any process is one in which the frequency distribution is the same at the beginning and end. See also EQUALIZATION.

FREQUENCY MODULATION (FM). A method whereby the information in an audio signal is carried on the much higher frequency of a radio wave. The frequency of the audio signal is represented by the rate of change of carrier frequency; audio volume is represented by amplitude of frequency swing. The maximum deviation permitted for FM transmission is set at 75 kHz. Transmitter and receiver equipment is engineered to this standard, which is arbitrarily regarded as constituting 100% modulation. Overmodulation does not necessarily cause immediate severe distortion, as with AM, and limiters are not needed to avoid overloading transmitter valves. Noise, which appears as fluctuations of carrier amplitude, is strongly discriminated against, though it does produce phase-change effects that cannot be eradicated. Pre-emphasis of top (i.e. prior to transmission), with a corresponding de-emphasis at the receiver, helps to reduce the noise level still further. Unless two carriers on the same wavelength have almost the same strength, the stronger 'captures' the area: there is only a small marginal territory between service areas.

FREQUENCY RESPONSE. Variation in gain or loss with frequency.

FUNDAMENTAL. The note associated with the simplest form of vibration of an instrument, usually the first and lowest member of a harmonic series.

FUZZ BOX. Used in the pick-up and reproduction circuitry of 'electric' instruments (electric guitar, piano, etc.). This deliberately heavily overloads the system, thereby filling in the texture of the sound with a dense array of distortion products. A buzzing effect is achieved.

FX (indication in script). Effects.

G   GAIN. Amplification: ratio of output voltage to input voltage. It is most conveniently calculated in decibels.

GAP WIDTH (*Am.*: Gap-height). The distance between poles of magnetic recording (or reproducing or erasing) head at the point of contact with the tape.

GATE. A switching circuit that passes or cuts off a signal in response to some external control, e.g. to whether or not an applied voltage is above or below a given theshold.

GRAPHIC FILTER. Filter in which the signal is divided into narrow bands, of an octave or less, each controlled by a slide fader. Side by side on the face of the instrument, they form a curve approximating to the response of the filter.

GRID. A framework below the roof of a theatre or television studio from which lighting and microphone leads may be suspended. A television studio normally has some of its microphone points in the grid.

GROOVE. Track on record which carries the audio signal in the form of a lateral displacement, or in the case of stereo a combination of two 45° displacements. *Coarse groove*. The groove that was used for 78 rpm recordings. The pitch was approximately 100–150 grooves per inch (*Am.*: lines per inch). *Fine groove, microgroove, minigroove*. The groove normally used for $33\frac{1}{3}$ and 45 rpm recordings. The pitch, about 250–330 grooves per inch, varies with modulation.

GROUP FADER (*Am.*: Sub-master fader). One to which the output of several individual faders is fed.

GUIDE TRACK. A second track on a twin-track recorder which is replayed to artists to assist synchronization, but is not itself included in the finished performance.

GUN MICROPHONE. Moving coil or electrostatic microphone fitted with an interference tube leading out along the axis. Sound enters the tube through a series of ports. That approaching off-axis reaches the diaphragm by a range of paths of different lengths, and mostly cancels out. The microphone is thus highly directional except for sound of wavelengths substantially greater than the length of the gun.

H HAAS EFFECT. When a sound is heard from two loudspeakers in different directions and there is a time-delay on one path all the sound seems to come from the other loudspeaker unless the delayed sound is increased in volume to compensate. The effect grows rapidly to a maximum as the delay increases to 4 or 5 milliseconds (equivalent to a difference in path-length of about 5 feet or 1·5 metres). At the maximum, an increase in volume of 10 dB in the delayed sound re-centres the image, and a greater volume swings it to the louder source.

HALF-TRACK RECORDING. A recording occupying the upper 40% of tape (the tape moving left to right across the heads).

HARMONICS. A series of frequencies that are all multiples of a particular fundamental frequency. They are produced by the resonances of air in a tube (e.g. woodwind, brass, organ) or of a vibrating string, etc.

HEAD. Transducer that converts electrical energy into magnetic or mechanical energy or vice versa. Thus we have tape recording and reproducing heads and disc cutter and pick-up heads. The electromagnet used for erasing tape is also called a head.

HEADPHONES. A pair of electro-acoustic transducers (e.g. moving coil) held to the ears by a headband. Alternatively, devices similar to hearing aids may be used in a single ear (e.g. for listening to talk-back instructions during a programme). Earphones are efficient and produce the best quality when the channel from transducer to ear is completely closed (as with moulded plastic ear-fittings). But when headphones are used mainly for communication purposes, high quality is of little importance. Some degree of control of volume can be achieved with telephone receiver type phones by moving them a little off the ear, but with the ear-fitting, it is desirable to have a volume control in circuit.

HEARING. Essentially, the ear acts like an instrument for measuring frequencies and volumes of sound logarithmically (so that they appear linear in octave scales and decibels). The subjective aspect of frequency is pitch: judgement of pitch is not entirely independent of volume. The subjective aspect of sound intensity is loudness. Below about 1000 Hz the ear is progressively less sensitive to low volumes of sound; above 3000 Hz the hearing may also become rather less sensitive—but not

524

necessarily following a smooth curve. The upper limit of hearing for young ears may be 16 kHz or higher, but with increasing age this is gradually reduced. No audio system needs to exceed the range 20–16,000 Hz (the signal may be cut off at this upper frequency). The acoustic part of the ear (the outer and middle ear) is relatively simple; essentially, it consists of a group of bones the purpose of which is to provide efficient coupling, i.e. the matching of mechanical impedances, between a diaphragm in contact with the air and a second diaphragm which transmits sound to the liquid of the inner ear. The physiological construction of the inner ear is known, but the mechanism of aural perception is complex.

HERTZ (Hz). The measure of frequency (q.v.) formerly expressed as cycles per second. It is more convenient for mathematical analysis to consider frequency as an entity rather than as a derived function.

HIGH-LEVEL MIXING. See MIXER.

HISS. High frequency noise.

HOWLROUND or HOWLBACK. Closed circuit (wholly electrical, or partly acoustic) in which the amplification exceeds the losses in the circuit. In a typical case the loudspeaker is turned up high in a monitoring cubicle and the microphone in the studio faded up high for very quiet speech, and then if the acoustic treatment is inefficient at any frequency (or if both connecting doors are opened) a howl may build up at the frequency for which the gain over the whole circuit is greatest.

HUM. Low frequency noise, at the mains frequency and its harmonics.

HYBRID TRANSFORMER. A transformer with two secondary windings, so arranged that cross-talk directly between them is as small as possible.

HYPERCARDIOID. Cottage-loaf-shaped polar response of microphone, intermediate between figure-of-eight and true cardioid.

I   IDLER. On a tape deck, the idler presses the tape against the capstan when the drive is switched on (but does not itself transmit rotation).

IMPEDANCE. A combination of d.c. resistance with inductance and capacitance, which act as resistances in a.c. circuits. An inductive impedance increases with frequency; a capacitative impedance decreases with frequency. Either type introduces change of phase. See MATCHING.

INDIRECT SOUND (in microphone balance). Sound is reflected one or more times before reaching the microphone.

INDUCTANCE. The resistance of (in particular) a coil of wire to rapidly fluctuating a.c. currents. The field built up by the current resists any change in the rate of flow of the current; and this resistance increases with frequency.

INSERT TAPE. A spool containing one or more pre-recorded programme segments ready for insertion into a production.

INTENSITY OF SOUND. The sound energy crossing a square metre. Relative sound intensities, energies, or pressures may all conveniently be measured in decibels. See DECIBEL, WAVE.

INTERMODULATION DISTORTION. See DISTORTION.

J JOINT. Point on a tape at which two physically separate butt ends have been joined together.

JOINTING TAPE. A specially prepared, non-oozy adhesive tape, slightly narrower than magnetic tape, used to back two pieces of tape that have been butted together.

JUMP CUT. A cut in replaying a disc, made by lifting the stylus and replacing it in a later groove (at which the cue has been checked in advance). There is a momentary loss of atmosphere while the replay is faded out. In film, the term is used to describe a cut between scenes or two separate parts of the same scene in such a way that continuity of action is deliberately lost.

K KC/S. Kilocycles per second. Now written kHz. See also FREQUENCY, HERTZ.

L LAVALIER. Personal microphone originally worn suspended around the neck, like pendant jewellery; now a microphone in any similar position.

LAZY ARM. Simple form of boom consisting of an upright and a balanced cross-member from which a microphone may be slung.

LEADER. White uncoated tape that may be cut on to the start of a spool of recorded audio tape, and on which may be written brief details of the contents of the sound recording. See also FILM LEADER.

LEVEL. Volume of electrical signal as picked up by the microphone(s) and passed through pre-amplifiers and mixer faders. At the BBC this volume is calculated in decibels relative to a *reference level* of 1 milliwatt in 600 ohms (also called *zero level*). Zero level corresponds to 40% modulation at the transmitter: 100% modulation is 8 dB (approx.) above this. To *take level* is to make a test for suitable gain settings, in order to control the signal to a suitable volume for feeding to transmitter or recorder. This test may sometimes be combined with the balance test. *Voice level* is the acoustic volume produced by a voice in the studio.

LIMITER. An automatic control to reduce volume when over-modulation occurs, e.g., to prevent dangerously heavy peaks of power reaching a transmitter that might be damaged by it. The most usual form of operation uses feedback: the signal is monitored by the limiter and any wave that exceeds a certain volume causes a corresponding increase in feedback, which reduces the signal. After a while, the operation of a recovery device allows the gain to return to normal. Limiters are necessary in AM transmitters, and in the input to disc recorders in situations where overmodulation may occur by accident. They are also used in pop music.

LINE. A send and return path for an electric signal. In its simplest form a line consists of a pair of wires. A *landline* is a line (with equalizing amplifiers at regular intervals) for carrying programme across country. (c.f. radio link, broadcast).

LINE MICROPHONE. Gun microphone (q.v.).

LINE UP. Arrange that the programme signal passes through all components at the most suitable level. In a broadcast chain this is normally at or about zero level (see under LEVEL).

LINE-UP TONE. Pure tone, usually at 1000 Hz, fed through all stages of a chain. It starts at zero level, and should read the same on a meter at any stage. A drop or jump in the level of the tone between successive points in the chain may be due to a fault in the line or in other equipment.

LIP-RIBBON MICROPHONE. A noise-cancelling microphone placed close to the mouth, the exact distance being determined by a guard resting against the upper lip. The microphone's directional properties discriminate in favour of the voice; close working also discriminates against unwanted sound, and bass is reduced still further by the compensation necessary when working so close to a directional microphone.

LIVE ANGLE. Angle within which reasonable sensitivity is obtained. (See CARDIOID and BI-DIRECTIONAL MICROPHONES.)

LIVE SIDE (of microphone). The face that must be presented to a sound source for greatest sensitivity.

LIVE TRANSMISSION. Broadcast, none (or little) of which has been prerecorded.

LOGARITHMIC SCALE. See EXPONENTIAL.

LOOP. Continuous band of tape made by joining the ends of a length of tape together. A tape loop may be used (*a*) to provide a repeated sound structure or rhythm (in radiophonics), (*b*) for an 'atmosphere' track where this is regular in quality, (*c*) in tape delay techniques. Magnetic film loops are used for continuous 'atmosphere' in film dubbing.

LOUDNESS. Subjective aspect of sound intensity. See METER, DECIBEL.

LOW LEVEL MIXING. See MIXER.

M M SIGNAL. The combined A + B stereo signal. Corresponds to the signal from a single 'main' microphone. See S SIGNAL.

M AND E. A pre-mix, nominally of music and effects. In practice, in documentary it is a mix of all but commentary.

MAIN GAIN CONTROL (*Am.*: Grand Master or Overall Master Control) Final fader to which the combined outputs of all group (*Am.*: sub-master) or individual faders are fed.

MASTER. This is the second stage in the processing of a record. The direct-cut original is sputtered with a finely divided conductor (e.g. gold) and then a copper electroplate is grown. This is stripped away from the original and nickel plated. The master has ridges instead of grooves. In half processing (when only a small run is required) the master is also used as a stamper; otherwise, for full processing, a mother is grown, and then a stamper.

MATCHING. Arranging that the impedance presented by a load is equal to the internal impedance of the generator. Unless this is done there will be a loss of power, and the greater the mis-match the greater the loss. Often, when there is adequate gain in hand, some degree of mis-match is not critical, but the input impedance should be lower than that of the following circuit: 'low into high will go'. However, in the case of microphones and similar generators, the signal is low to start with and any loss will result in a poorer signal to noise ratio. Matching is done by means of a small transformer. Where a microphone impedance is strongly capacitative (e.g. in an electrostatic microphone) its output voltage controls current in an external circuit.

MATRIXED QUADRAPHONY. Methods of combining the four quadraphonic channels (A, B, AR and BR) into two for recording on disc or transmission by conventional channels. AR and BR are changed in phase and added in different proportions to the A and the B signals. Special decoders are required. In all systems there is substantial cross-talk in the decoded signal, so that positional information is lost at the sides. Commercial systems differ in the distribution of losses incurred. After studying the deficiencies of the existing rival SQ and QS systems, the BBC proposed an improved system for its own quadraphonic radio transmissions.

METER. Device for measuring voltage, current etc. In audio, several types of meter are used for measuring programme volume. The *VU* (*Volume unit*) *meter* is used on much American equipment. Over its main working range it is linear in 'percentage modulation'. It is not, therefore, linear in decibels, and this means that for all but a very narrow range of adjustments of level the needle is either showing small deflections, or flickering over the entire scale. The VU meter is not very satisfactory for high quality work where a comparison or check on levels (which are not always close to the nominal 100% modulation) is required. In Britain the *Peak programme meter* (PPM) is used by the BBC. It is linear in decibels over the main working range.

MICE. See MOUSE.

MICRON (μ). A thousandth of a millimetre.

MICROPHONE. Electro-acoustic transducer. A microphone converts the power in a sound wave into electrical energy, responding to changes in either the air pressure or the pressure gradient (q.v.). Principal response patterns are omnidirectional, figure-of-eight, cardioid; principal types, moving coil (dynamic), electrostatic (condensers), ribbon, crystal, and carbon (q.v.). *Microphone sensitivity* is measured in dB relative to 1 volt/N/m². See NEWTONS PER SQUARE METRE.

MICROPHONE CHANNEL. The pre-amplifier, equalization circuit, fader, etc., in the mixer which are available for each microphone. The channel may also include facilities for 'pre-hear', and feeds for echo, fold-back, and public address.

MIDLIFT. Deliberate introduction of a peak in the frequency response in the upper-middle frequency range (somewhere between 1–8 kHz say). A group of mid-lift controls may be calibrated according to the frequency of the peak (e.g. nominal values, 2, 3, 5, 8 kHz) and degree of lift (e.g. 0–10 in 2 dB steps).

MIL. A thousandth of an inch. About 25 microns.

MIX. Combine electrically the signals from microphones, tape and gramophone reproducers, and other sources. To *mix down* or *reduce* is to combine separately recorded tracks in a multi-microphone balance. In *low level mixing* each source is fed directly to an associated fader without pre-amplification. Low level mixers are relatively inexpensive, but are now rarely used professionally. *High level mixing* with a pre-amplifier preceding each source fader gives a better signal to noise ratio at the input to the fader. *Computer mixdown* is an aid to mixing multi-track recordings. A trial mix is fed to the memory and then successive changes are made to improve it. This ensures that each individual stage is operationally simple: complexity does not grow, and so does not become a limiting factor.

MIXED-MINUS (*Am.*). Clean feed (q.v.).

528

MODULATION. Superimposition (of sound wave) on a carrier, which may be a high frequency signal (e.g. by amplitude or frequency modulation, q.v.) or (on a record) a smooth spiral groove which, when it carries no recorded signal is described as *unmodulated*. 100% *modulation* is the maximum permissible amplitude for any recording or transmission system. A *ring modulator* has two inputs and one output. (In radiophonics a useful type multiplies the instantaneous amplitudes together instead of simply adding them.)

MONAURAL SOUND. Alternative term for monophonic sound suggested by the analogy that listening with one microphone is like listening with one ear—which is not strictly accurate. See MONO.

MONITORING. (*a*) Checking sound quality, operational techniques, programme content, etc., by listening to the programme as it leaves the studio (or at subsequent points in the chain, or by a separate feed, or by checking from a radio receiver). A *monitoring loudspeaker* in the studio is usually as good as the best that listeners might be using (but it must be remembered that adverse listening conditions might radically alter the listeners' appreciation of sound quality—also they may be listening at a level lower than that at which the monitoring loudspeaker is set.) (*b*) Listening to other services for information. The BBC monitoring service listens round the clock for news to services all over the world, and the BBC news is itself monitored widely.

MONO (monophonic sound). Sound heard from a single channel. This is defined by the form of the recording or transmission, and not by the number of speakers. A number of microphones may be used and their outputs mixed; several loudspeakers may be used, and their frequency content varied, but this is still mono unless there is more than one channel of transmission. Multiplex radio transmissions and the single groove of a stereo disc each contain more than one channel. In mono the only spatial movement that can be simulated is forward and backward. There is no sideways spread; in particular there is no spatial spread of reverberation, or of ambient noise (see COCKTAIL PARTY EFFECT). The balance of sound in mono is therefore not natural but worked out in terms of a special convention. Working within, and recognizing the limitations of this convention, considerable artistry is possible. NB. In television, 'mono' is used in a different sense, to mean monochromatic, i.e. black and white, as distinct from colour pictures.

MOOD MUSIC. Undistinctive background music that does not distract the listeners' attention from foreground interest, but which is intended to guide the attitude of mind that the listener directs towards it.

MOUSE. Microphone laid flat on floor (e.g. of stage) inside neutrally coloured foamed plastic shield that is flat on the underside. As the capsule is very close to a hard reflecting surface, interference effects are limited to the very high frequency range and may be imperceptible on voice.

MOVING COIL MICROPHONE, LOUDSPEAKER OR PICK-UP. (*Am.*: Dynamic). These all use a small coil moving in the field of a permanent magnet. In the microphone or pick-up the movement generates a current in the coil; in the loudspeaker the current causes movement that is transmitted to a cone (q.v.) which drives the air.

MULTIPLEX. Radio transmission carrying A − B stereo information on a sub-carrier above the A + B signal.

MUSIC LINE. Broad-band circuit for carrying programme (including speech), as distinct from a telephone line which may occupy only a narrow band.

MUSIQUE CONCRÈTE (*French*). A work in musical form constructed from natural sounds that are recorded and then treated in various ways.

MUTE FILM. Scenes shot without sound.

N NARTB CHARACTERISTIC. In tape recording, the pre-emphasis and subsequent equalization standards used in America and Japan. (Standard set by the American National Association of Radio and Television Broadcasters. See also CCIR and RIAA.)

NETWORK OPERATION. A broadcasting system involving many local stations and transmitters that may join together or separate at will.

NEWTONS PER SQUARE METRE (N/M^2). The unit of sound pressure. This replaces a unit formerly used, dynes per square centimetre: $1 \ N/m^2 = 10 \ dynes/cm^2$. A common reference level, $2 \times 10^{-5} \ N/m^2$ approximates to the threshold of hearing at 1 kHz. Microphone sensitivity is calculated in dB relative to $1 \ volt/N/m^2$: this gives values 20 dB higher than those using the older reference level, $1 \ volt/dyne/cm^2$. Characteristically, microphones have a sensitivity of the order of -50 dB relative to $1 \ volt/N/m^2$ or -70 dB relative to $1 \ volt/dyne/cm^2$.

NOISE. This is generally defined as unwanted sound. It includes such things as unwanted acoustic background sounds, unwanted electrical hiss (e.g. caused by the random flow of electrons in a transistor, or the random placing and finite size of oxide particles in tape coating), or rumble, hum or unwanted electromagnetic noise (background noise picked up on a radio receiver). In all electronic components and recording or transmission media the signal must compete with some degree of background noise, and it is vital in radio and recording work to preserve an adequate signal-to-noise ratio at every stage. In general, noise consists of all frequencies or a band of frequencies rather than particular frequencies (hum is an exception to this). *White noise* contains all frequencies in equal proportion. *Coloured noise* is a band of noise that exhibits some coloration. (The term is used by analogy with coloured light.) In radiophonics and electronic music such forms of noise are sometimes used deliberately. Acoustic noise levels are often measured in dBA (or SLA). 1 dBA = 40 dB relative to $2 \times 10^{-5} \ N/m^2$ at 1 kHz, and at other frequencies is weighted (electrically) to be of equal loudness. PNdB (perceived noise decibels) use a weighting function that can be used to place aircraft and other noises in order of noisiness. The analysis of sounds in PNdB can be complex; a similar analysis uses an electrical network giving adequate results in units that are designated dBN.

NOISE REDUCTION SYSTEMS. Applied mainly to tape recordings, and essential to multi-track, these add some 10 dB to the signal-to-noise ratio, of which part is used to hold down recording levels that might cause print-through. The signal is encoded by splitting into frequency bands that are separately compressed. An alternative system uses digitally encoded audio signals, which are intrinsically less susceptible to noise and distortion.

O OBSTACLE EFFECT. Obstacles tend to reflect or absorb only those sounds with a shorter wavelength than their own dimensions; at greater wavelengths the object appears to be transparent to the sound. For example, a screen 27 in (67 cm) wide is substantially transparent to frequencies below 500 Hz, but will absorb or reflect higher frequencies. 15 kHz is equivalent to a wavelength of about 0·9 in (just over 2 cm); a microphone containing parts of about this size is subject to effects that begin to operate when this frequency is approached.

OFF-MICROPHONE. On the dead (i.e. insensitive) side of the microphone, or at much more than the normal working distance on the live side.

OMNIDIRECTIONAL MICROPHONE. One that is equally sensitive in all directions. In practice, there is a tendency for this quality to degenerate at high frequencies, with the top response progressively reduced for sounds further away from the front axis. Modern microphones with sufficiently small capsules do not suffer from the fault to a marked extent.

OMNIPRESSION. Proprietory term for a process combining the functions of expansion, compression and dynamic inversion in a single continuous operational range.

OPEN-AIR ACOUSTIC. See DEAD ACOUSTIC.

OPTICAL SOUND. A film recording system that is replayed by scanning a track of variable width (or, sometimes, density) by means of a lamp, slit, and photocell. Magnetic systems are to be preferred for all work up to and including the final sound mix. For finished film, optical sound retains certain advantages, such as convenience of handling (particularly for commercials) and economy (where cost of stock is important) which may be set against the higher quality promised by magnetic 'stripe' sound. See COMOPT.

OSCILLATOR. A device that produces an alternating signal, usually of a particular frequency (or harmonic series). An audio oscillator produces a pure sine tone at any frequency in the audio range. *Square wave* and *sawtooth generators* produce waveforms of roughly those shapes (these correspond to harmonic series). Other oscillators (e.g. tape bias and r.f. oscillators) provide signals at higher frequencies.

OUTPUT (from a studio). This should consist of the completed programme, fully controlled and ready for feeding to the transmitter (or recorder). The output which may be monitored during a recording is the product of a replay head.

OUTSIDE SOURCE (*Br.*). Remote (*Am.*). A source of programme material originating outside the studio to which it is fed, and appearing on an individual fader on the mixer panel just as any local source does (except that no pre-amplifier is needed as it is fed in at about zero level).

OVERDUB. Added recording (usually on a separate track) made while listening to replay of tracks already recorded.

OVERLAP CHANGEOVER. A type of changeover from one recorder to the next in sequence which may be used when the two have half a minute or so of material in common. The overlap is used to adjust synchronization before crossfading from one to the other; before changing over, the first recording is heard on the loudspeaker, and the second prefaded on headphones, or on a loudspeaker of different quality.

OVERMODULATION. Exceeding the maximum permissible amplitude for recording or transmission. Distortion may be expected, and in certain cases damage to equipment or to the recording itself (limiters are used where this could occur).

OVERTONE. A partial in a complex tone, so called because such tones are normally higher than the fundamental.

P PAD. Attenuator of fixed loss.

PANNING or STEERING. Splitting the output from a monophonic microphone between stereo A and B channels. *Panpot*. Potentiometer (fader) to do this.

PARABOLIC REFLECTOR. A light rigid structure (of aluminium or other material) that reflects sound to a focus at which a microphone is placed. The assembly is very strongly directional at frequencies for which the corresponding wavelengths are less than the aperture of the reflector. It differs from gun microphone systems in that it is not degraded by interference from reflecting surfaces.

PARTIAL. One of a group of frequencies, not necessarily harmonically related to the fundamental, appearing in a complex tone. (Bells, xylophone blocks, and many other percussion instruments produce partials that are not harmonically related.)

PATCH (*Am.*). Cross-plug.

PCM. Pulse code modulation (q.v.).

PEAK. A period of high volume.

PEAK PROGRAMME METER (PPM). A device for measuring the peak values of programme volume. In Britain it is the main programme control aid. See METER.

PERFECT PITCH. The ability to judge frequency absolutely, i.e. without comparing it with another frequency, and to do so instantaneously.

PERMANENT JOINT. Cemented join in slightly overlapped tape. It is permanent only in the sense that it cannot be undone as a temporary joint can.

PERSPECTIVE. Varying the levels and the proportions of direct and indirect sound in order to suggest variety of distance. This can be done by the actor moving on and off microphone. In dead acoustics the ratio of direct to indirect sound cannot be varied, as indirect sound must be kept to a minimum. In this case it may help if an actor 'throws' his voice, simulating raising it to talk or shout from a distance. In television, sound and picture perspectives are often matched by the adjustment of boom microphone distance, or by placing a fixed microphone sufficiently close to the camera that as a performer moves toward the camera the sound also appears closer.

PFL. Prefade-listen. See PRE-HEAR.

PHASE. The stage that a particle in vibration has reached in its cycle. Particles are *in phase* when they are at the same stage in the cycle at the same time.

PHASE-SHIFT. The displacement of a waveform in time. If a pure sine tone waveform is displaced by one complete wavelength this is described as a phase-shift of 360°. If it is displaced by half a wavelength (i.e. through 180°) it has peaks where there were troughs and vice versa. If two equal signals 180° out of phase are added together, they cancel completely; if they are at any other angle (except when in phase) partial cancellation occurs. Some electronic components introduce phase-shift into a signal, and the shift is of the same angle for all frequencies. This means that the displacement of individual component frequencies in the wave is different (depending on their wavelength) and distortion of the waveform results. This will not normally be of importance, because the ear cannot detect changes in phase relationship between components of a steady note. Interference between two complex signals, similar in content but different in phase, results in a very serious form of distortion: the loss of all frequencies for which the two signals are 180° out of phase. Electrical cancellation may occur when two recordings are played slightly out of synchronization (this is used creatively in popular music), or when a signal has to be sent by two different paths (this can make the transmission of stereo signals by land-line difficult, when lines with broad transmission characteristics are not available). It occurs in radio reception when a sky wave interferes with a direct signal, etc. In a studio, cancellation may occur when one of a pair of bidirectional microphones has its back to a sound source. Care must always be taken when there is any possibility of pick-up on two such microphones at the same time. A check can be made by asking someone to speak at an equal distance from both, fading both up to equal volume, and mixing. If the sound appears thin and spiky, or direct sound is completely lost, one of the microphones should be reversed. (Studio reverberation and random sound generally are not affected by cancellation.) Pairs of loudspeakers may also be out of phase. If a monophonic signal is fed to an in-phase pair the sound appears to come from behind them: if they are out of phase the sound appears to be thrown forward to a point between speakers and listener. Correct phasing of speakers is, of course, vital to true stereo reproduction.

PHON. A unit of loudness. Phons are the same as decibels at 1000 Hz, and at other frequencies are related to this scale by contours of equal loudness.

PICK-UP. The electromechanical transducer of a gramophone. The movement of a stylus in the record groove gives rise to an electrical signal. A very large variety of principles have been applied to this: some of the most important include crystal, moving coil and variable reluctance (q.v.).

PILOT TONE. See SYNC. PULSE.

PILOT TONE SYSTEM. Stereo broadcasting system in which the $A - B$ signal is transmitted on a subcarrier, and a pilot tone is also transmitted to control the phasing of the two signals.

PITCH. The subjective aspect of frequency (in combination with intensity), that determines its position in the musical scale. The pitch of a group of harmonics is judged as being that of the fundamental (even if this is not present in the series). Dependance of pitch on intensity is greatest at low frequencies. Increase in loudness may depress the pitch of a pure tone 10% or more at very low frequencies, although where the tone is a member of a harmonic series the change is less apparent. Pitch does not depend on intensity at frequencies between $1-5$ kHz, and at higher frequencies increase in loudness produces a slight increase in pitch.

PLAYING WEIGHT. The effective weight bearing down on the stylus tip in the groove. It should be sufficient to maintain the stylus in contact with the groove, but not greater. Counterbalancing of the arm should ensure that the optimum weight for the type of pick-up is adopted. Styli with very high compliance can track at very low playing weights.

POLAR CHARACTERISTIC, POLAR DIAGRAM. (*Am.*: field pattern). The response of a microphone, loudspeaker, etc., showing sensitivity (or volume of sound) in relation to direction. Separate curves are shown for different frequencies, and separate diagrams are necessary for different planes. Such diagrams can also be used to indicate the qualities of reflecting screens or the radiation pattern of transmitter aerials, etc.

POPPING. Causing breakup of the signal from a microphone by blowing the diaphragm right out of the gap (for example, in a ribbon microphone). This may occur when explosive consonants such as 'p' and 'b' are directed straight at the diaphragm at close range.

PORTAMENTO. Used in musical performance, a slide in frequency to reach a note, or from one note to another. Also provided in some synthesizers. Measured in octaves per second.

POT (POT'METER, POTENTIOMETER). Fader (q.v.).

POT-CUT. Editing a short segment of unwanted material out of a programme without stopping the replay, by quickly fading out and fading in again. Results in a momentary loss of atmosphere; tape editing is preferable if time is available.

POWER (of sound source). The total energy given out by a source (as distinct from intensity, which is energy crossing unit area). Power is the rate of doing work, and in and electrical circuit equals voltage times current.

PPM. Peak Programme Meter. See METER.

PRACTICAL. A prop (property) in film or television that works partly or completely in its normal way, e.g. a telephone that rings, or an office intercom that is used normally.

PREAMPLIFIER. Amplifier in circuit between a source and the source fader. See MIXER.

PRE- AND POST-ECHO. An 'echo' of a particular programme signal which, on a disc, may appear the groove before or after that which carries the signal. This is due to the gradual relaxation of molecular tensions that occurs after the record has been pressed, and causes plastic deformation of the groove walls. On tape it occurs one turn of tape before or after the normal signal, and is caused by printing (q.v.).

PRE-EMPHASIS. Increasing the relative volume of part of the frequency response (usually h.f.) in order to make the best use of some segment of a recording or transmission system (e.g. record, VHF radio). This is compensated by matched de-emphasis after the link or component in question.

PREFADE, DEADROLL. Playing closing music from a predetermined time in order to fit exactly the remaining programme time, and fading up at an appropriate point during the closing words.

PREHEAR. A facility for listening to a source either on headphones or on a loudspeaker of a quality characteristically different from the main monitoring loudspeaker. The source can thereby be checked before fading it up and mixing it in to the programme.

PREMIX. A mix made of several but not all components of a final mix, e.g. a music, effects and dialogue mix for a documentary (the commentary being added subsequently). Sometimes used for complicated effects sequences or dialogue with a lot of cuts and quality matching.

PRERECORDING. Recording made prior to the main recording or transmission, and replayed into it.

PRESENCE. A quality described as the bringing forward of a voice or instrument (or the entire composite sound) in such a way as to give the impression that it is actually in the room with the listener. This is achieved by boosting part of the 1–8 kHz frequency range. In fact, emphasis of a single component (or several, at different frequencies) in this band gives greater clarity and separation, although at the expense of roundness of tone. Presence applied to the entire sound (e.g. by a distorted loud-speaker response) achieves stridency but little else.

PRESSING. A commercial gramophone record or other disc is made by stamping a plastic material such as polyvinyl chloride (PVC) in association with other components that vary from manufacturer to manufacturer. PVC-based pressings have low surface noise (provided they have not been played with a heavy pick-up) and are not breakable. They are easily damaged by scratching or heat. Formerly, shellac was used for pressing records and having much greater elasticity, was suitable for record materials when only very heavy (low compliance) pick-up heads were available. The shellac was combined with a large proportion of inexpensive filler (e.g. slate dust) which made them hard, served to grind the stylus to the shape of the groove, and also contributed the characteristic surface noise of 78s.

PRESSURE GRADIENT MICROPHONE. One with a diaphragm open to the air on both front and back, and which therefore responds to the difference in pressure at successive points on the sound wave (separated by the path difference from front to back). The microphone is 'dead' to sound approaching from directions such that the wavefront reaches front and back of the diaphragm at the same time. (See FIGURE-OF-EIGHT and CARDIOID MICROPHONE.) A pressure gradient microphone measures the rate of change of sound pressure, i.e. air particle velocity. This is not quite the same thing as measuring intensity (as the ear does) but differs from it essentially only in phase, and as the ear is not sensitive to differences in phase, this does not matter. Pressure gradient operation begins to degenerate to pressure operation for wavelengths approaching the dimensions of the microphone. This may help to maintain the response of the microphone at frequencies such that cancellation would occur due to the wave-length being equal to the effective path difference from front to back of the diaphragm.

PRESSURE MICROPHONE. One with a diaphragm open to the pressure of the sound-wave on one side and enclosed on the other. If the diaphragm and casing is sufficiently small, the microphone is omnidirectional (q.v.).

PRESSURE PADS. Felt pads on spring loaded arms which press tape against the heads. They are not used on professional recorders, the feed spool back-tension (and curved path of the tape over the heads) being adequate to ensure satisfactory contact.

PRINT-THROUGH. The re-recording of a signal from one layer to another in a spool of tape. The recorded signal produces a field that magnetizes tape separated by only the thickness of the backing. (Other factors affecting printing are temperature, time and physical shock.)

PROGRAMME. (a) Self-contained and complete item. (b) The electrical signal corresponding to programme material, as it is fed through electronic equipment.

PUBLIC ADDRESS (PA). A loudspeaker system installed for the benefit of a studio audience. The output of selected microphones is fed at suitable levels to directional loudspeakers.

PULSE CODE MODULATION (PCM). A highly efficient means of using available band-width. The signal is sampled at frequent intervals and encoded in digital form. The coded signal is less susceptible to noise and distortion. On a multitrack recording it can be used for noise reduction (q.v.). A coded signal can travel considerable distances, and television sound may be interleaved with the picture signal: the signal is reconstructed at its destination and broadcast in the normal way.

PVC (Polyvinyl Chloride). Plastic commonly used in disc pressings and some tape backings and electrical insulators.

Q   QUAD, QUADRAPHONY. A system providing four-channel sound surrounding the listener. Two speakers are nominally to the front and two to the rear. The latter may be used to enhance the apparent acoustics of the listening room, or all may carry direct sound as well as the acoustic enhancement. The terms '*quadrophonic*' and '*quadrasonic*' are used by two of the rival systems used to encode the four signals into a single groove of a disc.

QUALITY (of sound reproduction). The faithfulness with which the original sound (or a monophonic representation) is reproduced in terms of frequency response and lack of distortion.

QUARTER-TRACK RECORDING. One that occupies about 15% of the full width of the tape. The tape runs from left to right and the top track is recorded first, and then the third. To record the other two tracks the tape is turned upside down and once again fed left to right. For stereo, the first and third tracks are recorded at the same time, using a stacked head (one with both gaps in line). Quarter-track recording has a signal-to-noise ratio poorer than that of half or full track recording in proportion to the relative widths.

R   RADIO LINK. A radio transmission focused into a narrow beam and directed toward an equally directional receiver placed in line of sight. Used in place of a landline.

RADIO MICROPHONE. Microphone and small transmitter sending a signal that can be picked up at a distance of up to perhaps several hundred yards (provided that the two are not screened from each other).

RADIO TRANSMISSION. A system for distributing audio information by modulating it on to a high frequency carrier at a particular frequency that is then amplified to a high power and broadcast toward the receivers by means of an aerial. Transmitter and receiver aerials act in a similar way to the two windings of a transformer; they are coupled together by the field between them. (The field at the receiver is, of course, very tiny: it diminishes not only as the square of the distance, but also by the action of other 'receivers' along the path. In passing over granite, for example, a great deal of a medium-wave signal is mopped up. For VHF, which does not penetrate so deep into the ground, the nature of the terrain does not matter—but high ground casts a 'shadow'.) This highly inefficient transformer action is improved if the receiving aerial is so constructed as to resonate at the desired frequencies of reception, and it will discriminate against other signals if it is made directional. It is important that the aerials should be parallel (both vertical or both horizontal). Systems of carrier modulation in use are amplitude modulation and frequency modulation (q.v.).

RADIOPHONICS (*BBC*). Electronic sounds or effects that are formally arranged, as in *musique concrète* or electronic music, but which are not usually intended to be heard independently of other radio or television material.

RAM. Random access memory: an electronic component storing digital information that can be sampled at any time and in any order.

RECORDING. An inscription of an audio signal in permanent form, usually on magnetic tape or on disc. The term *record* implies commercial gramophone record,

536

as distinct from any other pressing or other form of recording. A *recording engineer* (*BBC*) is a professional engineer whose job includes the technical recording of sound and the editing of tape, but not microphone balance and control. A *recordist* is a member of a film crew who is responsible for sound.

REDUCE. See MIX.

REINFORCEMENT (in sound balance). The strengthening of direct sound reaching a microphone by the addition of indirect sound. This adds body without adding appreciably to volume. See RESONANCE, REVERBERATION.

RELATIVE PITCH. The ability to judge one pitch by reference to another. Total lack of this ability is 'tone deafness'.

REMOTE (*Am.*). Outside broadcast or source (q.v.).

REPEATING GROOVE. An occasion when a stylus jumps back a groove. This may be due to a fault in the groove wall, grit in the groove, an excessive resonance in the pick-up arm, or a sticky pivot. A *groove run* is a run on to a following groove, due to a scratch across the grooves or similar cause.

RESISTANCE. The ratio of e.m.f. (electromotive force) to current produced in a circuit; the ratio of voltage drop to current flowing in a circuit element.

RESONANCE. A natural periodicity or the reinforcement associated with it. The frequencies (including harmonics) produced in musical instruments (e.g. vibrating strings or columns of air) are determined by resonances.

RESPONSE. Sensitivity of microphone, etc. See FREQUENCY RESPONSE, POLAR CHARACTERISTIC.

RETAKE. Re-recording of part of a programme, to be edited in subsequently.

REVERBERATION. The sum of many reflections of sound in an enclosed space. This modifies the quality of a sound and gives it an apparent prolongation after the source stops radiating. *Reverberation time* is the time taken for sound to die away to a millionth of its original intensity (i.e. through 60 dB).

REVERBERATION PLATE. A metal plate, held under stress and fitted with two transducers, one to introduce sound vibrations, and the other to detect them at another point on the plate. By this means the decay of sound in an enclosed space is simulated.

RIAA CHARACTERISTIC. Recording characteristic used on gramophone records. (standard set by the Record Industry Association of America). See also CCIR and NARTB.

RIBBON MICROPHONE (or loudspeaker). The ribbon is a narrow strip of aluminium alloy foil suspended in a strong magnetic field provided either by a powerful horseshoe magnet with polepieces extending along the length of the ribbon or (in a much smaller assembly) by ceramic magnets, which are made from a compressed magnetically orientated magnet powder. In this microphone the ribbon (which is corrugated for greater flexibility) is made to vibrate by the difference in pressure between front and back of the ribbon. If both sides are open to the sound wave, the resulting motion is in phase with the velocity, and not with the amplitude of the sound wave. Vibration of the ribbon in the magnetic field produces an alternating current along its length. (See FIGURE-OF-EIGHT, PRESSURE GRADIENT.) In the loudspeaker the same principle is used in reverse, but is not suitable for handling considerable power, and so is used only in a tweeter. A flared (exponential) horn is provided to improve coupling.

RING. Undamped resonance.

RING MODULATOR. See Modulation.

ROCK AND ROLL. A facility for discontinuous film sound re-recording (dubbing) in which the recording is stopped after an error is made, the picture and tracks run back in synchronisation and a new recording is begun from an earlier point. An essential characteristic is that the join must not be perceptible.

RUMBLE. Low-frequency mechanical vibration picked up by an audio system.

RUSHES. Work-print taken from camera master and processed, printed and screened as quickly as possible (often overnight) in order to check picture quality.

S S SIGNAL. The stereo difference signal A − B. The S does not stand for stereo (of which it is only part) but for 'side' (bi-directional) microphone — used sometimes in combination with a 'main' microphone to produce stereo.

SATELLITE. In this context, a stage in the transmission of audio or television signals from one part of the globe to another by two line-of-sight paths. Using a synchronous satellite (i.e. one for which the orbital speed is the same as the earth's rotational speed, so that the satellite remains stationary with respect to a point on the surface of the earth) there will be a delay of nearly a quarter of a second.

SCALE. Division of the audio frequency spectrum by musical intervals (i.e. frequency ratios). An octave has the ratio 1:2, a fifth 2:3, a fourth 3:4, and so on: common musical intervals are derived from series of ratios of small whole numbers. The *chromatic* or *twelve-tone scale* is a division of the octave into twelve equal intervals (semitones in the equal-tempered scale). On this scale most of the small-whole-number intervals correspond (though not exactly) to an integral number of semitones, which may, of course, be measured from or to any point. Certain scales omit five of the twelve notes of the octave, leaving seven (plus the octave) into which most of the small-whole-number ratios still fit—but it is no longer possible to start arbitrarily from any point. Instead, the interval must always be measured from a *key* note, or a note simply related to it. Music that for the most part observes the more restricted scales is called *tonal*, while that which ranges freely over the chromatic scale is called *atonal*. In *twelve-tone music* an attempt is made to give each of the twelve notes equal prominence.

SCENE. A single continuous film shot or any repetition of it.

SCREEN. A free-standing sound-absorbent or reflecting panel that may be used to vary the acoustics locally, or to cut off some of the direct sound travelling from one point to another in the studio. It may be moved about the studio at will. An object (such as a script) is said to be *screening the microphone* if it lies in the path of sound coming directly from a source.

SCREENING. A protection from stray electrical fields. It may take the form of an earthed mesh wire surrounding a conductor carrying a low level signal. Valuable tapes (particularly videotapes) may be screened in a metal box when sent by air.

SCRIPT RACK. An angled rack on which a script may be placed in order to encourage a speaker to raise his head. It should be transparent to sound.

SEGUE (pronounced 'segway'). Musical term meaning follow on.

SELF-DRIVE STUDIO. One that is operated by the user without continuous technical assistance.

SENSITIVITY. The ratio of response to stimulus, usually measured in dBs relative to some given reference level. See NEWTONS PER SQUARE METRE.

SEPMAG. Separate magnetic film sound, i.e. on a separate spool, but recorded with frame-for-frame synchronization. See COMMAG, COMOPT.

SEPARATION. Degree to which each of several microphones discriminate in favour of the sources or groups of sources associated with it, and against unwanted sound or that to be picked up by other microphones. The purpose of separation is to allow individual control and treatment of the sources.

SIBILANCE. The production of strongly emphasised 's' and 'ch' sounds in speech. These may in turn be accentuated by microphones having peaks in their top response.

SIGNAL. The fluctuating current that carries audio information (programme).

SIGNAL-TO-NOISE RATIO. The difference in decibels between the signal and noise levels. The quoted signal-to-noise ratio of any item of equipment is that available when the signal is as loud as it can be without significant distortion.

SINE TONE (Pure tone). A sound (or electrical signal) containing one frequency, and one alone. This corresponds to an air particle executing simple harmonic motion, and its graphical representation (waveform) is that of s.h.m. (i.e. a sine wave). In principle all sounds can be analysed into component sine tones. In practice this is only possible for steady sounds, or for short segments of irregular sounds; noise contains an unlimited number of such tones. Sine tones are useful for studying frequency response and for lining up equipment.

SLEW. Frequency shift, portamento (q.v.).

SLUNG MICROPHONE. One that hangs by suspending wires or by its own cable from a ceiling or grid fitting (or from a boom or lazy arm).

SOLID STATE DEVICE. A circuit element such as a transistor (q.v.) or a complete microcircuit combining a number of circuit elements and their connections. It is characterized by small size, low power consumption, and high reliability.

SOUND. A series of compressions and refractions travelling through air or another medium, caused by some body or bodies (*sound sources*) in vibration. At any place it is completely defined by the movement of a single particle of air (or other material). The movement may be very complex but there are no physically separate components due to different sound sources. Such contributions may be isolated by mathematical analysis, and the brain, too, acts as a mathematical computer which perceives the different components as separate entities. See HEARING, DECIBEL, LEVEL, FREQUENCY, WAVELENGTH, PITCH, PHASE, FORMANT, SINE TONE, VELOCITY OF SOUND.

SOUND EFFECTS. See EFFECTS.

SOUND SUBJECT (in *musique concrète*) A segment of treated sound material, to be assembled with others into the finished work.

SPACED PAIR. Two separated microphones used to pick up stereo. Phase distortion effects occur but may be tolerable.

SPACER. Uncoated tape, which may be yellow or other colours (other than white or red which are used mainly for leaders and trailers), cut into a spool of tape to indicate the end of one segment and the start of another.

SPILL. (*a*) To allow sound to be picked up on a microphone other than that intended, thereby reducing separation. (*b*) To unspool a quantity of tape by accident.

SPIN. The combination of original and delayed signals with multiple repetitions. Decay (or continuation of the effect) is controlled by a fader in the feed-back circuit. Eventually the quality changes to express the frequency characteristics of the feed-back circuit itself.

SPIN-START. Quick-start technique for disc, requiring no special equipment, in which the record is set up with the stylus in the groove and the motor switched off. On cue, the motor is switched on and the turntable boosted to speed by hand. This boost is not usually necessary for turntables with rim drive.

SPOOL. Reel for carrying tape. *Ciné spools* for tape are similar in design to 8 mm. film spools. The most common types are made of clear plastic in a variety of sizes. Metal spools are available in larger sizes, and are more often used on professional decks. Some also have larger hub size than the ciné spool. Transcription tape decks are normally equipped to play either type. (A large hub is used in order that the tension does not vary so much as it would with a large diameter ciné spool. Some recorders can be switched to provide reduced tension when ciné spools are used.) Another design consists of a hub and a one-side-only backing plate, but this gives the operator less security against spillage than the double-sided spool.

SPOT EFFECT. A sound effect created in the studio. It may be taken on a separate microphone or on the same microphone as the main action.

SPOTTING. Reinforcement of a particular element in a stereo balance using a monophonic microphone. The balance is usually very close, to avoid 'tunnel' reverberation effects and other problems.

SPRINGS. A reverberation-producing device. High quality springs rival reverberation plates. Each spring has changes of thickness, etc., along its length to introduce multiple reflections. For stereo two springs are used. The combined $(A + B)$ signal is applied to both, and separate A and B signals are derived at the other end.

STANDING WAVES. See WAVE.

STEERING. See PANNING.

STEREO (Stereophonic sound). A form of reproduction in which the apparent sources of sound are spread out. The word 'stereo' implies 'solid', but in fact the normal range of sound in two-channel stereo is along a line joining the loudspeakers —to which an apparent second dimension is added by perspective effects. This may be used to simulate the spread of direct sound of an orchestra or a theatre stage very well. And whereas each individual source may be fairly well defined in position, the reverberation associated with it is spread over the whole range permitted by the position of the loudspeakers. But even this range is small in comparison with the situation in a concert hall, in which reverberation reaches the listener from all around him. *Four-channel stereo* (quadraphonics) uses four independent sound channels (from 4-track tape or other systems). Two loudspeakers are in front of the listener and two behind in X-formation. *Stereophonic sound in the cinema* uses a multi-track, multi-loudspeaker system, partly to ensure that members of the audience who are not ideally seated for two-channel stereo still hear sound that is roughly coincident with the image.

STING. Musical punctuation pointing dramatic or comic mood.

STOPS. Stud positions on a stud fader, and the markings associated with them, or corresponding arbitrary divisions of a continuous fader. Thus, to lift programme level 'a stop' is to increase it by moving the fader (potentiometer) from one stud to the next (usually about $1\frac{1}{2}$–2 dB), or, by analogy, a similar amount on a continuous fader.

STRAY FIELD. Unwanted a.c. field that may generate a signal in some part of the equipment where it should not be. The use of balanced wiring discriminates against this (equal and opposing e.m.f.'s act in two wires), and so also, where necessary, does screening (in which an earthed conductor surrounds parts that might be affected).

STROBOSCOPE. Since a.c. electric lighting pulsates in intensity (at twice the mains frequency) such light can be used to illuminate a disc with bars (or spots) on it. When the speed is at an appropriate setting these move a distance equal to their spacing in the time from one pulse of light to the next. The number of bars for $33\frac{1}{3}$, 45 and approximately 78 rpm, can be easily calculated—the European mains frequency being 50 Hz and the American, 60 Hz (this difference means that exact standardization for 78 rpm is not practicable.) Stroboscopic indicators can also be devised for checking tape speed, but if the indicator used is on a guide pulley the number of bars depends on the diameter of the pulley as well as the speed of tape. Stroboscopes work best with neon tubes; and not at all in sunlight. When the dots move onward the speed is too fast; when they move backward it is too slow. Stroboscopes are very sensitive to the slightest deviation of speed from the normal.

STUDIO (sound studio). Any room or hall that is primarily used for microphone work. Its most important properties lie in its size and its acoustics—the way in which sound is diffused and absorbed, and the reverberation time (q.v.). A *studio manager* in BBC radio is the balancer in operational charge of the broadcast or recording. (At the BBC he is not an engineer, which is a separate function.)

STYLUS. The needle of a pick-up. Materials most used are diamond and sapphire. Wear depends on playing weight (and record material) and is most rapid in the earlier hours of playing, and in any case, different users tolerate different degrees of wear before replacing: it is therefore difficult to set a precise lifetime on styli. However, if a sapphire is badly worn after 50 hours use, the corresponding diamond would last over 1000 hours. There is therefore a considerable saving to be made by using diamond styli. But this saving (on styli, if not on record wear) may in many cases be only theoretical, as incautious users may be prepared to change a sapphire no more often than the careful user changes a diamond. The cost of a diamond depends on the time spent and equipment used in polishing. The tip radius of the cutter used is smaller than that of the reproducing stylus in each of these cases (and the included angle greater), so that the stylus tip rests at two points in the groove. A mono cartridge used on a stereo disc should have sufficient vertical compliance to ride the hill-and-dale (A − B) element of the recording without damage.

SUBHARMONIC. A partial of frequency $\frac{1}{2}f, \frac{1}{3}f, \frac{1}{4}f$, etc., lying below the fundamental f. The subharmonic $\frac{1}{2}f$ can be generated in the cone of a moving coil loudspeaker.

SUPERIMPOSITION. The recording of a second signal on a tape without passing the previous recording through the erase-head field. The h.f. bias on the new recording reduces the volume of the earlier signal. The method is not used professionally.

SWARF (*Am.*: Chip). The filament thrown up when a lacquer disc is cut. It has to be carried from the head by an air suction system. Cellulose nitrate is very inflammable.

SYNC PULSE (PILOT TONE). A signal related to camera speed that is fed to the tape on which the associated sound is recorded. When the sound is subsequently transferred to magnetic film, the pulse controls the speed of rerecording.

SYNC TAKE. Film shot with sound, using a synchronous recording system.

T   TAKE. An individual attempt at shooting a scene (film) or sequence (radio or television) that may be tried several times.

TALKBACK. Communication circuit from control to studio, used mainly for the direction of performers. *Reverse talkback* is a secondary circuit for communication from studio to control. Both forms of talkback are independent of live programme sound circuits, although in unfavourable circumstances breakthrough (or cross-talk) can occur.

TAPE. Magnetic recording medium consisting of a ferro-magnetic coating on a plastic backing (see COATING and BACKING). *Long Play tape* gives 50% more recording time on a spool than *standard play*, and *double play*, of course, gives double. Thinner tape is more susceptible to printing, and its use does not save money (for comparable quality); but it does save storage space, and permits fewer reel changes for a given spool size. *Videotape* is a similar medium, but is generally two inches (50·8 mm) wide; sound is recorded along one edge. Metric equivalents: The standard width, $\frac{1}{4}$ in = 6·25 mm, $\frac{1}{2}$ in = 12·5 mm approx., and so on. Cassettes use a narrower tape, 3·8 mm wide.

TAPE DECK. The mechanical part (plus heads) of a tape recorder or reproducer.

TAPE JOINER. Film joiner using a guillotine and polyester tape. As the film is not lapped, no frames are lost. This type has replaced the cement joiner.

TAPE RECORDING AMPLIFIER. Differs from an ordinary amplifier in that it includes an oscillator for bias and erase.

TAPE SPEEDS. Are all based on the early standard of 30 in/s (inches per second) for coated tape. Successive improvements in tape, heads and other equipment have permitted successive reductions in speed to 15 and $7\frac{1}{2}$ in/s (used professionally for music and speech) and $3\frac{3}{4}$, $1\frac{7}{8}$ and $\frac{15}{16}$ in/s (used domestically). Metric equivalents: 15 in/s = 28 cm/s, $7\frac{1}{2}$ in/s = 19 cm/s, $3\frac{3}{4}$ in/s = 9·5 cm/s and so on.

TELEPHONE ADAPTOR. A pick-up coil that may be placed in the field of the line transformer of a telephone or in some similar position where a signal may be generated.

TELEPHONE QUALITY. A frequency band between 300–3000 Hz. Simulated telephone quality should be judged subjectively according to programme needs.

TENT. A group of screens, arranged to trap (and usually to absorb) sound in the region of the microphone.

TIMBRE. Tone quality. The distribution of frequencies and intensities in a sound.

TIME CODE. A recorded time signal that can be electronically read and displayed. It may be the real time at which the recording was made or, alternatively, built up from an arbitrary time recorded earlier. It is used for automatic control and synchronisation, primarily of videotape; and also for timing duration, automatic logging, etc.

TIME CONSTANT. For a capacitor of C farads, charging or discharging through a resistance of R ohms (as in a PPM, limiter, etc.) the time constant, $t = CR$ secs. (Similarly, for an inductance of H henries and resistance, R ohms, $t = L/R$ secs.)

TONE. Imprecise term for sound considered in terms of pitch (of frequency content). A pure tone is sound of a particular frequency. See SINE TONE.

TONE CONTROL. Pre-amplifier control for adjusting frequency content of sound (usually bass or treble).

TOP. High frequencies in the audio range, particularly in the range 8–16 kHz.

TOP RESPONSE. Ability of a component to handle frequencies at the higher end of the audio range.

TRACK. (a) To move a camera or boom toward or away from the acting area. (b) An individual recording among several on a record. (c) One of several (typically, up to 8, 16 or 24) recordings made side-by-side on multitrack tape.

TRAILER. (a) An item in the continuity (link) between programmes that advertises future presentations. (b) Uncoated tape, usually red, that is cut into a tape to indicate the end of wanted recorded material.

TRANSDUCER. A device for converting a signal from one form to another. The system in which the power is generated or transmitted may be acoustic, electrical, mechanical (disc), magnetic (tape), etc. Thus, microphones, loudspeaker, pick-ups, tape heads, etc., are all transducers.

TRANSFORMATIONS, TREATMENT OF SOUND (in radiophonics). Changes in sound quality, pitch or duration, by any continuous or discontinuous process that may be used to convert the content of a sound into any other form.

TRANSIENT. The initial part of any sound, before any regular waveform is established. The transient is an important part of any sound and in musical instruments helps establish an identifiable character. *Transient response.* Ability of a component to handle and faithfully reproduce sudden irregular waveforms. See DIAPHRAGM.

TRANSISTOR. A semiconductor device that performs most of the functions of a valve (vacuum tube), but differs from it principally in that (a) no heater is required, so that the transistor is always ready for immediate use and no significant unproductive power is consumed, (b) it is much smaller in size, (c) input and output circuitry are not so isolated as in a valve, and (d) there is normally no phase reversal in a transistor, as the control voltage is used to promote flow of current, and not to reduce it. A range of designs and functions of transistors (as with valves) is available. The circuit associated with a transistor is somewhat different from that for a valve. Transistors are more sensitive to changes of temperature than valves. Power transistors, which generate heat, need to be well ventilated.

TRANSMISSION, TRANSMITTER. See RADIO.

TRANSMUTATION. Changing the timbre of a sound, but not necessarily its dynamics. This includes transposition in pitch.

TRANSPORT SYSTEM (of a tape deck). The drive motor, capstan and idler, the feed and take-up motors and spool mountings, and the guide pillars and pulleys round which the tape passes to draw it over the heads.

TREBLE. Higher part of the musical range; say, 1 or 2 kHz and above.

TREMOLO. A regular variation in the amplitude of a sound, e.g. of electric guitar, generally at a frequency between 3 and 30 Hz. Sometimes confused with VIBRATO.

TURN OVER. In filming, the director's instruction to run camera and sound.

TURNTABLE. The rotating plate of a record player. Besides supporting and gripping the record, it acts as a flywheel, checking any tendency to wow and flutter. It should therefore be well balanced, with a high moment of inertia (this is highest for a given weight if most of the mass is concentrated at the outer edge).

TUNNEL EFFECT. Monophonic reverberation associated with an individual source in stereo.

TWEETER. High frequency loudspeaker used in combination with a low frequency unit or 'woofer' and possibly also a mid-range unit (sometimes called a 'squawker'). The problems of loudspeaker design are different at the two ends of the audio spectrum and in some are easier to solve if handled separately. A single unit becomes progressively more directional at higher frequencies; a small separate unit for h.f. can maintain a broad radiating pattern.

TWIN TRACK. Two half track tape recordings used for different purposes: to record the separate stereo channels, to record mono plus a guide track (for television), or to make individual recordings in opposite directions.

U UNDERMODULATION. Allowing a recorded or broadcast signal to take too low a volume, so that it has to compete to an unnecessary extent with the noise of the medium (and has to undergo greater amplification on reproduction, risking greater noise at this stage also).

UNDIRECTIONAL MICROPHONE. This may refer either to a cardioid (q.v.) or near-cardioid type of response (live on one face and substantially dead on the other), or a microphone with a more strongly directional forward lobe. See also PARABOLIC REFLECTOR, GUN MICROPHONE.

V VALVE (*Am.*: vacuum tube). An almost completely evacuated glass envelope within which electrons released by a heated electrode (the cathode) are collected by a seond positively charged electrode (the anode). In this, its simplest form, the valve is a *diode* and it conducts electricity whenever there is a flow of electrons into the cathode (on every other half cycle of an alternating signal). In the *triode* a grid is placed in the path of the electrons and variation of voltage on this controls corresponding fluctuations in the flow of electrons, producing an amplified version of the signal on the control grid. Additional grids may be added (*tetrode*, *pentode* etc.) and these further modify the characteristics of the electron flow.

VARIABLE RELUCTANCE (pick-up). One of the principles that have been applied to pick-up design. The stylus armature (mounting arm or shank) forms part of a circuit of magnetic flux between the poles of a permanent magnet. Movement of the stylus produces variations in the magnetic flux, which in turn generates a current in a coil (or 2 coils situated on paths favoured alternately, and operating in push pull).

VELOCITY OF SOUND. In air at room temperature this is approximately 1120 ft/s (or 340 m/s). It can be calculated roughly as $1087 + 2T$ ft/s where T is the temperature in degrees centigrade. Humidity also makes a slight difference: in fully saturated damp air is 3 ft/s faster than in dry air. In liquids, solids much faster than in air.

VELOCITY MICROPHONE (*Am.*). Ribbon microphone (q.v.).

VHF (Very High Frequency). See RADIO.

VIBRATO. Rapid cyclic variation in pitch at a rate of about 5–8 Hz, used by musicians to enrich the quality of sustained notes.

VIDEOTAPE. See TAPE.

VIDEOTAPE CLOCK. Clock mounted on a board showing programme details. Shown in vision before the start of a television recording between about minus 30 seconds and minus 3 seconds, after which the picture cuts to black. This picture is accompanied in sound by a countdown, '30 . . . 20 . . . 10–9–8–7–6–5–4–3' with reference tone between minus 20 and minus 10.

VOCAL STOP. A short break in vocalized sound that precedes certain consonants. These help in the exact location of editing points on tape, and sometimes provide a useful place to cut at. For example, in the words 'to cut at' there are several stops: '/to/cu/ta/t'. It would therefore be possible to cut in before 'to' or 'cut', but it would not be possible to remove the word 'at' cleanly from the end. However, the same result might be achieved by cutting from stop to stop in 'cu/ta/t'. It is sometimes possible to lose the sound after a stop completely, e.g. when cutting 'bu·' (for 'but') on to the beginning of a sentence.

VOLUME CONTROL. See CONTROL, COMPRESSION, FADER.

VOLUME METER, VU METER. See METER.

VOLUME OF SOUND. See DECIBEL, LEVEL.

W WAVE (sound wave). A succession of compressions and rarefactions transmitted through a medium at a constant velocity. See VELOCITY OF SOUND. In representing this graphically displacement is plotted against time, and the resulting display has the appearance of a transverse wave (like the ripples on a pool). This diagram shows the *waveform*. The distance between corresponding points on successive cycles (or ripples) is the *wavelength* (λ) and this is related to the frequency (f) (the rate at which ripples pass a particular point) and sound velocity (c) through the relation $f\lambda = c$. Wavelength can thus be roughly calculated as 1120 ft/s or 340 m/s. As sound radiates out from a source it forms a *spherical wave* in which intensity is inversely proportional to the square of the distance. When the distance from the source is very large compared with the physical dimensions of any objects encountered this effect becomes less important; the loss in intensity is small and the wave is said to act as a *plane wave*. See BASS TIP-UP for illustration of this. In a *standing wave* the nodes occupy fixed positions in space. In a *progressive wave* the whole waveform moves onward at a steady rate.

WAVE ANALYSER. An instrument incorporating a selective amplifier of narrow band-width. It operates like a very sharp pass band filter.

WEIGHTED and UNWEIGHTED. Different ways of indicating levels of noise or hum relative to signal, with particular reference to their bass content. Programme meters do not normally give any frequency information, and low frequencies do not sound as loud as a VU meter or PPM indicates, as the ear discriminates against bass. For this reason, quoted noise levels are sometimes 'weighted' against bass according to standard loudness contours. Weighted and unweighted measurements may differ by 20 dB or more at low frequencies.

WHITE NOISE. See NOISE.

WIGGLE or FLICKER. The momentary displacement of a stereo image that occurs when one of the faders on the individual sound channels is not making perfect contact. In a mixer with studded faders it occurs when the sliders do not make simultaneous contact with successive studs.

WILDTRACK. Film sound recorded without picture.

WINDSHIELD (*Am.*: Windscreen). Shield that fits over microphone and protects diaphragm from 'rattling' by wind, and also contours the microphone for smoother airflow round it.

WIPE (tape). Erase.

WOOFER. Low frequency unit in Loudspeaker. See TWEETER.

WOOLLY. Sound that lacks clarity at high frequencies and tends to be relatively boomy at low.

WOW. Cyclic fluctuation in pitch due to mechanical faults in recording or reproducing equipment (or physical fault in a disc). The frequency of the variation is below, say, 5 Hz. See FLUTTER, VIBRATO, TREMOLO.

Z ZERO LEVEL. See LEVEL.

BIBLIOGRAPHY

Alkin, Glyn Sound Recording and Reproduction. *Focal Press* (1981). A comprehensive guide to all aspects of studio sound recording, reproduction systems and their use.

Alkin, Glyn Sound with Vision. *Butterworth* (1973). A substantial work on television sound—based on BBC practice.

Borwick, John (ed.) Sound Recording Practice. *Oxford University Press* (1976). Comprehensive but uneven collection of articles (some very good) with emphasis on techniques employed in the British recording industry.

Hilliard, Robert L. (ed.) Radio Broadcasting. *Hastings House* (2nd ed., 1974). Describes the job of the audio operation in relation to American local radio.

Millerson, Gerald The Technique of Television Production. *Focal Press*, London and Boston (11th ed., 1985). A highly analytical study of the medium, including the contribution of sound, videotape, electronic effects and on-location news-collecting.

Nisbett, Alec The Use of Microphones, *Focal Press*, London and Boston (2nd ed., 1983). A concise handbook on microphones, balance and control.

Oringel, Robert Audio Control Handbook. *Hastings House*, New York (4th ed., 1972). A simple and useful introduction to the subject (a little fuller in this edition than in the first three). There is a strong emphasis on American equipment.

Potter, Kopp and Green-Kopp Visible Speech, *Dover Publications*, New York, and *Constable*, London (1966). Useful when considering how to record, treat and edit speech and song.

Reisz, Karel, and Millar, Gavin The Technique of Film Editing. *Focal Press*, London and Boston (2nd ed., 1974). Concentrates largely on the general principles of picture editing.

Robertson, A. E. Microphones. *Butterworth* (2nd ed., 1963). Describes the engineering principles behind many types of microphone.

Stockhausen, Karlheinz Study II (Score). *Universal Edition.* See this and the scores of other works of a similar nature for illustration of the problems (and purpose?) of the notation of electronic music.

Wood, A. B. The Physics of Music. *Methuen* (6th ed., 1962). A standard primer on the subject.

INDEX

548

555

Sypher, 462